Memorial Book of David-Horodok
(Davyd-Haradok, Belarus)

Translation of
Sefer zikaron Dawidgrodek

Original Book Edited by: Y. Idan et.al., Tel Aviv, Former Residents of David-Horodok in Israel

Originally published in Tel Aviv, 1957

JewishGen
מרכז עולמי לגנאלוגיה יהודית
The Global Home for Jewish Genealogy

A Publication of JewishGen
Edmond J. Safra Plaza, 36 Battery Place, New York, NY 10280
646.494.2972 | info@JewishGen.org | www.jewishgen.org

MUSEUM OF JEWISH HERITAGE
A LIVING MEMORIAL TO THE HOLOCAUST

Memorial Book of David-Horodok (Davyd-Haradok, Belarus)
Translation of *Sefer zikaron Dawidgrodek*

Copyright © 2025 by JewishGen. All rights reserved.
First Printing: March 2025, Adar, 5785
Original Yizkor Book Edited By: Y. Idan et.al., Tel Aviv, Former Residents of David-Horodok in Israel
Project Coordinator: Gayle Justman
Cover Design: Irv Osterer
Layout, formatting and indexing: Jonathan Wind

Library of Congress Control Number (LCCN): 2024935031

ISBN: 978-1-954176-98-0 (hard cover: 516 pages, alk. paper)

About JewishGen.org

JewishGen, is a Genealogical Research Division of the Museum of Jewish Heritage - A Living Memorial to the Holocaust, serves as the global home for Jewish genealogy.

Featuring unparalleled access to 30+ million records, it offers unique search tools, along with opportunities for researchers to connect with others who share similar interests. Award winning resources such as the Family Finder, Discussion Groups, and ViewMate, are relied upon by thousands each day.

In addition, JewishGen's extensive informational, educational and historical offerings, such as the Jewish Communities Database, Yizkor Book translations, InfoFiles, Family Tree of the Jewish People, and KehilaLinks, provide critical insights, first-hand accounts, and context about Jewish communal and familial life throughout the world.

Offered as a free resource, JewishGen.org has facilitated thousands of family connections and success stories, and is currently engaged in an intensive expansion effort that will bring many more records, tools, and resources to its collections.

Please visit https://www.jewishgen.org/ to learn more.

Vice President for JewishGen: Avraham Groll

About the JewishGen Yizkor Book Project

Yizkor Books (Memorial Books) were traditionally written to memorialize the names of departed family and martyrs during holiday services in the synagogue (a practice that still exists in many synagogues today).

Over the centuries, as a result of countless persecutions and horrific atrocities committed against the Jews, Yizkor Books (Sefer Zikaron in Hebrew) were expanded to include more historical information, such as biographical sketches of famous personalities and descriptions of daily town life.

Following the Holocaust, the idea of remembrance and learning took on an urgent and crucial importance. Survivors of the Holocaust sought out other surviving residents of their former towns to memorialize and document the names and way of life of those who were ruthlessly murdered by the Nazis. These remembrances were documented in Yizkor Books, hundreds of which were published in the first decades after the Holocaust.

Most of these books were published privately, or through *Landsmanshaftn* (social organizations comprised of members originating from the same European town or region) that still existed, and were often distributed free of charge. The languages used to document these crucial histories and links to our past were mostly Yiddish and Hebrew. JewishGen has undertaken the sacred responsibility of translating these books into English so that the culture and way of life of these communities will be preserved and transmitted to future generations.

In 1986, a group of farsighted JewishGenners started a project to pool their efforts together in groups based upon their ancestors' towns and donate funds to translate the Yizkor books of their ancestral towns into English. As the translated material became available, it was made accessible for free at https://www.JewishGen.org/Yizkor . Hardcover copies can be purchased by visiting https://www.jewishgen.org/Yizkor/ybip.html (see section below).

It is our hope that the translation of these books into English (and other languages) will assist the countless Jewish family researchers who are so desperately seeking to forge a connection with their heritage.

Director of JewishGen Yizkor Book Project: Lance Ackerfeld

About JewishGen Press

JewishGen Press (formerly the Yizkor Books-in-Print Project) is the publishing division of JewishGen.org, and provides a venue for the publication of non-fiction books pertaining to Jewish genealogy, history, culture, and heritage.

In addition to the Yizkor Book category, publications in the Other Non-Fiction category include Shoah memoirs and research, genealogical research, collections of genealogical and historical materials, biographies, diaries and letters, studies of Jewish experience and cultural life in the past, academic theses, and other books of interest to the Jewish community.

Please visit https://www.jewishgen.org/Yizkor/ybip.html to learn more.

Director of JewishGen Press: Joel Alpert
Managing Editor – Peter Harris
Publications Manager - Susan Rosin

Notes to the Reader

The images in the original book were reproduced from photographs from the time of the first edition. These reproductions were already of poor quality, most being pre-war and others at least 60 or more years old. As a result, the images in the book are the best achievable.
A reader can view the original scans of the book on the websites listed below.

The original book can be seen online at the Yiddish Book Center website:

https://www.yiddishbookcenter.org/collections/yizkor-books/yzk-nybc313739/eidan-yitshak-sefer-zikaron-david-horodok

OR

at the New York Public Library Digital Collections website:

https://digitalcollections.nypl.org/items/7b823960-6a1a-0133-3ca8-00505686a51c

To obtain a list of Shoah victims from **David-Horodok (Davyd-Haradok, Belarus),** the reader should access the Yad Vashem web site listed below; one can also search for specific family names using family name option. These lists are continually updated by Yad Vashem, so it is worthwhile to periodically search them.

There is more valuable information (including the Pages of Testimony, etc.) available on this website: https://yvng.yadvashem.org/

A list of all books available from JewishGen Press along with prices is available at: https://www.jewishgen.org/Yizkor/ybip.html

Additional Sources of Information:

The JewishGen Belarus Database at https://www.jewishgen.org/databases/Belarus
The Community of David-Horodok website: https://david-horodok.org
The Descendants of David-Horodok Facebook page:
https://www.facebook.com/descendantsofdavidhorodok

\

Cover Photo Credits

Cover Design by: Irv Osterer

Front Cover:
Dov Ber (Berl) Eisenberg (b. 1853) in David-Horodok, son of Gershon and Sara Leah (Schwartz) Eisenberg. He was murdered during the Holocaust. Courtesy of Gayle Justman.

Background map: *David-Horodok* – [Preliminary pages in the original book, Page 4 in this translation].

Back Cover:

Top left:
Aharon Ladezky and friends boating on the Horyn River in David-Horodok. Aharon is second from the left, holding a pair of oars. Submitted to the Organization of the Descendants of David-Horodok in Israel by Aharon Ladezky.

Top right:
Hakoach Soccer Team 1927 – [Page 45 in the original book, Page 72 in this translation]

Right, second from top:
The Helman Family: Standing in back row (left to right) Charles and Leo Helman. Front row: Bessie, Anna (Osnay), Sara-Dina (mother), Dorothy, Isaac (father), and Rachel Helman. Submitted to the Zekelman Holocaust Center in Farmington Hills, Michigan by Eileen Aboulafia.

Right, third from top:
The Great Synagogue – [Page 90 in the original book, Page 124 in this translation]

Bottom right:
Noach (b. 1932) and Mirele (Miriam) (b. 1929) Mishalov in 1935 in David-Horodok. Both children were murdered during the Holocaust. Submitted to the Zekelman Holocaust Center in Farmington Hills, Michigan by Norma Gorosh.

Geopolitical Information

Map of Belarus showing the location of **Davyd-Haradok**

Davyd-Haradok

Horodło, Poland is located at 50°53' N 24°02' E and 161 miles SE of Warszawa

	Town	District	Province	Country
Before WWI (c. 1900):	David-Gorodok	Mozyr	Minsk	Russian Empire
Between the wars (c. 1930):	Dawidgródek	Stolin	Polesie	Poland
After WWII (c. 1950):	David-Gorodok			Soviet Union
Today (c. 2000):	Davyd-Haradok			Belarus

Davyd-Haradok is located at 52°03' N 27°13' E, 129 miles S of Minsk

Alternate Names for the Town:

Davyd-Haradok [Bel], David Gorodok [Rus], Dawidgródek [Pol], David Horodok [Yid], Davidgrodek, Davidgrudek, Dawid-Gródek

Nearby Jewish Communities:

Remel 5 miles E
Rubel 9 miles SW
Lakhva 13 miles NNW
Kazhan-Haradok 14 miles NW
Belogusha 15 miles WSW
Mikashevichi 16 miles NE
Stolin 19 miles SW
Stachava 21 miles W
Turov 22 miles E
Luninyets 22 miles NW
Lenin 23 miles NNE
Plotnitsa 24 miles W
Bukcha 27 miles SE
Drozdin, Ukraine 28 miles S
Zhytkavichy 30 miles ENE

JewishPoulation: 3,087 (in 1897), 2,832 (in 1921)

Project Coordinator Introduction

The town of David-Horodok holds a special place in my heart. It was the home of my maternal ancestors, documented back to my third great-grandfather. My grandfather was born there in 1881. My grandmother was originally from Starobin, a small town about 48 miles away, but moved to David-Horodok after her arranged marriage to my grandfather in 1911. My grandmother's sister had married one of my grandfather's Olpiner cousins and was already living in David-Horodok when my grandmother arrived. In 1912, following the tragic drowning of his beloved brother-in-law in the Horyn River, my grandfather decided to immigrate to America. My grandmother followed in 1914, bringing their young daughter with her. Growing up in Detroit, I often heard stories about the Horodokers and the David-Horodoker Organization. As an adult, I became a member of the organization, and in 2016, I had the privilege of visiting David-Horodok. It was an unforgettable experience to participate in a memorial service at the mass grave site alongside fellow Horodokers from the United States and Israel.

The original Yizkor book was published in 1957 by the Organization of David-Horodok Descendants in Israel with the support of the David-Horodok Women's Organization of Detroit and the David-Horodok Organization of New York. It serves as a permanent memorial to the town's lost Jewish community. Written in Hebrew and Yiddish by former residents, the 487-page book was compiled and edited by Yitzchak Zeldin-Idan, Yosef Lifshitz and Yaakov Mor (Kopel Moravchik). I was deeply moved to discover that I am related to one of the editors, Yosef Lifshitz, who was the son of my great-grandfather's sister. The editors repeated some of the articles in both the Hebrew and Yiddish sections, but it was decided that text would not be repeated in this publication. All of the content in the original book is preserved, just without duplication. Coordinator's notes explain how this was accomplished. The original page numbers of the text, indicating the Hebrew and/or Yiddish section, are included. Additionally, extensive footnotes and bracketed information have been added to the translation to enhance the reader's understanding. The Table of Contents in this book reflects the English translation, not the original Yizkor book.

The Yiddish section of the Yizkor book, beginning on page 327, was translated by Dr. Norman Helman z"l. Born in Detroit on July 27, 1934, he was the son of Horodokers Leo (Chaim Leib) and Anna (Hashke Glassman) Helman. Both his mother and his grandmother were active in the David-Horodok organizations of their time. In 1981, *David Horodoker Memorial Book*, his 126-page translation, was published in Oak Park, Michigan by Bessie Chase and the David-Horodoker Women's Organization. In the final paragraph of his translator's note, Dr. Helman wrote, "Much of the Hebrew original is duplicated in Yiddish. However, some is not, and this has not been translated – a project for the future, perhaps for another descendant of David-Horodok."

As a descendant of David-Horodok, I was inspired by Dr. Helman's words and decided that I would be responsible for guaranteeing that the translation was completed. Over forty years after Dr. Helman finished his Yiddish translations, the entire book has finally been translated. With this publication, English-speaking descendants of David-Horodok can learn more about the Jewish life of the town as well as read stories about their ancestors and landsmen. The complete translation offers the opportunity to discover names, biographical details, and historical information that may not be available elsewhere.

The story of David-Horodok's vibrant Jewish community before the Holocaust is fascinating, while the recounting of its destruction is horrifying. I hope that this translation will help keep the memory of David-Horodok's Jewish community alive for generations to come.

Project Coordinator Acknowledgments

The Yizkor book translation and publication project was a labor of love for me, made possible by the collective efforts of many individuals. I am very grateful for their contributions.

- The members of the David-Horodoker Organization, whose financial support demonstrated their commitment to preserving the history of the town. Special thanks goe to Roz Komisar Blanck, one of the co-presidents of the organization.
- Dr. Norman Helman z"l, who translated the original Yiddish text, and the translators who worked with JewishGen's Yizkor Book Project, including Gloria Berkenstat Freund, Ala Gamulka, Sara Mages, and especially Jerrold Landau. Jerrold translated all of the Hebrew text and provided extensive footnotes. A skilled translator of both Hebrew and Yiddish, he reviewed the entire book to ensure its accuracy and completeness.
- Lance Ackerfeld, Director of JewishGen's Yizkor Book Project, whose advice, experience, and patience were invaluable throughout this process.
- The team at JewishGen Press, including Joel Alpert, Bruce Drake, Sondra Ettlinger, Jonathan Wind, and Irv Osterer, who designed the book's outstanding cover. Special thanks to Susan Rosin, JewishGen Press Publications Manager, for her unwavering support, guidance, and friendship.
- And finally, to my Israeli cousin, Rachel Lelzizky, who patiently helped me to understand the meaning of certain words and ideas as well as shared my passion for our family history. She made this project even more meaningful.

Project Coordinator Dedication

In honor and remembrance of the men, women and children of David-Horodok who perished during the Holocaust, including my great-grandfather, Dov Ber Eisenberg, and my three great-aunts and their families:

- Gnesha Eisenberg Lelzizky, her son Yisrael Yosef and his wife Chaya and their children, and her daughter Zelda.
- Rivka Eisenberg Magidovitz, her husband Yitzchak, their sons Gershon and Yeshayahu, and their daughters Feiga, Elka, and Dvora.
- Sara Marmor Olpiner, her husband Meir, their son Gedalyahu and his wife Rachel and their children, their daughter Etel and her husband Arke Lifshitz and their children Gershon and Sara, and their daughter Chaya.

Now that I know, I will never forget. May their memories be for a blessing.

Gayle Justman
February, 2025

Table of Contents

Tarbut School

Told by the Elders

Personalities

Passed Away in Israel

The Holocaust

After the Holocaust

The Small Community (Rubel)

Memorial Book of David-Horodok
(Davyd-Haradok, Belarus)

52°03' / 27°13'

Translation of
Sefer zikaron Dawidgrodek

Editors: Y. Idan et.al., Tel Aviv, Former Residents of David-Horodok in Israel

Published in Tel Aviv, 1957

Acknowledgments

Project Coordinator:

Gayle Justman

**Our grateful thanks go out Ala Gamulka
for her technical assistance and translations.**

**Our sincere appreciation to Yad Vashem for the submission
of the necrology for placement on the JewishGen website.**

This is a translation of: *Sefer zikaron David-Horodok* (Memorial book of David-Horodok),
Editors: Y. Idan et.al., Tel Aviv, Former Residents of David-Horodok in Israel, 1957 (H,Y, 487
pages)

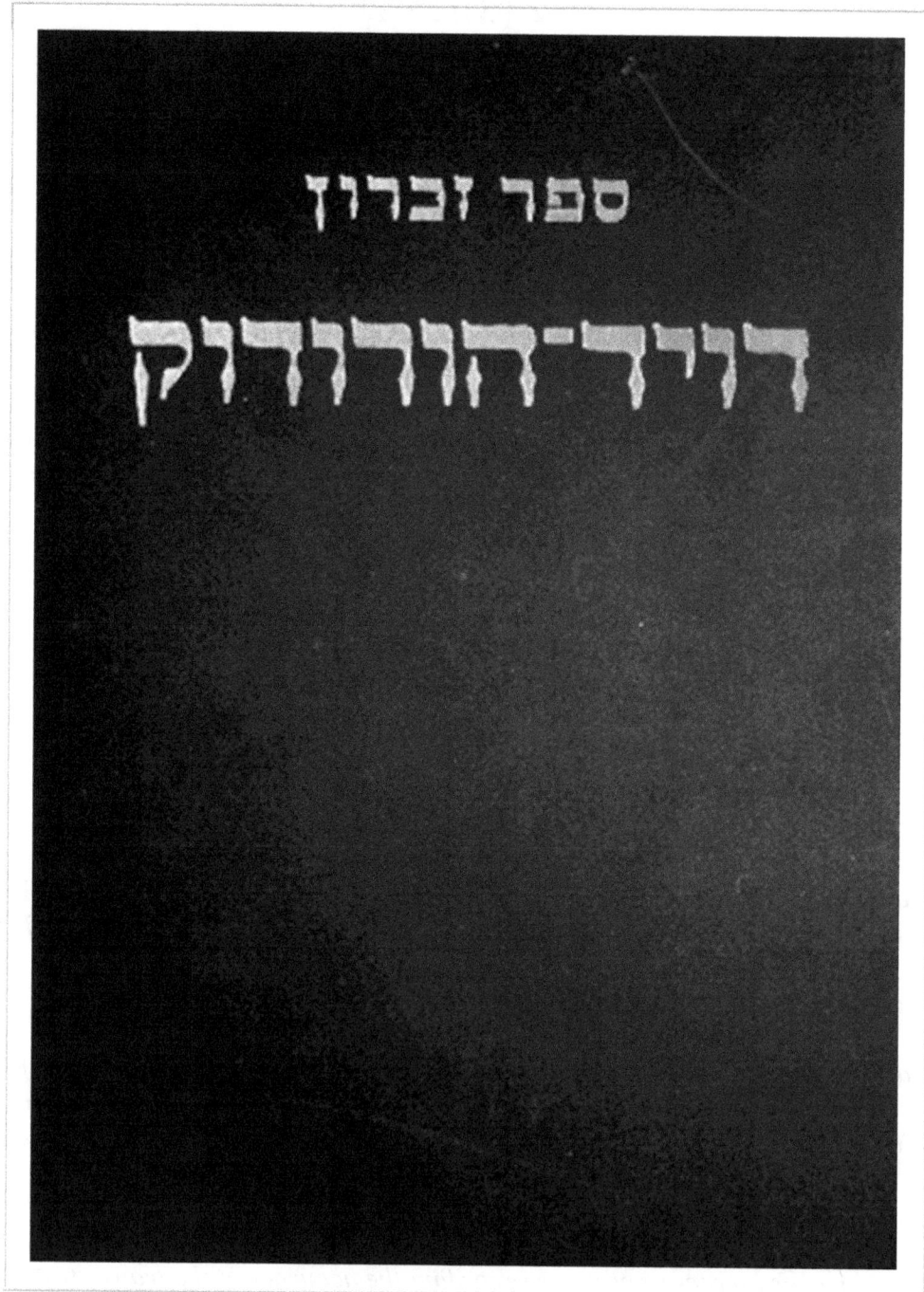

country map

Antopol
Dragichin
Gorodets
Yanov
Pinsk
Porakhonsk
Luninets
Mokros
Kozan Gorodok
Lakhva
Zhitkovichi
Orl
David Gorodok
Turov
POLESIA
STOLIN
Goryn
Polish border
Pripyat
Nobel
Gorodno
Lyubashevo
Steir
Vysotsk
Ubort
Kamen Kashirskiy
Dombrovitsa
Lishnevka
Berezhnitza
Streltsk
Nesukhoyzhe
Rafalovka
Sarny
Tomashgorod
Rokitino
Kovel
Gulevichi
Chartoriysk
Gorodetz
Sluch
Olevsk
Melnitsa
Stepan
Turiysk
Sokul
Kolki
Berezno

50 40 30 20 10 0 km

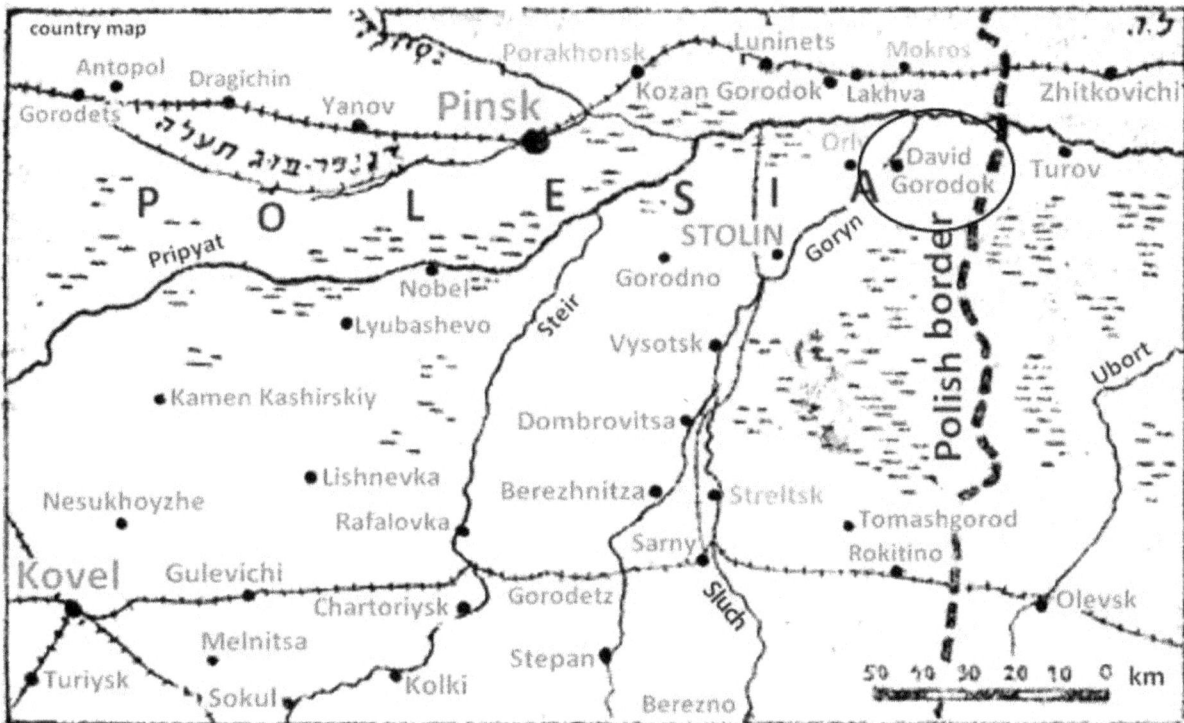

Uncaptioned. Map of the vicinity of David-Horodok, Stolin and Pinsk pre-WWII

Molnikos (Gentile Neighborhood)

Bridge

Carpenter Way

Lakhva Way

N →

14

The Horin River

Machus' Shore

Jerusalem or "Egypt" St.

Bridge

The Greble

8

6

12

7

4

5

10

Synagogue Courtyard

3

16

15

1

Olpene Street

Old Marketplace

11

2

To the new cemetery

10

Retail Stores

New Marketplace

Viallamitch Street

Raditch (Gentile Section)

The Marshes

Olshon Street

9

13

Second Alley

First Alley

The Shishka River

To the Grave of Our Brothers and Sisters

David-Horodok
Places of Note

1. City Hall
2. Court House
3. "Big" or "Cold" Synagogue
4. Study House
5. Stoliner Prayer House (Hasidic)
6. Study House of the Rich
7. Study House of the Rabbi
8. Old Cemetery
9. Tarbuth (Hebrew Language School)
10. Polish Elementary Schools
11. Russian Orthodox Church in Market
12. Russian Orthodox Church on Hill
13. Catholic Church
14. Electric Plant
15. Fire Station
16. Bathhouse

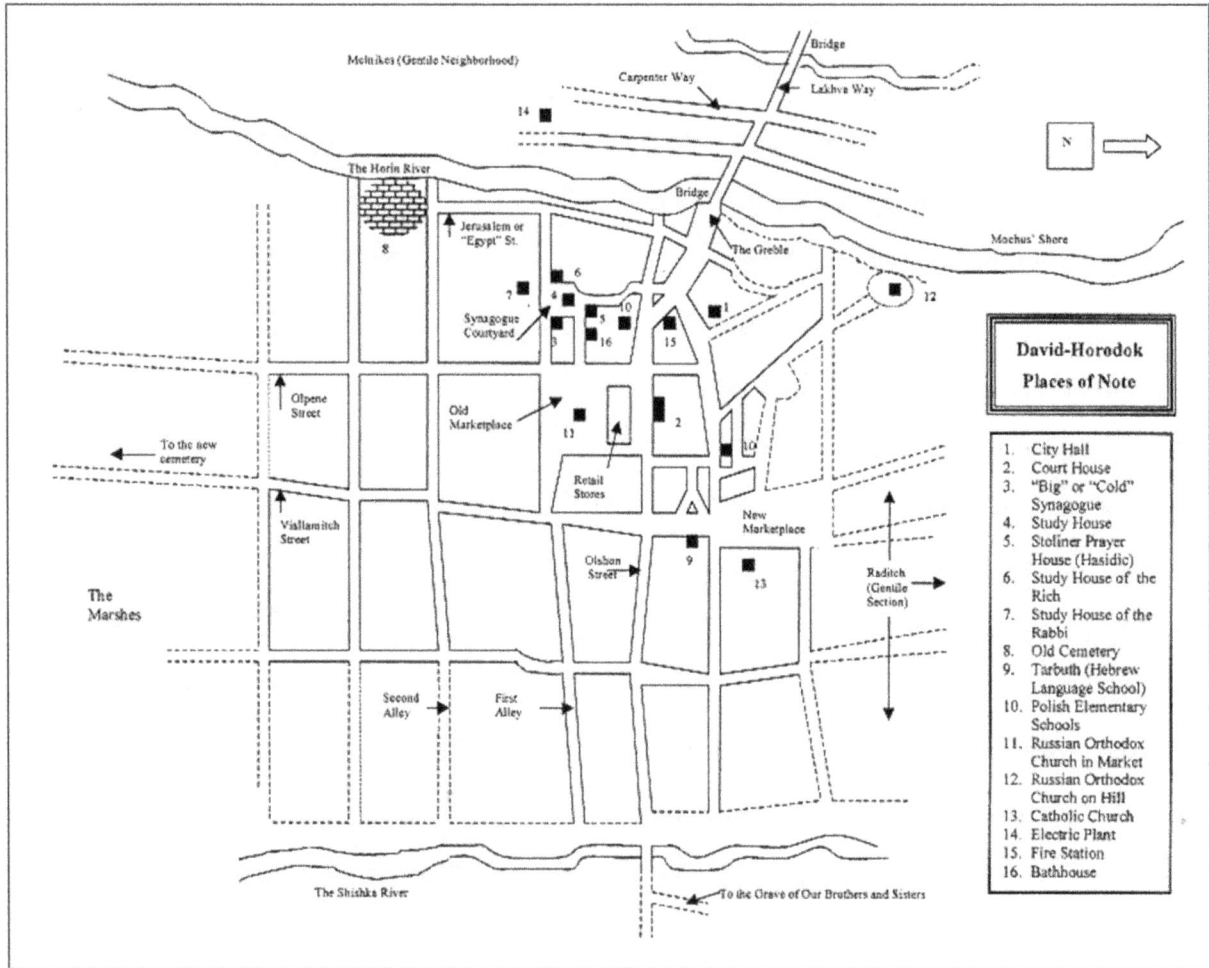

Uncaptioned. David-Horodok street map

[Page 3]

With the Book

Translated by Jerrold Landau

O that my head were waters,
And my eyes a fountain of tears,
That I might weep day and night
For the slain of the daughter of my people.

(Jeremiah 8:23)

… And as long as my heart beats
And as long as I do not know why and wherefore
The cause of all that was done –
I cannot forget
I do not want to forget…

David Shimoni (5707 – 1947)

[Page 5]

… And the blood shall pierce the depths
The blood of the murder shall leap
The blood of the child shall return to your cloak
And not be erased forever, forever…

(Ch. N. Bialik – On the Slaughter)

… And the sun shall turn into the stain of your innocent blood
The mark of Cain on the forehead of the world, the sign of failure
Of the broken arm of G-d…

(Ch. N. Bialik – I Knew on the Dark Night)

Introduction

Translated by Norman Helman z"l

In this book we are together with the holy memory of our dear David-Horodok sisters and brothers who were cruelly murdered by the Nazis.

Let this book serve as a holy permanent memorial for the lives that were cut off without mercy. At the same time, let this book be an unforgettable mark of Cain on the brows of those who, like wild beasts, spilled the innocent blood of men, women, children, the aged and the sick – peaceful and defenseless Jews.

* * *

In this book we have aimed an attempt to revive and relive the town's business and work activities as well as to give a picture of the effervescent and sparkling life in all its forms and in all its epochs.

Future generations will find in this book as well as in all memorial books a reflection of Jewish life in the Eastern European Diaspora in the period before the terrible Holocaust.

This book does not pretend to reflect the entire many-sided colorful Jewish life in David-Horodok. In fact, it contains only a small part of the original David-Horodok reality.

Our town was not uniquely different from all other Jewish towns in pre-war Poland but for those who were born in David-Horodok and for those who spent their youth and a great part of their lives there, this town is an inexhaustible source of unforgettable experiences, of memories and stories. What once was, is now gone forever.

* * *

We want to sufficiently emphasize that our town is one of the few communities whose chief murderers amongst the indigenous Byelorussian population, the *Horodtchukas*, were arrested and imprisoned thanks to the untiring and self-sacrificing efforts of our compatriot Aharon Dov Moravchik.

Fifteen years have passed since the tragic and horrible day of the 17th of Av. 5701, the day of the mass murder in our town. The wound has not healed nor will it ever be healed.

The only thing that we could do to perpetuate the memory of the martyrs was to write this memorial. Therefore, let this memorial send its heart-rending cry to the heavens for all generations.

This memorial book is a product of collective efforts of our survivors in Israel and the various countries of the Diaspora. The descriptions were written by Jews who never were and do not pretend to be writers. That is the special merit of this book which is an expression of unassuming simplicity.

Congratulations to all in Israel and elsewhere who wrote their recollections, gathered documents and photographs, devoted time, energy and effort, obtained the necessary funds and helped the editors fulfil the holy mission imposed on them.

The Editors

* * *

We extend our gratitude and acknowledge all those who helped us publish the memorial book to commemorate the martyrs of David-Horodok and vicinity.

1. The David-Horodok Women's Organization of Detroit and Mrs. Anna Grenadier Spielberg who was responsible for a large share of the group's accomplishments.
2. The David-Horodok Organization of New York and Mr. Yaakov Kitay who accomplished a great deal in gathering material and collecting money for the book.
3. Our friends Yitzchak Zeldin-Idan, Yosef Lifshitz and Yaakov Mor (Kopel Moravchik) who participated in writing, editing, translating and correcting the book.
4. All of those who devoted time and effort so that the book could be published.

Let this book be a source of contemplation, both in detail and in general for the entire surviving David-Horodoker family, both in sadness and in suffering.

Let this accomplishment, this book to commemorate the David-Horodoker martyrs, represent a permanent memorial until the last generation.

Committee for David-Horodok and Vicinity in Israel

[Page 7 - Hebrew] [Page 329 - Yiddish]

The History of David-Horodok

By Yosef Lifshitz

Text translated by Norman Helman z"l

Yiddish captions translated by Jerrold Landau

Coordinator's note: This article is repeated on pages 7-59 in the Hebrew section and on pages 329-401 in the Yiddish section. The text of the two articles is equivalent, but the illustrations in each section are different, except for one repeated photograph of the steamboat docking area in David-Horodok. Because the article was translated from Yiddish to English, the Yiddish pagination as well as the photographs and illustrations from that section have been given precedence. Illustrations from the Hebrew section are placed at the end of the equivalent subheading in the Yiddish section.

Foreword

I have been assigned the task to write a narrative history and give a picture of our town, David-Horodok in general and of its Jewish population in particular.

I am not a writer and certainly not a historian. I have no pretensions to either. Therefore, I do not know how successfully I can describe the historical facts correctly and in their proper order.

For this book, I have used the materials from *The YIVO Letters*, *History of the Lithuanian Jews* by S.A. Bershadski, *The Settling of Jews in Lithuania and Poland in the Past, Until the End of the Eighteenth Century* by I. Shipair and the anthology *One Thousand Years of Pinsk*.

Unfortunately, we were separated from the materials and archives which would have given us a more accurate and clearer picture of David-Horodok.

The history of the town in the last 70-80 years was derived from the recollections of our town elders, supported by my own memories and also from all those who could add and contribute something.

I have attempted, as much as possible, to report only facts and data, avoiding judgments. I have also attempted to verify these facts.

I am certain that this work is not an exhaustive one. Possibly certain important events will not be reflected in this work. It could be that certain moments should have been described in greater detail and others abridged. For these flaws, I beg the pardon of my dear readers and compatriots.

I have written this work with reverence and a trembling heart. I consider it my holy duty to perpetuate on paper the history of our town; how our ancestors lived for hundreds of years, built their homes, raised their families, practiced their customs and habits, experienced times of joy and sorrow, and finally, tragically perished along with the great majority of European Jewry at the blood-soaked hands of the murderous Nazis.

I believe that I would not commit the sin of local patriotism if I venture to say that David-Horodok was an unusual town, distinct from surrounding cities and towns.

It was a town in which the Jews were pious but not fanatic and were concerned with both Jewish and general education. The Jews were not ashamed to do any sort of work but they considered it a disgrace to be ignorant.

[Page 330 - Yiddish]

It was a town that was Zionistic throughout, with an organized and productive youth who studied and aspired to education and knowledge.

It was the only town in the entire Diaspora where, in the pre-war years, the youth spoke Hebrew exclusively between themselves, with adults and even with the gentile servants.

It was a town that possessed one of the best Tarbut [culture] Schools in Poland, many cultural institutions and organizations and libraries with avid readers. All public readings and lectures were presented at fully packed halls.

It is painful to write of all this in the past tense knowing that it has all disappeared and perished in such a tragic manner.

Therefore, my dear compatriots let me offer you this work as a small and modest memorial to our martyrs.

[Page 8 - Hebrew] [Page 330 - Yiddish]

The General History of David-Horodok

We have no clear idea as to when or how the town was established or when the Jewish community began. This chapter will deal with what little historical data is available, with the geography of the region and with the naming of the town as based on current evidence.

David-Horodok is in the heart of Polesye by the Horyn River, 10 kilometers before the Horyn spills into the Pripyat River. The Pripyat River is 570 kilometers long and it connects Volhynia with Polesye. As a result, Volhynia and Polesye are linked with Ukraine on one side and Lithuania on the other side.

Returning to the question as to when David-Horodok was founded, we must get help from the general history of Polesye which will enlighten us a little. The first historical reference to Polesye is in the year 988. *The Chronicles of Sidzdaler Farayaslov* describes the portion of Russia that was divided between the sons of Vladimir the Great. It says that one of his sons, Sviatopolk acquired Pinsk, Turov and their surrounding villages.

In 1005, a church center was established in Turov and vicinity. Pinsk was included in this Turov diocese.

In those days, all Russian towns were periodically attacked by the Tatars. In 1185, one such Tatar attack so completely destroyed Turov that it never regained its former eminence.

In 1240, the Tatars devastated the entire region to the east of the Horyn and the Pripyat. All of the inhabitants fled to the other side of the river and gathered mainly at Pinsk where Michael, Prince of Chernigov, concentrated the remnants of his army together with the Prince of Volhynia.

[Page 331- Yiddish]

The Tatars stayed in Polesye for a long period of time. They developed the area and they were responsible for the establishment of David-Horodok. They also built the hill by the riverside which served as a fortress. In later years, a Greek Orthodox Church was built on this hill.

That this was indeed an artificial hill was proven by excavations in 1936-37 which found a variety of implements and graves under the hill.

Uncaptioned. Written on photo: Dawidgródek

Where does the name David-Horodok come from? There are numerous legends. One says that it is the name of a duke's child, David. The second legend, a Polish one – that the Roman Ovidius was exiled to the region of the Black Sea and the town where he died was named after him. A third legend says that the name David is widespread among the Tatars and that they gave it the name David-Horodok.[1]

To this day, there is a remnant of the Tatar race amongst the inhabitants of David-Horodok who are called *Horodtchukas*. They are distinguished from the neighboring gentiles by their broad Tataric nose, their clear brown coloration and by their body-build.

[Page 332 - Yiddish]

David-Horodok was established and developed by the Tatars at the end of the 11th century or the beginning of the 12th century.

The first historical reference to David-Horodok is from the 14th century in regard to the treaty between the Crusaders and the Lithuanian Grand Duke Vytautas, who became recognized as the independent ruler of Lithuania. In the treaty papers, it mentions that Pinsk, David-Horodok and Ludmir [Volodimir Volinsk] were transferred from Vytautas to the Starodubian Duke, Sigismund Kastutovich.

This shows that in those days David-Horodok was an important town. From then on, David-Horodok was linked to the Pinsk duchy which in that time included all of Polesye.

In the 15th century, David-Horodok went over to Duke Yuri Semyonovich Olshansky who was the governor of the Lithuanian grand duchy for the Polish King Casimir Jagiellon.

After the death of Duke Yury, the governor of the grand duchy became Ivan Sviatoslavich and after his death, the Pinsk duchy reverted for a short time to the Polish crown.

In 1427, Duchess Maria became the ruler of the Pinsk duchy. She ruled with her son Vasily until 1495. After Vasily's death, his sister Yelena ruled with her husband Fyodor.

In 1521, Baron Fyodor died and the Pinsk duchy then went over to King Sigismund I. On October 8, 1523, this king gave his wife, Bona Sforza, the Pinsk region including Kletsk, David-Horodok and Rogatchev.

During the era of Bona Sforza, she developed Polesye. She brought in Polish colonists and gave them free land to settle. She cleaned out the rivers and dug canals. She levied a special tax on the inhabitants of Pinsk for the purpose of creating a permanent communication link between Pinsk, Nobel and David-Horodok.

In 1556, Queen Bona Sforza left Poland ending her rule over the Pinsk duchy.

The Polish king and the Lithuanian Grand-Duke Sigismund August took over the region abolished the Pinsk duchy which then became united with Chomsk, Zhavia and Broditza and they were annexed to the Lithuanian duchy.

1569 was a turning point in the affairs between Poland and Lithuania. In that year, during the reign of the Lublin National Assembly, a loose confederation was created between Poland and Lithuania. This union opened the doors for Polish immigration into Lithuania. Polish culture, especially the Catholic clergy, permeated the entire area. There was a two-fold purpose: to Polonize the Russian region and to convert them into the Roman Catholic faith.

With the support of the Roman Catholic King Sigismund III, the Catholic clergy took to their task with great fervor.

[Page 333 - Yiddish]

Nothing kept them from their work. They destroyed Greek Orthodox churches and monasteries. They let all the people know that as Roman Catholics they could do anything, but as Greek Orthodox, they would have no rest or safety.

In order to ease the conversion of the Greek Orthodox people to Catholicism, the so-called Uniate Church was created which was supposed to be a bridge between the two churches. The Uniates allowed the Greek Orthodox Church to use their own ceremonies, their own language and many of their own rites and most important, they recognized the Pope as the head of their church.

As an example that vividly illustrates the fight between the two churches, take the story of the marketplace and shops in David-Horodok. It is a fact that in the spot where the marketplace and its shops stood, there was once a Greek Orthodox cemetery. So how did there come to be a marketplace with shops? Who permitted this? It is only understandable within the context of the fight between the two churches; it being permitted through the Catholic authority in order to wipe out the traces of the Greek Orthodox property.

When the energetic priest Yuchnevich came to David-Horodok, he immediately began to repair the injustice which had been done to the Greek Orthodox Church and, in the middle of the marketplace, he built a church which stands to this day.

The Pravoslavic Church in the David-Horodok market square

[Page 334 - Yiddish]

The fight between the Greek Orthodox Church, one the one hand and the Roman Catholics on the other hand, was very bitter and it remained strongly ingrained in the memories of both sides.

We felt the remnants of this even in most recent times. After World War I, when David-Horodok had gone over to Poland, once again the Uniate was brought up which hadn't been heard of during the Czar's times. The Greek Orthodox priests began to feel less secure both in their rule over the masses and with their possessions. Quietly, the war between the churches resumed.

This was would have taken sharper forms had the Poles not been afraid that this would be oil for the wheels of the Communist propagandists in the vicinity. At this time, David-Horodok was 30 kilometers from the Polish-Soviet border.

Interesting to note that in the religious controversy between the Greek Orthodox and Catholic churches, the Jews quietly supported the latter.

The era of the Lublin Union brought great changes in Polesye in political, religious and economic life.

In 1648, there were great and bloody happenings in the region of Polesye. The Cossack uprising under the leadership of Bogdan Chmielnicki did not overlook Polesye.

The Polish Kingdom never had full control over its eastern provinces. The reasons for this are many and varied; for example: the character of the colonists that were brought there.

For the most part, those who came had left their homes for political, social or religious refuge; or they were seeking an easy livelihood or were simply criminals.

The rebels were not alone in their fight. They were joined by the oppressed peasant masses who wanted to throw off the yoke of the hated nobility. This rebellion was taken up in Polesye.

The years of the Cossack rebellion were inscribed with bloody letters in Jewish history. The years 1648 and 1649 were years of destruction and devastation for Eastern European Jewry.

There is no clear knowledge as to how the Jewish community of David-Horodok survived the destruction. There is, however, evidence that the David-Horodok community took a loan in order to rebuild the devastated town institutions.

Concerning this, there is some accurate information regarding the part played by the David-Horodoker Christians in the Cossack uprising. In the history of Pinsk, it is told that the greatest destruction occurred with the attack of the Cossacks, Tatars and the peasants from David-Horodok and Turov. Three times, it is told, Pinsk suffered from the Cossack uprising, but the greatest destruction occurred

[Page 335 - Yiddish]

when the David-Horodok Christians participated. The Jewish community in Pinsk was almost extinguished completely.

In 1707, the Swedes appeared in Polesye. However, because of difficulties with lines of communication, they did not stay very long in Polesye. They even began building bridges over the rivers but quickly stopped and left the area.

The elders of David-Horodok tell the following story: Once, three Swedish soldiers came to David-Horodok on patrol. They went into a whiskey distillery and began drinking from the huge casks that were standing there. One of them became so drunk that he fell into a cask of whiskey and drowned. The local people were afraid of the vengeance of the Swedish army and they hid in the surrounding forest for three months. The Swedes, however, did not come because they soon left Polesye altogether.

In 1793, Poland was divided a second time and David-Horodok remained part of Russia until 1920. From 1920 to September 1939, David-Horodok belonged to Poland. The Red Army entered David-Horodok on September 19, 1939. In July 1941, David-Horodok was taken by Hitler's armies and in 1944, David-Horodok was reunited with Russia.

View of the Horyn River in David-Horodok

[Page 8 - in the Hebrew section]

The church fire on the hill

[Page 10 - in the Hebrew section]

[Page 11 - Hebrew] [Page 335 - Yiddish]

The Christian Population

As previously mentioned, the David-Horodok Christians, the so-called *Horodtchukas*, were exceptional in all of Polesye.

The typical person from Polesye had a mild character, phlegmatic and pessimistic comportment. In contrast, the *Horodtchuk* was far from mild, feisty and energetic, more sturdily built and taller. The Christians of the nearby village of Olpen also had a reputation, having stemmed from Lithuanian forebears and never having assimilated with the surrounding people.

The narrow-mindedness and hatred that the *Horodtchukas* had for the surrounding peasants was no less than they had for the Jews. It is interesting to note that they never married outsiders. They went on business throughout the country but for marriage, they came home to David-Horodok. Because of this and for years, they did not assimilate and remained the direct descendants of the founders of David-Horodok with Cossack-Tatar blood flowing in their veins.

Their Cossack-Tatar heritage was also noted in the way they made a living. They were not farmers and had no desire for working the land. The gardens which their women worked were for personal use only. If there was any surplus, the wife would sell the produce at the market and the money would belong to her. In general, the *Horodtchukas*, with the exception of a small numbers of merchants and artisans, had no stable occupation.

[Page 336 - Yiddish]

They did everything. For the most part, their occupation depended on the season of the year.

They were fishermen. They were great experts in forestry. Winter they spent finishing wood products and in spring, they prepared and hauled the wood that they had worked on during the winter in the surrounding forests to the river banks. They were experts on water, good navigators of steamships, berlinas [river barges] and rafts which they would take from Danzig all the way to the other end of the Dnieper River.

In the last years prior to World War II, as the surrounding forests became smaller, they worked farther away. In David-Horodok, there were special brokers who interceded between the lumber dealers and the boatmen and they would assign the workers to the merchants.

They were good builders, painters, masons, shipbuilders of various sizes and especially good shoemakers. They were also skilled merchants.

Most of the *Horodtchukas* in spring would travel to fairs selling seeds; in summer they would sell ice cream throughout the land; in autumn they would deal in red berries, mushrooms and boots and in winter they were occupied at home with shoemaking.

It is noteworthy that they always avoided dealing with middlemen. In shoemaking, they would prepare their own raw material and in the worst case, they would purchase their materials from the first source. They would also go to the fairs throughout Poland to sell their own wares.

The same is true in the meat and wurst business. They went to the local villages to buy meat, prepared it themselves and sold it themselves. The *Horodtchukas* had the sausage business in all the larger train stations in Poland.

This was a specific people. They wandered throughout Russia before World War I and between the two wars, throughout Poland. Nowhere did they assimilate. One could recognize them anywhere because of their unique clothing, speech and mannerisms.

Since the time of Czarist Russia, they had a higher social-political status than the neighboring peasants and this enabled them to improve themselves somewhat. They were strongly given over to Czarist Russia and were called monarchists.

After the 1905 revolution, there was a Black Hundred organization founded. It was a reactionary terrorist group which had the responsibility of supporting the Czar against the revolution. They also established a strong and tight Black Hundred organization in David-Horodok and it existed until 1917. On a certain Sunday, they even attempted a pogrom. Thanks to the self-defense organization of the Jewish youth in particular, and the entire Jewish population in general, and also because of the opposition of

[Page 337 - Yiddish]

the magistrate, Ovchinnikov, who had business dealings with Jews, they came through with only a few wounded.

Their monarchist reputation remained with the *Horodtchukas* even after the 1917 revolution. A portrait of the Czar continued to hang in many houses. They were lukewarm to Kerensky's uprising and they were outspoken opponents of the Bolshevik Revolution.

At the first opportunity, they set up an armed resistance against the Red Army. At that time the Jews also helped and they paid dearly for it, as will be described in a later chapter. In the district headquarters of the Bolshevik authorities, the Christian people of David-Horodok were considered a counterrevolutionary element.

During the 20-year reign of the Polish power in David-Horodok (1920-1939), the status of the *Horodtchukas* strengthened, but this did not drive them to assimilation despite the fact that the Polish authorities did not allow them to open a Russian school and their children were compelled to learn in Polish schools. However, they kept their Byelorussian language and Greek Orthodox faith. They would teach their children the Russian alphabet in their homes. When the Bolsheviks returned to David-Horodok on September 19, 1939 they were met with the hateful looks and enmity of the *Horodtchukas*. With few exceptions, they did not become members of the Communist Party and did not take part in political life. They were very disappointed that instead of the nearby Nazi regime, the Bolsheviks had taken over.

Once more, as the Bolshevik regime became established and began requisitioning and nationalizing everything, their hate for the regime grew and they waited for Hitler even more. This was demonstrated at the election which occurred in western Beylorussia for the national assembly which was supposed to confirm the annexation of western Beylorussia to eastern Beylorussia. They threw slips into the ballot boxes with the following written on them: "Death to the Communists and Jews," "Down with the Bolsheviks" and "Long live Hitler."

More than once, they threatened the Jews that when Hitler would come, they would settle accounts with them.

They kept their word. In the beginning of July, 1941, when the Bolsheviks retreated from David-Horodok and Hitler's forces marched into town, the *Horodtchukas* were the first in all of Europe to assist the Germans in undertaking an aktion. On the 17th of Av, 5701, they murdered all of the men in the town.

The entire time of the German occupation, they served Hitler faithfully and they in turn enjoyed the full trust of the Nazi authorities.

When in 1944 the Red Army freed David-Horodok from the murderous Nazi occupation, they found not a single living Jew in the town. They also did not find any of the gentile leaders of the town. They had left with the retreating German army.

A Christian's home at the back of the town

[Page 12 - in the Hebrew section]

[Page 13 - Hebrew] [Page 338 - Yiddish]

The Jewish Community in David-Horodok

It is difficult to answer the question as to when the Jewish community of David-Horodok was founded. There is not a single remaining historical document that would clarify the question. The records of the community, even if they had survived, would not have enlightened us much because it was only 200 years old and there exists much prior knowledge of the Jewish community in David-Horodok.

To establish approximately when a Jewish community was founded in our vicinity, we must consult the history of the Jews of Lithuania and follow the settling of the Jewish communities.

In S.A. Bershadski's overview of *The History of Lithuanian Jewry* which was published in 1883 in St. Petersburg, and in Y. Schiffer's *History of the Jews of Poland Until the End of the 18th Century* published in 1914 in Moscow,[2] it shows that the years 1500-1550 were a period of growth for the Jewish community in Lithuania. In those days, many new communities were founded and the existing ones were expanded.

The stream of Jewish immigration was from west to east. Thus, the first Jewish communities were in the western part of Lithuania. It is clear that, for example, Grodno, Brisk, Lutsk and Volodimir Volinsk came before David-Horodok, Luninets, Stolin and others.

It should be noted that the community of Volodimir Volinsk was established in 1388 and David-Horodok, together with Volodimir Volinsk were part of the Starodubian duchy in those days. It is not definite that there was a Jewish community in David-Horodok at that time.

The immigration stream to Lithuania was even stronger at the beginning of the 16th century due to the flight of the Jews from Germany.

The new Jewish communities in Lithuania were founded in the following manner. Around each larger community, there would rise smaller settlements. In such fashion, the Jews pressed ever further into Lithuania. Jewish historians are of the opinion that if you look at a map of old Lithuania, you can pinpoint which Jewish settlements were older. The older settlements are in western Lithuania and the younger settlements are in eastern Lithuania.

In conclusion, we cannot reckon on an organized Jewish community in David-Horodok before there was one in Pinsk.

An organized Jewish community was created in Pinsk in 1506. That would mean that an organized Jewish community in David-Horodok came later. That does not rule out the possibility of some isolated Jews in David-Horodok before that time.

In those days, Jews would drive through the entire land on business. Besides this, they leased monopolies for whiskey making, salt merchandizing, inn keeping and tax collecting. It is possible, therefore, that in David-Horodok,

[Page 339 - Yiddish]

which certainly already existed since 1190, Jews lived there long before the establishment of an organized Jewish community.

The first accurate historical knowledge concerning the David-Horodok Jewish community is from 1667. In that year, the Pinsk community took a loan from the Lahishin Church for its own needs and for the needs of the surrounding communities. As collateral for the loan, they collected goods from the surrounding Jewish communities amongst which is mentioned David-Horodok.

This occurred after Bogdan Chmielnicki's uprising which destroyed the entire Jewish community of Eastern Europe. Those who had fled returned to their destroyed homes. The poverty and distress were great. Everything had to be set up anew and there was no available money broker. They, therefore, had to go to their gentile neighbors for help. The gentiles came to the Jews and loaned them money, not out of charitable feelings but rather out of pure commercial calculation. They made very good business from these loans. They took as guarantee the study-houses, the bathhouses and even the cemeteries. More than once, for not paying the interest on time, they would tear apart the study-house or not allow a burial in the cemetery.

Besides that, the law assured the rights of the lender. For not paying a debt, there were severe penalties, even death.

In the Lithuanian court records of those times, there are a great number of death sentences given to individuals, to groups and even to entire Jewish communities. This shows the great poverty of the Jewish communities in those times. In truth, the death sentences often remained on paper because there was a large gap between the handing out of a death sentence and its execution. The Polish authority in those days was riddled with anarchy. Its power to act was paralyzed and rebellion against the authorities was a daily occurrence. The Jews also did this but only as individuals. The community debts had to be paid.

· In the realm of these debts, there was great friction and controversy between the small communities and the large communities. They could never agree among themselves as to how much each community had to pay. There were religious court suits at the "Council of the Four Lands," and the disputes even resounded in the government courts.

This situation changed abruptly with the Cossack uprising. The prestige of the central government authority was greatly diminished. The hardship of the small towns was immense and they were in no position to contribute their share to the central communities since they didn't even have the ability to rebuild their own ruined communities.

Then the fight intensified between the small communities against the large communities with the purpose of getting rid of their guardianship. In the vicinity of Pinsk, the following communities began to fight: David-Horodok, Stolin, Slutsk, Turov, Chomsk and Drohitchin.

The controversy was prolonged and very severe. The central government stood on the side of the large communities

[Page 340 - Yiddish]

because it wanted to be paid in a centralized manner. The Lithuanian war minister gave an order that the military should aid the large communities in collecting taxes from recalcitrant small communities. However, the soldiers were of no help. The frequent religious court decisions were also of no avail because of the weakness of the central power which was caused by the separatist strivings of the Polish nobility and especially because of the new confederation adopted by the Central Assembly in 1764 which canceled the general tax on Jewish communities and replaced it with an individual tax of two gulden per head (beginning with one-year-old children. Thus, the large communities lost the battle and the small communities became independent.

Concerning the new tax system in Poland-Lithuania, there was a census taken of the Jewish people, giving us some idea of the number of Jews at that time. The census was taken in 1766 and here are the results (excluding children less than one year of age) in the following towns:

David-Horodok	408 people
Turov	316
Horodno	109
Stolin	408
Yanov	422
Drohitchin	510

We must accept these numbers with some reservation because, for purposes of taxation, the number is not entirely correct. Either the Jews gave smaller numbers in order to pay less tax or the officials gave larger numbers in order to collect more tax. To show that the tally was not correct, we can use the second census which was taken in 1784. The second census gives us a completely different picture:

David-Horodok	386
Turov	319
Horodno	47
Stolin	207
Yanov	261
Drohitchin	248

It is unlikely that the number of Jewish people in all the towns would decline in a span of 18 years. This is an indication of the incipient decline of the Polish Kingdom and the officials did not carry out their jobs carefully, not believing themselves in the usefulness of the census.

In general, the last years of the Polish reign were difficult for the Jews of Lithuania. The central authority was weak and demoralized; the taxes great; the local noblemen dominated, each in his own way; the Jewish communities tore at each other and rivalries arose between Jewish merchants. All of this impoverished the masses and the distress was great.

[Page 341 - Yiddish]

In that time, two things occurred that had a great influence on the lives of Lithuanian Jews. The first occurrence was of a general political character which had an indirect effect on the lives of Lithuanian Jews, namely that in 1793, Poland was divided a second time and the region went over to Russia. This brought a tremendous change in the economic and cultural life of the Jews in Lithuania. The second occurrence was of an internal nature and of religious Jewish significance: the founding of the Hassidic movement.

The Hassidic movement began to develop strongly at the end of the 18th century. It embraced great masses. It came as a result of the poverty of the Jewish masses on the one side and from the internal Jewish reaction from the other. This was also a protest against the severe hand of the community and the powerful.

The new Torah resonated in the hearts of the poor village Jews, tenant workers and merchants.

It is interesting that the Hassidic movement did not have a great influence in David-Horodok. David-Horodok was not affected by the nearness of Pinsk wherein Rabbi Levi Yitzchak (of Berdichev) resided for a while as well as the eminent Rabbi Aharon the Great, of blessed memory. Pinsk was the scene of a controversy between the Hassidim and the *Misnagdim* [rationalists.] David-Horodok did not participate in the controversy.

Stolin, Zhlobin and Dombrovitz came to help the Hassidim of Pinsk in the fight against Rabbi Avigdor who stood at the forefront of the battle against the Hassidim. They forbade Rabbi Avigdor to visit their communities. David-Horodok did not forbid him.

It seems that David-Horodok was strongly under the influence of the Vilna Gaon who stood at the head of the fight against the Hassidim. In David-Horodok, even in modern times, the religious would observe the anniversary of the death of the Vilna Gaon and many had his picture hanging in their homes.

In general, David-Horodok was greatly influenced by Lithuanian Jewry and the struggle concerning the rabbis was greater in David-Horodok than in all the surrounding towns.

From this, one should not conclude that there were no Hassidim at all in David-Horodok. There were also Hassidim there. Of the five study-houses in David-Horodok, one was Hassidic – the so-called *shtibel*. The relative number was not great and they did not have a great influence.

[Page 16 - Hebrew] [Page 342 - Yiddish]

The Economic Structure of Jewish David-Horodok

We have no certain knowledge of the economic structure of the David-Horodok Jews in the first years of the Jewish settlement there. In order to clarify the question, we must use the material of the surrounding towns and from the general economic structure of Lithuanian Jewry. We must remember that the Lithuanian government opened the gates for Jewish immigration from Germany, not out of humane feelings, but because this accorded with their policy which visualized in the Jewish immigration an element that would revitalize and activate the stagnant economy of the country.

They, therefore, gave the Jews many rights. Jews were considered free men (not royal servants such as the peasants) along with the nobility and the landowners. For killing or wounding a Jew, the penalty was death. One could not interfere with their prayers, call them to court or make them pay debts on the Sabbath. They were allowed to deal in whatever they wanted and they were free to move throughout Lithuania.

In old Lithuania, the government did not collect its own taxes. They gave the job to tax agents. Understandably, Jews were the tax agents.

In almost every town and village, Jews leased the following functions: collecting taxes, whiskey monopoly, beer and mead – both wholesale and retail, salt monopoly, the official weights, inns and toll booths.

This last one was a tax which each merchant had to pay before he could sell his goods. This tax was called mita. The merchants had to drive along the roads where the toll booths were. That was how the Jews of that era made a living. In all likelihood, this is also how the David-Horodok Jews subsisted.

David-Horodok Jews also had probably begun dealing in wooden articles such as joinery, material for ship building, potash and tar which were plentiful in the region.

Jews also took to farming and cattle raising. Until modern times, David-Horodok Jews were accustomed to keeping one or more cows. Jews also took up gardening.

Because of the strong restrictions by the ruling guilds as well as their strict religious character, there were no Jewish artisans in those days. It was only after the Cossack rebellion when a large part of the land was destroyed and that there was a great shortage of craftsmen did King John Casimir permit the Jews in 1669 to organize their own guild. Then, for the first time, the Jews who had been ruined by the Cossack rebellion began to learn crafts.

It should be mentioned that the standard of living was very low in those days. They were poorly clothed. Boots were only worn on the Sabbath and in winter. In summer, they went barefoot.

[Page 343 - Yiddish]

They would go through mud in sacks. The clothing was made of canvas. Meat was only eaten on the Sabbath and sometimes, not even then.

A Jewish home at the back of the town

[Page 17 - in the Hebrew section]

[Page 17 - Hebrew] [Page 343 - Yiddish]

Business in the 19ᵗʰ Century Until World War I

After the Napoleonic Wars there was an improvement in economic development for Polesye. Victorious Russia became the great power in Europe and began gradually rebuilding the land especially South Russia. Ukraine developed a great movement to build new colonies, a fleet of ships for the Black Sea and railroad lines. The nearest source of timber for all this construction was Polesye. A broad-based business developed with Ukraine. This, of course, affected David-Horodok which lay by the Horyn River and in the center of the forest region. In the second half of the 19ᵗʰ century, a merchant class developed in David-Horodok for lumber production as well as so-called watermen.

The David-Horodok lumber merchants were, with few exceptions, not wealthy but they and the so-called watermen together caused a marked improvement in the merchant business. Lumber dealing was not simple. It required much knowledge and skill. Buying the raw material required expert examination of the quality and making a precise calculation of how to work the wood, transportation, etc.

The watermen were referred to as berlinshetzkim because they used berlinas [river barges] as the chief means of transportation on the water. In bygone days, they used baidaks which were wide and heavy boats.

However, they were not very convenient and by the middle of the 19th century they were no longer in use. They were replaced by barges and berlinas.

The barges were usually open and had the following dimensions: 15-19 sazhen [one sazhen equals 7 feet] long; 7-8 arshins [one arshin equals 2⅓ feet] wide and 24-28 vyershok [one vyershok equals 1¾ inches] high. They carried a load of about 4-5,000 pood [1 pood equals about 36 pounds] that is 80 tons. The barges were mostly used for carrying firewood and boards.

The berlinas were covered and large: 17-20 sazhen long x 3 sazhen wide x 2 arshins high. They were divided into three or four sections in which they transported a variety of goods. Such a berlina required as many as 18 workers plus a captain.

In spring, they were mostly loaded with firewood or other wood material and went downstream as far as Kiev and in recent times, as far as Ekaterinoslav. A trip from David-Horodok to Kiev would take, in normal circumstances, two weeks. In the summer, the berlinas would work at the banks of the Dnieper for hauling various loads from one point to another.

In the fall, they would load up with a variety of food items from the rich Ukraine or with salt and go upstream to David-Horodok. The return trip

[Page 344 - Yiddish]

would take about 40 days. Not uncommonly, winter would come early and they would be forced to remain somewhere along the route. In such a case, they were understandably far from their source of income.

This was not an easy business. One was separated from home for 8-9 months of the year. One was dependent on weather conditions such as winds, water depth in the rivers, etc. The business required great skill and knowledge.

Until World War I, this business was a major source of income for the towns along the banks of the rivers. This was a multifaceted business with brokers, agents and warehouses.

The larger merchants bought the material and sold the products while smaller businessmen earned their income through transport.

In this regards, it is worth mentioning the Bregman family of David-Horodok which had, at the end of the 19th century, a large business. The Bregmans owned many of their own berlinas and from time to time would make deals with outsiders to transport merchandise for them. They had warehouses in many places. Later, they had their own steamship called the *Montefiore*. They had agents all along the way from Pinsk to Ekaterinoslav who would buy and sell for them, hire workers, procure food for the workers and also determine the prices of produce, sugar, salt, etc. They would also investigate the condition of wood reserves in Ukraine.

The Horyn [River]

[Page 345 - Yiddish]

This was a large firm with wide-ranging interests and thereby enjoying boundless credit and trust.

The water business created a shipbuilding industry in David-Horodok from which many Jews and Christians earned their livelihood.

The class of wood merchants and watermen had a strong effect on the development of the town and especially for the youth. The elders endeavored to give their children not only a Jewish education but also a broad secular education as was required for their businesses.

As a result of the extension and development of the water commerce and the lumber business in Polesye in general and in David-Horodok specifically, a Jewish community was founded in Nirtcha at the beginning of the 19th century.

Nirtcha is situated at the confluence of the Horyn and Pripyat Rivers and is 12 kilometers from David-Horodok. The water transportation between David-Horodok and Ukraine, between Pinsk and Ukraine, between Pinsk and David-Horodok as well as the water link on the return trips, had to pass this particular point. In those days, when business between Polesye and Ukraine began to develop and water was the cheapest and sole means of transportation, Nirtcha became important from a commercial point of view. It was a place that could give a large number of families sustenance.

Some of the Jews of Nirtcha in David-Horodok

[Page 346 - Yiddish]

Just after Napoleon's defeat in 1812, when Russia began to heal the wounds of war, when they began feverishly building and developing and when commerce began to develop, the Jewish community of Nirtcha was founded in those days.

It was a unique community. It was begun by the one family of Yossel Moravchik and in the scarcely 100 years of the existence of the Nirtcha community, it expanded and attained a population of 100 at the time of the dissolution of the Jewish community. These included sons and daughters, daughters-in-laws, sons-in-laws, grandchildren and great-grandchildren of the same Yossel Moravchik.

The Moravchiks ran a unique business in Nirtcha, employing both peasants and merchants. Their existence was based on horticulture which they worked themselves, fishing, raising cattle and especially dealing in lumber and wooden articles. They themselves would haul firewood by transport ships to Kiev. They would provide food for the workers on the steamships, rafts and berlinas. They also prepared food for travelers on passenger steamships.

The inhabitants of Nirtcha were examples of hardy and plain folks. They had daily contact with the Jews of David-Horodok and thanks to contact with a variety of business people, they were not ignorant villagers. They brought the very best teachers for the children who, incidentally, were quite willing to go there.

The land which they occupied and worked belonged to the Duke Radziwill. They paid him rent. As mentioned, the community of Nirtcha existed for almost 100 years. In 1906, the community was liquidated and all the inhabitants of Nirtcha moved to David-Horodok. The cause of the liquidation of the Jewish community of Nirtcha is as follows: Duke Radziwill chose this place to build a sawmill. He was certain that, at such an important transportation point, he would make a good business. The extraordinary efforts of the Nirtcha Jews to annul the decree were to no avail. They received compensation from the Duke and with great bitterness left the place where they had lived and earned a respectable livelihood for almost 100 years.

At first it was a great tragedy for these Jews. They had to start building anew in the town, seeking a means of existence. Later, they were very pleased with the change. They became involved in the town. They bought houses with the compensation money. In 1914 when World War I broke out, they would have had to flee anyway, out of necessity, and naturally without compensation.

The Duke had not made a good exchange because the sawmill did not develop and he had to close it.

Shops were an important part of David-Horodok life. Having

[Page 347 - Yiddish]

a Christian population which purchased everything it needed [the *Horodtchukas* were mostly merchants and laborers], and having a large number of surrounding villages, there was room for many shops in the town. In time, a large shopkeeper class developed in town. In truth, few became rich and without the help of the bank and credit unions, most would not have been able to exist.

The competition between the shops was considerable. In such a manner they persevered, more or less.

A corner in the new market in David-Horodok

Many families in David-Horodok earned a living in the meat business. The town was surrounded by farm country, many grassy meadows for pasture and the vicinity was rich in herds of cattle and oxen. The butchers of David-Horodok would buy these cows and oxen both for the town's needs as well as for export, especially to Warsaw.

Amongst the David-Horodok butchers were some bigger merchants who would travel to Ukraine, mainly in the Poltava region, purchase shipments of cattle and send them to Warsaw. It is of interest that these shipments along with their attendants went the entire way on foot.

This was a risky business because there were no standardized prices. The prices depended on the supply and the bidding of the Warsaw merchants. Not infrequently the profit on half the transport sold on a certain day would barely cover the loss on the sale of the second half of the transport on the following day.

The great majority of the butchers were not involved in business dealings. They earned their bread with great difficulty. Three to four days a week, they would go around

[Page 348 - Yiddish]

the local villages to try and buy something. Bringing it home was also not easy and selling it involved intense rivalry between the butchers and not infrequently an animal was found to be unclean.

The meat business brought much money and contributed greatly to the economy of the area, especially for the peasants. It also created the basis for the tanning industry which bought the great quantities of hides in the region. From the processed hides, the shoemakers of David-Horodok produced boots for the entire region.

The meat business also produced tallow which was used to manufacture soap and candles.

The fish industry was very important in David-Horodok. It was a source of income both for the Christians who were the fishermen and for the merchants. In this regards, it is noteworthy that the fish merchants did not bother with selling fish on the spot. The fish merchants would buy up the surplus of fish which the town was not capable of consuming and then sent it to Warsaw.

There were six or seven merchants who would bargain for the right to purchase fish from Radziwill's lakes. The Christians would catch the fish there and the Jewish merchants would send them to Warsaw. This was not an easy business but it was profitable.

In David-Horodok there were a large group of drivers who would go throughout the land with their wagons from David-Horodok to Pinsk, Minsk, Vilna, Brody and Odessa.

As in other towns, they were organized in David-Horodok into a "company" and they worked in partnerships. Along with other Polesye wagoners, they participated in the fast which they decreed at the opening of the Polesye railroad line in 1888.

Incidentally, it is important to emphasize that the development of the railroads bypassed David-Horodok. To this day, the town has no rail connection. The nearest train station is at Lakhva on one side, 25 kilometers from David-Horodok and on the other side of the Horyn - Stolin - over 30 kilometers from David-Horodok.

In 1898, a group of five drivers organized and purchased a small steamboat called *Vienna* which shuttled back and forth between David-Horodok and Nirtcha, delivering David-Horodok passengers to the large steamships that shuttled between Pinsk and Kiev. Not all the drivers were trustworthy enough for this business and most of them abandoned the partnership. The first years, the drivers who purchased the steamboat continued to work with horses in the winter. Gradually the business developed. They sent another steamboat to Stolin and Gorin and they completely abandoned their previous vocation. Later, Pinsk Jews joined the partnership and a steamboat link was established between Pinsk and David-Horodok.

World War I did not affect the steamboats and their owners and afterwards

[Page 349 - Yiddish]

when David-Horodok went over to Poland, they succeeded in returning the steamboats which were left in the Russian rivers.

After the war when Ukraine was shut-off due to the new Soviet-Polish border, the development possibilities became somewhat reduced and there remained only the transport routes of David-Horodok and

Stolin and David-Horodok and Pinsk. The existence of the steamboat owners was secured by these two routes.

After the World War, as automotive transportation developed, a larger group of wagoners organized, purchased an auto and began plying over the route between David-Horodok and Gorin. This time, however, the venture was unsuccessful.

The steamboat docking area in David-Horodok

[repeated on Page 21 - in the Hebrew section]

The two reasons for this were the rapid deterioration of the auto because of the poor Polesye roads and the huge taxes imposed by the government.

The David-Horodok wagoners were well organized. They were divided into two groups. One group, which worked in the town, transported the wares arriving on the steamboats to the businesses and warehouses, and the second group would travel to the train stations at Lakhva and Stolin and in the winter, they would also travel to Pinsk. They all worked in partnership and they would divide their earnings each week.

It was not an easy way to earn a living but, with a few exceptions, it was a respectable trade and a few of them were well-to-do.

* * *

[Page 22 - Hebrew] [Page 350 - Yiddish]

Craftsmen

David-Horodok was a town with many craftsmen who worked independently. There was no special item produced that was characteristic of David-Horodok. However, having a population of 10,000 and many surrounding villages, there was room for a variety of tradesmen who earned a respectable livelihood working for the populace.

The major trades of the David-Horodok craftsmen were as follows:

Tailors who were divided into two categories: those who worked for the Christian population on order or prepared finished products for shipment to the fairs in the town and nearby villages; and those who fashioned finer things for the Jewish population.

Shoemakers worked only for the Jews and for a few Christians. The Christian populace was provided with boots chiefly by Christian shoemakers who sold their products not only to the local Christians but also throughout the entire land.

Blacksmiths and locksmiths worked mainly for the peasant farmers. They would repair wagons, forge ploughs and axes and make a variety of other tools for construction work in the town.

The greatest number of craftsmen were in construction work. These were: architects, carpenters, bricklayers, glaziers, painters and roofers.

Jews also found work in shipbuilding. However, the majority of shipbuilders were Christian.

There were a few who had two trades: one in summer and one in winter. These were the trades in David-Horodok until the outbreak of World War I.

There were a number of strata amongst the tradesmen. There were some who were quite well-to-do, others who barely had enough to exist and the great majority who led a modest but secure and respectable living.

[Page 22 - Hebrew] [Page 350 - Yiddish]

The Villages Around David-Horodok

David-Horodok was surrounded by many villages populated by Jews until World War I. These Jews existed from working and dealing with the local peasant populace. It is not certain how long these villages were in existence. We have historical knowledge concerning only two of these villages, that is: Olshan which was founded by Duke Yuri Olshanski who ruled in Pinsk from 1447-1492 and Olpen which was named after a Lithuanian boyar [aristocratic landowner] who ruled in Polesye in 1341.

Jews began to settle in these villages after the freeing of the peasants. In general, the village Jews led an unassuming life. Their

[Page 351 - Yiddish]

living standards were not much higher than the local peasant populace. The Jews' main concern was to satisfy the religious and educational needs of their children. Even with the smallest number of families, the village Jews would make every effort to keep a teacher for the children.

Some sent their children to learn in town. For a time before the outbreak of World War I, the number of Jews in the villages began to diminish. The youth did not want to remain in the village. They were impressed by the town. The outbreak of World War I accelerated the tempo of migration of Jews from village to town.

The Jewish population was completely dissolved in the following villages: Nirtcha, Chovorsk, Holatz, Liadetz, Bekaisk, Great-Orly [Bolshiye Orly] and Vialamitch [Velemichi]. Jews remained in the following villages: Olshan, Remel, Choromsk, Lesser-Orly [Malye Orly], Samihostitch [Semigostichi], Tarablitch

[Tereblichi], Azdamitch [Ozdanichi], Malishev, Karatitch [Korotichi], Talmatchav [Tolmachevo], Ludka, Kalk and Chrapun. Understandably, their number was somewhat diminished after World War I.

There was hardly any change in the number of Jews in Olpen which was considered a suburb of David-Horodok. The village Rubel had a Jewish population like that of a small town. Just before World War I, there were 80 families with a rabbi and two study-houses.

There was an organized and Zionistic youth movement. *Hechalutz* [The Pioneer] was very strong and the first *Hechalutz* convention in Polesye was held in Rubel in 1924. The youth, seeing no future in the village, began to leave. The largest number made *aliya* to the Land of Israel. Thanks to this, there is now in Israel a reasonably large number of Rubel Jews.

* * *

The above description of the economic structure of David-Horodok until World War I shows us that the town did not have any really wealthy men among the merchants or any really poor among the laborers. In general, living standards were not high and their demands not very great.

Summer in the town was quiet. The majority of the Christians were occupied in the fields and the Jewish merchants were on the rivers. The tradesmen would work in the villages. In such a manner, the town was at a standstill in the summer.

In the fall, things began to liven up. The fairs would begin. The peasants would bring their surplus produce into the town and purchase their needs for the winter. The berlinas would arrive from Ukraine with flour, salt and a variety of food articles which they sold in and around the town. The lumber merchants and watermen would arrive in order to confirm the arrangements of prior years and to acquire new business. The Christian people would also come before winter and buy supplies. Winter was for them the season of marriage. All of this revived the town and its business. If

[Page 352 - Yiddish]

the winter was normal and the byways (both water and land) established in the right time, the lumber industry would be strongly revived and it was a great source of income for the town.

That is the way David-Horodok carried on a normal existence until the outbreak of World War I which shook up the well-established living patterns.

[Page 23 - Hebrew] [Page 352 - Yiddish]

David-Horodok in the Years of World War I

The outbreak of World War I had an unusually severe effect on the town. The mobilization which called up a large part of the population, the cry of those families separated by the mobilization, the new martial laws, and the requisitioning of numerous wagons and horses for the war needs were all indications that it was taking on an ominous character. "Experts" were predicting that the war would not last more than two or three months, but everyone was nevertheless upset.

The effect was particularly oppressive because, since the times of Chmielnicki, the town could remember no war. The Swedish bypassed David-Horodok. Napoleon's armies never saw David-Horodok, people in the town scarcely heard of the Russo-Turkish War and the same is true in the time of the Russo-Japanese War.

At first, after those mobilized had gone off for military training, the town did not feel the effect of war so strongly. Only later when the Russians had begun wreaking destruction on the Galician front was the entire horror of war felt.

The head commander, Nikolai Nikolaevich, gave an order that the Jews in the districts of Suwalki, Lublin and Chelm must leave their homes in 24 hours. Hungry, worn and unfortunate refugees fled through David-Horodok. Looking on helplessly at the Jewish refugees had a shocking effect on the David-Horodok Jews. Understandably, an assistance committee was immediately organized and the entire Jewish population received the refugees wholeheartedly. They accommodated them in schools and private houses and provided them with clothing and food.

At the same time, evacuated Germans began passing through David-Horodok from the region of Volhyn. These had been driven back by military force. They came to David-Horodok with their own wagons and from there, they took boats on the river deeper into Russia. Waiting for the boats, they loitered on the banks of the river in the town. This resulted in epidemics of disease which spread to the townspeople.

People began to show up who were fleeing from Brisk and Pinsk. Some David-Horodok Jews began looking around for evacuation routes. The Slonimer Rebbe and a few other families actually left. Many families bought horses and wagons

[Page 353 - Yiddish]

from retreating Germans and prepared for departure. Others drove to Pinsk with the purposeful intention of staying with the Germans so as to avoid being mobilized into the military.

The front came even closer. Panic increased. Cossacks appeared in the town. They took down the bells from the churches so that they wouldn't fall into the hands of the Germans. At night, cannon shelling could be heard. However, the Germans, having taken Pinsk on September 16, 1916, stayed there. Subsequently, almost a month passed and the front had not moved. As the fall rains and mud came, they began to realize in David-Horodok that the front would not move during the winter and they gradually began to adjust to the situation.

This was not greeted happily by the David-Horodok evacuees. These Jews who had bought horses and wagons from the German refugees in order to have something to evacuate with, sold them back. They became accustomed to the nearness of the front. The presence of military garrisons in the town gave a fresh source of income. They had profitable dealings with them and the economic situation improved considerably.

This situation continued for over a year until early 1917 when the Kerensky revolution broke out.

* * *

Even the remote areas far from the center of David-Horodok felt the new refreshing winds that began blowing in distant Petersburg. From mouth-to-mouth, in the stillness and with eyes gleaming expectantly, rumors were spread that the hated Czarist regime was toppling. Jews silently prayed that it should be true. Then came the information that some duke had poisoned Rasputin in Petersburg and that the royal court was turbulent. One waited from day-to-day for fresh news. No one yet believed that the dream would come true. Was it possible that Czarism that had been entrenched for hundreds of years could come apart? Was this not an empty dream?

Then came surprising news. The uncensored Russian newspaper which came to town reported that Czar Nikolai had abdicated his throne in favor of his son.

It was not believed. One was afraid to talk of it aloud for fear that it might turn out to be a lie. Then something happened in town which showed everyone that the previous information was correct. The royal representative in town, Ovchinnikov, went out into the marketplace and, in front of everyone, tore off the epaulets from his uniform.

It is impossible to describe the great joy that encompassed all of Russia. Understandably, the rejoicing was even more among the Jews who freely opened the gates of their towns and offices to all citizens. The first honeymoon of the Russian Revolution in the beginning of 1917 gave reason

[Page 354 - Yiddish]

to believe that they were standing on the threshold of a new epoch of equality, friendship and brotherliness between the common people and the landowners and that, under the wings of this revolution, there could freely develop in greater Russia the economies and cultures of the numerous national minorities.

There was a great enthusiasm and tremendous rejoicing as they waited to celebrate the international workers holiday - May 1 in David-Horodok.

[Page 24 - Hebrew] [Page 354 - Yiddish]

May 1, 1917 in David-Horodok

The preparations for the holiday were in full swing. A first of May committee was established jointly between the Jews and the Christians. A special delegation was sent out to the Hussar cavalry regiment which was stationed not far from David-Horodok, in order to invite them with their orchestra for the holiday.

The plan envisioned that the orchestra would play *La Marseillaise* and *Hatikvah* at the celebration. However, it turned out that the orchestra did not have the music for either of the two hymns. The musician, Velvel Karpel Hlerchiks came to the rescue. He wrote out the notes for *Hatikvah*. Thanks to the help of the old 1905 revolutionaries, the notes of *La Marseillaise* were also put together. In truth, that which the orchestra then played was not very similar to *La Marseillaise*. However, the proper feeling was there and everyone understood that it was supposed to be *La Marseillaise*.

The day of the first of May was a full holiday in town and everyone participated.

The first demonstration occurred in church. Jews, who would usually pass the hill on which the church stood with a certain anxiety, went inside freely with red flags. There the ceremony was led by a Christian, Misha Tukin. Thanks to the revolution, he was freed from prison where he was serving a fifteen-year term.

On leaving the church, a small incident occurred. An old peasant woman stood on the small bridge leading to the church and screamed, "Enjoy yourselves; enjoy yourselves as you will yet seek and beg our father Nikolai that he come and restore order for you." Needless to say, they quickly took her away and had a good laugh.

From the church, they went on to the synagogue. There the demonstration encountered Rabbi Rabinsky with Torah scrolls. He invited the general and the officers inside. The orchestra played *La Marseillaise* and *Hatikvah*. The rabbi gave a sermon and pledged, among other things and in the name of the Jewish people, that together with all the peoples of Russia, they would wage war against the outside enemy until final victory. He added that all youth who had not volunteered to serve in the military of Nikolai's regime would now willingly go into the army.

After the street demonstration there followed a reception for the officers. They

[Page 355 - Yiddish]

prepared lunch and, after eating, there was dancing to the sound of the military orchestra.

For the first time in the history of David-Horodok, Jewish girls danced with Russian officers.

In the evening there was a solemn convocation. In the name of the Jews, Anshel Zaitshik appeared. He was not a David-Horodoker but he happened to be there as a guest of his relatives. He gave an inspired talk concerning the great friendship and brotherliness between the peoples which the revolution had engendered. He then kissed the gentile Yosif Onoshko who stood next to him. This made a tremendous impression on all the onlookers. Many people wept with joy.

May 1, 1917 was the happiest day in the entire history for the Jewish community of David-Horodok. The dream was being realized that "the wolf would dwell with the lamb" - actually the time of the Messiah.

Who would have believed then that 25 years later, in the early autumn of 1941, the same Yosif Onoshko and all the *Horodtchukas* who were onlookers at that meeting would take sadistic joy and pleasure in sending to the slaughter their Jewish neighbors with whom they had lived for hundreds of years?

* * *

In those days there was a strong development of Zionistic and communal activities in David-Horodok. This will be described in another chapter. It should be mentioned that economic conditions had improved somewhat. Jews could move about freely and there were no job shortages.

The honeymoon of the revolution quickly passed and gray reality arrived. The front had not moved. The war had become sickening and ugly. All of Kerensky's offensives had failed. The people were tired and wanted no more war. The army was becoming increasingly demoralized. Soldiers appeared in town and began selling revolvers, rifles and even machine guns. The Bolsheviks drove out the Constituent Assembly and seized power.

The situation in the town became unstable. There was no firm power in David-Horodok and, in the meantime, everything was done by the system of the prior regime.

In the autumn of 1918, the Germans entered the town. They united David-Horodok to Ukraine. This did not cause any significant change in the economy of David-Horodok because the town was already economically bound to Kiev and Ukraine. They felt a little more secure with the Germans and they began to do business with them making some good deals. The German rule over David-Horodok did not last long. A revolution had broken out in Germany and the German military began to leave Ukraine.

In Ukraine there appeared Petlyura and his bands and

[Page 356 - Yiddish]

pogroms began against the Jews. However, the Petlyurians bypassed David-Horodok. Indeed, one day a group of Dombrovitz gentiles, who called themselves Petlyurians, showed up in town but then they quickly left.

The town remained without governing authority. Train transport became irregular and dangerous. Many David-Horodokers were stranded in various Ukrainian towns and were unable to return home. All business came to a standstill and there was no available work.

Lakhva, on one side, was occupied by the Germans. Stolin on the other side was occupied by the Petlyurians. Only David-Horodok was without a government. The town affairs were managed at the municipal court with the aid of several policemen.

It should be noted that there were no assaults or thefts in the town. The municipal affairs were concerned with straightening out land disputes between the peasants, recording land sales, giving out birth certificates, marriage contracts or divorce decrees for the Christians. The Jews took care of all these formalities with the rabbi.

Characteristic of the times was an original punishment which the court authority of those days imposed on a David-Horodoker Jew named Berl Eisenberg for not obeying the law. They caught him driving illegal whiskey. In those unsettled times even that law was obeyed in David-Horodok. The punishment was as follows: They hung the kettles in which he distilled the whiskey on his shoulders and a town gentile named Adam Pavuk went in front beating on a drum as they led him through all the streets of the town to the laughter of all the residents.

In this manner, the town led a quiet existence, a calm island in a stormy sea of war. The affairs between Jews and Christians in the town were peaceful and normal.

This calm did not last long. The Bolshevik military forces captured Lakhva and Luninets and then something occurred that shocked and interrupted the idyll of David-Horodok. The leaders of the town, both Christian and Jewish, then made a blunder for which the town paid dearly both in human and material sacrifices.

Teachers of the first Tarbut School in David-Horodok 1917-1918

Seated right to left: 1. *Unknown* 2. Yosef Begun
Standing: 1. Yehuda Kashtan 2. Avraham Durchin

[Page 25 - in the Hebrew section]

[Page 27 - Hebrew] [Page 356 - Yiddish]

The Punishment Expedition

The Bolshevik military detachment in Luninets sent out a group of soldiers into the surrounding area to requisition food for the troops. They also came to David-Horodok. In Visoka, 4 kilometers from David-Horodok, there were herds of cattle belonging to the landlords which the Bolsheviks wanted to requisition. Until today, it is impossible to understand what provoked the *Horodtchukas* to set up

[Page 357 - Yiddish]

resistance against the Bolsheviks and, even more unbelievable, why the Jews then stood alongside the resistance.

It is, however, a fact that they organized a defense. They went to the priest and convinced him that he should ring the church bells and persuade the gentiles to join the resistance and not allow the removal of the cattle herds from the town.

The rationale for the resistance was as follows: if they would allow the removal of the landlord's cattle today, then tomorrow, private cattle would also be taken.

The Jews, and especially the youth, helped organize the resistance. With joint effort, they actually succeeded in their opposition and prevented the removal of the cattle. Some shots were exchanged by the two sides and, as a result, one of the Christian members of the Revkom [revolutionary committee] was killed and one soldier was wounded.

They foresaw that the Bolshevik military power would react on learning the events. There was a warlike mood. They removed the bridge on the road to Chovorsk, erected barricades and then waited for the enemy. At the same time, they sent a delegation to Stolin where the Petlyurians were stationed and asked them for help. However, the Petlyurians could give no help since they themselves were preparing to retreat.

The author of this chapter and his brother were in Luninets at the time, running a restaurant. They were acquainted with the staff that had sent the squad of soldiers to requisition the cattle. The staff knew that the brothers were from David-Horodok and they came to inquire as to what sort of town it was.

They could not understand what reason the Jews had to oppose the Bolsheviks. In those days it really was madness. Indeed, the Bolsheviks had ruined the economy of the Jewish middle class, but they were also the only ones who fought against anti-Semitism and against all the gangs that carried out anti-Jewish pogroms. In those days, there were thousands of Jews who joined the Red Army in order to fight against these gangs.

The staff in Luninets was manned by some very competent students from Great Russia who had no feelings of anti-Semitism. There were also Jews on the staff. Thanks to these Jews, the town came out reasonably well. Under the circumstances, there could have been many more casualties.

They sent a strong disciplinary detachment of soldiers with cannons to David-Horodok. Understandably, the town quickly surrendered and the youth fled. The punitive expedition entered the city. The soldiers were given free rein to take anything they wanted except, naturally, not to lay hands on the people. That was the exclusive right of the commandant and the political commissar who happened to be a Jew.

Three David-Horodoker residents were executed by the punitive expedition in proportion to the population – two Christians and one Jew, Betzel Yudovitz. Besides this, they emptied out the town. They took out

[Page 358 - Yiddish]

everything that was movable. At that time there were large food reserves in town that had been brought in from Ukraine over the summer. This was all requisitioned. They even took good shoes right off people's feet. The David-Horodoker people were forced to take all their requisitioned things themselves to the trains at Lakhva and Luninets.

The destruction was great especially the needless sacrifice of B. Yudovitz who was a well-known personage, the victim of a foolish and poorly conceived action which was not in the interest of the Jews.

The death sentence was carried out in the Christian cemetery and that is where they buried B. Yudovitz. A few weeks later, in Luninets, the author extracted permission from the military to bury the martyr in a Jewish cemetery.

This is how David-Horodok paid for trying to resist the authorities. After this episode, the town was put on the blacklist of the Bolsheviks and the *Horodtchukas* became the deadly enemies of the Bolshevik regime.

The Bolshevik authority was strengthened in the region. However, the economic situation deteriorated. The town was impoverished. There were no business opportunities and no work. People began to suffer from hunger. They went out to the villages to swap clothing for food. The peasants would accept only gold as currency. A pood of grain was acquired with the greatest of difficulty.

At that time, they began to organize cooperatives. They acquired parcels of land and they planted it themselves with rye and potatoes. There was no lack of land.

The Bolshevik authority then declared a mobilization. It was rumored that the Poles were not far away and, therefore, no one wanted to be far from home. In order not to go into the military one could volunteer for forest labor in Sankovitz. This work freed one from military service. Hundreds of David-Horodoker youth volunteered for this work in which they produced firewood for the trains.

However, in one month, the Bolsheviks evacuated and the Poles entered David-Horodok.

[Page 28 - Hebrew] [Page 358 - Yiddish]

1920-1921. David-Horodok Passes From Hand-to-Hand

With feelings of dread and fear, the David-Horodok Jews received the Poles. Rumors regarding the behavior of the Polish military, particularly the *Hallerczykes* [General Józef Haller's soldiers] towards the Jews and the prior reports of a pogrom in Lvov, gave them reason to be very worried. The sad and shocking news arrived that the Poles had, without reason, shot 35 innocent young Jews in Pinsk. Even though under the Bolsheviks life was very difficult and they were half-starved, they looked toward their new future with dread.

The Poles entered David-Horodok. The Jews could barely look up at them. The regime of the town was very harsh. First of all,

[Page 359 - Yiddish]

they condemned to death a Jew named Krapivka who was the head of the town's professional union under the Bolsheviks. People were seized for forced labor. Organizational and Zionist activities ceased. Fear enveloped the entire town.

A little later, the regime became somewhat milder. They had begun to receive protests from America regarding the persecution of Jews. Morgenthau came to Pinsk on a fact-finding mission and an investigating commission arrived. The persecution diminished for a while.

David-Horodokers began to accustom themselves to the new life. The frontier was more distant – as far as Kiev. It became possible to communicate with Pinsk. They slowly began to do business. The chief item of trade was salt. With this item, they determined the worth of all other articles of trade. One pood of salt was exchanged for three poods of rye.

A link was established with America. Delegates came with help. The Joint became active. An American committee was formed which distributed goods and clothing to the poor. Prior to Passover, the committee received flour for making matzo and the matzo was then distributed to the people.

The schools were opened. Organizational life began to develop. An orphanage was established. However, this did not last for long. In the early summer of 1921, the air was once again filled with gunpowder. The Poles suffered a stunning defeat near Kiev and began a rapid retreat.

Then began nightmare-filled days for the Jews of David-Horodok. Day and night, for two consecutive weeks, retreating groups of Polish soldiers passed through the town. People were afraid to go into the street. Eventually, the Poles burnt down the bridge and were left on the other side of the river. That was the worst day. In the course of that day, the Polish soldiers would cross over the river to loot the houses. Things finally quietened down at nightfall. The Bolsheviks had arrived at the outskirts of town and they entered David-Horodok the following morning.

The Jewish population greeted the new authority with mixed feelings. On the one hand they were glad to be rid of the Polish authority which had revealed its anti-Semitic character in the short span of its rule. They were particularly pleased that the tension of the past month had finally ended. However, on the other hand, the advent of the Red Army meant that David-Horodok was now cut off from the rest of the world. The link to America was broken and the way was blocked to the Land of Israel where many of the youth had planned to immigrate.

Food provisions which had been sufficient under the Polish rule seemed to disappear overnight. The situation became difficult. Business came to a standstill and there was no work available. Authority was in military hands. They began organizing

[Page 360 - Yiddish]

cooperatives but, in the meantime, most of the time was spent in meetings, assemblies and concerts. What would they say in David-Horodok? "They are poor and happy."

However, before long and before one could look around, there came news of the Red Army defeat near Warsaw. Things again became unsettled. The Red Army began a rapid retreat. There was tremendous chaos.

The Jewish populace became terrified when they heard that among the first detachments of the advancing Polish army were the Balachowiczes. This was a Russian military group from the White Army under the leadership of General Bulak-Balachowicz which fought alongside the Polish military against the Red Army.

Retreating with Polish military from Kiev, they became infamous for the terrible massacres which they committed on the Jewish population of Volhyn.

The Bolsheviks retreated from David-Horodok during the intermediate days of Sukkot 1921 and a detachment of Bulak-Balachowicz's troops entered the town on the night of Hoshana Rabba.

There was great terror. The youngsters and particularly the women hid themselves and no one wanted to go out in the street. A few of the bolder ones who tried to go outside quickly returned indoors terrified. The Balachowiczes were adorned with plumed hats embroidered with death's-heads, and they ran about the streets like greedy beasts. The first ones to be assaulted were Rabbi Dovidl and Motel, the shopkeeper who had gone early Shemini Atzeret morning to pray at the synagogue. Afterwards they began to pillage the houses and beat up the Jews.

By noon, a larger number of troops had arrived in town and they were quartered in Jewish homes. The Jews catered to them hoping that they would prevent the other soldiers from entering and looting them. In many houses this was the case. There were other homes, however, where the soldier would initially look around to see what was in the house and, on departure, he would either himself or send other soldiers to remove all the valuables.

The last night that they were in town before going to the front was particularly severe. There were many casualties that night. Several women were raped and many Jewish homes pillaged.

The few weeks with the Balachowiczes in town were a terrible nightmare for the Jewish populace. They tried to associate themselves with the Polish military authority but the few Polish officers in town would either not help or could not help.

In those weeks the situation would change from time to time. Several times military detachments passed through David-Horodok who were former Red Army soldiers that had been captured by the Poles. They had willingly enlisted in Balachowicz's army for the sole purpose of returning home. These detachments were well behaved.

[Page 361 - Yiddish]

The staff of Balachowicz's army with Bulak-Balachowicz at the head passed through David-Horodok. When the David-Horodoker Jews complained to him about the behavior of his soldiers, he replied that he had ordered that civilians should not be harmed but that he could not be held responsible in this town where there were many Jewish Communists who were the foes of the soldiers.

When the last remnants of Balachowicz's army left town and the Polish troops were supposed to enter, they thought that the nightmare was over. Unfortunately, it was destined that the David-Horodoker Jews would have to endure a death threat which they would commute by paying a large ransom.

When the last of Balachowicz's army left David-Horodok, a small detachment of their cavalry returned, rode over to Rabbi Rabinsky and arrested him along with several more Jews. They demanded a payment of 100,000 rubles within two hours. If not, they would shoot everyone. The rabbi was freed so that he could collect the money and valuables.

It was horrible to see how the rabbi had to go over the streets with two sacks hanging from either side and pleading with tears that everyone should give as much as he could. The Jews began bringing golden rings, chains, watches and whatever they had. With this, they were ransomed from the hands of the bandits.

The David-Horodoker Jews later experienced a special boost in their morale. The Balachowiczes, having advanced further, suffered a defeat and were forced to retreat. However, at that time, the Riga peace treaty was signed and the Polish-Soviet border was established between Turov and David-Horodok. At the border, the Poles disarmed the retreating Balachowiczes. Without weapons they passed through David-Horodok on the way to the concentration camps. The Jews went out into the streets especially to laugh and mock at those bandits.

With that, ended the sorrowful chapter of that gang which had caused hundreds of Jewish casualties and had economically ruined thousands of Jewish families.

[Page 30 - Hebrew] [Page 361 - Yiddish]

Under Polish Rule (1921-1939)

After the Riga treaty, David-Horodok was situated within the borders of Poland. The border passed through the town of Malishev, 20 kilometers from town. The economic situation was very difficult. The town had been pillaged by the Balachowiczes and had been impoverished by the war. The Poles instituted a severe martial law in the town. No one was allowed on the streets after eight o'clock in the evening. It was forbidden to leave town without a special permit. Because of the newness of the border, the movements of the people were restricted. The town had been torn away from Ukraine with which it was economically bound. Because of the conditions of martial law, it was difficult to adapt to the new life.

[Page 362 - Yiddish]

After about half a year, the regime became more lenient and life became somewhat easier. They could move more freely and it was easier to get about. The Joint began its relief activities. Delegates came from America who, among other things, brought help from American relatives for David-Horodoker inhabitants. They also helped in the immigration process for those families whose fathers and husbands had already preceded them to America.

There began a great stream of immigration. After surviving the horrors of the war, they did not want to remain in David-Horodok. At first, the immigration stream went to America. Afterwards, when it was more difficult to get into America, they went to Canada, Cuba and Argentina. They went wherever they were allowed. A pioneer group was also formed to immigrate to the Land of Israel. However, because of the events in the Land of Israel in 1921, *aliya* was halted and the group remained in David-Horodok.

The economic situation gradually began to improve. The Polish mark became devaluated and goods became more expensive from day to day. Almost everyone began business dealings, shops grew like mushrooms after a rain. They began to earn "millions."

This is how things were until there was stabilization of the Polish currency. The worthless marks could not be exchanged for full-valued Polish zlotys. The orgy was over. All the new merchants were forced out of business and it became difficult to earn a groschen. To this was added the well-known tax system of the then Polish finance minister, Grabski who levied on the Jewish merchants and craftsmen an impossibly high tax which impoverished the Jews.

In the meantime, organizational and political life developed in the town. They established political parties, youth movements, cultural societies and charitable institutions. The Jewish people of David-Horodok and especially the youth threw themselves into these tasks with fiery zeal and exceptional devotion. They established a Hebrew Tarbut School which in time became one of the best in Poland. They established banks such as the People's Bank and the Merchants' Bank. They developed an excellent study-houses committee which gave rise to multifaceted activities. They founded libraries, sports clubs, drama circles, etc. However, we will not dwell anymore on all these institutions as we will describe them in more detail in later chapters.

After the Pilsudski upheaval, conditions began to stabilize. The Jews led a more or less quiet existence. They could earn a livelihood from commerce and handicrafts. However, life was monotonous and uninteresting.

Hitler's coming to power in Germany served to intensify the anti-Semitism in Poland. In Polish towns, there were pogroms against Jews. They began beating Jewish students. There was instituted the new infamous *Ovshem* politics [allowed boycott policy against the Jews] in economic life.

[Page 363 - Yiddish]

This policy was to boycott Jewish businessmen, shops, craftsmen and factories. In David-Horodok, several Poles were imported to open up shops and compete with the Jews. The air was saturated with primitive anti-Semitism. Yet, this anti-Semitism was not expressed in as vivid a form in David-Horodok as it was in other Polish towns. This is explained by the fact that the Poles constituted only 5-10 percent of the population in David-Horodok while the remaining 90-95 percent were Jews and Byelorussians and the *Horodtchukas* who also felt abused by the Polish authority. Despite the calm in the town, the Jews felt quite alarmed.

The conditions of the youth seemed particularly hopeless. Those who could took every possible way out of town. Most of them made *aliya* to the Land of Israel. The majority of the town's youth could not make *aliya* because of immigration restrictions and they saw no way to get themselves out. The Jews waited for better times, not knowing and not believing that they would ever come. They were embittered and full of hate for the anti-Semitic Polish authority.

Meanwhile, the danger of a Polish-German war approached with giant steps. After Hitler's friendship gesture towards Poland and with his poisoning the atmosphere in Poland with the spirit of anti-Semitism, he diverted the attention of the Poles away from the true danger that was approaching them. He then began to make his territorial demands to Poland.

The danger of war was on the horizon. The Jews felt like they were living under a black cloud. They forgot their previous score with the Poles. They put themselves in the service of the Polish government in order to fight against the common enemy.

On September 1, 1939, Friday morning, Hitler's troops invaded Poland. The Jewish people of Poland, amongst them the Jews of David-Horodok, stood and fought the Nazi enemy.

The sad ending of the Jewish community in David-Horodok approached.

We will now interrupt the chronologic narrative of events in David-Horodok and take it up again at the end of this work. Now we will return to describing the political, organization and cultural institutions in the town during the time between the two World Wars.

Translator's footnotes:

1. The author assumes that we know that Gorodok or Horodok means 'small town' in Russian.
2. A current reference source in English is: *The Jews of Poland* by Bernard D. Weinryb, Jewish Publication Society of America, Philadelphia, 1973.

[Page 32 - Hebrew] [Page 363 - Yiddish]

Political, Cultural and Organizational Institutions in David-Horodok

1. The Zionist Movement

David-Horodok was pro-Zionist since the times of the *Chovevei Zion* [Lovers of Zion]. As mentioned previously, the town was under the influence of Lithuanian Jewry. The *Haskalah* [Enlightenment] movement came to David-Horodok from there at the end of the 19th century. The Zionist movement also came from there.

[Page 364 - Yiddish]

Peretz Smolenskin's *The Wanderer in the Paths of Life* and Abraham Mapu's *The Love of Zion* and *The Guilt of Samaria* adorned the shelves of David-Horodoker households alongside the Talmud.

They read the Hebrew press in David-Horodok. They collected and bound *Ha-Tsefirah* [The Dawn]. Nachum Sokolov's Friday evening articles were not only read but also studied. They also tried to educate the younger generation in the spirit of Zionism. For that purpose, they brought the best teachers to David-Horodok who introduced classes where they taught Hebrew by speaking Hebrew. After World War I, there were youth circles in which they spoke Hebrew exclusively. In 1915, the youth of David-Horodok took the initiative and arranged an illegal memorial service for Dr. Herzl.

Keren Kayemet [Jewish National Fund] stamps were sold at David-Horodok weddings as soon as they came out. Shimon Leichtman and Shlomo Rozman would come to every wedding and sell these stamps.

The eve of Yom Kippur, they would sit in every synagogue with a collection plate for the National Fund. Whoever donated 25 kopecks had his name inscribed in a special book.

The Slonimer Rebbe used to donate a ruble.

Because of the war and the Czarist regime, it was difficult to develop diversified Zionist activities. However, under various pretexts, they would hold assemblies and celebrations on a variety of Zionist themes.

Vigorous Zionistic activity began after the Kerensky revolution in February 1917. It was as if they had been in a lethargic sleep of latent energy and they wanted to make up for the lost years of inactivity by throwing themselves into Zionist activities with wholehearted zeal and energy, filled with the hope and belief in the great possibilities that the Russian Revolution promised for the Jewish people.

The entire population of the town became involved in organizational and political activity. It was a disgrace not to be associated with a party. It was as if they forgot their worries about livelihood and existence in their preoccupation with party work.

With all their zeal, they threw themselves into the election campaign for the Constituent Assembly that was taking place in Russia. They set up the Jewish communal organizations, opened a large Hebrew school, founded a library, established cooperatives and were active in every realm of town and community life.

Organizational life quieted down when the Bolsheviks seized power. However, as soon as the Germans entered David-Horodok, Zionist activities resumed. At that time, news arrived of the Balfour Declaration which encouraged Zionist activities even more.

However, this did not last long. The Germans retreated; the Bolsheviks reentered and once again, all the Zionist work came to a halt.

Following the stormy period of the Polish-Bolshevik War and after a civil government was installed, there was renewed intensification of Zionist activities.

The first visit from *Keren Hayesod* [Foundation Fund] representative, Dr. Chaimson in 1923, was transformed into a magnificent demonstration for Zionism. The campaign for the *Keren Hayesod*

[Page 365 - Yiddish]

was conducted by the entire Jewish population of David-Horodok. There was not a single Jewish family, even the poorest, which did not support the *Keren Hayesod*.

The visit by the Jewish National Fund representative, Yehoshua Manoach from Degania made an even stronger impression. The town was ruled by a complete holiday atmosphere. No small thing – a delegate from the Land of Israel! People were curious to have a look at him. They wanted to see what a real Jewish farmer looked like. An extraordinary enthusiasm had seized the inhabitants of the town. The Jews in David-Horodok were then simply breathing in the air of the Land of Israel. The visit of Y. Manoach had strengthened the Jewish spirit and consciousness. This was the first direct contact with a Jewish farmer from Israel and it gave feelings of courage, national pride and self-worth to the Jews of David-Horodok.

Through the visit of Y. Manoach, a "unit" of the *Keren Kayemet* was organized in town. It existed until the outbreak of World War II and it conducted widely ramified activities for the *Keren Kayemet*. They gathered Zionists from all directions, young and old.

At that time, they had begun *aliya* to the Land Israel. The pioneers that left David-Horodok included entire families such as: A.Y. Shafer, Noah Grenadier, A. Turkenitz, A. Shostakovsky, L. Dushnik, D. Rimar, A. Lachovsky, S. Mester, Z. Pain and others.

The second "unit" of the *Keren Kayemet* in David Horodok

[Page 366 - Yiddish]

The first *Chalutzim* in David-Horodok

Right to left: 1. Shoshana Ziporin-Leib of blessed memory, 2. Baruch Blizhovsky,
3. Ester Olpiner-Beit Aryeh, 4. Zalman Gloiberman of blessed memory

The Committee of the General Zionist Organization in David-Horodok - 1922

Right to left: 1. Sorokin, 2. Reuven Mishalov, 3. Leibel Lachovsky, 4. Yossel Vaks, 5. Yankel Gelman, 6. Shalom Kvetny, 7. Meir Moravchik, 8. Yehoshua Yitzchak Matorin

[Page 367 - Yiddish]

A *Hashomer Haleumi* group in David-Horodok

A *Hanoar Hatzioni* group in David-Horodok. April 7, 1934

[Page 368 - Yiddish]

With the onset of normal organizational life in David-Horodok, the political parties became active in the town. The first to renew their activity were the General Zionists and *Tzeirei Zion* [Youth of Zion]. These were the principal parties in town during the entire span between the two wars. They were the most influential, had the largest memberships and were the most active.

When the General Zionists renewed their activity, they zealously threw themselves into multi-faceted enlightenment activities. They worked for the *Keren Hayesod* and the *Keren Kayemet*. They opened a new library which was not used during the Polish-Bolshevik War. They held frequent meetings and lectures. They assisted in the rise of the Tarbut School in David-Horodok and later also founded their youth movement, *Hashomer Haleumi* [National Watchmen] later called *Hanoar Hatzioni* [Zionist Youth]. The General Zionists took an active part in the various election campaigns in town such as: election for the Sejm, town council election, Jewish *kehila* [community] election, Zionist congress election, etc. For a short period of time there was a training kibbutz of the *Hanoar Hatzioni* in the town. This was run by a youth group from outside David-Horodok who had to spend their training period in David-Horodok. This training kibbutz did not last long, scarcely a year in 1934, because of a job shortage in the town. The youth

The party committee of *Poalei Zion* (left leaning) in David-Horodok, 1927
Sitting right to left: 1. Chaim Lansky, 2. Baruch Slomiansky, 3. Yosef Lifshitz, 4. Yitzchak-Leib Zager, 5. Meir Lifshitz, 6. Yerachmiel Rimar
Standing: 1. Yasha Kagan, 2. Yaakov Olpiner

[Page 369 – Yiddish]

from this kibbutz went away to train in kibbutzim in other towns and there they waited for approval to make *aliya*.

The General Zionists recruited mainly the well-to-do homeowners. The artisans, craftsmen, laborers and especially the youth constituted the bulk of the *Tzeirei Zion* party.

The *Tzeirei Zion* just as the General Zionists renewed their activities and regained their feet once normal living conditions were established.

The *Tzeirei Zion* was a party of the youth right from the onset, that is, its activists as well as its general membership were all young people between 18 and 25 years of age. This gave their work a dynamism which was felt in every campaign.

Full of youthful zeal and temperament, full of self-confidence and youthful idealism, they threw themselves into party work and they strove to encompass ever widening circles, not allowing any area of organizational life to pass without their influence and involvement.

Lectures, assemblies, elections, night classes, *Keren Kayemet* work, conferences, etc. were their daily bread. The local hall was filled every evening with members who were ready to do any sort of work

Uncaptioned. An announcement of a gala evening to celebrate the five-year anniversary (1925-1930) of the Y.L. Peretz Folk Library, on Tuesday December 2, 1930, in the firehall. Signed by the Jubilee committee.

[Page 370 - Yiddish]

that they were given. The *Tzeirei Zion* really developed a nice and diversified group for all realms of organizational life.

The *Tzeirei Zion* had great success in conducting a tool campaign in David-Horodok. This was the first great demonstration on behalf of the workers of Israel and all gladly gave tools for the laborers of Israel.

An especially selected commission of *Tzeirei Zion* took on the task of helping the pioneers who came out of the Soviet Union.

Through the initiative of the *Tzeirei Zion*, the activities of the orphans' committee were renewed.

In 1923, the *Tzeirei Zion* founded the *Hechalutz* [The Pioneer] and in 1924 they established a training kibbutz in Lisovitz.

In 1925, the *Poalei Zion* [Workers of Zion] founded a library named after Y.L. Peretz which developed very well both in numbers of worthwhile books and in the number of readers. In the last few years before World War II, it was the only active library in the town.

The first committee of *Freiheit* in David-Horodok - 1926
Sitting (First row right to left): 1. Tziva Magidovitz, 2. Chaichik Lansky
(Second row): 1. Shmuel Zezik, 2. Yosef Lifshitz, 3. Sheindel Ziporin
Standing: 1. Rachel Ziporin, 2. Chanan Gotlieb, 3. Tzvi Durchin, 4. Moshe-Aharon Olpiner

The youth organization of the *Poalei Zion* was *Freiheit* [Freedom]. It was established by the party in 1926 and it developed a nice educational function for the youth, helping to teach vocational trades. At the same time, they brought many of the youth to *aliya*.

[Page 371 - Yiddish]

First convention of *Freiheit*, Pinsk District, in David-Horodok — 1928, June 14

[Page 372 – Yiddish]

A group of lumberjacks in a *Hachshara* Kibbutz of *Hapoel Hamizrachi* in David-Horodok, 1933

A Hashomer Hatzair Group in David-Horodok, 1932

[Page 373 - Yiddish]

Agricultural *Hachshara* Kibbutz of *Hechalutz Hamizrachi* in David-Horodok in 1924

Sitting (First row right to left): 1. Moshe Friedman, 2. Shraga (Feivel) Shatsky, 3. Motel Dubrovitsky (Second row): 1. Masha Dubrovitsky, 2. Masha Baruchin, 3. Velvel Lachovsky, 4. Shapira — from the leadership of *Hechalutz Hamizrachi* in Poland, 5. Gershon Gloiberman, 6. Chaya Chertok, 7. Tzivia Fishman Standing: 1. Moshe Dreizin, 2. Butza Katzman, 3. Shalom Lachovsky, 4. Baruch-Hershel Kolozizky, 5. Yosef Bregman, 6. Simcha Chover, 7. Moshel Plotnitzky, 8. Chaim Kolozny, 9. Leibke Perberozky, 10. Simcha Fishman

In 1931, the party organized the town craftsmen into a group called *Haoved* [The Worker]. Many members of *Haoved* made *aliya* to Israel.

Unfortunately, the activities of the *Poalei Zion* were sharply curtailed in the few years before the onset of World War II because of the current reactionary fascist government. As an example, in the last *kehila* election in 1937, the list of *Poalei Zion* candidates was canceled.

The most important Zionist work amongst the religious people of David-Horodok was done through the *Mizrachi* [religious Zionist movement] and the *Hapoel Hamizrachi* [Mizrachi Workers]. In 1925 the *Hapoel Hamizrachi* founded a training kibbutz in Dobrin and most of the members made *aliya* to the Land of Israel. *Mizrachi* and *Hapoel Hamizrachi* took an active part in working for the *Keren Kayemet* and the *Keren Hayesod*.

In 1925, a party called *Hitachdut* [The Union] was established in David-Horodok. However, with the *aliya* of its founding fathers to Israel, the group ceased to exist.

[Page 374 - Yiddish]

Leaders of Beitar

Beitar chapter in David-Horodok, October 26, 1935

[Page 375 - Yiddish]

Besides the above-mentioned youth movements of *Freiheit* and *Hanoar Hatzioni*, there were two other active Zionist youth movements in David-Horodok: *Hashomer Hatzair* [Young Watchmen] and Beitar [abbreviation for Berit Trumpeldor or Covenant of Trumpeldor, the Revisionist Youth Movement].

The *Hashomer Hatzair* was established in the town in 1927. They did a good job of educating the youth of the town. At the same time, they were active in all aspects of *Keren Kayemet* work. They were involved in the League for Workers in the Land of Israel and they took part in all of its activities. The *Hashomer Hatzair* sent many members for training and most of them succeeded in making *aliya*.

Beitar was founded in David-Horodok in 1929. They also sent their members for training and most of them made *aliya*.

As already mentioned, David-Horodok was an absolutely Zionist town. There was no Bund [The General Union of Jewish Workers in Lithuania, Poland and Russia] in the town during the period between the two World Wars.

As a result of the reactionary and anti-Semitic policies of the Polish regime and the bad economic and helpless situation of the Jewish youth, there developed a small group of Communists in David-Horodok. Their number probably never even reached ten. They had no influence in town. The group was completely dissolved after a few of them were arrested. Some of those who were freed from jail later went to the Land of Israel. The others remained in David-Horodok but refrained completely from Communist activities. When the Soviets first came into David-Horodok in 1939, they became involved again as Communist activists and they caused considerable trouble for the Zionist concerns. As a result of their denunciations to the N.K.G.B., many of the town Zionists were arrested.

The teacher Shimon Leichtman and his wife Sheina, among the first teachers of "Hebrew in Hebrew"

[Page 32 - in the Hebrew section]

Administration of the library of the Zionist Organization in David-Horodok — 1917

Seated: 1. Yossel Moravchik, 2. Asher Zager, 3. Yoshke Friedman
Standing: 1. Vichal Friedman, 2. Leibel Lachovsky, 3. Zalman Olpiner, 4. Shalom Kvetny, 5. Bina Gorin

[Page 33 - in the Hebrew section]

The first "unit" of JNF in David-Horodok

Seated: (first row from right to left): 1. Itka Lifshitz, 2. Chava Gurevitz, 3. Baruch Slomiansky, 4. Tzipa Ratner, 5. Shoshana Gloiberman, 6. Sonia Baruchin, 7. Ester Mester
Second row: 1. Sonia Slomiansky, 2. Sara Volpin, 3. Zalman Slomiansky, 4. Pinye Novak, 5. Yehoshua Manoach - emissary of JNF from the Land of Israel, 6. Yitzchak-Leibush Zager, 7. Chaim Finkelstein, 8. Leichik Moravchik
Standing: 1. Meir Lifshitz, 2. Avraham Pain, 3. Dov Rimar, 4. Shmuel Zezik, 5. Leibke Reznik, 6. Arke Lifshitz, 7. Yaakov Olpiner, 8. Simcha Chover, 9. Gershon Gloiberman, 10. Feivel Shatsky

[Page 34 - in the Hebrew section]

Family of Aharon-Yonah Shafer near the ship in Constanza as they were making *aliya* – 1925

[Page 35 - in the Hebrew section]

The General Zionist *Hechalutz* in David-Horodok

[Page 36 top - in the Hebrew section]

Preparatory kibbutz of the *Hanoar Hatzioni* and the committee for the kibbutz in David-Horodok —
1934

[Page 36 bottom - in the Hebrew section]

A group of *Poalei Zion* (left leaning) members in David-Horodok – 1928

Seated (from right to left): 1. Chaim Lansky, 2. Shmuel Zezik, 3. Yashe Kagan, 4. Goberman, 5. Yosef Lifshitz, 6. Yitzchak Leib Zager, 7. Yankel Olpiner
Standing: 1. Moshe-Aharon Olpiner, 2. Sheindel Ziporin, 3. Chaim Volpin, 4. Chaichik Lansky, 5. Wolf Durchin, 6. Reuven Mester, 7. Reuven Friedman, 8. Zelig Yudovitz, 9. Rachel Ziporin, 10. Gedalyahu Olpiner

[Page 37 - in the Hebrew section]

Administration of the Y.L. Peretz library in David-Horodok - in front of the library

From right to left: 1. Y.L. Zager, 2. Yashe Kagan, 3.Yosef Lifshitz, 4. Reuven Mester, 5. Chaim Lansky, 6. Zelig Yudovitz

[Page 38 - in the Hebrew section]

Branch of *Hitachdut* in David-Horodok — 1930

Seated row one - right to left: 1. Yitzchak Olpiner, 2. Bracha Lutzky, 3. Leah Shostakovsky, 4. Tzivia Rappaport, 5. Chaim Basevitz
Row two : 1. Avraham Toplinky, 2. Leah Teitelbaum, 3. Avraham Olshansky, 4. Riva Moravchik, 5. *Unknown*, 6. Shoshana Lutzky, 7. Itzel Moravchik, 8. Chaya Durchin
Standing: 1. Motzani, 2. Meir Rappaport, 3. *Unknown*, 4. Moshe Ronkin, 5. Tzivia Ziporin, *[Unnumbered* and *Unknown]*, 6. Yehudit Katzman, 7. Rachel Shtofer, 8. Shlomo Shapira, 9. Miriam Basevitz

[Page 39 - in the Hebrew section]

[Page 39 - Hebrew] [Page 375 - Yiddish]

2. The Socialist Movement in David-Horodok in 1905

Unfortunately we have no material to enlighten us about the year 1905 in David-Horodok. We have no alternative but to draw on the memories of people who had not even taken an active part in the happenings of that stormy epoch.

From these memoirs, we learn that in 1905, a small group of the Bund was organized in David-Horodok under the leadership of the well-known A. Litvak, a Bundist who was rumored to have been banished to David-Horodok.

There was also a group of Socialist Territorialists. Concerning this group, we even have a historical reference. In the American *Forverts* [The Jewish American *Forward* newspaper] a picture was printed of 20 members of the David-Horodoker Socialist Territorialists (The picture is printed in our memorial book.)

The *Poalei Zion* [Workers of Zion] party also existed in David-Horodok at that time.

According to these stories, all of these socialistic movements were embraced by a great number of the youth. For a certain period, they were the rulers of the town. They had developed

[Page 376 - Yiddish]

self-defense organization and had weapons. They demanded a 12-hour work day. The laborers themselves did not want that "little" work but the revolutionaries would come and force them away from their work. There were cases where the children revolutionaries would come to their employer parents and take away the last workers. Aside from this, the revolutionaries were occupied with the distribution of wealth and self-education.

With the downfall of the revolution, all these organizations dissipated in David-Horodok. Some individuals were arrested and sent away. Many fled to America. The remainder left town during the period of danger.

In reference to this, it should be noted that after the Kerensky revolution of 1917, leftover members of *Poalei Zion* reestablished their organization. All the old revolutionaries again became very active and devotedly participated in the work. They tried to organize all the workers and sympathizers and they were very active.

Their activity was widely diversified: organizing readings, night classes, drama circles, a library, cooperatives and managing professional movement.

In those days the town was divided in two: the General Zionists and the *Poalei Zion*. At the election of the Constituent Assembly in Russia, the General Zionists received 120 more votes than the *Poalei Zion* – 740 to 620.

With the turnover of David-Horodok to the Bolsheviks, the situation changed. A few of the *Poalei Zion* leaders joined the Bolsheviks. The great majority of the leaders along with the entire membership did not follow them. They died off politically. From the entire powerful *Poalei Zion* organization of those days, there remain only memories.

A group of Socialist Territorialists in David-Horodok — 1905

[Page 40 - in the Hebrew section]

[Page 41 - Hebrew] [Page 376 - Yiddish]

3. Cultural Institutions

As indicated in a previous chapter, David-Horodok was culturally under the influence of Lithuanian Jewry. The *Haskalah* [Enlightenment] movement had permeated the town in the last century through the boys who had gone to Lithuanian yeshivas and especially through the Jewish merchants of David-Horodok who encountered in their travels the new winds blowing in the larger Jewish centers. They were also the ones who felt that their practices required that they give their children a broader and more general education that that given by the *cheders* and yeshivas.

To that purpose, A. Y. Shafer, M. Y. Lifshitz and others brought the renowned Y. S. Adler to teach in David-Horodok. He introduced a new instructional system and he laid the foundation for a modern and Zionistic education.

The other teachers in town attempted to adapt to the new times and they began to teach Hebrew in Hebrew. These included S. Leichtman, S. Zagorodski

[Page 377 - Yiddish]

תרבות,,

בית הספר העברי בדויד׳הורדק, תרע״ח.

Tarbut Hebrew School in David-Horodok, 5678 - 1918

and Y. Begun who were not the most eminent of the Jewish instructors but they were teachers who felt that they had a nationalistic and Zionist mission to educate a new Jewish generation. They were the carriers of Zionism in those days.

The elders also tried to open a high school in town. This was eventually opened as a government school. That was the town school in the Russian language which did a good job in helping the youth get into the intermediate and higher institutions and thereby acquire a higher education.

After the February Revolution in 1917, a Hebrew school was opened in David-Horodok under the directorship of the teacher Manevitz. With the assistance of teachers Yosef Begun, R. Shafer, Y. Kashtan and Y. Margolin, the school was established at a very high level. The school fulfilled a double purpose. It taught the children and, at the same time, it was a center for Zionist activities and national consciousness.

The Hebrew school existed until 1920. During the stormy war years

[Page 378 - Yiddish]

when David-Horodok was passed from hand-to-hand, it was impossible to carry on a normal educational system.

After the Polish-Bolshevik War, when normal life was restored in the town, the first concern was to set up the school.

Laying of the cornerstone of the new building of the Tarbut School in the year 5687 - 1927

In 1924, a Hebrew Tarbut [culture] School was founded anew under the direction of R. Mishalov.

There is not enough space in this book to detail in full the blessed activities of this Tarbut School in David-Horodok. It started with three classes and in time, it became a seven class school and one of the best in Poland. Until its closing in 1940, there were eleven ceremonies which graduated hundreds of children.

It was not easy to strengthen the Tarbut School to a point where it could stand safely on its own feet. The school did not get any subsidy from the government or the municipal agencies. The various expenses of the school as such were laid on the shoulders of the parents of the students. The teaching personnel existed only on their wages from tuition. Remembering the grave poverty which ruled the town, we then begin to understand the great difficulties with which the school struggled every moment. It was a credit to the remarkable commitment of a group of concerned individuals in the town to the loyalty of the teaching staff and the principal R. Mishalov and to the national consciousness of the parents. The parents were almost 100% in sending their children to the Tarbut School despite the fact that they had to pay tuition when, at the town Polish government school, the studies were free.

[Page 379 - Yiddish]

These three factors: the employers, the teaching staff and the parents, were responsible for the existence and the thriving of the Tarbut School.

The second director of the school, the teacher Avrasha Olshansky, elevated the school to such a high level that it became one of the best Tarbut Schools in all of Poland. After finishing the Tarbut seminar in Vilna, he first, as a teacher and later as director, devoted his entire energy and time to the school, leading it from year-to-year higher and higher. He was the one who, in 1931, founded the *Bnei Yehuda* [Sons of Judah] of David-Horodok, the Hebrew speaking youth of Poland.

Afterwards, the movement spread to other cities and towns in Poland but nowhere was it treated more earnestly than in David-Horodok.

It is worthwhile dwelling briefly on the *Bnei Yehuda* movement in David-Horodok. It began through the initiative of the director of the school, Avrasha Olshansky. He persuaded several school children that pupils of a Hebrew school who planned *aliya* to the Land of Israel ought to speak Hebrew not only in class but also at home and in the streets among themselves, with their parents, brothers, sisters, neighbors, friends and, in a word, with everyone. From a small group of children, the movement spread to all the school children.

Kindergarten affiliated with the Tarbut School in David-Horodok, 5688 - 1928, 29 Av

[Page 380 - Yiddish]

A child who had joined the *Bnei Yehuda* movement was obligated to speak only Hebrew at home, in the street or in the shop where he would buy a book. A *Bnei Yehuda* would always speak Hebrew to a Jewish companion. Understandably, at first, it was very difficult for the parents who did not understand Hebrew and it would often tax their interest but it was not long before the parents, the shopkeepers and the grown-ups in the street began not only to understand Hebrew but also began to answer in Hebrew.

Christian servants in Jewish homes also began to understand and speak Hebrew. Babies were taught Hebrew from the beginning.

Once David-Horodok was visited by Yosef Baratz. Before he came to town, he had heard the wonder of the "Tel Aviv of Polesye" as David-Horodok was called because of the spoken Hebrew. He could not believe that it was really true. To demonstrate to him that it was true, they took him out into the street. When he happened to meet a child, he would address the child in Yiddish expecting the reply would also be in Yiddish. No matter how many children he met, everyone replied in Hebrew.

A child who belonged to *Bnei Yehuda* always got a "5" (very good) for his grade in Hebrew class no matter how bright he was.

At first, the children organized a special intelligence unit whose task it was to verify that the new members of the *Bnei Yehuda* were keeping to their oaths to speak Hebrew exclusively. The intelligence officer would sneak into the new member's home and lay under a bed for hours in order to ascertain that the member was keeping his oath.

The Tarbut School existed until the onset of World War II. When the Soviets entered David-Horodok at the end of September, instruction in the school began once again but the language was Yiddish and not Hebrew.

An unforgettable moment occurred at the beginning of that schoolyear. The director, Avrasha Olshansky was forced, under the dictate of a Communist activist who himself was a graduate of that school, to assemble all of the children. Sobbing spasmodically, he announced that the school would no longer teach Hebrew but only Yiddish. The Communist activist then gave a lecture that the children had been duped in the past. He wanted to convince them that their Hebrew language was the language of the Jewish counterrevolutionaries.

Avrasha Olshansky, until then, had been the devoted and faithful father of the school but now he could no longer bear teaching there. He could not ethically tolerate the change. He and his wife, who was also a teacher, moved to Bialystok. He, his wife and children met their death at the hands of the Nazi murderers. Honor to their memory!

[Page 381 - Yiddish]

Through the initiative of the same A. Olshansky, a course in Tanach [Hebrew Bible] was initiated. It went under the title of "Every Day a Chapter of Tanach." This course was intended for the grown-ups in David-Horodok. These lectures were extremely popular. The course was attended mostly by the older youth and the adults. The lectures would pack the large hall in the school. The people who attended the lectures were from all social levels and from all political directions, both religious and freethinkers.

Teachers with a variety of beliefs taught the Tanach. A rabbi would teach and give an overall religious interpretation in his lecture. A *maskil* (adherent of the *Haskalah*) would lecture, explain the chapter with the use of new interpretations. There was a lecture from a member of the free atheistic circles who interpreted the Tanach from a purely historical-cultural viewpoint.

It was most interesting that each lecturer's special point of view was listened to with tolerance and patience.

These lectures began in 1937 and continued until the beginning of World War II.

* * *

In 1927, the *Mizrachi* [religious Zionist movement] initiated a religious Yavne school. This school did not exist for long having closed after only two years.

* * *

Besides the schools, there existed well-organized libraries in David-Horodok.

The teacher, S. Zagorodsky organized a library for children and school youngsters even before 1905.

In 1917, the Zionist organization in town founded a library which developed well. Unfortunately it was not active during World War I.

Following World War I, the libraries in David-Horodok developed vigorously. In 1925, the *Poalei Zion* founded a library named for Y.L. Peretz. In the last years prior to World War II, this was the only active library for adults in the town. There was a large library for the students at the Tarbut School.

[Page 382 - Yiddish]

Publications with Zionist and literary themes always had a wide audience. There were also self-education groups in town sponsored by the various parties and youth movements.

* * *

David-Horodok also had a long-standing amateur drama group which would give performances from time-to-time. There had long been an inclination towards theater and acting in David-Horodok. Even in the time of the 1905 revolution, such amateurs as I. Opingandin, Y. Gotlieb and Helman would excel in readings from the masterpieces of Sholem Aleichem, Peretz, Bialik, Frishman and others.

Later, a group of amateur artists were trained and they gave two or three performances each year for the Jewish populace. The most outstanding among them were the dentist Edel, Zelda Finkelstein and the midwife Kreinin.

Purim celebration in the kindergarten affiliated with the Tarbut School in David-Horodok, 5699 - 1938
Translator's note: one of these years is off by one, as Purim 5699 would be in 1939

[Page 383 - Yiddish]

After the 1917 Russian Revolution and later after the Russo-Polish War, the drama circle developed somewhat further. Fresh forces arrived and they would give a serious performance from time-to-time. The proceeds of the performances were for various charitable purposes. At times, they would use a percentage of the revenues for a variety of purposes.

In praise of the drama circle, it must be said that the amateurs had little interest in how to divide the money. They were only interested in artistic success.

In 1936, another youthful amateur group was founded. They gave several successful performances. Unfortunately, the outbreak of World War II ended the activities of both drama groups. It should also be mentioned that the children of the Tarbut School would give a successful annual performance under the leadership of their teachers.

Performance of *The Dybbuk* by a group of young amateur actors in David-Horodok, 1938

* * *

David-Horodok also had a sport club, Hakoach [The Strength] which developed a very good football [soccer] team. The football team competed for a couple of years but it was disbanded after their best players made *aliya* to the Land of Israel

The first staff of teachers in Tarbut School in David-Horodok

Seated (from right to left): 1. Shmuel Papish, 2. Chaim Branchuk, 3. Reuven Mishalov, 4. *Unknown*, 5. Moshe Erlich
Standing: 1. Yosef Begun, 2. Abramovitz, 3. *Unknown*

[Page 41 - in the Hebrew section]

The seventh graduation class of Tarbut School in David-Horodok

[Page 42 - in the Hebrew section]

Students of Tarbut School in David-Horodok preparatory class and kindergarten. They spoke only Hebrew and were nicknamed "Cubs of the Sons of Judah" – 1934

[Page 43 - in the Hebrew section]

The teacher Shlomo Zagorodsky - one of the first to spread Hebrew in
David-Horodok

[Page 45 top - in the Hebrew section]

Hakoach football team in David-Horodok — 1927

[Page 45 bottom - in the Hebrew section]

[Page 46 - Hebrew] [Page 384 - Yiddish]

4. The Orphanage

David-Horodok was ruined and impoverished after World War I. The Joint [American Jewish Joint Distribution Committee], which had begun its aide activity throughout Poland, also opened a branch in David-Horodok. One of the Joint's most important accomplishments was the founding of an orphanage in the town.

There were many orphans in town. There were 32 orphaned children up to the age of 14 who were kept in the orphanage which was founded in a comfortable dwelling with three bedrooms, a large dining room which doubled as a lecture hall and a large courtyard where the children played a variety of games. The orphanage was well-equipped with such items as comfortable beds, good bedcovers and a sufficient quantity of food and clothing. The food was good and the children were well fed and appeared healthy.

The entire maintenance of this house was paid for by the Joint. The local people could be of no assistance except for supplying teachers who worked without pay.

That was the situation until the Bolsheviks recaptured David-Horodok during the Russo-Polish War. Then there was a radical change. The management of the orphanage was transferred to a branch of the social service department of the Revkom [revolutionary committee]. They gave much advice but little practical help. There were no food reserves in town. The children became hungry and began to scatter.

When the Bolsheviks left town, they took the entire inventory of the orphanage despite the protests of the David-Horodoker Jews.

After the Russo-Polish War, all efforts to reestablish the orphanage were unfortunately unsuccessful. Instead, an orphans' committee was founded which undertook to place the orphans in homes.

The chief priority was to enable them to learn a trade. Through the committee's efforts, the orphans were well cared for in private homes.

The money to support the work of the committee was raised by selling flowers ["flower days"], special campaigns and proceeds from performances of the drama circle. The main reason that the committee was able to exist was due to the support it received from the David-Horodoker Women's Committee of Detroit.

This support was achieved through Yitzchak-Leib Zager who had personal family ties with America. Thanks to his concern, the committee received regular support from America throughout its existence.

The orphans' committee existed throughout the period of Polish rule in David-Horodok. In 1939, when David-Horodok was taken by the Bolsheviks, the orphans' committee was closed along with all other institutions.

[Page 46 - Hebrew] [Page 385 - Yiddish]

5. Bank and Credit Institutions

In David-Horodok as in all other Jewish communities, credit was a common problem. There were always Jews who needed cash for business purposes, for a child's wedding, to build a house or because of misfortune.

In by-gone days, there were the so-called usurers [the Yiddish word is vokhernik because payment was due each week] who would loan money on a pledge and for considerable interest. Each Friday, the debtor would have to bring the usurer both the principal and the interest. The usurer was usually an influential Jew with considerable authority in the community. If the principal and interest were not paid on time, he would not hesitate to keep a pledge which might have been as much as ten times more valuable than the borrowed money. Understandably, going to the usurer was a last resort when there was no other way out.

When loan and savings funds began developing in Russia, one such fund opened in David-Horodok and later, a second fund as well. These two funds had the same purpose but had different names. One was named after the bookkeeper, Shlomo Rozman's Fund and the other was named after the bookkeeper, Pinye Sheinboim's Fund. Many merchants had accounts in both funds.

The funds enjoyed the complete faith of the populace and were entrusted with their savings. As a result, the funds had enough cash for loans to those needing them.

In 1909, the larger businessmen in David-Horodok founded a Merchants' Bank under the management of Noah Grushkin. The bookkeeper was Meir Olpiner. The bank developed very well.

With the outbreak of World War I, all the financial institutions failed.

After World War I when David-Horodok went over to the Poles and normal life had resumed, another Merchants' Bank was formed in 1923 under the management of M. Kventy, and a People's Bank was founded in 1924 under the management of S. Papish.

These banks developed very well and they were a significant factor in the economic life of the town. There was also a charity fund in David-Horodok which gave free loans to small businessmen and handworkers.

The charity fund was managed by a committee headed by Y. Gotlieb. This committee would control the requests and set the amounts of the loans.

The Administration and first managers of People's Bank in David-Horodok — 1933

Seated (from right to left): 1. Mendel Reznik, 2. Pesach Pilchik, 3. Gevirtzman, 4. Yankel Volpin, 5. Shmuel Papish, 6. Chaikel Freiman
Standing: 1. Yudel Shnur, 2. Moshe-Yitzchak Eisenberg, 3. Moshe Katzman, 4. Moshe Veisblum, 5. Unknown, 6. Unknown, 7. Unknown

[Page 47 - in the Hebrew section]

[Page 48 - Hebrew] [Page 385 - Yiddish]

6. Firefighters

One of the most useful institutions in town was the fire brigade which was 99% Jewish.

[Page 386 - Yiddish]

David-Horodok, like most small towns, was composed of houses built out of wood and with thatched roofs. These often fell victim to fires. Fire, the unbidden and undesired guest, would pay a visit almost every summer and cause considerable distress. Homes were burnt as a result of a variety of mishaps: carelessness with fires, placing a hot iron outside, going out at night to the stable with a torch, throwing away unextinguished cigarettes, children playing with fire and arson.

Fire was a nightmare for the masses. Summer was the most beautiful and the most interesting time in the life of the town. However, it was often spoiled by the frequent fires. In many homes, they would pack up the valuables in summer and carry them away to one of the town's few brick houses which were fireproof. An alternative was to keep the valuables at home in packs which would be easy to remove in case of fire.

In order to fight this plague and even in former times, a firefighters brigade was established. The town administration then built a large station to hold the equipment and the water buckets. The town administrator levied a special chimney tax with which to finance the building of the station. The insurance companies also helped pay the expenditures.

Almost all the Jewish youth were enrolled in the firefighters brigade. They considered it a civic obligation to belong to the firefighters. Even though the Christian populace was in the greatest danger because of their thatched roof houses, only three or four were enrolled as firefighters.

In summertime, the firefighters would periodically hold drills. In the olden days, this was quite an event in the life of the town. Massey, the station watchman, would go around all the streets with a special bugle to signal that the firefighters should come out for the drill. The firefighters would put on their special uniforms and gather at the station which was in the center of the town. After a few callisthenic exercises, one of them was secretly sent out into the streets to pick out a house which was supposedly burning. He would then give a signal and they would begin to "extinguish" the fire. The firefighters would pick the house of someone against whom they bore a grudge. After the drill, the firefighters would have a beer.

After World War I, the firefighters brigade expanded. The town council allocated more money to enlarge the inventory and to teach the firefighters better techniques of extinguishing and especially containing the spread of fires. However, when a fire broke out during a wind or in the vicinity of thatched roofs, the firefighters were unable to localize the fire. That is what happened in 1936 when a fire broke out in the middle of the day in the Christian

[Page 387 - Yiddish]

part of town. One third of the town, along with the Greek Orthodox Church on the hill, burnt down.

In the last years before World War II, the town administration directed the firefighters. The management remained in the hands of Jews. The most active managers were Y. Yudovitz and M. Rimar.

[Page 49 - Hebrew] [Page 387 - Yiddish]

7. The Municipal Government

The David-Horodok populace had the status of town citizens [called *meshchane* with more political rights than the typical peasants] since the time of the Czars. They would vote every three years for a town council consisting of three persons: an elder (starosta) and two assistants. One of the assistants was a Jew.

The election would take place as follows: each street voted for a representative and the street representatives would then vote for the elder and his two assistants. This election process was far from democratic and those who wanted to be elected took advantage of family ties, neighbors. For the most part, the Christians would be "elected" through a bottle of liquor, etc. – and anyone who brought more would be elected.

That is the way things were until the revolution of February 1917. Then the town council was enlarged. However, as a result of the stormy revolutionary times and the frequent changeover of ruling powers, these elections were also not very democratic. When the Bolsheviks appeared in town, they appointed a Revkom and the Poles appointed the town council. During the entire period that the Poles appointed the town council, the Jewish representatives were always the same: M. Lachovsky, M.Y. Lifshitz and S. Katzman.

The appointed town council managed the town until 1928. In that year, elections for town council were held throughout Poland and naturally in David-Horodok as well.

That was the very first democratic election for town council in the history of David-Horodok. The Jews took an active part in the election and it was a vigorously fought campaign. Eight Jews were elected representing 40% of the town council. They were: Dr. Zholkver, M.Y. Lifshitz, M. Lachovsky, Y. Yudovitz, R. Mishalov, S. Reznik, H. Zipin and Y. Lifshitz.

The hope that they could use the town treasury to support the Jewish institutions was shattered. Every proposal suggested by the Jews to give financial aid to the Tarbut School, the Jewish libraries or even the orphans' committee, were rejected by the Christian representatives and the one Pole who was the chief representative.

The only Jewish operated institution that received a subsidy from the town council was the fire department. This was because it served the Christian populace as well.

The town council did finance the Polish public schools in town, paved the main road and built the

[Page 388 - Yiddish]

power station in 1929, providing light in the houses until midnight.

When the term of office ended for the town council, new elections were not held. The reactionary movement had strengthened in Poland and the government was not interested in new elections. The result was that an agreement was reached without an election and a new town council took office with only six Jews: Dr. Zholkver, Y. Yudovitz, M. Kvetny, D. Rimar, M. Lachovsky and S. Mishalov.

By then, the town council had no power because the actual town authority was the district administrator in Stolin.

During the scant two years (end of 1939 to June 1941) of the Soviet rule in David-Horodok, there was no elected town council. It was run by appointed Bolsheviks sent by the Communist party.

[Page 49 - Hebrew] [Page 388 - Yiddish]

8. The *Kehila*

Unfortunately, we have no reference sources on the activities of the Jewish *kehila* [community] in David-Horodok. There are no remaining books or documents either from the past or from the last years before the Holocaust.

There was an organized Jewish *kehila* in David-Horodok just as in all Polish-Lithuanian cities and towns. Until the last partition of Poland, the David-Horodok *kehila* was linked to the Pinsk Great *kehila* and they paid taxes to Pinsk.

We do not know how the *kehila* was organized and when it became independent under the Czarist authority. We know only of certain sources of revenue for the *kehila*, for example: the *karavka* [a special tax] on meat; the selling of yeast which the *kehila* gave as an exclusive concession to the rabbis and the *chevra kadisha* [burial society] which was supervised by the *kehila*. The *chevra kadisha* was a well-organized and closed institution in which membership would pass by inheritance from father to son.

The First World War abolished everything and the various *kehila* affairs were taken over haphazardly by individuals. One would take care of the bathhouse and the *mikveh* [ritual bath], another the poorhouse and yet another the cemetery.

The old cemetery lay at the edge of the Horyn River and the water would often wash away parts of this cemetery. Every year, they would have to spend money to repair the holy ground. The expenses were covered by the *chevra kadisha* who had their own special source of revenue.

There was no official town rabbi in David-Horodok. There were several rabbis in town, about four or five in number, each supported by its own circle which had given it its rabbinical chair. From time-to-time, there were conflicts between the various sides especially when it came to dividing rabbinical funds which flowed in from general sources.

[Page 389 - Yiddish]

In 1917, after the Kerensky revolution, the first democratic election to the Jewish *kehila* was held in David-Horodok through the initiative of the Zionist organizations. However, this *kehila* could not accomplish anything because of the Bolshevik revolution and the disruptive transfer of power from hand-to-hand in war time.

In the first years of the Polish reign in David-Horodok, after the Polish-Bolshevik war, there was no Jewish *kehila* in the town. The nominated town council representatives served as semi-official agents of the *kehila*. These were: Moshe Lachovsky, Shlomo Katzman and Moshe Yehuda Lifshitz.

As a result of a Polish government decree, elections were held for the Jewish *kehilas* in 1928.

However, the election ordinances were quite reactionary. Only those over the age of 25 had voting rights and those over 30 only had a passive right. Women had no voice at all. The jurisdiction of the *kehila* was severely restricted so that it had no responsibilities except for rabbinical matters, the bathhouse and the cemetery.

In David-Horodok, where the number of rabbis was relatively not small, the elections caused disputes and discord. They did not even avoid slander to the government. People and lists were invalidated, and there was no shortage of disgrace and wrath. Meetings of the *kehila* became arenas for conflict and dispute. The battle surrounding the election of a chief rabbi for the city of David-Horodok was particularly harsh. Rabbi Shapira was the first chief rabbi.

Elections for the *kehila* took place twice during the period of Polish rule. The first time was in 1928. Meir Moravchik was elected as head of the community. Kaplinsky was elected head of the community during the second time in 1936.

The old cemetery in David-Horodok

[Page 50 - in the Hebrew section]

[Page 51 - Hebrew] [Page 389 - Yiddish]

Years of Turbulence and Death

1. The Eve of War

What will be? Will the efforts of the world's statesmen avert war? Will the great world powers such as England, the Soviet Union, America and France not succeed in curbing the Hitleristic appetite and will the world really be flung into a dreadful slaughter? These questions traveled from mouth-to-mouth in the early summer months of 1939. The tension grew from day-to-day. The situation became more strained from minute-to-minute. The air smelled of gunpowder. Here and there shines a ray of hope and everyone walks around with optimistic smiles on their faces; and just as suddenly, the sky clouds over and the people walk around worried and gloomy all over again.

What will be? So the David-Horodokers ask one another. They listen to the radio day and night, clasping at information from the entire world. They search for

[Page 390 - Yiddish]

a ray of hope but the next day invariably demonstrates the increasing hopelessness of the situation.

Presently, there is a breakdown in the talks between the Soviet Union and the western powers and then comes the astounding information with regards the Ribbentrop-Molotov treaty.

A mobilization was declared in Poland. The question that occupied people's minds was not whether there would be a war, of that they were sure, but they asked only when it would break out! One waited with fear and dread of that unfortunate day. Who knows what that day would bring with it?

[Page 51 - Hebrew] [Page 390 - Yiddish]

2. The Polish-German War

Friday, September 1, 1939. The announcement came over the radio like thunder. At dawn, the Nazi military forces had crossed the German-Polish border and attacked Poland without a prior declaration of war.

David-Horodoker Jews could not sit still in their homes. Wherever one turned, there were groups of people with questioning looks and worried faces, talking about the great misfortune. Intuition predicted that the outcome would not be good. Who knows? Who knows how it will end?

The town was proclaimed on war status. At night, all windows were to be shaded so that no light could be seen from the outside. The electric street lamps were no longer lit. Darkness ruled the streets in the evenings, just like the darkness in Jewish hearts, both night and day.

Economic life in the town died down immediately. They soon began to have shortages of products, the first being salt and matches.

One day passed and then another. There was no pleasing news from the front. The Polish army was retreating. Entire armies were surrounded by the German military forces. Rumors spread of betrayal by Polish military leaders. There were reports of extraordinary espionage involving highly placed Polish personalities. Despite the boasting on the Polish radio, one felt that the decayed demoralized card-house was collapsing.

One sought a ray of hope, waiting impatiently for England and France to honor their pledges and come to the aid of the Polish army.

September 3, 1939. Everyone's face lightens. A ray of light and hope appears. England and France declare war against Germany. Everyone imagines that now the situation will change. From now on, the

German military will suffer defeats. Unfortunately, these hopes vanish. The murderous Nazi hordes advance and the Polish military is crushed. Soon, Warsaw is surrounded; then the Germans are in Bialystok, Grodno and Brisk. Hundreds of Jewish refugees begin to arrive in town. They describe

[Page 391 - Yiddish]

the horrors of the war. They fear the day when the Germans will enter David-Horodok. The heart portends evil.

What will be? From where will salvation come? How can we save ourselves?

[Page 52 - Hebrew] [Page 391 - Yiddish]

17 September 1939

Rumors begin circulating that the Red Army has crossed the Soviet-Polish border in order to free the western region of White Russia and Ukraine.

Is this really true or is it, perish the thought, only a rumor? Every Jew wants with his entire being for the news to be true. They were afraid to talk about it too loudly while the Polish authority was still in town. They waited impatiently for the day that the Red Army would march into David-Horodok.

No small matter. They would, at the same time, be rid of the hated anti-Semitic fascist Polish government as well as avert the great danger of a certain death under the rule of the Nazi murderers.

The Poles began leaving David-Horodok, retreating towards the west, certain that the Red Army was advancing from the east. On the night of September 10th to the 19th, the Polish military detachments that were stationed at the Polish-Soviet border began to withdraw.

The Jews of David-Horodok did not sleep the entire night. They were afraid of acts of vengeance by the Polish detachments on the Jewish population. Fortunately, the Poles retreated without causing any harm to the Jews.

At dawn on September 19th, after all their detachments had crossed the Horyn River which divided the town in two, the Poles tore down the bridge and they set up barricades on the other side of the river. Right behind them came the assault forces of the Red Army. At the river there was a brief exchange of fire between the two sides. One Red Army man was shot to death and another wounded. The Poles quickly retreated. A Soviet sapper detachment quickly set up a pontoon bridge over the river and the Red Army troops continued on their way.

[Page 52 - Hebrew] [Page 391 - Yiddish]

3. Under Soviet Rule (September 1939 to June 1941)

Without question, September 19, 1939 was the happiest day in the lives of the David-Horodoker Jews in the course of the last several years. After the shooting between the Poles and the Red Army detachments had ended, the entire Jewish population (and not only the Jews) came out into the streets with happy smiling faces and they received the Red Army detachments that had unceasingly attacked from east to west.

Young and old, small and large, man and wife – all stood on the sidewalks of the main street through which the army troops passed. With smiling faces and waving hands, they greeted the Red Army men.

[Page 392 - Yiddish]

The Red Army men, in turn, greeted the inhabitants in a friendly manner.

One is reminded of how a high officer, who was at the head of a detachment, noticed the elderly Velvel Raishke's who stood with the others on the sidewalk. He called to him with the following: "Nada zhit staritchak, nada zhit!" [We must live old man, we must live!] What an enthusiastic response these few words brought. That day, everyone was simply intoxicated with joy and happiness.

In the afternoon, a meeting was held under the open sky and the representatives of the Red Army made speeches in which they pledged a free and blissful life for the inhabitants of the freed regions of West White Russia and Western Ukraine. "Oppression, people-hatred and poverty will no longer be the destiny of the freed brotherly people of Western Ukraine and West White Russia. Henceforth, they will work under freedom, brotherhood and love and they will work under the rays of the sun of the great leader of the people, Comrade Stalin." That was the quintessence of the speeches which were given at that meeting.

Understandably, the chief celebrants who acted as if they were the hosts were the few Jewish Communists in town who were joined by several *meshchane* [town citizens] of David-Horodok.

All day and until late at night, everyone stayed in the streets conversing with the Red Army men about how the Poles had suppressed the national minorities and especially the Jews.

They were astonished at the approachability and simplicity of the Red Army men. They were impressed by their thoughtfulness and sympathetic expressions and they were thus even more encouraged by their promises and reassurances that from then on, the Jews would no longer know of such trouble.

On the night of September 19, 1939, the Jews of David-Horodok slept peacefully, blissfully and full of hope for a brighter future.

The first weeks of life under the Soviet authority began in David-Horodok. By edict, all the businesses were reopened and people began besieging them trying to stock up on clothing, footwear, produce, etc. Especially conspicuous was the attitude of the *vostochniki* which was the name given to the arriving Soviet citizens. They went from shop to shop buying everything they laid their eyes on, paying whatever price was asked. They would come away from the shops with large bundles.

At first, it was thought that they didn't bargain because they were accustomed to the fixed prices of the government stores. However, no one could understand why they bought so much. Gradually, it became apparent that they could not obtain these things at home. This brought on an even greater buying spree.

The Polish zloty became of equal value to the Soviet ruble

[Page 393 - Yiddish]

so that the zloty was not annulled and remained as currency. The town authority was in the hands of local Communist activists. The Soviets allowed them to run things in the first few months. About 6-7 Jewish and 3-4 Christian Communist activists dominated the town during the course of the first few months.

These few Communist activists inscribed a sad chapter in the history of the town: on the one hand, because of their denunciation to the N.K.G.B. [Soviet security organization] and subsequent arrest of the majority of the Zionist workers in town, and on the other hand, because of their inciting the majority of the *Horodtchukas* [Christians of Tartar descent from David-Horodok] against the entire Jewish population.

In the meantime there were many meetings, entertainment evenings and theatre performances and the youth did not have a bad time. As a result of the large stream of refugees from greater Poland, the Jewish population of the town swelled, reaching some 7-8,000.

Slowly the holiday mood dissipated and people began to think about a livelihood especially since the reserve of supplies was depleted prematurely. There were no fixed Soviet undertakings or bureaus as yet and there were no jobs either. So people began bartering. Both Jews and Christians began trading. Everything was an item of trade: salt, cigarettes, matches, produce, clothing, shoes, etc.

There was a unique trade in Polish zloty. Inasmuch as the zloty was also currency in the part of Poland occupied by the Germans and was then worth more than the ruble, here they would exchange two or three rubles for each zloty on the black market and then, they would smuggle the zloty to the German side. The refugees from Greater Poland were particularly adept at this business. They would, themselves, smuggle back and forth across the Soviet-German border.

The situation of almost free trade existed until the end of 1939. In the meantime, the Soviets arrested and exiled several Polish families who had not escaped in time with the Polish army. A Jewish family from a border village was also exiled and one of the Communist businessmen who had been active until then was banned.

Over ten Jewish youngsters from town secretly left David-Horodok and reached Vilna which the Soviets had ceded to Lithuania. Their goal was to go from there to the Land of Israel.

In November 1939, there were two conferences in Bialystok and Lemberg [Lvov] attended by elected deputies of Western White Russia and Western Ukraine. They decided to turn to the "Supreme Soviet" – "the Soviet Upper House" with the request to officially annex the regions of Western Byelorussia and Western Ukraine to the Soviet Union.

They prepared for over a month to arrange these elections

[Page 394 - Yiddish]

with meetings, assemblies and entertainment evenings. Special propagandists taught the people the Soviet constitution. The elections arrived with great pomp and a holiday atmosphere.

David-Horodok elected two deputies to the Bialystok (Byelorussia) conference, a Jew and a Christian. Understandably, they were Communist activists who were appointed by the Soviet authority. These were the first elections in David-Horodok during the Soviet reign. Already at these elections, one saw the enmity of the *Horodtchukas* for the Communist authorities and the wild and blind hatred for the Jewish populace of David-Horodok.

Counting the ballots later, they found notes with the following inscriptions: "Down with the Soviet rule," "Death to the Bolsheviks and the Jews," "Long live Hitler," etc.

Gradually the Soviets began to arrange and organize a normal life in the Soviet manner. All the local Communist activists who had run the town until then were replaced by imported Soviet citizens.

The town president, the police chief, the leaders of the various economic, cultural and social institutions were all replaced by *vostochniki*. Also, the other, more or less, responsible posts were occupied by Soviet citizens.

The heretofore local Communist town leaders were then employed in second rank posts and they were used by the N.K.G.B. to give information about each and every inhabitant.

These local Communist activists willingly took on this "honorable" mission, transforming into simple informers, devising false accusations against their victims.

The first result of their calumny was the dismissal of certain people from their posts because of their social origin. Naturally, the Jews were the first in line to be affected along with a few rich *Horodtchukas* who were not overlooked. This action was called "nationalization." The larger businesses and enterprises such as tanneries, the sawmill, flour mills, etc., were nationalized. The *finat diel* [financial department] took these over and the Jewish Communist activists managed the work with great zeal.

Understandably the nationalized *Horodtchukas* figured that the Jews were most to blame for this and hate for the Jews grew from day-to-day. They would say that a day would come when they would "pay back" the Jews in full.

However, life in town began to normalize. All three tanneries in town united and a single, large tannery was created employing over one hundred workers. Next to the tannery, a shoe factory was founded which employed over one hundred and fifty shoe workers.

The saw mill with its building enterprises which previously had belonged

[Page 395 - Yiddish]

to Moche Rimar, was enlarged and employed over 400 workers. Various cooperatives were organized. All the various Soviet organizations and institutions began to function. A full-blooded and intensive life began to pulse in the economic domain.

There was also an intensification of work in the field of culture. The schools resumed their classes. Instead of the two previous Polish public schools, two intermediate schools were organized; one in the

Byelorussian language and the other in Russian. The Hebrew Tarbut School was transformed into a Yiddish-speaking school.

All the existing libraries in David-Horodok were united following which, all objectionable books were confiscated and replaced solely by Soviet publications in Russian, Byelorussian and a few in the Yiddish language.

For the first time in the history of David-Horodok, a hospital was established with a special maternity ward. Women no longer had to give birth at home but instead, had a well-organized hospital with careful medical supervision.

For the first time in the history of David-Horodok, there was a permanent movie theater established in which the newest films were shown each evening. Needless to say, the theater was packed every night.

They were proceeding to build a large, modern-designed culture house with halls for lectures, performances, recreation, etc.

The majority of the David-Horodoker inhabitants settled down to work. A bare minimum took to speculation on the black market.

In order to frighten speculators, they arranged a show trial for the David-Horodoker, Herzl Zipin, who was caught speculating with wurst and he was sentenced to four years in prison. This sentence made a strong impression on the town's inhabitants.

However, life flowed on as the Jews began to adapt to the new regime, not looking at the shortages in produce, clothing and footwear. The situation was calm and more or less normal until summer of 1940 when there was a political arrest.

Yosef Yudovitz was arrested. He was the son of Betzel Yudovitz who was shot along with two Christian citizens at the time of the Bolshevik Revolution during the punishment expedition. This first political arrest shook up the Jewish population of David-Horodok and it forecast eventual further arrests.

Many people were then called up by the N.K.G.B. for "a talk." Later, these people never said what the conversation was about. Shortly after the detention of Yosef Yudovitz, Leizer Ronkin was also arrested. He was the owner

[Page 396 - Yiddish]

of a tannery that was nationalized by the Soviet government. Immediately after him, they arrested Yanye (Yosef) Baruchin, a revisionist worker.

The mood of the Jews was very depressed. They understood that the N.K.G.B. used not only the local Communist activists but also other disguised local agents and informants who gave them information concerning every single town inhabitant.

In reality, there were those in town, including also upstanding and elderly Jews, who worked along with the N.K.G.B., giving them information and carrying out their assignments.

In order to solicit these informants, the N.K.G.B. used the following device: They would call in someone who was above suspicion, who was subject to become an informer, reckon up his former sins and propose that he be rehabilitated by working with them for a period of time. In case of refusal, he was told that he must suffer for his sins and be arrested. Understandably, without thinking of the outcome of this conversation, the summoned individual would have to sign an oath that no one, not even his closest, must know about what the N.K.G.B. had discussed with him.

Unfortunately, there were those who surrendered to the threats and accepted the proposed "work." Thus, there were amongst the informers, people of various ages, political hues and social strata. No one knew for sure who was working with the N.K.G.B. and, therefore, everyone was suspect at being a possible agent. This mutual suspicion resulted in the fear of speaking a word in front of others.

The culmination of these political arrests came on the night of February 10, 1941 when ten workers were arrested. They were: Chaim Branchuk, Yashe Yudovitz, Archik Moravchik, Berl Rimar and Shia Kantor, who were leaders of the General Zionists; Shmuel Zezik, Arke Lifshitz, Kopel Moravchik and Mendel Kravchik, who were *Poalei Zion* workers and Berl Kaftan, one of the most capable of the, till then,

Communist activists who was charged with working for the Polish security organization.

These arrests had a shocking effect on the David-Horodoker Jews. No one was sure of his safety. The still-free Zionist workers anticipated further arrests and waited fearfully for their turn. There was a mood of panic in town. People would avoid passing the building containing the N.K.G.B. bureaus. This building cast terror on the inhabitants. Who knew how many more victims it would swallow up? Gloom and dread befell everyone. Several Zionist workers left the town and moved to other places where no one knew them.

[Page 397 - Yiddish]

People stopped attending organizations. Everyone spent the after-work time in the narrow circle of their family.

During this time, several *Horodtchukas* were also arrested.

The outcome of the political arrests of the thirteen David-Horodoker Jews is as follows: Five men: Shmuel Zezik, Yosef Yudovitz, Archik Moravchik, Mendel Kravchik and Kopel Moravchik (now Yaakov Mor) are now in Israel. Shia Kantor is in Poland and Kaftan is in America. Leizer Ronkin escaped from the prisoner transport deep in Russia. He returned to David-Horodok where he was killed with all the David-Horodoker Jews. Five men: Chaim Branchuk, Yanye Baruchin, Yashe Yudovitz, Arke Lifshitz and Berl Rimar starved to death in the various Soviet prison camps. Honor their memory!

* * *

Despite the fear and dread, there were no further political arrests or exiles until just before the German-Soviet war. As things began to quieten down, a new mood of alarm emerged, far more horrible than detention by the N.K.G.B. Rumors began to spread about the eventual possibility of war between Germany and the Soviet Union. The fear of this eventuality was unusually intense. The town's Christian population, the *Horodtchukas*, became self-confident and waited impatiently for the day when the Germans would march into town. It became apparent that they were preparing for vengeance.

Then there began the movement of large Red Army detachments from east to west, giving the impression that war was approaching at giant steps. Just before the outbreak of war, several Jewish families were arrested and exiled.

On June 22, 1941, Hitler's hordes treacherously attacked the Soviet Union without a declaration of war and thereby began the sad and horrible end of the Jews of David-Horodok.

The sawmill of Moche Rimar in David-Horodok - in the picture M. Rimar, his wife Bushke, daughter Rachel, and son Berl, as well as three foremen

[Page 55 - in the Hebrew section]

[Page 56 - Hebrew] [Page 397 - Yiddish]

4. Destruction and Holocaust

There was great panic. The Jews were frightened to death. The *Horodtchukas* were confident. The Soviet authorities in town were agitated.

The town's youth were quickly mobilized. However, not everyone was taken into the army. Those who had unacceptable social status were later released.

[Page 398 - Yiddish]

German airplanes appeared over the town and although they dropped no bombs, they created a terrible panic. The German troops continued onward with immense power. The Red Army retreated in disarray and confusion. The Soviet town leaders began evacuating.

Hundreds of Jewish youth and entire families fled to the previous Soviet-Polish border with the aim of evacuating to Russia in order to escape the murderous hands of the Nazis. Unfortunately, they encountered a strong Soviet guard at the old border that only let those with special permits to pass. The remainder were not allowed to cross over and they were forced to return to David-Horodok. The Soviet town authorities were also sent back with orders to remain until the last minute.

The Germans had already captured Pinsk, Luninets, Lakhva and Mikashevitz but they had not yet entered David-Horodok. The town was in fact without a government. David-Horodok was not captured because it was not near a railroad line or a highway. The *Horodtchukas* could not wait until the Germans came and on their own accord, they sent a delegation led by the feldsher [paramedic] Maraiko to the German military authority in Pinsk, requesting that the Germans speed up their arrival in the town. They thereby declared the willingness of the *Horodtchukas* to work alongside with the Germans. They wished to make a quick end to the Jewish population of David-Horodok.

The delegation returned pleased with the "positive" results which they had achieved. After the return of the delegation, the rumor was spread that the Red Army had begun assaulting and repelling the Germans. The delegation was terrified and they fled back to Pinsk. Unfortunately, in a couple of days, the news was proven false and the delegation returned to the town accompanied by the Germans.

That same day, the *Horodtchukas*, led by the above-mentioned Maraiko, the brothers Tania and Liava Kasarev, Kuloga, Yavplov and others, arranged a meeting under the open sky in honor of the "great historical day." The Germans gave over the civil authority into the hands of the *Horodtchukas*, appointing Maraiko as town mayor and Liava Kasarev as commander of the civil police. The Jews were ordered to wear the Star of David.

On the 16th of Av, 5701, an order was delivered that a six o'clock the next morning, all Jewish men over the age of 14 were to gather at the marketplace opposite the Catholic Church, taking shovels with them. It was implied that they would take them to work.

Early the next morning, the Jews began assembling at the marketplace which was surrounded by armed German SS troops and many *Horodtchukas*.

[Page 399 - Yiddish]

After all had gathered, the *Horodtchukas* spread around town checking for holdouts.

The brothers Isser and Hershel Gurevitz, who were found in a hiding place, had their eyes gouged out while being taken to the marketplace.

All those gathered at the marketplace were led away on foot by a strongly armed SS detachment, accompanied by hundreds of *Horodtchukas* to Chinovsk, a village seven kilometers from David-Horodok. There, the graves had already been prepared.

Surrounded on all sides by artillery and machine guns, every single man was shot to death. The cries and the screams of the unfortunate victims carried through the air and reached as far as David-Horodok.

The gathered *Horodtchukas* had fulfilled a triple mission: they made sure that no one fled from the field; they removed the gold rings, watches, clothing, shoes, and boots and even tore out gold teeth. Finally, they carried out the job of throwing the victims into the graves, not looking to see if they were really dead or still half alive.

Only two children succeeded in escaping unnoticed from that frightful slaughter. Wandering through the fields, they joined a partisan group and thus survived.

* * *

In town, the second part of the frightful tragedy took place. After the men were led out of town to the slaughter, the women and small children were ordered to leave David-Horodok within an hour.

The few men who had succeeded in hiding out and did not go out to the "work," among them Rabbi Moshele, Chaim Moravchik and others, changed into women's clothing and they went along with all the women and children. However, there were *Horodtchukas* at the bridge checking for disguised men among the women. All the disguised men were recognized by the *Horodtchukas*. They were brutally beaten and then thrown from the bridge into the river. Thus a group of several thousand women and children set out on a horrible path of wandering, not knowing where to go.

They wandered for two weeks over fields, roads and trails. Not one town would take them in despite the efforts of the local Jews. Only a few dozen women and children succeeded in getting accommodations with relatives in the surrounding towns of Lakhva, Stolin and Luninets. The remainder kept wandering for two weeks, suffering hunger, cold and the hatred of the peasants who would beat and rape them.

[Page 400 - Yiddish]

During those two weeks, all the deserted Jewish homes with their possessions were pillaged. Many Jewish houses were dismantled by peasants from surrounding villages, bringing them back in pieces to their own villages. The *Horodtchukas* moved into many of the houses.

After two weeks of wandering, the women and children returned to the gates of David-Horodok which "deigned" to receive them. It was understood that they were no longer permitted in their own homes and a ghetto was created for them on a few streets where there were gentile hovels. This ghetto existed for a year. In the course of that year, more than half died from epidemics, "accidental homicides" and starvation. Officially the ghetto inhabitants received 100 grams of bread per person per day, but, in fact, no bread at all was distributed at least two days a week.

After a year of extraordinary suffering and frightful existence, all those women and children still alive, including three or four grown men such as Velvel Kushnir, whom the Germans spared from the slaughter of the men because he was an expert in the repair of new machines, were led out on a certain day (unfortunately the date is unknown) to the same place where the men had been murdered the previous year, and they too were shot to death.

Thus ended the close to 500-year existence of the Jewish community of David-Horodok.

* * *

During the three years of Nazi occupation of David-Horodok, a partisan group paid almost daily "visits" to David-Horodok causing much damage to the Germans and many headaches to the *Horodtchukas*.

The partisans burnt almost all the Jewish houses in town so that the *Horodtchukas* would not benefit from Jewish possessions. They blew up the town's power station. From time to time, they raided the town, killing both Germans and *Horodtchukas*. They kept the town under tension throughout the entire period.

In this partisan group, there was a Jewish girl (whose name and fate are unfortunately not known), who was distinguished by her extraordinary courage and daring. In every partisan raid, she was always the first to go in and the last to withdraw. With her heroic deeds, she threw terror into the Germans and the *Horodtchukas* and at the same time gave courage to her partisan comrades.

* * *

In 1944, the Red Army freed David-Horodok of the murderous Nazi occupation. Unfortunately, there was no longer a living Jew in the town.

[Page 401 - Yiddish]

A few dozen leaders of the *Horodtchukas* fled along with the German army.

Several of the Jews were saved because they were in the Soviet Union during the war: Hershel Korman and his two sons, Neta and Matityahu (today in Israel); Itzel Nachmanovitz (now in the United States of America); Mendel Kravchik (now in Israel) and Litman Moravchik (in Israel) visited David-Horodok and encountered a ravaged and scorched town without one living Jew and an immense common grave where the tortured David-Horodok Jews rested.

In every *Horodtchuka* house, they found Jewish furniture and possessions. In the marketplace, the *Horodtchukas* sold Jewish clothing with kaftans. The *Horodtchuka* women wore kerchiefs made of Jewish prayer shawls.

However, they all had nothing to say. They laid the entire guilt on the Germans and the escaped leaders of the *Horodtchukas*. They themselves "know nothing," "regretful," "was not in the town at the time," "also suffered from the Germans," and in a word: "entirely innocent sheep – almost martyrs!"

* * *

Today, there is not one Jew in David-Horodok.

* * *

The saving remnant is mostly in Israel. Several remained in the Soviet Union, some in Poland and a few immigrated to America.

Member of our town Yitzchak (Itzel) Nachmanovitz (in army uniform) at the mass grave in David-Horodok in 1945, on the fourth anniversary of the tragic destruction

[Page 59 - in the Hebrew section]

Way of Life

[Page 63]

The City of David (David-Horodok)
Sections From My Memory, From the Period of the Diaspora

Dr. M. Zagorodsky (of Blessed Memory)

Translated by Jerrold Landau

Dr. M. Zagorodsky of blessed memory

a) A Section From the Introduction to the First Volume of the Book of Memories, From the Chapter "Twilight and Dust"

It was August 1, 1950. That day, I was 83 years and seven months old. I had been thinking thoughts and pondering ideas for about seventy of those years, now as an elderly man. Of course, everything was in its era and situation. I spent about half of those 83 years in the Diaspora and half in the Land. However, even throughout the forty years that I spent in the Diaspora, I thought about the Holy Land, for my mother of blessed memory, who was the daughter of one of the Yeshiva heads of the holy community of Mir, the daughter of Rabbi Leib Kunem, knew all the prayers by heart. When I was already about three years old, she taught me to recite the *Shema, Shmone Esrei*, and Grace After Meals, and I would repeat several times a day "And rebuild Jerusalem the Holy City speedily in our days," "Have mercy upon Zion," etc. "Please O L-rd our G-d have mercy upon Your nation of Israel, and upon Jerusalem Your city, and upon Zion Your honorable sanctuary." When I got a bit older and became proficient in Torah, David-Horodok became "the City of David"; every river in the Diaspora became the Jordan, Jabbok, or the Arnon; every hill – the Lebanon; and every tree an acacia tree or the cedars of Lebanon.

"The City of David" was a town during my childhood "at the beginning of its founding." It was small, with about 300 Jewish families living in its center, around a field of shops. The houses were built of wood, with uneven boards; the windows were without shutters; the roofs were covered with bales of hay, or for the wealthy people, thin pieces of wood; the streets were without sidewalks or thoroughfares. During the spring, when the snow was melting, the streets would turn into bogs or even streams of water. The part of the town close to the riverbank was literally a pond, to the point where boats could travel from the houses to the marketplace. Aside from the houses of the Jews, gentiles lived in huts surrounded by vegetable gardens, pigsties, and areas for other domestic animals.

The Jewish community was poor and destitute for the most part. There were many teachers of young children and butchers; but in particular, there were very many shopkeepers. They owned general stores, in which the residents would be able to purchase whole salted fish – because for the most part, the salted fish was sold in pieces – as well as other diverse products apparently needed by city dwellers. On the other hand, one could obtain all the needs for one's household and farm, for the "payment" of the gentile was the "fat portion" of the Jew…

[Page 64]

b) The *Melamdim* [Teachers]

The majority of the Jews of David-Horodok had one aspiration: that the sons (not the daughters) would study Torah and become rabbis, or at least rabbinical judges or cantors – that is general clergymen in the Diaspora communities. Therefore, there were many *melamdim*. The parents went hungry and with meager clothing, so long as their sons would study Torah. One can portray "the Pohoster" [a person from Pohost] as a typical *melamed*. He "fathered" four children; fathered, but did not concern himself with their livelihood. As soon as they grew up a bit, he sent them to study Torah. And who would support them? He would say, "He Who gives life will give sustenance." During his childhood, he too certainly ate from "his toiling in Torah", and was supported at the table of others. He "ate his meals on a rotation basis" when he studied in Yeshivot and *Beis Midrashes*. He was a great scholar, ordained as a rabbi, and graced with all good traits – albeit "traits" that did not produce bread to satiety or education for his children. On Thursdays, Mother, that is the wife of "the Pohoster", would purchase rolls (potrochi in Russian), and sometimes also a part of large intestine that had been pressed and cleaned, and filled with various stuffing – and this was our treat. To our good fortune, we were not sensitive to odors, and we did not sense it… On Fridays, she would sometimes cook kasha soup with some sort of inferior meat. Our father would cut the meat into small pieces, but he could not control himself, and as he was slicing, he would toss a piece into his mouth while we, his children, stared at him with thirsting eyes. Only on the Sabbath did we get more appropriate servings of cholent.

c) The Poverty

Who can describe the poverty? Who can find the precise words to describe the full depth of suffering of the impoverished Jews in the towns of Polesye!? Is it a wonder that poverty sometimes drove upright people out of their minds – and they sinned! The poverty of the residents of the remote towns 80-100 years ago requires a quick scribe and a lamenting pen to describe, as Jeremiah in Eicha [Lamentations].

There is the story of a certain prayer leader who did not receive his wages from the community, so he stole the synagogue candlesticks. (His wife nagged him to death, saying "Men do not despise a thief, if he steals to satisfy his soul when he is hungry[1] (Proverbs 6:30) – and how much more so to satisfy the souls of his many children who are shouting for bread, but there is none!" I recall

Velemitsher Street in David-Horodok

[Page 65]

that prayer leader when he covered his head with his tallis at *shacharit* of Rosh Hashanah and walked to the prayer leader's lectern [*amud*] with important steps. He stood, powerfully recited *Hamelech* [The King] and continued in the standard melody, "sitting on the throne"... A shudder passed through my childlike bones, as if I was indeed seeing "the King" sitting on the high and lofty throne...

The disgraceful poverty! There was a cobbler in town named Sopliak. He earned his livelihood from the poor people who wore torn, worn-out shoes, and would bring their shoes to him to have the patches replaced. This Sopliak, as a typical tradesman, lived with his family in a corridor that he rented from the homeowner (This house had one room for the family of the owners.) The corridor was the pen for the cow that stood tied in one corner. The other corners were set up for the family of Sopliak the cobbler... The cold penetrated the corridor in the winter, but the cow also warmed up the Sopliak children. He did not know of a comb or soap throughout all his days, and his appearance was like a destructive demon. His mustache and lips were always wet and full of tobacco – the only pleasure that this poor man ever knew in his life. He used it to his heart's content. With two fingers blackened by tar, Sopliak would pinch a small measure of tobacco from the box that he prepared with the horn of a cow. He would push it into his nostrils and breathe with force, thrust and breathe until he began to sneeze loudly. His roommate, the cow, also began to tremble and free itself from its rope. The wet tobacco hung from the thick hairs that stuck out of his nose, and added a garland of grace to his face... When this Sopliak came to the synagogue on Shemini Atzeret and Simchat Torah and saw that they were giving Torah honors to every child but skipping over him, as if he was not alive and existing, he would raise his hand to the *shamash* [beadle] and scream: "To me, to me!" This poor man did not pass over the pleasure of embracing the Torah and circling the *bima* with it. My father, who educated me according to the methodology of King Solomon, "chastise your son" etc.[2] would also use the threat: "I will send you to Sopliak as an apprentice..." This had its effect...

d) My Age

My mother kept track of my birthday by a unique type of count: according to the fires! My mother told me that I was born on the third day of Chanukah in the third year after "the great fire". This is the matter of the fires: A hundred years ago, there were towns in the Polesye area surrounded by forests from the time of creation. Most of them were coniferous: pines, firs, and the like, all of which are rich in tar. All the houses were built from these tar trees (the walls, ceilings and floors). The roofs of the few wealthy people were covered by wooden shingles. All the rest were covered with bales of rye hay. All this was very flammable. Not one summer passed without a single fire in the towns. A fire might destroy the entire town if it was large, or only a sizable portion of it. A large fire would be announced in the nearby towns, and the Jews, merciful people that they were, would hasten to collect loaves of bread to send to the people afflicted by the fire. (According to my research about the community, it is possible that the "large fire" was in the year 5627 (1867), even though, according to the head of the "community", there was a significant fire also in 5628 (1868).)

To this day, after the age of 80, I recall the plan of the towns – a plan that was not very different in all the towns of the district of the forest of Polesye. There was a square yard with the shops of the Jews: that was the market. Small streets without names spread out from there. The homes of the Jews surrounded the market, and behind them were the huts of the gentiles with the vegetable gardens and pigsties. The pigs would wander around outside throughout the day, and they would conduct the sanitation task in the yards of the Jews – cleaning the garbage. The underground water in that area was shallow, and almost every yard had an unfenced well. I recall that when I was about three years old, we children played in the yard, and when we returned home at sunset, a child was missing. His mother went to look for him, and I showed her that he was playing in the well...

At that time, a *Desiatnik* (ruler over tens!) ruled in town. When I was three years old, I was given over to the teacher. We were about ten children in the room of the rebbe. Whoever was outside shouted aloud: "*Desiatnik*!" The doors would creak,

[Page 66]

we would then all climb up on the oven, as the rebbe himself would crawl to the chickencoop beneath the oven and frighten the chickens… We did not know what happened, but we were all afraid of the *desiatnik*. The fear of him remained in our imagination until we came to the Land (The Jewish policeman did not frighten us: on the contrary, he was afraid of our lads…)

e) The *Tzadikim*

There was a rabbi living in David-Horodok who was a *Tzadik* in his generation. People did not come to him from other towns to receive his blessings, and he was not wealthy like the other *Tzadikim* with their "courtyards and assistants". Nevertheless, even the small donations from the Hassidim of the City of David were sufficient to sustain him more or less appropriately. My father, a native of Lithuania, was a *Misnaged* [non-Hassid] who did not believe in the Rebbe. However, he did not separate himself from the community and did not force his ideas during unusual occurrences. For example: When I was born, Reb Ahrele Karliner, a well-known *Tzadik* and kabbalist came to town. He had Hassidim in towns as well as cities (Pinsk-Karlin). Even though my father was a *Misnaged*, he invited Reb Ahrele to circumcise me. (When I take a bath, I always recall Reb Ahrele and think: how good is my lot.) Once on the Sabbath, my father went to listen to a Torah lecture from the local *Tzadik* (with the goal of proving it incorrect, as was his manner). This time, I went with him. The Rebbe blessed me and placed his hand on my head. (I am now close to 90, and have no baldness on my head. This is certainly in the merit of the Rebbe – The *Tzadik*…)

Along with the faith in *Tzadikim* (good Jews), there was also great faith in prayers, belief in the evil eye, belief in demons, spirits, witchcraft and other nonsense. (Due to a lack of cleanliness, children had *kilkim* (*kilk* is kolton in Russian) on their heads – long hairs that stuck together and were impossible to comb apart, but rather a clump that would not separate, and needed to be cut.) My older brother had such a *kilk* on his head. My mother did not remove it from his head, for she said: "This child is a great scholar and bright as the sun, and if I remove the *kilk*, the evil eye will overtake his wisdom and beauty. When he got older and went to *cheder*, the children embittered his life, "The one of the *kilk* has arrived." He cried and pleaded with his mother to have mercy upon him and remove his disgrace. My mother finally cut off the *kilk*, but the child was punished: he began to squint with one eye.

f) Wagon Drivers

Wagon drivers would come and go every week from the City of David to nearby cities. They would bring merchandise for the shopkeepers as well as letters. My mother told about the wagon drivers that they decreed a fast day on the day that the first train arrived on the railway, bringing letters and merchandise for the shopkeepers and robbing the livelihood from the "class of wagon drivers", who were separate from the rest of the community and had their own house of worship as well as a rabbi and rabbinical teacher. One wagon driver asked his rabbi on the Sabbath: "I recited the entire Book of Psalms today, must I still recite *Barchi Nafshi* (sections of Psalms recited on winter Sabbath afternoons)?"[3] The rabbi deliberated, but then finally said, "If you transport a house full of tar, must you place tar on the wheels of your wagon?"

g) *Haskalah* [Enlightenment] in the Town: The *Melamdim*

There were many *melamdim*. If there was no chance of opening a shop, many would open a *cheder*. I recall several of them. I recall my rebbe whose name was Kadish. He was poor throughout his entire life: he wore worn-out patched clothes, with multi-colored patches. He would stand next to the table dressed in an apron of pads, peer into the Gemara, and shake his body: clumps of old cotton would shake off of his simple apron. He would shake his body, and read from Tractate *Ketubot*: A virgin gets married on Wednesday and a widow on Thursday... oy, oy, master of Abraham! *Tali tania bedelo tania; oy oy ha tania ve ha tanya, oy oy...*"[4]

The rebbe Kadish prepared his class for his students in that manner. I was among the students, and I was eight years old... I did not understand any of Kadish's words. All of us lads sat on a low wooden stool. I, being small, could not see what was written in the Gemara. I would lift myself up from time to time to peer into the Gemara on the high table. My friends then shouted: "He lifts himself up to look at the virgin who is getting married..." The rebbe Kadish would get angry.

[Page 67]

Once when I lifted myself up, he approached, grabbed me by two hands, shook me, and forcefully placed me on the bench, to the point where my nose started to bleed. One student burst out shouting: "He who spills the blood of a person!"[5] (Kadish panicked and called the rebbetzin to dry up the blood.) I stopped studying in Kadish's *cheder* at the end of the term. He was a negative character among the students.

My father the *melamed* was a positive character. He explained the structure of the Tent of Meeting, the Tabernacle, and its vessels to the lads who studied in his *cheder*. He drew for them the clothing of the priests with the bells, the miter on the forehead, the menorah with the knobs and flowers. However, a group of those students had been "poisoned" by the "culture" that was brought in by the lads who visited the large cities. Those lads would make mocking gestures, and stick out a finger... When my father caught a child in his iniquity, he would send him home to his father to punish him, for he did not know any other ways of teaching... But, with his healthy intellect, he understood that beatings would not uproot the evil...

My family lived in the house of Hillel the butcher. His son Wolf did not succeed in his studies. His father told him, "My son! You will not be a rabbi among Israel, and you will also not be a butcher. Go do something for yourself, and you will be a *melamed*..."

There was one other *melamed* who disseminated *Haskalah*: the *melamed* Moshe Zaika. He was called that because he had difficulty with words. He taught in accordance with the new methodologies. He imparted education to the children of strangers, but he left his own son out on the street. On the day after Yom Kippur, the city was in uproar: The son of Moshe Zakika played on the street with the daughter of a neighbor on the holy festival.

h) The Sabbath

It is said that the Sabbath protects the Nation of Israel more than the nation observes the Sabbath (Ahad Ha'am). This was true with respect to the Sabbath in the towns. The poverty, denigration and atrophy were only felt in town during the weekdays. When Thursday arrived, the awakening toward the Sabbath began: women began to concern themselves with flour for challahs, wine for *kiddush*, and meat. Lamentations began in the houses of the poor about the lack of money for the needs of the Sabbath. The men ran about, some to obtain a loan, others to oppress a debtor, and still others lifting their eyes to the mountains, from whence will their help come...[6] The butchers organized their tables with meat, innards and intestines, and the market was full of the shrieks of the women. On Friday, the town filled up with its residents, for those who were returning from the villages and the fairs hastened to return to their homes and prepare for the Holy Sabbath. They returned, some in a wagon laden with produce from a village; some on foot, worn out from carrying a sack over their backs filled with the goods of a village. The tailor exchanged his work with the needle, and the shoemaker with the anvil. Anyone sitting in the empty market, for G-d had not prepared anything for him – prepared to hear the curses of his wife and her complaints about her "wage earner". He would go straight to Chaya-Tzipa (see further on) and promise to pay next week. Will G-d not cast off forever?[7] If only not to return to "his dear partner" emptyhanded…

Friday: In every house they were baking, cooking, scouring, cleaning, scraping; shampooing the children's heads, organizing and setting tables, preparing candelabras and candles. The dwelling places of poverty were turning into sanctuaries of rest, to splendid holiness, to a place where it was possible "to sanctify the Seventh day as appropriate to it."[8] Even the mistress of the house was resting after a week of wandering, worry, resentment and curses. She wore her dress from the time of her wedding, recited the blessing on the candles, added her tears, the tears of blessing, over and above her tears of the entire week – and sent her shampooed and combed children to the synagogue to pray, and to answer Amen.

i) The Bathhouse

The men had just emptied their sacks or closed their shops. They immediately took their laundered cloak in one hand, and the "broom" into another hand, and rushed to the bathhouse. The barbers sat in the anteroom of the bathhouse. For two kopecks (one mil or prutah in Israeli currency) the barber would cut the hair. For three kopecks, he would also give a shave. Along with his wages, he would also take the hair that was used to make cushions or mattresses for weddings. There, one could obtain wind horns, they would let blood for those suffering headaches, and for any ailment…

[Page 68]

They would get undressed, fold their outer clothes and make a bundle, take the cloak and the dirty pants (used as a "zoo"), take the "broom", and go inside. They would hang the dirty clothes on rods beneath the ceiling, where the heat was burning, and begin to wash their bodies, scrubbing and cleaning in water that was almost boiling. They would beat themselves with the leaf-broom until they ran out of energy. Then they would pour cold water over their bodies. They would take their folded clothing, get dressed, and return home with a rejuvenated body, drink a warm drink, and hasten to the Welcoming of the Sabbath service. (The bathhouse served as a place of healing for all diseases, and fortified the body so that it would not weaken from the change of atmosphere. People lived, had many children, and lived long.)

The Sabbath helped the Jews forget the bitterness of the exile, for when they considered the situation, with a hidden assertion, the Jewish soul mourned for the fact that permission was given to the wicked ones to damage the chosen of G-d, who were created in the Divine image. The Sabbath made them forget this disgrace.

j) The Gentiles

The exile was especially felt on the day of *Nitl* or *Nitla.*[9] I recall that day from my childhood days in Horodok. *Nitl* was a holiday for the Christians, the birthday of Jesus. The gentile lads would arrange *Koladi* – they would go out at night with torches and burning wooden sticks. They would make bonfires, jump through the bonfires, and sing inciteful religious songs. Woe to a Jew who encountered these celebrants. It would be better for him to encounter a mad dog. On that night, the Jews would hide and close themselves within their innermost rooms. They would not learn, however. On *Nitl*, they would play cards. The next day, they would tell about a shattered Jewish window, about Reb Yankel the *Melamed* being hit by a large, heavy snowball, for he went out to attend to his bodily needs (for due to his illness, he could not hold back until the wrath passed…).

k) People Who Comported Themselves Well, and Others

The settlement of the City of David had various characters: those who comported themselves well, and rotten ones whose livelihood forced them to swear falsely, to lie, to impinge on the honor of their fellow, to create ruses for livelihood. From those who comported themselves well, I will note Shaul-Ber the *Maggid*. He earned his livelihood from selling raisin wine for *Kiddush*, *Havdalah*, and the four cups [of Passover]. He would prepare it with his own hands with scrupulous kashruth, protecting it from the eyes of a gentile.[10] From this source of livelihood, he merited a fine house, full of sons and daughters. On the Sabbath, after an afternoon nap, Shaul-Ber would go to the *Beis Midrash* filled with Jews who were waiting for him. He would sit in his place next to the Holy Ark, roll up his white sleeves, expose his hairy arms up to the elbow, rise, stand up straight, and lecture the audience on the *Midrash* of the weekly Torah portion or *Ein Yaakov*. He had a pleasant, somewhat nasal voice. He would emphasize his words from the *Midrash* with hand gestures. The congregation paid close attention, absorbing every clear, full word from his mouth. Shaul-Ber lectured until he got tired. Then a member of the congregation approached the prayer leader's podium and declared *Ashrei Temimei Derec*,[11] etc. He would recite it verse by verse, and the congregation would respond, until the conclusion of this eightfold chapter, by confessing his error: "I have strayed like lost sheep." Then someone would lead the *Mincha* service in a glorious, moving voice. After that, the worry began to return to the hearts of those who had observed the Sabbath… the worry for the upcoming week did not grant rest. Sometimes, the rest was interrupted with the cracking of the ice in the river, the sound of trees breaking because of the heaviness of the snow, the breaking of wood and beams, etc.

Chaya-Tzipa also belonged of the ones who "comported themselves well". She was a middle-aged woman, childless because G-d had closed her womb.[12] Her husband managed the property of the landowner [*poretz*] and spent every weekday on the estate, returning home on Friday for the Sabbath. Chaya-Tzipa was a G-d fearing, goodhearted and merciful woman. Since she did not have a family, she occupied herself with good deeds. On Thursdays, she would take sacks and make the rounds to collect leftover bread from the homes of the wealthy people, so to speak, for on that day, they would already be preparing dough for the upcoming week. Chaya-Tzipa would collect in her sack the morsels that the children had bitten and left over, along with morsels of pastry, cake, charred bread,

[Page 69]

etc. She would collect one or two sacks worth, load them on her bent back, and go around the next day to distribute her loot to the homes of the "needy" – that is the families who had become impoverished but were embarrassed to extend their hand. Chaya-Tzipa did not distribute this as a gift, but she rather sold it on loan that was to be paid back when they regained their means… Her husband would return from the estate on Fridays, bringing sacks and bags of the finest produce of the estate. A sack of potatoes for the rabbi, a sack for the rabbinical judge, a small sack for the cantor, and similar for all the rest of the clergy. The rest was for his wife, who hastened to give it to the families "under her protection". In return she received blessings on her head, and wishes that G-d should open her womb…

Among the rotten ones were numbered the poor people who took advantage of the fires that broke out in the houses, partaking of the booty during the panic that arose in the town with every conflagration. There were also the parents who could not afford to marry off a daughter, so they sent her to the big cities to earn a livelihood. One such person in Horodok was Moshe the Drummer, who played the drum while the musicians were performing at weddings. He raised a daughter who came of age, but nobody had mercy on her. She traveled to the city of Pinsk where such girls would find a place to stay in certain houses. She got old there, and they sent her away, for there was nobody interested in that worn out person. When she returned to her parents' home, she continued on as was customary in the "guest house" in Pinsk. Anyone who passed by the house of the drummer and saw this licentious woman would spit and curse in his heart on account of the promiscuous woman.

I remember other families whom I knew while I was still a child in the City of David. There was the family of Eli Kon: The head of the family got the name Kon (horse in Russian) during the year that he purchased a small steamboat that was able to float through the shallow water of the Horyn River after the snow and water swells melted in the spring. The jokers of the city called him "Kon" as they thought it was appropriate for his steamboat. The Yudovitz family was known as one of the wealthy families of the city. They lived in a house that was plastered even on the outside, and we children would look with jealous eyes on his children who would come with their father to services on the Sabbath, always late. There was also the Katzman family, one of whom was a defense attorney for the justice of the peace in civil cases. (There was a case where someone purchased a bull, but they gave him a steer, and the defense attorney could not explain the difference between them to the judge, because he did not know the translation of the word "castration" in Russian.) The other Katzman brother had a son who was a student in Berlin. When he was interested in a girl from a strictly Orthodox family, the parents of the girl refused to look at him – they would not give their daughter to a goy [gentile], who eats non-kosher food and goes around bareheaded. It would be better to give her over to Molech.[13] Getzel the student did not give up, and, it is said, he explained the matter based on the foundations of realities.[14]

l) Conclusion

This was the way Horodok or, as I call it, the City of David, was during my childhood, seventy or eighty years ago. When I got older, I always thought: I wish that I had wings like a dove,[15] I would fly and see the place of my childhood cradle! How great was my desire for such when girls and boys from the City of David came to the Land of Israel and told me that the town was already a city, a city like all cities: sidewalks, streets, water in the houses, physicians, a pharmacy, bogs and pits that had been cleaned, and a Tarbut School! O! Who would have thought, who could believe the news? I said that the day would come when I would visit it again, my town. But then the Holocaust came. A weakness[16] overtook the gentiles, and they destroyed the town, to the point that not one survivor remained! My eyes weep over the loss of my town along with all the towns in the area where my people had lived. I can find no comfort by justifying their punishment in that they did not heed the call of the prophets, and did not hasten to leave the vale of tears and go to our Land, which was awaiting its children so that they could settle it and build it up.

Translator's footnotes:

1. Translation of this verse from Mechon Mamre. The reference in the text states it is Proverbs 10:30, but this is a typo – it is actually Proverbs 6:30.
2. Proverbs 19:18.
3. Psalm 104 is *Barchi Nafshi*, then the *Shir Hamaalot* Psalms (120-134) are recited.
4. Seemingly a nonsensical droning on of Talmudic words that do not make sense. (A reasonable English translation would be: Yadda, yadda, yadda.)
5. Genesis 9:6.
6. Paraphrased from Psalms 121:1.
7. Paraphrased from Lamentations 3:31.
8. Paraphrased from the *Kol Mekadesh* table hymn [*zemer*] of Friday night.
9. Referring to Christmas. *Nitla* means the hanged (or crucified) one.
10. It is forbidden by Jewish law to drink wine that has been touched by a gentile. Some are scrupulous to avoid wine that was even looked at by a gentile. (Note, this prohibition does not apply after wine has been boiled or pasteurized. Hence, in modern times, there is little issue once wine has been commercially bottled and pasteurized.)
11. The opening words of Psalm 119. Psalm 119 is an eightfold alphabetic acrostic. The final verse of this psalm is noted in the next sentence.
12. Based on Samuel I 1:6.

13. The pagan god of child sacrifice.
14. Hard to interpret this – but I believe it means that the girl was interested in him as well, so he ignored the parents and continued to pursue the relationship.
15. Psalms 55:6
16. Probably referring to a failing on the part of the gentiles – a desire for bloodshed.

The Progressing Town

Yitzchak Ben-Yosef

Translated by Jerrold Landau

1.

To what can our settlement between Stolin and Horodok be compared? To a child growing up in a home in the shadow of an adult brother or sister. He jealously raises his eyes toward him, and they serve for him as an example in all their ways and deeds: He attempts to study Torah, knowledge, manners, and character traits from them.

[Page 70]

Our connection to Horodok was greater than to Stolin. Letters and newspapers reached us in Rubel via Horodok. Lipa Finkelstein's shop was the "postal authority" and letters from all corners of the earth reached us in his name.

These two towns were different from their founding, and certainly from the beginning of this [i.e. the 20th] century. The former was noble, aristocratic, sated, joyous, fully like a bright spring day. Its proximity to the railway station and its centrality to thousands of Hassidim left its mark upon it.

In contrast, the population of David-Horodok was composed primarily of toilers. It was all grumpy and gloomy. It was full of bogs. The marketplace was a bog, the streets were bogs, and one could only move from street to street with difficulty. In my eyes, it was like one long, rainy day.

2.

This gloominess of Horodok was the positive moving force for the youth. The youth of Horodok did not freeze on their guard. They were bustling, storming to find a way to leave this mud. They aspired to the breadths and to progress.

It was natural that the modern *cheder* that taught Hebrew in Hebrew, would arise first in Horodok. Aharon Yonah Shafer was the one who would bring the praiseworthy, famous teacher Yishai Y. S. Adler to Horodok. This was in the early days of the Zionist movement, in 1900. From that year until the modern Tarbut School arose in 1917, the old *cheders* in Horodok with their vapid methodologies disappeared in stages, and a new order and spirit pervaded in local education. This was something that other places did not merit.

It was as if the gloom of this town was saying to the youth: "Don't sink in the mud. Search for a way, and rise up." Talented lads, not only the sons of the wealthy, left their parental house for the wide world – to obtain a matriculation diploma and to go to university. Even a local public school, where elementary fundamental knowledge and education was taught together with gentile children, was opened in Horodok. The people of Stolin, for example, were unable to rise above the poverty of their lives, for they bore their souls in that manner.

3.

The city was not graced with a beautiful landscape. However, nature graced it with a large river that sent its waters afar, to the cities of the valley – Niz – and the large ones: Kiev, Kremenchug, Ekaterinoslav. It exported lumber, and in return imported flour on large and small rafts filled to the brim.

The large bridge spread over the river said to the youth, so to speak: "See, how great is the power of man, and how manifold are his possibilities with science and technology to assist him." The steamboats would come and sail at the side of Horyn to the railway station or to Nirtcha on the Pripyat River – bringing news and reminding the youth that there is still a large, wide world there in the distance – a world of breadth and light, of enlightenment and praise.

There were boys and girls who returned to their parents' home for the Passover holiday, bringing from the wide world the pulses of rich life, the spirits that were blowing there, the spirits of freedom and struggles, penetrating the hearts with disquietude and dissatisfaction, feelings of incompleteness with the current reality, and seeking for the new and the good. In time, that discontent penetrated the spirit of the students of the Tarbut School. They called themselves *Bnei Yehuda*, and declared Hebrew as their language at home and on the street, like the deeds of the great Ben-Yehuda. There was nothing like it in any city or town in the Diaspora at that point. Students in the schools in other places followed and took hold of this later on.

The *Bnei Yehuda* who are today in Israel certainly are able to tell of this splendid chapter in the annals of the town that was wiped out and destroyed, as if it never was.

4.

In Horodok, the parents followed after the children. From the time of the rise of the Zionist movement, the important householders did not hold back from participating in gatherings and activities with their children, even though the youths were directing

[Page 71]

everything. Nobody stood as an obstacle before the seekers. There was no person of authority who raised their voice against the youths (for example, like the Rebbe in Stolin). The rabbis in Horodok did not act with strength, and were even lacking in influence to mix in with communal affairs. They stood at the side or, inadvertently, assisted the new movement.

Distant Sights

A. Yisraeli

(From *Mibifnim*, August 1950)

Translated by Jerrold Landau

a. What Is Unique About David-Horodok?

In essence, there was nothing unique about it. It was like several hundred other towns in the former Pale of Settlement. Look into Mendele, Peretz, Sholem Aleichem, Sholem Asch, Bialik, and all others from the group of writers of that generation, and David-Horodok will appear before you as it was, with its Jews and gentiles, wealthy people and paupers, with its parties and organizations. Absolutely everything is as written. However, it had one hidden trait – my native city. A person is born only once during their lifetime, and a person only has one native city. The farther away one gets from it, the more one senses its reality. Even if one moves away from it, it lives within you. It is a portion of your essence, and a flood of water will not wash it away.

b. Houses and Streets

As a child, I walked on the ground of my town, and I saw it through the eyes of a child. I did not know then that somewhere in the wide world there were mansions, buildings of stone and concrete, paved roads, gardens, and meadows. I accepted my town as it was, with its thatched roofs, its "ponds" of water on its streets, its alleyways and passageways, and all its charms. I saw it as a complete whole, containing everything. It was whole in its style of building, both with the houses of the Jews and the houses of the gentiles. A child who grew up there absorbed its tastes and styles, and united with it.

I recall that there were two-story houses in my town. In order to see the upper story, one had to raise one's head upward, with the concern that one's hat might fall to the ground. It was the work of Satan that the Pravoslavic Church rose up close to those houses. Its gold crosses sparkled in the sun and whitened in the snow, casting oppression over the heads of the Jewish children.

One such house was owned by Aharon Slomiansky. As customary, the first floor was a shop for manufactured goods. In times of emergency, which occurred with some frequency, it served as a place of refuge. Those who lived on the street would turn their heads toward the Singer sewing machines, the Fraget products and various bundles of bedding and moveable objects. At a time when the church bells rung and sounded the alarm for a fire, the store took in everyone. There were wicker baskets containing dowries for daughters who had come of age, wooden chests with iron rings filled with all sorts of finery, holy objects of the rabbis, and all sorts of utensils. Everything was mixed together, and the valuable could not be discerned from the cheap. That was the first floor. The upper story was only open to the public once a year, when the Rebbe of Stolin would be hosted there when he came to visit his flock. I too was among his flock. At that time, the youngsters did not know where to look: whether on the throng of Hassidim who crowded into the rooms, awaiting with awe the Rebbe, who was in an inner room; whether to look upon the baked goods, desserts, and jams that were brought in and removed in cycles. Or perhaps to touch the heavy furniture and valuable ornaments that decorated the rooms.

The second house was splendid, fully secular, and mainly private. You could look from afar, but could not enter. This was the house of Yudovitz, an elderly Jew, perhaps a wealthy man, perhaps not. However, he was a complete *apikores* [heretic],

[Page 72]

almost an unbeliever to vex[1] – this is what the adults who knew everything said. He brought in a building plan from outside the country that was not known in our place. The "stately" roads that spread out from the house were not like the height of the house. There was a slightly arched balcony in the front, flower bushes in the corners, and a wonderful chair on the balcony – if you wanted, it could double over and stand, and if you wanted, it could be a half chair and half sofa. I later found a house and furniture of this nature in drawings in a textbook of the German language. It was as if it was copied from there, and presented for viewing in the market square in our town.

I never peeked into this holy of holies. Below, amongst the rest of the rented shops, there was a very popular pharmacy. The pharmacist was the son of the elder Yudovitz. He spoke to every person in their own language: to gentiles in gentile language, to the common folk in Yiddish, and to the maskilim [enlightened ones] in a language which was a blend of half Yiddish and half intelligentsia-style Russian, peppered at times with Latin names. I was a visitor there at certain times to obtain pills, creams and various types of "leaves" prescribed by Wolf the medic. The pharmacist often served as a sort of physician, for the minor illnesses of the Jews and gentiles were known, and there were medicines established from the six days of Creation.

These mansions jutted upwards, arousing curiosity and wonder. However, they were exceptions. Who is so ignorant as to turn their eyes upward at a time when everything is lovely and close to the range of vision of a child: you open your eyes and see everything. Even the street is entirely before you – as a shortcut, for jumping over an abandoned fence, for "sailing" over the greenish water. When nobody was looking, one could also take a reed off of the roof of a cottage, and escape before the gentile would find out or before his dog would start to chase you. The builder knew what was wonderful to the soul of a child. He left a place on the pathways, placed ladders on the roofs, and placed barrels of water next to every house as a protection against fire. He made pits under the ovens and the entrances to the houses. How good were your houses, O Horodok!

We once ran about on those streets and in those houses. Some did so for a few years, and then escaped to the "wide world", and others walked upon them until the end of their days, until they were carried to the place outside the city where the sky and the ground kissed together.

c. Jews and Gentiles

The *Chumash* and the *Siddur*. Tisha B'Av and Passover nights. The rebbe in the *cheder* and grandmother in the house – all of them declared: "Exile, exile!" However, I will admit, and I am not ashamed: I did not see the exile at that time, and I never even saw a proper pogrom during my childhood. For some reason, the uncircumcised ones, many of whom "understood all speech" are etched in my imagination like the Gibeonites,[2] drawing water and hewing wood for us. They removed the manure from our barns, they lit the ovens on the winter Sabbaths so we would have heat, they put out the lights on Sabbaths and festivals so that we would not, heaven forbid, fall into a sin. They did every difficult job for us. At the end, they stood at our doorways as paupers to receive challah on the eve of the Sabbath, and matzos on Passover. They drank the wine of the "ten plagues" for their own enjoyment, etc. The *Beis Midrashes* and houses of worship stood on the roads in splendor. Hundreds and thousands of Jews comported themselves in the manner of freedom, and worshiped out loud to G-d, the Creator of the world. For some reason, it seemed to me that the wooden cross standing at the corner of the street was bent and embarrassed, cancelled with the Jewish sense of holiness breathed around me. For indeed, what was that wooden plank. It had no form or splendor in contrast with the Torah scrolls adorned with silver crowns, pointers, and checkered covers. It was not clear to me at that time what exile was, and what was its essence.

After time I heard, and also read in books, that the sun and the trees, the gardens and the broad areas, the joy and happiness of life – the gentiles took everything and left nothing other than asphyxiation and slime, the bare street, without shade or protection. The books were indeed telling the truth. As for me, however, when imagining my native city before my eyes, cherry orchards appear before me, apples and pears giving of their bounty, and the trees rustling. The waves of the river caress the ground of my town, and boats sail in it. Groves encircle it, and the wide, high sky is spread above me. I see children running about, fighting, and making up. Battles are conducted

[Page 73]

between the sons of the covenant [i.e. Jews] and those who were not sons of the covenant [i.e. gentiles]. There were "wounds, bruises and sores"[3] – when such an event took place to a youngster in the wide world.

The sages further stated: The gentiles took the dew of the heavens and the fat of the earth,[4] and only left the Jews the businesses of oil, kerosene, salted fish, and all types of haberdashery. However, by your life, I saw succulent fruits growing on "Jewish" trees, ripe vegetables in our yards, and animals that are kosher by the most stringent view, with split hoofs and who chew their cud. Various kinds of kosher fowl waddled in our precincts. Indeed, the gentile tilled the soil, making furrows, and even planted seeds and saplings. Indeed, the gentile guarded the cattle. At times, they would even bring the calf born in the meadow – however, the furrows in our yards were witnesses that we pulled out the weeds with our own hands, we broke apart the clods of earth, we placed stakes for the beanstalks, and we recited our blessing to the fruits of the ground. The red crests and speckled feathers were witness to the adventures of the children on the leather plucked from the fine wagons – for the mooing of the cow was heard in our barns, and the clucking and pecking in our houses. Indeed, the books exaggerate in their words, that a miniature Noah's Ark was in the town, containing everything.

d. The Revolution Arrives

During my childhood, I did not know what socialism was or the meaning of class struggle – as it came to be called with the passage of time. The concept of tycoons and paupers, homeowners and tradespeople was clearer. In accordance with external signs, very picturesque, socialism then appeared to me: polished gardens as if they emerged from a bath with reddish white chimneys rising above, and covered gardens growing greenish moss; straight walls and crooked walls; glass windows of one piece, and patched windows with a blanket stuck into a hole that had enlarged specifically during the harsh winter. Also many *kapotes* [cloaks] passed before my eyes: black, shiny and rustling; and dull, yellow, and worn-out. Various beards fluttered. Some covered a difficult life and pale face, while others covered a full life with a red face. Looking at them aroused feelings of confusion. The ears absorbed complaints about one who disappeared, that such-and-such happened to somebody, and another thing to someone else. After time, these visions took on names in the vernacular, but in their time they were inexplicable mysteries.

Various events took place then in the kingdom of my childhood, without being able to find a common thread. Cut-off pictures rise before me now as if from the fog. On one Thursday, at 10:00 p.m., my sister suddenly appeared before me, emotional, fiery, panicky, with news: certain lads broke in noisily to Motel the tailor's workshop, declaring, "From this day forward, we will not work nights for this exploiter." They "removed" the girls from work. Neither the household or the "girl laborer" knew whether to rejoice over an additional night of undisturbed sleep, or to be concerned that the meager livelihood was further reduced. I recall a loud knock on the window of our house one Saturday night, with the voice outside declaring: "We do not work on Saturday night!" These lads once made a mistake and came to take down someone in her own house, without permission from the master of the house – someone who blinded her eyes at the sewing machine in order to provide bread and clothing to the members of the household. Indeed, they did not continue to "knock" and the machine continued to click during the nights without interruption despite Karl Marx, and, to differentiate [between the deceased and the living], Senderka, the son of the town blacksmith.[5] One dark night, he entered the large *Beis Midrash*, right opposite the window of our house. That time, there was no voice of the *Maggid* [Preacher] or the weeping of women in the courtyard, but rather high talk and song. Suddenly a shot flew through the air, and shouts of *Doloi* (Forward!) shook the street. The light in the house was extinguished. Someone ran for his life to lock the door of the hallway with a wooden beam, and told the children, "Sleep in your clothes tonight."

The next day, the children told each other that the "sisters and brothers" were wreaking havoc, because they have fists and *yurks*,[6] and when the "*Distnik*" (an unarmed civilian guard) Lybonko appeared with the copper stripe on the flaps of his clothing, with the symbol of the regime

[Page 74]

on them, they were shouting, "*Doloi Samodirjzovetz*!" (Onward individual ruler!) They especially told about a certain dwarf, called not to his face "Shpentser" [undershirt]. He was brave, imposing fear upon the gentiles and even upon the various *Strazniks*[7] who appeared in town from time to time.

The truth be told: This was both frightening and enchanting. It was frightening because of the gentile-looking faces of the lads, wearing blue pants and tall boots, with forelocks peeking out backwards from their hats, which were tilted a bit to the side. It was said that there was an abundance of these types in the city of Kiev, which was known for its gentile thugs and gangs. However, here, it was Jewish lads, and it was dangerous to be in their presence. They were not afraid of their parents, and did not honor the Rabbi or other honorable individuals. They even acted against the Czar. There was also a great charm with these hooligans. The competed successfully with the children of our forefather Jacob, with the acts of bravery described in *Sefer Hayashar*,[8] and with the mighty Samson who pulled down the posts of the building and cut up a lion – for we witnessed with our own eyes acts of bravery taking place outside with nobody to disturb.

Just as they suddenly appeared, they suddenly disappeared. It was said, "they escaped to America." Only one of them, specifically the legendary dwarf, the aforementioned "Shpentser", remained in town. We later saw him with his posture bent even more, thin and weak, as an ancient, weak tower, with a beard, and a raspy voice. It was said that he returned to religious observance. He afflicted himself, prayed a great deal, slept on the floor with a wooden board at his head, in order to purge his sins. With the setting of the splendor of the dwarf, the final spark of the "revolution" in my childhood area also set.

e. The Land of Israel

It is said that the Land of Israel is embedded in the hearts of Jewish children by the *Chumash*, the *Siddur*, *Selichot*, and *Kinot*.[9] It is said that the carobs of Tu B'Shvat, and the gourds and grapes of Rosh Hashanah imparted a love of the Land. It is possible that this is so. However, in my city – it was sanctified through song. Even before Frischmann told about Rachel's Tomb, the celebrations in Meron and the Western Wall, even before Tchernichovsky's "Velvele" set out to "walk" to the Land of Israel, and even before Bialik's "Bird" returned from the hot lands to our window – the Land knocked on our doors. Eliakum Zunser, Dolitzki, Imber and their comrades echoed in our place with clear, pleasant voices of boys and girls. That which prayer and belief in the advent of the Redeemer did not do was accomplished by glorious song, from the embrace of the poets of Chibat Zion. That which the *Mizrach*,[10] embroidered by the Jewish girls with their own hands and hung for display, did not do, was accomplished by the illustrated pamphlets that reached us in a wondrous fashion, with the name Mishmar Hayarden written upon them, as well as Rechovot and Kastina; and was also accomplished by the album of dried flora of the Land of Israel with names from the Song of Songs written upon them. The love of Zion and the love of life, the adventures of the Land of Israel and the adventures of life – both of them were one, and imparted vitality to each other.

In our place, the Land of Israel could be found in many corners, first of all in the modern *cheders* of Shlomo Zagorodsky and Shimon Leichtman, where Hebrew was read with the correct "melody" [i.e. pronunciation], and the first lessons were from an illustrated book with wonderful stories, even some of the fables of Krylov and La Fontaine, and adages of our sages. The name of the book was *Safa Chaya* [Living Language]. It lived up to its name. It imparted life to the child. Even those who did not merit to study Torah from them, for the "methods" frightened G-d fearing, observant Jews, and their sons continued to warm themselves in the light of Torah in the *cheder* – these children also came to the Land of Israel through the library of Shlomo Zagorodsky, full of books such as "The Heroes of our Nation", "The Complete Legends of Israel", etc.

Even regular story books, in which the Land is not mentioned or noted, these too only told about the Land of Israel, and the story was only about the Land of Israel.[11] Thus a story touches upon a song, and a legend upon a melody, and the hearts of the children were won over to Zion as the song about Jerusalem in the vision.

Once, the Land of Israel visited us, literally, in its own reality and essence. This was a Zionist "preacher" who came to town and caused excitement. I have completely forgotten his name, his appearance. I only remember that large gathering.

[Page 75]

On that occasion, the women did not weep in the women's gallery, the elderly did not groan, and the children stood with open mouths to hear the words. That preacher had a rod, a wonderful stick, with verses from the Bible and images of Jerusalem etched upon its back. The entire Land of Israel was, so to speak, folded over this rod, and came to us. When the preacher reached the pinnacle of his enthusiasm, and pointed to the audience with the stick, it seemed that it was like Moses our Teacher raising his stick, splitting the sea, and bringing Israel through it, etc. etc. That preacher had a very wise soul, and he knew that listening is not the same as seeing. Therefore he "showed" Zion to the people. When he finished speaking, he cast his rod to the audience. It passed from hand to hand with holy awe. My hands also touched it, and I felt that I was one sixtieth in the Land of Israel.[12]

* * *

Houses and roads, gentiles and Jews, Cossacks and firefighters in uniform, songs of Zion and the pealing of bells – all of these were a dream and reality, until one day the child left his place and traveled afar. The child left and a young man returned. It seemed as if everything changed: the streets, the houses, the people, the trees. The war, the revolution, the change of regime, and the disturbances heaped up furrows before the people. New centers of life were found: parties, organizations, libraries, schools. However, for some reason, it seemed that everything was hanging on nothing, for even electric lighting reached here, although it could not disperse the shadows cast around. He arose and left his childhood place forever.

Translator's footnotes:

1. A halachic term for a person who rejects Jewish religions practice not out of laziness or convenience, but rather out of conviction (as if to anger G-d).
2. A Canaanite tribe that made peace with Joshua, rather than submitting to the Israelite conquest. See the ninth chapter of the Book of Joshua.
3. See Isaiah 1:6.
4. From the blessing of Isaac to Jacob (intended for Esau), see Genesis 27:28.
5. Senderka must have been the town Socialist activist.
6. I suspect that this means batons or rods.
7. A person whose job is to prevent people from escaping.
8. A medieval book of Midrash, with a historical bent.
9. *Selichot* are special penitential prayers for the High Holy Day period as well as fast days. *Kinot* are the dirges of Tisha B'Av.
10. A decoration placed on the eastern wall, pointing toward Jerusalem.
11. An obscure sentence. I believe it means that the youths were so in love with the concept of the Land of Israel that they read it into stories that were not about that topic.
12. A rabbinic expression for a small but not negligible amount. Jewish tradition states that sleep is one sixtieth of death, for example. (i.e. there are small but non-negligible aspects of similarity)

Thoughts

Yosef Lifshitz

Translated by Jerrold Landau

Fourteen years have already passed since the bitter day when the Jewish community in our town was murdered, and it is still difficult for me to come to terms with the thought that this indeed took place, and that I will never again see my native city, in which I spent the years of my youth, years of fine dreams and great hopes.

Greble Street in David-Horodok[1]

***

[Page 76]

On occasion, a ray of hope arises in me that some day I will return to visit all those places.
And at times it even seems to me that I am once again walking on the streets of David-Horodok.

The Eve of the Sabbath

Most of the shops are closed. The last of the wagon drivers are passing quickly through the streets of the city, for the hour is late. Reb Dovidl, may the memory of the righteous be blessed, left the bathhouse fully clean, with water still dripping from his *peyos*.

He ran, with his long *kapote* [cloak] constantly dragging on the sidewalk, to the shops and especially to the barber. He quickly warned them to shut their doors while there was still time. Quiet pervaded on the streets.

The first worshippers were already coming from all corners of the city. They walked calmly to the center, to the *Shulhof* [Synagogue courtyard]. A festive, holy atmosphere pervaded on everything.

The bridge in David-Horodok

Sabbath Night

After the meal, people went to stroll on The Greble and on the Horyn Bridge outside the city. Friends and acquaintances met there to discuss all the issues of the world. On such moonlit nights, we would go out to sail a boat on the Horyn.

Sabbath

We strolled as a group behind the large garden that Mordechai Zelik had leased from the Kniaz [nobleman].

Among the grain fields, between the tall stalks, we met with people older than us, such as: Z. Olpiner, Zeev Basevitz and, may he live, Sh. Kvetny. They were reading the recently published poems of Tchernichovsky or Bialik. They were discussing and arguing about every word and title. Sometimes, we went to the new cemetery on the other side of the city. We walked amongst the graves and the brave ones from among us turned, approached the graves of the *Tzadikim* and read the *kvittels* [Petitionary notes] that were placed in the burial canopy of the *Tzadik* [righteous person].

There, in their time, gatherings of the youth and various other gatherings were arranged, beginning already with the revolutionaries from 1905.

[Page 77]

A springtime flood during the time of the melting of the snow
and the overflowing of the river in David-Horodok

The Eve of the Festival of Shavuot

It was the time of year with the most pleasant weather. We went out to stroll on Tchipiasker Alley – the romantic area of the city. We sat on the small bridge next to the church. It was quiet all around. Under the bridge, the water remaining from the overflowing of the Horyn during the spring flowed leisurely. The entire area was a single garden. Nighttime birds raised their voices in song. They were joined by the croaking of the frogs. The air was suffused with intoxicating aromas of the blossoming of the trees and gardens in the area. Everything was lively and vibrant. It was hard to part from such a night.

These images and many other similar ones from the days of my childhood and youth rise before my eyes. Then, I am overcome with an aching longing and a strong desire to peer once again into that corner.

Apparently, this is the power of one's childhood cradle.

Indeed, what was this Horodok in essence?

It was a small town in the heart of Polesye, far from the highway, from a main road, and from the train. It was immersed in mud for five to six months a year, often weighing down on the body and the soul together. There was even a very difficult struggle for existence during the final few decades.

Nevertheless, as has been said, the power of one's childhood city is so great, that one cannot control it.

How painful that, of the memories of childhood and youth, only a large, communal grave remains on the road to Olshan.

Translator's footnote:

1. The inscription on the photo indicates it is Ulica Pilsudskego – i.e. Pilsudski Street

Sections of Memories

Moshe Meiri (Moravchik)

Translated by Jerrold Landau

In town, there was a street corner next to Kaplinsky's pharmacy.

If you stood in that corner, you could see the town divided into its main street, fanning out to its four corners.

The streets were straight, and you could see them from beginning to end in one glance.

On a weekday, the market was bustling with lots of people. Cattle and fowl were brought for sale. Farmers with their wagons came from

[Page 78]

the many villages in the surrounding area, bringing their merchandise to the center, from where they spread out to the streets and alleyways. They brought from the good of the land and the fruits of the ground, and in return they received clothing, shoes, and other necessities that the soil did not provide them.

The commercial center of David-Horodok[1]

The main source of livelihood of the Jews was from these farmers. Most of the Jews earned their livelihood from what they bought and sold.

The bustlingness of the marketplace reached its pinnacle during the afternoon hours, and subsided toward sunset. When the electric lights were lit and the stores and workshops closed, the wide area that bustled with life all day rested, and prepared itself for nighttime life to the light of the rising moon.

* * *

Toward evening, the population went out to the streets, setting out toward the main street leading to the bridge and the river.

Were you to stand in the corner of that street, all the residents of the city would pass before you as if in a procession. At the head were the boys and girls who did not yet bear the yoke of livelihood on their shoulders. Therefore, they were able to devote themselves to their studies, to youth group activities, and to spending evenings without any burden or worry – as is appropriate and fitting for that age.

Lads stood at the corner of the street, surveying all the passers-by. They would lean on a wall or a post upon which a large light fluttered. It was as if they were standing on a stage, conducting an investigation through jokes and mirth.

Everyone knew each other in this town, not just by name and surname, but also by unique nicknames. The nickname would resonate with you more than the surname, the name of the father, or the profession – for the nickname was the profession.

[Page 79]

It was sufficient to point with the finger to someone walking and approaching, and to call him by his unique nickname – and all the lads would burst out in laughter, as if the single word told everything...

Night by night, after the movement subsided and most of the people went to bed, the boys and girls continued to wander about in the corners of that street, and to enjoy themselves with highlights, jokes, and stories about many various matters, about matters between a girl and a boy and about matters about important world events.

Those who tarried late into the night would spend these late hours in song and music. Many of the youths were able to play musical instruments of all types. They would bring them to the corner of the street, and the echoes would resonate afar.

The corner of that street fell asleep after the last of those out for a stroll left. It would rest from the bustle of the previous day, so it could arise and awaken to new life the next day. That is how things continued on, without accounting and without purpose.

At the Bridge

It was a wide river, and on Sabbaths and festivals, the residents of the city streamed to stroll atop the bridge.

The bridge was the central meeting place of the city – on a warm Sabbath day as well as on a harsh winter day.

The great river flowed beneath it. Its head could be seen somewhere among the trees, and it continued endlessly, until it flowed into a second, larger river, and then to the sea within the bounds of greater Russia.

On the water beneath it sailed boats filled with youthful mirth and song, the echoes of which could be heard from afar.

The movement was especially great toward evening, when the heat lessened and work and studies concluded – when laziness fell upon the face of the earth...

For many hours after the town fell into its slumber and the streets emptied of people, the river was still filled with boys and girls moving about – sailing like long shadows under the moonlight on a clear night.

In the summer, the river also served as a place for bathing and swimming throughout all the hours of the day.

In the summer, before the ice rose upon the river, it served as a connection between the town and the larger world. Boats would come and go from morning until night.

The second whistle sounded, all the travelers boarded the boat, and those accompanying them remained on the shore. The third whistle sounded – and the boat set out. The travelers waved. It sailed and moved toward the horizon, until it disappeared behind the great circle. Only then did all those who gathered to say goodbye to the travelers decide to leave, turn their backs, and return to their homes. However, the idle ones who always came to watch the boats setting out continued to stand and watch from afar, as if they were waiting for another new thing to once again capture their interest.

All this was in the summer.

In the winter, the river was covered with thick, heavy, hard ice. Then, those out for a stroll left the bridge above and moved to the white bridge below – the natural bridge, solid and wide.

Day and night, they enjoyed themselves with skates and winter sleds. The movement along the ice was especially great on clear, moonlit nights, when a mantle of mystery enveloped all living things.

We spent many hours of our lives upon the bridge – the bridge that was destroyed from time to time on account of the battles and wars that came through on both sides. The bridge both separated and united. The bridge was an attractive force and the most popular meeting place – who can forget it?

The *Shulhof* [Synagogue Courtyard]

What was the most known place in the town? Pleasant to both children and adults together?

This was the large, broad square in the center of town, upon which all the synagogues of the place were built.

[Page 80]

That place was constantly bustling. Every morning at dawn or late in the evening, Jews would enter and exit through the doors of these synagogues that filled the yard.

The movement was especially great on Sabbaths and festivals, in the morning hours and even in the afternoon hours.

For what would good Jews do after the festive, pleasant afternoon meal and the nap that followed? To where were they attracted, if not to the synagogues to hear the *Maggid* [Preacher] and to gather together in a crowd – one large, diverse congregation, separated and distinct on all the days of the week, with each person going about their work and livelihood, hitched like slaves to the wagon of life. However on Sabbaths and festivals, they were angels, the children of angels…

Nevertheless, the *Shulhof* was not only a place of Torah. It also served as a valuable place of culture, where lectures and speeches by Zionist emissaries would be arranged. These emissaries were also emissaries of the new life arising at the corners of the East.

In the yard and inside the synagogues, Jews would gather not only for prayer and supplications, but also for outcries and protests against the travesties perpetrated against the Jews throughout the wide world, and for preaching about the path to new life – the path to national revival, which struck roots in that place.

The synagogues were served not only by rabbis and preachers of Torah, but also by the various parties – the Zionist parties, the workers' parties, and even the parties that preached against Zionism.

Therefore, we will remember that *Shulhof*, which attracted many of the town residents, and became a place of education and guidance not only for the love of the nation, but also for the changing face of that nation.

The *Shulhof* with its many synagogues stood in the center of the city. Roads and alleyways were next to it from all sides. All of them led to one place – like streams flowing into the sea, the Jews of the town flowed from all sides into that yard.

Translator's footnote:

1.   The inscription on the photo says: Rynek – i.e. town square.

My Parental Home

Y. Lifshitz

Translated by Jerrold Landau

The gathering place for the youth of the Workers in the Land of Israel, the center of Zionist activity, and the center of political and communal life in our town – such was my parental home between the two world wars.

Father received this house as a dowry, and with it also the center and meeting place of the large, wide-branched family – that is the family of Gershon Eisenberg of Olpen.

Our family was one of the largest in the city. Grandfather left behind 126 children and grandchildren when he died. On Sabbaths and festivals, everyone would gather at Grandfather's. The house was always open to all the residents of the city.

When Grandfather sensed that his days were numbered, and that he was about to leave "the foolish world" and pass to the world of truth, he sent me to call Lipa Finkelstein and Moshe Kolozny. He had business connections with them throughout all the years. Therefore, he wished to ask them for forgiveness. He was concerned lest he ever overcharged them by accident or on purpose, and whether he owed them anything, or whether they remained in debt to him. From that point, all debts and obligations were nullified and canceled.

His life was interlocked with religion and religion with life. It seemed as if life was only created to fulfil the commandments, to observe the Sabbath and festivals. In this manner, it was easier to endure all the difficulties of livelihood and existence, the wounds of the bitter exile. When the Sabbath arrived, all the signs of the weekdays disappeared – the toil and suffering. The dust of the week was removed; the weariness of the six workdays was assuaged.

b. The Sabbath

Life centered around that which is called the Sabbath. On Friday, while it was still the middle of the day – before noon – Grandfather would leave work at 11:00 a.m. and prepare

[Page 81]

himself to greet the Sabbath Queen. He cut his nails, took a clean cloak with a towel, and went to the bathhouse. Once or twice a year, during the hot summer days, he would permit himself to go to the Horyn River to immerse himself in its waters. When Grandfather returned from the bathhouse, the final preparations to greet the Sabbath were already taking place. The holiness of the Sabbath was sensed in the air, slowly expelling the mundane out of the house. A white, clean tablecloth appeared on the table, with a candelabra with the Sabbath candles on top. The women concluded their work in the kitchen. They were clean and sparkling with white kerchiefs on their heads, as they prepared to recite the blessing over the candles. Grandfather finished his cup of tea from the eve of the Sabbath, and began to recite "The Song of Songs that is Solomon's" in a festive, joyous voice. The aromas of the cholent and the chicory rose from the oven, and the pleasant aroma of the warm food enveloped you, as if it was preparing you to greet the Sabbath.

"Good Sabbath," said grandfather in a festive, high voice, as he returned from the synagogue. He immediately began singing "*Sholom Aleichem Malachei Hasharet Malachei Elyon*" [Welcome, ministering angels, the angels from on high]. At that moment, it seemed to you as if all the good angels were fluttering about, as they came to celebrate the Sabbath with us – fluttering over the candles atop the table and over the chandelier below the ceiling.

The time for *Kiddush* and the meal arrived. Everyone was obligated to hear the *Kiddush*, to taste the wine, and to gather around the table.

The meal was pleasant and festive, accompanied by hymns and melodies in honor of the Sabbath. Of course, a Sabbath guest was not lacking.

After the meal, Grandfather would review the weekly Torah portion twice, with the *Targum* [Aramaic translation of *Onkelos*] once[1]. A spiritual calm fell upon us on the Sabbaths of the long, cold *Tevet* nights. A snowstorm was taking place outside. The wind was howling through the chimneys of the house and the windows. However, there was warmth and calm in the house, with only the unique voice of Grandfather chanting "And Jacob lived in the Land of Egypt for seventeen years"[2] being heard.

During the warm summer nights of *Tammuz*, Grandfather would permit himself to go out to the balcony after the meal to breathe a bit of fresh air. He would review the weekly portion in the morning at sunrise. At that time, it was quiet on the street. Only a third of the residents of the city were Jews, but on the Sabbath it felt that the entire city was Jewish. The voice of Grandfather chanting about Balak the son of Tzipor[3] burst forth outside through the open window, to the clear quietude, and blended with the voice of the birds. This song was powerful for the Sabbath, for nature, and for the Creator of the World.

The entire Sabbath passed in calm and study. Even a thought of matters of work and livelihood was forbidden. Sadness was also forbidden.

I recall the first Sabbath after the passing of my uncle Chaim-Baruch Olpiner. My uncle died in far-off Berlin during the prime of his life. He left behind three daughters, two of whom had come of age, and four sons, the oldest of whom was in the army. Grandfather did not change his custom one iota, and did not permit anyone to mention even a single word about the tragedy. "It is the Sabbath today," he said. It was only after *Havdalah* that he was not able to control himself, and he burst out weeping. The atmosphere of the Sabbath continued in many houses even after *Havdalah*.

Even during the weekdays, everyone searched for islands of calm and salvation from the day-to-day life through the fulfilment of the commandments and the observance of the festivals. In this manner, it was easier to live and exist.

c. The Passover Holiday

The most important and pleasant of all the holidays was, of course, Passover. First of all, because it fell in the spring, and the summer would follow, when life was infinitely easier than it was during the winter. Second, because of the great change from *chometz* [foods with leavened ingredients] that Passover brought into the house.

One would prepare for Passover through virtually the entire year. In the summer, people would prepare cherry preserves and pickled cucumbers for the holiday. In the fall, they would prepare horseradish, beets, and potatoes. In the winter, they would prepare pickled beets and wine. The main preparations took place after Purim.

[Page 82]

The first week was devoted to general laundry. The second week, to whitewashing, which was very difficult work due to the rainy weather that almost always pervaded before the festival. The third week was devoted to the baking of matzos. The final week was devoted to general cleaning and the kashering of the utensils.

This was a month full of work, in which there were many expenses. The special preparations for the festival and the vacation from studies inspired great interest in us children. We helped, like the adults, in all matters, and even received our part: new clothes and shoes, nuts, and various sweets. The preparations for the festival were difficult, but everyone waited impatiently for its arrival. All the days of the festival were dedicated to rest, relaxation, visits to family, and even arranging of matches.

The jokers of the generation would say that all the revolutions in the synagogues against the *parnasim* [administrators] of the community took place on Passover, since there was no concern for livelihood during that festival and there was time to devote to communal affairs. They would also say that it was much easier after Passover than after Sukkot, for after Sukkot, one had to prepare the house for winter, bring in the double windows, and check if there was enough soil for the foundations. One also had to prepare vegetables and potatoes for the people and the cattle, and warm clothing and shoes for everyone. After Passover, on the other hand, there was no need for any preparation. At home, there were leftovers from the holiday: matzos, fat, wine, eggs. The weather was warm. The cattle were going out to pasture. There was sufficient milk and butter, and a week or two after Passover, there already was sorrel, green onions, and radishes, and the expenses were low. The "summer-love" began after Passover. Indeed, festivities and weddings were forbidden during the *Omer* period. However, in the words of our friend Bania Katz: "We will give over the *Sefira*[4] to the rabbi, Reb Dovidl. Of course, he will count properly. And the spring is the spring." It did not take long before the preparations for the Shavuot festival began. Our fathers told that, in their time, this was the festival of the lads, for they demonstrated their prowess in arranging all types of decorations from greenery and eggshells. The preparations for Shavuot already began from Lag B'Omer. This was the only holiday in which greenery was brought into the house.

d. The Shavuot Festival

The festival of the giving of the Torah was an easy, pleasant festival. The weather was pleasant. Everything sprung to life, and everything was blossoming and flowering. It was difficult to restrict the festival solely to the confines of the giving of the Torah and the yoke of the commandments. Nature had its influence also upon the Jews of the Diaspora. However, the pleasant summer days passed quickly, and the period of mourning between the 17th of Tammuz and Tisha B'Av began. Tisha B'Av was a day of mourning for all the Jews of the city. Almost everyone went to the old cemetery to supplicate upon the graves of the righteous ones.

The mood changed after Tisha B'Av. Summer was approaching its end. The weather became colder. The sound of the shofar already cut through the air. Then it was the Sabbath of *Rosh Chodesh Elul* – the Days of Awe were approaching.

e. The Days of Awe

This was a special month in the life of the town. In the latter years, the sting of fear and awe was blunted. However, several decades previously, people would be careful about even the smallest of sins starting from *Rosh Chodesh Elul*. Everyone was obligated to investigate their deeds and to supplicate at the graves of ancestors, asking that they be righteous intercessors for the new year.

The situation of the Jews in the surrounding villages was especially difficult. We all recall only the jokes about the *Yishuvniks* [i.e., the residents of small settlements]. However, Father of blessed memory would relate that the Jews of the villages would [have liked to] live in the town during the Ten Days of Repentance so that they would not be among the gentiles during those days. Rather, since they could not leave their homes, they concerned themselves with arranging for a minyan, cantor, Torah reader, and shofar blower for those days.

I still bring to my memory the fear that fell upon everyone during the final week before Rosh Hashanah, when the first *Selichos* were recited. It was dark, cold, rainy, and muddy outside. However, everyone went before midnight with flashlights

[Page 83]

to the synagogue. On the evening of Rosh Hashanah, the Hassidim of Stolin, Turov, and Olevsk would pass through our city on the way to the Rebbe in Stolin. Moshe of Chorsk [Chorovsk in the text] would be the last to travel. He relied on his postal horses, which would arrive on time to Stolin. On Rosh Hashanah, almost all the time would be spent in the synagogue or in reciting Psalms.

The women felt it a special holy task to prepare the memorial candles for Yom Kippur. In the latter period, the candles were already preprepared, but about fifty years previously, each woman would prepare candles in her own home. Grandmother told me the following: During the Ten Days of Repentance, people would take cotton wicks and go to the cemetery. There, they would go to the graves of family members, and invite them to take part in the preparation of the candles. This was called *"Tzien a Kneitl"* [moving or tying a knot]. The weeping and screaming that accompanied the special petition composed for that purpose penetrated the heavens. All the wicks were taken home. Wax was heated up, and each wick was placed into the wax, for the souls of all the family members who were invited from the cemetery. A single memorial candle was braided from all those candles. It would burn throughout the entire Yom Kippur.

It is difficult to describe the fear and awe that fell upon all the residents of the city on the eve of Yom Kippur, and on the day that the Sabbath of Sabbaths was sanctified. Everyone gathered in the synagogue. Only babies remained at home. Even the Christians were afraid of wandering about the city on that day. The great awe was assuaged somewhat on account of an incident that took place during the time of the First World War. On Yom Kippur of 1915, the Cossacks entered the town, forced Shlomo Finkelstein to open his shop, and even purchased something from him. When a year passed, and nothing happened to Shlomo, for on the contrary, he amassed greater wealth, the youth began to act a bit lighter on that day.

After the *Neila* service, everyone would take their memorial candle from the synagogue and go home with it. They would recite *Havdalah* over it. The leftovers would be saved until the Intermediate Days of Sukkot, and the *Hoshanot* of Hoshana Rabba would be recited to its light.

There was an incident with Grandfather, who went after *Neila* to fetch his candle, and found that it was extinguished. He immediately lit it from another candle, and acted as if nothing had happened. However, his face turned pale, and it was obvious that he was somewhat perplexed. He gestured at me to be quiet. The next morning, he traveled to the Rebbe in Stolin, and indeed returned calmer and happier. However, that entire year, until *Rosh Chodesh Elul*, he was very careful about any action that might pose a risk of danger.

Everyone breathed calmly after Yom Kippur. The "danger" had passed, and preparations for the Sukkot festival began.

A Sukkah was set up in almost every house. The joy on Sukkot was great after the tension of the Days of Awe. The joy was especially great on Simchat Torah. There was great weariness from all the holidays. The autumn days were approaching, with rain and mud. The great expenditures that were needed to arrange the house for winter, including to provide clothing and food, clouded the joy of the festival somewhat.

The gray days began after Sukkot. The rain almost never stopped. Sometimes, we spent the entire day in the house, for we were unwilling to go outside in the rain and mud. This continued until winter when snow covered everything. With it also came the Festival of Lights – Chanukah. This was primarily a holiday for the children, for they did not study in *cheder* during the nights [of Chanukah]. Things were a bit more joyous next to the Chanukah candles. They ate latkes and played with the dreidel, while the adults played cards. However, this was an isolated island of joy in the long, tiring sea of winter, until *Adar* came. Purim was approaching. Light winds began to blow. The snow lost its hard form, and became soft and black. The ice began to break up. The song of birds could already be heard on the street. Spring was approaching, bringing with it a bit more freedom for living and growing things. Purim was the holiday upon which an ordinary Jew would legally permit himself to drink "until he does not know the difference."[5] The masks and Purim plays also gave expression to the joy of the holiday.

The giving of food gifts [*mishloach manos*] was customary on Purim. I recall that three people worked with us to accept the communal *mishloach manos*. This was a responsible job that had to be carried out with great tact: to know what to do to send to every person in accordance with their honor and appropriate to their degree of closeness to the family.

[Page 84]

The breaking up of the ice of the Horyn River
near the bridge in the spring

We would conduct the Purim feast together. I still recall one Purim feast in which about 80 people, including children and grandchildren, took part. The main joy was from this large crowd. It is no wonder that tragedies affected many families when members of some families turned away and began to arrive in America. One *Maggid* [preacher] who came to our city expressed this well: One can earn one's world with the women of the city through one verse: "And your life will hang in doubt before you."[6] Don't read this as your "life" but rather as your "children", for there is no life without children, and your children are hanging in doubt before you – the pictures of your children are hanging opposite you on the wall, but the children are not there. The birds flew away from the warm nest of mother and father, with only pictures and pieces of paper of a letter remain. The women wept and even the men shed tears.

f. The Revolution of 1905

The Revolution of 1905 caused a great upheaval in the life of the town. The youth, who played a very active role in the revolution, where forced to emigrate after the revolution failed. The emigres included many of Grandfather's grandchildren. Grandfather's house, which had always been a constant fortress for the family members, was emptied somewhat. Our house again filled with people during the time of the First World War. That time, it also included many of the residents of the city, including some of my friends, and the friends of my brothers and sisters. Our house remained open to everyone until Father made *aliya* to the Land.

[Page 85]

Father always had an inclination toward communal work. During the time that he lived outside the city, when he would come home for only two or three months, he would only get involved with cultural and rabbinical questions. However, when he settled in the city, he began to take interest in everything that took place in the city. Then, he was also elected as a representative to the city council. He took interest in issues of the community and rabbinate. He was an enthusiastic Hassid of the Rabbi of Slonim, may the memory of the righteous be blessed.

Four generations of David-Horodok [women]

From left to right: 1. Tzipa Baruchin – the mother; 2. Sara Olpiner – the daughter; 3. Shoshana Ladezky – the granddaughter; 4. Beila Ladezky – the great-granddaughter

The important problems of the city were deliberated upon in our house. Thus, our house turned into the center of the city. There were no halls in the city at that time. The youth from all strata and groups gathered at our place. My brother Avraham's friends from the Russian school would come to visit him, and my friends from the Hebrew and Russian schools came to visit me. The following were among those who came: Yitzchak Olpiner, Yisrael Shostakovsky, Yankel Olshansky, Moravchik, and others. Students from the modern *cheder*s also came, including: Ch. Finkelstein, Z. Lutzky, Sh. Mishalov, Matorin, N. Filbin, and others. Even the Yeshiva lads would come, including P. Novak, Y. L. Zager, and Sh. Reznik.

There were no dance parties at that time. There were evenings spent in reading and debates for many hours, each person according to their area of interest. Shostakovsky would read from the works of Pushkin, Lermontov, or Tolstoy. Nechemia Filbin was a great expert in reading and declamation. He surprised us once by reciting by heart Bialik's "The Diligent Student" and "In the City of Killing". He was also an expert in reading the works of the Hebrew and Yiddish writers, which began to reach us at that time: the writings of Mendele, and the exchange of letters between Menachem-Mendel and his wife Sheina-Sheindel.[7] "A Night in the Old Market" by Y. L. Peretz, as well as his writings on Hassidism, made a great impression upon us. Sh. Reznik organized communal singing. He was a singer with the cantor of the synagogue, and was talented in music. Zeev Lutzky was a great expert in Bible [Tanach] and he would bring a verse for a proof of anything. He even proposed that we should only speak Hebrew amongst ourselves. However, not everyone agreed to this, especially the students of the Russian school. At times, adults also participated in the readings, especially of the writings of Sholem Aleicheim.

[Page 86]

g. The First World War

The order of the world was overturned when the war broke out. Many of the residents of the city were without work or livelihood. A great deal of time remained for politics. Our house became one of the centers for discussions and debates about world politics. It seems that the magnitude of the tragedy that was coming upon the world was not yet felt during the first year of the war, or even a bit later. However, out of great hatred for the Czar, people were happy about the defeat of the Russians on the front. Even Grandfather was satisfied with the results of the war. He brought signs and portents from the holy *Zohar* that this was the war of Gog and Magog, and the coming of the Messiah would follow.

When the Jewish newspapers were closed in Russia, we subscribed together with Sh. Katz to the liberal Russian newspaper *B. Vedomosti* [*Birzhevye Vedomosti* or *The Stock Exchange Gazette*]. The post office was next to our house, and when the newspaper arrived, everyone gathered around to hear the news. Chaim-David Katz was the chief reader, and Eizel Schuster was the "political commentator".

This Eizel Schuster was a shoemaker by profession. However, not many people of the town, including his neighbors, ever saw him working. Nobody knew how that Jew earned his livelihood. We always saw him on the street with a stick in his hand, a circle of people around him, as he was the chief spokesman. He did not know how to read and write, other than a bit of Yiddish, and the prayers. Nevertheless, he knew everything that was happening in the wide world. Every day, he showed on a Russian map every detail of the situation at the front.

He hated the Czar without bounds. There was no end to his joy at every Russian setback. When the Russians captured Lvov all of his acquaintances gave him a nickname from a verse of the *Kabbalat Shabbat* [Welcoming the Sabbath] service, *Am Toei "Levov" Hem* – which means that the Russian nation got lost and entered Lvov.[8] *Hem* sounds like *Heim*, which means "house" in Yiddish – he felt that they would remain there as if at home. However, *Vehem Lo Yadu Drachai* [And they do not know My ways] – when they wanted to go home, they did not know which way to go, so they ran along a path that led to nowhere. Indeed, that is how it was. There was no end to Eizel's joy when the well-known German General Mackensen began his attack on Galicia, and the Russians fled for their lives.

Eizel knew a great deal about what had happened in the city many years earlier. Among other things, he owned a ledger that was 200 years old. Despite his great friendship with us, we did not succeed in obtaining the ledger from him.

The old post office in David-Horodok

[Page 87]

Only in the latter period did my brother Meir succeed in peering into this ledger, related to his articles about the history of the city in the *Pinsker Shtime* [the newspaper Voice of Pinsk].

Eizel related a great deal about the history of the city. Many very interesting things have been forgotten from my memory. He was graced with great talent to talk about everything with great speed. It was as if the incident was standing before your eyes. Among other things, he described the strong impression that the residents of the city had when they brought the first gramophone to Nissan Gurevitz. Everyone went on Saturday night to see and hear the great wonder. An extended debate broke out at that time regarding the source of the voice – whether it emanated from the record, the needle, or the speaker. The gentile neighbors were astounded at this new machine, and they fled for their lives.

The first sewing machine made a similar impression upon all the needleworkers in the city. People understood how the top stitch was done from the result, but, regarding how the bottom stitch was made – this they could not understand at all. Eizel came to our house every day when the newspaper arrived. When the revolution broke out and the city was divided into two, Zionists and *Poalei Zion* [Workers of Zion], Eizel was also forced to choose his path. Ideologically, he did not affiliate with *Poalei Zion*. He was a sort of anarchist. He went out to the street with the masses of people, and conducted publicity about everything and against everything.

h. After the 1917 Revolution

After the outbreak of the revolution, our house became a center for communal and Zionist activity in the city. Father was chosen as the vice chairman of the "Rabkom". The government of all Russia was in the hands of the Rabkoms, for the laws of the Czar were annulled and new laws had not yet come in their place. At that time, the civic government was both the legislative and executive authority combined. There was a case of a Christian couple who came to the Rabkom to get divorced. Father signed the bill of divorce since the chairman was not in town at that time. One Christian woman who saw this went out screaming and weeping, "Woe to the eyes who have seen this, that Moshe Yehuda has authorized a bill of divorce for proper Pravoslavs!"

Father was also chosen to the city council through the General Zionists. In this way, he was the regular spokesman of the Jewish community of our city until close to the time that he made *aliya*. Whether during the times of the Bolsheviks, the Germans, or the Poles, they always turned to him as the elected authority of the city. He passed through all the stormy days in this city in peace only thanks to his honesty and his dedication to the public. (He was only imprisoned on one occasion by the Hetman's people.)

His main communal activity was during the time of the Polish occupation of the city. During those days, the issue of passports cut through the space of our world. Many Jews fled Russia and crossed the Polish border. It was impossible to move without an identity certificate, because David-Horodok did not have a ledger of registration of residents, for the Bolsheviks had taken the books of property ownership and registry with them during their retreat. It was possible to receive a provisional identity card based on the signature of two citizens of the city. This granted them the right to remain in Poland. Father's signature was regular and obligatory.

Many of those who requested passports had very weak connections to David-Horodok. Nevertheless, Father did not hesitate to help them obtain the certificate. On more than one occasion, the regional authorities asked how it was possible for a Pole born in Mozyr to receive a passport from David-Horodok. Go tell them that, according to Sholem Aleichem, a Jew could have been born in Kiev, registered in Mozyr, and receive a passport in David-Horodok. Nevertheless, the authorities trusted Father's signature.

Father did all this without expectation of remuneration, despite all the danger associated with this. The sole reward was that – the *Keren Kayemet* [Jewish National Fund] box in his house was always fuller than the other boxes in the city. Aside from his interest in Zionist work, Father took an interest in the question of education, even though his children were no longer of school age. He was among the supporters of Rabbi Shapira of blessed memory, and was one of those who was involved in bringing him to David-Horodok. With all this, he was able to maintain good relations with Rabbi Moshele Ginzburg, may the memory of the righteous be blessed. Despite being a fervent *Misnaged* [non-Hassid], he also maintained strong friendly relations with the Rebbe of Stolin, Rabbi Moshele Perlow, may G-d avenge his blood.

[Page 88]

Whenever he was in Stolin, he would visit him for a friendly conversation. He would also go to the Rebbe of Stolin on his visits to David-Horodok and the Rebbe always greeted him with great joy.

There was no communal activity in the city in which Father did not play an active role.

It was only for the communal council during the time of Polish rule that he did not agree to register his candidacy, due to the smell of reactionism and coziness with the authorities that emanated from that institution. Communal activity took a great deal of Father's time. This had a negative effect on his business activities, which were not always successful.

i. During the Time of Polish Rule

After the Treaty of Riga between Russia and Poland, when the military situation in the city eased somewhat, the youth began once again to take interest in Zionist activity. Then, an arrest took place in our house. This was in 1921. The border between us and Russia was closed and well sealed. Nevertheless, several people of David-Horodok who remained in Russia succeeded in coming home. Avraham Durchin may G-d avenge his blood, who studied at the university in Kiev, was among the returnees. He was one of the primary members of the Zionist movement, and was already a member of *Tzeirei Zion* [Youth of Zion] in 1917. We youths ran to hear from him what was taking place in Russia, particularly with respect to the Zionist movement. During those days, the internal battle among the Jewish youth was difficult: Zionism or Communism? – that was the question. During the first years of the revolution, the Jewish youth were enchanted by the opportunity to take revenge on the various pogrom perpetrators and anti-Semites, with the help of the Communists. The revolution also opened up a broad field of activity for workers' rights and Socialism. Nevertheless, the issue was fraught with certain, absolute assimilation within the large ocean of the peoples of Russia.

On the other hand, it was the time of the Balfour Declaration, and the first commissioner in the Land of Israel was a Jew. It was possible to maintain the connection with the wide, open world, and there was the possibility of *aliya*, of actualizing the Zionist dream. Several of the youth of our city became attracted to Communism and left for Russia. Some are there to this day, and others became sorely disappointed and returned. The majority, however, remained faithful to Zionism. It is therefore no wonder that when A. Durchin came home, we were anxious to hear what he had to say. Everyone gathered in our house, and Durchin told us about the life of the Jews in Russia, about the possibilities of Zionist activity, and about Communism. The hour was already late. Many of our friends had already left. Father had gone to sleep. We remained sitting there, my two brothers Meir and Aharon, Dov Shafer, A. Moravchik, and me. Soroka of Turov (his sister was a teacher in the Tarbut School, and he remained in David-Horodok) also remained with us. In the meantime, two Poles entered and requested beer. I fulfilled their request, and we continued our conversation. It became clear only later that the Poles were from the secret police, and when they heard that we were talking about Zionism and Communism, they called the police and we were all arrested. This was on a Sabbath eve.

The next day, the city was in turmoil. The accusation of Communism in a city situated on the border between Russia and Poland at that time was no simple matter. Furthermore, Avraham Durchin, who had just come from Russia, and Soroka of Turov were among those arrested. The deeds of the Poles in Pinsk when they killed the 35 were still well remembered.[9] The fear in the city was great. They began to collect signatures from the residents of the city testifying that we were not Communists. Some of the residents were reluctant to sign. We did not know about all this fear, and aside from Soroka who had a miniature passport,[10] we were happy to be political prisoners. We were taken to Luninets on Sunday morning. The entire city came out to accompany us. Father, Aharon-Yona Shafer, and Dov Moravchik traveled with us. With the assistance of M. Muzikant, the owner of the hotel, who had connections with the police chiefs, we were freed after three days of imprisonment. This imprisonment put an end to the Zionist activity of the youth in our city for several months. However, it renewed with greater force after that. Our house once again became the center of activity until we made *aliya* to the Land. Even when permission was given to open a meeting place, all the decisions and major activity related to the Workers in the Land of Israel were decided in our house.

The first meeting of the group regarding the founding of *Tzeirei Zion* in David-Horodok, with the participation

[Page 89]

of Y. L. Zager, P. Novak, Z. Lutzky, and may they live, A. Veiner and Dov Shafer was at our place. Virtually every Zionist activity that took place in our city by *Tzeirei Zion*, and later by the left-leaning *Poalei Zion*[11] was centered in our house. There was a small house in our yard that served as a sausage factory during the war, and later stood empty. The first meeting of *Hechalutz* [The Pioneer] took place in that house. There, the decision to form a *kvutza* [Zionist preparation group] in Lisowitz took place. That house also served as a warehouse for work implements that were collected in the city and sent to the Land of Israel. The decision to found the Y. L. Peretz Library was also taken there. Every emissary who came to the party and to *Hechalutz* came to us. The first permits for *aliya* from *Hechalutz*, with the participation of the late Hershel Pinsky, also took place at our house.

Our house was the central meeting place for most of the organized youth. Everyone could come and go at any time without asking.

If there was a need for an urgent action in the party, someone would always be at our house.

The "Asiria" [Group of ten] is a story of its own. This consisted of: my two sisters, the two Rimar sisters, Beila Moravchik, Mania Cohen, Sonia Kolodny, the two Lifshitz sisters (daughters of Shmuel Lifshitz), and Etel Olpiner (All of them, with the exception of my sister-in-law E. Olpiner, are in Israel.) These people were non-factional, but they openly supported the Workers in the Land of Israel. They were very active in the "brigade" for the *Keren Kayemet LeYisrael* [Jewish National Fund] and served as our backbone. For the most part, they gathered in our house with their friends.

It should be noted that all this activity was carried out with the agreement and great support of Father. He supported the Workers in the Land of Israel even though it cost him money and time, and greatly interfered with his livelihood.

I recall the elections for the city council. Father stood at the head of the workers list, and I was at the head of the list of the left-leaning *Poalei Zion*. Nevertheless, Father won people over to our list and even helped us in the elections. He also always voted with us in the city council on issues in which we had a direct interest.

Thus was my parental home, until we made *aliya* to the Land, and Father merited to rejoice in the establishment of the State of Israel, even though the joy was not complete since Father did not succeed in bringing our entire family to the Land. Three of his sons as well as grandchildren perished at the hands of the murderers, may G-d avenge their blood.

Translator's footnotes:

1. It is customary to review the text of the weekly Torah twice, with the Aramaic commentary once, each week. This is called *Shnayim Mikra Veechad Targum* [Twice the Biblical text, and once the translation].
2. Genesis 47:28 – the opening verse of the Torah portion of *Vayechi*, generally read about two weeks after Chanukah.
3. The Torah portion of *Balak* begins with Numbers 22:2. It is generally read in the early part of the summer. Note, the name Tzipor means 'bird' (which explains the play on words in the rest of the sentence).
4. The word means 'the counting' referring to the period of the counting of the 49 days of the *Omer* between Passover and Shavuot. Traditionally certain festivities are forbidden during all or part of that period.
5. One who does not know the difference [between cursed is Haman and blessed is Mordechai].
6. Deuteronomy 28:66
7. By Sholem Aleichem.
8. Psalms 95:10. The portion of the verse is "And they are a nation that err in the heart". *Levov* means "heart" and sounds like Lvov.
9. Referring to the Pinsk Massacre of April 5, 1919.
10. An internationally recognized refugee travel document that was issued to stateless people. The document was known as a "Nansen passport" after the Norwegian explorer and statesman Fridtjof Nansen.
11. *Poalei Zion* at one point split into a right-leaning faction and a left-leaning faction.

In the Diaspora in Polesye

by D. Tannenbaum

From the *Pinsker Shtime* [the newspaper Voice of Pinsk]

Translated by Jerrold Landau

I checked and found that there was no town dearer from the perspective of Zionism than David-Horodok. The Hebrew language was fluent in the mouths of everyone there, and at times, you could hear its echoes on the streets among the youths. The greeting with which passers-by greeted each other was "Shalom" (a seemingly insignificant point, but testifies to the spirit that pervaded). The Tarbut School that existed there could serve as an exemplary Hebrew school from all perspectives. It had more than four hundred students. From the words and relationship of the students to Zionist activity, one can determine that the school was not only a house of learning for them, but rather an environment and atmosphere of Israeli life.

There were youth organizations and organizations for older people of all types there. A kibbutz of *Hanoar Hatzioni*[1] also existed. It was maintained by and benefited from the moral and material support of the Jews of the town. Individuals as well as entire families made *aliya* from there. Those Jews became fed up with a half-Diaspora and half-Hebrew life, so they chose to make *aliya* and prepare for a full Hebrew life in the Land of Israel.

[Page 90]

Synagogue of the Hassidim of Stolin: "Stoliner *Shtibel*"

The large Beis Midrash

The Great Synagogue

[Page 91]

The Nagid Beis Midrash

The Rabbi's *Beis Midrash*

Translator's footnote:

1. In this context, a kibbutz refers to a farm or an institution for preparation for *aliya* (also known as a *Hachshara* kibbutz).

[Page 92]

From the Way of Life of the Town

by A. Lahav Lachovsky

Translated by Jerrold Landau

Rabbis and Torah greats among the residents of David-Horodok: Rabbi Yosef Reizin, *Moreh Tzedek*[1] (later moved to Slonim), Rabbi Pesach, Rabbi Yaakov Yeshayahu Rosenblum, known as the Slonimer, Rabbi David Berkovitz, Rabbi Baruchl, as well as the rabbis and Rebbes of the Ginzburg family. The following is the family dynasty from Rabbi Wolf, the elderly *Tzadik*: Rabbi Wolf, his son Rabbi David, his son Rabbi Yosef, his sons Rabbi Velvele and Rabbi Alterke, Rabbi Velvele's sons Rabbi Yaakov David and Rabbi Moshele (The former served as the rabbi in Luninets, and the latter as the *shochet* [ritual slaughterer] in David-Horodok.) Rabbi Moshele, the last of the sons, was murdered at the hands of the Nazis, Rabbi Yitzchak (Itzikl) the son of Rabbi Alterke (His son Rabbi Velvele currently serves as a rabbi in the United States.)

Ritual slaughterers and rabbinical judges include Reb Shalom the son of Reb Yosef Lachovsky of blessed memory, the *dayan* [rabbinical judge] from Minsk.

There were five synagogues in the town: The large *Beis Midrash* built by Zeev Yudovitz; the Great Synagogue, built with the assistance and dedication of Pinchas Novak the glassmaker; the *Beis Midrash* of the Rabbi (of the Ginzburg family); the Synagogue of the Hassidim of Stolin (built of brick in the latter years); and the Synagogue of the *Nagidim*. There was also a synagogue in the house of Reb Itzikl, in which his Hassidim worshipped.

There were many known prayer leaders in David-Horodok. The following were the main ones known from the large *Beis Midrash*: Yonah Rimar, Moshe Lachovsky, Yosef Mekler (the butcher), Leibele the cantor, Shlomo Novak (the Torah reader), Meir the son of David (David's).[2] In the Great Synagogue: Noach Zager the blacksmith, Reb Shmaryahu Lansky the cantor with his choir of singers. In the Synagogue of the Rabbi: Wolf the Aleinik, Lipman Dreizin, Noach the son of Pinchas Dobrushin. In the Synagogue of the Hassidim: Avraham Moshe the *Melamed*, Yosef Chasha-Bashe's (Shatzki), Izel Kolozny, Moshe Kolozny, Yosef Kolozny, Yudel Shatzki, Asher Margolin, Yaakov Begun (for Sabbath *Mincha*), Yaakov Milman the blacksmith, Mordechai Begun. In the Synagogue of the *Nagidim*: Reb Yehuda the son of Rabbi David Berkovitz. Many came to hear his prayers (at times, Reb Dovidl would invite him to the Great Synagogue, where he worshipped) Avraham Horvitz, Shachna Moravchik, and Yisrael Meir Lachovsky.

They would study between *Mincha* and *Maariv* in several synagogues. Reb Berl the *shamash* was the main teacher in the large *Beis Midrash*. After him, Rabbi David Berkovitz and Avraham Velvel Lutzky would give a class. Reb Shimon Ronkin would give a class in *Mishnah* and *Ein Yaakov* between *Mincha* and *Maariv* in the Great Synagogue. Yaakov Rabinovitz, a merchant of manufactured items, gave a class in the Synagogue of the Hassidim. He moved to Nesvizh after the First World War and served in the rabbinate there.

The Jews of David-Horodok were observers of tradition in general, but they did not forego the *Haskalah* [Enlightenment]. In 1900, the teacher Y. Sh. Y. Adler set up a modern school. Zionism was also strong in David-Horodok. The heads of the Zionists were: Yisrael Friedman, Moshe Yehuda Lifshitz, Eliezer Pinchuk, Aharon Kagan, Aharon Yonah Shafer, Moshe and Noach Grushkin, Yisrael Meir Lachovsky, Tzimrinsky, Aharon Dobrin, Shimon Leichtman, Shlomo Rozman, Shlomo Zagorodsky, Asher Zager, Moshe Aharon Mishalov, Mosheke the son-in-law of Yerachmiel Shifman, Shmuel Lifshitz, Shimon Opingandin, and Yitzchak Katz, who later moved to Luninets.

The Jews of David-Horodok formed the majority of the population in the center of the town, including its business center. Many of them were wealthy, including forests merchants, owners of transport ships, and cattle and fish merchants. The Jewish merchants of Horodok marketed their merchandise as far as Warsaw and other large cities. Some also had fishing rights in the ponds of the region.

David-Horodok was surrounded by forests, and there were lumber merchants there. The largest of them was Yaakov Friedman, who moved to Kiev in 1906, but did not stop supporting the rabbis and the needy of the city. He would send his generous donation twice a year before the festivals. He established the endowment,[3] which later became the locale of various communal institutions: the Zionist council, the library, etc. Mordechai (Moche) Rimar was the owner of a shipyard that built

[Page 93]

transport ships. He employed many workers, both Jews and Christians. He also owned a sawmill. There were three flourmills in town, one owned by Asher Zager, one by Avraham Baruchin, and one by Yehuda Berkovitz (who also owned an oil mill), and A. Z. Lutzky. There were also tannery owners, including the hide factory of Shlomo Finkelstein, who was one of the philanthropists who responded generously and willingly to every request. He also set up a charitable fund for all those in need.

Yaakov Friedman

There were also dairy owners in David-Horodok, as well as various tradespeople (builders, blacksmiths, shoemakers, etc.). Every Sunday, the residents of the villages of the area, Jews among them, would come to sell their agricultural produce at a fair and to purchase products for their homes. There was a special place at the side of this center for the thirty butcher shop owners.

Most of the houses of the city were made of wood, but there were also a few two-story stone houses. One of them was the house of Zeev Yudovitz, which served as a first-class hotel. From 1909, that house served as the government public school for all the townsfolk. There were shops on the first floor. Meir Eliyahu Kushnir, Aharon Gorin, and Alter Friedman also had restaurants. David-Horodok and its environs received their provisions for winter, including salt, flour, and salted fish, from ships that returned from Kiev and Yekaterinoslav after they brought them firewood in the spring.

David-Horodok was also not lacking in common folk, poor people, widows, and orphans, who needed support and assistance. There were people of action and emissaries for mitzvos who would make the rounds to the wealthy people and people of means on Sabbath eves to collect challahs, cakes, and cooked meat and fish to distribute to the needy. The women of the house, for the most part, would prepare the portions and donate them generously. One of those occupied in this mitzva was Shimon Leib Katzman. When he got older, he began his mission on Thursday afternoon so that he would be able to finish it on time. There were families, especially of the neediest, who were supported on all the days of the week, and were given double portions for the Sabbath.

Yaakov the son of Shimon Leib and Malka Katzman

[Page 94]

When Reb Shimon-Leib died, his son Reb Yaakov followed his path and continued the *Matan Beseter* [giving donations discreetly]. He would collect money and distribute it among the needy. It once happened that someone knocked on his window close to midnight. Reb Yaakov went out and arranged what he could. When he returned home, his wife Malka asked him: "Who and for what?" Reb Yaakov responded, "If the person would have wanted you too to know who he was, he would certainly not have come at midnight." She did not ask further.

Several of the householders supported those who fell upon hard times with significant donations in the form of loans that were never paid back.

Like most Jewish towns, the town was quiet with its traditionalism until the First World War. During the wartime, many refugees passed through the city and were generously supported by the Jews of the town. One of them, Rabbi Rabinsky, even served there in the rabbinate. After the war, during the Ukrainian times, there were also Germans in town, and they felled one of its first victims: Zeev Zager (Velvel the Smith). Early in the morning, when he went out to worship, the soldiers of the guard shouted at him, "Halt!" He did not understand their language, and they stabbed him to death. During the time of the Bolsheviks, Bezalel Yudovitz was murdered (1919?). At the end of that year, Leibel Krapivka was murdered by the Poles. The number of victims in David-Horodok during the Balachowicz times was relatively smaller than in other towns, but there were victims.

The Balachowiczes entered David-Horodok on Shemini Atzeret. Baruch Dubrovitsky (Baruch Pesha Kreina's) went to hide in the synagogue on the advice of his wife. There were four or five other Jews there, including Reb Dovidl, who was standing in prayer. When morning came, Reb Dovidl was surprised that nobody had come to worship. Baruch told him what had taken place in the city and added that they should not wait for a *minyan* [prayer quorum]. At this point, three soldiers entered the synagogue and demanded money. Only Baruch had three hundred rubles in his pocket. The soldiers took the money and did not harm them. When Reb Dovidl asked him how he dared to have money with him on the festival, Baruch replied, "I prepared a ransom for my life." When Reb Dovidl returned to his home enwrapped in his tallis, the Balachowiczes captured him on the street and commanded him to dance before them if he wished to keep his tallis. Reb Dovidl acceded to them, devoting himself to the honor of Simchat Torah.[4] During the time of the Balachowiczes, the following people were murdered: Shmaryahu Shirmuk, Chana the wife of Yosef Broder, and the young girl Roshka the daughter of Dov Moravchik. There were many more victims in the villages, where there were also instances of rape. In Chorovsk they hanged Yosef on the doorpost with a towel. Similar incidents took place in Malishev and most of the villages of the area.

Many Jews (Lipa Finkelstein, Shmuel Motzolsky and others) were saved from hanging by Asher Berman, who knew one of the Balachowicz captains.

Translator's footnotes:

1. A term for a rabbi who was not necessarily the primary rabbi of the city. It literally means "a teacher or guide of righteousness".
2. In the text, the name is spelled daled vav gimel. However I believe this is a typo, and David was intended.
3. The term can also refer to the poorhouse – i.e., the place for housing indigents.
4. When it is customary to dance.

About What Was and Is No More

by Itka Veiner-Zeldin

Translated by Jerrold Landau

After fifty years, it is very difficult to sail back to the distant past, to one's far-off childhood, and dredge up memories and impressions. Many things were forgotten. Many impressions have been pushed aside and erased from the memory. That which was good and nice, or the opposite – now appears in a very different light. I will attempt to tell something about the way of life during those days. I will begin with the closest – our street.

Our street was no different than the other streets in the town in its external appearance. It did have extra holiness because all the synagogues were centered there. This gave it its nickname, the *Shulhof* (neighborhood of the synagogues). Our street was constantly bustling with Jews coming to worship, especially on Sabbaths and festivals, and even more so on the High Holidays, *Bein Kese Le'esor,*[1] on the days about which Grandmother said, "The fish tremble in the water" (i.e. the fish in the water are overcome by fear and trembling out of fear of the Day of Judgment...). There was another thing that added taste and grace to our street – the Yeshiva lads whose singsong echoed from morning until evening as they were studying their lessons: "Oh, the rabbis taught – if one gathers sheep into a pen..." etc. etc.

Every stratum and group had its own synagogue. I can see the Great Synagogue before my eyes. There,

[Page 95]

the common folk worshipped: tradespeople, builders, tailors – simple Jews, upright Jews, "Jews from the entire year" as they were called by the people.

The *Beis Midrash*, "Yudovitz' *Beis Midrash*" stood opposite our house. It was named for one of the wealthy people of our town, named Yudovitz. Most of the worshippers there were Jews whose fortunes had declined somewhat, but who still maintained their external appearances, ensuring that their clothes would not have any stain, as a final remnant of their former status. The *Nagidisher Beis Midrash* stood in another corner. Its worshippers were in accordance with its name:[2] most of its worshippers were the wealthy people of the town. It was also noted for its appearance and cleanliness. In addition to all this, there was the Hassidic Synagogue [der Chassidishe *Shtibel*], in which the Hassidim of Stolin worshipped. There were several more houses of worship on the street.

Most of the clergy desired to live on our street: three *shochtim* [ritual slaughterers] including my father of blessed memory, and three rabbis. They were not actually rabbis, but rather Rebbes, scions of dynasties of Admorim for generations. Each of them had their own congregation of Hassidim. Hunger was their lot as well as that of their Hassidim who supported them. When I grew up and began to understand the qualities of the houses of the Rebbes, I especially held Rebbe Velvele of blessed memory in esteem. He was a proper, upright Jew, who did not get involved in politics, and was beloved by his fellows. His congregation of Hassidim was also larger than the others. His wife, Liba-Reizele was a woman of great energy. Grandmother related that Liba-Reizele was very beautiful in her youth, and when they brought her from afar to our town after her marriage, people camped at the door of her house to witness her beauty. During my childhood, I too saw the remnants of the beauty in her face. Apparently, the life of poverty and suffering left their mark upon her. They had three sons and an only daughter, my friend Tziporale. All were of fine appearance and fine spirit. It can be said in truth: there were many girls in our town, and people set their eyes upon the daughter of the clergy. More than once I heard mothers and grandmothers whispering: the *shidduch* [match] is fine and proper, but "two dead people do not go out to dance together..." Indeed, poverty pervaded in the houses of these members of the clergy.

There was a pond of turbid water (called *koloza* in the vernacular) on our street, between the Great Synagogue and the *Beis Midrash*. This pond never dried up, even during the hot days of *Tammuz*, and never froze during the cold days of *Shvat*. It always remained with its filth. A sort of green shell always covered it. Frogs croaked there on pleasant summer evenings. The pigs of the gentiles of the town wallowed there to their pleasure and warmed up in the sun, spraying water or mud upon the passers-by. When the mothers caught us in our "disgrace" – bad and bitter was our fate. Nevertheless, we always returned to our place...

The Physician Who Escaped

It was told in the town that a young physician once came to settle. When he saw the wonderful pond with its slimy water, he became disgusted. He stood up, gathered the Jews of the city, and told them, "Jews, pack your bags and escape from here!" He described for them in full color the danger that was lurking, as he had just studied in medical theory, and what the puddle might bring upon them: the black plague, cholera, and other such diseases. I do not know if anyone listened to him and left the town. The one who did so was the physician himself. The day after the gathering, he packed his bags and disappeared. For many years, the Jews told the story about that strange physician and his black prophecies. As they told this, they burst out in laughter, and the puddle with its filthy water remained in its place as always. The frogs continued to sing their croaking song. Their song blended in with the glorious song of the Yeshiva lads.

Pranks

A legend spread among the Jews that every Saturday night exactly at midnight, the dead rise from their graves and came to worship in the Great Synagogue. Anyone passing by the synagogue at that time would be called by the dead

[Page 96]

to receive an *aliya* [Torah honor] – and this would be a sign that his time has come. The Jews were careful to avoid passing by the Great Synagogue at that time. The youth knew that our neighbor, Saneh the butcher, was about to return very late on Saturday night from the home of Rebbe Velvele of blessed memory. What did the pranksters do? They hid in the women's section of the Great Synagogue, and as Saneh the butcher approached his house, which stood exactly opposite that synagogue – they began to recite prayers with great devotion and with a coarse voice, like the voice of the dead from their graves. They called out, "Reb Saneh the son of Reb so-and-so, come up to the Torah!" The Jew became agitated and petrified. He opened the door of his house with difficulty, and in a weeping voice, told his wife Sara-Leah about the disaster that had taken place to him. He went about perplexed and downtrodden, not himself, for a few days. He stopped working and awaited the verdict. Who knows what his end would have been, had my grandmother Dvosha-Necha not told him the truth. Of course, she did not tell him that "children of good families" were involved in this, including one of her family members...

The Revolutionaries

Years passed. The children grew up and became lads, and the lads became adults. Slowly, they began to leave the town, some for Torah, and some for livelihood. When they returned, they brought back with them the song of freedom. Revolutionary songs began to echo through the air:

> Brothers and sisters, take yourselves by the hand,
> Let us go to the prisons, and tear down the walls, etc.

Or a mocking song such as this:

> Nikolai is our Czar
> He is a large dog!
> Hail Czar, Hail Czar,
> *Nosh Roseiski Gosudar!*[3]

The New Cemetery in David-Horodok

Those who came back not only brought new songs in secret, so that the police would not notice. They began to convene meetings next to the cemetery that was outside the city. There, they spoke of great changes that were about to take place, and about the revolt

[Page 97]

against Czar Nikolai. Illegal books were distributed, and people began to look into them. They were not just rebelling against the rule of the Czar, but against tradition. On Sabbaths and festivals, one could encounter in the church alleyway boys and girls wearing embroidered black shirts and shiny black boots, walking arm in arm, with cigarettes in their mouths. They were called "brothers and sisters" and they imposed their fear upon all the townsfolk. One Saturday night, these boys and girls gathered in the large *Beis Midrash*, delivered lectures, and spoke about "God and his Messiah". At the end of the speeches, they shot a shot into the air. Grandmother whispered into the ear of my mother, "These are the brothers and sisters." The next day, the city was in turmoil. It was said that the police came and arrested them all. One bright day, the door opened, and someone shouted to my mother loudly, "Menuchale, Nikolai is now an ex-Czar!" With a powerful voice, he began to sing the rest of the song, with the echo responding, "Nikolai is now an ex-Czar…"

Translator's footnotes:

1. A term for the period between Rosh Hashanah and Yom Kippur.
2. *Nagid* is a term for a wealthy person.
3. I left this phrase in the original. *Nosh* means to snack. *Roseiski* means Russian. *Gosudar* is a Lord or sire. Together it may mean "snack on the Russian sire!"

Memories

by Tzipora Kunda-Ginzburg

Translated by Jerrold Landau

Rabbi Moshe Ginzburg of David-Horodok in the company of New Yorkers

Even today, when I close my eyes, I see with great clarity the long street that extends from the marketplace to the riverbank. It was called the *Shulhof* [Synagogue Street] by the Jews. The Great Synagogue and *Beis Midrash*es of the town stood honorably on that street.

[Page 98]

If you just exited the marketplace, the Great Synagogue would be before you, surrounded by a spacious yard, into which couples would be led to the wedding canopy accompanied by the musicians. The *Beis Midrash*, rising on the other side of this yard (it was built through the initiative and generosity of the wealthy Yudovitz, and was called Yudovitz' *Beis Midrash* in his name), and the small *Beis Midrash* next to it, served as the places of worship for the *Misnagdim* [non-Hassidic people] of the town.

The family of Rabbi Moshele, may the memory of the righteous be a blessing

The Synagogue of the Hassidim of Stolin stood behind the *Beis Midrash*. The *Beis Midrash* of the elderly rabbi stood opposite the old *Beis Midrash*, across the street. It was also surrounded by a spacious yard, which contained the houses of the two sons of Rabbi Yisrael Yosef, may the memory of the righteous be a blessing.

This district served as a sort of spiritual center for the Jews of the town. Primarily on Sabbaths and festivals, the street was filled with Jews in festive garb, hastening to services or coming back from services.

Chapters of Psalms and the melody of *Gemara* and prayer burst forth from all corners. I especially recall the nights of *Elul*, when the Jews walked to *Selichos* at midnight, with flashlights lighting their way.

The Jews of the town were upright and straightforward. Most of them were tradespeople or merchants, pure in their ways and straightforward in their comportment. In their opinion, a thief or a drunk could not be found among the Jews, for there was only a commandment to drink on Purim and Simchat Torah. Indeed, it was joyous with us on Purim. The "ensemble" of the Hassidim of Stolin would arrive, along with Avraham-Moshe the matchmaker, an enthusiastic Hassid and expert scholar. He would be wearing a cylinder hat on his head. We knew that he had partaken of several drinks. The "ensemble" would drink *Lechayim* with us, and the people would entertain us with melody, song, and dance until the conclusion of the feast.

That was David-Horodok, from which images of my dear family members rise and soar. I do not recall my grandfather, peace be upon him, Rabbi Yisrael-Yosef, may the memory of the righteous be blessed. However, he was talked about in our home. He had great talent. He had already received rabbinic ordination at the age of thirteen. He served as a rabbi in town, and the Rebbe of the Hassidim of David-Horodok. Many people would come to be near to him, especially on Rosh Hashanah and Yom Kippur, when he would serve as the prayer leader.

Father Rabbi Velvele, may the memory of the righteous be blessed, was very upright, and an unequalled fearer of Heaven. He ascended the seat of the Admor after the passing of Grandfather. He dedicated all his time to prayer and Torah. He donned two pairs of tefillin, and kept them on until after the *Mincha* service. He recited all his prayers with great intention, dedication, and feeling.

We always lived in a meager situation, with a restricted livelihood. Nevertheless, Father was happy with his lot, and did not complain. I never saw him get angry. He died the death of a kiss[1] on 3 Adar I, 5781 [1921]. He rose to worship, as was his custom, then suddenly removed his tallis and tefillin, went outside, fell down, and died.

[Page 99]

The Rebbetzin Liba Reizele Ginzburg

Mother of blessed memory, Liba-Reizele, was a fifth generation descendent of Rabbi Levi Yitzchak of Berdichev. She was the helpmate of Father. She was very meticulous in the observance of the commandments. She was murdered in Pinsk along with the entire holy community, may G-d avenge her blood.

My sister Chayale died in her prime.

My eldest brother, Rabbi Ahrele of blessed memory, served in the rabbinate in Luninets. He was a Torah scholar and a fearer of Heaven, with a splendid countenance. He was happy with his lot, despite his difficult life. He would serve as a prayer leader on the High Holy Days. He was murdered with his son Shamai and daughter Miriam by the Nazis, may G-d avenge their blood. His wife (a descendent of the Baal Shem Tov and Rabbi Aharon Karliner, may the memory of the righteous be blessed) died in Pinsk.

My second brother, Rabbi Yaakov-David of blessed memory, was a *shochet* [ritual slaughterer] in David-Horodok. He was a fearer of Heaven, with a generous heart, wholesome in all his traits. His wife Henia was the daughter of one of the Hassidim of Stolin. They, along with their daughters Miriam, Rachel and Sara, fell at the hands of the murderers in David-Horodok, may G-d avenge their blood.

My third brother, Rabbi Moshe-Yehoshua, may the memory of the righteous be blessed, inherited the rabbinical seat of Horodok from Father, may the memory of the righteous be blessed. He was a great scholar, a fearer of Heaven, and a preacher of renown. He was a graduate of the Volozhin Yeshiva. His wife was the daughter of the rabbi of Ostra. They were murdered in David-Horodok along with their three children: Chanale, Feigele, and Velvele.

I recall them all – and my soul aspires to revenge.

Translator's footnote:

1. Referring to a sudden, peaceful, painless death. According to tradition, Moses and Aaron both died through a kiss from G-d.

Refugees - "*Bezhentsy*" - in David-Horodok
(During the Time of the First World War)

by Y. Zeldin

Translated by Jerrold Landau

David-Horodok was not on a main road. The wartime fronts (1914-1917) were far from it, and the echoes of the battles only reached us from the pages of the newspaper.

Entire large Jewish communities were destroyed by order of the high command of the Russian army. Many communities in the border areas close to the fronts received sudden deportation edicts, to leave their places within 24 hours. The cruelty of the Czar and his uncle Nikolai Nikolaevich, the chief commander, was known for a long time before the outbreak of the war (through expulsions from the villages, the Beilis blood libel,[1] etc.), so these things did not surprise us. We knew that this was their nature and their manner throughout all times.

One ray of light shone for us in the darkness. This great thing was the feeling of Jewish brotherhood that was shown at that time during the times of the expulsions. We knew from the newspapers that many communities extended to the refugees (*bezhentsy* in the vernacular) faithful and timely brotherly aid. We were encouraged by the fact that there, in the capital city, a central committee of mighty and powerful Jews arose, and acted with exemplary dedication in aiding the refugees. (It was called YEKOPO – Yevreiski Komitet Pomoschi – the Jewish Aid Committee.) Emissaries of the central committee accompanied

[Page 100]

myriads of refugees. They enlisted local Jews at every station and did their best to extend urgent aid to the refugees.

When we read about these benevolent deeds in the newspaper, we did not imagine that we too, the residents of a remote town, would be called into the aid activity and would stand up to it with wholesomeness and honor. One Friday close to candle lighting time, a steamship – the Parachad – brought a caravan of over a hundred refugees from Minsk to David-Horodok all at once.

Later, the secret became known that a young native of our town, Yehuda Kashtan of blessed memory, went to the district committee in Pinsk and recommended that they send a number of refugees for us to take care of, while everyone thought that they came by surprise.

Through a high command, we, the youth, girded ourselves to take care of those who came. We housed them in the synagogue of the Hassidim of Stolin, who agreed to worship in the Great Synagogue on that Sabbath. The aforementioned Yehuda Kashtan was the head and chief doer of all this effort. He organized, he arranged things, and everyone listened to him. Within a few days, a shelter and roof above the heads of all the refugees was already arranged in the houses of the town. They were received with good relations and a warm heart in every home. We immediately went out to collect the first dishes and food provisions, and a civic committee was set up to provide constant care for these brethren. This committee was comprised of prominent householders, such as Reb Yaakov Rabinovitz as well as the youth. The Rabbi, Reb Baruchl, stood at the head of the committee.

The living sprit of the committee, the instigator, who found new ways daily to collect money and to help the refugees, was once again that Yehuda Kashtan of blessed memory. He negotiated with Cantor Shmerl Lansky to arrange a festive service with a choir on one of the Sabbaths. Notices were posted, and a large congregation filled the synagogue. *Aliyot* [Torah honors] and Mi Sheberach blessings for donors were sold. Thus, a significant sum was collected for the refugee funds.

The cantor of the city, Shmaryahu Lansky and his group of singers

Since the event in David-Horodok was successful, the cantor took several of his singers with him to the nearby "large" community of Rubel. There were two synagogues in Rubel, at the two edges of the village. The prayer service was divided into two. Once again, there were pledges, and donations of cash and food provisions were collected after the Sabbath for the benefit of the refugees. They next day, a wagon brought all that was collected to David-Horodok. This was during the winter. A simpler event was arranged in the summer. Zaitchik was asked to come to Rubel to speak before the congregation. Zaitchik, as we all recall, was unparalleled in his oratory skills. The congregation filled the synagogue to the brim to hear his lectures in David-Horodok. Once again, the residents of the villages were asked to donate for the benefit of the refugees.

[Page 101]

The sense of communal consciousness arose and knitted itself into communal activity. It found its first arena to display its strength through the work on behalf of the refugees. The arena grew and broadened after some time with the liberation from the Czarist rule and the beginning of Zionist activity in David-Horodok.

Translator's footnote:

1.   In 1913, the Russian government conspired to accuse an innocent Jew, Menahem Mendel Beilis, of the ritual murder of a 12-year-old boy.

David-Horodok During the Time of the Balachowiczes
(In Memory of Reb Asher the Son of Reb Yitzchak Berman of Blessed Memory)

by Gershon Berman (Canada)

Edited by Chaim Kolozny

Translated by Jerrold Landau

It was 1920. The Balachowicz brigades came through the towns of Polesye like thieves. They robbed, extorted, raped, and murdered in every place they went.

They arrived in David-Horodok on the eve of Simchat Torah. When the news of their arrival spread, and the bearers of feathers appeared in the city – a great fear fell upon the Jews, and everyone sought refuge in the houses of the gentiles or some other secret place. All the property was left wanton, if only to save their lives. The Polish priest who hid tens of Jews in his house, in the church, in front of the organ and in other secret places, should be remembered positively. He did not permit the destructive forces to come inside.

However, the salvation of the Jews of David-Horodok during those difficult days came primarily through Reb Asher the son of Reb Yitzchak Berman of blessed memory. Reb Asher was a supply contractor. He supplied the infantry brigade of Czar Nikolai, and he had many acquaintances among the high command of the brigade in Brest Litovsk.

Several of the captains of that brigade joined the camp of the enemy Balachowicz, may his name be blotted out. One of them, the captain of the unit, who knew Reb Asher, came to his house when he arrived in town. He extended his hand in greeting, even kissed him, and said, "Berman, Berman! Do not worry. Everything will be good! I know about the attitude of our troops to the Jews, but – do not fear! I will ensure that everything will be proper." A notice was immediately posted on the house that the commander desired to stay there, and Reb Asher was given a document of free passage to wherever he wanted.

When the situation grew worse and the hooligans began to act destructively, Reb Asher went to the commander, described the situation to him, and demanded assistance. The commander promised to place guards on the streets of the city, but the killing did not stop on the side alleyways. Reb Asher's family urged him to remain in his house, but he did not listen to them, and continued to wander through the city in the company of the soldiers given over to him, so as to save anyone that he was able to.

"Shall I sit hidden in my house if I am able to save Jews from death? And what am I if I fall victim in exchange for all the city?" The gentiles were greatly astounded at his great brazenness to wander outside at the time when the Jews were hidden in their hiding places, but he mocked them.

Many Jews found refuge in the attic of his house. Among them were Rabbi Rabinsky and Reb Yosef Kolozny. The members of the household brought food to those in hiding and provided for their needs. This hiding place was also hidden from the eyes of the commander. Its existence depended on boundless energy and strength, and constant vigilance.

Then a day came when there was an alarm call issued from the house of Reb Lipa Finkelstein: the rioters were about to hang him. Reb Asher did not deliberate for long. Like an arrow from a bow, he hastened with his troops to the home of the tormented one. He cut the rope of the gallows and saved Reb Lipa just in time. The rioters were brought to the captain, who determined their punishment and warned them not to repeat such deeds. In this manner, Reb Asher also saved his brother-in-law Shmuel Motzolsky from hanging.

They summoned him to the home of Aharon Dvorin: the rioters were threatening to cut off Reb Aharon's ears. Reb Asher hurried and saved him. He had just returned from there when he was called by his father himself, Reb Yitzchak of Choromsk: they had killed his son and a lad from Rubel. They must be brought to a Jewish burial, and the survivors must be helped. Within a few hours

[Page 102]

Reb Asher hastened with soldiers, weapons, and wagons that the commander left in his charge, and he brought the Jews of Choromsk to a secure place, and the slaughtered people to burial.

The winds calmed somewhat in David-Horodok itself. However, there was fear in the villages and on the roads. A "save us" call came from Turov. In the words of Baruch Lutzky: "We are dying of hunger!" Reb Asher immediately loaded a wagon full of grain, brought it in peace to Turov, and saved its Jews from the disgrace of hunger. News reached him that they were plotting against him. He hid for several days until the danger passed. When he returned to his home, he did not tell anyone what had happened.

During the final days of the rule of the rioters in the city, a report reached their high command that there were Communists hiding in the home of Asher Berman. Two captains were sent to conduct a search. There was a dark room in Reb Asher's home where Jews were hiding. The captains turned their attention there. Reb Asher opened the door for them. They room was dark. He lit one match and then a second one before the eyes of the captains. The light blinded their eyes, and they did not see anything. They left from there saying: "*Pravda nikova nyet.*" (Indeed, there is nobody there.)

After the wrath passed and Polish rule took hold in the city, Reb Asher became known to them. He received an order from them to provide meat for their army in Luninets. During those days, it was difficult to obtain wagons. Reb Asher approached the Balachowicz overseer and asked for vehicles to travel to Kozhan-Horodok. The commander gave him his vehicle and its rider. Reb Asher set out on the journey but never returned. The rioters ambushed him on the route and murdered him.

This was during the days of Chanukah, 33 years ago. The man suddenly disappeared and was no more. Those who searched for him came up with nothing. On Purim, a notice was received from the police of Luninets that a hunter who passed by during the time of the melting of the snow not far from the cemetery of their town found a murdered corpse, which was identified as Reb Asher Berman, may G-d avenge his blood.

Thus did the saviour of Israel fall. Fortunate are you, David-Horodok, that you had such sons. Shed tears, mourn, O survivors of David-Horodok, for this pure martyr who perished.

Memories

by Tzivia and Bracha Fishman

Translated by Jerrold Landau

The home of our parents Sara and Zalman Fishman "der Drebsker" [the person from Drebsk] stood next to the river as well as the bridge. It was a large, long house with many rooms. It served as the first meeting place and library for the General Zionist youth in the town. The Mizrachi [religious Zionist movement] organization of the town also had its headquarters in our parents' house. It also became a house for tending to guests, and served as the center of life in the town.

We were four boys and five girls. Only two of us survived the great murder. The survivors, some of them living in Israel, tell about the many deeds of rescue by our eldest brother Moshe. He lived in Lakhva, and earned his livelihood from the boat that sailed in the river. Many Jews were saved through our brother's boat, but he himself did not merit such.

Institutions and Organizations

[Page 105]

About Our Community That Is No More

by Sh. Kvetny

Translated by Jerrold Landau

a. The Remote Community

It is a difficult task to write about the events of a remote community that was situated among vast bogs stretching for hundreds of kilometers, a community that is far from important centers, without paved roads, and without secure means of communication. It was a community that did not leave behind any markers regarding its communal life. Its history left no firm traces fitting for special attention. It produced no famous people of renown. It was a poor, impoverished community whose means of existence did not deviate from the ways of life known during that period – the period of Polish rule followed by Russian rule. It was like other communities in the Pale of Settlement.

From an administrative perspective, David-Horodok was incorporated in the country of Poland (region of Brest Litovsk, district of Pinsk). Its official name in Polish was Dawid Grodek. It had a population of 408 in 1766, six years before the Russian conquest.

b. The Communities and Their Protocols

The term *"kehila"* [community] implies independent governance recognized by the authorities, and given complete authority over issues of religion and education, which could be arranged in its own spirit and in accordance with its own will. Such a governing structure was not a new phenomenon in Jewish communal life. Throughout all their years of exile, the Jews had a certain degree of independent authority over matters of religion, education, and the like, even though this independence did not always have that same meaning, and was not always founded upon such principles. In Poland, the communities had the special attention of the Polish kings, who granted them broad rights through special proclamations, serving as a broad foundation for their development. The community represented the people before the central government, and had the rights to impose taxes, to set up courts of law and justice, which all granted power to the authorities. These protocols of governance imparted their stamp upon the population, and forged the manner of societal life.

Elections to the communal council took place annually on the third day of Passover, and received the approval of the government. The electoral process was democratic: every taxpayer had the right to vote and be elected. They were especially careful that relatives not be elected. The elected people were called *parnassim* [communal administrators]. Every *parnas* would direct communal affairs for a month, in accordance with a rotation. From there came the term *"Parnas* of the Month".

The villages and settlements in which the Jewish population was too small to establish an independent community were affiliated with nearby communities. In this manner the residents of nearby villages were affiliated with David-Horodok. It in turn was subordinate to the central council of communities, which represented the communities before the central Polish authorities.

There were the fundamental principles upon which David-Horodok was based, until a radical change in its history began.

c. From Poland to Russia

In 1772, the eastern regions were cut off from Poland and annexed to Russia. Their Jewish residents became Jewish citizens of Czarist Russia.

David-Horodok was annexed to the region of Minsk, district of Mozyr. According to the census conducted in Russia in 1847, the number of its residents, along with the residents of the nearby villages, reached 1,572.

The Russians maintained the status of the communal structure, but only as an apparatus for tax collection. The communities were to

[Page 106]

collect from every Jew "registered" in the community one ruble for the benefit of the Russian treasury. Anyone who did not pay would not receive a "passport", which was a certificate without which it was impossible to move from one place to another or even to leave the city. The community collected taxes for the high institution and oversaw the movement of the population. Everything else was neglected.

d. Snatchings

The democratic regime in the communities turned into a despotic authority. The communal officials took advantage of their positions to the detriment of the residents. They hardened their hearts toward the poor, and raised the tax burden. Various strongmen ruled over everything. The suffering especially increased from the year 1827 and onward. By edict of Czar Nikolai I from that year, the communities were obligated in military service. Every community was obligated to send a specific number of soldiers. People of means and influence utilized all means, both proper and improper, to evade service. With the help of the communal structure, lovers of profit were hired to snatch people, especially from the poor, and give them over to the army to fulfil the quota imposed upon the community. The "snatchers" instilled fear and trepidation throughout the entire Pale of Settlement. No small number of old-time residents of David-Horodok recall one of the "snatchers", a native of the town, who was called "Shlomo Der Yoven" – that is Shlomo the Soldier. He was snatched during his childhood. The name of the son of one of the strongmen of the community was connected to him, and he was sent to the army in his place. He suffered many torments in the army, and was afflicted with all sorts of suffering. They even attempted to force him to change his religion. However, he maintained his stand, and remained a Jew who was faithful to his religion and his people. After a service of 25 years, he returned to his native city already married. The family name Yudovitz remained with him all his life, and was even transmitted to his children and grandchildren. He died in 1906. Several of his grandchildren are living in Israel.

An anti-Semitic Russian writer who traveled through the Pale of Settlement in those days wrote a report to the central government regarding the suffering caused to the population by the communal strongmen:

"The administrators rule over the community with unbounded obstinacy. The community collects sums of money by imposing taxes. The administrators do not give over an accounting of the income and expenditures of the community. The citizens of the Pale of Settlement are very poor and indigent. Their physical appearance evokes feelings of disgust. On the other hand, the administrators are very wealthy. They live lives of wealth and plenty. They have double authority: over religion and taxes. Through those two aspects, they rein in the masses from revolting against them." Yalag[1] raised a bitter outcry over this.

e. After the 1917 Revolution

The Revolution of February 1917 instilled hope into the hearts of the Jews of Russia. The yoke of the Czars who oppressed for 145 years was cast off. A life of freedom appeared on the horizon.

The leaders of Russian Jewry attempted to organize the communities on democratic foundations in the spirit of the times. The center of political life was in Petrograd. From there a call went forth to all the residents of the Pale of Settlement to form elected councils. They received directives from there, and emissaries were sent. An emissary from Minsk named Pinchuk reached David-Horodok. An electoral committee was set up through his initiative, consisting of representatives of the parties and leaders of the synagogues. Bezalel Yudovitz was elected as chairman, and Shalom Kvetny as secretary. The secretariat of the council compiled a detailed list of all those with voting rights. The voting took place in the Great Synagogue headed by Bezalel Yudovitz. There were three lists, Zionists, *Poalei Tzion* [Workers of Zion], and non-partisans headed by Yosef Berkovitz, son of Rabbi David Berkovitz. Stormy debates regarding the character of the community preceded the elections. The General Zionists promised to concern themselves with all the communal needs, both secular and religious. On the other hand, *Poalei Zion* claimed that religious affairs must be separated from communal affairs, and the community should not be responsible for maintaining the clergy, synagogues, etc. through the money of the taxpayers – everything in accordance with the winds of the times that were storming during those days. Two of the eight administrators chosen were General Zionists and six were from *Poalei Zion*. The non-partisans suffered a downfall. The following were elected from the Zionists: Bezalel

[Page 107]

Yudovitz and Moshe Yehuda Lifshitz. From *Poalei Zion*: Yekutiel Shkliozier, Papish Zipin the father and his son, Yosef Burshtein, and one other whose name has been forgotten from the memory of the writer of these lines.

However, the communal council did not last long. Before it managed to convene its opening meeting, the Bolsheviks seized the government in Petrograd. Tribulations came one following the other. Changes took place from one day to the next. The council was invalidated in the wake of the Bolshevik Revolution even before it began its activities. Nevertheless, a short article about the elections in David-Horodok and the number of those elected was written in one of the issues of the *"Rasvit"*, published in Petrograd.

f. Numbers

According to the census of 1897, the population of David-Horodok was 7,815, of whom 3,087 were Jews. In 1917 their number reached 4,500, and in 1941, the year of the Holocaust, the Nazis slaughtered 7,000 Jews. Apparently, this number included Jews who were residents of the nearby villages as well as refugees who came to live there from various places in 1939.

Translator's footnote:

1. Y. L. Gordon, known by the acronym of his initials, was a prominent Hebrew Enlightenment poet and author who advocated for religious and social reforms.

The Maccabi Organization in David-Horodok

by Yaakov the Son of Yosef Kolozny

Translated by Jerrold Landau

The first sports organization, called "Kraft", was founded in David-Horodok in 1928. After a brief time, the members Zeev Shafer of blessed memory and, may he live, Shlomo Kolozny approached the principal of the Tarbut School at that time, Reuven Mishalov, with a request to take upon himself the directorship of the sporting group. After several meetings conducted in the Hebrew language, a unified opinion was not formed, due to minor differences of opinion. However, in 1930, an agreement was forged in the merit of several members – Dov the son of Mordechai Rimar, Shlomo Kolozny, and others – and the Maccabi sports organization began to be organized.

All of the Zionist organizations and the leadership of the Tarbut School were invited to the founding meeting that took place in the school building. Hundreds of residents of David-Horodok participated in that event. The atmosphere was festive and full of enthusiasm. Th result was a public declaration regarding the founding of Maccabi in David-Horodok. The following were elected as members of the leadership: Avraham Olshansky of blessed memory, principal of the school; Chaim Branchuk of blessed memory, teacher at the school; Dov Rimar of blessed memory and, may they live, Chaim Treshansky, Chaya Farber, and Shlomo Kolozny. To our great dismay, no practical activity took place, and all the festive proclamations remained on paper alone. No Zionist organization in the city displayed the understanding and the will toward sporting matters of the Jewish youth, with the exception of Beitar, which extended its full assistance to Maccabi.

During the few winter months, the writer of these lines approached the members Dov Rimar and Shlomo Kolozny to serve as heads of a soccer team. He said to them that if they wish to maintain Maccabi, they must not rely on others, and they should begin activities through their own efforts. The approach was not for naught, and as a result, a small-scale meeting of sports enthusiasts took place in the Beitar hall. A committee was chosen, headed by Dov Rimar. Shlomo Kolozny was placed as head of the sporting branches, Yitzchak Lansky as secretary, Nachman Yonush as treasurer, and Yaakov Kolozny as convenor.

With the assistance of the Beitar movement in David-Horodok that placed itself at the disposal of Maccabi, the committee succeeded within four months in raising the necessary means to purchase sports equipment. Money was collected through fundraising campaigns, membership dues, flower days, and dance parties.

The teachers of the Tarbut School – Motzny, Blumenkof, and Oltz – ran various sporting practices three times a week in the stadium of the Polish army. The captains of the Polish army in the city extended their help to us beyond the call of duty, in a proper and pleasant fashion. All the sporting equipment, uniforms, shoes, and other items were given to us in an honorable fashion, and, above all – the military field was placed at our disposal.

On May 1, 1929, a sports competition between the sporting teams of the city and those outside of it took place at the military field. The best of their members competed. The Maccabi members Shlomo Kolozny, Yosef Olpiner, and Asher Baruchin excelled and won medals. They added honor to Jewish sports activities.

[Page 108]

In 1930, a regional competition took place in the city of Stolin. The sports committee affiliated with the regional captain also invited the Maccabi of David-Horodok. We sent the best of our people. Shlomo Kolozny won three gold medals, and Yosef Olpiner won two silver medals. These competitions also added honor and praise to the Maccabi organization.

At that time, sporting competitions of the entire region were organized in the city of Brisk. We sent district representatives. Shlomo Kolozny and Yosef Olpiner, among others, represented the district of Stolin. Through their merit, the district won second place – 105 points as opposed to the 105 ½ points earned by the Briskers.

In 1931, a competition of light athletics and various sports was arranged in David-Horodok between Maccabi and the Christian sports organization of the city. The Christians were ordered to take first place and defeat the Maccabi team, but after a strong, stubborn battle, the brothers Shlomo and Yaakov Kolozny won first place. They were given medals and diplomas.

The representatives of soccer in David-Horodok in 1937, composed of Maccabi players as well as players from the Polish army who were camped in David-Horodok

(Right to left): 1. Nachman (Chona) Yonush, 3. Yeshayahu Magidovitz, 5. Yitzchak (Idel) Friedman, 8. Shlomo Kolozny, 10. Feivel Finkelstein, 11. Yaakov Kolozny

Exemplary work took place in the branches of soccer, basketball, and croquet. From time to time, competitions with teams from the Polish army took place. The Nordia team from Pinsk, the Maccabi of Luninets, and Steshlitz of Mikashevitz also visited David-Horodok. A joint team of the Maccabi of David-Horodok and the Polish army soccer team was formed when the Maccabi of Pinsk came to visit. The Maccabi of David-Horodok visited Mikashevitz and Stolin.

One of the successful activities of the Maccabi of David-Horodok was the receipt of ten places to travel to the Land of Israel to participate in the second Maccabiah in 1935. Ten residents of David-Horodok then succeeded in making *aliya* to the Land. Had it not been for that opportunity, their fate might possibly have been the same as that of the rest of the residents of David-Horodok.

[Page 109]

Organizations and Economic Institutions in Our City

by Shmuel Papish

Translated by Jerrold Landau

The composition and sources of livelihood of the Jewish population was largely similar to that of other towns in the district of Polesye. As usual, the majority of the Jewish population worked as merchants, shopkeepers, and peddlers who purchased agricultural goods from the farmers of the villages in the area. It should be noted that a considerable proportion of the Jews earned their livelihoods from productive work. These included builders, experts in building wooden or brick houses, sawmill workers (*filchikes* in the vernacular), carpenters, dyers, locksmiths, tailors, shoemakers, smiths, and others. Christian residents of the town also worked in the two latter trades. The products of these tradespeople not only supplied the local markets, but also supplied the businesses in nearby Pinsk as well as other cities in Poland.

The economic situation of the various small-scale shopkeepers and tradespeople was generally meager. However, there were several families whose income allowed them a higher standard of living. The lumber merchants, flour mill owners, tanners, and lessees of estates and fishing ponds, hide and flax merchants, some of the textile shop and shoe shop owners, and others, were among those.

The flour mill of the Baruchin family of David-Horodok

Business connections were forged with nearby Pinsk as well as other commercial centers such as Warsaw and Lodz. Large quantities of processed and unprocessed lumber from the nearby forests, agricultural products, wagons of cattle, shipments of fish, wagons of hides, flax and other such products were sent.

Flour, sugar and salt were imported from the region of Volhyn. Textile products, agricultural equipment and shoes were imported primarily from Warsaw.

Two organizations were set up in our town, a union of tradespeople and a union of merchants. Through their efforts, two cooperative banks were set up: the Merchants' Bank by Chaim Diatlovitzky and Mordechai Kvetny, and the People's Bank by the writer of these lines. These banks were located in fine dwellings in the center of town. The Merchants' Bank was in Kaplinsky's house, and the People's Bank on the first floor of Moche Rimar's house, in large rooms that had previously served as the courthouse hall.

[Page 110]

Almost all the heads of families of the Jewish community of the town, as well as of the Jewish settlements of the area, were members of the two banks.

Our town had a tradition of cooperative activity in this area as well. Decades previously, there existed two cooperative funds in town called "Lending and Credit" (or some similar name). One was directed by Pinchas Sheinboim, and the second by Shlomo Rozman.

The activities of these two banks encompassed all areas of economic life in the town. They maintained connections with the economic institutions and private and government central banks. The relationship of the Jewish community to those institutions was vibrant and proper. The number of participants in general meetings always reached a very high percentage.

The Zionist organization was also alert to what was transpiring in the economic institutions. A recognizable number of its active members were among the directors.

It should be noted that the Merchants' Bank, in its time, helped build the new school building via a special loan. During difficult times, especially at the end of the school year and before a new school year, the two banks assisted the school leadership to avoid a crisis.

There was a difficult economic crisis of Polish Jewry in the years 1933-1935, and the cooperative banks were also affected. The Merchants' Bank, which underwrote the merchandise shippers to a larger degree than customary, was forced to interrupt its regular activities. The People's Bank, the majority of whose members were small-scale merchants and tradespeople, did not engage in underwriting large quantities of merchandise, and also conducted its activities with caution, fulfilled its obligations even during the years of crisis, and continued its activities until the conquest of Poland.

The following were among the council members and directors of the People's Bank: Pesach Pilchik, Meir Milman, Mendel Reznik, Yehuda Shnur, Chaikel Freiman, Aharon Eisenberg and his brother Moshe Yitzchak, Yaakov Volpin, Moshe Katzman, Moshe Veisblum, Meir Morel, Avraham Zeev Lutzky, Litman Kolozny, Nissan Leib Treister, Chaim Branchuk, Yosef Friedman and others. The bank workers during its period of existence included Shmuel Papish director, Meir Rappaport, Yaakov Olpiner, Asher Milman and Yonah Baruchin.

The directors and working committee of the People's Bank in David-Horodok

(Right to left): Sitting (right to left): 1. Yoshke Friedman, 2. Meir Milman, 3. Chaim Branchuk, 4. Pesach Pilchik, 5. Shmuel Papish, 6. Litman Kolozny, 7. Chaikel Freiman, 8. Nissan Leib Treister. Standing: 1. Yisrael Moravchik, 2. Yosef Baruchin

[Page 111]

The following were among the members of the council and directors of the Merchants' Bank: Shlomo Finkelstein, Tzvi Mester, Aharon Shostakovsky, Moshe Aharon Mishalov, Yaakov Beilin, Yosef Yudovitz, Reuven Mishalov, David Rimar, Zeev Moravchik and others. The following were among the workers of the building during its period of existence: Chaim Diatlovitzky and Mordechai Kvetny. The directors were Yisrael Moravchik, Chaim Lansky and Zelig Neiman.

The *"Kupat Gemilat Chasadim"* [Benevolent Fund] engaged in constructive activity. Loans were given in small sums, with bi-weekly or monthly payments. Those who turned to them and benefited were people of meager means who were unable to receive credit from the banks. This was not a charitable fund in the usual sense among Jews. Its basis was communal and societal, and those who received loans did not regard this as an act of benevolence or charity. The money of the fund came primarily from the Joint [American Jewish Joint Distribution Committee]. With all this, it was based on the principle of membership. Even those who received loans were counted among the members. From a membership perspective, it was a form of mutual aid. The leadership would authorize the requests for loans and the recipients were meticulous with their payments. The fund operated for many years, until the conquest of the town. It assisted many families of meager means in no small fashion. It was a modest institution that complemented the credit activity of the two cooperative institutions.

The life of the Jewish community was gray and difficult. The Zionist movement, with all its streams, was the sole anchor of salvation for us. The activities for the funds, for the upbuilding of the Land, Hebrew culture, the schools and the gathering of the youth around it, and above all the desire and hope for *aliya* – all these were rays of light for us in the darkness that enveloped us in our town in the bogs of the remote district of Polesye.

The Firefighters Organization of David-Horodok

by Yosef Yudovitz

Translated by Jerrold Landau

The founding of the organization was in 1904. Its founders were Zeev Yudovitz, his son Bezalel, Mordechai (Moche) Rimar, Nissan Gurevitz and Liba Friedman. The gentile founders included Captain Chereisky and Petroskovitz. The many fires that took place moved the founders toward that step. The first donation was given by Zeev Yudovitz, who gave over his private well and two barrels. The residents of the town, both Jewish and gentile, all gave their donations. The insurance society of Minsk, which took great interest in the minimization of fires, also donated funds to purchase equipment.

Captain Chereisky was chosen as the first commander of the organization, and Petroskovitz as secretary. Chereisky's assistants were Bezalel Yudovitz and Nissan Gurevitz. During 1911-1912, when Chereisky was sent to the front, Mocha Rimer accepted the role of commander, assisted by Bezalel Yudovitz and Nissan Gurevitz. In 1919, Bezalel was murdered, and Nissan became ill. Yosef Yudovitz and Simcha Mishalov were appointed in their stead. Petroskovitz continued his role as secretary until 1920, and then Aharon Moravchik took his place.

In 1935, when Moche Rimar was getting old, his role was transferred to Simcha Mishalov, assisted by Yosef Yudovitz and Yaakov Matosvitz. Two years later, in 1937, Yosef Kozak replaced Simcha, assisted by: Yosef Yudovitz, Simcha Mishalov and Yaakov Matosvitz. They continued until the entry of the Red Army.

The president of the communal committee for firefighters was Zagernkorn. Members of the committee were Yosef Yudovitz, Simcha Mishalov, Yaakov Matosvitz and Aharon Moravchik.

Five extinguishing pumps and eighteen barrels were in the hands of the organization until the Poles entered (in 1920), over and above other vital equipment needed by firefighters. During the Polish period, two benzene motors were added, which transported kilometer-long rubber hoses. At first, a small building was erected for the needs of the organization. During the Polish period, the area of the building was increased. The second half housed the theater, the proceeds of which were dedicated to the needs of the firefighters. In 1937, a 25-meter tower with a siren on top was set up next to the building. If a fire broke out, the siren would sound and 35

[Page 112]

wagon drivers would be summoned to the site, riding on their horses and prepared to do anything asked of them. There were 63 volunteer firefighters of whom 10 were Poles.

In 1938, a brick theater (the first theater was constructed of wood) was set up with the money of the organization. Its entire income was dedicated to its expenses, which continually increased.

The fame of the organization spread afar, and more than once, the firefighters went out to extinguish fires in the villages in the area.

The large fire of 1936 in David-Horodok

The Zionist Movement
in David-Horodok

The Beginnings of the Zionist Movement in David-Horodok

by Yitzchak Idan

Translated by Jerrold Landau

a. The Silent Memorial

Open Zionist activity began immediately following the Russian Revolution (February 1917), since the fear of the government ceased, and there was no more fear of the police. We sought to do that which was good in our eyes, and especially to convene meetings and to speak to the people about what was in our spirits. That was the main matter: to speak to the people!

To clarify, I will describe here an incident that took place before the revolution, in the summer of the year 1916… It was decided to organize a memorial for Dr. Herzl on the night of the 20th of Tammuz. We informed each other in our small group that we would be gathering at the home of the teacher in Avigdor's house, opposite the synagogue. About ten of us male and female friends sat together, including Avraham Durchin, Sara Gloiberman, Masha Yudovitz, Chaim Finkelstein, and others. This was the first time that we talked to the gathering in Hebrew. We were all astonished that our efforts had borne fruit: we spoke about the movement and the leader in clear Hebrew, without stumbling and error. Our eyes were turned toward the windows throughout the entire period of the memorial to ensure that no policeman hat could be seen on the street. How content were we when our modest memorial concluded without mishap.

That was the way things were then, prior to the revolution. Then freedom came to the country. All the public efforts that were locked and stifled for many years burst forth in strength, calling for communal activity and serious activism.

b. Gatherings

We went to gatherings with holy trembling, as a pious Jew hastening to the house of worship to pour out his words before his Creator. I recall the first Zionist gathering in Horodok, organized in Ladezky's large hall. It was as if that hall was designated from the outset for its holy task. It stood desolate for years, with no living soul crossing its threshold. It was only with the revolution that streams of vibrant, stormy life poured into it. Anyone moved by the spirit of G-d spoke within it, even the mute among us who did not dare to utter "a few words" before the crowd. I do not recall whether the prominent householders also participated in the speeches – many of them did have a national spirit, and collaborated with us youths – or if the speeches were delivered solely by the youths.

One fact is etched in my memory: one of the young speakers uttered his words in a flurry, emitting the following words from his mouth: "The state of the Jews will not arise in one generation. Perhaps the efforts of generations will be required for this. However, finally, it will surely arise and become the safe place…"

A storm of opposition, disagreement, and bitterness of spirit broke out in the world. The community was pre-empting the conclusion… They wanted to believe that the redemption would come speedily in our times, and that the state will be served immediately, without preparation, on a silver platter. We must not forget, this was prior to the Balfour Declaration, the news of which reached Russia quite late.

c. Winning Over the Street

We maintained contact with the central committees. Any flyer that we received evoked new waves in our stormy souls, vibrant and aspiring to national activity. An emissary, or an instructor – in our language of that time – from the headquarters would visit us from time to time. Our entire interest was to have many gatherings, to increase our activity, to become stronger publicly, to win over the opinions of the community, and to attract it to our side. This was at the head of all goals and desires. We had not yet reached a higher level of Zionist activity. The year was 1917. There was in this a sort of fulfilment of the known command of the leader, who demanded at one of the congresses: "Win over the communities!" We stormed to win over the street.

[Page 116]

Our opponents also did not sit with folded arms and no activity. Speakers and instructors also came to them at times, and called their listeners to war against the bourgeoisie and Zionism, with intensive language, etc. etc. ... There was not an insignificant number of them in town, and their power was not small. Our town was a settlement of laborers.

d. The Large Step of the Chairman

We had a Zionist council locally with a chairman, a secretary, a treasurer, etc. We also had an office space in a set place. Everything was as customary and accepted. It was necessary to reply to the flyers that were received, to call meetings, to keep minutes, and to set the daily agenda. In short, it was an organized chapter in all its details. Asher Zager was the chairman of the committee and Avraham Durchin, may G-d avenge his blood, was also one of the most active members of the committee.

One night, a committee meeting was held. At first, differences of opinion between Avraham Durchin and the chairman became evident, and the meeting passed in a stormy spirit. We returned home silently after the end of the meeting, each person immersed in his thoughts. We walked a long way, quiet, without uttering a word. Finally, Asher Zager turned to me and said, "You will see, Zeldin, that Durchin is a *Poalei Zion* [Workers of Zion] man..." These words were uttered in such a depressed spirit, as if we were, Heaven forbid, standing at the threshold of an impending disaster.

e. The Large Convention in Petrograd

Asher Zager was a good friend, even though he was older than us and of a different social class. We appreciated him and liked him. He too returned the love, and encouraged us with his simplicity and dedication.

After some time, he went to the large Zionist convention in Petrograd. That was the first and last convention of the Zionist council in Russia. We did not have the means of sending a delegate to that important convention, and we did not even think of doing so. It was a convention of all the Zionists of Russia, and who were we, people of a small town. However, Asher Zager informed us that he was going to Petrograd for business matters (perhaps that was merely a pretext), and he wanted to participate in the convention. Nevertheless, he required the mandate of a delegate. We were very happy, and the secretary prepared an official letter of authorization for him in diplomatic terms, and signed it with a fine signature. Asher Zager was accepted as a delegate among all the delegates.

After he returned from Petrograd, a general meeting was called to hear a report on the convention. This was his desire, and we too were eager to hear what the heads and greats of Zionism had to say. His report aroused great astonishment here and there in the hall. As was known, our delegate did not have higher education, and was not among the speakers. Perhaps this was because this was a communal innovation for us: For it would only be a journalist who would look on from the side and know what was going on in the convention and what opinions were expressed there, who would be able to give a report of a national convention of this nature. The writer of these lines was sent by our chapter to the regional convention that took place sometime later in Minsk. I recall how difficult it was for me afterward to produce some sort of report of the convention to our community. Communal experience was lacking. Everything was still new, like "the work of creation." The members from Bialystok later told me, as a joke, that Rabbi Fajans, one of the heads of Mizrachi and the chief rabbi of the city, would begin with a description of the journey and what took place in the hotel in which he was staying when he returned from the convention. He would discuss the people whom he met and what he discussed with them, and many more such things. He never would get around to the report on the congress itself.

f. Shiva After the Death of Borochov

There was another *Poalei Zion* party in David-Horodok. Its members were the nationalists from among the commonfolk. During that period, we did not yet have a common language with them, and there was a sort of partition between us and them, even though matters did not come to a public dispute and hatred.

A *maskil* [a follower of the Haskalah [Enlightenment] movement] named Papish, who was a teacher from the village of Orly, stood at the head of that movement. Through the years,

[Page 117]

it was said that he attained a high-level career in Russia. At that time, at the beginning of the Zionist movement, during the first year of the Russian Revolution, he stood, as had been noted, at the head of the *Poalei Zion* movement in town. With the sad news that Ber Borochov passed away in December 1917, the members of *Poalei Zion* arranged a memorial, and sat shiva as a token of mourning over the death of the teacher and dear leader.

Of course, we did not know who Ber Borochov was. We were still standing within the bounds of the pure general Zionism of Herzl without the addition of colors and without "*shaatnez*,"[1] to use the euphemistic term of Jabotinsky for Socialist Zionism. Things had had not reached that point yet. The doctrine of Jews as a nation had a unique way of developing, different than any nation. First, we must move the masses of Jews, weak people of the air,[2] toward a life of creativity and labor. We would first have to create a large stratum of working people within the nation – work in the literal sense of the term. This doctrine, which was watered and nurtured in the Land through the people of the Second Aliya, came to us years after the era discussed here. Then, at the beginning of the legal Zionist activity in our town, after the disbanding of the Czarist regime in Russia, and the transition from slavery to civic freedom – this was our Zionism. That is, the pure Zionism of Herzl, even though we did not call it general.[3]

News from the Land regarding the struggle of the workers for Hebrew work had not yet reached us. We knew that Zionism in the Diaspora refers to the shekel [token of membership in the Zionism movement] for the congress, the Hebrew language, and money for the *Keren Kayemet* – Jewish National Fund. Our concepts for the future were vague. One of the honorable people of the town remembers well that after one of the Zionist meetings, our eyes were open to this. This was Betzel – Bezalel – Yudovitz. He turned to us youth, and said, "Why are you sufficing yourselves with coins. The building of the Land and the formation of a state demand large sums, and not what you are demanding from us." He did not say these things as a man standing at the side, but rather as a man whose heart was close to the idea, and who was also prepared to participate in its actualization. His words surprised us at that time. Apparently, he was closer to the sources than we, the youths of that time, were.

Translator's footnotes:

1. A halachic term for prohibited textile mixtures of wool and linen. Here it refers to intermixture of extraneous ideas and concepts.
2. i.e. a luftmensch – a person whose ideas are impractical and theoretical
3. i.e. it was not referred to as General Zionism

About Zionist Activities in David-Horodok

by [Shmuel Papish][i]

Translated by Jerrold Landau

I wish to present here, and not in general terms, something about communal life, regarding the wide-branched Zionist movement and educational institutions, from the culture and economics that marked the Jewish settlement of our town during the final ten to fifteen years prior to the Holocaust. Only now, after everything that was and is no more, can we appreciate what our dear town of David- Horodok was to us.

The Zionist movement and Hebrew culture in our town – the roots of tradition and Hebrew culture were deep in their foundation. There were quite a few Jews of David-Horodok for whom ancient Hebrew literature was not foreign. The six synagogues, centered on the *Shulhof* [Synagogue courtyard], symbolized that ancient culture and served as the center for the spiritual life of the fathers. Quite a few Jews who studied Torah were concentrated within them, and there were always groups of Jews attending a class in Talmud, Mishna, *Ein Yaakov*, or the weekly Torah portion. There was always someone who was delivering a lecture appropriate to each group.

The *cheders* in which the children of our town studied Torah and knowledge: There were the *cheders* of Reb Avraham Moshe "Der Melamed" [the Teacher] and of Rabbi Avraham Yitzchak "Der Malachl" [the Angel], and the period of the modern *cheder* that preceded the Tarbut School. Its teachers included Yosef Begun, Chaim Katzman, Yehuda Kashtan, Yechiel Margolin, Manevitz who was the principal of the Tarbut School in 1918, Yitzchak Zeldin, and others. They all served as a strong foundation and a natural transition point to the Zionist movement and the activities of the Zionist organizations during the twenty final years. They were fertile soil for Hebrew education and the establishment of the Tarbut School in our town.

It is no wonder that the Zionist movement in our town had deep roots and broad horizons. The General Zionist Organization, *Poalei Zion* [Workers of Zion], and *Hitachdut* [The Union] were the Zionist parties. In time, youth movements and *Hachshara* [pioneer training] kibbutzim were also established.

[Page 118]

Hebrew tradition and culture based on the forefathers, the Zionist movement, the pioneering and youth movements, hundreds of students educated in the Tarbut School – all these were brought to the Land by hundreds of youths from the town and the area. Those who merited in making *aliya* along with those after that, and who brought their parents and family members with them, were absorbed in cities, villages, and working settlements.

However, it was not only the members of the young generation, the members of the parties and movements – the youth, who bore the yoke of the Zionist activities and the efforts for the funds. Many of the veteran Zionist activists were in their 50s or 60s, burdened with livelihood concerns. They also worked to the best of their ability for the funds, in the committee for *Keren Hayesod* [Foundation Fund], and the like. The merchants, shopkeepers, and tradespeople also played an active role.

It was a great source of satisfaction to us, the members of the parties, to see in our midst, in our Yeshiva, Rabbi Shlomo Zalman Shapira of blessed memory, Moshe Yehuda Lifshitz of blessed memory, and Moshe Aharon Mishalov of blessed memory, who later merited to make *aliya* to the Land.

I will remember here one of the donors to the funds, Reb Avraham Zeev Lutzky, may G-d avenge his blood. His family was known in our town with its modest way of life. His donations for the funds were always given in a generous fashion, and beyond his means. They served for us as a support for our activities and an example for others. Reb Avraham Zeev Lutzky did not merit to make *aliya* to the Land – the aspiration of his soul for many years.

The members of the *Keren Hayesod* committee during the latter years included, among others: Shlomo Finkelstein, Pesach Pilchik, Yosef Yudovitz, Mordechai Kolozny, Tzvi Mester, Aharon Shostakovsky, Reuven Mishalov, Chaim Branchuk, Avraham Olshansky, the writer of these lines, and others.

The Committee of the Zionist Organization in David-Horodok in 1936

Seated from right to left: 1. Yosef Gloiberman, 2. Dvora Geier, 3. Chaim Branchuk, 4. Shmuel Papish, 5. Chaya Geier, 6. Berl Katz
Standing: 1. Unknown, 2. Yaakov Durchin, 3. Chana Papish, 4. Berl Rimar, 5. Golda Baruchin, 6. Unknown, 7. Sonia Baruchin, 8. Yossel Moravchik, 9. Sonia Olpiner, 10. Neidos

Constant, vibrant, and wide-branched activity was conducted by the committee for issues of the *Keren Kayemet LeYisrael* [Jewish National Fund (Israel)], in which

[Page 119]

all the parties and youth organizations participated. Successful and unceasing competition took place in that field of activity among all the parties throughout all the latter years. Most of the factions competed with each other for the responsible positions regarding the fund.

Those in responsible positions during the final years included the scholar Yitzchak Leib Zager of blessed memory, Meir Rappaport, Chaim Kolozny, Yosef Gloiberman may G-d avenge his blood, Dvora, and others.

Our school also excelled in its educational activities and achievements for the *Keren Kayemet LeYisrael*.

The visits of emissaries from the Land formed a special chapter in the Zionist era of the town. Emissaries came on behalf of the funds or the parties. At such time, the Zionist tension rose to a high level, and left its impression upon communal life and the party activists. Veteran Zionists would donate and make efforts for the success of the enterprise.

Regarding this, I will relate an episode from the time of the visit of Comrade Manoach from Degania. He spent several days in our town at meetings, discussions with members, singing, and dancing. During the final moments, when he parted from the members, and the feelings of the Israeli nationalist atmosphere reached a pinnacle, Comrade Toplinky called out to him with emotion: "Comrade Manoach, to whom are you leaving us?" The visit of Meir Haezrachi of blessed memory on behalf of the *Keren Kayemet LeYisrael* also left an impression.

The registration of the two cooperative banks in the Golden Book [of the *Keren Kayemet LeYisrael*] was among the activities on behalf of the *Keren Kayemet LeYisrael*.

The following were among the members of the committee of the General Zionist Organization during the final era: Reuven Mishalov, Chaim Branchuk of blessed memory, Meir Moravchik of blessed memory, Yaakov Helman, Mordechai Kolozny may G-d avenge his blood, Berl Katz may G-d avenge his blood, Tzvi Mester of blessed memory, Shoshana Gloiberman, Sonia Baruchin may G-d avenge her blood, Yosef Moravchik may G-d avenge his blood, Yaakov Yudovitz of blessed memory, Dov Rimar of blessed memory, Chernomoretz may G-d avenge his blood, Avraham Gurevitz, and others.

Coordinator's footnote:

i. The author's name was in the Table of Contents, but was not included with this article.

Poalei Zion (Left Leaning) – in David-Horodok[1]

by Sh. Zezik

Translated by Jerrold Landau

The movement began in David-Horodok during the years 1919-1920, when Dr. Meir Peker served in the unit of the Polish army that was camped in the city. He was the first to organize the "People's Faction of *Tzeirei Zion*" in David-Horodok, a small circle of older youths full of energy and thirsting for factional and communal activity. They enthusiastically began activity.

An important turn began in the party work with the visit of Comrade Ritov in David-Horodok in 1921. His visit gave an impetus for organized work in all areas of communal life in the city. The first committee of the chapter of the party was then chosen, composed of: chairman – Yosef Lifshitz, secretary – Menachem Novak, treasurer – Yitzchak-Leib Zager, members of the committee – Baruch Slomiansky, Yaakov Cohen, and Aharon (Arke) Lifshitz.

Through the efforts of the members of the committee, *Hechalutz* [The Pioneer] was re-established. Most of its members belonged to the *Tzeirei Zion* [Youth of Zion] party. Through the leadership of the party, *Hechalutz* set up a *Hachshara* [pioneer training] group in Lisovitz in 1924, most of the members of which made *aliya* in 1925. The *Tzeirei Zion* youth group and *Hechalutz Hatzair* [The Young Pioneer] were organized as well that year, in 1924.

In 1924, when the party convention of *Tzeirei Zion* took place, there was already a well-organized chapter of the party in David-Horodok. The chairman of the local council, Comrade Yosef Lifshitz, represented the chapter at that convention.

The party was very active in the area of culture. A public meeting of the party took place almost every month. Parties, literary judgments, and publicity meetings on various topics, which took place on very frequent occasions, focused the best energies of the youth in our city, and significantly influenced the character of communal and political life. The party carried out most of the cultural activities with its own energies, and from

[Page 120]

time to time, also with the participation of the leaders of the headquarters. The members Yaakov Olpiner, Yaakov Cohen, and Yosef Lifshitz bore the burden of and successfully executed most of the cultural activity of the chapter.

The cultural activity of the chapter of the party spread out even further in 1925. That year, two valuable cultural enterprises were set up by the party, fulfilling a very important education mission in David-Horodok. These were the *Undzer Vinkel* [Our Corner] dramatic club, and the Y. L. Peretz Library.

The dramatic club earned a good reputation not only in David-Horodok itself, but also in the entire area. Its performances, which were carried out at an above average level, always attracted a large audience. The dramatic club was liquidated when most of its members made *aliya* to the Land.

The chapter invested great energy and much work in establishing the Y. L. Peretz library.

The first books were purchased with the money of members of the party, and the books were bound through the independent work of the members. The members spent days and nights within the walls of the library. The acquisition of each new book brought with it joy, and was a celebration for the party.

At the celebration marking the first anniversary of the founding of the library, the chairman of the library committee, Comrade Yaakov Cohen, was able to announce that 700 Yiddish, Hebrew, and Polish books were available to the readers.

Thanks to the dedication of the members and the thirst for books by the many readers, the library developed, and its collection of books grew from year to year.

With the *aliya* of most of the veteran active members of the party, a crisis affected the library, and there was concern over its existence. However, in 1935, a group of youths, including Kopel Moravchik, Chaim Moravchik, Chaim Farber, and Tzvi Shklaver as the head, took over the running of the library. The library again began to flourish and develop. The circle of readers grew from day to day, and new books from the finest of Yiddish, Hebrew, and Polish literature were added to the library every month.

The library was closed with the entry of the Soviets to our town. The library and archives were destroyed during the years of German Nazi occupation, along with all the Jews of the city.

The unification of *Tzeirei Zion* with *Poalei Zion* [Workers of Zion], which took place in 1926 in Poland, was barely felt in David-Horodok. There was no *Poalei Zion* chapter in the city, and therefore there was no organization with which to unify. Y. L. Zager was the delegate to the district convention of *Poalei Zion* (left leaning) in Pinsk, which was set up after the unification.

That year, a youth organization of the Freiheit [Freedom] party was founded in the city. It quickly gathered in the youth of all the classes of workers in the city. Freiheit conducted worthwhile educational work amongst the working youth, and many of its members made *aliya* to the Land after some time.

The extent of the growth of the influence of the party can be seen from results of the first elections to the city council of David-Horodok that took place in 1926. From among the eight Jews who were elected to the city council, there were three representatives of *Poalei Zion* (left leaning): Yosef Lifshitz, Shmaryahu Reznik, and Tzvi-Aryeh Zipin.

The participation of the members of *Poalei Zion* (left leaning) in the *Keren Kayemet LeYisrael* [Jewish National Fund (Israel)] and Keren Hayesod [Foundation Fund] was large and great. The activities in the funds were expressed in the daily work of gathering money as well as in the leadership of the funds. The party was very active, and was the life force of the League for Workers in the Land of Israel.

In 1934, *Haoved* [The Worker] was created by the party. It was active among the tradespeople of the city, and organized them for *aliya*.

The League list reached 60% of the voters in the elections to the Zionist congresses.

Delegates of the chapter of David-Horodok participated regularly in the national conventions of the party as well as of the League. The daily agenda of the convention served as a topic of deliberations in meetings of the chapter before and after the conventions.

In 1935, a *Hachshara* group was organized in David-Horodok as a chapter of the *Hachshara* group of Klisov. The group had 25 people. The female members worked in home economics, and the males in all sorts of heavy labor in the city. To our great dismay, the group was not able to maintain its stance in the city due to a lack of work.

[Page 121]

The activities of the party weakened to a noticeable degree after most of the activists made *aliya* to the Land. However, within a short period, they overcame the crisis in the chapter, and the members Y. L. Zager and Shmuel Zezik, who headed the party activity at the time, succeeded in organizing anew regular activity of the chapter.

In the elections for the communal council in 1938, *Poalei Zion* (left leaning) appeared on a joint list with the tradespeople. The veteran member of the party, Y. L. Zager, was at the head of the list. His integrity, honesty in action, and scrupulousness were well-known in the city. There was every chance that this list would attain a decisive majority in those elections. However, the district governor (Starosta) of Stolin invalidated the list literally at the last minute, without giving a reason. Thus, the possibility of the party directing the communal affairs in the city was ruined.

The fascist regime of Poland did not look kindly upon the development of the party in a border city such as David-Horodok, and the members of *Poalei Zion* (left leaning) also suffered in the final period (before the Second World War) from persecution by the police.

When the Soviets arrived in the city at the beginning of the Second World War, the party work ceased entirely, and its finest activists were imprisoned by the N.K.G.B.

At this juncture, we have a duty to recall the veteran, active member of the party, Aharon (Arke) Lifshitz, who was imprisoned by the N.K.G.B. and died in a Soviet concentration camp. Honor to his memory.

Party members Mendel Kravchik, Kopel Moravchik (today Yaakov Mor), and Shmuel Zezik, who were imprisoned at that time, succeeded in surviving their period of imprisonment in Soviet Russia, and made *aliya* to the Land after the Second World War.

Translator's footnote:

1. The *Poalei Zion* organization split into a left leaning and right leaning branch at one point.

A Story About a Notebook

How *Tzeirei Zion* Was Founded in David-Horodok
Memoirs of A. Veiner – (Yisraeli-Givat)

(From *Mibifnim*, August 1953)

by A. Yisraeli

Translated by Jerrold Landau

It was a notebook that was not thick, covered in blue, traveling "the journey of forgiveness"[1] from the Land of Israel to the Diaspora. It arrived in the town one day at the beginning of the 1920s.

The notebook, in which political surveys and plans are described, is an overflowing treasury that was revealed incidentally. We perused that notebook, and poured through it, and everything became clear to us: the numbers, the professional concepts, the awakenings, the vision. We felt: This is it!

So perhaps it is worthwhile to tell about it according to the [chronological] order.

The Balfour Declaration was now celebrating its fifth anniversary. The mandate of the Land of Israel, which was set up "to establish a national homeland for the Jews in the Land of Israel" was certified by "fifty-two nations." However, the honeymoon in the Land of Israel was quickly severed, and reddened with the blood of Trumpeldor and his comrades, with the blood of Brenner and his comrades. *Aliya* to the Land of Israel was restricted by a command of "the first high commissioner of Judea." The weekdays, the six gray days of toil, arrived. The situation stalled, delayed – what was delayed in coming! These that were going to happen, how mistaken were the visions and the dreams of the kingdom of Israel to the point of drunkenness and personal forgetfulness: Some were perplexed and afflicted with somnolence regarding the dream of redemption that had been killed, and the sanctity that had been violated. There were also those who suddenly saw that the prophesied ideals that they had woven and about which they had preached for some time already, those ideals will no longer be recognized in their place in secular life.

On the other hand, not far from the town – there was a border and a sign: Proletariat of all the lands, unite! Not long ago, thunder thundered from there, and reached the town: Comrade: a new world: Long live Socialism: Brothers, a strong Socialist and human "earthquake." Dams have been burst. Joy. Perplexity. A feeling of the end of days and the beginning of days. Hunger for bread, and hunger for life. One sixtieth of the redemption, and its birth pangs are like the birth pangs of the Messiah. Thick darkness, and you do not know what will happen the next day, until, one autumn day, the flag of "Independent Poland" spreads over the town.

[Page 122]

And suddenly – from one side, the east of Poland, there is the town: from the other side – western Byelorussia. East-not-east, west-not-west, a remote corner next to borders, cut off from yesterday, cut off from today, an in-between creation in the space of the world.

That was the geographical mark of the town on the world map. And its history?

Ask the wind, and it will tell you. Do not ask the boys and girls of the town, for whomever wanders through its streets, alleyways, paths, and hiding places; whomever dips in the golden fields decorating it all around: whomever wanders in its green groves; whomever wades in the waters of its rivers lapping at the edge of its ground; whomever knew their residence, their names: their family trees, their worries, their joys, secrets, from inside; whomever saw the sun and the color of the sky for the first time there – the eternity of their life and the eternity of the city, and the images of its people are one. Before you is everything, after you there will be everything.

b.

And I will recall my sins: Even today I do not know who, how, and when this town arose, and what the name David-Horodok means ("The City of David"?). Even to this day, I do not know how to classify its Jews by type. Its classes and social formations are fenced in. I will recall one thing: very many of them were toiling folk. Behold my neighbor on the right, the one on the left, and those on such-and-such a street, and on a certain lane. Here are the apprentices of Herzl the carpenter and Eizik the smith: I saw them while they were still apprentices, aspiring to become independent tradespeople. Here are the up-and-coming tailors, builders, locksmiths, and store assistants. Here are the friends of Pandry,[2] the butchers, and the wagon drivers. Here is the eternal *shamash* [beadle], bowing on his knees before every wealthy person and every mitzvah. Not few were the numbers of householders, half wealthy people, clergy, and shopkeepers. These and those "measured" the streets with their feet, feet that were lacking in work. They went around idly, looking for employment and support in life.

It seems that the town was frothing toward a social revolution, frothing indeed. A small group of wealthy people, a number of youths, and a large mass of people, each to his trade, people in difficult circumstances, and indigents. Some were petite bourgeoisie, others were proletariat, and others were of the unrestricted class. Apparently, the Marxist doctrine did not particularly resonate with the Jews of the town. The Jews of those social classes basked in the shade of the "higher structure" – and some became involved with Zionism, some with Socialism, and some with the "strategic basis" of the town, and lived as they lived. Indeed, it was no coincidence that living here at the beginning of the century were Yishai Y. S. Adler, and A. Litvak, one with his "Hebrew in Hebrew"[3] and the other with his Bundism, heresy and revolt. It was not in vain, that the bells of revolution and the news of Zion pealed forth in the year 1917. A trace of this was absorbed and gained followers, supporters, and like thinkers.

Nevertheless, the town was Zionist. Despite the anti-Zionist sprouts of Bundism and Communism, despite the community of Hassidim and the abundance of rabbis, despite the rage of America that swept up everyone. For there was nothing other than Zionism, even if it was the supernal Zionism, of Sabbaths and festivals, of activity, mitzvot, and scholarly individuals.

Within the community of Zionists, there was a group of youths, friends for progress, complaints, thoughts, and dreams. It was a variegated group. One was the son of the butcher; another was the son of a merchant and communal administrator; one was the son of a smith and another from a wealthy family. One was the son of an agent, the apprentice of a carpenter, a watchmaker, and a bookkeeper. Some were destined to be students, and salespeople in the shop of their parents. There were about thirteen other such "pairs." The circle was completed by girls, who also had their family trees, friends, and friends of friends who walked in the paths of the time, knowing wars, revolutions, and changes of regimes. They were surrounded by the boredom and routine of the town, sated with the doctrine of Zionism, searching for a grasp upon the future.

In those days, the notebook arrived.

The notebook opened as follows:

"The old social group and the old culture is tottering, not to arise again. Humanity bound in fetters is struggling with its material difficulties and traditional shame. In the bosom of labor, new creative forces are bursting forth and growing, calling for the final battle against the rule of the classes and social inequality.

[Page 123]

"And now, in the era of social revolution and national revolutionary change, the struggle between the world of yesterday and the world that is bursting forth and rising – specifically now, the pressures on the masses of the House of Israel have increased and reached their pinnacle. The realities of the exile, the dependence upon foreign soil, foreign economy, foreign culture, and the benevolence of strangers – have now become exposed in their full tragedy." Furthermore:

"With the victory of the Socialist movement, the forces that will also lead to the liberation of the Jews are also rising and strengthening. With the victory of the international proletariat comes the hope for the redemption of Israel. The hope is not in heaven, and not in the bosom of the distant future.

"To become the active force, the primary forger in the process of the upbuilding of the Land of Israel, and the settling of the masses of the people on Socialist foundations – that is the goal of the Jewish proletariat."

c.

We will leave our group of youths for a little while. Let us read the notebook. It is quite necessary for them. Necessary, and not only for one hour. We will yet see its readers moved, enthusiastic, reluctant, and the cycle repeats. Now, we will unite a bit with the notebook and its writers.

When the historian comes to talk about the era, he will not pass over the notebook. He will relate approximately as follows:

In July-September 1918, emissaries of the world covenant of Poalei Zion gathered in the city of Stockholm for their convention. They decided to send a delegation to the Land in order to construct a plan of activities for the future.

These emissaries certainly knew: the time was a time of the "birth of the world." The year 1919 in the world at large and the Jewish world. The path to redemption is not paved with roses. Life is tottering and life is being built. From the enthusiasm one can establish a new, different world. The great hour is also knocking at the doors of the Jewish world. Every moment is precious, and is not to be wasted. The historian will certainly add:

After two years, a schism arose within those camps. "The era of social revolution" slowly evaporated from them, and disappeared from them completely with the passage of years. And those – the "strength of all energies" was deferred to the end of days, with the belief that the stychic[4] forces will break through the circle on their own, and will pave the way for mass settlement, etc." As the years go on, they will return from casting their desires solely upon the historical process. New forces from here will lead to the realization of the task. They will warn the new "heirs" who are making efforts in old doctrines. However, in the interim, in the year 1919, this camp was complete. The committee set out to its desired place.

And when it came, among its members were – economists, communal workers, villagers, activists working in the city, writers, teachers, and others – "a brain trust" in the entire country placed itself at the disposal of the committee. The committee researched, inquired, deliberated, built, and bound its statements in a notebook with the prosaic, official name: "The Work for the Land of Israel."

The notebook reached the Diaspora in the language of the Diaspora, in Yiddish.

d.

What was the notebook, and what was it not?

A Bible and not a Bible. New "Knowledge of Palestine," different from that in the usual Zionist booklets. Resonance of the soil emanated from it, the color of soil, literal ground. Zionism such as this, vibrant, the voice of the past, the voice of the era,

[Page 124]

and vision of the future. And cruelty. Only people connected in their vision to life and death. Only great believers enveloped in several covers of romantic and delusion, itching with wounds but not being concerned about it, imbued with trust, faith, and love.

The "researchers" related, proved, demanded, and encouraged. Our readers read.

Suddenly, the veil was lifted from Petah Tikva, Rishon LeZion, Ness Ziona, and others – from all that photographed and drawn romanticism that was once common on actual images decorated with verses from Isaiah and Amos. The sounds of *Ya Ha Li Li, Mechorati*, and *Am Shachar, Ura, Yeled Chen*[5] – which symbolized the closing of the paths of the sea and land, came to the town and were sung with devotion in the gloom of the twilight in the *cheder*, in a shady grove, or on a lovely boat on the water – were lowered. The Biluists, the Colonists, those who conquered the desolation and the bogs, consumed by fever and planters of trees – this entire great epic that had not yet been written, but was guarded in the depths of the heart – this epic lost its luster. New hymns were heard: Jewish effendis,[6] apologizing, confiscating workers and liquidating workers, violators of the dream of the Hebrew village, of Hebrew work. That is the type of thing that the notebook described.

The readers – "One by one without seeing" were moved, became agitated, and struggled as if in a nightmare. And there were also those who thought that this must be a jest, a pernicious joke to distract and to foment discord: perhaps a new incarnation of Kamtza and Bar Kamtza,[7] and what remained of the hope was as if hanging by a thread.

But behold, there was a bit of comfort. Small beginnings, simple hints. "A group." "A cell of a Socialist group in the Land of Israel." Such an exotic creation, but it was tangible, with a future and a hope. Revolt, work, equality, the battle of the classes, brotherhood between nations – under the blue skies and upon the desolate ground. Our tiny Socialist revolution, with our own hands, for us. We jumped up as if Bialik, Gorky, A.D. Gordon, Herzl, Peretz, Tchernichovsky, Borochov, and Lenin all together jumped into the lines of the publicity prose forged into the book, blended into the plan, and stood on the birthstool.

Our youths became enthusiastic once again for news of a different life – they were enthusiastic and afraid of it. They were revolted in a state of stagnation and emptiness, and they did not gird the strength to break it. They certainly understood revolution, a change of values, the creation of something new. These were true, certainly true, but they could not make peace with the fact that this was the reality. They were pursuers of newness, being eaten up by traditionalism and gnawed by doubts. They breathed that atmosphere, and absorbed it to their innards, the Socialist reality, "the voice of the blood" – was not easily given up.

And the covenant was forged… The members gathered "far from the city," at the side of the slope, in the shadow of the tall, thick trees that formed a canopy over the Jewish cemetery. Unintentionally, the place was a symbol of connection, continuity, revolt, life. There, the "brothers and sisters" who were rising to revolt against the regime gathered before, after and during the year 1905. There they learned the doctrine of parades, revolutionary songs. There they learned the art of the gun. From there, one by one, they returned to their houses, their dreams, their battles, along tortuous routes, for a little respite and free time. Our group of youths gathered there on one Sabbath morning.

This time, without saying anything, it is summed up: this is it! "The revolt" was planned in all its details and particulars: the conquest of the local Zionist chapter and turning it into a Socialist-Zionist chapter. Tasks were allocated. The participants were informed with decisive debate. The candidates for the new committee were determined. The activities for the near future were outlined, etc.

And when we dispersed, we knew, indeed, these were comrades in a "revolt." They were rebelling against their past and present. They were rebelling against their parents and against themselves. They were aroused, people aroused late, who had been consumed during the times of dispute and frightful civil war, but they were aroused, renewed, enthusiastic. The way opened: from the movement to *Poalei Zion, Hechalutz, Freiheit*, a *Hachshara* kibbutz, a Y.L. Peretz Library, communal activities in the explicit name of Socialist Zionism, even the beginnings of *aliya* to the Land. In their paths and following them – *Hashomer Hatzair*, and others, which existed, burst forth, and were vibrant in all the Jewish towns of Poland. This also took place in our town.

Each person from the first group, with their bags packed for the journey to the Land of Israel. In them were bound precious, vibrating papers of the notebook, with a blue cover.

[Page 125]

Now I stumbled across the notebook by chance. I found it among other precious personal belongings, belongings that everyone hid from onlookers and themselves for some reason. I stumbled across it, and read it for the second time. I saw: many of the members of that committee, as well as their assistants and advisors, had passed away: N. Sirkin, A. Ribotsky, B. Katznelson, D. Ramaz, Ch. Kalvarisky, A. Ettinger, M. Wilbushevitz, and others. Some of those captains are now in Israel and in the State of Israel. Who knows whether this notebook is to them a reminder of the sins of their youth, a reminder of iniquity. Only isolated ones maintain their faith now as it was then, for the era was an era of social revolution, and there was oppression of Jews, etc.

And the notebook itself: it was truth and vision, straightforward and a dream, the flame of the youthful era in the world. Its prose is poetry, and its dream – reality. Its recommendations are reality, and its realities are better than its recommendations. I said that it would be appropriate to attribute a soul to that notebook, for it was a sort of "brief course" for a great many people in the Jewish towns of Poland regarding a very broad topic, longer than the exile, like the length of oppression and slavery in the world, like the length of the faith in good, the hope of the struggling and building man.

Translator's footnotes:

1. I am unsure of the meaning of this mysterious phrase, but it seems to relate (and uses similar terms) to the tradition that the bodies of those Jews buried in the Diaspora will make the journey (i.e. roll through tunnels) to Israel prior to the Resurrection. In this case, the notebook is going in the opposite direction.
2. Seemingly a reference to "Pandry Hagibor" [Pandry the Hero], also known as Noach Pandera, a Yiddish novel by Zalkind-Zalman Shneur.
3. A methodology for teaching Hebrew by using only Hebrew in the classroom.
4. The term "stychic" means natural, objective, or dynamic, and is part of Jewish Socialist terminology.
5. These seem to be old-time Zionistic songs.
6. A man of high social status as a result of wealth, education, or position in government.
7. A reference to the Talmudic legend regarding the cause of the destruction of the Second Temple, based on baseless hatred between Kamtza and Bar Kamtza. See Tractate Gittin 57a.

About the Youth That Was and Is No More

by Moshe Meiri (Moravchik)

Translated by Jerrold Landau

The foundations for the life of the youth organized into its organizations was laid in the school. From there and onward, the path is known. That is: the pioneering path to the Land of Israel.

Seemingly, everything was usual and straightforward as it was in many cities and other countries of Eastern Europe.

However, there was something about the youth in our town that was unique. They attempted to forge their path in life with their own energies for they did not want to follow the paths of the parents.

Grade 7 of the Tarbut School with the teacher Blumenkof (Ben-Yosef) in 1931

[Page 126]

By the time they were of school age, the youth spent most of their time outside their parents' houses. That is what imprinted its stamp upon communal life of the entire city.

The history of the youth in the small towns of Poland has not yet been written. If that chapter of history will ever be written, it will be possible to choose the youth of David-Horodok to serve as an example and material for the research that will be done.

Almost all the youth were organized into various organizations and groups. Most of them were pioneering organizations and groups of the Zionist Movement. *Hashomer Hatzair* [Young Watchmen] was the largest in size. The local *Hechalutz* [The Pioneer] was the largest in scope and activity.

Even though the aims of the Zionist movements were different than the others, the common thread among them was revolt against the present and the desire to set up new imprints for the Jewish people.

The paths that lead to that goal were many, however, the central path was that of *Hechalutz*, even though that path was more difficult than all of them.

The male and female youths who were members of the *Hechalutz* movement had to leave their parents who often were in a difficult economic situation, and go toward physical labor to which they were not accustomed. The difficulties of becoming acclimatized were great, and at times unbearable.

However, this path always illuminated the holy idea of redemptive Zionism, and most of the youths who chose that [path] ended up making *aliya* and living a new life in the Land of Israel.

Even though the youth were always thinking only about that path, most of the sons who arrived in the Land dreamed about bringing their parents to them. Through this, they concerned themselves with a solution to the family life that remained in the town. Many of them even succeeded in bringing their parents to the Land.

The influence of the youth on that town was great even when they were of a young age. Societal and communal life was borne mainly on their shoulders: with Zionist activity, activity for the *Keren Kayemet* [Jewish National Fund], and especially Hebrew education and the study of the Hebrew language, in which not only the youths but also the mothers and fathers participated eagerly.

The *Bnei Yehuda* [Sons of Judah] movement – that was the movement that urged its members to speak Hebrew from when they were young – became an important educational factor in the town. The Tarbut School, whose name went before it, also contributed honorably to that.

After the war, there was a particularly dismal accounting. Survivors remained, brands plucked from the fire, one from a family and two from a street.

After the war, they wandered from country to country. Many of them reached the Land of Israel.

However, some set their steps to other countries.

These youths,[1] who are now in Israel and in other countries of the Diaspora, are the sole and final remnant of a long, unique period of life.

These youths have the duty to establish a memorial monument to the life that was and is no more, to the mothers and fathers who brought them into the light of the world and did not merit to the contentment, to the brothers and sisters who struggled with the bitter fate and did not overcome it, to the many memories before they are erased from the heart, to the friends who went along that path but did not reach the end. To all of these, let a memorial monument be erected, and let it be transmitted from father to son and from mother to daughter until we too, the youth of that time, will only be memories.

Translator's footnote:

1. Clearly no longer youths – the author is looking back to the time that they were raised as youths in David-Horodok.

Youth Clubs

by Moshe Meiri (Moravchik)

Translated by Jerrold Landau

If you heard the sounds of song or echoes of dancing in unison coming from some place late at night, you would know that you were in proximity to a youth club.

When all streets were slumbering and the lights were extinguished in all the windows, light would still come through the windows of the

[Page 127]

youth clubs. In this manner, every day after the conclusion of studies or after finishing work and having a quick dinner, the youth would come to their clubs.

There, they would meet for discussions on current events. There, they would meet for a light conversation and meetings of friends. There, they would gather to enjoy themselves and remove all yokes.

There was almost no boy or girl in the that town who were not involved in a youth movement. The number of organizations was large, and they included all colors of the rainbow of those days, starting from *Hashomer Hatzair* [Young Watchmen], *Freiheit* [Freedom], *Hashomer Haleumi* [National

Watchmen], and *Gordonia*[1] – to the *Hechalutz* [The Pioneer] movement that encompassed all the Zionist youth organizations.

These clubs were maintained through the funds of the male and female youths who paid membership dues to support them, as well as to cover all the other expenses involved in existence, study, sporting equipment, etc.

It was interesting to look from close upon these clubs, with their internal structure and form.

Each group was headed by a leadership committee that was responsible for filling all the needs and roles of the movement, and to educate the boys and girls in the path that the movement had set.

The daily regimen of the various organizations was not filled solely by fun and games. They would also study the doctrines upon which the ideological foundations of the movement were constructed.

More than once, such an organization raised the banner of revolt. In the event that the parents did not agree to the path that their son or daughter had chosen, the counselors would appear at the house of the member and describe the entire doctrine to the father and mother in brief.

In many cases, the parents were convinced, and agreed to part from the son or daughter. In cases where they did not come to an agreement, the children would escape from the home and go to the *Hachshara* [pioneer training] places through their own energies, until the parents finally made peace with the situation and stopped resisting.

These youth movements bore the communal tasks on their shoulders. They were involved with the people and played a role in every activity that took place in that place.

At committee meetings or meetings of the leadership council of the institutions, one could see a boy or girl representing the youth organization, and enthusiastically deliberating with the adults who were participating in that meeting.

Therefore, it was only on rare occasions when neighbors came to complain about the clubs who were having a late party and making noise on the streets, for they knew that in this town and in those clubs, the new soul of the Hebrew youth was being forged, and these clubs were educating the young generation for a different life, more independent, and more beautiful.

These clubs will now be in our memories as points of light and comfort remaining for us survivors.

Translator's footnote:

1. A Zionist youth movement based on the beliefs of A.D. Gordon.

The *Hechalutz* Organization in David-Horodok

by Yehoshua Begun

Translated by Jerrold Landau

Dedicated in memory of: father, Mordechai Zeev the son of Aharon Begun; mother, Etel the daughter of Aharon and Guta Abrin; sister Elka; brother-in-law Dov (Berl) Turkenitz (the son of Noach of Stolin); their children Gittele, Brachale; sister Tzirel. May G-d avenge their blood.

It is impossible to dredge up and write on paper about the era of *Hechalutz* [The Pioneer] in David-Horodok. It is not within the power of my memory or ability. However, I still recall well the period during which I was a member of *Hechalutz*.

The *Hechalutz* chapter in the city grew continually, even though it did not include the graduates of the youth groups such as *Hashomer Hatzair* [Young Watchmen], Freiheit [Freedom], etc. The youths who were not yet organized, who were "ordinary *chalutzim*" knocked on our doors. They were attracted to the movement not specifically because of idealism, but rather simply out of a desire to be able to go to *Hachshara* [pioneer training], to be able to merit to later make *aliya* to the Land of Israel. Therefore, the chapter grew and developed, and became an

[Page 128]

important factor in the city and amongst the youth. The veterans went on *Hachshara*, and the newer ones took their places. When the veterans made *aliya* to the Land, the newer ones went on *Hachshara*.

During those days, the number of certificates (*aliya* permits) for *Hechalutz* members increased. The *Hachshara* places quickly emptied of their members, and new members were required from the chapters. The *Hachshara* places sent emissaries to "win over" additional workplaces in the near and far region. Tens of *Hachshara* places were thereby set up in the cities and in the villages, in manufacturing and in agriculture. Almost all of them lived in meager straits and in poverty. *Hachshara* places such as these were also set up in David-Horodok by the emissary woman from the Kibbutz Klosova. After a short time, an emissary woman came from the Kibbutz *Hashomer Hatzair*. However, neither of these maintained themselves, and they left the city to seek a more appropriate place after a short time. There were two reasons why they left: a. the lack of local industry, and b. the fact that the Jews of the city pitied a Jewish tree cutter. From ancient times, Jews knew that tree cutting and being a servant in Jewish homes were jobs for gentiles.

Nevertheless, *Hachshara* kibbutzim were set up. Thousands of male and female youths prepared themselves in manufacturing centers in large cities, as well as in agriculture.

This was the peak period, but it did not continue. The Mandate government reduced the quotas. As a result, the people in *Hachshara* remained in their places for a year or two, three years, or even more. Many returned to their homes. The chapters dwindled. Some returned to David-Horodok, but most of them continued to wait for their turn.

In light of this situation, new avenues for *aliya* began to be sought. This was known as *Aliya* Bet [Second *Aliya*]. The way was not easy and not short. The secrecy of the situation required great caution. I too was among them. Apparently, I returned home as if separating from *Hachshara*, but actually, I prepared for *aliya* for eight months. I returned to my previous workplace with Sh. Finkelstein. When the day came for me to travel to Warsaw, only my family members, and Shlomo Finkelstein and his brother knew. Their task was to create the impression and to respond to any questioner that I was traveling to Warsaw for work. When Yossel Der Geler came with his wagon to pick me up from my home – I did not bid farewell to my family members. That had already taken place previously, in a room inside a room.

Father made several plans, searched for several routes, and made several efforts to reach the Land. How did he dream and pine for the day when his only son would make *aliya* to the Land, and open the gate for the rest of the family. I recall his words to the people with whom he was discussing this topic. "First, I will transfer my heart to the Land of Israel (he was referring to me, the son), and then I will come. I will certainly do so." At the time of parting, tears poured from his eyes, and his prayers accompanied me on the journey. The wagon moved from the house, with the eyes of the family accompanying their only son and brother with the hope that they will quickly follow him. But, they did not merit.

The family with a Zionist Jewish tradition, honest and working, one of the many of David-Horodok, all of whom formed a vibrant Jewish community in the Diaspora, for Zionism and the Land of Israel – Amalek waved its impure sword over them to destroy them and annihilate them.

May their souls be bound in the bonds of eternal life.

With the *Hachshara* Kibbutz in Lisovitz

by [Rivka Aharoni-Ziporin][i]

Translated by Jerrold Landau

Fifteen male and female members (I among them) joined together in 1925 into a *Hachshara* [pioneer training] group before our *aliya* to the Land. We were allotted a plot of land of two dessiatin[1] in Lisovitz. Yosef Lifshitz and Zager were the main ones who assisted us in this.

We quickly got used to *Hachshara* life: rising at dawn, working a full day (with breaks for eating, the appetite was great!). After work, several members studied Hebrew (with Baruch Slomiansky). Others spent time singing and reading (*Davar*[2], *Hapoel Hatzair*[3], *Alt-Neuland*[4]).

Many guests visited us on Sabbaths. Some were our friends from the older *Hechalutz* [The Pioneer] and members of *Hechalutz Hatzair* [The Young Pioneer].

[Page 129]

They did not hold back from helping us during a time of need. Everyone who came encouraged us. A double dose of encouragement came via the words of astonishment from the elderly farmer and landowner who helped us in all the work of planting and harvesting. He was astonished at the sight of how quickly we had become competent in agricultural work, in contrast to the many years that it would have taken a gentile to learn how to handle a work implement.

We all eventually joined the Pinsk group (Givat). Hershel Pinsky was our main counselor. However, due to the serious recession that pervaded in the land at that time, we scattered in different directions after our *aliya*.

Yaakov Olpiner, Zelig Lamdan, his sister Hinda, and Yisrael Moravchik fell at the hands of the Nazis. Aharon Lifshitz (Aku)[ii] died in Siberia.

Aryeh Shostakovsky fell in defense of the Land. The rest are in the Land.

Translator's footnotes:

1. A unit of measure for area in Czarist Russia (equivalent to 1.09 hectares).
2. A Hebrew-language daily newspaper.
3. The newspaper of the *Hapoel Hatzair* [The Young Worker] movement.
4. A utopian novel by Theodor Herzl.

Coordinator's footnotes:

i. The author's name was in the Table of Contents, but was not included with this article.
ii. I believe that "(Aku)" is an error in the text. Aharon Lifshitz was my relative and his nickname was Arke.

The *Hachshara* Kibbutz in Lisovitz

Hechalutz Hamizrachi in David-Horodok

by G. Gloiberman[i]

Translated by Jerrold Landau

Rabbi Dines, a member of the *Mizrachi* [religious Zionist movement] headquarters, visited David-Horodok in the summer of 5683 (1923). He came on behalf of *Keren Hayesod* [Foundation Fund]. In the meantime, he seized the opportunity and delivered an enthusiastic lecture in the large *Beis Midrash* on the topic of the revival of the nation in the Land in the spirit of Torah, as was the aspiration of *Mizrachi*, to realize the prophetic vision, "For out of Zion shall go Torah, and the word of G-d from Jerusalem" [Micah 4:2].

Among his other words, he said, "If our entire strong desire is to revive our Hebrew language and to turn it into the language of education and life, the language alone will not impart to us the light of Torah and the love of our ancient literature. The Torah is the primary source and fruitful kernel of Judaism, and it must not be exchanged with various streams."

When I recall those moments, it is as if I am again living that pleasantness, an exaltation

[Page 130]

of the soul, and the feelings of joy that filled the hearts. A holy silence pervaded in the hall, and warm seriousness was etched on the faces of all those gathered.

After that meeting, it was decided to found *Hechalutz Hamizrachi* [The *Mizrachi* Pioneer].

The member Chaim Kolozny, who was a very talented orator, lectured with simple, clear words about Zionism and *Mizrachi*, and especially about the meaning and doctrine of *Hechalutz Hamizrachi*, and the great work that we will be responsible for. The general feeling was "we will do and we will heed." A committee of five members was chosen: Chaim Kolozny as chairman, I as secretary, and Simcha Chover, Feibush Shatzky, and Tzfasman as members of the committee. We made contact with the headquarters of *Hechalutz Hamizrachi* in Warsaw, and received directives regarding how to organize the work and fill the special tasks related to it. Even though we were still quite young, sixteen and seventeen years old, we knew how to get organized. Those first days of our movement were beautiful, full of meaning and rich in dreams. New horizons were opened for us. We accepted with enthusiasm and joy every piece of information, every piece of news in the newspapers that were brought to us from the Land. The debates were vibrant and full of energy. All the members participated in them. We obtained a meeting place at first from the principal of the Tarbut school, Mr. Reuven Mishalov, until we succeeded in obtaining a large, spacious room by ourselves for meetings and debates. We then also began to organize the Young *Mizrachi* organization for those who were not yet prepared for *aliya* to the Land of Israel and who did not yet have the necessary means for *aliya*. Thus, we reached the year 5684 [1924]. At the beginning of the summer, we decided to prepare a *Hachshara* [pioneer training] place in agricultural work for our members who were ready for *aliya*. Instead of traveling to other places, we set up an agricultural farm in our region. For this purpose, we leased a large plot of land near Dobrin. We planted barley and set up a large vegetable garden. We built a large bunk that was divided into a large kitchen, a mess hall, a meeting hall, and bedrooms. Some of the female members worked in the kitchen, and some in the garden, by rotation. We requested financial support from the *Hechalutz Hamizrachi* headquarters in Warsaw. They sent us from there a member of the headquarters, Shapira, who delivered a major speech on *Hechalutz Hamizrachi* and the tasks of *Hachshara* prior to making *aliya* to the Land of Israel. He praised our efforts in setting up the agricultural farm without support from *Hechalutz Hamizrachi*, and promised to work for our benefit at the headquarters.

We also began efforts for the benefit of the *Keren Kayemet LeYisrael* [Jewish National Fund (Israel)]. We organized a delegation of the best of our members to work for the redemption of the Land. A general organization was created, which included people of influence from all the various parties in our city. We did not neglect any appropriate occasion and did not forgo any opportunity to work for the *Keren Kayemet LeYisrael*. We would go to any circumcision, *Tenaim* [engagement celebration], or a wedding in the city, and never returned emptyhanded. Some gave more and others gave less, but we asked and they gave. Boxes for the *Keren Kayemet LeYisrael* were distributed to all the houses, and we would go around to empty them every month. We should note that in many houses, there were other charity boxes for the benefit of Yeshivot or other institutions. That summer, the emissary of the *Keren Hayesod*, Bunim Mordechai, came for a visit. He also visited our agricultural farm.

In the winter of the year 5685 [1924-1925] we organized a large party, a farewell celebration for our members who were making *aliya* to the Land. We wished them that their *aliya* should be successful and that tens and hundreds of others will follow them.

The party made a great impression on all those present. The dedication of our beloved chairman, Ch. Kolozny, who succeeded in all his public appearances, should be noted. He was sent to organize chapters of *Hechalutz Hamizrachi* in other places, including Baranovich, Nesvizh, and Pinsk. Letters of acknowledgment of the success of these visits were received from all the places. He also traveled to various conventions of *Hechalutz Hamizrachi* in Warsaw. After the first ones made *aliya*, a new committee with seven members was chosen, including our dear member, the late Sander Margolin.

The tasks were many, and the new committee had the responsibility for a great deal of work for the benefit of our idea. Our parents did not look favorably upon our dedication with heart and soul for the movement, for we neglected the study of a page of Gemara every day.

We decided that comprehensive explanations of all the important questions that stood before us would only take place three times a week.

[Page 131]

From time to time, we would put on a flower day for the benefit of the *Torah V'Avoda* [Torah and Work] fund. Our member Sander Margolin was also sent often to the various conventions of *Hechalutz Hamizrachi* and Young *Mizrachi* in Warsaw. We received long reports and detailed descriptions from him of all the proceedings that were discussed.

Hechalutz Hamizrachi chapter in David-Horodok

Sitting (right to left) 1. Shmaryahu Ziporin, 2. Masha Dubrovitsky, 3. Sheindel Kitain, 4. Yafa Chover, 5. Simcha Chover, 6. Shoshana Lichtenstein. 7. Leah Ziporin
Standing (row 1); 1. Moshe Dreizin, 2. Pinya Shreibman, 3. Tova Shulman, 4. Baruch-Yankel Lichtenstein, 5. Chana Mekler, 6. Lichtenstein, 7. Chana Baruchin, 8. Meril Yudovitz
Row 2: 1. Gudel Vager, 2. Miriam Gloiberman, 5. Motel Dubrovitsky, 4. 5. 6. Sonia Baruchin, 7. Freidel Tzfasman, 8. Michael Lichtenstein

Certificates, protocols, and reports of all the meetings throughout the seven years that I served as the secretary of *Hechalutz Hamizrachi* and Young *Mizrachi* in David-Horodok are preserved in the archives. I finally decided to leave everything and make *aliya* to the Land of Israel, and my decision was carried out, with the help of G-d, after a brief time.

Coordinator's footnote:

i.   The author's first initial was printed in the book as *nun* (N). However, the correct initial is *gimel* (G) for Gershon.

The League for Workers in the Land of Israel

by Shmuel Zezik

Translated by Jerrold Landau

The League for Workers in the Land of Israel was among the active organizations in David-Horodok. This was due to a group of members who dedicated themselves to this work.

In addition to the *Poalei Zion* [Workers of Zion] (left leaning) party, the *Hitachdut* [The Union] party, as well as the *Hashomer Hatzair* [Young Watchmen], *Freiheit* [Freedom], *Hechalutz* [The Pioneer] youth groups and others, there were also separate groups and individuals who dedicated themselves to the work of the League

[Page 132]

from the day that the League was founded in December 1927 with the visit of Ezriel Begun from Pinsk. The league encompassed all the populist strata in David-Horodok, who took it upon themselves to pay a monthly payment. Even though the income was not that great, the essence of the living connection of the League for Workers in the Land of Israel with the community was of great importance.

With time, there were many visits and lectures from the league headquarters. The most successful visits were those of E. Berdichevsky (now Bigur), Yochanan Morgenstein (one of the fighters of the Warsaw Ghetto who fell in battle), Pinchas Rashish, Yosef Baratz, and others. The work of the members of the League during the times of elections for the Zionist congresses especially stood out, for they brought the concept of the *Histadrut* [Organization] to the broad community of David-Horodok.

It is appropriate to note the many activities of Gedalyahu Olpiner (secretary of the League), Arke Lifshitz, Rivka Moravchik, and Leah Rozman, who were the supporting pillars in all activities. The display of torches on Saturday night on the eve of the 18th Zionist Congress was the first display of torches in the annals of Zionist activity in our city (and also the last one). Members of all the youth groups of the Workers in the Land of Israel and their supporters participated in it. The residents of the city accompanied them with shouts of appreciation.

Translator's footnote:

1.   There is an obvious typo in the caption here, which I fixed. Number 6 is repeated twice, and there is no number 7.

From right to left, standing: 1. Tzvi Shklaver, 2. Yissachar Kirzner (Curacao), 3. Kuba Moravchik, 4. Zelig Geier (Jerusalem), 5. Leah Rozman of blessed memory, 6. Elchanan Gotlieb, Tel Aviv, 7.[11] Mendel Kravchik, Haifa, 8. Yaakov Mazer and Rafael Moravchik (Givat Rambam)
[sitting] 9. Gedalyahu Olpiner of blessed memory, 10. Shmuel Zezik, Tel Aviv, 11. Yosef Baratz, Degania, emissary from the Land of Israel, 12. L. Zager of blessed memory, 13. Yaakov Shulman

The Revisionist Movement in David-Horodok

by Ch. Kolozny

Translated by Jerrold Landau

The Revisionist Movement took an honorable and important place in Zionist David-Horodok. Its difficulties during its beginning period were very hard, but with constancy and persistence, slowly but surely the *Beitar* movement was created and organized in David-Horodok.

[Page 133]

This youth covenant began to forge its path in accordance with the concepts of activist Zionism on the basis of a healthy soul and a healthy body.

Nationalistic education and tradition were the principles of the activity amongst the youth. In this spirit, every group and cell broadened its knowledge of the Nation of Israel and dedicated themselves to the concepts of sacrifice for the future.

A *Beitar* group in David-Horodok

The ranks of the youth grew from individuals to tens. A *Tzah'ar* [Revisionist Zionist] group was also organized that doubled its ranks within a brief period, and gained supporters.

Aside from the cultural work and various sporting activities, money was collected for *Keren Tel-Hai* [Revisionist Fund].

A non-insignificant part of the ranks of *Tzah'ar* and *Beitar* succeeded in making *aliya* to the Land. The rest were caught up in the annihilation.

May their memories be a blessing.

About the *Keren Hayesod* Fundraising Campaign in David-Horodok (1922)

by Aryeh Lachovsky

Translated by Jerrold Landau

After the public meeting that took place in the town with the participation of Dr. Chaimson, a member of the national council of the *Keren Hayesod* [Foundation Fund] in Poland, approximately fifty important householders gathered in the home of Reb Moshe Aharon Mishalov for the purpose of an individual approach to each of them. The lowest donation was set at twenty dollars. It was decided to begin with the wealthiest people (20-25 people) – and each of them donated 40-50 dollars. When they reached the wealthy people of lesser means, it was as if a competition broke out among them: if these gave 40 – we are exempt. However, since the minimum is twenty dollars, we will give more (25-30), and the rest will give according to their means: 200, 300, 400 and more.

When he heard these words, Dr. Chaimson became enraged in his place, tore up the documents,[1] tossed the torn pieces onto the table, and called out, "You have cheated me, indeed! A Jew who is obligated in hundreds suffices with tens? Let Greenbaum

[Page 134]

come and conduct the appeal with you." He rose up, put on his coat, and turned to leave. The youths, faithful to the *Keren Hayesod*, did not let him leave. After much urging, he agreed to return to his place. This time, the donations started with the lesser wealthy people. They stood by what they said, and each of them donated 25-30 dollars. When the turn of the wealthier ones came, each one donated 300, 400, or 500 dollars. The signatures on the documents were sent to Pinsk for collection. (There was no bank yet in David-Horodok.)

When the time for payment came, I went with Yaakov Gelman as the delegation to redeem the documents. An announcement was publicized that anyone wanting to save effort for themselves should provide the money, and the documents would be brought to them from Pinsk. A long row [of documents] was immediately collected – to the point that the departure of the ship had to be delayed until the inflow of money had ended.

Translator's footnote:

1. The documents would be donation contracts or pledge cards.

A Son of David-Horodok in the Jewish Legion
(Memories)

by Chaim Yachnitz

Translated by Jerrold Landau

This was at the beginning of the year 1918. At that time, I was on my way from Detroit to Los Angeles, and I stopped in San Fransisco for a few days. The first thing I did was wander through the street to find a shop that sold Jewish newspapers, so I would know what was going on in our Jewish world. Traveling for a few days without a Jewish newspaper in hand was beyond human capabilities in those days. When I obtained a newspaper, I immediately noticed that a Jewish Legion for the Land of Israel had been created. It even mentioned the names of the first volunteers. A flash of lightning went through my body and shook my bones. I immediately made a firm decision: to volunteer for the Legion.

A few weeks later, I appeared on the road in an army uniform. I did not take this step out of love of might or to pursue honor. I certainly knew that the Legion did not have any military value or importance. However, its value was immeasurable from the moral and nationalist perspective.

Even though the number of Jewish soldiers in all the armies of the war was sufficiently large – thousand of lads had volunteered for the Legion of their own good will, from pure nationalist feelings.

The Jewish Legion was the kernel of a national army in the full sense of the term. All strata of the people were represented within it, and all had one single goal: the return of the Land of Israel to the People of Israel. I recall the day of April 21, 1918, the day we traveled to Canada and began our training. New volunteers were added all the time. The only thing that separated us from the rest of the soldiers was the Magen David on our sleeves.

Chaim (Harry) Yachnitz. A soldier in the
Jewish Legion during the First World War.

A few weeks later, we set out for England. We did not tarry there for long. We were transferred to the Land.

We arrived in the Land in August. Our first stop was Tel El Kebir. I recall the desert heat of the Land of Israel in August, which oppressed us greatly. We were three brigades: brigade 38 whose captains were solely English; brigade 39 whose captains were mixed; and brigade 40, which was completely of the Land of Israel. One day, while we were stationed in Rafiach [Rafah], Zeev Jabotinsky appeared before us dressed in a captain's uniform. The battalion was filled up, and we moved from Rafiach to El Arish.

[Page 135]

We reached Lod in October, and were able to visit the moshavot [agricultural colonies] of Rishon LeZion, Ness Ziona, and Beer Yaakov. In 1918, we reached Jerusalem, where we celebrated the day of the Balfour Declaration. I was discharged in August 1919 and sent to recuperate. After that, they did not want to take me back.

How I Obtained My *Aliya* Permit

by Leibush Dushnik

Translated by Jerrold Landau

I was the first to make *aliya* to the Land from David-Horodok along with my family in 1924, even though I was not an enthusiastic Zionist. This happened by chance. As I was once walking along a street in Pinsk one evening, the shouts of a watchmaker to Feinstein, the secretary of the office of the Land of Israel in Pinsk reached me: "I want to make *aliya* to the Land of Israel." Feinstein responded, "We only send agricultural workers." I approached Feinstein, and the sudden idea that flickered within me enticed me to tell him, "If I will bring you a certificate from Prince Radziwill, for I am an agricultural worker, will you permit me to make *aliya*?" "You will make *aliya*," he responded. I immediately rushed a letter to my brother-in-law Hershel Zezik in David-Horodok, and the permit arrived about three days later. I made *aliya* to the Land about a half a year later.

How We Made *Aliya* to the Land

by [Dov Dushnik][i]

Translated by Jerrold Landau

(*In memory of the martyrs of David-Horodok, of blessed memory*)

Exactly thirty years ago, we left David-Horodok and the cradle of our childhood, on our way to the Land of Israel. I was fifteen years old at that time.

We set out to Pinsk on a steamboat on Saturday night. In the morning, our entire family went to the synagogue. We were honored with aliyot to the Torah, and we recited the wayfarer's prayer to Zion.

The worshippers of the synagogue accompanied us to a kiddush. Men, women, and children streamed by us all day, bringing us

Jews of David-Horodok accompany a family making *aliya* to the Land of Israel in 1929

[Page 136]

their blessings as we set out on our journey to afar, for we were the first family of David-Horodok, a family of eight people, who dared to set out for the Land of Israel.

I am proud to note the energy and spiritual strength of my dear father, may he live, who endangered himself and took on the great responsibility without a coin in his pocket, without any plan, and without any relative or friend to greet us when we arrived in the new place.

We faced a very difficult problem in our first year. Every day, we received tens of letters, in which people requested our advice as to whether it was worthwhile for them to leave David-Horodok and make *aliya* to the Land, and whether they would succeed in acclimatizing. The situation at that time was very difficult, but we responded to everyone in the affirmative.

We endured many trials and tribulations until we acclimatized and got used to the life and conditions of the Land. This was thanks to our wise, refined mother, Chaya Sara, the daughter of Reb Zeev of Dolfin of blessed memory, who passed away before her time. She always encouraged us and imbued us with the pioneering spirit.

Perhaps I would not be exaggerating if I state that we were helped from Heaven, and we served as guides for all those from our town who succeeded and are now together with us in our dear Land. Our hearts are pained for all those who did not merit to make *aliya*. May their memories be blessed!

Coordinator's footnote:

i.   The author's name was in the Table of Contents, but was not included with this article.

Tarbut School

[Page 139]

Tarbut School

by Sh. Papish

Translated by Jerrold Landau

The educational and cultural enterprises in the town were organized by the Zionist organization. They also took responsibility for its budget. The school buildings stood on a public lot next to a grove of trees. A new building was erected over and above the two old buildings that were fixed up and rendered appropriate for their purpose. The eight classes and the kindergarten were housed in spacious rooms, full of light and fresh air. We can attribute an honorable place in organizing the educational institutions in our town and ensuring their ongoing success to Reuven Mishalov, who served as the first principal of the school. His organizational talent, energy, and influence on both the communities of parents and children, his dedication and talents in forging proper relationships also with other factors, even taking a strong stance at the time of need, along with the assistance of active members of the Zionist organization and some of the teachers, were all factors that helped overcome the many obstacles, and ensured the development of our educational institution to a high organizational level, and even to an educational level fitting for its name, already during the first years of its existence.

The first building of the Tarbut [culture] School as it was being constructed — 5687 [1927]

[Page 140]

The second stage of the development of our school and raising it to an educational-pedagogical level that brought it fame as one of the finer schools of Poland came with the change of guard, the growth of the teaching staff and the hiring of young teachers who were graduates of Hebrew high schools and of the Hebrew seminary in Vilna. This was under the leadership of Avraham Olshansky. This was the era of splendor of our school, which was the pride and glory of the Hebrew community of our town.

Hundreds of students were educated in the school. The classes were always filled to the brim. Children from the settlements of the region, from the nearby village of Choromsk to the village of Chrapun on the border of Soviet Russia, a distance of fifty kilometers from the town, would come to continue their studies in the upper grades.

The leadership of the school, most of the members of which were members of the Zionist organization, already they actualized to a significant degree the principles of the law of compulsory education. Tuition fees were graduated. Those of meager means, whose numbers were not small, paid from 25% to 50% of the regular tuition fees. Many parents who were unable to pay were completely exempted from tuition fees.

Many of the graduates of our school continued their studies in the Tarbut Gymnasium in Pinsk, in the Hebrew Teachers Seminary in Vilna, or in other upper-level and professional schools.

Throughout the years, a club for knowledge of the Land functioned in the school under the direction of Chaim Branchuk of blessed memory, one of the dedicated teachers, who served as the secretary of the Zionist organization for many years. His entire life was dedicated to educating the young generation and the building up of the Land. His desire to make *aliya* to the Land was strong, but he did not merit such. He oversaw with dedication the *aliya* of many of his friends. With the conquest of Poland, he was exiled along with the members Yaakov Yudovitz and Dov Rimar, members of the final Zionist council, and died on route to far-off Siberia.

Classes in Talmud for the students of the upper grades took place in the school for many years. The teacher was Rabbi Shneur Zalman Shapira of blessed memory. He would explain his lessons in Hebrew. The late rabbi was the chairman of the *Mizrachi* organization, a dedicated Zionist who participated in activities for the benefit of the funds and in other Zionist activities.

In 1933, the *Bnei Yehuda* [Sons of Judah] organization and *Bnei Yehuda* Cubs were founded alongside the school. This was the youngest Zionist organization in our town, and in the Zionist movement in general. Its members were the children of the first grade: the children of the kindergarten as well as four-year-olds who were still pre-kindergarten. Members of the Hebrew organization for young children kept faith with the Hebrew language. They refused to speak Yiddish. There is a story that one of the mothers urged her four-year-old daughter to speak to her grandmother in Yiddish, for the grandmother did not know Hebrew. The child responded, "Mother, how can I speak Yiddish? I have taken an oath to speak only Hebrew." Even the shopkeepers, including those of the candy stores whose owners were gentiles, became comfortable with the Hebrew language, out of fear of losing their young customers.

During that period, Hebrew on the Jewish street in our town was not only the daily language for hundreds of youths and children, but also in every house where the children lived.

At the end of the summer of 1935, when Yosef Baratz of Degania returned to Warsaw by train after visiting our town, he told those travelling with him about his impressions of his visit, with enthusiasm and appreciation. He described the wide-branched Zionist activity, discussed the achievements of the school, and especially of the *Bnei Yehuda* Cubs and the living Hebrew languages that had taken root in one of the towns of the remote district of Polesye. He told about Pablo, the guard of the school, and the maid in the home of the school principal, who both spoke Hebrew.

Our school was a ray of light in the gray, day-to-day life of the Jewish community of the town. Every celebration in the school – the Lag B'Omer parade, the year beginning, the distribution of report cards – turned into a holiday for the entire Jewish community. The streets filled with people, and the faces of the Jews beamed with joy and national pride at the site of hundreds of school children walking all together along the streets of the city.

The celebration of a decade of the existence of the school was an unforgettable event. The beautiful ceremony was prepared with exactitude and precision, and was carried out with success. The magnitude of content turned the celebration into a national festival for all the Jews of the town. Dr.

[Page 141]

Zweigel, the principal of the Hebrew seminary in Vilna, participated in the celebration on behalf of the Tarbut headquarters in Warsaw. On his way from the railway station, he passed through the streets of the city in a fine wagon hitched to beautiful horses, as the schoolchildren holding flags and the Jewish community greeted him with joy. The impression was strong. This was a very impressive demonstration of Hebrew education in one of the veteran communities of the towns of Polesye. These were moments of full satisfaction for the Zionist movement in the town. The gentiles whispered that the Jewish minister had come to visit the school of the Jews.

The tenth cohort of the Tarbut School in David-Horodok, 1938

The Zionist library and the Zionist hall, which was opened in the latter years with brief interruptions, served as meeting places for the members to organize mutual activities. The active female members during that period included Nechama Friedman, Batya Shtofer, Shoshana Gloiberman, Musia Geier may G-d avenge her blood, Sonia Baruchin may G-d avenge her blood, Chaya Geier may G-d avenge her blood, and others.

During festivals, a "Zionist minyan" was held in the school. It always had many participants, even some who did not regularly attend synagogue. For that as well, we did not require any outside help. The entire "staff" was from amongst our members. Yerachmiel Rimar and Shmaryahu Reznik, may G-d avenge his blood, served as the prayer leaders. Moshe Erlich served as the Torah reader. Berl Katz would bless us with the Priestly Blessing. We also had a group of Levites.[1] The Zionist minyan imbued the members with a unique festive spirit.

Translator's footnote:

1. The Priestly Blessing is recited on festivals in the Diaspora, and daily in Israel. Prior to the recitation, the Levites wash the hands of the Kohanim.

The School

by P. Dobrushin

Translated by Jerrold Landau

The days of my childhood in our town pass before my imagination as if in a dream. The nicest memories are from the school. At first, we learned in the *cheder* with the *melamed* Shimon Leichtman. The *cheder* was large and spacious. Tens of students were hunched over the long tables, repeating enthusiastically: *Kometz aleph oh.*[1] The teacher walked among us, ensuring

[Page 142]

that the letters of the Holy Tongue would be absorbed well in our young minds. He derived pleasure from a diligent student who would go to the blackboard and recite his section properly. He did not spare threats from an indifferent or lazy student.

We got older, and transferred to the *cheder* of Reb Yosef Begun. There, we learned arithmetic and *Chumash*, and Rashi's commentary was not strange to us. We were already scholars to no small degree… Others of our age studied with Reb Shweidel. We were diligently engaged in our studies almost without a break during all hours of the day. We came home at night by the light of a lantern. This was over the course of many months.

One day, the appearance of the *cheder* changed. News of the opening of a school spread on the street and at home. This became the topic of conversation of the day. What was this all about? None of us children knew. Our parents toiled to establish that institution, and the future principal visited the *cheder* to inform us of the impending change. We were to become the third grade, the highest grade in the school when it was to open.

I recall how Father of blessed memory discussed the school with others. He had many meetings with his committee, until that splendid institution, in which we first and many after us were educated to love the nation and the Land, became firmly based. What feelings pervaded on the street when the benches were carried to the school building on the shoulders of the parents. I will never forget the first day of classes. At first, we studied in the old building, which seemed to us like a palace at that time. New worlds were revealed to us, and they were especially attractive and interesting. It was good to exchange the *cheder* for the Tarbut School.

The school flourished from year to year, and its students were successful in their studies. Teachers came from outside the city. A kindergarten was opened. At first, the kindergarten was looked upon with distrust by the parents. However, it quickly gained admirers. We became a modern city of culture, bustling with "scholars" of school age. Our teachers suffered from a delay in salary more than once. Our parents lovingly signed the contracts that were given to the teachers as an advance.

The students of the school quickly turned into warriors for the Hebrew language. A brigade of Hebrew speakers was formed, which spread through the outskirts of the city and its shops. They stubbornly spoke Hebrew, and "forced" the adults to answer them in that language.

Years passed, and grade three became grade seven – the first graduating cohort, "the most important students." The founders, builders, teachers, and workers on behalf of the school merited to celebrate with joy the graduation of the first cohort, to which I had the pleasure of being part of.

The first graduating cohort of the Tarbut School, 1929

[Page 143]

The parents, teachers, and many guests gathered in the yard, and the ceremony of distribution of diplomas turned into a festival for the city. We graduates had a multiple dose of joy. Our exam period had ended. These were literal matriculation exams, which took place in the hall of the firefighters, and they left a great impression upon us with their seriousness. Now, we were happy that we had gotten through them.

The teachers and the parents' committee sat next to a decorated table. With holy awe, we approached one by one to receive our diplomas from our dear school. At this sight, tears flowed from the eyes of many who knew us well. The people of our city were used to seeing us going out on excursions with the song of *Chazak Veematz* [Be Strong and of Good Strength] on our lips. On occasions, we provided them with pleasure as excellent actors in the performance of *Shnei Nigunim Li* [I Have Two Tunes] by Y.L. Peretz. We also astonished them by exercising before their eyes, and we visited their homes on occasions for matters of the Jewish National Fund.

The community was proud of us, and participated in our joyous occasion with a full heart. It is unfortunate that they did not merit to see us among the builders of the State, actualizers of their great dream.

Translator's footnote:

1. The beginning of the traditional chant of the alphabet.

Ten Years Since the Establishment of the School in David-Horodok

(from the *Pinsker Shtime* [the newspaper Voice of Pinsk], 1934)

by Litman Gotlieb

Translated by Jerrold Landau

The years of existence of the Hebrew school were difficult. It had to fight with the Orthodox from one side, and with the Yiddishists from the other side. It had as many internal opponents as it had external opponents.

In addition, it also had to struggle with the indifferences of the parents and the enticement to send the children to other schools.

Today, the school has 400 students. All the students, from the second grade to the seventh grade, speak Hebrew amongst themselves at home and on the street. When they enter a store, they speak to the shopkeeper in Hebrew. He speaks Yiddish and they respond in Hebrew.

A wall newspaper is put out by the students (with the help of the teacher) every week. Student clubs for literature, history, and the like are organized. There was a carpentry shop for the students of the upper grades. Graduates of the institution also worked there. There was also a sewing course for the female students and graduates.

To this day, the school has graduated five cohorts (more than 100 individuals). A large portion of them continue their studies in Tarbut institutions such as the gymnasium, seminary, technion (of Vilna), and trade schools. A portion have made *aliya* to the Land of Israel, and a portion work in kibbutzim.

All the graduates of the school are organized into a special club under the guidance of the principal of the institution, Mr. Olshansky. Constant contact is maintained between the club and the graduates who left David-Horodok.

Now, they will be celebrating the decade of the existence of the school, with the participation of the teachers of the institution, its graduates, and its students. An exhibition is being prepared (through the efforts of the supporters and the students), and a celebratory newspaper will be issued.

However, the great depression with the accompanying impoverishment has brought difficulties to the institution. Nevertheless, we can hope that all those who bear the burden of the school to this day will continue with their work into the future – work that is difficult, but blessed and with significant results.

Tarbut School

by Moshe Meiri (Moravchik)

Translated by Jerrold Landau

The Hebrew school in the town was renown throughout all of Poland. That school educated an entire generation in the spirit of Hebrew culture and the ideas of national revival.

[Page 144]

How pleasant it was to see hundreds of boys and girls hurrying and running to school every morning, with their schoolbags on their shoulders and joy rising from their mouths.

The school that stood in the large yard on a side street was a first-degree cultural center of this town.

The school and its large yard served as a meeting place for boys and girls not only during school hours, but also in the afternoon. They spent many hours in the yard playing or participating in games.

This splendid school, with hundreds of male and female students, was the largest enterprise in the city from old times until the destruction.

The teaching staff, who were carefully chosen, did not just see their role in teaching. They also saw themselves as bearing a loftier task – the education of the younger generation to a new life, and raising them as faithful children to the Hebrew nation, and guiding them along the path that leads to Zion.

Indeed, very many of the students of the school followed that path in which they were educated. Very many of them recall that study hall with great appreciation, awe, and honor. To this day, it remains as one of the finer memories of the life that has passed and the reality that is no more.

How the *Bnei Yehuda* Society Was Established

by Yaakov Hochman

Translated by Jerrold Landau

Abrasha Olshansky, the principle of the populist Tarbut School in David-Horodok, had a strong desire for his students to speak Hebrew in their day-to-day lives, rather than only at school. The objective that he preached day and night was not simple, and he found many ways to influence the people of David-Horodok. For example, the Hebrew teacher promised celebratorily that any student who would speak Hebrew outside the walls of the school would get a boost in marks – that means, a student who was fitting for a "satisfactory" mark would get "good," and a student who was fitting for "good" would get "very good." However, all the enticements, requests, and speeches did not help: not because of the refusal of the students, but rather because of the environment in which they lived. Meetings and activities in Hebrew were held at the youth movements of *Hashomer Hatzair* [Young Watchmen], *Hashomer Haleumi* [National Watchmen], Beitar, etc. However, at home, at the grocery store, and in every place where one had to meet with adults and not just youth – this was virtually impossible. How could one approach Mother and speak to her about food, clothing, etc.? It would be as if you were speaking to her in Chinese. It was somewhat easier with the men, for some of them understood but did not speak, and others spoke a bit. There were a few who were fluent in Hebrew, and one could "get along" with the help of the hands and feet [i.e., gestures]. The objective was more difficult with the women.

Thus, it was both ridiculous and interesting to see Meir Plotnitzky, a twelve- or thirteen-year-old student, decide suddenly – I believe this was at the end of the major vacation of 1934 – to speak Hebrew with every Jew, whether or not they understand. Meir was stubborn and strong-willed, and he did not care what people would say about him. He fulfilled his word. He did not give in, and did not utter even one word in Yiddish. He spoke Hebrew with everyone. If someone did not understand him – they would go and learn.

This behavior was strange in the eyes of the other children (whose day-to-day language was Yiddish), and therefore, they mocked him. One day they even hurt him. Meir went to the principal, Abrasha Olshansky, and told him what had happened. The children were called to the principal for clarification, and he rebuked them. Eliyahu Veinstein, the son of the cantor, and Motele Shneidman were among those who hurt Meir. As a sign of full regret over their deeds, the children decided to join Meir in speaking Hebrew.

Several other students joined them within a brief period, and they founded the Bnei Moshe [Sons of Moshe] Society.

After some time, its name was changed to the *Bnei Yehuda* [Sons of Judah] Society, for the name of Eliezer Ben-Yehuda.[1] This was a society

[Page 145]

that was zealous for Hebrew, and only accepted into its ranks members who proved that they would only speak Hebrew.

It was not easy to join the society. One of the students would come and announce that he had decided to speak only Hebrew, and that he had spoken Hebrew for a certain time. After they heard his announcement, they told him to wait for an answer. In the meantime, they would send a group of students to spy on him and inform them whether indeed he spoke Hebrew at home, with the neighbors, etc.

I recall that I once went with a group of children for the final act of espionage about a student who announced that he wanted to join the society, and that his language was only Hebrew. It was clarified that he indeed spoke to everyone in Hebrew. However, the matter was suspicious, since his mother did not understand Hebrew at all. We visited him at night. We sat and chatted. When we left the house, one of us, Beryle Veinstein, a student in our class, remained there, hiding under the bed of the "candidate." Nobody in the household noticed that, and Beryle followed matters from his position under the bed. Before he went to bed, he argued strongly with his mother, who did not understand him. He used various means, including threatening language, to explain his desire – and he did not utter one word in the vernacular. When Beryle saw the behavior and suffering of the candidate, he was convinced that he was fit to join the society. He immediately came out of his hiding place to the surprise of all the members of the household, approached the lad, tapped him on the shoulder, and declared: "You have been accepted!" (That is what the group did when it was determined that a candidate had passed the test.)

The society, the planning, and the various committees were run only by the students, under the guidance of the principal Abrasha Olshansky, who was full of satisfaction. His dream had been realized.

A member who was accepted to the society was not always certain about his membership. Members would supervise each other lest they stray, Heaven forbid. There is a story about my sister (a member of the society and a student in grade four or five). She had returned from an agricultural exhibition in the nearby village of Chovorsk. Because of her great impressions, she said to my mother, who did not understand [Hebrew], in Yiddish: "I saw there a giant ox with very large horns." Suddenly, the heads of several of her classmates appeared from behind the window, and declared in Hebrew, "Speak Hebrew!" They escaped, of course. Because of their testimony, my sister was removed from the society to her dismay and sorrow.

The society, which at the end encompassed almost all the students of the Tarbut School, also left its impression upon the students studying in the schools based on other languages, and even upon the youths who were not studying – everyone joined the circle of Hebrew speakers. The wonder was actualized, and, having no choice, the parents also began to understand the language, some more and others less.

The news of the founding of the *Bnei Yehuda* Society in David-Horodok took on wings. The Hebrew schools in the nearby cities began to take interest in the matter. The two mockers, Eliyahu, the son of the cantor, and Motele Shneidman, later became the pillars of support of the society. To this day, I am surprised how Motele Shneidman, short in stature and thin, only twelve years old, spoke amongst men, and lectured in a convincing manner with enthusiasm. Eliyahu, the son of the cantor, was like him. They were both sent to make the rounds in the Hebrew schools in the nearby cities of Stolin, Luninets, and others. Their enthusiasm slowly caught on to the people of those cities, even though at the outset they did not believe what their ears heard: "How is it possible to speak Hebrew all the time?" "Do you even think in Hebrew? And when you wake up, are you first words in Hebrew?" they asked. We also asked such questions at the beginning of the formation of our society…

Translator's footnote:

1.   1858-1922, considered to be the founder of modern Hebrew.

[Page 146]

Bnei Yehuda,
Pioneers Who Revived Our Language

by Yerachmiel Morstein, Ramat Gan

Translated by Jerrold Landau

We are getting more distant from the era of the Second World War, when a third of our people were annihilated in a cruel fashion, including our closest relatives. Therefore, it is indeed appropriate to extend double gratitude to the dedicated activists, natives of David-Horodok, for their efforts to erect this memorial monument. To my dismay, my native town did not succeed in such. May your hands be strengthened!

The town of David-Horodok, with its Jews who are no longer, with their lives and customs, is typical of a large portion of the towns that I had visited and knew well on account of my work. The natives of that city were indeed blessed for their great dedication in the perpetuation of that path for our children. You should know, they are the place from where we were forged. Those good Jews did everything, but to our sorrow did not merit to be with us and to participate in the realization of their vision and our vision – the establishment of our state, to which they helped lay the foundations.

Already today, during the era of the rise of the state – most of the youth who were raised in the Land do not recognize the importance and place of the Diaspora Jewry from which we stemmed. To those youths, the concept of the Diaspora refers to weak Jews, lacking in power, afraid and trembling before all gentiles, who tear up decrees through the recitation of Psalms and fasting, closed in their four cells,[1] awaiting the arrival of the Messiah… Our children cannot imagine for themselves that all the dreams and dreamers of the establishment of our state – the pioneers in all manners – stemmed from there, and that it is to their merit that we have attained that which we have attained.

As the director of the Jewish agricultural cooperative in Pinsk, founded by the I. C. A. [Jewish Colonization Association], I visited towns in the area and searched for the Jews. Outside my job I investigated their past. I arrived at the railway station of Lakhva in the spring of 1932, and began to search for a wagon driver to take me to Horodok. How great was my pleasant surprise when I heard one of the wagon drivers, a young lad, calling out *bevakasha.*[2] I did not believe what my ears heard, so I turned to the wagon driver and said, "Did you say something in Hebrew?" "*Amnam ken,*"[3] he responded, and boasted that he was a member of *Bnei Yehuda* [Sons of Judah]. During the journey, he explained to me the purpose of the society that was set up by the youth in the town: to learn and speak only in Hebrew so that it will become the language of the masses in time, and not the heritage of a restricted group – mainly *maskilim* [followers of the *Haskalah* [Enlightenment] movement] – as it is today. To my questions as to whether this could be realized, he responded with self-assurance that he and his friends are very proud of their achievements to this point, and he would prove this to me when we reached the town. Indeed, he proved it to me, and I was convinced!

Their oath when they joined the society, to refrain from using any other language, was fulfilled with the enthusiasm that is typical of youth. The Hebrew language struck roots thanks to the stubbornness of these youths.

Translator's footnotes:

1. The translation of the Hebrew word *amot* is cubits or ells, a Biblical measure. There is a common phrase in Rabbinic literature of someone being within the four *amot* of halacha, or enclosed in their four cubits or ells, meaning that they are only interested in their spiritual life and are cut off from the world.
2. Please or thank you in Hebrew.
3. Indeed so in Hebrew.

About the Teacher Branchuk of Blessed Memory

by Mendel Kravchik

Translated by Jerrold Landau

At the end of 1922, a youth dressed in festive clothing appeared in the town. Because of his clothing, it was immediately recognized that this man was foreign in town. News quickly spread through town that this man was a teacher who intended to set up a *cheder* in town.

The first deed of the teacher was to invite parents to a meeting in the home of Shlomo Rozman. Out of curiosity, several youths, including the writer of these lines, chose a hiding place in one of the rooms next to the meeting, and listened to what was taking place at the meeting. The young teacher spoke at length about the new subjects that he intended to enter into the curriculum: about his desire to teach nature, geography, and history. Many of the parents expressed their willingness to send their children to the new *cheder*. They even promised a means of livelihood for the teacher, and he decided to settle in the town. A few parents objected to the *cheder*, and regarded the changes and innovations as heresy and a deviation from the straight path.

[Page 147]

At the beginning of the studies in the *cheder*, the news spread that one should come with a head covering only for Bible classes. For the rest of the classes, one was to come with an uncovered head. The teacher introduced another custom – the obligation to knock on the door. This modern *cheder* was maintained by the teacher Branchuk until the establishment and renewal of the modern Hebrew school in 1924. He was appointed as a teacher there as well. Very many people studied Torah from him until he was imprisoned in 1941, starting from studies of Bible and ending in classes in history and music.

I remember our teacher when he appeared at the first music class with a violin in his hand. His appearance elicited our laughter. We were embarrassed to open our mouths, and he helped us by starting to sing.

He was my first counselor in the classroom at school. Every week, the counselor had to record notes regarding the behavior and studies of each student in a special ledger maintained by the institution. We had to bring these notes to the attention of our parents on the Sabbath, and they had to certify it with their signature.

Since we knew what would happen to us at home if our parents were to read negative reports, the writing of these reports served as an expert pedagogic tool. Because of this, along with the influences of his explanations, we were very diligent in good behavior.

He knew no weariness. His body was weak, but he bore the yoke of all the tasks imposed upon him. The number of students in the school was large. The school building of that time could not accommodate them all, so the classes were given in two shifts. He himself taught in both the morning and the afternoon. After the classes, he would organize the school choir and student performances, take care of the library, etc.

Aside from all this, he himself was forced to continue his studies, since the government educational authorities demanded a teaching certificate from him. Therefore, he had to prepare for the exams.

A Lag B'Omer parade in David-Horodok in the year 5692 – 1933[1]

The pioneering Zionist idea slowly began to penetrate the circles of the older youth of the town. A Jewish National Fund brigade was organized, and pioneering youth groups were established, mainly from amongst the students of the school. In that period, the school was a "factory for the souls of the nation," and the youth groups filled up what was lacking in it.

[Page 148]

Branchuk played a large role in the youth groups, and we always met him there, whether it was a "celebration of questions and answers" (in vogue at the time) or public meetings of the youth groups. He would always come, lecture, explain, and guide. He spared no effort, and often accompanied us on our hikes to the forest near Borok.

In the autumn of 1931, Branchuk was chosen by us as a delegate to the Tarbut convention in Warsaw, in which Ch. N. Bialik participated. Afterward, he gave over details of that convention with great emotion at a public meeting that was called in town after his return. He told us about the ways of the Zionists at the convention, and the lectures of the poet Ch. N. Bialik. Our emotions grew stronger when he told how the poet thundered against the leaders of the Jewish community of Poland by shouting, "*Shkotzim* – to the *cheder*!"[2]

In the spring of 1932, most of the youths were organized into Zionist youth groups. The older ones were registered for the most part in the Zionist parties, and we decided to demonstrate our collective power in the town through a mass demonstration that was to take place on Lag B'Omer. We also invited the youth groups from the nearby towns of Stolin and Lakhva. Almost all the Jews of the town participated in the demonstration. The students of the school marched at the front. Behind them marched the members of the parties and youth groups, with their flags. This was an impressive sight. The national flags fluttered in the air. The shirts and ties stood out from all sides. After several speeches delivered from the porch of Mordechai Rimar's home in the marketplace, we began to dance the hora. Branchuk, who by chance was standing next to me, told me with emotion, "Behold, this is Tel Aviv and not David-Horodok. We will yet merit to see the blue skies of the Land of Israel."

The Soviet army entered David-Horodok in the autumn of 1939. The communal activists began to worry about the fate of the Hebrew school. The students were required to return to their studies after the vacation. The local authorities had not yet solved all the government issues in the town – so for now, there were no classes. Finally, a directive was issued regarding the ban on the Hebrew language. It is hard for me to forget the image etched in my mind: there are rows of students standing in the long corridor of the school, and the teachers were explaining to them that the Hebrew language is now strange to us – and from now we will learn in our mother tongue of Yiddish. Branchuk's throat was choked with tears as he said, "From now on, it will be good for us here, and we must not think about aliya to the Land."

It was the night of February 11, 1941. I was among the prisoners arrested in the town that night. We began to surmise the reasons for the imprisonment. After they hauled in Shmuel Zezik and Kopel Moravchik – the political background, Branchuk suddenly appeared. Nervousness and fear overtook us. Aharon Moravchik burst out weeping, and Branchuk encouraged him, "The sun shall yet shine for us. Our only sin is that we were Zionists. We did not sin one iota against the Soviets. I am certain that they will free us." He concluded his statement. After the end of the investigation, they transferred us from the interrogation cells to the central prison in Pinsk, and we met again. The cell was full of prisoners, mainly of the worst kind. We Jews found a corner in the cell and avoided all meetings and conflicts with the worst of them.

Branchuk approached them, explained some geography to them, and earned their appreciation. Things came to the point where they sat around us with special awe, listening to his explanation, and ensuring that nothing bad will happen to him or his belongings. Through his merit, we too were helped.

A sack of tobacco, like a treasure, was tied to his neck, and he gave some to whomever would request. They began to speak of his good heart with great admiration.

We were in prison in the heart of Russia, and the days were at the beginning of the Russian-German war. Soviet troops were retreating. There were alarms and bombardments several times a day – and we were locked up in a room. The prisoners began to guess, and some said, "Would it be that the enemy will arrive, and we can get out of jail." Branchuk quietly expressed his opinion to the Jews, "Heaven forbid for us to think that the Germans will be our saviors. Even though we are prisoners, we must not request their arrival." He spoke with fear about the fate of the families who remained in David-Horodok, "My heart tells me that the path that seems short – is the long path."

[Page 149]

It was August 1941. We were once again brought by trains from the prison to the heart of Russia. Branchuk took comfort, "Perhaps there we will survive. Would it be that they will also bring our families." That time, the journey was difficult and tiring. There was a serious lack of water. The food was salty, and when a flask of cold water was brought at one of the stations, people fought over it, and the strongest won. Branchuk became ill on the fourth day of our journey. According to the medic who was with us, this was dysentery and intestinal spasms. Those on the train treated him with respect and patience. We changed his clothing, and helped him eat, but his energy dissipated from day to day. We arrived in Kyruv on August 16, 1941. We received a notice to prepare to disembark. We dressed him in warm clothing. We packed his sack and took him off the train. It was difficult to recognize him. He was dying. We laid him down on the grass quietly. He was trembling all over. The policeman prodded us to join the ranks of the healthy ones who were continuing their journey on foot. I looked behind me to see where the grave of my teacher was being dug.

Toward evening, we met a Jewish doctor from Pinsk who certified his death to us. It took place about an hour after we took him off the train.

May his memory be blessed.

Translator's footnotes:

1. The Hebrew and secular years are both noted in the original caption. There is an error in one of the years, as Lag B'Omer (generally in May, but could be at the very end of April) of 5692 would correspond to 1932, not 1933. This becomes clear further on in the text.
2. Intended as a mocking statement. *Shkotzim* is a derogatory term for gentiles, but here it refers to Jewish heretics who have followed more modern educational paths.

In Memory of My Loved Ones
(My Uncle Asher, Aunt Beila, and Brother Abrasha Olshansky)

by Sara Rimar Olshansky

Translated by Jerrold Landau

Father of blessed memory was a Zionist, and he did not want his children to assimilate among the gentiles. Therefore, he took us to Pinsk, so we would be among Jews, and mainly so we could study Hebrew.

I was seven years old at the time, and my brother was six. That night when Father informed me that he must part from us and return to his home will never leave my memory.

I wept bitterly all night, and my aunt and uncle were unable to console me. How great was our joy the next morning when we saw our father return to us. He did this intentionally. He wanted to see how we would behave in his absence. He spent a week with us until our aunt and uncle earned our trust, and our hearts began to love them.

We did not lack anything in our new house, including the love, dedication, and care of a mother. Our childless aunt dedicated her whole heart to us, and we returned the love to her bosom. During the time of the German occupation of the First World War, when the command came to register the population, our aunt and uncle registered us as their children – and from that time, we called ourselves by their family name.

Their dedication to us was exemplary. Even during the times of famine in Pinsk, when our uncle's material situation was quite poor since his entire business was in Kiev in the Russian zone, leaving him in complete lack – they went out to work in the fields at the risk of their lives so that we would not suffer, Heaven forbid, from want. Most of the children left their studies for the schools were closed, but we received our lessons from private teachers even during the difficult times. They dedicated their whole hearts to us.

We moved to David-Horodok, my uncle's native town, when the borders opened in 1918. I made *aliya* to the Land seven years later, and my brother Abrasha traveled to Vilna to continue his studies in the seminary. Abrasha knew that our uncle could not afford to bear all the expenses, so he tried to the best of his ability to earn a livelihood from giving lessons. Nevertheless, our uncle gave him the main portion of his sustenance. When Abrasha finished his course of studies, he started teaching in the Tarbut School of David-Horodok, and was appointed as its principal a short time later. He imparted the best of his strength and energy into the school. He was loved by both the teachers and the students. He won over souls for Zionism amongst the students, and organized the youth into his primary task: speaking Hebrew wherever they were. Even the parents were forced to speak Hebrew with their children.

In 1937, my brother visited the Land, and decided to return there with his family. However, the war thwarted his plans, and he remained stuck in David-Horodok. When the Russians entered the city, he could have moved to our parents in Russia, but he was concerned that such a step would put an end to all possibilities of ever making *aliya* to the Land. The Tarbut School turned into

[Page 150]

a Soviet school. Abrasha was fluent in Russia, but the new form of education was disappointing to his spirit. In one of his lectures on behalf of the authorities, he had to speak to the students and parents about the Soviet regime and the new education. He began his speech, but did not have the energy to continue, for tears choked his throat. It was difficult for him to preach Communism instead of Zionism. Thus, his fate was sealed. The new regime regarded him as an untrustworthy person. The period of his wandering and tribulation began. He was forced to leave David-Horodok, and he sought refuge in Bialystok, but there too he did not find rest. He moved with his family to Luk, and from there we lost track of them. Apparently, the hand of the murderers reached them there. May their memories be blessed.

Told by the Elders

[Page 153]

My Memories

by Moshe Yehuda Lifshitz

Translated by Jerrold Landau

a. One Hundred Years

I am eighty years old today. I do not exaggerate when I say that I have memories from seventy years ago. I can add that I know things that I heard from my ancestors from another thirty years previous – so you have information from a hundred years ago, that is from the 5610 – 1850 until the destruction.

Moshe Yehuda Lifshitz. He was the first active societal worker in David-Horodok (Stolin district). He was a former deputy in the "Oprava"[1] during the time of the Czarist regime. After the revolution of 1917, he was the assistant chairman of the civic "committee" until the Bolshevik Revolution.[2] Under the Polish regime, he was elected as a councilor in the local "Rada" [Council] as well as in the civic "Rada." He was recognized by the Starosta as a first-class citizen in the region.

* Photo is from Illustrious Guard, Warsaw 1925.

b. Hassidim

The truth can be said that our city of David-Horodok was divided into several factions from the time of its founding until its last day. The Hassidim of Stolin were a sizable portion of the citizens of the city, and they had their own synagogue. Among them were Hassidic people with precious souls, and I will tell about them later. Now we will deal with the main thing, the rabbinate of our city, which is the large and important Ginzburg family, which connects to the rabbinate and *Admorim* [Hassidic masters] from many generations. I recall the honorable names such as The *Tzadik*, from whom the rabbinate was transmitted to the rabbi and Rebbe Yisrael Yosef, may the memory of the holy be blessed. Many who are here certainly knew him. He served as a rabbi and Rebbe, and he had the burden of sustaining his entire family. These included Reb Alterke and his sons and daughters, as well as Reb Velvele with all his children, for they had not attained rabbinical ordination, and even if they had, there was no place for them – thus they remained dependent and counting on the support of their father, Rabbi Yisrael Yosef, as they occupied themselves with Torah, Divine service, and the fear of heaven. They indeed merited to have important children: Alterke had a son named Itzikl, who was also fit to be a rabbinical teacher. Like the father Reb Velvele was the son Reb Moshele, who was graced with all fine traits. His mouth would exude pearls of commentary, and he was also an excellent prayer leader. However, with regard to halacha and rabbinic decisions – they had to stand back, for "one does not stand in the place of great ones."

In truth, until Rabbi Moshele's turn came to sit on the rabbinical seat, two preceded him, Rabbi Itzikl from one side and Rabbi Baruchl from the other side. All of them were accepted to the rabbinate and the Ginzburg [Hassidic] court only and in opposition to the other Ashkenazic side,[3] against the rabbi and Gaon Rabbi Yeshaya Rozenblum, who was indeed fitting and graced with all the traits necessary for a city rabbi.

[Page 154]

c. *Misnagdim*

Shimshon Leib Katzman

Now I will begin with my memories of the *Misnagdim* [non-Hassidic people] in our city. These are: the family of Reb Shalom who was called Reb Shaulke at that time; the family of Reb Arke HaKohen; the Katzman family, to which Reb Shimshon Leib, whose photo is included here, belonged; the Tiktinsky family; the Friedlander family all of whom united and came to the conclusion that they must have their own rabbi, so that they would not be like a flock without a shepherd. They began to search within their family to see if there might be a young man who would be fitting to accept such a position. Then without any effort, the found a modest young man, Rabbi Yosef Reizin, a Gaon who was expert in Torah, whose end testifies to his beginning, for within a brief time he was taken from amongst us to become the rabbi in the city of Telz. From there he went to Stolin in the place of the known Gaon Rabbi Eizel Charif. There as well, not far from us in Stolin, was one of the important people of the generation, Rabbi Pesach Frenkel, a man of morality with fine traits. He did not last long in that post, for he was close to the age of eighty, and died at an old age in great honor. He was eulogized by the entire city, for he was dear to them all. They were left once again without a rabbi and guide.

d. The Rabbis Rabbi Berkovitz and Rabbi Yaakov Yeshaya Rozenblum

It is known that the Holy One Blessed Be He prepares the cure before the affliction. In this case, before the sun of Rabbi Pesach set, the sun of Rabbi David Berkovitz appeared on the horizon. He was a native of Lakhva, the son of Rabbi Dov Berkovitz. At the age of eighteen, he married Pesil the daughter of Avrahamel-David Yudes. Rabbi David had a large family in David-Horodok from his father's side, that is: Yonah Rimar, Itza Rimar, Reb Zeev Yudovitz the Great (grandfather of the Yosef Yudovitz who is with us), as well as the second Reb Zeev Yudovitz, the grandfather of Berl Yudovitz, and others such as them. They placed their Rabbi David in the large *Beis Midrash* in the place of Rabbi Pesach of blessed memory, against the will of the entire Jewish community. Rabbi David himself was a righteous, just, and upright man, meticulous in all ways of holiness down to a thread of a hair. There was no matter of Jewish custom that he did not observe. He made the rounds to all the synagogues and made sure that the worshippers were putting on their tefillin in the correct position. On Sukkot, he would make the rounds to all the yards to see who had a Sukkah with a wing, that the wing should stand straight and not bent.[4] During the time of the baking of the matzos prior to Passover, he would make the rounds to all the bakeries several times a day to oversee the kashruth of the bakery. There is no matter of a mitzvah that he did not deal with completely. He himself pushed aside the rabbinate, for he did not want to get involved in questions regarding the butchers, divorces, marriage, and the like. Therefore, all the city notables had to search for a rabbi fitting for this. They found the rabbi and Gaon Rabbi Yeshaya Rozenblum, the grandson of the late Rabbi Yosef Reizin the author of the book *Edut Biyehosef*. This was the Rabbi Yosef whose rabbinate began with us. He was known as the Ma'tz–the acronym for *Moreh Tzedek*.[5] Thus, there were two rabbis with us, that is two kings serving under a single crown. Nevertheless, with all this, they did not argue about any matter related to the rabbinate. Rabbi David would elongate his recital of the *Shemone Esrei*, and Rabbi Yaakov Yeshaya would shorten it, so they waited for Rabbi David to finish.[6] In other matters, they would honor Rabbi

[Page 155]

Rozenblum – in that they would give him precedence for an *aliya* to the Torah on festivals, and he would oversee the shofar blowing on Rosh Hashanah and the *hakafot* [Torah processions] on Simchat Torah. All these matters took place calmly and quietly, with no disputes. I will tell of the merits of Rabbi David, who was very stringent in all matters of uncertainty for him. Rabbi Rozenblum was lenient in doubtful cases, certainly not based solely on his own opinion. There was a halachic question with the new, modern *mikveh* that was built at that time in a new building that endured in David-Horodok during this destruction.

Note from the editor: the author of these memories did not complete his memoirs, for he got sick in the middle and died at an old age in the year 5711 [1951]. May his memory be blessed!

Translator's footnotes:

1. The Memorial Book of Slonim describes the Oprava as "A civic leadership authority appointed by the regional minister."

2. This sentence stounds strange unless one realizes that there were two Russian revolutions in 1917, the Menshevik revolution in March and the Bolshevik revolution in October. This sentence is evidently referring to the Menshevik period.
3. In contrast to the Hassidic side.
4. The laws regarding what makes a Sukkah valid or invalid are quite complex. I am unsure of the meaning of a "Sukkah with a wing." The term here used for a wing is *fligl*.
5. Literally "Teacher of Righteousness" – a title for a rabbi who deals with halachic questions and teaching, but is not the official rabbi of a city.
6. It is customary to not begin the recitation of the repetition of the *Shmone Esrei* aloud until the rabbi has concluded his recitation of the silent *Shmone Esrei*.

Wonders and Miracles

From the Mouth of Reb Mordechai Kotzikovitz

Translated by Jerrold Landau

The dynasty of the Rabbi Reb Wolf found their resting place in the cemetery of David-Horodok. The custom of this dynasty was similar to that of the descendants of the Baal Shem Tov in their time. The first was a rabbi and Rebbe, the second generation – only a Rebbe – the third generation again a rabbi and Rebbe; and this repeated. The son of Rabbi Reb Wolf was Rabbi Dovidl, and his grandson was Rabbi Reb Yisrael Yosef the *Tzadik*. Rabbi Yisrael Yosef had two sons: Reb Alterke and Reb Vova (Zeev). Reb Alterke was the father of Rabbi Levi Yitzchak, known by people as Reb Itzikl.

a.

During the time of the Rabbi Reb Wolf, there was a story about a Jew from the town who used to go out of his house on Sunday mornings and make the rounds to the gentile villages all week. He would return to his home on Thursday evening. One Thursday, he did not return as usual, and the members of his household were full of worry. They waited until Friday morning – and he did not come. The sun was almost setting, and the Sabbath was just about to start – and he wasn't there. They went to Rabbi Reb Wolf – and at that time, the Jews were already going to the synagogue to welcome the Sabbath – and ordered the rabbi to recite *Kaddish*! A great tumult was made, and they closed the synagogue and did not let anyone worship. They even complained to the Rabbi that he was being brazen against the Rambam.[1] The Rebbetzin entered and said, "Do you see what you caused!" "What can I do?" he responded, "I see what the Rambam saw. He is lying outside the town under a certain tree."

They went and found him there.

b.

Rabbi Yisrael Yosef would travel to Rabbi Motele of Chernobyl for the High Holy Days. When he went, he brought with him the petitionary notes from his Hassidim. (Since he was a Levite, he would say that they gave him *Leket*[2] (Lakhva, Kozhan-Horodok, Turov), the towns in which his Hassidim were scattered.) News spread in Stolin that the Rabbi of Horodok was accepting petitionary notes. The Stolin [Hassidic] house (who stemmed from the Chernobyl dynasty) hinted that it was appropriate for the Chernobyler to point this out to Rabbi Yisrael Yosef.

Rabbi Motele of Chernobyl treated Rabbi Yisrael Yosef with honor, and drew him near and seated him at his side. That year, he did not invite him to sit with him on the night of the festival. Rabbi Yisrael Yosef was seated at the edge of the table. The guest felt uneasy, but he thought that the Chernobyler was immersed in his thoughts. The next day, after the shofar blasts and the conclusion of the entire service – and night was already coming – he again did not draw him near. Then he understood that there was something the matter. He even did so on the second day [of Rosh Hashanah]. After the Fast of Gedalia, when the masses of Hassidim came to say goodbye to the Admor and return to their homes – Rabbi Yisrael Yosef did not dare to enter to him. He requested that the *Gabbai* inform his son (the sons of the Chernobyler were also leaders in the court of their father) that "the Rabbi of Horodok wishes to talk with him." The *Gabbai* did as he was asked, and the son responded, "Tell the Rabbi of Horodok that I am sleeping now." The Horodoker sent the reply, "Tell him that if he does not let me enter, I will do so forcibly." He then permitted him to enter. "Sit down, Horodoker Rabbi," said the Rebbe.

[Page 156]

He gave him some wine and cake, and added, "What is upon your mouth?" [i.e., what do you want to say] "I want to know, why is this year different than all other years? For on all other years, your father received me with love and joy, seated me at his side, and did not let me sit in any other place. This year – no – what happened?" "You reminded me," said the son. He ran to his table, opened the drawer, and told him the story of the letter from Stolin.

"It is true," said the Horodoker. The son rose from his place in astonishment, for he was awaiting a different answer. "If that is the case, indeed, there is a Jew here who is childless, and who has come to Father for ten consecutive years already. Can you help him?"

"Bring him in," said the Horodoker. When he entered, the rabbi asked him, "What is your name?" "Michael." He took his hand and said, "Michael is your name. Oh that thou wert as my brother, that sucked the breasts of my mother! When I should find thee (Song of Songs 8:1).[3] Travel home in peace. In one year at this time, you will bring me cake from the bris."

The son saw this and was shaken, "Father was not 'permitted" from Heaven to respond to that Michael, and that Horodoker was permitted." He hurried to his father and told him the entire story. The Chernobyler responded, "I know who and what he is. He is great. So why did I distance him this year? He is a vessel that is lacking only a little. It is impossible to fill it from up close. It must be done from a slight distance, so I distanced him."

He immediately called the Horodoker and said to him, "Come to me no longer. Conduct your own court."

c.

In the village of Lakhovka there lived a Stoliner Hassid named Reb Moshe. There were many fishponds in that village, but there was no church. The gentiles of the villages took council and decided to lease the ponds to Reb Moshe Lachover permanently on the condition that he erect a church for them. They drew up a contract and sent it to the regional minister for certification. He signed it in gold letters.

The church was built and called by the name of its builder: Moshe's Church.

Moshe amassed a great deal of wealth. At the time of his old age, thoughts began to bother him: How would he get *there*?[4] He appeared before the Stoliner Rebbe, asked about practicalities – and was not answered. He expressed his bitterness to his friend Moshe Mordechai Drepsky of Koreni, a resident of Kozhan-Horodok, who was a Hassid of the Horodoker and also had fishponds. He advised Moshe Mordechai to travel with him to the Horodoker on Rosh Hashanah, for perhaps he will be saved.

Reb Moshe Lachover took his sack and traveled to Rabbi Yisrael Yosef in David-Horodok. At *Zechor Brit,*[5] Moshe Mordechai asked the rabbi to draw Reb Moshe near and do good for him. "Now it is *Zechor Brit*, and we have time. Let us yet see," responded the rabbi. On Rosh Hashanah, Reb Moshe approached the rabbi to wish him *Lechayim*. He waited for a word from him, but the rabbi was silent on both days of the festival. On the Fast of Gedalia, Reb Moshe asked for mercy and wept. The rabbi said, "Remain here until Yom Kippur." In the meantime, his fortune was spent, and his wealth melted away. Yom Kippur came, and the rabbi was silent. The eve of Sukkot arrived, and the rabbi pushed him off until after Sukkot. He continued to plead, and he pushed him off until after Shabbat *Bereishit*.[6] That day, he went to the Rebbetzin and beseeched her. She went to the rabbi and asked for mercy. At the conclusion of the Sabbath, prior to *Havdalah*, the rabbi suddenly said, "Moshe, is the contract here?" "Yes." "Show it to me." He took out the contract from his briefcase. The rabbi looked at it and said, "Can you give up on it and forgo it?" "Yes, rabbi." "And you will have no benefit from it, you or your children?" "No!" The rabbi took the contract and burnt it in the flame of the *Havdalah* candle. Immediately the sound of mighty thunder was heard – and all of David-Horodok shook. Immediately after that, fire was seen from the direction of Lakhovka. The church went up in flames.

d.

This was on the eve of Rosh Hashanah. As he did every year, Rabbi Yisrael Yosef arrived in Chernobyl along with a list of Hassidim that was given to Rabbi Motele. The Chernobyler reviewed the list and suddenly called out, "What is your opinion, Horodoker,

[Page 157]

about Reb Shlomo Leizer, the smith from Kozhan-Horodok. Is he at all a proper person?" "Certainly," responded Rabbi Yisrael Yosef. The Chernobyler continued to peruse the list and suddenly repeated the question. Rabbi Yisrael Yosef once again responded in the affirmative. When Rabbi Motele did this for the third time, Rabbi Yisrael Yosef realized that there was something going on here, but he remained silent. He impatiently awaited his return home. Immediately upon his arrival, he asked about the wellbeing of Reb Shlomo Leizer the smith. "A miracle happened to him," they told him. "On the eve of Rosh Hashanah, he traveled by boat on the Pripyat to purchase fish from the gentiles. The boat capsized. He began to drown, and he struggled with the bitterness of death." During that time, the conversation was taking place between the two rabbis. When it finished – they pulled him out of the Pripyat healthy and hale.

e.

This Shlomo Leizer had the custom of going to the synagogue of Rabbi Yisrael Yosef every Friday night after the Sabbath meal, and resting there until after midnight. Then he would get up, and knock on the shutters of the slumberers, "Arise for the service of the Creator." He did this summer and winter, and did not miss any Sabbath eve. A large kerosene lantern was burning in the hall of the synagogue. One winter Sabbath night, a fire broke forth and burnt the ceiling. Even the walls caught fire. Without impediment, the fire spread around and drew near to the Holy Ark, while Reb Shlomo Leizer was sleeping soundly. Rabbi Yisrael Yosef came to him in a dream and called out, "Shlomo Leizer, what is with you, sleeping? The Beis Midrash is going up in flames." He did not wake up. He pulled him and said, "Get up quickly! You too will go up in flames!" Reb Shlomo Leizer suddenly woke up and saw himself surrounded by flames. "I did not know what to do," he related after that. "I approached the lantern and breathed upon it, and the fire was completely extinguished."

Every year when he came to Kozhan-Horodok, Rabbi Yisrael Yosef would be hosted by Reb Yisrael Chaim Kotzikovitz. This took place from after Passover until Shavuot, and at times even though the festival of Shavuot as well. During his last time, everyone sensed that this was his last visit to them. Chaya, Reb Yisrael Chaim's mother, sensed this with particular clarity.

Everyone came to accompany him before he left. The old woman stood in her doorway, leaning her body on the doorposts. She extended her hand and did not let him leave. "What do you want?" he asked. "You know, rabbi, how great is our effort for you throughout the entire seven weeks, from early morning until late at night. Now I want to know, what provisions should I take with me for my final journey?" "I beg of you, leave me be," called out the rabbi. "I will not let you be until you answer me." When he saw that he could not escape, the rabbi said, "Prepare the lulav rings, they are your provisions." She died on the third day of Sukkot, and they placed the rings on her fingers. (The shrouds were prepared for her in her casket.)

f.

On a Friday morning after midnight in the winter, this took place. The rabbi (Itzikl) was sleeping in his bed in the home of Reb Yisrael Chaim in Kozhan-Horodok during one of his visits there. Suddenly a knock was heard on the door. Reb Yisrael Chaim hurried to the door. Avraham Yoel the shoemaker (Latucha) was standing at the door. He begged that he awaken the *Tzadik*. His daughter was going through a difficult childbirth, and this was the third day. She was dying, and only the rabbi could save her. Reb Yisrael Chaim said, "How can it be? Is it polite to awake the rabbi? What will be with the honor of Torah?" They were still talking when the voice of the rabbi was heard, "Who is there? Let him enter!" Reb Yisrael Chaim allowed him, and they entered. The rabbi raised his hands to the light of the candelabra that was burning all night, and asked: "What is wrong?" Avraham Yoel poured out his heart and begged for mercy. "Don't scream," responded the rabbi, "Go home. She has given birth to a boy!" "But rabbi, when I left there, her soul was departing." "Go home, she has given birth to a boy! Mazel Tov!"

That is what happened. Avraham Yoel hosted a *kiddush* that Sabbath, and joy pervaded in his house.

The aforementioned Rabbi Levi Yitzchak, nicknamed Reb Itzikl, the grandson of Rabbi Yisrael Yosef, would also go to Kozhan-Horodok from time to time to stay with his Hassidim.

[Page 158]

When the decree of Nikolai to expel the Jews from the villages and estates to the towns was issued (this was in 1904/5, the residents came to the rabbi in Kozhan-Horodok (on the Sabbath of the Torah portion of *Beha'alotecha*) and brought their pleas before him. They informed him that they must leave the villages by a certain time.

On Friday night and during *Shalosh Seudos* [the third Sabbath meal], the rabbi would speak words of Torah. On that Sabbath he said, "Eldad and Medad are prophesying in the camp[7] is the acronym for: Nikolai is a treacherous person, he will die, and nobody will sit on his throne. There will be great bloodshed and the King Messiah will come. Would it be that I will merit [to see] that day."

Translator's footnotes:

1. I am unsure of the reference here, but likely referring to the impropriety of delaying or preventing the service of welcoming the Sabbath.
2. *Leket* – literally gleanings – are the dropped sheathes that are left for the poor. Here, more colloquially, it seems to be referring to the agricultural gifts given to the Levites. And of course, it is used as an acronym for the three towns.
3. I took this translation of the difficult verse from the Mechon Mamre site. The first few words of the Hebrew version form an acronym for Michael. And the verse itself makes a reference to a child.
4. This word is italicized in the original, and I believe it is referring to the World To Come.
5. The title of the *Selichot* service of the day before Rosh Hashanah, and, more generally, a name for the day before Rosh Hashanah. Specifically, it is the opening words of the signature piyyut [liturgical hymn] of the *Selichot* service of the day before Rosh Hashanah.
6. The first Sabbath after the Sukkot festival, named for the first Torah portion read that day.
7. Numbers 11:27, from the Torah portion of *Beha'alotecha*.

Told by Reb Kopel Lichtenstein

Translated by Jerrold Landau

a.

I came to Horodok in the year 5661 (1901). Calm pervaded in the town during my first four years, but the gentiles began to torment us in 1905. My brother-in-law Leizer Kreines, a Bund [The General Union of Jewish Workers in Lithuania, Poland and Russia] member, called to the youths to join the independent defense organization. I, as a locksmith,[1] taught them how to shoot. We gathered in Baruch Kesler's cellar, lit a candle, placed a bottle of beer in a corner of the room, and shot at it. This training continued for a half a year, until that day when Livonko the policeman informed me of the searches that were about to take place. This Livonko would come to me from time to time. We became friends since I would service the guns of the police. One day, Livonko innocently told me that the police were coming to Horodok to search for and imprison members of the independent defense organization. I hurried immediately and informed all the members that if they desire freedom, they should make haste and escape. Leizer Kreines fled to Slutsk, and was arrested there. He was there for four weeks, and made the acquaintance with a young woman whom he later married. Members of the independent defense organization who did not heed my warning were arrested that night. After I warned everyone, I secretly moved all the weapons and hid them next to the bridge.

b.

About a year after the slaughter of the Sosniks[2] in "Lesser Ochli"[3] (incidentally Nissan Horvitz and others, I among them, hastened there that Sabbath after the terrifying news reached the synagogue), I was informed by gentile friends whose guns I repaired (from the mouth of a farmer from Choromsk whose sister lived in Ochli) – that preparations were being made for a pogrom. This was on Friday. I stated such in the synagogue. (A short time earlier, a pogrom took place in another town in the vicinity.) After the Sabbath, Shlomo and his sons: Itzele Yudovitz, Noach Yudovitz, and Asher Yudovitz, gathered together. Itzele said, "I am already prepared." Michael Riterman refused to join the preparations. Ezra Friedman and his brother Shimel were summoned to the synagogue. Ezra registered immediately and also intended to register his brother ("Is he a dog?")[4] Moshe Feivel the butcher and Orla Zager the butcher also registered. Itzele stuck the handle of an axe into his pants and stood on guard. After about half an hour, I went out to see if anything was happening. Itzele told me that they already saw several gentiles next to the house of Turkenitz in the market. The butchers were in their butcher shops at that time. In the meantime, several more gentiles gathered, and their numbers reached about 25. Itzele asked them what they were doing. "What business is it of yours?" responded one of them, "Nobody asked you, disgusting Jew!" Itzele took hold of the stick in his hand and called out, "Brothers, come here," and threatened to crack his head. At that moment, another gentile approached. Itzele did not hesitate. He raised the axe handle and cut off his hand. The gentiles scattered in all directions.

We stood on guard until midnight, and no living soul was seen.

c.

Nachman Cohen was a simple smith. He prepared the bellows (the *blozk*) to fan the flames. As he worked, he would turn from time to time to the small stool upon which the [Mishnaic] *Order of Zeraim* laid open. He would learn a few sections and return to his work.

It was that Reb Nachman who composed the known melody for the Priestly Blessing.

[Page 159]

d.

When I was seventeen years old – it was in 1896 – I was honored by Reb Ber of Lakhva, Reb Dovidl's father, with an unusual honor. I brought him a fine shofar for the High Holy Days. He liked it very much. He suddenly told me, "Come, lad, come and I will show you something." I went with him to the synagogue. He took out the communal ledger of Lakhva and opened it to a certain page. This is more or less what I saw written there.

In Ozernitsa next to Lakhva there lived (around the year 1796) Reb Chaim David with his family in great poverty and straits. He earned his livelihood from selling various kinds of tags to the gentiles of the area. He earned his livelihood with difficulty. When he would go out at the beginning of the week, he would also take the rest of the liquor from the Sabbath to sell to the gentiles.

The situation was difficult, for there was not enough food for the children. One Saturday night, when his wife was bothering him, he left the house with the rest of the liquor with him. It was a dark night. Along the way he suddenly stopped, turned to the Holy One Blessed Be He, and said:

"Master of the Universe, You know that I have walked with You with a pure heart all the days. However, You have made it bad for me. I am not asking for mercy from You, but rather business. I propose to You: everything I earn from now on, half will be for You and half for me. Do You agree? Indeed, we have agreed and concluded. Now, let us drink *Lechayim* in honor of the occasion."

Reb Chaim drank from the bottle, and immediately turned around and returned to his home. "Our salvation has come," he calmed his wife, "From now on, we will not know want."

That night, one of the gentiles knocked on Reb Chaim David's door. When he opened it, he said that he had no liquor. The gentile responded, "It does not matter, here is a bundle of money! My children do not allow me to drink. Give me liquor on another occasion." And he left.

Now his fortune changed. Reb Chaim David purchased various kinds of haberdashery and business merchandise, made a great profit, and did not forget his promise. He would go to the rabbi of Lakhva on Fridays and give him half of his income for the week.

After some time, Reb Chaim David left Lakhva and opened a manufacturing business. He succeeded in all his endeavors. He would sit in the synagogue or the *Beis Midrash*, while his wife would stand in the store. He had a custom: when a *Maggid* [itinerant preacher] came to lecture in the synagogue, Reb Chaim David would accompany him to the householders, who would give him money according to their generosity.

One day, one of the *Maggidim* came and delivered his lecture, and nobody came to accompany him. He went to the rabbi and expressed his surprise. The rabbi sent for Reb Chaim David. The *Maggid* responded, "He was in the audience and did not get up to accompany me." "Tell him that I sent you to him," added the rabbi. Rabbi Chaim went to accompany him. They went from house to house, as was the custom with *Maggidim*. They passed by one of the houses, into which people were careful about entering because a *dybbuk* [malicious spirit] had entered the woman of the house. "Let us go in," said the *Maggid*. At the door, the wife greeted them with the following:

"You should know, *Maggid*, that the man who is accompanying you has had an exchange of opinions with the Holy One Blessed Be He." The *Maggid* was astonished. However, Reb Chaim David called out, "Through the power of this agreement, I decree upon you, the *dybbuk*, that you must leave this woman." The woman immediately calmed down, and they entered in a pleasant fashion. She gave her portion. The *Maggid* was moved, and would not leave Reb Chaim David until they went to the rabbi. When the rabbi heard this, he was also filled with surprise. They were not satisfied until ten notables of the city gathered together, and Reb Chaim David told them the entire story.

e.

After eight of his twelve children died, Father of blessed memory went to Reb Ber, the father of Reb Dovidl. He told him this and poured out his bitterness. Reb Ber told him, "Go home, and you will find a black splotch on a ceiling panel. Change that panel!" After he did so, death stopped entering his room!

[Page 160]

Gershon, Reb Moshe Yehuda Lifshitz's father-in-law, owned a liquor business. Once, when I was still young, I went to him and remained there. The door opened. One of the gentile neighbors entered and told him in a subdued voice with soft language, "Gershonke, give me a glass of liquor." After he finished drinking and left, Reb Gershon told me, "Do you think that he always acted in this manner? The story is as follows: This gentile would always enter with shouts and curses, and demand his glass. He would threaten with the force of his magic if his wish was not given to him. One day, the gentile came in his usual fashion, cursing, swearing, and demanding his liquor. He again threatened his sorcery. I pondered, decided, and told him, "The power of my magic is greater than your magic." "How?" he asked. "Let us see." We immediately shook hands in agreement that on Saturday night, we would go outside the city, each of us with our demons, and see whose power is greater. Do you know Chaim and Berl? – my sons, may they live. I ordered them to wear the garb of demons, to dress up, and to hide in a secret corner. When they hear my call, they should rise and leave, armed with 'proper' rods that can be used easily. They should beat him until I tell them to stop.

"On Saturday night, the gentile appeared as we discussed. "So Ivan," I called out, "Call out, he will answer you quickly." The gentile immediately opened his mouth and called out again and again. There was no power to his magic.

"So," he called to me angrily, "Show me yours!" Immediately, I called out, "Chaim smash, Berl cut." The two "demons" appeared and beat Ivan soundly, until I told them to stop. From that time, he would drink his glass of liquor at my place calmly and peacefully."

Translator's footnotes:

1. From the context below, it seems that locksmiths were also adept at gun repairs.
2. See page 239 for reference to the murder of the Sosniks.
3. It seems that there is a typo here, and the village is actually Malye [i.e., Lesser] Orly. Perhaps this is an issue of dialect and pronunciation.
4. This is likely a sarcastic expression of dismay as to why his brother had not registered in the first place.

Personalities

[Page 163]

A. The Pure and the Holy, May G-d Avenge Their Blood (Murdered by the Nazis)

Rabbi Yisrael Yehuda Kula of Blessed Memory

(the Galician *Shochet* [ritual slaughterer] in David-Horodok)

Y. Ben-Yisrael

Translated by Jerrold Landau

There are people for whom the stings of life do not influence them and do not affect their mind, and they maintain themselves, even though life is difficult, and their shade is more than the sunlight. However, these special individuals see everything through a clear lens and utilize every opportunity and possibility to bring rays of light and happiness into their lives. They are imbued with a refined, strong faith in G-d. Their faith is a solid foundation that pervades their lives. They draw their strength to overcome all obstacles from their faith, and it serves as a protector and salvation to them in the darkness of their world.

This idea floats and comes before my mind as I recall the wonderful, noble personality, full of good traits and clear character. This is the enthusiastic Hassid and scholar, the well-known musician amongst the Hassidim of Stolin-Karlin and beyond, who served as the *shochet* in David-Horodok for six years – Rabbi Yisrael Yehuda Kula of blessed memory, may G-d avenge his blood.

He arrived in David-Horodok in the year 5686 [1926], through the influence of his rabbi, the Admor of Stolin, the rabbi and *Tzadik* [righteous person] Rabbi Moshe Perlov, may the memory of the righteous be blessed, may G-d avenge his blood. He was one of his enthusiastic Hassidim who held him in great reverence. He left his city of Bielic in Western Galicia (that is why he was called the Galician *shochet*). He lived with Mr. Boaz Schuster (Boaz the *Perechodchik* [Translator]) on Olshaner Street for the entire time he lived in David-Horodok. His way of life in that town was not a hedge of roses, and his success came after that time.

As was the way with most of the small Jewish towns in the Diaspora, dispute did not skip over our town, and indeed found its victim. The dispute between the various strata and between the *shochtim* and the butchers took on a very unfortunate form. Someone saw the new *shochet* as a person unsuitable for his role, and for the customary protocols in the town and its institutions, for he was concerned lest he be too stringent. That person perhaps regarded him as serious competition who might impinge on his livelihood in the future. Jealousy was also aroused in him, for his prayers and his sweet voice made a great impression in the town. On the first Passover, as he led the Prayer for Dew in the synagogue of the Hassidim of Stolin, the worshippers in the synagogues on the *Shulhof* [Synagogue courtyard] left their places and came to hear the new cantor. The elderly rabbi, Rabbi Dovidl of blessed memory, was also among those who came – and the impression was very strong. This poured oil on the bonfire. The dispute became harsher and reached Pinsk and Vilna. Reb Yisrael Yehuda's suffering due to the dispute was great, but his spirit did not fall. Not only was his reaction not negative, but it was even decisively positive.

Reb Yisrael Yehuda of blessed memory was graced with a deep sense of melody and music. He composed many melodies even though he was not able to read musical notes, and he invested a great deal of his soul, the feelings of his heart, and his yearnings into them. Apparently, these were simple spiritual concepts, but nevertheless, they served as an expression of complete and deep life, for he drew their tones from the source of the spirit of his life, from the unique world in which he lived.

Most of his melodies were stamped with the imprint of religious feeling. They had an effect on their listeners like chapters of prayer and hymns, which were pleasant to those who recited them, along with the understanding of the content and the meaning of the words. No less, they had an outpouring of the soul, overflowing with agony and joy, absorbing the atmosphere of their composer. Many knew how to ascend to the heights of the world, to sublime enthusiasm, in a holy flame.

His creations were influenced primarily from the treasury of Hassidism to which Reb Yisrael Yehuda was bound with a permanent knot. He absorbed into them all the beauty and pleasantness of Polish and Galician Hassidism, especially of the character of Stolin-Karlin Hassidism, with its enthusiasm, warmth of heart, internal essence, and dynamism, in accordance with "all my bones shall say."[1]

[Page 164]

His melodies were primarily calm, with a special charm, caressing the ears and imbuing the listeners with light pleasure. (As an example, the *Pesukei Dezimra* of *Shacharit* before *Hamelech*.)[2] However, as the melody continues, its resonance strengthens, "heats up," and ascends with a flame of holy fire, an internal fire that penetrates the heart and soul with extra devotion, leading to the central, high point, to a world that is full of holiness, glory, and splendor.

His faith and devotion to his Rabbi was deep and strong. When the Rebbe commanded him to compose melodies, he did not know how to desist: he was like an overflowing wellspring, spilling over its brim, with its waters spreading outside. Thus did the steams of melodies flow forth in honor of every holiday and event, for hymns and Hassidic dances, for the High Holy Days and for all the days of the year.

When Rabbi Yisraelke, may the memory of the righteous be blessed, the *Yenuka* [Child] from Stolin, passed through Warsaw on his final journey to Frankfurt, where he died, he met Reb Yisrael Yehuda after not having seen him for many years (because Reb Yisrael Yehuda of blessed memory escaped from Russia in 1905, when he was drafted to the Russian army during the Russo-Japanese War). It was 1920. The Rebbe listened to his song, and it made such a great impression on him, so he said, "Let him sing as a sign of his soul, for he is a professional, he knows his trade." He even commanded him to send him special tunes for the High Holy Days, for *Vayeetayu*[3] and *Hayom Harat Olam*.[4]

Reb Yisrael Yehuda sent his Rebbe the notes to these songs. When the Rebbe died a year later, he kept his command stringently, and continued to compose melodies for the High Holy Days that were always sung in Stolin. [He also composed melodies] for all the Sabbaths of the year (for example, *Menucha Vesimcha*[5] on the eve of the Sabbath, and the holy hymn *Ka Echsof*[6] sung by the Karlin-Stoliner Hassidim on Sabbath eves and the third Sabbath meal). This was their custom until the terrible Holocaust that brought destruction upon Polish Jewry, and also silenced the holy, pure voices and resonance.

Reb Yisrael Yehuda was murdered on 4 Cheshvan 5703 [1942] along with his wife Beila Chaya, and their daughter Chana by the Nazis in the city of Kobrin. His melodies are sung to this day among the rest of the Karlin-Stolin melodies on Sabbaths, festivals, and the High Holy Days.

Avraham Zeev Lutzky

by A. Ziporin

Translated by Jerrold Landau

He was born in Kozhan-Horodok to his parents Moshe and Chana-Sara. He received a religious education and was ordained for the rabbinate; however, he did not wish to use the rabbinate as a means of earning a living. He got married in Nirtcha on the Pripyat to Rachel, the daughter of Tzvi (Hershel) Moravchik of blessed memory. During the early period, he worked with his father-in-law in the fish business. After several years, they were expelled from Nirtcha and moved to David-Horodok, where he started a business in lumber, forestry, etc.

He was pleasant with his fellow, an enthusiastic Zionist from his youth, Orthodox in his faith, while also dealing with *maskilim* [followers of the *Haskalah* [Enlightenment] movement] with patience and understanding. Truth was his guiding light. He was the symbol of honesty. He pursued peace and loved his fellow. He never entered a dispute. He did not want to be an arbitrator for one side unless it was for both sides. One could trust his honesty.

He was a follower of the methodology of the G'ra [Vilna Gaon] of blessed memory in his study and behavior: simplicity, modesty, not wanting to praise his children for that would be as if he was praising himself. He loved the poor and never forgot about them. His wife helped him in his charitable deeds.

[Page 165]

His way in business was with truth. He would relate: When I studied in Yeshiva, we heard the rabbi (the Yeshiva head) saying: Rabbi Meir says, "What should a person do to become rich?" All the students were eager to hear the advice for attaining wealth. The continuation was: "He should conduct business in honesty." At that time, I did not understand the advice of doing business with honesty. However, through my life experiences, I have found this proper, and I guide my children along that path.

His life was a life of Torah and divine service. He attended a Talmud lesson every day, and he never wasted a moment of his time.

During his final years, he opened a manufacturing business. Despite the difficult years, his business flourished thanks only to the great trust that both his suppliers and customers had in him. The gentiles would urge each other to shop in his store since "here is the truth."

His entire family was murdered together with him.

Surviving him are: A son who left for Cuba in 1922 (Chaim Lutzky), and his daughter Yentl who made *aliya* to the Land in 1933 along with her husband.

May his memory be blessed.

My Father Reb Yosef
the Son of Moshe Kolozny of Blessed Memory

by Chaim the Son of Yosef Kolozny

Translated by Jerrold Landau

Yosef was a fruitful vine,[7] modest and humble a friend to old and young, to the rich and the poor alike.

He was a man of deeds, with imagination and ideas, a believer the son of a believer, who always said: Fortunate is the believer, how good is his lot and how beautiful is his heritage. The good, and also, Heaven forbid, the bad, everything is from He Who Is Blessed.

A sizable portion in forging the spiritual image of my father goes to Rabbi Avraham Yitzchak Koltin, who was called "*Der Malach*" [The Angel] by the people of the city. Rabbi Avraham Yitzchak had exceptional influence on all his students, who were the finest of the city. Aside from studies in Talmud and commentaries, Rabbi Avraham Yitzchak worked to imbue the hearts of his students with pleasant traits, love of one's fellow, love of fellow Jews, etc.

There, in a narrow room, next to the table crowded with a number of students, they would learn Torah for its own sake with his large eyes filled with mercy, his high forehead shining like rays of lights, and, most important, his mouth exuding pearls – there, Rabbi Avraham Yitzchak imprinted his seal, the seal of truth, love, and righteousness in the hearts of his students. My father of blessed memory remained his faithful student, listening to the stories of his Rabbi about *Tzadikim*, who served as lessons in morality forging proper behavior between man and G-d, and between man and his fellow – and he made efforts to fulfill them.

The main part of his education came from Grandmother and Grandfather Reb Moshe and Leah of blessed memory. Grandfather was G-d fearing, diligent in observing commandments, a man of truth, who lived from the toil of his hands. Grandmother was righteous, and not a day passed without her giving charity. They gave their part in educating their son, who was a source of pride to them and their Creator.

They cannot be counted! I cannot write on paper all the fine traits with which he was graced. He read, learned, did, acted, studied, taught, worshipped, and sang with feeling, sweetness, and devotion.

He was a Hassid with all strands of his soul. He was connected to his Admor and to his Father in Heaven with an unbreakable bond. What is the difference between us, the Hassidim, and those who attend the cinemas and the theaters? We Hassidim receive, influence, and are sustained throughout the entire year. The

[Page 166]

spiritual sustenance that we absorb, spread, and disseminate is pleasant, beautifies the soul, and leads to spiritual sublimity. Whereas they: at that moment they laugh or cry, and later everything passes, as if it never was, like smoke that flies away.

He would explain Hassidic song as follows: Our songs are deep. They have content and life. Everything is feeling, joy, and longing. They have levels, and everything is in accordance with the level. When we sing *Ka Echsof*[6] the longing and desire is great and endless. The splendor and glory in them to greet the pleasantness of the Sabbath continues until "Your souls shall long." The pleas emanate from the depths of the heart. The effervescence, the storminess, and the pleading of "May Your mercy be aroused" and "Let us find shelter under the shade of Your wings" – are the content, the primary matter, and the faith. One lives by them. He continued: The melody is not abstract. It is expressed and comes forth in the spirit of *Atah Echad, Dror Yikra*, and *Ata Nigleita.*[8]

Not only did he preach nicely, but he also fulfilled everything with his entire body and soul. His sweet prayers that emanated from the heart penetrated the hearts of all those who knew him, both Hassid and *Misnaged*. Even though he was weak in body and was not considered as one of the mighty ones, he girded himself like a lion at *Ezkera Elokim Vehemaya* and *Yareiti Biftzoti*[9] in the synagogue of the Admor of Karlin and in David-Horodok. Above all was the *Ya'alot* and *Neila*. Those who knew him often wondered from where he drew such energy.

The Admor of Karlin, may the memory of the righteous be blessed, told me that on the final Rosh Hashanah, my father of blessed memory came to Karlin weak and subdued. On the first day of Rosh Hashanah, as always, he was sent by the Admor to serve as the prayer leader, and he stumbled on account of his weakness. The Admor told him, "Go! G-d will help you." The Admor continued: "I saw him, I heard him, and I knew very well the order and style of his prayers, but I will never forget that final *Yareiti Biftzoti*.

I will remember it for my entire life. It was the power of a pained heart with feelings to rise up 'Before the Mighty, Awesome One,' and to storm with super-human energy in accordance with 'My insides are stormy as I commence' so that 'I will find forgiveness and pardon for those that sent me.' "[10]

From melody, song, and prayer to study. The Talmud with the Levush was his daily bread. Even though he was busy with matters of livelihood, no day passed without studying Gemara or looking into a book.

He was expert and knowledgeable regarding matters of the day. He would read Yiddish, Russian, and Hebrew newspapers to find out what was taking place in the world. His reactions to world events were based on a religious outlook, were interesting, and beyond dispute.

All of this, and even more so, was between man and his Creator, but what about between man and his fellow? Who can enumerate and who can count the level of concern he had for his fellow? He gathered, collected, took from one person, and gave to another. To fulfil the needs of the poor he would collect sums of money during his many travels and hasten to give them to the designated recipients. There were such people who knew that they had someone who concerned himself with them, and he never failed them, Heaven forbid.

His chief concern was the bathhouse, which was a burden and expense on the Jews of the city. "We have been commanded regarding purity and cleanliness," he would say, "and especially about family purity.[11] How can we eat our daily bread without concerning ourselves with family purity among the people of Israel? Is this not our pride and greatness?"

He was an advisor in matters of the individual and the public. He would answer everyone willingly. He would think deeply. He turned the topic of discussion on all its sides. He would reach a judgment and forge a path. Even though he could not satisfy everyone, the majority would heed his advice. He especially excelled as an arbitrator.

Despite the tribulations that he suffered, the illness of his young daughter Risha of blessed memory, who was bedridden for several years and died at the age of eighteen, and the tribulations of the individual and the public that pressured his heart, his shine did not dull. He would explain: "The righteous lives by his faith[12] – he who comes to terms with everything and that is his faith – shall live!"

When his friend Rabbi Shneur Zalman Shapira of blessed memory left David-Horodok about a year before the destruction and the Holocaust – and his situation was already unbearable – he told Rabbi Shapira as he bid him farewell, "Your departure is difficult on me. Who knows if the agony, the longing, the situation, and my wife's illness will not crush the remainder of my heart. I take comfort in that three of my sons are in the Land of Israel. I wish that I had a wing like a dove, and I would fly to our Holy Land in order to enjoy the splendor of the Divine Presence that flutters over the Land of the Patriarchs."

[Page 167]

A stream of hot tears burst forth from the pure, glowing eyes. The words emanated from the holy mouth, and the heart was emotional and stormy, without finding relief…

And he did not merit… His soul ascended heavenward along with the entire holy community of David-Horodok.

How is it, my holy father, how did you fall, Heilel the son of the morning star?[13] You, your daughter Chava and her three children, your son Litman, your brother Litman, his wife Gittel, and their sons Yaakov and Yisrael, your sister Feigel her husband Chaim and their children, your mother Leah, pure, upright, and modest – how is it [that this happened to] the entire community of the Children of Israel in David-Horodok?

Your blood boiled for three days and was not calmed. Was this your final protest on the earth, with nobody to listen and nobody to give comfort?

May your memories be etched in the hearts – not to be forgotten, and may revenge come and avenge the honor that was desecrated and the dear souls that perished in an untimely fashion. May G-d avenge your blood!

May your souls be bound in the bonds of eternal life.

Avraham Durchin,

May G-d Avenge His Blood

by Y. Lifshitz

Translated by Jerrold Landau

A memorial candle

"Be careful with the children of the poor, for Torah shall emanate from them"[14] – this statement was not applicable to us.

We were not poor like the "children of the poor." In any case, there were such people, old and young. In a small community, there was relatively more of such than in a large city.

Regarding such children of the poor, who broke through toward a path with their independent powers, and went out to the wide expanses, the poet writes:

"Luminaries shall arise for us from among the luminaries. And geniuses shall descend upon us from the gardens…" (Bialik, *Hamatmid*)

Avraham Durchin was the son of poor people. His father was a peddler who went about the villages and returned to his home for the Sabbath. His mother also did everything to sustain the household. Avraham was a talented youth, thirsty for knowledge and education. When a public school opened up in the city, he was recommended to the director of the school, who agreed to accept him without paying tuition.

Not only tuition but it was not proper that this student should sit in the classroom among his friends without wearing the same uniform as his friends, as was customary at that time in all government schools. Therefore, the director made an effort to organize a celebration for the school with the income being dedicated to the student, to purchase books for him, and to sew a uniform for him.

The student passed from class to class successfully until graduation.

He could not think of high school, even in a dream. The only place where it would be possible to study for free was the Teachers' Institute in Vilna. Perhaps he had an inclination to teaching. We never had the opportunity to speak about this. It seems that only the thirst for education brought him to Vilna. The tall lad returned to his town for vacations, wearing the cap of the Institute's uniform on his head. He would return to the place of learning when the time came. This is the way it was every year. In the meantime, there was communal work and dreams about the Jewish community of the future, about autonomous institutions, about national education and culture, and about all

[Page 168]

nice things seen in the distant horizon. This is the way Avraham was. We would meet during the gloomy time of war during the time of the Czarist regime, and dream of spring, about a change of ways in Russia, when we would be able to organize our lives according to our aspirations.

Then the revolution of 1917 broke out. Vibrant communal life began in the town, especially in the local Zionist organization. Durchin was alert and active. He appeared in public gatherings and was chosen as a member of the local Zionist council.

Durchin's activities during that period will be described in another place.

Durchin left the Institute, not to go to teaching, but rather to continue his education abroad. He chose the chemical profession.

Later, we found out that he had entered the circles of Torah and science. He married the daughter of the well-known Sh'y Ish Horowitz. Durchin lived in Warsaw and was occupied in his profession of Doctor of Chemistry.

He visited the Land and wished to settle there but did not succeed. The war broke out and he perished along with all the Jews of Warsaw.

Yaakov Olpiner

by Y. Lifshitz

Translated by Jerrold Landau

He was modest, inobtrusive, and somewhat shy. That was Y. Olpiner. He joined the party through the ranks of *Hechalutz* [The Pioneer]. We immediately sensed that he would be successful, and he joined the party directly. He was nicknamed "the living encyclopedia" for what did he not know by heart? – whether it was Jewish or general history, or Hebrew Yiddish, Russian, German, or Polish literature. He knew the exact date when Ivan the Terrible, Tolstoy, Julius Caesar, and Louis XIV were born. He also knew the birthdates of Maimonides and Rashi, and the dates of every important event in Hebrew history.

He knew when Tolstoy wrote *War and Peace* and when Dostoevsky wrote *The Brothers Karamazov*, and of course dates in the annals of Yiddish literature. Furthermore, he knew about the personal relations between Mendele and Bialik or Ahad Ha'am, and about everything done behind the curtain among people of science, literature, and politics.

Of course, the party made use of his talents. He ran every cultural activity of the party, especially among the youth. He related to political opponents with great honor. It was fascinating to see him during a political debate: he surprised his opponent with his knowledge of everything that took place within his party, and it was as if he agreed with their ideas. However, along with this, he tore the arguments of his opponent to pieces. He did all this with seriousness, with a level head, with the appropriate honor, and with a smile on his lips. He made *aliya* to the Land in 1926, but he left since he was weak and was unable to become accustomed to physical labor. There was no room for such a talented lad in any office in the Land.

When he returned to Poland, he got married and moved to Stolin. There, he met his tragic end along with the community of Stolin.

May his memory be blessed.

[Page 169]

Aharon the Son of Moshe Yehuda Lifshitz

by Sh. Zezik

Translated by Jerrold Landau

He was a Zionist from the time of his youth. He lived and worked on behalf of labor Zionism and dedicated his entire life to it. Such was Arke Lifshitz.

He was born in 1905 to his father, the important communal activist and dedicated Zionist. From his youth, he absorbed the national and Zionist spirit that pervaded his home.

In 1915, he was already a member of *Chovevei Sfat Ever* [Lovers of the Hebrew Language], an organization that was founded in their home and functioned clandestinely, like all the communal organizations and societies in pre-revolutionary Russia.

After the revolution, Aharon was active in the Zionist youth. When the *Tzeirei Zion* [Youth of Zion] party was formed, he was among its first activists and dedicated workers. He distributed the newspapers of the party. Later, when the party united with *Poalei Zion* [Workers of Zion], he distributed the newspaper of the united party, *Dos Vort*, to the members.

He was especially active in *Hechalutz* [The Pioneer]. He displayed great dedication to the work of the *Keren Kayemet* [Jewish National Fund]. Similarly, he did so to the Y.L. Peretz Library and the League for Workers in the Land of Israel. Aharon was the doer, activist, and initiator in every political or financial activity.

In 1925, when the *Hachshara* [pioneer training] unit was formed in Lisovitz, Aharon was among its founders. He was elected by the members as the labor director. Through his dedication and faith, he served as an example and guide to all the members. He merited, and made *aliya* to the Land in 1928, but he was not able to settle there. For various reasons, he was forced, to his great dismay, to leave the Land temporarily, with the hope of returning in good time. This idea and hope never ceased in his heart even for one minute.

In 1938, he was certified for *aliya* once more, but his *aliya* did not come to fruition due to the lack of *aliya* permit certificates.

In 1941, he was imprisoned by the Soviets and deported from the town with eight other members for the crime of Zionist activity.

A long series of wanderings from prison to prison to prison and from concentration camp to concentration camp began. This wandering was replete with tribulations that put an end to his young life. In 1942, he died without meriting, as did some of his imprisoned friends, to survive to the end of the war and arrive in the Land of his aspirations and his hopes of all the years.

May his memory be a blessing.

Sara Gloiberman-Plotnitzky

by Her Sister, Shoshana Gloiberman

Translated by Jerrold Landau

It is hard to believe that Sara, who loved life so much, was cut off during the mass murder along with her dear husband and children!!!

It seems to me that I saw her only yesterday: walking among us full of life. She knew how to draw people close and make a difficult moment easier. She was a dedicated mother and a good daughter to her parents. She did all this with a wonderful blend of simplicity and good heartedness.

Anyone who came close to her immediately recognized her character and loved her. She was alert and attentive to everything that took place in our town and in our Zionist world. She dedicated her best years to communal work. She was an expert in the history and development of the movement. I recall that already then, more than 24 years ago, she would gather us together in her home after a grueling day of work – in a narrow room with the light of a lamp and read newspapers to us. She would guide people and organize them for *aliya*. She was active, and urged others to be active to pioneering and the upbuilding of the homeland…

We have merited a flourishing Land of Israel.

[Page 170]

And a large nation returned to it!
But she did not merit to see her dream actualize…
Sara, Aharon, and their children fell victim to the mass murder in David-Horodok.
Meirke, Nechamale, Yisraelke, and Chaimke, may G-d avenge your blood!

Musia (Devora) Geier-Gloiberman

by Shoshana (Gloiberman) Zilberstein, Hadera

Translated by Jerrold Landau

She was the most active of the active members of the city.

She was a communal personality immersed in her day-to-day activities. Throughout all the years of her work, she had almost a single theme: cultural work among the group of mothers and friends. Musia was what is called in our community a "Tarbutnik" … and she lived up to this name. She worked in it with all the strands of her soul, with her understanding and love of the human spirit. Her intellectual talents were suffused with a deep humane attitude. This was the charm of her personality and her force of influence upon those who came in contact with her. I see her as then, as a girl flying through the storm of influence. She was self-assured, chic, but also simple.

Her love for the homeland was strong, but she did not merit actualizing this… May her memory be a blessing.

About My Dear Girlfriends

by A Friend

Translated by Jerrold Landau

Among the other members of the Y.L. Peretz Library committee, the following especially stood out with their dedication and activity – Chaichik Lansky, Sheindel Ziporin, and Rachel Ziporin who worked in all areas, as librarians, organizing performances, plays, celebrations, flower days, etc. with the income dedicated to the maintenance and growth of the library.

Coordinator's note: According to my research, the women pictured are, from left to right, **Sheindel Ziporin, Chaichik Lansky, and Rachel Ziporin.**

[Page 171]

In addition to the activities in the library, they also devoted their time to party work for the *Keren Kayemet* [Jewish National Fund] and the League for Workers in the Land of Israel, especially during the times of the Zionist Congresses. Even at a later time, when they were already busy with families and children – to whom they gave a proper Zionist education – they did not stop their activity. Until the final period, they planned to make *aliya* to the Land, but they were unable to actualize their dream.

May their memories be a blessing.

Translator's footnotes:

1. A quote from the *Nishmat* prayer, indicating that one praises G-d with all one's limbs.
2. This is evidently referring to the beginning of the main part of the *Shacharit* service on the High Holy Days, which starts with a loud shout of *Hamelech* [the King].
3. This prayer, in the *Musaf* service on Rosh Hashanah and Yom Kippur, looks forward to a time when all people will be united in the service of G-d.
4. This prayer, recited after the shofar sounding in the *Musaf* service on Rosh Hashanah, connects the holiday with the creation of the world and asks G-d for just and compassionate judgment.
5. This Sabbath hymn praises the Sabbath and those who properly sanctify the day.

6. The words of this Sabbath hymn evoke longing for the sweetness of the Sabbath.
7. Genesis 49:22
8. *Ata Echad* [You are one] is from the Sabbath *Mincha Amida*. *Dror Yikra* is a Sabbath hymn. *Ata Nigleita* is the opening of the *Shofarot* section of the Rosh Hashanah *Musaf*.
9. The former is from the *Selichot* service two days prior to Yom Kippur, as well as from the Neila service, and the latter is from the chazzan's petition at the beginning of the Shacharit Amida on the first day of Rosh Hashanah.
10. These are quotes from *Yareiti Biftzoti*, a liturgical poem said at the beginning of the repetition of the *Shacharit Amida* on the first day of Rosh Hashanah
11. Referring to the monthly visit to the mikveh following a woman's period of menstruation.
12. Habakkuk 2:4.
13. Isaiah 14:12.
14. From Tractate *Nedarim* 81:a.

B. From the Old Generation (and Also From the New)

Rabbi Yeshayahu Rozenblum
– "The Rabbi From Slonim"

Y. Lifshitz

Translated by Jerrold Landau

Who am I that I shall come to portray and present a complete picture of the personality of the Rabbi from Slonim, may the memory of the righteous be blessed. I did not merit to know him well.

I wish only to present in brief that which my father of blessed memory always told me about the Rabbi. Thereby, I can also fulfil the request of my father to erect a monument in his memory in the book of David-Horodok, as he was one of his most fervent Hassidim as well as his right hand.

I merited to be a frequenter of the home of the Rabbi from Slonim regarding the yeast business that grandfather ran in partnership with the Rabbi.

He never gave the impression of a rabbi or a member of the clergy, but rather that of an aristocrat, a member of the nobility. He was a scholar, with a unique countenance that evoked honor.

I recall the impression that he left on me on the eve of Yom Kippur when I sat with the charity plate to benefit *"Hachshara for the Yishuv."* He entered and began to distribute charity into every plate with great generosity and breadth of heart. It was clear from his face that he had complete joy from this mitzvah. He would give me a ruble, and his name would be printed in the book of *"Hachshara for the Yishuv"* every year.

Today, I believe that it is possible to regard him as a scion of Lithuanian Jewry who received a traditional religious education as well as rabbinical ordination. With all this, he absorbed sparks of Hebrew *Haskalah* [Enlightenment] and love of Zion. This was the face of the era at the end of the 19th and beginning of the 20th century. I will bring another statement of the Rabbi regarding this, that Father always told me.

Once, a dispute came up before the Rabbi between the *Gabbai* Moshe Lachovsky and the *Shamash* Velvel. Moshe Lachovsky did not want to increase the salary of the *Shamash*. The Rabbi decreed, with the agreement of the Gaon of Vilna of blessed memory, that the *Gabbai* must give a raise to the *Shamash*, since he was a unique personality. These are the words of the Rabbi:

"The dividing line between day and night is twilight. The dividing line between a plant and an inanimate object is a stone, which does not grow. However, if it remains in the same place for years, it grows. The dividing line between a *Yomtov* [festival] and a weekday is Purim, which is not a *Yomtov*[festival] even though it has great value. Nevertheless, it is not a weekday.

The dividing line between a Jew and a gentile is the *shamash*. On Friday evening, everyone goes to the synagogue for the Sabbath, but the *shamash* is still working in the synagogue. And at the conclusion of the Sabbath, while everyone is still in the synagogue, the *shamash* is already working: His Sabbath has ended." This was the verdict of the Rabbi.

[Page 172]

He apparently said this in the name of the Gaon of Vilna, but it was actually his own idea. Father heard this from his mouth in Slonim when he was learning there. However, the Rabbi was modest and avoided honor,[1] and never demanded his livelihood from his Hassidim. On the contrary, he supported many families of his Hassidim with money that he earned from his medical inventions.

Translator's footnote:

1. Therefore, he said it in someone else's name.

Rabbi Yeshaya Aryeh Leib
the Son of Rabbi Yeshaya Aryeh Leib Rozenblum

by A. Lahav

Translated by Jerrold Landau

He was born in the year 5627 [1867] and died in the year 5684 [1924].

The rabbi was born after the death of his father of blessed memory. He was raised and educated by his maternal grandfather, the true rabbi and Gaon Rabbi Yosef Reizin, may the memory of the righteous and holy be blessed, the head of the rabbinical court of the communities of Telz and Slonim, and the author of the books *Edut Biyehosef* and *Porat Yosef*. He raised him and taught him Torah. Under the influence of that mighty Gaon, he was appointed to teach Jewish law and proper deeds, and to respond to thousands of questions that were posed to the Gaon from the entire Jewish Diaspora. The paternal grandfather of this rabbi was the rabbi, the luminary of the Diaspora, wonderful and excellent in his Torah, fear of G-d, and diligence, Rabbi Elchanan Yaakov Rozenblum, may the memory of the righteous be a blessing, of Pinsk, who was known as Rabbi Choncha of blessed memory. He was an honorable businessman all his life, great in action and charitable deeds. He was especially involved with the charitable fund of Rabbi Meir Baal Haness[1] to support those who live before G-d in our Holy Land, may it be built up. Rabbi Yaakov Elchanan of blessed memory excelled in Bible, was steeped in tradition, and was an unequalled grammarian. He would read the Torah, blow the shofar, serve as a *mohel* [circumciser], all in one. He was the son of the rabbi and *Tzadik* Rabbi Shmuel David, may the memory of the righteous be blessed, of Kobrin. He was appointed as rabbi in the city of David-Horodok in the year 5650 [1890].

(From *Oholei Shem*, edited by Sh. N. Gottlieb, 5672 [1902]).

Translator's footnote:

1. Founded in 1796, the charity allowed Jews in the Diaspora to provide assistance to needy Jews in the Land of Israel.

Rabbi David Berkovitz

by Yitzchak Ben Chana

Translated by Jerrold Landau

They called him Reb Dovidl, either out of love and esteem, or because he was short in stature, thin, and scrawny, like the fig of Rabbi Zadok.[1] Only his dark eyes were deep and sparkling. He lived for most of his life on milk, tea, and biscuits, and died at an old age.

He was a rabbi, the son of a rabbi. His father Rabbi Avraham Ber was a rabbi in Kozhan-Horodok and Lakhva. He was a rabbi and *Tzadik* [righteous person], in the style of a worker of portents. We will include stories and legends about him in another part of this book. In the early days, Kozhan-Horodok was a central place, like a community mentioned in the ledgers of the Council of the Four Lands. Later, when the Brisk-

Baranovich railway line was laid, the railway station of nearby Luninets emptied Kozhan-Horodok of its Jews.

Kozhan-Horodok remained like a trap without fish, in the style of "My sons left me and are no longer here."

Reb Dovidl's father, Rabbi Avraham Ber, made *aliya* in his old age to die and be buried in the Holy Land. His son Reb Mordechele also made *aliya* to support him along the long, difficult journey, for the rabbi was old and weak. He took his Torah scroll with him to the holy city of Jerusalem. We were young children at the time when Mother brought us from Rubel to Reb Dovidl's house to receive a blessing from the elderly Rabbi who was making *aliya* to the Holy Land, a blessing of an elderly grandfather to his descendants.

The old man placed his hand on the head of each one, gave us his blessing, and gave everyone eighteen coins.

[Page 173]

Rabbi Avraham Ber reached Jerusalem, and died after a short time. His son settled in with the *Beis Midrash* attendees in the Old City.

The two of his sons who were rabbis remained in the Diaspora. One, Rabbi Itche, was a rabbi in Lakhva, close to David-Horodok, and the second, the elder one, Reb Dovidl, was in Horodok.

When the two rabbinical brothers would meet, they would use the second person plural [*atem*] when addressing each other, as if they were strangers and not brothers. Once they were asked, "Our rabbis, you are brothers, why do you talk to each other in the plural, and not the singular [*atah*]?" They responded, "This is because of the honor of the Torah."

Indeed, they were great in Torah.

They did not bask in glory about this, especially Reb Dovidl. He never stopped his learning, day or night, at home or on the road. Even on a journey, his lips would be moving and dealing with a discussion in one of the tractates, for he knew them by heart. He was a man typical of the students of the *Gr'a* [Vilna Gaon]. "You should delve into it"[2] is everything. This is the purpose of life and the destiny of those on earth. Anything else is all vanity. Therefore, he was far from the city and the crowds. He was not involved with people. He did not know the wisdom of life, how to be sociable with powerful people. He was modest in his ways, a pure upright man. His "simplicity" was known in town, and at times aroused laughter among the more sophisticated townsfolk. The Jewish population in the town was indeed large, but the number of rabbis and rebbes was more than average and more than needed. It is no wonder that almost all of them suffered from poverty and want.

He earned his livelihood in ways customary for all the rabbis, by selling candles for the Sabbath, yeast for challahs, and wine for Passover.

One Passover eve, the number of purchasers who came to the house of the Rabbi to purchase wine for the four cups was very large.

In the afternoon, the members of the household realized that the cask would soon be empty, so they added water to it.

Somehow, the Rabbi found out about this. Perhaps one of the grandchildren said something in his innocence. The Rabbi reproved the members of the household for this deed, for if the amount of water is over a certain amount, the blessing over the wine changes to *shehakol* from *borei pri hagafen*. The Jews would then be reciting a blessing in vain. He knew no rest all day. Is it possible that the members of his household had caused the masses to stumble, and he knew and would remain silent?

Such a thing must not be! He must inform them and warn them so that the masses will not stumble on the second Seder night. The congregation concluded the *Maariv* service in the synagogue. He ascended the bima and announced clearly and publicly that such a deed was perpetrated in his house without his knowledge, and one must be suspicious of a blessing in vain, it would be best if all those who purchased wine in the afternoon recite the *shehakol* blessing rather than *borei pri hagafen*, so as not to stumble in a sin, Heaven forbid.

This announcement aroused great laughter among the congregation. However, he, the Rabbi, breathed calmly. What did their laughter and mocking matter to him. He fulfilled his duty to his Maker and warned the masses lest they stumble in a blessing. He did what was required of him.

Yehuda Berkovitz

This was the person, and this was his way. He was the head of the Yeshiva for many years, and concerned himself with it. When they had to obtain a permit from the Polish authorities to open a Tarbut School in 1925, a meeting of parents was organized in the synagogue with the participation of the Polish supervisor. He, the Rabbi, addressed the students in the presence of the inspector, stating that they must be G-d fearing, upright Jews, that the boys will fulfil the commandments, and the girls will not go about with uncovered arms. The permit was granted.

Yosef Kashtan of blessed memory relates: When he came during his youth to the town of Radin to study in the Yeshiva of Rabbi Yisrael Meir Kagan, known as the Chofetz Chaim on account of his books (in Israel, there exists a Kibbutz by that name, run by Poalei Agudat Yisrael, on the route from the south to Gedera), the rabbi asked him from where he came. Y. K. responded, "From Horodok." At first,

[Page 174]

the Chofetz Chaim did not know which Horodok (for there were several towns in Lithuanian areas with that name). Y. K. told him that it was Horodok near Lakhva. The Chofetz Chaim then asked him "This is the Horodok where the honorable *Tzadik* Rabbi Dovidl lives?" That is how the Chofetz Chaim referred to Reb Dovidl the rabbi.

Reb Dovidl left behind a manuscript of Torah commentaries. After his death, his son Rabbi Yosef, who inherited his position, published the manuscript along with his own additions. He dedicated the publication to his unmarried sister Chana who died in her youth.

Translator's footnotes:

1. An obscure Talmudic reference based in the story in *Gittin* 56a.
2. Joshua 1:8.

The Rabbi Reb Dovidl

by A. Lahav (Lachovsky)

Translated by Jerrold Landau

The rabbi, Reb Dovid was the eldest son of the rabbi and Gaon Rabbi Avraham Dov Ber, may the memory of the holy be blessed, Berkovitz. He was born in the year 5609 [1849] and died on 30 Kislev 5696 [1935]. He was a combination of splendorous perfection and refined traditionalism. He was modest with people, and very particular that no eulogies be delivered after his death. He would review and study the entire Talmud and Mishna literally by heart. He never stopped his learning, even during his illness, until his last day. He would come to the *Beis Midrash* early, with great alacrity, before dawn and would remain there until a late hour of night, as he studied Gemara, halachic decisors, *tosafot*, and the early sages. From the time he came of age, he was never late for the time of reciting the *Shema* in the morning and the evening, and he never missed any communal prayer service. He would remain in the *Beis Midrash* all day studying, enwrapped in his *tallis*, and wearing his *tefillin*. He would intentionally afflict himself, and never ate anything aside from bread and milk. He did not sleep with a blanket other than on Sabbaths and festivals, when he would use something soft. He kept himself away from all pleasures of this world. He did not wear woven clothes out of fear of *shaatnez* [forbidden textile mixtures]. He was careful in both easy and difficult commandments. He was especially careful with the commandment of hosting guests. He was very careful not to speak any evil, gossip, or meaningless talk. On Sabbaths and festivals, he refrained from any excessive talk. Many related to him with love and honor. Even those who saw him from afar during their youth and did not fully appreciate him finally recognized his hidden, modest purity and splendor in his latter days, and honored him. He left behind novellae on the Talmud, Mishna, Maimonides, and responsa from many Gaonim of his generation with whom he maintained correspondence.

His main rabbi was his honorable father, the aforementioned rabbi and Gaon, who was the rabbi of the city of Lakhva near David-Horodok. He was educated under his influence and trained for giving halachic decisions. In the year 5650 [1890] he was appointed as rabbi in the nearby town, and he served as rabbi there until his final day. He left behind three children. The youngest, Rabbi Yosef, was appointed after him as the local rabbi. His oldest son Rabbi Yehuda moved to Canada in 1925, where he served as a *shochet* [ritual slaughterer]. He was an excellent prayer leader, as well as Torah reader and shofar blower.

His brother Rabbi Yitzchak Tzvi served as the rabbi in the city of Lakhva from the year 5659 [1899], when his father, the Gaon and *Tzadik* [righteous person], made *aliya* to the Holy Land along with his youngest son Rabbi Mordechai (the son-in-law of Rabbi Chaim Teitelbaum, who was the son-in-law of the true Gaon Rabbi Elazar Moshe Halevi Ish Horowitz, may the memory of the righteous be blessed, the head of the rabbinical court of Pinsk). Rabbi Mordechai died in Jerusalem. A large manuscript of Rabbi Avraham, which was never published, remains in the hands of his descendants in Jerusalem.

When I made *aliya* to the Land in the year 5685 (1925), and went to take leave of Rabbi David, he asked me to visit his brother, Rabbi Mordechai and ask him to make efforts to enable him to make *aliya* to the

Land. However, his brother lived here on charity, and it was not possible to arrange for his *aliya*. It is unfortunate that Rabbi David did not merit to see the Land, and was only able to dream of it from afar.

(From *Oholei Shem* edited by Sh. N. Gottlieb and the booklet *Chana David* by Rabbi Yosef the son of Rabbi David).

The father of Rabbi David and the brother of Rabbi Itche of Lakhva, the rabbi, Gaon and *Tzadik* Rabbi Avraham Dov Ber the son of Rabbi Yosef, may the memory of the righteous be blessed, was born in the year 5585 (1825) in our city David-Horodok to honorable, G-d fearing parents.

When he was a young child, the spirit of G-d began to resonate with him. The lad then began to abandon his folly, for he would become a Nazirite to the L-rd, and was created for greatness. He distanced himself from becoming friendly with children of his own age, and did not participate in their game and entertainment.

With his sublime talents and his vast diligence, this excellent child gained renown while he was still

[Page 175]

ten years old. At that time, he was examined by the mighty Gaon Rabbi Yaakov Meir Padwa, may the memory of the righteous be blessed, the head of the rabbinical court of Brisk, when he was in Pinsk at the time.

At the age of twelve, the desire for Kabbalistic studies was already aroused in his tender heart. One could often find that man-child studying with his full senses the Kabbalistic book *Eitz Chaim* by Rabbi Chaim Vital, may the memory of the righteous be blessed. At the age of fifteen, Kabbalistic study was already one of his regular lessons.

The lad continued to grow, and to complete himself with the revealed and hidden [i.e. mystical] Torah of G-d. Then he married the modest woman Beila-Chaya the young daughter of Rabbi Nachman Yaakov Lifshitz, may the memory of the righteous be blessed. She was a granddaughter from her mother's side of the famous person through all of Volhynia, known as Reb Hirsch Chasid, may the memory of the holy be blessed. He was supported at the table of his father-in-law, who loved Torah, for eighteen consecutive years. The father-in-law provided for all the needs of his scholarly son-in-law. Throughout that time, he never stopped studying day and night. Regarding the extent of his great diligence, the elders of that generation tell about the means he used to prevent sleep from overtaking him. When he would sit and study late at night, he would hold a lit candle between his fingers, close to the flame. In order to wake up early along with the members of the household, when he would lie down for his brief sleep, he would place the utensils most important to the members of the household close to his head – for alarm clocks did not yet exist in those days.

In the year 5619 [1859] he was accepted as rabbi in the city of Lakhva, where he served in the rabbinical post until the year 5659 [1899]. He bequeathed the rabbinic seat to his young son, Rabbi Itche. For many years, he had a strong desire to make *aliya* to the Land. In the year 5659 (1899), he was able to do so. He was 74 years old then, and was able to carry out his will despite his increasing weakness. All efforts by his children, friends, and the many people who held him in esteem to dissuade him from his journey came to naught. "If not now, when, and I am sure that the good G-d will bring me to my desired place in peace," was his brief, strong answer. On Tuesday, 2 Elul 5659 [1899], the *Tzadik* bade farewell to his rabbinical sons and the masses who held him in esteem who had gathered to receive his farewell blessing. At that time, those gathered beheld a wonderful sight for the last time: This weak, elderly man, who could barely get out of bed, suddenly girded his strength on the day of his journey, ran to the synagogues and *Beis Midrashes*, as in former days, and parted from the Torah scrolls with holy awe. He blessed all those gathered, every person with his relevant blessing, and according to the wishes of his heart for good. He set out in peace on his journey. He Who Fulfils the Will of Those Who Fear Him led him to our Holy City of Jerusalem in peace. However, to the sorrow of all those who revered him, and of his dear sons, he was summoned to the Heavenly Yeshiva one month from the day he arrived. He died on Wednesday, 28 Tishrei 5660 [1899] and was buried in honor at the heights of the Mount of Olives. May his merit protect us.

The rabbi made *aliya* to the Land with his son Reb Mordechai'le. Rabbi Mordechai was among those studied Torah in the Old City. He established a family in Jerusalem. A large manuscript by Rabbi Avraham Ber, may the memory of the righteous be blessed on halacha and exegesis, which he did not succeed in publishing, remains in the hands of his heirs.

(From *Oholei Shem*, edited by Sh. N. Gottlieb)

To the Wonderful Personality of Rabbi Avraham Yitzchak Koltin,
May the Memory of the Holy Be Blessed

by Yaakov Kolozny

Translated by Jerrold Landau

David-Horodok merited that Rabbi Avraham Yitzchak, *Der Malachl* [The Angel], may the memory of the righteous be blessed, was numbered among its great personalities, full of splendor and grace. He was known as *Der Malachl* in David-Horodok. That is his name and his memory, and that is what he was called by the Hassidim of Stolin and Karlin.

He was a noble personality, with his beard flowing down over his cloak. His eyes exuded purity, mercy, and tenderness. He had clear thought, a wonderful memory. He embraced the pillars of Torah and Talmud, and explained them simply and fundamentally. He endeared his listeners to their Creator through the means of "Love your neighbor as yourself."

The love of Israel and the love of G-d were his support pillars, upon which he sustained the People of Israel. Given this, he had to fulfil these morning and evening, day and night, as it is written: "When you sit in your house, when you go on a journey,

[Page 176]

when you lie down and arise."[1] It was through this path that Rabbi Avraham Yitzchak approached both the old and the young. His modesty knew no bounds. He was graced with fine traits. He was careful with his speech, and especially strict about quoting matters in the name of the person who said it, in order to bring redemption to the world.[2] He toiled in Torah, Talmud, rabbinic decisors, the early and latter sages, mussar [books on morality], and stories of *Tzadikim* [righteous people] – to explain them and elucidate them appropriately.

He learned and taught Torah for its own sake, in all its details and minutiae. His students always drew from this unfailing wellspring, which was the mouth that exuded pearls.

He was revered and honored without bound, by the young and the old, by the believer and the freethinker, by the Hassid and *Misnaged* all together. The pleasantness of his mannerisms, his manner of speaking, the sharpness of his intellect, and the clarity of his thoughts acquired for him friends of the soul, who were thirsty for the words of his mouth. One hundred fifty people in the synagogue of the Hassidim of Karlin and Stolin in David-Horodok would wait with holy awe until he concluded his silent *Shmone Esrei*, which he recited with feeling and deep devotion. The congregation of worshippers knew that it was not for naught that Rabbi Avraham Yitzchak took a long time for his prayers, both when he stood on his two aching feet and after they amputated one to save the second – he never changed from his custom, and he accepted his suffering with love. On Sabbath eves after the meal as well as on Saturday nights, the Hassidim of Karlin would gather with him. The melodies, hymns, and Hassidic stories would join together into a mighty spiritual force, to the point where materialism was overcome. The warmth, love, and brotherhood would burst forth from the house. All those who passed by would remain in their places, even on cold, frosty days. The following fact testifies to his greatness.

Once, when a crowd of Stolin Hassidim gathered for Rosh Hashanah – the *Yenuka* [Child],[3] may the memory of the righteous be blessed, approached Reb Yosef Kolozny of blessed memory and Reb Natan Gloiberman of blessed memory, and said to them: "With you are living fish with large heads. Why did you not bring them to me?" The innuendo was very clear: they were referring to Rabbi Avraham Yitzchak of blessed memory. During the latter days of the *Yenuka*, before he left for Frankfurt am Main, he asked Rabbi Avraham Yitzchak to come and bid farewell to him. Hassidic legend states that during that meeting, he informed Rabbi Avraham Yitzchak that he will not be returning from his journey. He even hinted to him which of his sons should serve in his stead.

He did not serve as prayer leader, due to his weakness, and also not to hold up the congregation. However, his rendition of *Akdamut*[4] before the congregation on Shavuot was unique. The congregation was standing, and was moved by the awe of his voice and the pleasure of his spirit. He would conclude this splendid song with deep enthusiasm, bursting forth with great faith in our Father in heaven and in the future of the Nation of Israel.

Rabbi Avraham Yitzchak underwent two difficult operations, one on his intestines and a second when they were forced to amputate his leg due to the cancer that had taken root there. They made an artificial leg for him. Thanks to Reb Ahrele, may the memory of the righteous be blessed, the son of the *Tzadik* Rabbi Yisrael of Stolin, Rabbi A. Y. was admitted to the largest Polish hospital. In an exceptional manner, he was permitted to bring kosher food with him. The joy in the city was great when he returned to Horodok after the successful surgery, and they arranged a large *kiddush* in his honor.

Three people concerned themselves with his livelihood and the sustenance of his family: Reb Yosef Kolozny, Reb Aharon Slominsky, may G-d avenge his blood, and Reb Natan Nota Gloiberman of blessed memory. When his granddaughter was with him, she used to cook for him. After she got married and moved to Luninets, Rachel Slominsky would cook his meals, and Reb A. Slominsky would bring them to him daily.

It was a great honor to bring him to the synagogue. Reb Hershel Molochnik, the son of Bina, was especially dedicated to this. He would leave his work and bring Rabbi A. Y. to the synagogue and then take him back to his home.

At the end, Rabbi A. Y. once again became ill with throat cancer. His situation was hopeless, and Rabbi Elimelech of Karlin, may the memory of the righteous be blessed, commanded to take bring him to Pinsk. Despite the good accommodations, the well-lit rooms, and the atmosphere at the home of Reb Yosef Bochtnik, of blessed memory, and despite the efforts of the local physicians, he did not recuperate. On Friday morning, his pure soul departed with severe suffering.

His death became known in Horodok via a telegram from Rabbi A. A. of Karlin, who requested that they come to participate in his funeral. However, people could not come on account of the distance.

[Page 177]

His final honors were given through the rabbi of Karlin, who carried his coffin, and did not permit anyone to swap with him. Thus did the wonderful, noble personality pass away.

Translator's footnotes:

1. From the *Shema*, Deuteronomy 6:7.
2. Based on *Pirkei Avot* 6:6.
3. Rabbi Yisrael Perlov became the leader of the Hassidim of Stolin-Karlin as a young child. The name *Yenuka* remained with him all his life.
4. A hymn recited on Shavuot prior to the Torah reading.

In Memory of Rabbi Avraham Yitzchak the Malach [Angel]

Translated by Jerrold Landau

Rabbi Avraham Yitzchak was a rare character. He served G-d with pure faith and fear of Heaven. He toiled and was diligent in Torah, and was an expert in Talmud and halachic decisors.

His influence in the synagogue of the Hassidim of Karlin and Stolin was very great. They would not begin the services without him. Even though he lived close to the synagogue, they used to call him and help him to come. He suffered greatly in his legs during his latter years, but he made the effort to come to the synagogue despite the great suffering that afflicted him.

He would follow a set order [of study] during the hours of the day and night. The *Beit Aharon* [1] was the candle at his feet, and he conducted himself according to it all his days.

Rabbi Avraham Yitzchak knew the greats of the generation very well, especially the Chofetz Chaim, may the memory of the righteous be blessed. When the Chofetz Chaim published his first book, and he made the rounds to disseminate the book, he also came to David-Horodok. He went to Rabbi Avraham Yitzchak and requested that he help him. Of course, he immediately agreed to his request. When they arrived at the home of Reb Asher the Scribe, the aroma of fresh bread that was being baked at that time in the home of the scribe wafted forth. The Chofetz Chaim, may the memory of the righteous be blessed, turned to Rabbi Avraham Yitzchak of blessed memory, and said: "Asher's bread shall be rich, and he shall yield royal dainties." [2]

Rabbi Avraham Yitzchak loved the Chofetz Chaim very much. He was effusive in his praise, and stressed the importance of conducting classes on the books of the Chofetz Chaim. The Stoliner Rebbe, Rabbi Yisrael, may the memory of the righteous be blessed, was effusive in his praise of Rabbi Avraham Yitzchak, and portrayed him as one of the great ones.

A sublime joy rested upon Rabbi Avraham Yitzchak on Sabbaths, festivals, and holidays. Even someone who saw him for the first time knew that this was no ordinary man in front of him but rather an angel in human form. He was often asked to pray for the ill. He was literally like a father to us, and his memory will never depart from us. It is unfortunate regarding those who are no more and are not forgotten. May his soul be bound in the bonds of eternal life.

Gershon Gloiberman

Rabbi Avraham Yitzchak was one of the Hassidim of Stolin. Nevertheless, he would always purchase a *shekel* [token of membership in the Zionist organization]. After he would purchase one, it was immeasurably easier to disseminate the *shekalim* in the town. He was not among the opponents of Zionism – as were most of the Hassidim, but he did express his concern that male and female youths were always gathering together. I succeeded in calming him by stating that "they" are acting properly.

Once, during an ordinary conversation, he told me a story about a Jew from Kharkov who spoke badly about the Land after he returned disappointed. When the Jew who left the Land died, they etched his name on the monument that he ordered. However, a bad odor emanated from that monument due to the bad report that he uttered about the Holy Land. That is what Rabbi Avraham Yitzchak told me.

A. Lachovsky

Translator's footnotes:

1. A Torah commentary by one of the Rebbes of Karlin.
2. From the blessing of Jacob to his sons, one of whom was Asher (Genesis 49: 20).

The *Maggid* Rabbi Shaul Dov

by Yeshayahu Magidovitz

Translated by Jerrold Landau

Many who came from our town as adults certainly remember Rabbi Shaul Dov the *Maggid* [itinerant preacher]. He was a man with a splendid countenance and a scholar. His name aroused honor and awe amongst the people of the town, including gentiles, because of his pure hands [i.e. honesty], great understanding of the paths of life, his loving relations to his fellows, his proper, good advice to anyone who requested [it], and his pleasant mannerism to anyone who approached him, as he eased the distress of anyone who turned to him.

On Sabbaths, festivals, and holidays, many of our townsfolk would gather in his regular *Beis Midrash*, in which his own

[Page 178]

Torah scroll stood in the Holy Ark, to listen and enjoy his wise words and explanations on the weekly Torah portion or the issues of the holy day. The audience would drink up his words with thirst.

His private life was very discreet. He satisfied himself with little, and the rest he donated and gifted to anyone in need. He would secretly give support to those in need.

All of his free time was dedicated to the service of G-d and the study of His holy Torah.

He earned his livelihood from the manufacture of homemade wine. He had great satisfaction and enjoyment from producing wine that was kosher for Passover, that the Jews could use to recite the *hagafen* blessing on the four cups. It was pure raisin wine. It was also used for *Kiddush* and *Havdalah*.

Many people of the town would stream to his house to purchase his wine that was excellent in quality and taste.

May his memory be a blessing.

Sara Ita Zager

by Chaim Kolozny

Translated by Jerrold Landau

She was one of the noble personalities of the town. Modesty and poverty were her hallmark through all the days. She was called "the blind." She would go around summer and winter with thick blue glasses on her eyes and nose. Through them, she could clearly see the needs of anyone in need of help and support. She would walk delicately, with a sack over her shoulders. She would go from door to door, taking from here and giving to there. She was a master of charity. When her strength weakened, the number of those in need increased, and she could not continue the daily rounds, she was very disappointed. She was doubly pained in that she knew that there was no replacement for her, and no emissary to fulfil her mission. When she found out in the winter that someone's oven was not lit, and the young children were freezing from the cold she would arise with the remainder of her strength, gather a wagon-full of wood, and bring it to them with warm blessings of encouragement.

Sara Ita was alone, widowed from her husband. However, she did not know loneliness. She was always involved with people, and rejoiced with all people regarding any mitzvah that came her way. She did so with all her limbs, to the point where she was always mumbling, arranging her plans almost aloud, responding with love and tenderness to all who were of bitter of spirit.

When the Sabbath or a festival came, all sorrow left her. She dressed in festive clothes and hastened to the synagogue to make her accounting with "He who spoke, and the world came to be." She presented all of her needy people before Him, asking that they no longer suffer want, Heaven forbid, and that they should not lack anything.

If there was a joyous celebration in the city, or Heaven forbid, a funeral or a fire, Sara Ita was among the first [to become involved], for she loved with her whole heart every Jewish person, young and old, rich or poor, simple or of great deeds. She would say that they all require mercy. She ignored the differences, and all were righteous in her eyes.

When *aliya* to the Land took place, she went to bid farewell to those making *aliya*. Her face was beaming, full of tenderness and warmth. She was jealous of those making *aliya*. Certainly, this was the only jealousy in her life.

She was a dear soul. Her entire life was dedicated to the public.

Passed Away in Israel

Rabbi Shneur Zalman Shapira,
May the Memory of the Holy Be Blessed

by Yaakov the Son of Yosef Kolozny

Translated by Jerrold Landau

When the Rabbi from Slonim, who had served in David-Horodok for many years, died, the householders and *gabbaim* [trustees] of the large *Beis Midrash* began to search for a replacement. At first, they brought the well-known Rabbi Hershkovitz to Horodok. However, after he spent two weeks in Horodok and noticed the cool relations toward him, he decided to leave the place, despite all

[Page 180]

the urgings that later came from the people of Horodok when they realized too late what type of an illustrious personality he was. It should be noted that Rabbi Hershkovitz was accepted as the rabbi of Frankfurt am Main.

The connoisseurs of Horodok relate that during the time that Rabbi Hershkovitz was in Horodok, Reb Shlomo Zagorodsky, one of the teachers of young children in Horodok, led the *Mincha* service on one of the weekdays and got mixed up. Rabbi Shlomo became shaken up and afraid, and could not calm down. When he was asked later what happened, he returned, "A strong deep fire," pointing to the place where Rabbi Hershkovitz was standing, "is present before my eyes." After a brief time, Rabbi Shneur Zalman Shapira, may the memory of the holy be blessed, the rabbi of Olshany near Vilna, came to serve as the rabbi in Horodok. He continued his role until the outbreak of the last war.

His first speech in the large *Beis Midrash*, which was filled to the brim, made a deep impression. It was a grandiloquent speech, full to the brim with heartwarming parables, Torah, and wisdom, all blended together. It should not noted that Rabbi Shapira of blessed memory was the first and only Zionist rabbi in Horodok. He was affiliated with *Mizrachi* [religious Zionist movement], and was very active in the field of Zionism.

He was tall, with penetrating eyes, a sharp mind, a warm heart, and was alert to everything that was taking place in the city. He was active and urged others to be active. He taught and educated, and fought strongly without playing favorites. He made himself available to everyone, religious and secular, Zionists and haters of Zion. Through his sharp explanations and reasoning, he would exert his influence based on the verse, "The Glory of Israel does not lie." [I Samuel 15: 29].

He was very active, and even stood at the helm of various institutions and organizations: *Keren Hayesod* [Foundation Fund] and *Keren Kayemet* [Jewish National Fund], the committee for the Yeshivot, the charitable fund, the orphans' committee, and various social institutions. He was always an example, and never refused to collect money for all types of needy people.

As a spiritual shepherd, he succeeded through his great influence in instituting the study of Gemara in the Tarbut School of Horodok. Despite all his efforts in civic matters, he himself served as the Gemara teacher, and succeeded, though his great devotion, in laying the foundations of the Oral Torah within the walls of the school.

[Page 181]

He preached Zionism from the synagogue pulpit. Thanks to that, the religious people drew near to Zionism. He was sent on missions outside of Horodok on behalf of the *Mizrachi* headquarters, and he delivered enthusiastic speeches on behalf of Zionism and the Land.

In his public appearances, he was almost the only one who appeared on behalf of the community on the national holidays of Poland, or during a visit of a Polish religious personality or the Minister of Education. He would deliver a benediction on behalf of the Jews of Horodok. He was also the official rabbi recognized by the authorities.

He would draw hearts close, despite the conflicts between *Misnagdim* and Hassidim. He would go the synagogue of the Hassidim of Karlin and Stolin on the nights of Passover to recite *Hallel* with the congregation, and he would also go there to participate in the *hakafot* [Torah processions] on Shemini Atzeret.[1] He would also go on Chanukah to take part in the celebration of the release from jail of the rabbi and *Tzadik* Rabbi Shneur Zalman of Liadi, may the memory of the holy be blessed.[2] On Simchat Torah, the Hassidic community would come to Rabbi Shapira for the *Kiddush* that he hosted in their honor. When the Admorim of Karlin and Stolin would visit Horodok, Rabbi Shapira would visit them, and they would pay a reciprocal visit.

Thus did he serve in honesty, faith, and uprightness as the renowned rabbi of Horodok. He led his flock as a merciful father who shields from issues – until the war broke out.

When the government of Horodok passed to the Soviets, Rabbi Shapira remained there for about two weeks. When Vilna was given over to the Lithuanians, he decided to go there with his wife in order to be closer to the Land of Israel.

On the final Saturday night before he left Horodok, the people of the city gathered to bid him farewell. Nachman Blizhovsky of blessed memory accompanied him to the Luninets station. He later said that when one of the Soviet commissars asked him who was traveling, and what were the books he had with him, he responded, "He is a lawyer, and the books are books of law and jurisprudence."

He remained in Lithuania for about three months. When he received a certificate [for *aliya*] from the *Mizrachi* headquarters, he made *aliya* to the Land in an airplane along with his wife.

He lived in the Land for about ten years until he became ill and suffered greatly. He maintained his stance thanks to his only son and daughter-in-law who supported him and helped him during his illness.

Rabbi Shapira died on 8 Tammuz 5708 [1948] during the siege of Jerusalem in the War of Independence. He was brought to burial in the holy city of Jerusalem under a barrage of bullets and shells.

The natives of Horodok in the Land were unable to give him his final honor. The spiritual personality passed away, alone and isolated, but his memory will never depart from the midst of the natives of our city.

Translator's footnotes:

1. The recitation of *Hallel* on Passover nights as part of *Maariv*, and the conducting of *Hakafot* on Shemini Atzeret night, are customs that are observed by Hassidim and the *Nusach Sephard* rite, but not by the Ashkenazic rite.
2. The actual date of this Hassidic celebration is on 19 Kislev, one week before Chanukah.

Reb Shimon the Son of Reb Chaim Leib Ronkin,
May the Memory of the Holy Be Blessed

[by Rabbi Techoresh][i]

Translated by Jerrold Landau

Reb Shimon Ronkin of blessed memory was a resident of Schunat Shapira neighborhood [a neighborhood of Tel Aviv] for several years. He died in the year 5693 [1938]. He was a scholar, upright in his ways, modest and humble, and very pleasant to his fellow man. He taught Torah in public in that neighborhood, and conducted classes in *Ein Yaakov* and Mishna. He even led them in a personal manner, with fine explanations that were easy to understand. He instilled in the hearts of his listeners the pure spirit of G-d, the love of the Land, and the love of Israel.

The worshippers of the central synagogue in Schunat Shapira and the neighborhood invited him to serve in a holy capacity there, but they did not relate to him as a *shamash* [beadle], but rather as a spiritual guide, and rabbi and a teacher. They absorbed from him a full dose of Torah, fear of Heaven, and proper conduct, all with the dedication to the Land of Israel and its upbuilding.

Rabbi Techoresh, the rabbi of the neighborhood, honored him greatly. Alongside with his holy service in the synagogue, the rabbi included him in his spiritual work, and consulted with him on all issues of the neighborhood.

[Page 182]

Reb Shimon was happy for the privilege of being able to live in the Holy Land. He was always smiling, and we never saw him angry.

He also had an influence upon the youth. He taught them, guided them, and served as a father and patron to anyone who approached him. He related to all of them with affection and a loving spirit.

Reb Shimon was a central personality in the neighborhood, injecting Torah and spiritual life and enthusiasm into the synagogue. He maintained the order and influenced the worshippers, who accepted his instructions willingly, since everyone honored and revered him.

He died at an old age. Rabbi Techoresh eulogized him with heartfelt feelings, stressing that the neighborhood had suffered a great loss, and that he himself had lost his right hand.

The neighborhood erected a memorial for him in the synagogue.

With his purity and uprightness, Reb Shimon Ronkin was a father and an example for the previous generation. Woe for the person lost who will not be forgotten.

May his soul be bound in the bonds of eternal life.

Coordinator's footnote:

i.   The author's name was in the Table of Contents, but was not included with this article.

Rafael Shafer of Blessed Memory
(On the Thirtieth Anniversary of His Passing)

by Ch. B.

Translated by Jerrold Landau

He was one of the first activists of the Third Aliya in Poland, from the splendid era of the Land of Israel offices in the Diaspora. He was active in their organization and activities. He fulfilled important roles in their leadership until the destruction and the Holocaust.

He was born in David-Horodok in 1892 and began his Zionist activity as a teacher in the district school. However, he did not find satisfaction in the life of the town, so he went to Warsaw after the World War. In 1921, he started his activities in the arena of *aliya*, as the director of the division of information at the central office of the Land of Israel in Warsaw. He did a great deal in organizing mass *aliya* from Poland via Romania. He concerned himself with the groups of *olim* [immigrants to the Land of Israel] and in improving their conditions of travel to the Land. In 1925, he was appointed as director of the central office of the Land of Israel in Warsaw. He served in that difficult role until the outbreak of the Second World War, and into the Nazi occupation period, until no further chance remained for people to save themselves and make *aliya* to the Land.

He went to Vilna in 1940 along with a group of Zionist activists, and remained in contact with the Land and the representatives of the *aliya* office in Kushta [Constantinople], until there was no longer a path toward *aliya*. He then made *aliya* through a tortuous route and arrived in the Land, while his family went out with the last *olim* from Trieste.

He did not rest when he arrived in the Land. He immediately went to Tehran to organize the *aliya* of Polish refugees who went from Russia to Persia, so that they could reach the gates of the Land. The era of the rescue *aliya* via Persia demanded efforts and organizational talents, with negotiations with high level foreign governments. There, he found an arena to work on great things. He was a man of *aliya* even after he returned from Tehran. He devoted all his energy and talents to work for the rescue committee, which was one of the pillars of his activity.

With the founding of the State of Israel, he was appointed as director of the supervisory division of the Ministry of the Interior. He contributed greatly to instilling order and methodology in the work of the local committees in the area of budget. Through this, he came in contact with the state audit office, and was appointed to an important organizational committee therein. In the final year, 1955, he was accepted unanimously as the auditor of the city of Tel Aviv, with all its divisions and activities. He founded and directed the audit office of that city, and was able to produce a report of his activities, which was accepted with great appreciation.

[Page 183]

In the final year, he was afflicted with a difficult illness, that he was no longer able to withstand. Even during his illness, he did not stop concerning himself with the oversight of the audit office that he had set up and founded with great effort and talent.

With his death, the personage of a faithful activist of the Third Aliya, from its beginning to its end, was taken from us. He went through all of its difficulties and adventures. He was one of those who held the helm in stormy Polish Jewry until its destruction. He did not rest or remain quiet, as he assisted and saved thousands of people until they came to the Land.

Blessed is his memory for all those who knew him.

Rafael Shafer of Blessed Memory

by M. Gurari

Translated by Jerrold Landau

His life was full of plots and decorated with deeds. From a young age, the train of his life galloped through many stations, barely stopping. As an extern in his native city of David-Horodok, his desire for education led him to far-off Moscow. Then came the period of the First World War, and Shafer was caught up in the Russian army, and from there, he became a German prisoner. When he returned from captivity, he pitched his tent in Warsaw. As he sat in its schools, he transferred from the language of enslaving Russia to the language of liberated Poland. These schools served as magnets for the youths who desired knowledge. Indeed, until his thoughts went from potential to actuality, he occupied himself in teaching Hebrew and turned his attention to the area of activism and civil service. He then started working at the office of the Land of Israel. When he was only 30 years old, the leadership of Zionism was placed in his hands, as he directed the office of the Land of Israel in large Jewish centers of Europe.

That office was no ordinary office, with limited and measured activity, a measured and balanced budget, and with work set out in an orderly fashion. His incarnations were many and extreme. The desire for *aliya* in the midst of the Jews of Poland burst forth strongly. Those who were failing in the enchantment of redemption, and those who were persecuted by tribulations would knock on the door of the office to request salvation and assistance. Then, the office would buzz like a beehive from the sound of the crowd of *olim* and the bustle of those accompanying them, and from the tumult of those making *aliya* "by force" and their recommenders, coming and going, making noise and causing noise; and from the bustle and businesses of hundreds of officials, issuing directions and instructions as attendants at the central station.

However, there were also cases when the gates of the Land were locked with seven locks, and the key was in the hands of the British masters of the Land. Or there was a serious crisis – political or economic – afflicting the Land, and the hearts of the *olim* hesitated as to whether it might be best to defer *aliya* until the wrath passed. Then the office of the Land of Israel stood cold and bored, with nobody visiting, nobody coming and nobody going. The hustle and bustle quieted. The workers were bare and empty-handed. Their splendor departed, as leaves before the autumn.

Shafer of blessed memory led it through the waves of the storm, and he did not let his ship descend to despair and helplessness. Degradation did not afflict him, and pride did not entice him. He saw into the distant horizons as a clear-sighted captain, as he guarded the kernel of the faithful and talented staff.

Shafer's appearance was something of the landscape of his native Polesye, like a branch of a firmly rooted tree: wide-boned, with a large head, as if he were planted upon his soil. He had a heavy step, lifting a foot and putting it down, lifting and putting down. His speech was like his appearance: with broad folios, wide-branched, and picturesque. As he spoke, a mischievous smile appeared between his eyes, as sunrays between the clouds. Therefore, his appearance was so convincing, and his words were heeded in the offices of the Polish government, at the consulates, and at the emigration institutions. Shafer did not stand at the doors of the rulers as an emissary of a poor, persecuted nation. Rather, he represented those who sent him with honor and strength.

[Page 184]

Thus was Rafael Shafer there in Warsaw in the midst of his nation, the Jewish nation of Poland.

When the eagle descended on European Jewry, and Polish Jewry was its prey, Shafer's world darkened. Nevertheless, he succeeded in escaping from the Nazi dragon and arriving in the land of his desires along with a group of Zionist leaders. However, he no longer found rest. He was apparently cut off from Polish Jewry, from which he had drawn his life force. His body became shriveled and bent, his face grayed, and the sparkle of his eyes dimmed. With immeasurable dedication, he placed all his energy in the rescue activities of the Jewish Agency. The Jewish Agency sent him on a mission to head the Land of Israel office in Tehran, which served at that time, during the Second World War, as an important transit station for saving Jewish refugees who had escaped from Poland and Russia. Apparently, the contact with brands plucked from the fire of the abyss[1] fanned the flames of his soul. However, the fire was quickly extinguished. He found no rest. The tragic fate of Polish Jewry did not escape him.

When the state was established, Shafer left the Jewish Agency, to which he had be bound with all the stands of his soul for more than twenty-five years. He went to follow after his teacher and master, Yitzchak Greenbaum, who served as the first Minister of the Interior of the State of Israel. Even there, the hammer did not meet its anvil. The severed branch was no longer able to strike roots.

It seemed that he had found his place for some time in the audit office. It was as if his wings opened up again to a bridge between the glorious past and the secure, busy present. However, his heart became a nest of worms. When he left the national audit office to serve as the auditor of the city of Tel Aviv, I asked him, "What indeed does your soul seek?" "My soul seeks my Jews; it seeks, but I do not find them…" And tears poured from his dimmed eyes.

The train of the life of Shafer of blessed memory galloped along, and did not slow down when it reached a remote station. Rather, it galloped on straight to the crossing of the border of life. It was not for Shafer to become bored or stagnate in a stop that he had no desire for. His life was woven as a book with much tension and a heavy plot; and when it reached pages that were devoid of plot, several pages turned at once, as a reader seeking a plot turns through pages devoid of meaning.

Even before he managed to become a burden upon himself, the redemption of death came upon him. May his soul be bound in the bonds of eternal life.

Translator's footnote:

1. Based on Zechariah 3:2.

About the Death of Yehuda Kashtan
(On the *Sheloshim* – Thirty-Day Anniversary of His Death)

by Tz. Rosenstein

Translated by Jerrold Landau

How can I lift up my words, for they are too poor to express the depth of sorrow in the heart of his many friends over his untimely death. For we all loved Yehuda Kashtan, the good, the noble and refined spirit.

He did not conduct himself in a grandiose style. He did not deliver speeches or write articles. He was modest, and conducted his work quietly. He did not wish to stand out, "to capture a place." With all this he stood out with his generous traits, pleasant mannerisms, upright heart, natural folksiness, and simple charm. It was good to be in his home, the home of Yehuda and Beila Kashtan, may she live long. Great warmth emanated from their home. How great was the cordiality that enveloped anyone who entered.

For us, the people of the Land of Israel who went to Poland for *Hechalutz* [The Pioneer] matters, the home of Yehuda and Beila Kashtan in Warsaw was like a home of the Land of Israel, through the Hebrew that was fluent on the mouths of the entire family, through the songs of the Land of Israel, popular and Hassidic tunes, and the Zionist atmosphere that pervaded there. I will always remember the grace of Yehuda and Beila's home, which calmed the hearts that were perturbed by communal affairs.

Even in Poland, he was close in spirit to the Workers in the Land of Israel movement. He joined the party of the Workers in the Land of Israel, in which he saw the primary force for the upbuilding of the Land.

[Page 185]

Yehuda was a Zionist and a Hebraist from his early youth. He was well grounded in fundamental Hebrew culture. He started out as a Hebrew teacher in our town, David-Horodok of Polesye. He continued working in the field of *aliya* until his last year. At first in the Land of Israel office in Warsaw, where he served as the secretary for many years. In its time, the office of the Land of Israel in Warsaw was the largest *aliya* office in the Diaspora. Myriads of *olim* [immigrants to the Land of Israel] passed through it, and very many of them remember to this day the loving care of Y. Kashtan, his great patience, and his pleasant countenance. He was happy when he could help someone in a practical manner, giving good advice.

After he made *aliya* to the Land at the beginning of the World War, he joined the *aliya* office of the Jewish Agency, at first in Haifa and later in Jerusalem. He fulfilled responsible roles. He worked with dedication and all his energy, for he saw his life's mission in this work. He had an alert eye and saw many things, including those that oppressed his spirit greatly. Nevertheless, he was not a man of war, and he did not know how to fight strongly, neither in communal matters nor in his personal affairs. He only knew how to pour out the bitterness of his heart in the ears of friends.

When many of his friends found out that Yehuda suffered from a heart disease, they were surprised: the quiet Yehuda, with such a pleasant disposition, was apparently not inclined to get angry, and never lost his temper – how could he have a heart disease? It was perhaps because of this, because his choked off the pain very deep in his heart, that his heart was damaged and slowly but surely became burnt.

Yehuda Kashtan of Blessed Memory
(On the *Sheloshim* – Thirty-Day Anniversary of His Death)

by Y. Ritov

Translated by Jerrold Landau

He was born on 29 Kislev 5655 [1895] in David-Horodok in Polesye, Russia – that same Polesye that played such a great, significant role in the upbuilding of our Land. It was that area that gave us Chaim Weizmann! It was its cities and towns – chief among them Pinsk and Brisk – that gave us the best human resources for Zionism, and the first of the finest of the pioneering movement and the movement for the Workers in the Land of Israel.

Life was bitter in desolate, impoverished Polesye, a region of broad bogs. The land was weak, and its entire body was bleak. Its people struggled hard for their existence. The battle for existence of the Jewish population of Polesye was sevenfold difficult. However, that battle forged and consolidated a sublime type of folksy Jew, who loved work, was diligent in deeds, was wise and understanding, pure of heart, following the straight path, and seeking Torah and knowledge. In this area of settlement, there were many farmers. There were Jewish farmers, among the few in the Diaspora.

Vibrant, strong, and broad spiritual and communal life flowed forth from Jewish Polesye. There were great rabbis of Israel there. Some were the leaders of *Misnagdim* [non-Hassidic people] – illustrious scholars, those who could uproot mountains – and others were Hassidic Rebbes. There were revolutionaries of renown there – from the cream of the crop of the Bund and other Socialist parties. There were various ideological streams, but Zionism took the top place. The longing for Zion, redemption, and pure life of labor on the soil of the Hebrew homeland burst forth and rose up above all the voices and ideas. Polesye was a fortress of Zionism, pioneering, and the Hebrew language.

In one of the veteran Jewish settlements of this Polesye, excellent in its folksiness and grace of dedication – in David-Horodok – Yehuda Kashtan was born and raised, with the handsomeness of his appearance, nobility of his soul, sweetness of his melody. His diligence and excellence in studies conquered all hearts. His city was honored because of him and proud of him, for he brought it great renown. He was a basket full of books,[1] fluent in Hebrew, and he knew how to express himself in that language with the fullness of its rich bounty. He absorbed all the Jewish values. He was an enthusiastic Hassid and, above all, a Zionist and a pioneer.

He moved to Stolin during his youth, where he married his friend Beila, may she live. He worked in teaching, and was quickly appointed as principal of the Tarbut School. To this day, his students recall with awe and love their time of studying in that school which he led and where he taught. Hebrew teachers and educators

[Page 186]

in Poland placed special hope in him. However, his period of teaching did not last long. When they were searching a "person of growth, of which there are few," an active Zionist, fluent in the Hebrew language, who works diligently and is pleasant in his mannerisms to serve as secretary of the central Land of Israel office in Warsaw, they found none better than Yehuda – the young man, modest and humble, eschewing fame and honor, doing his work for Zionism and pioneering, and disseminating Torah to the Jewish children in a remote corner of far-off Polesye.

He moved with his family to Warsaw and built his home there. This was the only Hebrew speaking home in Warsaw, with its 350,000 Jews. They only spoke Hebrew: both the parents and the children. A good spirit, the spirit of the additional soul, pervaded in that house. The home was a gathering point for wise people, writers, activists, pioneers, and regular fine Jews descended from fine Jews.

Y. Kashtan was a sort of institution in his own right in the office of the Land of Israel. He was an "institution" of grace, kindness, and love of his fellow man. Myriads upon myriads of candidates for *aliya* would frequent the office of the Land of Israel in Warsaw. They would come there, and mull about with noise and commotion – refugees from Russia and Ukraine, pioneers, regular people from all corners of Poland, Zionist activists – they were *olim*; every *oleh* is also an "immigrant" – a wandering person, uprooted from their land of origin and not yet rooted in the new land. The people were perplexed and nervous, with heavy spirits and hearts. They were searching for a good and helpful person – and they found such with the "institution" whose name was – Yehuda Kashtan. Masses of *olim* – residents of Israel – remember the man Kashtan with trembling and reverence. They remember his heartwarming relationships, his humaneness, and the bountiful help that he offered them.

At the beginning of the Second World War, Kashtan succeeded in escaping Nazi Warsaw together with his family. He made *aliya* to the Land and settled in Jerusalem, where he was immediately accepted as the secretary of the *aliya* department of the Jewish Agency.

From the day of his arrival in Jerusalem he blended in fully with the spiritual landscape. He became an inseparable part of the supernal Jerusalem. He knew all the recesses of the city. He frequented the communal gathering cases, the neighborhoods, and the synagogues, where he would from time to time reveal precious spiritual treasures – reveal them and disseminate them in public.

He was a faithful member of the Workers in the Land of Israel party.

The personage of splendor and glory, full of light, wisdom, and love, has disappeared. May his soul be bound in the bonds of the life of the nation and its land.

Translator's footnote:

1. This is a rabbinic, expression in Aramaic meaning: a man full of learning.

Yehuda Kashtan of Blessed Memory,
the Teacher During the Years 1916–1917

by Gloiberman

Translated by Jerrold Landau

The teacher from whom I gained a great deal of knowledge in Hebrew language and grammar, Bible, and the new Hebrew literature – was Y. Kashtan.

He was a never-ending wellspring of stories from the Talmud, Midrash, and other books, through which he captured our hearts. We sat bound to the table as he told us all sorts of stories in his innocence, and we listened with great intention. He did not know of administering beatings, as did the other *melamdim* [teachers]. Rather, he disseminated Torah and education.[1] He knew how to guide us and educate us with a proper methodology. He would give us "good" and "excellent" marks. He conducted a physical education class in military order. He would work wonders with his students. One does not even need to speak about quiet, talented lads, for he also did so with those of lesser ability.

When they informed me at home that my teacher would be the aforementioned teacher – I was very pleased, for my brother and sister had already been his students. I doubt that today one could find a teacher such as him who is so dedicated to the good of his students.

He did not just accept any child. He chose. I studied with him in 1916/17. Our progress in all areas was noticeable from week to week and from month to month. It is possible to say that the work of his hands was splendid. It is unfortunate that I did not study with him more than I did.

Translator's footnote:

1. In these two sentences, the Hebrew word for administering (a beating), and disseminating (Torah and education) is exactly the same. The play on words is lost in the translation.

[Page 187]

The Rabbi Reb Avraham Yitzchak
May His Soul Rest in Paradise

by Yosef Kashtan

(From the *Tipusim* [Personalities] Series)

Translated by Jerrold Landau

Indeed, our sages of blessed memory had stated, "the block of land is one."[1] This means the same as "there is the same thing in the pond as in the sea." This is the imprint of the "coin" – the Jewish essence – that is based upon the religion of Moses and Israel, and that is forged from one imprint, single and unique, complete and all-encompassing, the imprint of the Torah of Israel, its tradition, laws, statutes, customs, and minutiae that have been preserved with a full guarding as they have been transferred from fathers to children, from generation to generation. It includes heaps of fences and protections. That form has been crystallized with sparkling, shiny precious stones. It encompasses the entire Jewish people in its Diaspora,

and envelops every Jewish person from the time they emerge to the air of the world until the day of their passing from it – including those days themselves. It is everything and includes everything, including even Jews who sin – with the exception of those who curse the hearth that forged them, those who rebel against the covenant – they lived and live their lives within that reality.

Indeed, such is apparently the case: There is nothing in Brisk and Pinsk other than that which is in Trisk and Minsk, and there is nothing in Luk and David-Horodok other than that which is in Slutsk and Kozhan-Horodok: synagogues, *Beis Midrashes* here and there, and, to differentiate [between the holy and secular] bathhouses in all those places. There were rabbis, cantors, and *shamashim* [beadles] as well as musicians in all those places. There were circumcisions, *pidyon habens* [ceremonies of redemption of the firstborn], engagements and marriages, Sabbaths, festivals, and holidays, *cheders* and modern *cheders*, butchers and wagon drivers, merchants and tradespeople, old and new cemeteries, all sorts of groups, etc. etc. Absolutely everything was apparently such.

(This section, the beginning of the article of appreciation of the "Malach" [Angel] the rabbi Reb Avraham Yitzchak, may he rest in paradise, which was designated for the David-Horodok Book – has been found in the estate of Reb Yosef Kashtan, may his memory be blessed. To our great sorrow, he did not merit to finish it.)

Translator's footnote:

1. A Talmudic statement (Kiddushin 27b) meaning that a block of disconnected fields is considered as a single unit, so if one takes possession of one field of the block, the act of taking possession applies to the entire block of fields that was contracted for.

In Memory of Reb Yosef
the Son of Noach Kashtan of Blessed Memory

by Ch. Kolozny

Translated by Jerrold Landau

Yosef the son of Reb Noach and Tzira Kashtan, beloved and revered, with the alert and warm heart, was cut off in an untimely manner – the man died before his time.

Who was Yosef, and what was his power? What was his unique charm and grace?

He gained a love of Torah and his fellow man, reverence for those who study Torah as well as the "Tehillim reciter,"[1] to those who rise early and go to sleep late -- from his Hassidic educator, the rabbi Reb Avraham Yitzchak the "Malach" of blessed memory.

From his teacher, the sage of the generation, the Chofetz Chaim, may the memory of the holy be blessed, of Radun, he received the fundamentals of diligence, of delving deep into the sea of Talmud, and for studying Torah for its own sake.

From the Hassidim of Stolin, he absorbed Hassidic enthusiasm in all its manifestations – in prayer, in style of worship, and in melody.

From drawing close to educators and teachers, he raised himself to an elevated level – in generous traits and sublime manners, which not every person merits to obtain.

The regular conversation of Yosef of blessed memory was in Torah style, etched and embedded in the heart, spiced and woven with ideas of uprightness, propriety, and nobility.

His mannerisms were pleasant. He was a true friend, lighting up the faces of people and encouraging and assisting them in times of trouble.

His flaming soul, which knew the mystery of devotion; his Hassidic songs and melodies that were taken from the world of music;

[Page 188]

imbued with a spirit of enthusiasm, sublimity, and unity. As he would sing pleasantly, everyone was attracted to him, and the song and prayer burst forth like the waves of the sea, thanks to the great conductor, the possessor of extra spirit, sublime and lofty – forged drop by drop and decorated with emerald stones.

Anyone who had the merit of being his student will never forget his Torah, his lessons, his explanations and commentaries. With the faith he had for Zion and the Hebrew language, he nurtured and educated his many students to believe, like him, in the return of the nation to Zion and the revival of the language of the homeland.

He was one of the first in his native city of David-Horodok to lay the cornerstone of the Hebrew school, the Zionist youth, and those who rebel against the exile and servitude.

He merited to make *aliya* to the Land and to be among those who actualized. Despite everything he did not complain, but rather bore with love all the difficulties in taking possession of the Land.

Yosef of blessed memory entered the community of teachers, and later he took on the task of secretary of the teachers. He served there for thirty years and accomplished great things in a discreet manner.

With the death of Yosef, we, the family of David-Horodok natives in the Land, lost not only a friend, comrade, and teacher, but rather a personality – he was for us an embodiment of "and every difficult thing shall be brought to Joseph."[2]

Despite all the things keeping him busy, Yosef knew how to place himself at the disposal of the committee of the David-Horodok natives, and to help the survivors of the last war in Russia with all his energy and purity of heart. He supported them, assisted them, and encouraged them.

At gatherings and memorial events, he knew how to express the pain, agony, and general loss, and he always found words of comfort.

With his death, one of the fine, wonderful sons of David-Horodok was taken from us and from the synagogue of the Stolin and Karlin Hassidim. He was burnt by the flame of his soul, consumed by the flame of love and dedication to his fellow man.

He was young and fresh in his spirit and appearance. He was always full of life, brimming with energy, and was a leader in initiative. He was pleasant mannered, beloved and loving. He was a "basket full of books," full of content. He was both modest and a fighter.

The community of David-Horodok natives in the Land has been bereaved, and we have no comfort. The spokesman and guide of the family of David-Horodok natives has disappeared.

The sorrow is great, and the pain is plentiful. Along with his family, his wife – our exemplary friend – his dear children, and thousands of acquaintances and friends, we weep over the loss of Yosef, the dear man.

"Woe over this wonderful person who has been swallowed by the ground."

May his memory be blessed!

Translator's footnotes:

1. A term for a pious but relatively uneducated Jew, who spends his time reciting Psalms [Tehillim] rather than delving into Talmudic studies. The term can be derogatory, but here it seems to refer to an ordinary simple Jew.
2. An interesting combination of Exodus 18:22 (referring to Jethro telling Moses that all difficult matters should be brought to him), and Pharaoh's instruction to the people of Egypt to go to Joseph and listen to anything he said (Genesis 41:55).

From the Mourning Gathering at "The House of the Teacher" on the Seventh Day After His Passing

by Dov Yelin

Translated by Jerrold Landau

Dr. B. Ben-Yehuda, the principal of the Herzliya Gymnasium in Tel Aviv:

A friend and comrade of mine has died. I was in the home of the deceased for a few minutes about an hour and a half after he passed away. Relatives usually express their grief with tears and screams. Friends control and suppress their grief, but it is no less deep. For me and a few others, Kashtan of blessed memory was an exemplary friend. I knew him for the entire thirty years that he worked at the institution. I recall the day he started work at the institution. He understood himself, knew his place, and attracted our hearts. I believe I do not err if I state that the office of teachers in Tel Aviv that started that day, in a tiny room, using handwriting for there was not any office equipment, and has now become a significant office in Tel Aviv – can be attributed greatly to Kashtan of blessed memory.

He was only 59 years old when he was taken from us. How much did he desire to work and how he worked with love! Why was he taken from us in an untimely fashion? It is customary to say: A loss that has no replacement. Certainly, someone will be found to direct the office in Tel Aviv and lead it forward; but here was lost a precious combination of realities, the likes of which is hard to find. He was a scholar who honored scholars. He did not tolerate ignorance. He was refined, and he attracted our hearts with his refinement. I remember

[Page 189]

his handwriting, for there were not yet any typewriters. His flyers to the schools were works of craftmanship. He loved flowery language, out of a desire not to be cheap. At times it seemed to us, especially the younger of us, that this was something the time of which had passed. We requested that he write his communications in dry office language. However, his desire to express something nice and fine stood out in every letter of his. His style was not confusing, lacking relevance, or hasty.

Kashtan of blessed memory was a throwback to a noble era. He was honest in a unique fashion. This does not mean that he was unaware of the chicanery within human relations. However, he loved to prove his stance, and his reproof was always pleasant.

Another rare phenomenon with us should be noted. A talented man, a Torah scholar, sat in one place for thirty years. He did not wander or search for ways to ascend the rungs of the group. How great is our need to value this matter in our time. How much are we accustomed to searching for fortunes in new positions. This man spent thirty years in a single place. He started young, and died while still standing guard.

The loss of a man such of this is very sad. A blend such as this in a single person is a rare find. Today, we have technical tools: typewriters, telephones, offices. All this assures greater productivity. However, the question arises: is it not possible for a person today, in this state of technical productivity, to become lost in the meantime? With the death of our friend Kashtan of blessed memory, each of us feels as if a portion of ourselves died. May his memory be blessed.

A Memorial to the Departed

Yosef Kashtan of Blessed Memory (on the Seventh Day of His Passing)

by Yaakov Rimon

Translated by Jerrold Landau

He was a scholar and a fatherly figure, alert, pure, and heartwarming. He had a noble spirit and a refined soul. He was a true friend. His eyes lit up to every person, and he knew how to share in their pain and difficulties. He was a fighter from the soul, and knew the secret of devotion. He was a Renaissance man, with generous traits. He was humble in mannerisms, and pleasant in all his ways. He was a friendly man, who knew how to speak and urge others to speak. His love of his fellow man was boundless. He demanded much from himself and others.

I met him at conventions and parties, and I knew from up close the purity of his spirit and goodness of his heart. He was a master of rhetoric. His speeches were full of charm, and were listened to with attention and full seriousness, for the man was serious and a deep thinker.

He was a Stoliner Hassid. We enjoyed listening to his sweet Hassidic melodies at all festival parties. Everyone followed along as Yosef sang pleasantly. He revealed himself as a conductor of a large choir, with his face beaming and smiling. He was like a man living in the world of the spirit.

He worshipped in the synagogue of the Stoliner Hassidim on the morning of the bitter day when death suddenly overtook him. He studied a chapter of Mishna for the elevation of the soul of his brother Yehuda Kashtan. He chatted innocently before he said goodbye to the congregation of worshipers. "I will retire in another six years, and I will come to you regularly to worship and study." On a weekday night, one could find Yosef Kashtan standing in a corner of Heichal Hatalmud,[1] listening to a class on *Mussar* [Jewish morality]. He set times for the study of Torah, and astounded the congregation with the study of *Midrash Rabba*. His pleasant explanations excited his audience.

He was a good friend and true brother to all of us. He was dedicated to the religious labor movement in the Land with all strands of his soul. He worked in teaching for years, and then in the teachers' office in Tel Aviv. All the teachers who came in contact with him loved him boundlessly. Anyone who entered his office was received pleasantly. He was concerned with any teacher during their lifetime and with their family after their death.

We weep over his untimely death along with his many friends.

May his precious memory be blessed forever.

Translator's footnote:

1.   The name of a Yeshiva in Tel Aviv.

[Page 190]

In Memory of a Dear Friend Rivka Ziporin-Aharoni
of Blessed Memory

by Y. Ben-Shachar

Translated by Jerrold Landau

She was a member of the Lisovitz *Hachshara* [pioneer training] Kibbutz. She was dedicated and concerned about everybody. She made *aliya* in 1926. She was with her sister Shoshana Lev of blessed memory in Kfar Saba during the first period, but she moved to Tel Aviv and worked in a sock factory, and later in sorting oranges in an orchard. She gained a trade with great difficulty and effort, but she was able to overcome everything. She worked in tending to young orchards during the summer. She was honest, proper, and pleasant, and was able to attract friends. She married Yaakov Greenspan-Aharoni of Stolin and established a fine family, with two sons, a daughter, and an orderly home. A malignant disease put an end to her beautiful life, and she departed from us suddenly. How we loved her. She was the image of a pioneer who was able to overcome everything, to encourage anyone suffering, ad to help everyone in need. Only a short time ago, she came to ask for help for a sick friend. She always concerned herself with anyone who needed help.

Her strong, dear, charming personality will always remain before our eyes.

She died on 19 Tishrei 5717, October 5, 1955. A large number of people came to accompany her on her final journey. Peace be upon her remains. May her soul be bound in the bonds of eternal life.

Reb Natan Nota Gloiberman
of Blessed Memory

by Chaim Kolozny

Translated by Jerrold Landau

He was like his name.[1] He conducted business faithfully. He planted the love of friends and love of Heaven among his children, friends, and acquaintances.

He was born in the village of "Bilohosh" [Belousha] between David-Horodok and Stolin to his parents Reb Eliezer and Tauba. He excelled in his studies, in delving into his learning in depth, and in his diligence and consistency. He was considered as a wonder child by anyone who knew him.

And he did not disappoint! His quick grasp, sharpness of mind, and memory prowess were an example to everyone.

He began to work in business with great success while still young. His knowledge of the vernacular opened up for him the courts of the estate owners, with whom he maintained business connections.

When he was freed from military service, he married Ester, the daughter of Reb Avraham and Tzipa Baruchin.

He moved to David-Horodok in 1911 and was considered to be one of the pillars of support of the synagogue of the Hassidim of Stolin and Karlin.

Reb Natan Nota was a great believer, thanks to the education that he received in his parents' home and in the court of the Admor of Stolin. He absorbed numerous Hassidic stories into his soul and his essence.

His zealousness for faith, religion, and tradition was great. This was demonstrated through the staff of his mouth, from which he would preach morality and guidance. He concerned himself with the needy when he was in the Diaspora, and continued along that path as well in the Land. He never neglected any opportunity. He was always prepared to help, and there were many honorable people whose entire needs he filled.

Family purity[2] was at the top of his concerns. Along with his friend Reb Yosef the son of Reb Moshe Kolozny, he bore the burden of repairing and maintaining the city bathhouse in a proper, satisfactory manner.

Since he was sharp and learned, he was invited to all types of arbitrations. He succeeded in building bridges over the chasm and finding the golden path even in the most difficult cases.

Even though he was busy in business, he set times to study Torah and wisdom. He greatly appreciated the rabbi Reb Avraham Yitzchak. He was among those who tarried in his house while enjoying the pearls of wisdom from his mouth.

[Page 191]

Reb Natan Nota Gloiberman was the embodiment of a Jew of stature and pleasant mannerisms, with fine, refined traits. He possessed understanding and appreciated the good in a person and the honor of his soul.

He merited to make *aliya* to the Land together with his wife and part of his family, where he enjoyed the holiness of the Land. He reached a ripe old age,[3] and he fulfilled the commandment of Torah study until almost his final day. He died with a clear mind. His final words were "Read on! And I must go!"

All the natives of David-Horodok weep along with his family members over the death of this dear, prominent Jew, Reb Natan Nota Gloiberman of blessed memory.

May his soul be bound in the bonds of eternal life.

Translator's footnotes:

1. The name Natan means "given." The Hebrew term for conducting business, *Masa Umatan*, includes the same root, and literally means "taking and giving" (i.e. give and take). The nickname for Natan, Nota, is similar to the Hebrew word for "planting," although the nickname is based on similarity of sound rather than of meaning.
2. i..e. ensuring the presence of kosher *mikvehs* [ritual baths] so that the Jewish laws of family purity can be fulfilled.
3. The Hebrew term *gevurot* refers to an age above 80.

Persons From David-Horodok

Translated by Jerrold Landau

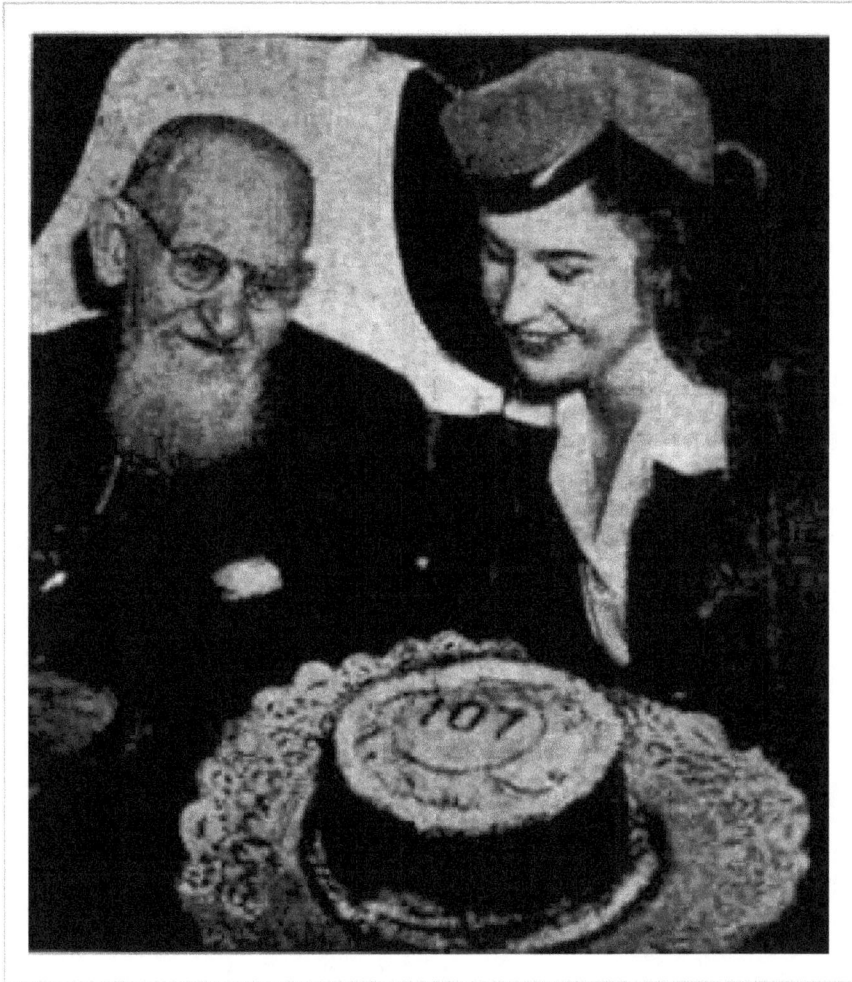

David-Shlomo Eisenberg of blessed memory. From among the David-
Horodok immigrants in the United States, on the occasion of his
107th birthday.

[Page 192]

Velvel Raishke's of blessed memory

This was really his name! That is what the David-Horodokers called him. His occupation was meager: small-scale trade in pig bristles, but his needs were few and he was mostly silent. He was a precious Jew, with good manners, a G-d fearing believer, who was among those who frequented the study-house. He was a devoted friend of Rabbi Dovidl. He was both humble and zealous for G-d and His Torah. He was an exceptional man, an honor to the David-Horodokers, and an example to many. He will be remembered positively, and his good name will remain forever.

Wolf Bielke's Eisenberg

He was a merchant who traded in textiles, a trade where many bankruptcies occurred. He did not fail. His energetic wife helped him, and they lived a quiet and honorable bourgeois life. He was considered a quiet, humble, and pleasant man. May his memory be a blessing.

[Page 193]

Wolf Hillel's Schechter

He was very poor. His livelihood was selling newspapers, but this did not provide an adequate income for him. One could meet him running about selling the papers, revisiting the few existing subscribers, and trying to enlarge the number of readers. However, most of his time was dedicated to the *Beis Midrash* – that was his real place. He would listen to the lesson, learn it by himself, and then complete the quorum of men who spent their entire day in the large *Beis Midrash*. He was a righteous, observant Jew. May his soul be bound in the bonds of eternal life.

Saneh the Butcher

He was one of the hundred butchers in the town, who earned their livelihoods with difficulty. He was an honest Jew with an upright posture and a leisurely pace. He accepted the difficulties of life without complaint, and endured everything quietly. He was considered one of the honest and faithful ones from among his trade. Let him be remembered positively among all the martyrs of Horodok.

The Holocaust

[Page 197]

Why???

Y. Idan

Translated by Jerrold Landau

A.

This vexing question penetrates into the depth of the soul. It has distressed us for fifteen years already, and it will continue to pursue us as a terrifying shadow and will disturb our rest until the end of days, having no answer.

As long as we deliberate over the question, we recall that a similar question was once asked, under different circumstances, when our ancestors were still cleaving and holding on in this land. A difficult cataclysm overtook them, and they asked themselves bitterly: (Psalms 74:1): "G-d, why have You cast us off forever?" This question has returned time after time.

The way of life of this nation is strange, and the path of its fate is wondrous. The binding of Isaac serves as a sort of introduction and symbol for it.

If we remember the "days of yore"[1] – we will definitively establish, without any question, the following things:

There is no other land in the entire world that is so soaked with the blood of its children as this land. There is no other nation in the world that has dedicated its soul to its liberty as this nation and has paid such a high price in blood. It was only on rare occasions that it received recompense for its large amount of blood.

B.

The tribulations that afflicted the nation have been many, and at every horrifying tribulation, the bitter question emanates from its mouth: Why?

It is not only the members of the nation that do not know why and for what reason. Even the G-d of the nation wonders about the fate of its children. In its manner, legend speaks in the language of humans, and knows how to tell: (*Sefer HaAgadah* I, 192):

"The Holy One Blessed Be He weeps." He laments and says: "Woe to the king who succeeded in his younger days and did not succeed in his old age"….

The forefathers appear and supplicate: Why? Moses comes and shouts: Why? And they are not answered. Only Mother Rachel evokes the mercy of the Holy One Blessed Be He, and only she received the sure, comforting response: "For you, Rachel, I will return Israel to its place." "And the children shall return to their boundaries." (Jeremiah 31: 14).

The meaning of these words is: The mother is the guarantor for the continued existence of this nation, and the nation will continue on the path of its life, the path of its wondrous destiny.

C.

The most difficult and frightful cataclysm was the conflict of the nation with Rome. Rome was the epitome of might, enslaving and subduing all who stood in its path. Tens of lands and nations were subdued, placing their necks under its yoke. Only Judea, small and poor, refused, and fought with all its might, and beyond its powers. "*Judea Capta*" [Judea is captured] boasted the victors.

There is no measure for the blood of our ancestors spilled in this land during their protracted clash with Rome, during the many revolts, the great war, and afterwards during the time of Bar Kokhba. "The blood moved boulders of 40 *seah*.[2] The nations of the world fortified their vineyards from the blood of Israel for seven years without need of fertilizer..." (*Sefer HaAgadah* I, 262). "Who in the world can be compared to us with our love for the land and freedom? Who is like you, O Israel, a singular nation in the land?"[3]

And Rome, that evil kingdom, wearied its soul from the illogical opposition of that small, stubborn nation,

[Page 198]

crucified for freedom. Hadrian, may his bones be ground up, decided to destroy the soul of that nation, saying, "Let us destroy them as a nation, so that the name of Israel will no longer be remembered."[4]

They perpetrated a great massacre of the intelligentsia of the nation, "the ten martyrs of the [Roman] government, Rabbi Akiva and his comrades. The life of the nation was hanging on a hair. Legend tells (*Sefer HaAgadah* II, 56)," The ministering angels said before the Holy One Blessed Be He: "This is Torah, and this is its reward?" The Holy One Blessed Be He responded, "What can I do for my children, it is a decree, and there is no one to mitigate it."

Rabbi Yishmael uttered a great, bitter scream, shaking the heavens and the earth. He uttered a second scream, and the Throne of Honor shook. A heavenly voice stated, "If I hear one more sound, I will turn the entire world to a formless void..."[5]

When Rabbi Yishmael heard this, he was silent. That is, he accepted the verdict. The meaning of the Heavenly voice is: The fate of the entire world is dependent on the state of this small nation...

We know of two meanings of the nickname that the historian Simon Dubno, may G-d avenge his blood, called the Jews: "A nation of the world."[6] One is: a nation that the entire world is full of its place.[7] Second: a nation whose days are like the days of the world, an eternal nation. Now a third meaning of this term has been revealed to us, as has been outlined by the poet, and as is implied by the legend.[8]

D.

If we wish to continue along our journey to "Remember the days of yore, and understand the years of generation to generation,"[1] our feet will take us against our will from the inheritance of G-d and bring us to far-off, foreign fields to various centers that the nation created in the east and the west, whether close to the Land of the Patriarchs or far from it, and served as a refuge for the body as well as a fortress for the spirit for many generations. At the end, they were uprooted from them after no small amount of bloodletting, especially in the center in the west. The center in Sura and Pumbedita lasted for 1006 years. The center in Grenada and Cordoba lasted for 1500 years.[9] We will skip over other small centers until we arrive at this latter center, which served as a refuge for 1,000 years, and was uprooted and destroyed before our eyes during our days, covering in its cataclysm one third of the nation in such a terrible and frightful manner that has no equal, whether in the center in Babylonia or the center in Spain.

How did the nation regard this center in the country of Poland. Legend states: "At a time when the gentiles were persecuting the Jew in the Diaspora greatly, and the Divine presence, so to speak, saw that there was no end and no purpose, and there was a possibility that the remnant of Israel might be lost, Heaven forbid, the Divine Presence immediately came before the Holy One Blessed Be He and raised her complaint, stating: Until when? You gave the dove that was sent from the ark during the time of the flood an olive branch so it will have a place to set its feet upon the water – but it could not withstand the waters of the flood and returned to the ark. You sent my children out of the ark to the waters of the flood, and you did not create any place for them where they could rest in their exile?"[10]

Immediately, the Holy One Blessed Be He took a piece of the Land of Israel that was hidden with him in the heavens from the day that the Temple was destroyed, lowered it to earth, and said:

"Be a resting place for the people of the Diaspora." Therefore, its name is Polin, meaning "Rest here [*Po Lin* in Hebrew] in the Diaspora." For that reason, Satan has no authority there, and Torah spread out throughout the entire country: synagogues, houses of study, and Yeshivas. Praise to His Name, may He be blessed!

And what will happen in the future? When the Messiah comes? What will happen to the synagogues and communities that we built in Poland? How is this? In the future, when the Messiah comes, the Holy One

Blessed Be He will certainly transport Poland with all its communities, *Beis Midrashes*, and Yeshivas to the Land of Israel." (From Kiddush Hashem by Sholem Asch: A conversation between the author Rabbi Yonah, and Mendel the Parnas of Złoczew.)

E.

These things were stated at the end of the era, the era of Jewish connection to the State of Poland under the shadow of merciful kings, from Kazimierz the Great until Zygmunt August (during the 14th, 15th, 16th, and half of the 17th centuries).

[Page 199]

Not a long time passed before a terrible tribulation affected that peaceful Jewry. The years of 5408-5417 (1648-1656)[11] uprooted the Jewish tree planted in Poland, Lithuania, and Ukraine. Approximately 700 Jewish communities and settlements were destroyed (some partly). That Jewry could not return to its strength for several generations after the great tribulation of the 5408.

Now, the latest cataclysm was most difficult and terrible, and final upon that same land of Poland. There, we had found a place of refuge for more than 1,000 years, even though our sojourn there during most periods was in accordance with the words of the poet: a sojourn "among scorpions, between the straits of the netherworld and the tribulations of the pit." From time to time, there was spilling of blood, whether great or small. However, the martyrs of Nemirov,[12] like the martyrs of Magentza [Mayence or Mainz] did not ask: Why? In their consciousness, their victims were not in vain. They knew why and for Whom they were giving their lives. There was a purpose in their deaths, just as there was also a purpose in their lives. This was not the case with our generation, with the cataclysm of our day on the land of Poland, a cataclysm that our nation, learned in experience, has not seen the likes of in form or scope. Before our eyes and in our days, this center has tottered and collapsed, and will not rise or return! Is this a coincidence or a twist of fate, that this land, which was called Po Lin [rest or sojourn here] at its outset – ended up being the eternal resting place for millions of our martyrs? Six million?

Once, the refugees of the Diaspora streamed there from the lands of Europe, to its protective, sheltering land. Now, before our eyes, death trains traveled upon its land from the countries of Europe. The vast majority of its residents collaborated with the enemy.

"Cursed are you, cruel gentile. Cursed be your name for ever and ever."

(Sh. Tchernichovsky)

F.

A future historian who will research our history during the current [i.e. 20th] century will blame that generation for shortsightedness, in that they did not realize what was coming and did not foresee the dangers to come. Did not Binyamin Zeev the son of Yaakov from Budapest[13] and before him Yehuda Leib the physician from Odessa,[14] and before and after them many other great people issued clear warnings, as scouts standing on their guard, as they blew the shofars and called to the people:

Arise, escape before it is too late, for the ground is burning under your feet, and the volcano is likely to erupt at any moment, any hour.

"There is no hope here, my brothers, the end has already been determined.
"There is no hope for the dove in the talons of the hawk…"

(*Iggeret Ketana*, Ch. N. Bialik)

The ears of many were blocked and heavy, and the few who heard the call and wanted to leave, woe, remained standing "behind the gate."

...How can I come through the gate	There is no voice, and no answer,
Of the treasured land,	And the dove with a lad
My key is broken	Refined, are knocking
And the door is locked.	On the door of the gate.

(Behind the Gate, Ch. N. Bialik)

G.

The ancients established in their visions that there will be the War of Gog and Magog prior to the redemption, and a large amount of Israelite blood would be shed. "It will be a time of tribulation for Jacob, and he will be saved from it."[15]

[Page 200]

Indeed, the great salvation arose before our eyes. Could it be that we paid the price through the loss of one third of the Jews off the face of the entire earth??

Translator's footnotes:

1. Based on Deuteronomy 32:7.
2. A *seah* is a Biblical / Talmudic unit of volume, equivalent to approximately 8.5 liters.
3. From the Sabbath afternoon *Amida*.
4. Psalms 83:4.
5. Based on Genesis 1:2. Note, this legend of the Ten Martyrs is graphically portrayed in the *Eileh Ezkera* section of Yom Kippur *Musaf*.
6. Usually translated as "an eternal nation" but here open to different meanings, so I gave a purely literal translation.
7. Seemingly: That this nation is significant for the essence of the entire world.
8. That the veritable existence of the world is dependent on the Jewish nation.
9. These timeframes are not exact.
10. A very difficult legend, with different aspects of the Divine speaking to each other, so to speak. A multiplicity of the godhead is not to be read into this legend [as per Christological views of the deity] – rather, from a human perspective, it appears that G-d has a more aloof form, as well as a more immanent form. Note, the author, Sholem Asch, is known for having interspersed some elements of Christological ideas in his writings.
11. The Chmielnicki uprising.
12. The site of one of the worst massacres during the period of the Chmielnicki uprising.
13. Also known as Theodor Herzl.
14. Also known as Leon Pinsker.
15. Jeremiah 30:7. For a Biblical description of Gog and Magog, see Ezekiel 38.

We Will Surely Remember

by Moshe Moravchik (Meiri)

Translated by Jerrold Landau

I still remember your image, O tiny town, that dwells far from the bustle of the world, and almost alone.

At a time when fates were being determined, you remained exactly within your bounds, and had a bit of this and that.

I still remember your streets, narrow and long, with low houses on both sides, as soldiers arranged in a row. Every house had an extended family, with one or two families, and children running about in the yards.

In the summer, the doors and windows were open toward the street, and one could look inside to the faces, and see everything that was going on in the rooms.

In the winter, the windows were covered up, and the houses were turned inwards, as if they were hiding their residents.

I still remember the days of summer, warm days of bright sunlight, when the entire town spilled out to the street – in the morning to work and in the evening to stroll.

How good and pleasant was it to get up in the morning and see the cows going out to pasture in herds, accompanied by the cowherd with his stick and faithful dog.

I still remember boys and girls rising early to go on excursions outside the city, to the meadows and forests, to set up camps there and spend an entire day in the bosom of nature. These were the youth who were preparing themselves for a new life. The center of that life was then the Land of Israel and the national renaissance movement.

I still remember boys and girls hurrying to the cheders and schools with their schoolbags on their shoulders and joyous laughter on their faces – who knew what fate was awaiting them?

I still remember parents going out to their work, some to commerce, some to trades, to concern themselves with sustenance for their families. Toiling parents bearing the yoke of life – who would have thought that such would happen to them?

I still remember rainy days, as if the windows of the heavens had opened, and the thunder shook the windows of the houses. Behold, lightning flashes, and fire breaks out in one of the houses in the suburbs. The sound of the alarm of the guard reaches one's ears to put out the fire. The rain even stops as if to give time to save the house, a cow, a horse, or anything that can be saved from the talons of the fire that spread quickly through the roofs of the houses and the surrounding hay.

I still remember clear, snowy winter nights, sparkling in the white that covered all existence. Inside, the family gathers around the hot oven with the steaming tea.

As those winter days approached, the heads of the families prepared themselves with food, firewood, animal feed, and warm clothing.

I still remember those peaceful days when the course of life flowed along at its own pace, as nobody foresaw that a Holocaust would come.

I still remember the days of spring and the days of Passover. Every corner in the entire house had been washed and cleaned. We enjoyed the splendor of the world, and were immersed in worldly life, without seeing that a disaster would break out.

I still remember many youths leaving the town to go to bastions of learning in the large city. When they would return home for holidays and vacations, they would be wearing the hats of *gymnazja* [high school] students, thereby arousing the jealousy of those in their age cohort who did not merit to leave the town and go afar.

I still remember boys and girls rebelling against the current realities of life, as they set out for places of *Hachshara* [pioneer training], so that they could join the camps of the pioneers making *aliya* to the Land of Israel when the time came, setting out for a new, difficult life.

I still remember this rebellion of children against their parents, of escape from home, of abandoning the school bench, of leaving elderly parents to their sighs, of forging a different life, of burning all bridges in order to build a new bridge through which the members of the generation who were yearning for their own homeland and their own life would pass.

I still remember the last days before the World War, when the pure Jews did not want to believe the footsteps

[Page 201]

of the approaching Holocaust, as they held their children back and did not permit them to make *aliya*, for that was fraught at that time with the danger of stealing across borders and crossing seas without permission.

Then suddenly, the screen fell, and everything that remained behind it was very far from us, separated by continents and seas.

I still remember the first tidings of Job that reached us about the slaughter and murder, and the atrocities of the Germans in the town, with the assistance of the gentiles who collaborated with them, and there was nobody to save us.

I still remember when I came to destroyed Poland after the Holocaust, my journey from city to city, and the hopeless attempt to save what was possible. At that time, the survivors were poor, sparse, and lacking of means.

I still remember the darkest of dark, worst of the worst, the information brought to us by the survivors, the last remnants, who told us about those who were about to be murdered digging their own graves, and the deportation of the residents of the town who were unable to stand before the bullets of the murderers and the knives of their helpers.

I still remember the day when I stood on what was once the famous death camp of Auschwitz, and on the gas chambers and crematoria that remained in their full awfulness and frightfulness, and the heaps upon heaps of bones of millions of people who were cremated in that place.

We will surely remember all this, and we will not allow ourselves to be silent until the end of all generations.

[Who Can Describe...]

by Chaim Kolozny

Translated by Jerrold Landau

Who can describe the magnitude of the destruction? Who of us has the power to put it all on paper? Indeed, a decade or more has passed since those bitter, unstable days.

I said: I will delve into the forgotten depths and dredge from there that which comes to my memory – day to day realities, holy and mundane, specific and general, about that which was and is no more.

I went from house to house, from one desolate, gloomy road to the next, from dawn until the stars came out: On every wall there were only shadows, and thousands of eyes shout out and supplicate on account of the fear of death that pervaded.

As I was walking there, a single living soul, uniting with the souls of thousands of our martyrs, old and young, big and small, fathers and mothers, members of all strata, who were united in a single communal grave as they fell. Beasts of the field consumed the flesh of all the others, who did not merit a Jewish burial.

I delved further into the echoes. Now I saw my native city as it was during my childhood and youth. I saw its many Jews at their daily work: some in education, some in culture, some for Zion, some for their day-to-day needs, some for whom the matters of *aliya* to the Land overtake their rest, some concerned about the difficulties of a daughter who has come of age – these matters concern them and do not allow for silence.

How lovely were your deeds, O residents of David-Horodok? You helped, gave support, assisted, made things easier, created something from nothing through the sweat of your brow. Your livelihood came through the mercies of Heaven.

Is there anyone who was satisfied with little in the material sense as you were; and who was as dedicated to and strove for the needs of the spirit as you were dedicated and strove? I recall the Hebrew schools, which suffered countless difficulties, and nevertheless maintained themselves and educated 90% of the children of the town. I recall the echoes of spoken Hebrew on the lips of the valiant "*Bnei Yehuda*," whose lives were dedicated to ensuring that it took root within the town and outside of it. Here is the orphanage, the libraries, the halls, the synagogues. The spirit of Zion pervaded every house. This dedication to Zionism and the Land of Israel was to such an extent that at times it seems that your feet were standing upon the ground of Israel.

But no, I cannot express your entire essence, realities, and destinies, O martyrs of my town. Words fail the mouth, and tears dry in the eyes. Woe!

[Page 202]

A Monument

by Zelda

Translated by Jerrold Landau

A strong desire moves me to erect a monument to David-Horodok, where I was educated and raised. It is a populated town situated in the Polesye district, covered with bogs and poorly connected to transportation. It was a town in which poverty and crowding were blended. On the other hand, Hebrew culture and life pulsated within it. Already about fifty years ago, Yishai Adler worked there in the dissemination of Hebrew enlightenment and the revival of the language. Many were helped by him and continued successfully even after his departure. There was enthusiastic Zionist activity in this Jewish town, and its residents were among the first to take part in the Second Aliya. They snuck over borders, and traversed the seven levels of hell in order to reach the Land. I will not dwell here on the description of this town. It seems to me that its name and memory are spoken of in the community.

A few months ago, at the time of the Russian conquest, pieces of information began to filter through from letters from Russia. Among them was the letter of a fourteen-year-old boy, the only one who survived from our entire city. The following is written in the letter, among other things: "The heart turns to stone at the sight of all the troubles, murders, tortures, and the burning of people alive. After I wandered around for three consecutive years without a roof over my head, without the right to life, filthy and starving, awaiting an unusual death at any moment – I cannot believe that I am here alone, that I alone remain of my entire large family and my unfortunate town. Woe, my death would have been better than my life." – laments a fourteen-year-old boy! "What more can I write. The matter is terrible and known. The wound in the soul is deep. You must certainly be wondering how I could write such, but it has already been some time since I had a human heart. The fire of revenge is burning inside me. I would drink their blood, and do to them what they perpetrated upon us – – – "

Indeed, the pain is great, and the chances of our brethren in the Diaspora are bleak. Nations will arise to new life, cities and houses will be built upon their ruins, but our dear parents and siblings will never rise again.

[Page 204]

From 1939 to 1945

by Yaakov the Son of Yosef Kolozny

Translated by Jerrold Landau

A. Declaration of War and We Guard the Order

On Thursday, August 27, 1939, four days before the outbreak of the war, announcements were posted on the streets of David-Horodok regarding a general draft. The Jewish community in the city was perplexed. People went around as shadows, knowing what was to come. Nevertheless, many believed that the war was not near.

On Friday, September 1, 1939, at 4:00 a.m., German soldiers crossed the Polish border and advanced as quick as lightening. The gloomy news that a portion of the Jewish and gentile population was drafted by the firefighters

[Page 205]

to ensure the fulfillment of the command and to stand on guard during the alarm was posted. I too was among the draftees. We stood on guard day and night.

One evening, we were summoned by the fire chief and informed that the Polish police no longer exists, and it was our duty to protect the order until the arrival of the new regime. Some of us were given axes and hatchets, and others were given live weapons. The residents of the surrounding villages organized themselves and armed themselves with anything they could get their hands on, with the aim of attacking the city and pillaging it. However, the villagers were stopped by the civilian police at the entrance to the bridge over the Horyn River. The police threatened to open fire, and they scattered.

B. The Entrance of the Red Army

The situation continued to be tense and we remained on our guard, with the exception of the time of shofar blowing on Rosh Hashanah. After about two weeks I found out from Moshe Margolin and Simcha Mishalov that the Red Army would shortly arrive in David-Horodok. Indeed, the Red Army entered the town on September 19 at 6:00 a.m. The Jewish community felt relieved. My unit of five firefighters who guarded the Olshan bridge was the first to meet the Red Army as it entered. They thought that we were Polish police, and their aimed their weapons at us, until we were able to prove who we were. They did not leave us, and we advanced together to the Horyn bridge at the other end of the city. Three Polish soldiers shot at us next to the house of Moshe Baruchin, for they did not want to give up the city without a battle. Two lieutenants of the Red Army fell in the ensuing battle.

All of the draftees and firefighters were commanded to advance with the firefighting equipment under a volley of bullets in order to extinguish the fire at the bridge that was ignited by the Poles. When the Russian tanks approached the river, we informed them that it was very deep, but they responded *"Nichevo"* [Don't worry; let things take their course]. They entered the water and crossed the river with the help of special wings.

C. Under the New Regime

The new regime did not particularly affect Jewish life. The religious and Zionist segments were most affected. Elders and people of faith, who had always been punctilious about the holiness of the Sabbath and festivals throughout their entire lives, were forced to worship at 4:00 a.m. on Yom Kippur and then go out to work at 7:00 below the riverbank of Moche Rimar. Everything that had existed was cut down and disappeared. Suspicion replaced friendship and brotherhood. The idea of leaving for Vilna slowly developed, as it would be an opening of hope for leaving for the free world. A free exchange of population continued for about two weeks. On one Saturday night in October, hundreds of Jews came to the home of Rabbi Shapira of blessed memory to bid him farewell as he left for Vilna with his wife. As I entered there, he approached me, and said: "Yaakov, I command you to travel to Vilna immediately, for your Zionist work will stand for you." I understood him, sighed with a broken heart, and said, "Rabbi – You are correct."

D. Going and Returning

My father of blessed memory wanted very much for me to leave Horodok. Since he was unable to express his will to me, he repeated this in front of my friends several times. It was not easy to come in contact with several of my friends, for it was impossible to tell this to anyone. The first group, numbering four individuals – Yosef the son of Moshe Baruchin, Avraham Gurevitz, Zeev Ronkin, and I – set out in the direction of Romania via Rovno and Lvov. We were forced to return since there was no crossing. The second time, we set out toward Vilna. When we reached Eishishok, we were told that they were sending people back from Vilna, so we returned. The atmosphere was very oppressive, and I decided to leave Horodok at any price.

[Page 206]

E. On the Way to Vilna

At 6:00 p.m. on September 22, 1939, toward evening, as I was standing next to the store of Yosef Basevitz, which served as a co-op for provisions, one of the trustworthy people of the new regime approached me and told me that I was given an ultimatum to bring the Beitar archives to the police station… My response was that the archives were completely destroyed at the beginning of the war, along with all the Zionist archives. I knew that my days in Horodok were numbered. Two days later at 8:00 a.m., I was informed by Yosef Gloiberman of blessed memory that his brother Yaakov and David Gurevitz had crossed the border from Vilna to transfer the Admor of Karlin. I hastened home, and after a brief consultation with my parents, sister, brother, brother-in-law, and uncle, I packed my belongings and set out on my journey. I also wanted to speak to my friend Yosef Baruchin and convince him to come with me, so that my conscience would be clear, but Yosef Gloiberman dissuaded me from that, saying that has already set himself up, is working in a bank, and has a red card. I went to Chaikel Freiman and asked that his son Leibel accompany me. He agreed, and we set out to Luninets.

We met up with Gloiberman and Gurevitz in Luninets. The Admor did not come, and we continued to Lida, and from there to Turgal, the last town at the border. After much wandering, tribulations, and difficulties on the fifty-kilometer trek through the mud and snow on our knees, we succeeded in crossing the border. Leibel Freiman was the weakest of us. As we ran across the border zone, a length of four kilometers, until the nearby grove, we realized that he was missing. I was certain that he remained on the way because of his weakness. I backtracked approximately one kilometer to look for him, but I did not find him. When I returned, I found him in the grove. When I asked him where he had disappeared, he told me that he had fallen because of lack of energy, but at that time, Rabbi Sorotzkin was crossing the border on a sled, and he took him across as well.

F. From Ponevezh to Kuybishev

Our situation was good when we were in Vilna, and after that in Ponevezh in the center of Lithuania. I wrote the following in my last letter home: "When the band starts playing, go out to visit your sister Rivka." I was in Ponevezh when the war between Germany and Russia broke out. Yaakov Gloiberman was in Vilna, Leibel Freiman in Kovno, and Zeev Shafer on the way from Pinsk to Sarny. They all met the same fate. One day I received a letter from home informing me that my mother of blessed memory had died on 3 Shevat.

There in Ponevezh, I worked with a Pole who had remained in Lithuania already from the time of the First World War. He was considered to be a very honest person. When I went to consult with him, he advised me to hide with him, and even promised to concern himself with obtaining Aryan papers for me. I did not lose my common sense. I thanked him and told him that his neighbors would certainly report me, and I did not want him to suffer because of me. Therefore, I decided to escape to Russia. Then the Pole gave me some money and wished me success. At 2:00 p.m. that same day I set out with several friends to Dvinsk [Daugavpils] on the way to Bogshiva in the Russian territory. We continued on through Polatsk and Vitebsk. The bombing was terrible. Everything was destroyed and burnt. The skies were darkened during the day from smoke, and were reddish at night from the fires. We survived only through a miracle.

We saw Smolensk going up in flames during the light of the day at a distance of seventy kilometers from us. Since we could not continue, we returned and traveled toward Kuybishev. After a journey of about one month on trains, we arrived in the Viznichok station, forty kilometers from Kuybishev. There, we worked in agriculture in the *Puti Socializma Kolkhoz* [collective farm]. Our nerves partially calmed down, but our nights passed without sleep, for we worried about our relatives and friends.

G. In Central Asia

After the Stalin-Sikorski agreement was signed, Polish citizens in exile in Russia were granted asylum. The largest group began to stream toward Central Asia, the concentration area for the armies of General Andras, with the hope of making *aliya* to the Land. Through great effort, we succeeded in leaving Kuybishev and reaching Zarbuloq in Central Asia.

[Page 207]

However, we did not succeed in moving from there on account of the well-known relations of the Andras brigades with the Jews. I remained in Zarbuloq for four years. I succeeded in establishing contact with my brother in the Land of Israel. How great was my joy and emotion when I received the first telegram from the Land. I also succeeded in establishing contact with David-Horodok natives in Russia: Kopel Moravchik, Yissachar Kirzner, Yosef Yudovitz, Yaakov Bregman of blessed memory, Shalom Kvetny, Asher Baruchin, Shmuel Zezik, Baruch Lelzizky, and others.

When we were in Zarbuloq, all the Jews there, who were from Poland, Russia, Latvia, Lithuania, and Bessarabia, organized themselves. A charitable fund was even set up to support those in need.

Not far from us there was a hospital. Most of the sick people, who mainly suffered from typhus, dysentery, and malaria, received milk and bread every day. Members of the committee would visit the sick twice a month, bringing them food packages and encouraging them. The committee also concerned itself with the religious needs of the refugees. A house was obtained to serve as a synagogue. We even received a Torah scroll from the Jews of Bukhara, which was twelve kilometers from Zarbuloq. A *minyan* was held every Sabbath. People would pledge money for the needs of the community fund during the *aliyot* to the Torah on Sabbaths and festivals. There participation was especially great on the High Holy Days. I served as the shofar blower for two years.

H. Tidings of Job From the Towns

When the awaited moment arrived, and the war ended, I contacted the town council of David-Horodok. After some time, I received their response: "The fate of your parents was the same as that of all the Jews of Horodok. All the Jews were liquidated, and their property was pillaged." At that time, Yissachar Kirzner visited me. We went to the post office together to get the responses of the town councils of David-Horodok, Stolin, Visotzk, Pinsk, and Nesvizh. The text of all of them was the same. Those moments were the gloomiest of our lives. We did not believe and could not come to terms with the bitter truth that was thrust in our faces.

I. The Voice of the Blood of Our Brethren Is Screaming From the Earth

The sense of despair was strong. The cold pained the hearts and souls. Loneliness and apathy pervaded all over. Humans were created in the [Divine] image, created to exist and live on the land in a state of blessing, to enjoy life in every place. However, the "enlightened" world that had advanced in giant steps from a technical perspective, accepted with equanimity the rivers of boiling blood of our brothers, sisters, wives, children, and infants who had been seized with vile force and in sadistic ways from the arms of their mothers and tossed upon walls and rocks. This world was still thirsty with a voracious desire relating to the tragic, unforgettable past. The ground had yet to be calmed from the blood of the victims that it had absorbed. It was screaming, calling out and warning: "The voice of the blood of your brother is shouting at you from the earth"[1] – and there is nobody responding as the voice calls out in the wilderness. Their final screams echo, but the ears are blocked and the brains are dulled – nobody is listening!

Were I to have been an inventor, I would have invented the proper medicine that could uproot the frothing poison. The time has come to "silence the accuser, and let the defender take his place."[2] They did not even come to a Jewish grave. The two mass graves of the natives of David-Horodok on the route to Chinovsk are orphaned. Nobody comes and nobody visits. Nobody sheds a tear, and nobody bats an eyelash.

The torture and suffering are etched deep in the wounded heart. There is no power in the world to cause them to be forgotten, and there is no way to ignore them. I was far from you during those terrible awful days and nights. Alone and abandoned, your souls expired collectively and ascended toward the heavens of the G-d who did not inquire about us, and who did not ask about us – this is what fate wanted. The impure iron fist was victorious…

May you rest in peace, and may your souls be bound in the bonds of eternal life, and be righteous intercessors for those that remain.

Translator's footnotes:

1. Paraphrased from Genesis 4:10.
2. From the *Amnam Ken* hymn of the Yom Kippur evening service.

[Page 209]

About Two Towns: Stolin, David-Horodok, and the Village of Rubiel [Rubel]

by Michael Nosanchuk

Translated by Jerrold Landau

(From a letter sent by one of the partisans of the Red Army to his sister in the Land. This letter contains first-hand testimony to the fate of two towns in Polesye, Stolin and David-Horodok, both known for their activities on behalf of the funds[1] and the Hebrew language. The Bnei Yehuda movement, consisting of school youths who took upon themselves to change over to the Hebrew language at home, on the street, and in every place, was formed in the latter, David-Horodok, approximately a decade prior to the war. They actualized this decision with exceptional consistency and dedication, and served as an example for many other Tarbut schools in the country of Poland.

The author of the letter, Michael N. lived in a village between these two towns, and he begins his letter with the fate of the Jewish community in that village. We bring characteristic sections from this letter, which open a window for us to peer into the darkness of the hell in which millions of our brethren in Poland found themselves.)

…For complete days and nights, there was only one thought in my heart: Do you at least know about our torment and the bitterness of our fate? When I escaped from the darkness of the ghetto and the accursed Germans, and wandered through the bogs and forests, in holes and hiding places, literally like a mad dog, only this thought was on my mind: How can I inform you, my brother and sister, so that someone from our family will know after my death what I went through? At times, I thought about taking my own life. It is only when your memory came before me that I girded myself with strength, and a spark of hope passed over me: Perhaps? And with the rest of my strength, I overcame everything, and my only aspiration was that the day will come when I will arise with weapons in my hands to take our revenge.

It was not easy for me to be accepted into the partisan brigade, and later into the Red Army. I passed through Lithuania and Latvia with the Russians. I fought on the front, and I finally even reached the impure Berlin, and took revenge for our spilled blood… However, the deep wound in my heart will never be healed…

In 1941, one week after Tisha B'Av, I remember that this was a Sunday, the great slaughter in David-Horodok took place. All the men were gathered into a field outside the town with the pretext that they would be taken to work. They were all murdered by gunshot.

I was then in the village of Rubiel, and we did not know anything. I always loved fishing. I arose in the afternoon and went to the river. I called my cousin Yaakov R. to accompany me. He joked and responded in his usual fashion: I will come to the river in an hour by horse and wagon to pick up your fish. I went myself. At 5:00 p.m., I heard the sound of gunshots, one after the other. I hid deep in the bushes, and I waited that perhaps

[Page 210]

someone from the village might come, and I will understand what was the meaning of this. One of the farmers passed by and brought me the terrible news. A few hours before this, nobody knew what was about to happen. Everyone was working at his work, one with his anvil, and another with his needle. Then suddenly – all were dead. Yaakov was among them. An hour earlier, he was still joking, and now he was dead. For what reason? 53 people were murdered in our village, including Motel Z., the father of our sister-in-law Chanale. Yaakov still said a few words before his death. All the Jews of the village gathered at the shed of the firefighters. They were chained in groups of threes, marched between the barns, and murdered.

Later, news came from David-Horodok about what had happened there.

I secretly snuck out of the village and set out to Stolin. The murderers sensed that I was not among those murdered, and they went out to search for me. However, one of the farmers who was my friend hid me, so that they would not find me.

It was still quiet in Stolin at that time. The wild S.S. men had skipped over Stolin for some reason. They only captured David-Horodok, and the Christian residents did their job. The *shkotzim*[2] among the local farmers also perpetrated their deeds in the village of Rubiel as well as the next village.

(Note from the publisher: The murderers from among the Christian residents were not so brazen as to also murder the women and children. This was a well-known form of restraint, a sort of Christian "righteousness" to not attack women. Even in 1920, when the gangs of Bulak-Balachowicz rampaged through Polesye, they maintained this Christian "righteousness".)

The unfortunate, bereaved women wandered through the fields and forests. They were pillaged of all that they had, and there was no place for them to go. The communal council of Stolin interceded strongly. After much effort and payment of high bribes, they were permitted to come to Stolin.

On the second day of Rosh Hashanah, two murderers entered the home of our brother Moshe, removed him from his house, and imprisoned him. After three days, we found out that he had been killed by torture. We only managed to bring him to burial a half a year later. We wrapped him in his tallis, and his son L. recited *Kaddish* for him.

From the time that my days of torture and torment began, I remained alone, surrounded by widows and orphans. I had to concern myself with restoring their starving souls. There was always a *minyan* in our home, and our father recited *Kaddish*, at first for the martyrs of Rubiel, and later for the souls of our brother and aunt. Our father did not speak. He held his lips and was silent. At times, when the women burst out weeping, he would warn them to refrain from lamenting, as he himself choked his tears in his throat.

And me – I was forced to show strength and fortitude, even though I was fully immersed in tears. At 7:00 p.m. it was forbidden to be seen outside. The house was closed. The blinds were drawn, and we sat closed in and talked about you again and again. Do you know our fate, and will you ever find out about it?

Thus did the winter pass. They expelled us from our home on the eve of Passover of 1942. Then, they began to mention that a ghetto would soon be set up in Stolin. Countless payments and fines were extorted from us. They literally ripped the skin off our bodies.

On the eve of Shavuot, they finished encompassing the ghetto with a fence consisting of fifteen metal wires, with three meters between each pillar. We were ordered to move into the ghetto. Each one of us took something along, for we had to sustain the wretched body. Our father took his walking stick and walked. We were all in a single room, as were the others.

In the ghetto, life began that was worse than death. We could not come or go. Every day, twelve people died. People lay down swollen from hunger. I saw the swollen feet of our parents and my heart burst inside of me. There was no other conversation on the lips, only food, and food. We found ways to sneak food into the ghetto. We heard the astounding news. The heart did not want to believe. Could it be possible? Children too? Would such a thing happen?

Then, the dark, dismal day came, the eve of Rosh Hashanah of 1942. There were 7,000 souls in the Stolin Ghetto, and all were murdered. The graves had been prepared beforehand. They were stripped naked, placed prone in the pits, and shot row by row.

[Page 211]

I will never forget the last night in the ghetto... We sat together with our parents until 3:00 a.m. We bid each other farewell, kissed and wept, kissed and wept. We bid farewell to your pictures, and held them close to our hearts. Our father recited the confession, and our mother bathed, donned clean white clothing, and prepared herself to greet death. She chased me out of the house: "Get out of here, leave, you will survive. Hide yourself. It should not be on our hands. At least, you will take revenge for our blood. You will tell about us!"...

At that moment, I did not believe the words of our mother. How can I escape death, we were surrounded on all sides. I finally left them, only to give them the illusion that I would survive, so as to ease their final moment of life. Thus did I part from them forever.

* * *

More than once, I cursed that moment when I left them. O, how I wished to die together with them, embraced in their arms, just like all the martyrs died bound together in an embrace. I lay in a narrow cellar with Zeev M. for eighteen days. I sought a way of leaving there. My heart told me that if I succeed in leaving the ghetto, I would not die. I told me friend that we should try to escape together, but his wife was still alive, hiding in one of the holes, as was his mother, brother N., and sister Batya, and he did not agree to leave them. His uncle Shalom D. and family also remained alive after the slaughter. I was the only orphaned one. I met them at night and attempted to change their minds and search for a way and means to leave the place. However, they waited, for perhaps a miracle would happen. Thus, they remained.

Then I began to search for methods on my own. On the eighteenth night after the slaughter, I snuck out of the ghetto in the darkness. The windows and doors were broken. Everything was desolate. Every moment, it felt to me that I would soon stumble into a body of one of those killed. The hair on my head stood on end.

Then I stumbled into a living person. I approached him, and I was quite surprised when I saw before me a tall gentile. (This was the head of the thieves of Stolin. Later I found out that he was in prison.) He brought me out of the ghetto.

All those who remained behind were dead within a few days.

* * *

At that time, days began that had no worth to me. I was an extra person on the earth! I do not have the power to describe what I endured. Only thanks to some of my friends, farmers from the village, did I succeed in going out to the highway. That means that I entered the partisan brigades, and from there to the Red Army. I will not tell about what happened to me after that, for it is no longer important.

I hope that you will receive a clear idea of everything that we, the residents of the village of Rubiel, endured. In the army, I met two other lads, brothers, the sons of A. Shulman the Levite.

Translated from Yiddish by Y. Idan
Davar, 19 Tishrei 5707 October 10, 1946.

Translator's footnotes:

1. This seemingly refers to the two main Zionist funds at this time: *Keren Kayemet* [Jewish National Fund] and *Keren Hayesod* [Foundation Fund].
2. A derogatory term for gentiles.

After the Holocaust

[Page 226]

After the Holocaust

by Sh. Tchernichovsky, Baruch of Magentza

Translated by Jerrold Landau

G-d is a G-d of recompense. He will surely repay.

(Jeremiah 51:56)

You will pursue them in anger and destroy them from under the heavens of G-d.

(Lamentations 3:66)

Cursed are you, O cruel nation
Cursed be your name
For ever and ever, a curse from on high
Shall lay upon you forever!

Cursed are you more than any person,
And a curse shall rest upon you
As long as you see the light still shining,
And it will descend with you to the netherworld!
Let your strength be erased, let your vigor be dried
Your soul shall bear your iniquity…

— — — — —

You will drown in the blood of your victims
The tears will ring in the sea
And you will be awakened at night, at night
By the screams of the victims, the atrocities…

[Page 227]

My Visit to David-Horodok After the Holocaust

by M. Kravchik

Translated by Jerrold Landau

1. From Moscow to Lakhva

A unique feeling overtook me when I entered the railway center in Moscow, to leave toward Homel. It seemed that from there, I would reach my city, my family circle, my friends, acquaintances, and relatives within another day or two.

The journey was not interesting until the Dnieper, and one could immerse oneself quietly in reading a book or a newspaper, or engage in conversation with the travelers in the car. The travelers began to feel nervous six or seven hours before the Dnieper Bridge. The year was 1945, the bridge of the Dnieper was temporary, and these were the first days after the war. A fear overtook everybody because the train tracks went over the floor of the bridge that was lacking support. However, we finally arrived in the Homel railway station. It was difficult to find the tickets for the train leaving in the direction of Brisk. At that time, the desire to already be in the Lakhva station grew stronger. In the Mikashevitz station, we began to peer into the eyes of those getting on and off, searching for a recognizable face. We already had heard the first stories from the eyewitnesses about the killings in the area. We arrived in Lakhva toward morning.

2. From Lakhva to Horodok

When I got off the train, it seemed to me that the wagon drivers would certainly be present, the ones who used to make the journey between Lakhva and David-Horodok, and that they would grab the baggage of the traveler, as in previous times. However, a deathly silence pervaded in the station. The station itself was not in its regular place, but rather in a small wooden hut. A steward sat inside. To my question, "How does one get to David-Horodok?" He responded, "By foot, there are no longer any *Zhyds* who will transport." While already in the wagon, I was made to realize that not one Jew remains here. Having no choice, I took my suitcase and marched by foot. At a distance of three or four kilometers from there, I met a gentile who knew me from home. He was employed in carrying the mail between the two towns twice a week. Success was with me, for specifically on the day that I arrived, the gentile was traveling with the mail.

The entire route from Lakhva to David-Horodok was partially paved during the wartime. The Germans had brought an electric grid with generators to the place. They cut the trees in the forests and turned them into boards, with which they had improved the road. The gentile Stachiko, in whose wagon I was traveling, told me on the way about what had happened to the Jewish community in David- Horodok. I sensed some strange reticence in his words, and it seemed to me that he wanted to hide the truth from me. "The gentile is behaving according to his manner," I thought, "I will come home, and I will know." The wagon reached the small bridge near the former house of Slobodnik. Stachiko asked me to get off since he was turning toward the right, to his house in front of the post office. When I got off, I felt homeless.

3. The Priest and His Wife

I continued on foot. The houses of the Jews between the small bridge and the large bridge were empty and locked. The windows had been removed from their frames and were boarded up instead. As I crossed the temporary bridge over the Horyn, built of barges and boards, the local priest recognized me and politely invited me to his home. I accepted his invitation and began to pester him with questions. His answers were evasive. Their essence was "We ourselves were afraid of the Germans. We were locked up in our houses and did not see anything. We only learned about the slaughter afterward." When I expressed my wish to go to my parents' home, the priest's wife said, "There is no placed to go. Your house was bombed by the partisans since it was used as a bakery for the German Army." Nevertheless, I went there.

[Page 228]

4. The Destruction

A fear overcame me at the sight of the destruction and ruin around. From the house of Kopel Lichtenstein, it was possible to see through an open-air line directly to Meir Milman's home. Between it and Rimar's home (a distance of 500-600 meters), there was Pitner's home, which remained intact. Next to the ruins of the stone store of Groshko I encountered gentiles who were taking down the remaining stones and loading them on their wagons to take them to "Raditch" [the gentile section of David-Horodok].

5. Two Jewish Souls

I approached the town hall, the offices of which were located in the house of Gottlieb-Meinkin on Luchnikovska Street. I found out from the officials that there were two Jewish women remaining in the city. The daughter of Eizik Furman (the wagon driver) had returned with her Jewish husband (a Soviet citizen) from the Caucasus to live in her native city. There was a young man from the village of Azdamitch named Gitelman (his father had owned the flourmill in the village) who was saved by a Christian woman who had hid him during the conquest. He married her as a token of appreciation. I set out to the house of Furman's daughter (in Boloto [the section of David-Horodok near the marshes]). She lived in the house of a Christian. I spent my two days in David- Horodok there.

6. The Christian Tells

The Christian homeowner was the only one who gave me details about what had transpired during the German occupation. The man began his story, "One day toward morning, they demanded that all the Jewish men present themselves on Kosciuszko Street. Within a few hours, all those summoned had gathered, apparently for work. They were ordered to march forward. Ten Germans were in charge of the operation. Their assistants were local gentiles who had been integrated with the Jewish community. They beat and pushed the Jews with sticks, some of whom were good acquaintances. Next to the observation outpost at the entrance to the town of Olshan, the caravan veered leftward off the main road. The murder aktion of the entire caravan took place a few meters from there. According to an eyewitness, the caravan numbered over 1,000 individuals. A few days later, some of the women were gathered together with the intention of taking them to Stolin. For unknown reasons, the caravan returned from there, and remained on the road next to Lisovitz for days. The cold and rain that afflicted them aroused feelings of bitterness and rebellion against those who were their sole guards. Yaakov Gertzulin's wife stood at the head of the revolt, demanding that they be taken back to David-Horodok. Then, they were all sent to the ghetto that was set up in the Boloto area of the town.

7. On the Streets and in the Market

On the first day of my visit, I began to pass through the streets of the city. The moment when I arrived at the house of Wolf Eisenberg (Bielke's) and the synagogue yard (*Shulhof*) will never be erased from my memory. All the synagogues were completely destroyed, only the four walls of the Hassidic *shtibel* remained. I stood in a corner, with the Pravoslavic Church jutting upward from one side in the center of the marketplace. Only its dome had been damaged. On the other side, there was the destroyed synagogue. It seems as if the church was opening its mouth to say: "You have come to the graveyard of your nation. See, your house has been destroyed. Your nation has been annihilated and will never rise again. Indeed, my head has been damaged, but my nation is with me. My wounds will heal and I will continue my existence. But you, you will not rise again."

Most of the Jewish houses that I passed were empty. Offices of the Soviet government were in some of them. Soviet officials lived in others. Gentiles from the suburbs of the city lived in several houses. The houses were standing in their desolation. The next day, I went out to the market that took place every morning as in days of old. I heard a gentile woman selling fish. She wished to praise her merchandise, and added, "Had the *Zhyds* been here, they would have paid nicely for them."

8. At the Grave

That day, I continued to the village of Olshan, the site of the mass murder. After walking for an hour,

[Page 229]

I found the lookout pillar (the only sign I was given for the location of the mass grave). I stood on the road and asked the passers-by about the exact place of the grave. I received no response. I decided to enter the village and I asked. In return for a significant payment, the first resident I met showed me the place. The victims were buried in four large graves. From lack of experience, the murderers did not cover the graves with sufficient soil. As the person accompanying me said, wolves appeared about ten days after the murder. They began to ransack the soil with their paws and remove body parts. Then, tens of Olshan residents were summoned to cover the graves with additional earth. The remnants of bones, pieces of cloth and hair that I saw there confirmed the words of my accompanier.

Tears flowed from my eyes. With difficulty, I overcame my emotions at that moment. I gathered some of the bones that I found and buried them in the ground. After an hour, I left the place and parted forever from this holy place, and from all the dear and beloved ones who remained there.

In David-Horodok in 1945[i]

by Meir Tzvi Korman

Translated by Jerrold Landau

A. Five Who Returned

Bas-Sheva Lin, the niece (daughter of the sister) of Meir Eliyahu Kushnir, was the only resident of David-Horodok whom I found in the city when I returned after Rosh Hashanah of 5705 [1944]. The water carrier who worked with me for four full years did not recognize me. Her house was full of Jewish goods. From there, I went to 1 The Greble Street. She sent me to a gentile who had taken over the house of Litman Nachmanowitz. "The gentiles of David-Horodok received a high medal of excellence for their proficiency in murdering Jews," that gentile told me. The next day, I requested a place of residence from the authorities. When they offered me a Jewish house, I refused and demanded permission to live in the place of my former butcher shop. My request was denied. However, I ignored the denial, and set up the butcher shop as a dwelling. The authorities even arranged a grocery store for me. In time, Noach, the son of Bezalel Yudovitz, assisted me. He had come to Horodok on crutches, and received full material and medical assistance from the government. After that, Zeev Shalom Lachovsky and Moshe the son of Yisrael Reznik also returned to Horodok.

A butcher shop in David-Horodok

In the photo: (from left to right) Meir-Hershel Korman — from the butchers of the city, Berl Farber — a customer

B. The Slaughter

Eliyahu Kushnir was the first victim of David-Horodok. After he was expelled from his house, he lived in Raditch [the gentile section of David-Horodok], and was murdered by the *Horodtchukas* [Christians of Tartar descent from David-Horodok] while he was walking to the marketplace during the time of the German occupation. After him, Zeev, the son of Grunya Kunda, was murdered on Olshan Street, next to Fleishman's house. On the 17th of Av, the Jews were gathered in the yard of the Catholic Church and transferred to Chinovsk, where the *Horodtchukas* had dug graves. It is difficult to describe the means of torment there. Clothes were removed, limbs were cut off, and the slaughter was perpetrated with whatever implements they had – sticks, stones, firearms. After that,

[Page 230]

they were tossed into the pits that were dug by the gentiles. Their blood flowed through the ditches for three days, and the ground lifted and moved from their death throes.

The father of the pogrom perpetrators was the medic Maraiko, who travelled specially to Pinsk to fetch the S.S. Before his journey, he gathered up and hid the gold of the Jews that was given to him to watch.

C. Those Who Hid

After the selection, the gentiles began to search for Jews in hiding. Avraham Slutsky the wagon driver was the first to be found. The son of Mendel Moravchik was found between the beds of beans, and was murdered on the spot. Reuven Kolozny was murdered in the toilet of the gentile Markovitz – and he remained there. Baruch-Yosef Katzman and his two sons who survived after the slaughter were murdered in their rooms by Dimitry Pozik. Isser Gurevitz was dismembered and his eyes were poked out. Yehoshua Zager from Tury was hiding in an oven. He was removed from there and murdered. Aharon Slomiansky was cast in the Horyn River, and was pulled out of there dead by gentiles who were hired by his wife Rachel. Thus, he at least succeeded having a Jewish burial.

My two children, Bracha and Baruch, who had been smuggled by a gentile woman to the Dubinitz Forest, were brought back to the city by the *Horodtchukas* and murdered by dismemberment in the market square. My son Yaakov succeeded in escaping the vale of murder.

Simcha Mishalov found refuge in a cellar. The maid of the house sustained him for four months there. Finally, she turned him in, and he was taken out to be murdered on The Greble Street. Before he expired, he succeeded in calling out three times : "Scoundrels, what do you want?" The children of Matityahu Korman later informed the Soviet authorities that Boris Sraiko murdered Simcha – and he was arrested and exiled to Siberia.

Rabbi Moshe Ginzburg was spared by the Germans, but out of fear of the *Horodtchukas*, he disguised himself as a woman. A year later, he met his death during the period of the existence of the women's ghetto. Yitzchak, the son of Berl Schmutz, also disguised himself as a woman, but he was recognized and was murdered.

After the slaughter of the men, the women of Horodok were expelled to nearby villages. Some were absorbed into them, and others died along the way. Those who remained and returned to Horodok were murdered by the gentiles and buried in the graves of the men.

Rabbi Moshele's daughter was with the partisans in the forests of Wysokie and was killed. The family members themselves were also subsequently killed.

Golda Rachel, the wife of Meir Eliyahu, met her death in the "chapel" in Choromsk, where she had been hiding.

Shmuel Katzman, Leibel's son, wandered about for four months after the slaughter. The gentiles captured him in the forests of Orly and tore him to pieces.

Nishka Kirzner, Chaim's wife, was found with two other women in their cowshed, and they were murdered there. Leah Kolozny was murdered by the gentiles on the bridge.

D. I Left the City of Killing

Day by day, wandering Jews came to me from the entire region, and I supported them. The gentiles plotted to kill me. One night at 11:00 p.m., a gentile came, dressed up. I warned him, threatened him, and shouted at him – and the police were summoned and saved me.

Finally, I could no longer maintain myself in Horodok due to the hostile attitude towards me – and I left.

Coordinator's footnote:

i.   This article is very similar to the article "Impressions" by Meir Hershel Korman on pages 447-449 in the Yiddish section. Both were written by the same person (Hershel in Yiddish and Tzvi in Hebrew are equivalent names.) However, each article contains unique information, so both have been included.

[Page 239]

The Murderer and His Punishment
(The Slaughter in the House of the Sosniks)

by Leibush Dushnik

Translated by Jerrold Landau

This took place on the Torah portion of *Bereishit*[1] in 1906.[i] Zuchter, Zenko, and Klini – a group of murderous friends – set their steps to the house of the wealthy Meir Leib Korman to murder him and pillage his property. When they reached Malye-Orly on the eve of the Sabbath, it was still early, so they went to Gedalyahu Sosnik, who owned a small tavern. They ordered liquor and got drunk. When Gedalyahu returned from the *Maariv* service, he kicked Zenko and Klini out of the house. Zuchter was dozing at the table. He woke up at night and murdered all the members of the house, five people in total, as well as their brother-in-law who had come from Stolin to invite them to a wedding. Even after he perpetrated this iniquity, Zuchter's drunkenness did not pass, and he remained asleep next to the victims. In the morning, a gentile woman arrived to milk the cow, and found the door closed. She summoned her family who lived in the village, and the police searched and arrested the murderer.

During the First World War, Zuchter was drafted into the army and freed. During the time of the revolution, Zuchter stole pigs from an estate owner in the area. His path led him to Malye-Orly, where the soldiers captured him. Sosnik's children pointed to him as the murderer of their family.

One of the soldiers tied him to his horse and galloped back and forth on the village road until his innards spilled out. Thus shall they be destroyed!

Translator's footnote:

1.   This is the first Torah portion after Simchat Torah.

Coordinator's footnote:

i.   Although this article is in the "After the Holocaust" section, the murders actually did happen in 1906 as reported.

The Small Community

(Rubel)

[Page 243]

A House in the Village

by Yitzchak Idan-Zeldin

Translated by Jerrold Landau

a.

The first of the householders in Rubel was Shlomo Zingerman. His father Moshe was called Moshe from Minkovitz by the Hassidim of his time, for the Minkovitz estate next to Stolin, which he leased from the *poretz* [Polish landowner], in accordance with the custom of the landowners of those days to lease their estates to be worked by a Jewish lessee. These were the famous lessees for whom Y.L. Peretz established a monument of witness in his books, with his wonderful creativity.

For the most part, these lessees were negative characters. Like their landowner masters, they too were of coarse spirit, people who pursued honor, haughty people who aspired for lordship, heavy-handed and hard-hearted – as their personality is portrayed by Peretz in *The Seder of Dogs* and *Mendele the Lessee* which was also performed in theaters, and other books.

However, there were also positive characters, who had a Jewish heart and a good eye, broad knowledge, and open hands. In short, like the students of Abraham our Forefather (and not the wicked Balaam).[1] Moshe, and especially his son Shlomo, were among the lessees of the second group.

Avraham Elazar Rabinovitz, the son of the first rabbi of Rubel, said the following about Shlomo Zingerman, after many years, when he was already among the chief teachers in Vilna: "When I remember Shlomo Zingerman of Rubel, the image of Rabbi Shlomo the Nagid of the author Sholem Asch floats before the eyes of my imagination."

Shlomo was like his father Moshe, having business with the landowners and the estates all his days. He had a horse and wagon, with a lad from Horodok, Moshe Baruch, riding with him. They would go out to the estate and the "court" in the morning and return home in the evening.

b.

Moshe's house was bigger than all the other Jewish houses in the village. (There were 70-80 houses.) The door of the house never closed. It was always open to passers-by. When someone entered, the woman of the house would invite him to the table. If she was not present, the maid would do so. "'Sir Jew' should go, wash his hands, and sit at the table." A Jewish young woman served as the maid in the house throughout all the years, and not, Heaven forbid, a gentile from the shiksas [non-Jewish women (usually derogatory)] of the village.

The young woman would work for several years until she had amassed enough money for a dowry. Then the owners of the house would marry her off to a man and arrange the wedding in their house, as if she were their own daughter and not a maid. They would give her presents, and she would then go with her husband to build her own home. A new young woman would come in her place, and this scenario would repeat.

The tablecloth would never be removed from the table, especially during the summer months when many people passed through the village: paupers from Horodok, peddlers, and ordinary poor people. The village was large, there were many farms, and the farmers always had something to sell. Sometimes, the guest would remain for the evening and dinner.

There was a very large room in the house. That room was larger than the other rooms, and was designated for honored guests. When the period of rabbis took place in Rubel, with a rabbi coming, a rabbi leaving, and a new rabbi appearing, the large room would serve as the venue for those who came to see him. The walls of that room were adorned with pictures of the great ones of Israel, *Gaonim*, and leaders of the generation. A picture of the holy city of Jerusalem, may it speedily be rebuilt, in an antique gold frame, hung over the door leading to the next room.

c. *Melave Malka*

On Saturday night after *Havdalah*, the young son Shmuel would take his violin from the wall, and begin to play. His friends Motel and Yudel Berman, the elder son of Shimon the *Shochet*, were next to him. He played the violin, and they played flutes, as they would play music and escort the departing [Sabbath] Queen.

[Page 244]

Other youths, children, and young adults would come to the large room. Girls would not come, for once a girl reached the age of 11 or 12, she was forbidden from being in the company of men. If a girl managed to escape from the eye of her own mother, she could not evade the eye of Gisha, the mistress of the house. Shlomo's wife Gisha was observant of the commandments, and stringent about the easy as well as difficult ones. She was exacting about matters of religion, and conducted herself as one of the righteous women. Under no circumstances would she allow any traditions of the ancestors to be taken lightly. Her eyes were even always upon her youngest son Shmuel, lest he stray, Heaven forbid, from accepted customs. There was no shortage of vexation in the house regarding this. If she would see her son, whose friends were leading him off the "straight path," shortening his prayers and being lenient about the morning washing of hands, she would be certain that he was not fulfilling the commandments, that he had not recited a legitimate Grace After Meals, and countless other complaints regarding the laxity of the younger generation. There should never be such a thing. The religious tradition as transmitted to her was to be transmitted exactly the same to her progeny.

During the winter, when the day was short and the evening was long, the oven would be specially lit on Saturday night to prepare a fourth meal in honor of the departing Sabbath Queen. This is the Hassidic feast of *Melave Malka.*[2]

Two barrels stood in the storehouse from the beginning of the autumn. One had pickled cabbage, and the other had frozen meat. It was not only the members of the household who were invited to that meal, for it was a meal of religious significance.

d. Hassidism in Rubel

The small community was connected to Horodok rather than Stolin in all matters. The vast majority of the people of the village were not Hassidim, even though they worshiped in the *Nusach Sephard* rite.[3]

The veteran *Misnagdim* [non-Hassidic people] in the village maintained their independence, and conducted an early *minyan* at sunrise on Sabbaths and festivals, as was the custom of the *Misnagdim*, unlike the Hassidim who would worship later. Nevertheless, there were roots of Hassidism in the village. The most prominent sign of Hassidism was the custom to come to the home of Shimon the *Shochet* before the end of the Sabbath to partake of the Third Sabbath Meal [*Seuda Shelishit* or *Shalosh Seudos*]. The Sabbath hymns of the father and young sons would burst forth through the low windows of Rabbi Shimon's house and be carried afar.

During the days of Passover, they would go to the synagogue in the afternoon and sing the well-known Haggadah songs.

The chief singer was a Jew who was not necessarily well off, Yossel Tzeitel's, a carpenter by trade. He would sing with all of his 248 limbs, in the sense of "all my limbs shall say."[4] He was given the rights to lead the second *Maariv* service on festivals.[5] The hearts of the women would literally depart from the sweetness of his voice, which was like "a violin player."

They would also come on the Intermediate Days of Sukkot for the *Simchat Beit Shoeiva*.[6] Shlomo would send for liquor and cakes from the house,[7] and they would drink *Lechayim* in memory of the days of yore in the Temple.

e. The Synagogue in Rubel

The synagogue stood at the edge of an alleyway, facing the fields. The synagogue was built many years before us, for its roof was already leaky during our childhood, and it was necessary to bring shingles and to hire a tradesman from Stolin to cover the roof with new shingles.

Two of the elders, Shlomo and Moshe (he was Moshe Durchin, the father of all the Durchins in Rubel) were still very young when they carried thick wooden beams on their shoulders to lay the foundations of the synagogue. They carried them from the river, through the entire breadth of the village, all the way to the fields, where the building site was. As they both walked, bent under the heavy load, they certainly saw themselves as carrying the hewn stones of the Temple Mount to build the Holy Temple in Jerusalem.

That synagogue was a witness to the double murder perpetrated by the band of Balachowiczes on Simchat Torah of 1920. It took place in the afternoon, when the festival was eclipsed, and the joy turned to bitterness.

They attempted to arrange the hanging of Moshe's son Yehuda Durchin, on the *bima* of the synagogue "in the same place where I had an *aliya* to the Torah in the morning" – as he later said.

They murdered someone in the anteroom of the synagogue a short time before. That was his nephew, Aharon Hershel Durchin. Shalom Boyer, a young man from Stolin, was murdered along with him in the anteroom. He had been spending the festival with

[Page 245]

his wife's mother in Rubel. When they had arrested the young man, his mother-in-law ran after him to save him. The murderers told her to bring a ransom of two hundred rubles, and they would free him. She went back, obtained the money, and brought it to them. They received the ransom from her, and returned to her a dead body rather than a living person.

The synagogue was a large, spacious building. Its tall windows declared to every passer-by that it was a holy place, and honor must be given to the House of G-d.

Even though the building stood near the fields, separate and far from the houses of the Jews, and the villagers would pass by it daily on their way to the nearby fields – they never dared to damage it at all, to throw a stone or to break the windows, as was their custom on their night of watching, the eve of Good Friday before Easter, to take revenge for their crucified messiah.

If they were angry or had a grudge against some Jew – that night would be a night of revenge, where they would break the windows of the Jew on their way home from church after the festival service. That night was also a night of watching for the Jews,[8] to pull down the shutters. In houses that had no shutters over the windows, they would cover and protect them with boards or doors that they took from the inside rooms.

There were no shutters over the windows of Yehuda Durchin's home. One year, there was a concern that the youths would throw stones at the windows as they passed by the house. The residents of the house went outside with lanterns in their hands to light up the way for the passers-by. Their son Aharon would light them and call out a verse from the New Testament, "Happy are the tormented, happy are the pursuers of peace, love your enemies, if you forgive a person for their sins – your father in heaven will also forgive you." This announcement was quite effective. The stone in the hand dropped to the ground and was not thrown.

We will return to talk about the synagogue: There were about eighty seats there. On festivals, when children would return to their parents' home from the city, the synagogue would be filled to the brim. People and children also crowded in the anteroom.

The synagogue also had another trait. It was flush with the open fields, and at times we would go out in the middle of the services to feast our eyes on the expanse of grain stalks swaying in the wind.

f. Disseminators of *Haskalah* in Rubel

When Shlomo's children got older, he would bring young teachers for them from Horodok. The teachers would teach the boys as well as the girls Bible, grammar, and the Russian and German languages. These teachers would bring to the village the spirit of the *Haskalah* [Enlightenment] of that time, the *Haskalah* writers and their books: *The Mysteries of Paris* by Kalman Schulman, and *The Painted Eagle, Guilt of Samaria*, and *Love of Zion* by Abraham Mapu. All of the writings that appeared in the Jewish world at that time also reached the remote village, *Hamagid, Hameilitz, Der Yud*, and the house was connected with the greater Jewish world, and lived a communal Jewish life. Along with the members of the household were their friends and relatives of the same age, and especially the children of Shimon the *Shochet*, the intelligent Motel and Yudel.

When the convention in Katowice took place in 1884, which led to the founding of the *Chovevei Zion* [Lovers of Zion] organization, the household followed what was going on there from across the border in Russia, and their hearts swore an oath of allegiance to Zion.

The children of Nachum Neiditz, the well-known teacher from Horodok, Eizik and his brother Yaakov, disseminated *Haskalah* in the village. Shlomo had brought them from Horodok to be teachers to his children. As is known, these brothers later went out to the wide world and gained worldwide renown.

After them Yosef Choroshchensky, the brother of Mordechai Choroshchensky, the father of the Choroshchenskys in Rubel, served as the teacher in the home. The children, along with the few other youths in the village became acquainted with the new winds that began to blow in our poor world, the winds of *Haskalah* and the winds of new nationalism. National songs and songs of Zion in Yiddish and Hebrew echoed through the roads of the village from the mouths of the youth. They knew about everything happening in the Jewish world. When the great tragedy of the Kishinev Pogrom took place in the spring of 1903, the members of the household read the newspapers, knew what had happened, and participated in the great sorrow that overtook "The House of Jacob" in Russia.

[Page 246]

g. Dr. Herzl is No More…

We were young children then in the summer of 5664 - 1904, when the illustrious leader died. We, a group of friends, including the brothers Avraham and Yosef Choroshchensky, were strolling through the roads of the village. This was on a Saturday afternoon. The Choroshchensky parents came to meet us along with their guest, their brother Yosef Choroshchensky, who had been the teacher in Shlomo's house some years earlier. Yosef the uncle decided to test us on our knowledge of Hebrew. He followed us in the middle of the street and asked this simple question: On the first page of *Hatzefira*, in a black frame, the words "Herzl is no more" are written. What does "is no more" [*einenu*] mean? Should it not have said "Herzl is dead" [Herzl met]? What is *einenu*? A poignant question! We stood astounded and silent. None of us found an answer to the question. There were very talented children amongst us. Then Choroshchensky explained to us: *einenu* means that there is none similar to him, no one like him.[9]

That week, we were studying the weekly Torah portion, *Matot-Masai* with the teacher Pesach Golombovitz, our first modern teacher after the *melamdim*. We read in the *Chumash* "And Egypt was burying the firstborns whom G-d had smitten…" [Numbers 33:4]. Our friend Baruch Berman, one of the young sons of Shimon the *Shochet*, was sitting amongst us. He burst out in laughter at the words "Egypt is burying." This was the laughter of revenge for the evil Egypt. We were wondering about this laughter. Our friend Avraham Durchin (living in the Land) reacted to this, "And on this day we will bury him…" an echo to the great tragedy that overtook the Jewish people with the passing of the leader.

The Sabbath came. The youths of Rubel, the older sons of Shimon the *Shochet*, Shmuel and their friends, decided to arrange a memorial ceremony for Herzl from the *bima* of the synagogue. When he time of the memorial came, the *shamash* Matityahu the Melamed pointed to the youths and began *Kel Male Rachamim*.[10] The pious from among the Hassidim, Shlomo's brother Yaakov and Leizer Gomer rose and protested: "No, it is not permitted to arrange a memorial in the holy place for their heretic Dr." The youths stood perplexed. As if the general tragedy was not enough, the small private tragedy was added. They were not even permitted to mourn the death of the leader... Yehuda Durchin, the president of the synagogue authorized by the government, decided in favor of the spirit of the youths and gestured to Matityahu to continue. The memorial took place. The youths were victorious over the darkened ones, who lacked the light.

h. Oh, All Who Thirst, Come to Water...[11]

These youths of Rubel did not sit with folded hands. They did not regard themselves as sitting on a remote island. Rather, they regarded themselves as part of the Jewish world. The newspapers that appeared in Russia at that time, *Hameilitz, Hamagid, Hatzefira*, and the Yiddish *Der Yud*, reached the village in order, and the youths of the village knew about everything that was taking place in the larger Jewish world, and saw it as their duty to do what was being done in all places for the sake of the new movement, the renaissance movement of the nation, first and foremost, in the area of education and culture.

Taking the example of the activists of nearby Horodok, especially of Aharon Yonah Shafer, who brought the well-known teacher Yishai Adler to the town and opened a modern school – our youths rose up and also founded a similar modern institution in their village, in which the children would not only learn *kometz aleph oh*,[12] but rather learn according to the modern methodology. The language of instruction was not a translation to Yiddish, but rather Hebrew in Hebrew. Furthermore, boys and girls studied together.

Who were the teachers in this new school?

Shimon the *Shochet* was greatly honored and important in the community. He had two older sons from his first wife. They, together with Shmuel the son of Shlomo, were the center of this new movement. Several other youths gathered around them, girls as well, which was an innovation to that generation. Of course, it was girls from the family.

When the modern school opened, Motel as one of the teachers. The second, who served as principal, was Yaakov Reznik, the son of Eizel the butcher from Horodok. He had a grandmother in the village, Hinda Rivka the wife of Meir Moshe the scribe.

They rented a home from a farmer, brought in benches (*skameikes* in the vernacular), and not simple tables as in the *cheder*. They placed them in rows. They brought in a podium for the teacher, a blackboard, chalk, and a bell – and behold, it was a veritable school.

[Page 247]

They hung an announcement in the synagogue, as follows: "O, all who are thirsty, come to water, and those who have money, go buy and eat" (Isaiah 55:1). This verse from the Bible served as the permit for the youths to talk in the holy place about the revolution that they were about to make in the education of the generation.

In the second year, the institution was transferred to a large house, and rays of light from the wide world penetrated the village.

i. The Library

These young activists also concerned themselves with culture. They gathered the books that they owned and donated them to the public library. They brought all the works of Peretz Smolenskin, and other children's books that were published at that time. At first, the library was in Shlomo's warehouse, for who would bring this *treif-pasul*[13] into the house – for they were not from among the sacred books? Later, when our turn came to stand on guard of the renaissance, the library was already housed in a private house. We paid rent and purchased a bookcase. Everything was as it should be.

Uncaptioned. Seemingly one of the library activists mentioned in the following paragraph.

The library activist was the greatest of our friends, Aharon Hershel Durchin, may G-d avenge his blood. He had the opportunity to obtain all the works of the Russan Turgenev, a large number of volumes at a low price, from Vintus the village medic. The works of Belinsky, the great Russian literary critic, were also brought to the library. There were also many Yiddish books for the many readers who did not know Hebrew. However, most of the books were in Hebrew. As the years went on, the library became a point of light for the youth. Generation after generation, guard upon guard, tended to it with love and dedication. In the final pre-war years, the library contained more than seven hundred books on six bookcases. The dedicated activists conducted various events to grow the income of the library and to obtain new books on occasion. The activists included Baruch the son of Noach Leib Zezik, Roza the daughter of Yaakov Lifshitz, may G-d avenge her blood, and, alive in the Land: Yitzchak the son of Motel Zingerman, and Yisrael Yaakov Kolodny.

The Polish teacher and Warsaw native, Rachel Feler, did great things. She was a teacher in the Tarbut School in the village. Through her connections to the capital city, she enriched the library with many books.

There was a period when the library in the village served the people of the nearby towns of Stolin as well as Horodok. The residents of Horodok recall that during the year prior to the revolution, there was a large library in the town, but it was shut and locked, until someone recommended that the library be transferred from the village to the town so that the masses could enjoy. However, the local residents objected, saying, "We prefer our poverty here over wealth in a different place."

j. Volumes of *Hashiloach*

Our friend Aharon Hershel, may G-d avenge his blood, found out from the activists in Horodok that one could obtain all the volumes of *Hashiloach* for the library for free. One only had to issue a certification from the responsible person stating that a public library exists in the place.

Who was the philanthropist who donated the issues of *Hashiloach* to distribute to libraries for free? It was the well-known activist Kalonymus Zev Wissotzky, the owner of the famous Wissotzky Tea Company. He was a great lover of Zion, one of the founders of the [*Chovevei Zion*] organization in Katowice in 1884. He was also once sent by the *Chovevei Zion* headquarters to the visit the Land and report on the situation of the settlements that were in a difficult position at that time. Those were the settlements of the First Aliya: Petah Tikva, Rosh Pina, Zichron Yaakov, and Rishon LeZion. Incidentally, it is worthwhile to note that this Zionist activist left a bequest of one million rubles to found the Technion in Haifa.

[Page 248]

Indeed, who was the person of authority who would be able to confirm the existence of a library in the village of Rubel? It is self-evident that it would be the rabbi. Aharon Hershel went to Rabbi Moshe Chaim Hechtman, who settled in the village after the Balachowiczes. The rabbi gave him the requested certification.

Before long, packages of books arrived from Odessa: dozens of *Hashiloach* booklets covered with green covers, enjoyable to the heart and attractive to the eye, enchanting, and calling out: "Take us and enjoy us." Indeed, we enjoyed them as "first fruits before summer." They were like sweet honey and intoxicating wine to us.

We gave the booklets over to be bound, and the library of the village was suddenly enriched with a large treasury of thought, poetry, literature, and science. These volumes opened for us a window to the wide world of Jewry.

We got to know Mendele the Hebrew and Brenner from these volumes of *Hashiloach*. It was a great enjoyment to read the *Thoughts and Deeds* feuilletons of "Rabbi Karov" at the end of every booklet. This "Rabbi Karov" was the merchant and author E. L. Levinsky, whose name is borne by the Teachers' Seminary in Tel Aviv. He was a central figure among the group of writers in Odessa. He published the utopian *Journey to the Land of Israel in the Year 5800*.

These feuilletons were offered to the readers as a sort of wonderful fruit soup or tasty dessert after the ample, fine meal of important articles in the booklet.

The taste of these *Thoughts and Deeds* is guarded in our mouths to this day…

Finally, we should remember in a positive way the houses which hosted the library in the village: Sara Leah the widow of Reb Shimon Berman the *Shochet*, Nachum Durchin, Zelig the Carpenter, Yehuda Baruch Frumkin, and the final host until the time of the Holocaust – the home of the ordinary Jew Yossel Plotnitzky, who related to the library with honor, as a holy matter. He only accepted a very small, symbolic rent payment.

k. Two Thousand Years Ago…

To complete the needs of the small community, a small bathhouse was built at the bank of the river through the initiative of the rabbi. That bathhouse had sweat boards, a *mikveh* for ritual immersion, as well as baths. During the winter, gentiles from among the local farmers or those of the nearby area would also come. On Friday afternoons, they would sweat along with the Jews in honor of the Sabbath.

On occasion, they had to make repairs on the bathhouse, and the appropriate sums of money were not always collected.

During the days of Rabbi Hechtman, there was a need for money for repairs, but money was not obtained. The community refused to give. The rabbi thought, and found a ruse to force the people to give their part. During services on the Sabbath, he announced from the pulpit that nobody would be permitted to bring their tallis home. The tallis would remain in the hands of the rabbi as a surety until the money would be brought. He spoke thus and did thus. After the services, he stood at the door to confiscate the tallises of the worshippers.

Another time when money was again needed, the important householders went down and the others went up. Those whose hearts were open had empty pockets, and those whose pockets were full had closed hearts, so the bathhouse remained firmly locked. Discussions regarding the bathhouse and the *mikveh* never ceased in the synagogue.

One day after services, a few people remained behind to conclude their prayers, Shlomo Zingerman among them. Yossel Plotnitzky, or Yossel "Samachdregas" as he was known in the village, stood in the second corner of the synagogue. He was childless, ignorant, and had a coarse spirit. Yossel began to speak on the issue of the times: the bathhouse. He opened his mouth and said in a cynical tone, "Of course, it will be good without a *mikveh...*" Shlomo heard his words, and responded with the following historical story:

Two thousand years ago, a Jewish woman gave birth to a son without a *mikveh* – and we have bundles of trouble from him to this day...

[Page 249]

l. The Second Synagogue in the Village

There was a second concentration of Jewish houses at the second edge of the village, in the direction of Stolin. These were working Jews, tradesmen, carpenters, shoemakers, builders, and sawmill workers – Pilshchikes. A large number of the houses of the farmers in the villages on the routes to Stolin and Pinsk were built by the callused hands of these upright workers. They would go out to the villages with their work tools at dawn on Sunday, and return on Friday afternoon. As their numbers grew, they built a small synagogue in their neighborhood, so as not to tire themselves with the long walk to the synagogue at the other end of the village. Only on Sabbaths when the rabbi delivered a sermon to the congregation, or when one of the *Maggidim* would preach his words to the community – and *Maggidim* did visit the village frequently – did these toiling Jews trouble themselves to go to the large synagogue at the other end.

The only one who lived in their neighborhood and who went on the long route to the first synagogue on Sabbaths and festivals was Shlomo Durchin, even though he had a place on the eastern wall of their own synagogue. He went either because of family connections or because he did not feel close with his Jewish neighbors. The common thread in that neighborhood was that this was pure Judaism, without excessive neighborly connections with the gentiles.

When the settlement dwindled and the bathhouse at the bank of the river was destroyed, they also built their own bathhouse in the courtyard of their synagogue.

The wealthy person in that neighborhood, the first in any communal matter, was Mordechai Nosanchuk. Any matter in the neighborhood was decided by his mouth. He would bring in a teacher for children. He continued in this role throughout all the years, even when the Tarbut School was built. He concerned himself with the school and the proper credentials of the teachers until he left the village to move to Stolin. He would bring in more than one of the *maskilim* of Horodok to the village to disseminate Torah to the children of those toiling families. They would partake of their meals at their tables in rotation, in accordance with the conditions of those times.

The writer of these lines also taught their children from time to time, until he left to nearby Horodok. Among those toiling Jews were several Jews like the Jews of Y. L. Peretz, the Sabbath and festival Jews, refined Jews with all their simplicity, with a way of life of working people that were upright and of the straight path. Ch. N. Bialik wrote his poem regarding such people: "May my lot be with them." He called them "Tormented of this world, with mute souls, you are the faithful guardians of the spirit of G-d in the world." We will bring here the memory of several of them: Yehuda Burshtein the shoemaker, Yosha Rimar the saddler, Moshe Feigelman the carpenter, and others.

m. Rabbis in Rubel

i.   The *Shochet* is the Rabbi

There was no rabbi in the village for many years. The number of householders was not yet large enough to sustain the family of a rabbi. In addition, there was no urgent need for a local rabbinical guide. There was a *shochet* living in the village, Rabbi Shimon Berman. He was a Hassid of Stolin and a native of Breznitz-Dombrovitz. He was the former brother-in-law of Shlomo Zingerman. He would fill the role of rabbi at times of need. He would provide guidance in the laws of women,[14] issue decisions related to issues of meat and milk, etc. He was a Torah-oriented person with generous traits. He was honored by everyone, and had major influence upon all the residents of the village, just like a rabbi in his congregation. Rabbi Shimon filled the job of rabbi for tens of people.

When the community grew, a rabbi was brought to the village. He was an actual rabbi, a man of stature, and possessing of authority. This was Rabbi Yechiel Michal Rabinovitz, the first rabbi of Rubel. Rabbi Rabinovitz ran his community with a strong hand. We were friends with his young sons Yosef and Chona in the *cheder* of Avraham the Melamed. His oldest son Avraham Elazar, who was noted in the early chapters, was a friend of my brother Yudel, may G-d avenge his blood (perished along with his wife and daughter in the community of Pinsk). Both of them studied Gemara with the rabbi.

ii.   The Man With the Angry Eyelids

When Shimon the *Shochet* grew old and no longer had the energy, he taught his oldest son Motel the laws

[Page 250]

of *shechita* [ritual slaughter], so he could take his place from time to time. This was logical and natural, and did not arouse any opposition. Everyone greatly honored Rabbi Shimon and related to his deeds with full trust. At that time, there was a man meticulous about religious matters, who was zealous for the L-rd of Hosts, who raised a racket and instigated a wave of protest.

Moshe Durchin had a brother named Wolf. That Wolf was an unparalleled zealot, a man of wrath with angry eyelids. He considered himself as a protective wall for G-d's Torah, with a character similar to the well-known *shochet* in the *Yosha Egel* play. We children knew his difficult spirit and did not like him. He used to suddenly appear in the *cheder* of our rebbe Avraham the Melamed, sit comfortably at the head of the table and act as the superintendent. He would test our knowledge of Bible. He would begin a verse and ask us to finish it. He brought a bad spirit in with him when he came to the *cheder*.

When this Wolf heard about the young *shochet*, he raised his voice, shouting, "Can it be that a lad who sits together with young women be a *shochet*? He will feed us non-kosher, *treif* meat! Such a thing will surely not be!" The village was in ferment. Some were opposed and others were in favor, and the Satan of discord celebrated its victory, as was common in Jewish communities during that time. However, the power of the *shamash* [beadle] was displayed with full strength later, when the saga of the rabbis of the village began.

iii.   The Contempt of Torah

Rabbi Rabinovitz lived in the village for six years, and then moved to Dombrovitz. The ship of the small community was left without a captain, but not for long. Candidates for the rabbinical seat began to stream to the village. A rabbi came, ascended the pulpit, delivered a sermon to the congregation, and made a good impression. It seemed that everything was straight and smooth. However, when the matter came down to action, everything disbanded and was as if it had not been. The rabbi left as he had come, and another rabbi came to try his luck. This happened repeatedly. Woe to the people for the contempt of Torah [*Pirkei Avot* 6:2]. How much disgrace, desecration of honor, how much oppression of the soul and contempt did these candidates for the rabbinical seat in "large" Rubel endure. The matter with the signatures on the writ. Local Jews were requested to sign their names that they install Rabbi so and so the son of so and so to guide, and judge in their community, and they obligate themselves to several obligations: To purchase Sabbath candles from the rebbetzin, as well as yeast for challah – all those were the monopoly of the rabbi. Those two primary sources of income, as well as the festival payments at the holidays, and other sporadic sources of income, such as for conducting weddings, rabbinical adjudications, and the like, were not great in this small community.

That is where the differences of opinions and discord began. Some said yes, others said no, and there was no end to the matter. This was the way things were in large and small Jewish communities. The matter never ended.

Several candidates came, delivered fine sermons, and left empty-handed. One winter, Reb Dovidl Berkovitz brought his son-in-law, the husband of his daughter Alta, to Rubel. He died in his prime. He was a young man great in Torah. Apparently, everything went smoothly. Reb Dovidl worked, wearied himself, and interceded, but he did not achieve success.

Another time, in the summer, his nephew Reb Baruch Zeldin, his sister's son, came. He too was ordained as a rabbi. He attempted to obtain the rabbinate of Rubel, but also did not succeed.

Two were accepted and settled there, but they left after a short period. One settled at the second end of the village. Mordechai Nosanchuk gave him a dwelling in his house. He lived as he lived, and finally left the village.

The second settled in the larger edge of the village. He also lived as he lived, and left at his first opportunity. He later initiated a lawsuit against the householders who signed the writ. The matter continued for several years. A rabbi came, a rabbi left, and there was no rabbi. Finally, a young rabbi from Slutsk came to Rubel. He was a man of stature, who excelled over the masses, and knew how to win over people's hearts.

iv.   A Rabbi, a Man of the People

He was also not accepted by everyone at first. A miracle such as that does not happen. He left the few, the well-pedigreed people, and went to the masses of regular people. He visited their homes and talked with them. The regular people were unaccustomed to such honor – especially the women. He won over their hearts. He brought his family. He rented a dwelling

[Page 251]

and settled in. He made no preconditions, and did not request signatures on the writ. He slowly but surely captured the hearts of the community. The number of his opponents dwindled continually, and, at the end, he was loved by everyone.

He also suffered from want during the first period, but he was supported by his father-in-law, a wealthy Jew from Slutsk, who from time to time fed anyone who reached the disgrace of hunger.

The young rabbi, Moshe Chaim Hechtman, conducted his small community with wisdom and understanding. He taught the chapter [of *Pirkei Avot*] during summer Sabbaths, and Mishnah between *Mincha* and *Maariv*. He frequently delivered sermons on Sabbaths. In time, he became endeared to everyone, including the youths.

Rabbi Hechtman led his small community during the days of the First World War, until the days of the great disaster of the Balachowiczes, may their names be blotted out (Sukkot 1920), in which he and his family also suffered greatly. After the community was shaken up by the disaster and many left, some to America and others to nearby cities, the rabbi found the opportunity to go to the city of Sarny, where there were several Rubel natives. He was appointed as the government rabbi with the support of the local Zionist community. He built a large house, married off his daughters, and lived a life of comfort and honor, until the arrival of the terrible Holocaust, in which he and his community perished among all the thousand communities in the country of Poland. May G-d avenge their blood.

Later on, several details about the last hour of the rabbi became known. He hid for some time, and was not removed from his house with all those who were found. After his hiding place was exposed and he was found, he was led bareheaded outside, where he was murdered. May G-d avenge his blood.

After the departure of Rabbi Hechtman, the community of Rubel did not remain without a rabbi. Yossel, the second son of Rabbi Dovidl came and served as a rabbi for many years. He returned to Horodok after the death of his father Rabbi Dovidl to take his place.

This ends the annals of the rabbis of Rubel. Now we will discuss rabbis from Rubel.

n. Rabbis from Rubel

The village did not produce many high school graduates. On the other hand, it did send many of its sons to Yeshivas, and many became ordained and occupied rabbinical seats.

Rabbi Hechtman, and his position in the city, served for many households, and especially for many mothers, as a fine example of how to build a career for the sons in Yeshiva and as rabbis in communities. We have before us a long list of rabbis. Most of them immigrated to the United States and Canada, following their fathers, to fructify the desolate fields of Judaism in the new world.

A more living and more instructive and practical example was the first two natives of our village, of our age, who became rabbis of renown thanks to their unusual talents and diligence.

The first was Yitzchak the son of Leib and Bracha Stollman, today a rabbi in Detroit. He was a deep lad with unusual talents, as well as an artist. Even when occupied in Talmudic discussions, he had the "evil inclination" to draw from chapter to chapter. When he was studying in Slobodka, he received regular monthly support from his father in America, so he would not suffer from the tribulations of a Yeshiva student, and not degrade himself to partake of his meals in rotation at the tables of strangers. His dress was splendid and elegant, literally

[Page 252]

not like a Yeshiva student. With his talents, he would have been able to successfully complete an upper-level school for sciences and become famous in the modern world. However, he did not, Heaven forbid, get enticed to leave the world of Torah and transfer to another world.

After some time, he visited the Land, and was even invited to direct a well-known Yeshiva in Jerusalem. He lived in the Holy City for one year. He returned to his former place for various reasons to lead his flock. From there, he went overseas.

The second was of the same age – Mordechai the son of Chana and Natan Elya Gertzulin the smith. He was from a home of literal paupers, and he was not graced with special talents. It was only because of his strong desire and diligence that he attained that which he attained. When these two natives of the village would come home for the holidays, they would treat the congregation to a lecture in the synagogue. The first, Yitzchak or Itzel Stollman, knew what he was preaching, and the second, Mordechai, preached what he knew. That Mordechai encapsulated the character that the writer Azar, Alexander Ziskind Rabinovitz, portrayed in one of his stories *From the Yeshiva*. Avraham Hirsch was the name of Azar's hero in his interesting story. Avraham Hirsch was not unique in the dwellings of Jacob. Our village also had one such as that.

Those two were guides to those who followed in the next generation. They are as follows, without giving details about them:

3.   Moshe Milman, the son of Yosef and Gruna Feigel, a writer for *Davar*. He lives in Hadera. Y. Shiv is his relative. He was a rabbi in Kostopol.
4.   Shimon Shulman the son of Motel, of the wide-branched Shulman family of the village. Another two sons of Avraham Shulman as well (who are mentioned in the book).
5.   Berl Budimsky the son of Moshe.
6.   Zeev the son of Nachum Durchin, grandson of Wolf, the religious zealot who was mentioned in earlier chapters.
7.   Shaul Rosenzweig the son of Chaim Leib and Rivel of the Gomer family. He was a rabbi in Pinsk. He has relatives in the Land. He is a cousin of Chaim Weizmann.
8.   His brother Berl Rosenzweig, a rabbi in Cuba.
9.   Moshe Hechtman the son of Rabbi Hechtman. He is in America.

10.   Hershel Stollman, a rabbi in Brooklyn. He is the son of Chava and Nachum who were murdered by the Balachowiczes in Rubel. He is the brother of Ada Stollman of the Teachers' Center, and her sister Zelda who participated in our   book.

11.   Aharon the son of Dov Bokov.

12.   Shlomo the son of Yeshayahu Bokov (a *shochet*).

o. Immigration to the Land

Then, in those generations, it was a great merit to immigrate to the Land of Israel and to be buried in the holy soil – but this was not a common occurrence. Only a few took hold of that merit. Only those who came to a general agreement, without a shadow of doubt or uncertainty, as if it is written about them: To him it is fitting, to him it shall be fitting.[15] Only such a person would leave his family and the people of his place during his evening years and make *aliya* to the Land of the Patriarchs, to return his soul to G-d there, and to be saved from the tribulation of rolling through the tunnels[16] at the time of the Resurrection of the Dead.

There would not even be one such person in a city, and there would not be such a person at all times. The writer Micha Yosef Berdichevsky enriched our book with a story about one such person who left for the Land of Israel from his city of Tolna, Natan Nota the *Shochet*. From the days of our childhood, we know about two such situations of *aliya*. One was the elderly Rabbi Avraham Ber of Kozhan-Horodok, the father of the rabbis Rabbi Itche of Lakhva and Rabbi Dovidl of Horodok.

We went to Horodok to bid him farewell. He placed his hand on our heads and blessed us, his great-grandchildren. He gave us each eighteen coins as a token of blessing.

[Page 253]

The second was Rabbi Meir Moshe the writer of Rubel. He traveled with his wife Hinda Rivka, the grandmother of the teacher Yaakov Reznik, who was mentioned in earlier chapters.

It was a lovely summer day. The wagon with their belongings drove in front of them. Walking behind it were the *olim* [immigrants to the Land of Israel], accompanied by women, men, and children accompanying them until they left the village.

When the entourage passed by the *cheder* of Avraham the Melamed, our rebbe interrupted his lesson, when out to the street, and told us to run to catch up with the old man and get a blessing from him.

We ran, and reached the head of the entourage, and we each stuck out our small hands and wished him "Travel in peace." The old man touched our heads with his hands as a sign of blessing. In the name of historical truth, we should add that there was one other *aliya* from Rubel. It was a literal *aliya*, not of old people on the verge of death, but rather of youths who traveled to the Land to try their luck there. It was not from inspiration and aspiration, like all those who made *aliya* on the Third Aliya, but rather because of some spirit that overtook them, for they were people who were very far from inspiration and idealism.

These were the two: Mordechai the glassmaker, a pure, upright man, from among the simple folk. He was poor and indigent all his life. The second was Moshe Kotsh, who made a living by his profession, but was also very poor in body and spirit. They used to travel to southern Russia to work there in the summer. Apparently, they were swept up with the stream of the Second Aliya to seek work in the Land. They remained there for the time they remained, and just as the Land absorbed them, it expelled them. They returned to the village, and nobody knew what was what. Nobody started up with them because their spiritual level was less than zero. It was well known that only few people of the Second Aliya withstood all the trials and remained in the Land. Approximately ninety percent left. Only ten percent remained in the Land. On the other hand, the village merited to serve as a host for the regional convention of *Hechalutz* [The Pioneer]. This was at the height of the Fourth Aliya. Approximately a hundred *Chalutzim* [Zionist pioneers] came from Stolin, Horodok, and the region in 5685 / 1925 to prepare for *aliya* to the Land.

Uncaptioned. A group meeting (caption unclear), from 5685 / 1925

[Page 254]

They were unable to gather in Stolin or Horodok because of the evil eye of the government, so they chose a place between the two cities.

p. The Class War

In its time, this was a matter of *shkotzim* [non-Jewish men (usually derogatory)] in our eyes, when the simple people burst forth against the honorable ones in a revolt against the people of the eastern wall in the synagogue.[17]

Of course, there were not workers and employers in the village. There were not oppressed and oppressors. As in any large or small community, there were classes. There was the class of shopkeepers and merchants, and the class of tradespeople and craftspeople, who earned their livelihoods from both the Jews and the farmers. These were the "householders" who sat at the "east," whereas the tradespeople sat on the northern and southern sides of the synagogue, or stood behind the *bima*.

There were apprentice youths who worked with the tailors, shoemakers, and smiths. These people once declared a revolt against their employers and demanded an improvement in their working conditions. This was several years before the incident that will be described later. One youth, specifically from among the better pedigreed ones of the village, became friendly with these poor people. He drew close to them and spread his protection upon them. He organized evening classes for them, and taught them reading, writing, arithmetic, and especially class consciousness. He also set up a small library for them, and led them toward their first act, their first class action.

One day, these apprentices stood up and declared to their masters: "Enough! You have the day, and we have the evening. We will not work for you endlessly."

In its time, this was a veritable revolution. The youths and apprentices succeeded through the power of their organization.

However, in actuality, this also had results that reached nearby Horodok.

There was a Jew named Shmuel Gomer in Rubel who would sail all summer on his berlina [river barge] to cities in Russia, as did many of the people of Horodok. As someone who came from the "wide world" who knew what was transpiring in the big cities, he placed himself at the side of the employers, and defended their rights that had existed from generation after generation.

When he found out about this rebellion of the apprentices against their employers, and who had incited them to such, he encountered the youth who instigated the rebellion, slapped him over the cheek, and warned him with reproof: "Hey you *sheketz* [a non-Jewish man (usually derogatory)], for you have mixed in to affairs that are not yours, and you should surely remember…"

The youths heard about this, and became very incensed. However, they could not deal with the strongman in his place. They rose up and informed their friends of the same class in Horodok about the travesty that had taken place to their patron and friend. They decided to react. When Sh. G. came to Horodok and crossed the bridge in the direction of his boat that was anchored at the riverbank, he found a large crowd of male and female youths blocking his path to the boat: "Why did you hit our friend and protector Shmuel Zeldin? We will not permit you to board your boat until you ask his forgiveness in public for the deed that you had done!"

After a long negotiation, he acceded to their demand. One day, an apology to Shmuel Zeldin by Sh. Gomer appeared in two newspapers, *Hameilitz* and *Hatzefira*. The matter became a topic of discussion among everybody.

The blood of a rebel revolutionary bubbled within that youth Sh. Z. from his childhood. When they stood him up in the synagogue to recite *Kaddish* for his father who had died while he was a youth, he refused and protested with the following words: "Why should I say *Kaddish* to a G-d who stole my father from me?"

After that, when he moved to Pinsk to study in the trade school, he joined the ranks of the members of *Tzeirei Zion* [Youth of Zion] and was among those who were most active in that organization. As is known, this was fraught with many dangers at that time, under the rule of the Czar in Russia.

On page 160 in the book *One Thousand Years of Pinsk*, published in America, it describes that young locksmith who lived in the attic of a certain house, and in whose dwelling the proclamations of the party were published. The "stash" of "weapons," so to speak, of those days was also in his dwelling.

One winter night, the owner of the house sensed that not everything was proper in the attic of his house. He rose up with the fear of death and demanded that he leave the room. What was to be done with the printing and the "weapons"? They took the letters – Yiddish and Russian –

[Page 255]

placed them in small bags, and distributed them among the members. Some of the printings were placed in chests and hidden in the cemetery. The implements of death were placed in the yard of one of the synagogues. The gunpowder was taken out, scattered in the snow, and covered on top. That is how the resident of the attic was able to escape the wrath of the police.

Eventually, that locksmith immigrated to the United States and became a member of the right leaning *Poalei Zion* [Workers of Zion]. He became one of the dedicated activists of the *Histadrut* Campaign in Los Angeles. He visited the Land after the rise of the state, and a second time this past Passover (5717 [1957]).

Let us return to the matter of the class war in the village. The war first broke out against the "owners of the east" in the synagogue, with the formula: "You have taken on too much. The entire congregation is holy, so why shall you raise yourselves up?" [Numbers 16:3]. It is logical that the revolt in the desert on the route to the Land of Canaan served for them as the first factor to jump up and call out: "Why shall you overload? We too want to "have rights." The revolution against the "ones with rights" in the Great Synagogue began.

We were small children, aged 7-8 at that time, when the event took place on a winter Sabbath, on the Torah portion of *Vayechi*. They were reading the Torah as customary, and about to conclude the Book of Genesis. Matityahu the Melamed stood to the left of the Torah reader and he called up for an *aliya* "Let Rabbi Yaakov the son of Rabbi Moshe come up for an *aliya*, *Chazak*!"[18] Two people jumped up from close to the southern wall, ascended the *bima* from the right side, and called out, "Let Rabbi Yeshayahu the son of Yosef come up for an *aliya*, *Chazak*!" From one side Yaakov, and from the other side Yeshayahu. Yaakov was the brother of Shlomo Zingerman, one of the well-pedigreed people. He was erudite. More than he was pedigreed, he considered himself of high pedigree. Even though he lived under meager straits all his life, he would announce that he was the only scholarly Jew in the synagogue – *Uchony Yevrei* as would be said in Russian.

And Yeshayahu was an ordinary person who rose to greatness. He began as a woodcutter, and ended up as a shopkeeper, trader, agent, filling all roles. He surrounded himself with his fellow professionals and family members, and was a "something" in the village. Now, for the first time in his life, he desired to be honored with the *Chazak* honor.

Needless to say, they did not recite the *Musaf* service in the synagogue. It was only with difficulty that they managed to put the Torah back in the ark. Then they congregation dispersed and went home, with the pain and anger about the dispute and the degradation of the Torah in the holy place.

There was someone who reported the incident to the authorities. The police chief came to the village, interrogated, and asked questions. There was a great suspicion that if these matters were to reach the high offices, the district governor and regional governor – the synagogue would be shut, and perhaps even worse things would happen.

The Jews utilized the well-known and tried method, from that time and previous, even from the days of Jacob our Forefather. They gave a present to the police chief, and the matter was covered over, as if it never happened.

However, the chasm that opened on that Sabbath never disappeared. The dispute and hatred never stopped for many years. It is possible that the echoes of winds blowing from Russia at that time, winds of revolt and revolution, reached even to the remote village.

Once, a dispute broke out in the synagogue in the middle of the holy Yom Kippur. The dispute was not limited to *Chazak* and synagogue honors, for it passed over to economic matters, competition in business, and other such matters. A new community of those jumping to the top stood opposite the small number of veterans, of old, well-pedigreed householders. There were times when the dispute took on a sharp form. Once, they even boasted that if they were to catch Chanchik the daughter of Yehuda Durchin, they would cut off the long braids of her head.

q. Good Morning Mr. Editor

There was a widow in the village, Sara Leah, who had been the wife of Rabbi Shimon Berman the *Shochet*. She was the daughter of the brother of Rachel Weitzman, the mother of the first president [of Israel]. She was left to tend to young children after the death of her husband. The widow suffered no small amount until the children grew up and went out to seek their luck in the wide world.

The older children scattered in different directions, some to Yeshiva and others to work. Only Baruch and the daughter Rivel were left with her. Baruch began to work as a teacher, and gave over his salary to his mother.

[Page 256]

The sole source of income that she had after the death of her husband was the "rights" to *shechita* [ritual slaughter]. The new *shochet* who came was obligated, as was the way in communities, to give over a portion of his earnings to her. Since the place was small, and there were few *shechitas*, the *shochet* did not earn enough to sustain two families, and the widow suffered from want and poverty.

After time, it was agreed that she would have the rights to the meat tax in the village, as was the custom in Russia for many years.

She leased the tax from the butchers of Horodok. They leased the tax from the government in the district city of Mozyr. The money was collected from the customers by the butcher based on every liter of meat. This is how things continued in the village for many years. Nobody would have thought about damaging the widow and her sole source of livelihood.

The revolutionaries looked jealously upon the tax that was in the hands of the widow. Prior to the beginning of the new tax year, they stood before the butchers in Horodok, added to the price, and received the rights to the tax. They returned to the village and imposed their fear upon the *shochet* to refrain from slaughtering without getting permission from them. They entered the house of the *shochet* and removed his *shechita* knives by force. Drunk with victory, they took them to their home.

At that time, I was teaching the Jewish children in the other side of the village. I returned home, and my mother told me about this scandalous deed. They had taken the knives from the *shochet* by force, and had removed the last morsel of bread from the widow and her children – all my blood was boiling. What could be done for these poor people? Who can adjudicate with someone stronger than themselves? I decided to publicize the matter. If there is no justice or judge here – there is justice and understanding in the world community.

The *Hatzefira* newspaper had a regular column called *Letters from the Remote Cities*.[19] I wrote a long description of the shameful event and signed it with the initials Y. Z. The letter appeared in the newspaper after some time. Of course, the perpetrators were not among the readers of *Hatzefira*, but they found out about the letter and the newspaper. Somebody informed them.

One morning as I was walking to work, Avrahamel Plotnitzky, the brother of the aforementioned Yeshayahu, met me on the alleyway of my classroom. He had been a participant in this entire deed. He greeted me, "Good morning to you, Mr. Editor!" It seems that they were generally satisfied with the publicity that I had given them in the newspaper. They did not have a lifegiving breadth within the narrow confines of the village. They were lacking the broad arena for the frenzy of their stormy activity.

In time, almost all of these "children of Korach"[20] immigrated overseas to the United States and Canada. First the men went, and then the entire family. There, in the land of dollars, their ebullient energy found broad horizons for activity. Like many other immigrants, many of them quickly ascended the rungs of the ladder and became very wealthy. Some became involved in positive communal activity in their overseas communities.

After years, they had the opportunity to give some sort of reparations for the travesty that they perpetrated to the widow. Her youngest son Sheika – Sam (who visited Israel in Elul 5715 – 1955 as a wealthy tourist from Los Angeles) – was received with honor by one of the Plotnitzkys, Arke the son of the aforementioned Yeshayahu, when he arrived in Canada in 1922. Sheika benefited from the support of his wife Malka during the first period until he got set up in the new country. This was a sort of atonement for the deed of that time in Rubel. Perhaps even at that time, the hearts of the son and his wife were not content with the deeds of the father.

Revolutionaries[21]

On a Sabbath afternoon, we would float over the fields, far from the village, at least, outside of the Sabbath boundary.[22] There, behind the fields, there was a long row of piles of grain bundles, *"fades"* in our language of that time. After the harvest, the farmer would gather some of the rye into the barn for a certain period. He would leave the rest next to the field, on top of four pillars pitched in the soil, at a height of more than a meter. We sat in their shade

[Page 257]

on Sabbath afternoons. There were paths among the furrows in the standing grain fields leading to the heaps. There was also a main route, which was the meeting place with the youth from the other end of the village.

One Sabbath, we gathered for a clandestine meeting in the shade of those heaps. An "agitator" that is an activist from the "democratic" revolutionaries as they were called at that time, spoke. All the youth of the village of age twenty and below, the children of the wealthier people as well as of the tradespeople, all gathered at the meeting. Guards were set up lest one of the villagers pass by and see a mass gathering of Jewish youth. Difficulties and tribulations were not lacking at that time. There were arrests, fines, and worst of all – exile to Siberia.

The meeting passed without mishap. The speaker uttered his statements not like dew, and not like rain. Rather, his words fell upon the ears of his audience like clumps of stones. These were strange words, not absorbed even though they were spoken in the Yiddish language. We knew Peretz at that time. We also known Sholem Aleichem and Mendele in Yiddish, but our ears still did not absorb a scintilla of his words, whether because the orator uprooted us to another world far from the world of our conception, or because his language was the languages of the brochures that were known in this days – brochures hugging the world and what is in it, people and groups, and written in a languages and style in which the German foundations were greater than the popular Jewish foundations.

The winds of revolution and revolt always blew toward us from Horodok. There was an unmediated influence from the youth in the town to the youth in the village, whether in relationship to the *Haskalah* [Enlightenment] or in ideological and factional affiliation.

The constant influence was known in the home of Eizel Beilin. Even though Eizel was a tradesman, spending his days with the hammer and anvil – he was an erudite man, a Jew who knew the book. In his development, he exceeded many of the wealthy householders, and his children even more so. His children served as examples and guides for our youths, especially after their sister married Michal the smith, the son of Shlomo Chaim Shulman, the Nikolaev soldier, in Rubel.

If sparks of connection to Socialism and Yiddishism, and opposition to bourgeoisism, Hebrew and the Land of Israel – this came from the energy of Beilin's sons.

… In time, the new ideologies caused a separation between the adherents. A schism arose between those faithful to Hebrew and their friends who were promoters of Yiddish.

One day, newspapers from Horodok reached the village. It told there that Dr. Chaim Zhitlowsky, the famous writer and ideologue, went to the Land of Israel and stood up to deliver a lecture in Yiddish in Jaffa. Students of the Herzliya Gymnasium came and arranged an obstruction in the hall. The audience was forced to disperse, and the lecture did not take place.

They said in dismay: "Oh, is this what your high school students do, to not permit a famous man such as Chaim Zhitlowsky to speak! You should be ashamed and embarrassed!" The response was:

"If one brings an idol into the sanctuary – should we be quiet?"

t. A Hand to the Pioneer of the Third Aliya

Who was that speaker in the secret meeting that we discussed above?

There was a man in Rubel named Baruch Kaplan. He was like an exception to the Jews of the village. He was not a peddler amongst the farmers, and he did not earn his livelihood from business or trade. He eventually immigrated to Canada. He remained there for a period of time, and returned to his home with a bundle of money. He went to Stolin, and could not find what to take hold of, so he took his family and returned to the New World.

Baruch had a brother, a young lad named Berl. Berl would come from time to time to the home of his brother as a guest. He would remain for some time and leave, and the cycle would repeat itself. Eventually, we discovered the mysterious secret, that the brother was hiding from the eyes of the Czarist police who were following his steps.

From Baruch's son Gershon Kaplan, who visited Israel in the summer of 5713 [1953], we learned interesting details about the adventures of his uncle Berl, who was the one who arranged the clandestine meeting in the field on the Sabbath. Like many of the other youths of that generation, he had studied in Yeshiva and was a candidate for rabbinical ordination. He left the Yeshiva and transferred to the *Haskalah* and the revolutionary movement.

[Page 258]

Berl continued with his revolutionary activities, in propaganda against the rotten Czarist regime, until the police caught him one day and brought him to trial. His verdict, as was the verdict of most of the revolutionaries of that era, was deportation to Siberia. They were a full group, and they succeeded in escaping from Siberia and coming to Canada. In Canada, the revolutionary had a field and a farm. Years passed, and the owner of the farm was successful and had amassed a significant sum of money. The days of the regiments arrived, and the days of Balfour, and of the "State for the Jews" fluttered in the air. It was not for a man such as Berl to sit on the fleshpots in the land of the dollars. His aspiration was to become a *chalutz* [pioneer] in the Land of Israel, a pioneer of the farm and Hebrew agriculture.

Fifteen families from Canada, with Berl at the head, made *aliya* to the Land at the end of 1921. Their aspiration was for agriculture – and this is proved by the fact that Berl brought a special species of Leghorn chickens with him.

The question arose: Where to go to establish an independent farm?

From Yaakov Metman, the brother of the well-known founder of the Herzliya Gymnasium Dr. Metman, and from the lawyer M. Talisman, we found out the following details of our acquaintance Berl Kaplan and his attempt at agricultural settlement in the Sharona German neighborhood.

In 1914, even before the outbreak of the First World War, several people of Achuzat Bayit – which is Tel Aviv – succeeded in purchasing a nearby plot of land for agricultural settlement.

The first of the initiators were the aforementioned Dr. Metman and Swerdlow – both were teachers at the Herzliya Gymnasium. Our own Dr. Zagorodsky, Dr. Slushtz, Yishai Adler, and several other activists founded a company called "*Ir Ganim*" to obtain land.

They negotiated with an Arab from the village of Salama who owned properties in the area, who gathered together plots from other Arabs, for a total of 1,800 dunams to the right of Wadi Musrara – which is Nachal Ayalon. The price was approximately two liras per dunam (At the time, the currency was the French franc.) Members joined the company and invested money as candidates for settlement in the new area.

In the meantime, the war broke out. Alongside came hunger, suffering, and the deportations of Djemal Pasha. Of course, the matter was abandoned.

When the new era came, and the Land was transferred to the Mandate government, negotiations were renewed regarding the purchase. The purchase was concluded in 1921, at the price of ten liras per dunam.

The area was all desolate sand dunes, with no sign of life, no tree or bush, a distance from the "Negev" in the Sharona German neighborhood.

Plots were sold to 270 people. They dug a well next to the wadi, which gave four cubic meters of water per hour.

While the residents of young Tel Aviv who owned the plots were thinking about taking hold of the land (it was not all that easy to leave the Achuzat Bayit neighborhood next to the city of Jaffa and to go out to the "desert" that had no roads, no [electric] light, and no regular flow of water) – new pioneers had made *aliya* from Canada, headed by our acquaintance Berl. As had been noted, this was at the end of 1921. Of the fifteen families who had come from Canada, eight remained that decided to settle. They were joined by another family who had been in the Land for a long time, and who had suffered greatly in the moshava of Qastina – today Beer Tuvia – and who could not maintain themselves in the heart of the Arab sea at the "edge" of the Land.

These were the first nine families who pitched the first tent peg in that area, which is now the location of the splendid Ramat Gan.

They brought money with them, and they also had goodwill. Furthermore, they were not lacking in agricultural experience. Therefore, they dreamed of establishing an agricultural settlement, a farm, near Jaffa-Tel Aviv.

The *Ir Ganim* company sold each of them fifteen dunams of land at the purchase price. Later, they also added to them an area that would, to their best estimation, be sufficient for maintaining a family.

They chose the strip next to the wadi. This was for two reasons: it was close to the water well, and the banks of the wadi were formed of heavy soil rather than sandy soil.

[Page 259]

The settlers set up huts in their new place and moved there, with various plans in their heads. This was on Chanukah of 5682 – 1921.

On Tu B'Shvat, the owners of the plots set out to a new place. Along with the Canadian settlers, they fulfilled the commandment of "When you come to the land – you shall plant" [Leviticus 19:23]. They prepared 5,000 saplings for planting. The giant eucalyptus trees that today obscure Nachal Ayalon – the polluted Wadi Musrara – from our eyes, are the work of the hands of these first pioneers, the splendid efforts of their hands.

And what became of the agricultural plans? They began to plant orchards. At that time, before the area was turned into fields (with the Fourth Aliya), Ramat Gan was one giant orchard, a spectacular area with its large, precisely measured, straight rows.

However, the orchard began to bear fruit only after four or five years, and in the meantime, our farmers had no source of livelihood. They had small farms of fowl, vegetables, and goats. That was the period of tobacco prosperity, and the entire ground from Petah Tikva to Rosh Pina set their hopes on that sector. Our agriculturists also took hold of this. They finally left with their hands over their heads.

The experience of our farmers from blessed Canada did not serve them well. In time, the money that they brought with them from Canada was used up, and the situation became quite bad. As the aforementioned Metman relates, "they were bound the earth," that is, they had reached the point of a morsel of bread.

In a letter that Berl sent to his brother in Pinsk, he writes the following:
(The letter was written in clear Hebrew: the former Yeshiva student, a *Haskalah* man, was recognized therein.) "This is a known matter in the Land of Israel, that it impossible to extract even a cent from a farm worked by others (Jews) – (the owner of the farm was sick for three years with fever) – Nevertheless, I am trying to do something this year (5683 – 1923) on my plot: I will plant a small vineyard, some fruit trees, and a few shade trees to improve the appearance of the place. He adds: my biggest lack now is the lack of [the contents of] a pocket, for not one coin remains from all the money that I have brought from Canada. I have already borrowed two hundred dollars from our relatives in Canada to purchase a cow..."

He purchased a cow for seventy liras. It later became clear that the cow was sick. He went through issues and court cases until he returned the cow, and only received part of the money back.

These were the issues in agricultural settlement, so to speak.

However, from the letter, a clear picture emerges from those days – the beginning of the Third Aliya, when the Land began to rejuvenate after the tribulations of the war.

Here are the words of Berl in a letter:
"Here the yoke of life does not oppress people as it does in the Diaspora. If a person only has his own dwelling and a bit of his own land for vegetables – he remains with very few needs." He adds: "Here in the villages, the difference between man and beast is indeed naught. There are no books, no daily newspaper, no theater, and no movie theater. And this is the wonder: there is not even any need for such... People wear torn, worn-out clothes, and are not embarrassed. They purchase on credit and do not pay. They promise and do not fulfill. At first, this dismayed me, but now I have gotten used to it."

"I am sorry that I do not have the ability to help you..."

Despite the lowly material situation, Berl was at the center. The youth gathered around him. His hut was a sort of gathering place. The man was joyous and full of life. He had no equal in hosting guests. As the lawyer Talisman describes him, "he was 100% a national man," "pleasant in his ways," "with refined soul," and "full of humor."

He was not burdened by family matters. When he took ill with fever, he took in a lad to work his farm, and the worker lived together with him.

At first, the local council would hold its meetings in Tel Aviv. Later, the opinion grew to "sit" for meetings in the place. A committee was chosen to direct the issues of the settlers, and Berl Kaplan was the first committee head

[Page 260]

of Ramat Gan during its infancy, at the beginning of 1923. M. Talisman, who later became a lawyer in Tel Aviv, was the secretary of the committee. The hut that served as the office stood at the top of a hill. Berl would go up to there from his hut on his donkey. The donkey forged a path with its feet, the first path on the sandy hill.

There was a large warehouse next to his bunk, in which all the tobacco of the members was collected.

Berl would urge his brother in Pinsk to send one of his daughters to the Land. This was worthwhile from all perspectives (there were five!), and he would have an assistant in his farm, for he was a bachelor, unlike the rest of the settlers who came with families.

The brother responded, and made a condition that he add a room to his hut, a special room for her. She made *aliya* in Sukkot 1924, but no longer found Berl.

One night the secretary Talisman was summoned to the chairman who was lying in bed, burning like a furnace. Talisman brought him to Hadassah [Hospital] by a wagon, and he never returned from there.

Berl was unable to withstand the difficult conditions of those days There was no communal support for those who settled, no *Keren Kayemet* [Jewish National Fund], no *Keren Hayesod* [Foundation Fund]. There was only their own efforts. The lot of Berl the bachelor was much more difficult. His energy was drained, and his heart could not withstand the difficulties of settling. He left his lot and his farm in 1924, and died childless…

After the eldest sister made *aliya* to the Land, the other sisters came one by one. His brother Asher also came in 1933 to take over the estate of his brother.

Berl's plot still exists to this day. It is an orchard, largely abandoned, the remnants of the large orchards from those days. It is a green area next to the road, past the bridge on the right side before Ilit.

Let these lines serve as a monument to that revolutionary from the bogs of Polesye, who was exiled to frozen Siberia, moved from frozen Siberia to Canada, and made *aliya* from Canada to the Land of Israel.

He was a pioneer of the Third Aliya. May his memory be a blessing.

Translator's footnotes:

1. See *Pirkei Avot* 5:19.
2. Three meals are eaten on the Sabbath: on Friday night, on Saturday at midday, and the *Seuda Shlishit* (or *Shalosh Seudos*) toward the end of the day. Many people also eat a fourth meal, called *Melave Malka* [escorting the Sabbath Queen] after the Sabbath ends on Saturday night.
3. There are several styles of prayer formats within Judaism. The true Sephardim (Jews of North African origin) as well of Middle Eastern Jews (e.g. from Iran, Yemen, etc.) use various forms of the Sephardic form. European Jews generally use the Ashkenazic form. Ashkenazic Jews who are influenced by Hassidim used a modified form of the Sephardic rite, called "*Nusach Sephard.*" This is not the true Sephardic rite of the Sephardic Jews – it can better be termed as the Hassidic rite.
4. Psalms 35:10, also incorporated in the *Nishmat* prayer of Sabbaths and festivals.
5. I.e. the *Maariv* service of the second night of a festival.

6. A Sukkot night celebration in commemoration of the water drawing festivities during the time of the Temple (see fifth chapter of Mishna *Sukkah*).
7. The celebration would be taking place in the *Sukkah*.
8. *Leil Shimurim* – also a term for Passover night – literally, a night of watching or guarding. See Exodus 12:42.
9. A play on the word *ein* [none or is not].
10. The prayer for the dead.
11. Isaiah 55:1.
12. The traditional rote rendition of the Hebrew alphabet with the vowel sounds, used in old-fashioned *cheders*.
13. Literally – unkosher and invalid. A reference to the religious objection to secular works.
14. I.e. laws related to the *nidda* cycle and ritual immersion in a *mikveh*.
15. This is the refrain of the *Ki Lo Naeh* hymn of the Passover Seder.
16. There is a tradition that at the time of the Resurrection of the Dead, those buried in the Diaspora will roll through tunnels to Israel.
17. The "*Mizrach*" people – i.e. e people who sit near the eastern wall – i.e. the wealthier people.
18. This is the formula for calling up a person to the Torah for an *aliya*. The final *aliya* of each of the five books of the Torah is called up with the term "*Chazak*" – "Be strong," since the phrase "*Chazak Chazak Venitchazek*" [Strength, strength, and let us strengthen ourselves] is recited at the conclusion of the reading of each of the five books. *Vayechi* is the final Torah portion of *Bereishit* [Genesis] and is generally read about two weeks after Chanukah.
19. Literally: Cities of the field.
20. Based on the Biblical character of Korach, who led a rebellion against Moses [Numbers 16-18].
21. This section header was not numbered. And the next one, on page 257, is numbered incorrectly.
22. There is a prohibition of walking more than 2,00 cubits (around one kilometer) outside the bounds of a human habitation (city, town, or village) on the Sabbath or festival.

Craftsmen in the Village
(Dedicated in Memory of the Martyrs of Rubel)

by Yitzchak the Son of Mordechai (May G-d Avenge His Blood) Zingerman

Translated by Jerrold Landau

A. Eli HaKohen

He was a tall Jew with yellow hair and a beard. He was a strong man. He earned his livelihood through the needle. He would travel through the nearby villages all week long and sew the clothing and garments of the farmers. He was like Ephraim the Tailor in David Frishman's story "The Sambatyon." However, Frishman's Ephraim was one of the *lamed vovniks*.[1] He sewed during the day and studied Torah during the night without anyone knowing, for he was discreet about it like all the hidden *lamed vovniks*. Our Eli HaKohen, however, was not among the hidden ones. On the contrary, he showed his face and essence on every occasion and opportunity as he pursued the cantorial arts. Some sort of a demon possessed him to serve as the prayer leader in the synagogue. He had his desire for the *amud* [prayer leader's podium] and the congregation was against him (His voice was not particularly pleasant, and his Hebrew pronunciation was not especially fine.) There was always a battle between Reb Eli and the congregation. In order to make him bitter, they would not honor him with the first *aliya*, which should have been his right as a Kohen, and they would call up a Levi instead of a Kohen.[2] This enraged him greatly. However, Reb Eli took the initiative and found an occasion to protest for his rights. During the Priestly Blessing on festivals, he would deviate from the accepted Hassidic custom in the synagogue and would elongate the melody once or twice, as he repeated the words after the cantor, in the manner of the *Misnagdim*. This would enrage the zealous Hassidim, especially Reb Yaakov Zingerman. He would rejoice in the synagogue on the festivals. On the Sabbath before the end of the day, prior to the *Maariv* service, he would recite the entire *Ashrei Temimei Derech*, Psalm 119, by heart.[3] He would treat this like an offering on the altar by a Kohen.

[Page 261]

He was very proud that he had a female relative in the Land of Israel, and that he would exchange letters with her. Who wrote his letters – this was his secret. However, he would request that one of the *maskilim* [followers of the *Haskalah* [Enlightenment] movement] of the city inscribe the address for him, and he would bless the writer heartily, "May you have a long life."

B. The Levites in the Village

There were two brothers. One, Shlomo Chaim, was one of the snatched people.[4] He was proud that he maintained his Jewishness throughout all the difficult tribulations that he experienced. Like all the snatched ones in those days, he loved to talk about his experiences. He would still march a soldier's march, strong and proper, left, right, left right, even when he reached old age. He was a scholar. He participated in the study of *Mishnah* with the rabbi between *Mincha* and *Maariv*.

His brother Leizer was also among those who studied. He was a modest, quiet man, G-d fearing in private and in public. He acted in a miserly fashion at his table, even though he was not all that poor. He sold textiles to the farmers, and his children were together with him. Avrahamel's two children were saved from the slaughter in the village and were part of the partisan army. The partisan Michael Nosanchuk met them there.

C. Kotsh

He was a whitewasher, and also made ovens and cleaned chimneys. At times he was white as snow, and at other times as black as a raven. He would instill fear in young children, but he also knew how to joke with children and make them happy. He excelled especially in Purim games. He would dress up as a Cossack. He would wear a Cossack hat on his head, have a Cossack sword on his side, and instill fear and trepidation to those around him, but within a moment he would start to sing and dance, run about and joke, bringing boundless joy.

We would gather around Grandfather's table for the Purim feast. However, it wasn't Grandfather's radiant face, Grandmother's pleasant eyes, not these that caught our heart and filled it with joy and the gladness of the holiday, not even the strong song in which we children took the main part – it was not all this, but rather the appearance of Moshe Kotsh with the Purim players – that was the main thing on the holiday. We waited for him impatiently and with longing all evening. To our great dismay, he would come to Grandfather's house very late, apparently at the end of his making the rounds to all the houses of the villages. When he appeared, we children went out of our minds with great joy and mirth at the appearance of the players, and especially of Moshe himself. This was Moshe Kotsh, who was poor and indigent all the days of the year.

We will also remember "positively" his wife Chaya. This Chaya was literally "an animal"[5] or even worse than that. She was like a stork standing on the top of the roof and chattering toward the sky with her beak pointed upward; or more accurately, like a frog croaking incessantly from evening to morning in the heart of the bogs. That is how that would go out to the middle of the street – their house was isolated next to the field – and send forth "blessings" without end or without bound. She would utter curses atop curses, each more terrible and frightful than the next. Upon whose head were her blessings cast? On the head of her husband? Her children? Her enemies? Nobody wanted to hear. If one heard them, the hair would stand on end and the heart would be overcome by horror. Everyone escaped and avoided her so that a trace of her "golden tongue" would not reach their ears. Even the gentile farmer women would be afraid of coming too close to her so as not to be hurt by the flames of fire bursting forth from the mouth of that frightful woman standing in the middle of the street and casting "her blessings" into the air of the village…

D. Mordechai Leib the Glassmaker

He was a short Jew, who worshipped G-d with a full heart and soul. His place in the synagogue was behind the *bima*, and he never made his voice heard in prayer in the manner of the Jews at prayer. Nobody even heard the voice of his speech. He was a taciturn person of the family of "Bontshe Schweig [Bontshe the Silent]" of Y. L. Peretz.

Both of them earned renown and a unique history. Speech came to them in another place in this book,

[Page 262]

(in the chapter "Aliya to the Land of Israel"). They did not have money for a train or ship ticket. They reached the port city of Odessa on foot, and they traveled to the Land of Israel on a rickety boat.

E. Yossel Tzeitel's

He was called by the name of his wife, like Peretz's Mendel Breina's. He was a modest man who avoided publicity, and she was a talkative woman with lots of energy, pleasant with other people and loved by the women. He was a carpenter by trade. He was graced with a special talent, and that is how he obtained his renown. He would serve as the prayer leader in the synagogue on festival nights. He would place his hand behind his ear, stamp his foot, and begin *Barchu*.[6] The entire place was filled with light. The congregation followed after him with holy devotion. Yossel's *Maariv* service was a great experience for the worshippers. The entire congregation joined in his devotion, and reached the sublimity of the soul and Hassidic enthusiasm that cannot be described in human language. The experience was especially great in the women's section. Even they, or especially they, were affected by Yossel's sweet voice. They would return home full of amazement from this prayer service. They say repeatedly: "He is a Jewish craftsman with a harp in his throat. Wonder of wonders, from where did he get this?" When children wanted to imitate the voice of a cantor in the synagogue, they would only imitate Yossel. His voice penetrated everyone's hearts deeply.

F. Baruch Yeshaya Bukov the Blacksmith

This Jew had an angry face. He was like the heaviness and hardness of the iron that he hammered with his heavy hammers every day. He was very exacting, and this too was from his trade. He also understood the "black dots" and had some knowledge of medicine. He would utter incantations for the "evil eye." He would peer into the throat of someone in pain, and he knew how to calm the sick person with his words. He also owned a thermometer, the only thermometer in the village. From whom did he learn the art of medicine? Perhaps from his neighbor, the goodhearted Vyncus the medic, who lived in the village for many years and worked as the director of the government liquor monopoly. That Polish gentile loved Jews, and his hand was outstretched to help anyone who turned to him in the event of illness.

Baruch Yeshayahu was one of the *Misnagdim*, even though the accepted prayer rite in the synagogue was *Nusach Sephard*.[7] There were years when he and his friends organized an early minyan on Sabbaths. It was said about him that his face was raging from his anger toward the Hassidim whom his soul hated. However, how joyous was his appearance, and how changed was his spirit when the Hassidim in the synagogue would begin to sing *Vayeetayu* and *Hayom Harat Olam*,[8] or *Ki Anu Amecha* on Yom Kippur.

During such moments, not only did he not object to the melodies during the services, but he encouraged the musically inclined youth to ascend the *bima* and sing together with the congregation.

He belonged to the group that studied *Mishnah* together with the rabbi between *Mincha* and *Maariv*. He was an expert in religious questions and answers, second only to the rabbi.

H.[9] Yehuda Burshtein the Shoemaker

He was a Jew with a fine appearance and a solid build. His beard was black and splendid, and his entire appearance exuded nobility and splendor. He was upright in his ways. Anyone who ordered shoes from him (ready-made shoes did not yet exist) was certain that the work would be done faithfully and with full diligence, for his work was a holy task, and the words of his mouth were more precious than gold. The youth in the village would be effusive in their praise of that craftsman, more so than the rabbi of the city, and certainly more than many of the wealthy, well-pedigreed Jews. In short: he was one of the Jews of Y. L. Peretz.

I. Mendel Nosanchuk the Holy

He was a Jew who was honest with his G-d and his work. He loved work (He was a lumber worker.) The idlers would say about him that if he were asked, "Reb Mendel, how are you?" He would respond, "I have the energy, but I am lacking wood and beams."

He was killed by a bullet from the Balachowiczes, may their names be blotted out, in the middle of the day of Simchat Torah, as he was defending with his own body the honor of a Jewish girl. May G-d avenge his blood.

[Page 263]

J. Aunt Devora

Jews and gentiles alike both called her Aunt Devora. She possessed the gift of words. She would pray every day, and she served as the prayer leader in the women's section. When wicks were placed in the candles for Yom Kippur, she would arrange the prayers and petitions for each wick, in accordance with the traits of the deceased man or woman.

On the eve of Passover, her house turned into a matzo bakery. She kneaded the dough. She instilled fear upon the women who were rolling the dough, telling them to wash their hands after every three matzos. She was especially meticulous during the baking of the matzo shmura. She was also a "medic" to the many ill people who turned to her.

* * *

Most of the residents of Rubel earned their livelihoods from manual labor. Even the merchants were upright individuals, and there was not even the hint of suspicion that they were using dishonest weights and measures, and the like.

Who can imagine your pain and agony, Rubel? Who can describe what happened to its residents during the times of murder and the Holocaust.

May the memory of your martyrs be blessed forever.

Jerusalem, Holocaust and the Ghetto Uprising Memorial Day, 5711 [1951]

Translator's footnotes:

1. According to Jewish mythology, there are 36 [numerically: lamed vov] hidden righteous people in every generation.
2. The formula used to call up the first *aliya* when a Kohen is not present.

3. This is the longest chapter of the book of Psalms, with an eightfold acrostic. Such a recitation would take a fair amount of time.
4. *Chatufim* [snatched ones] is the term used for those Jews forcibly conscripted to lengthy army service in Russia.
5. The Hebrew word *chaya* means a living creature, generally and animal as opposed to a human.
6. The opening word of the festival evening service.
7. The prayer rite used by those with a Hassidic background.
8. *Vayeetayu* is part of the *Musaf* service on Rosh Hashanah and Yom Kippur, and *Hayom Harat Olam* is recited following the blowing of the shofar during the *Musaf* service on Rosh Hashanah.
9. The letter *Zayin* (which would correspond to G) is skipped in the original.

Those Who Faithfully Engaged in Public Needs

by Yaakov Kolodny

Translated by Jerrold Landau

a. Mordechai Nosanchuk

He was a simple Jew, a builder who succeeded at his business, and an honorable householder in his community. He devoted all of his free time to communal work.

That Jew, portly and with difficulty breathing, would run from one end of the town to the other (a distance of two kilometers) collecting coins. He would call a meeting of parents (even though he himself no longer had children in school), sometimes standing alone at the event, and present contracts of obligation to the teachers, mostly signed by himself, to ensure that the classes would not stop and that the school would exist. No matter what, one would be full of reverence and honor for this purehearted Jew. When something had to be worked out, either with the authorities

[Page 264]

in Stolin, or, on the other hand, with the local rabbi who sometimes complained that the studies in the school were too much in Hebrew… that Jew would spring into action and engage others. He did not rest or quiet down until the matters were settled, and the work of the school was not interrupted, Heaven forbid.

With regard to helping relatives, his wife Sara Leah, may G-d avenge her blood, was as active as he was. If a girl from near or far reached marriageable age, the husband and wife would offer help with a wide heart and an open hand, as they would provide a fine, good arrangement for the bride, without even being asked. They perished in the Stolin Ghetto along with the entire community on the eve of Rosh Hashanah 1942. Their son Michael (today in the United States) who was hidden and survived and was among the partisans, tells about their many days in the ghetto and their final days. His words are included in *Davar* from October 14, 1946, and in our book.

b. Yaakov Rimer

He was a good friend. He played an active role in all areas of communal work in the village.

He always fulfilled the tasks he was given: whether it was the emptying of the *Keren Kayemet* [Jewish National Fund] boxes, setting up a stage for a performance, the income of which would be dedicated to the benefit of the local Tarbut school or for the benefit of the local library. He was always prepared to stop his work from which he earned a living so as to respond to the task that he was given.

His brother Feivel is in the Land, but Yaakov was too late and did not come. He perished with his family in an untimely fashion. May his memory be blessed.

c. Noach Leib Zezik

He was a Jew who feared sin, was dedicated to his G-d, was careful about the easy and difficult commandments, and was happy to fulfil any good deed when the opportunity arose. Every *Maggid* [itinerate preacher] and emissary who would come to the village, or even just a regular Jew in need, would be brought to all the Jewish houses of the village by Noach Leib to collect money. If there was a need to raise money for the *Keren Kayemet* or for any communal matter, this person was prepared to respond immediately.

[Page 265]

A poor person never left his home hungry. His wife Alta knew in which manner and with what to feed hungry people, for they themselves knew the soul of a poor person. When they sat around the table on the Sabbath (and there as not always wine for *kiddush*!)[1] he would elongate the hymns in honor of the Sabbath until he fell asleep at the table.

Their children traveled to Argentina. Only their oldest son Baruch, known to us as Bucha, remained with them. He was a good friend and a dedicated Zionist. He got sick and died, leaving behind a widow and three orphans, who remained with the grandparents until they were murdered.

May their memories be a blessing.

And These Did Not Merit...

1. Aharon Lifshitz

He was a resolute, faithful Zionist, a political man who knew how to debate about G-d, his Messiah, and their separation. He was a *maskil* [a follower of the Haskalah [Enlightenment] movement], a nationalist in heart and soul, who loved to peruse newspapers and Hebrew books. He taught his children beyond his capabilities, with his wife Tzipora assisting him. They sent their four daughters to the Land, and they themselves waited, waited more, and were too late to conclude their accounting with the gentiles in the city before they were murdered by Hitler's soldiers, may their names be blotted out.

May their souls be bound in the bonds of eternal life.

2. Shalom Durchin

Shalom was his name, and shalom [peace] was with him. He brought peace with him everywhere he went. He was a lad who made others happy and told jokes. He was always ready to assist with advice and guidance. He accompanied[2] those who were making aliya to the Land of Israel and those who were immigrating to various countries. He accompanied them all and wished them "a good journey." He deferred his own aliya numerous times until he perished with his family in the Stolin Ghetto.

May his memory be a blessing.

His mother Basha-Batya should also be remembered positively. She had a brave soul similar to Bruria, the wife of Rabbi Meir,[3] who comforted him on the loss of their two sons on a single Sabbath: G-d has given and G-d has taken. When her dear, most beloved son Aharon Hershel, a precious, pleasant lad, was murdered on Simchat Torah by the Balachowiczes, may their names be blotted out, in the anteroom of the synagogue â€" she accepted the tragedy with wondrous bravery. She buried her very deep sorrow in her heart. However, her heart did not persevere for a long time. A year did not pass before she returned her pure soul to G-d.

d. Sunya Lifshitz

He was a wise Jew and a great joker. He always appeared with his jokes, even when the situation was dire, and he did not have the ability to sustain his large family of nine children. His sharp witticisms were transmitted from mouth to mouth. His appearance and expressions on his face always aroused healthy laughter. He had some of the traits of Sholem Aleichem's Tevye the Milkman. He was a Jew "to whom it did not matter." He was always "I will rejoice and be happy." His income was meager. Even the gentiles liked him very much. They would say "*Jaka Sana Kasza*" which means "as Sunya says." He was among the last to remain when many left the village and moved to nearby towns. With his large family and meager belongings, he could not arrange things for himself in a different place. He perished with his entire family, and not a trace remains.

May his soul be bound in the bonds of eternal life.

Translator's footnotes:

1. If one does not have wine for the Sabbath, either by chance or because one cannot afford it, one is allowed to recite *Kiddush* over the challahs.
2. On their final journey out of town.
3. A Talmudic sage.

[Page 266]

Fragments of Memories

by Zelda Kagan-Stollman

Translated by Jerrold Landau

It was a summer night, and quiet around. We children were already lying in bed. A voice from across the river called out "*Leibe, Podvy from!*" (Leib, cross the crossing.) At times, the call was directed at us, "*O, shov tovi, zdorovya, podvy from!*"... (By your life, cross the crossing.)

The call repeated over and over again.

Alta and Noach-Leib were our close and best neighbors. We considered their home like ours. On winter nights, we would sit in their house at a late hour together with mother. Mother knitted, Alta plucked feathers and we children helped her. The house was full of farmers who were smoking and telling stories. Reb Noach-Leib would be perusing a book at the table. He did not take part in the mundane discussions. He was immersed in his own world. Alta told many stories, and how wonderful were her stories! We did not pay attention to the tobacco smoke or the steam from the oven, until my sister Meril gave the signal. She was the first to faint.

It was the Sabbath eve. The house was clean and shiny. We had bathed and were wearing our Sabbath clothes. Father appeared in the wagon hitched to two horses that he drove. He came only for a short while. He had to return the wagon. This was during the time that he taught in the Karlin House in Bobruisk. We accompanied him in the wagon when it was time to return. I wanted to travel with him. Mother admonished me, but it was to no avail – I was stubborn, and I did not get off the wagon. It seemed that father accepted this unwillingly. The journey was wonderful. Father prodded the horses, told jokes, and talked to me the entire way.

It was Lag B'Omer. A group of children, my sister Leah and I among them, went out to a hike on the other side of the river. We gathered berries. We returned in the evening. The crossing was full of people. The gentile women were chatting with each other. As we were holding on to the rope to do the crossing, I also placed my hand on the rope and pulled with all my strength. I was at the edge of the crossing. Suddenly, the ground shifted under my feet. I was over the water, holding onto the rope with both of my hands, and the crossing [i.e. the main group holding onto the rope] disappeared – it moved forward from me. The rope was dropping lower and lower, and the danger was approaching. Then, one of the farmer women noticed me. The gentile women began to make the sign of the cross, and with all the noise, the crossing returned and approached me. I was saved. Mother was quite shaken up, and did not calm down until they brought a *lachshan*[1] to recite an incantation for fears.

In the Russian public school, I was introverted, quiet, and afraid. Even the route to the school was full of scary things, *shkotzim* [a derogatory term for gentiles], dogs, and especially spirits and ghosts.

It was the first day in *cheder*. Chaim Baruch was my teacher. He was full of amazement, for he taught me the entire Torah on one foot [i.e. she absorbed the lessons quickly]. It was the first day of my Hebrew studies, and I could already read. Mother appeared, and he stressed my knowledge to her. A mishap occurred, and I made a mistake. He scolded me, "*Goya*!" [gentile].

I reached the book of *Bereishit* [Genesis]. My cousin Miriam Henie's, an older girl, teased me as a young girl. "*Vayitrotzetzu – in s'hobn zich geshtoisn, Habanim – di kinder, bekirba – in der boich.*"[2] She passed by the *cheder* and heard my studies.

Father taught me. I was the only girl in a large group of boys. My best friend was Velvel Leibe's. We reviewed our lessons together in Reb Leib Durchin's home. Reb Leib Durchin regarded our diligence positively, and he confirmed this by reciting a verse, as was his custom: "Two are better than one!"[3]

It was April 1. Mother stood next to the oven with enthusiasm. Suddenly the kitchen door opened, and the frightened voice of our neighbor Sobistinya was heard. "Chavanku, the Jewish children are drowning!" Mother ran to the river in a panic. This was an April 1 prank. Mother immediately took to her bed feeling ill, and I decided to take revenge. In the evening, I came to Sobistinya and informed her that Lipa Durchin had brought the mail, and there was a letter for them as well. She asked, "Is the address printed?" "Yes," I responded with certainty. The letter was addressed, however, to her daughter Yelena. She put on her boots and walked to Lipa Durchin's house at the edge of the village

[Page 267]

to get her letter. Apparently, they figured out what was going on, and sent her to Mordechai Nosanchuk at the other end of the village. I saw her returning after she had crossed the village from one end to the other, wandering about in the mud of Passover eve. "Wait, wait until next year, I will put you in your place," she threatened me.

I had nightmares that night: a tapestry of terrifying images, including Sobistincha chasing me with a long stick in her hand.

I was reading. It was very sad. I was crying. Is this not "Baruch of Mayence?"[4] Father was sitting next to me. He was describing that era in a graphic fashion. I was choking on my tears. The teacher Buchkin appeared, "What happened?"

Father was proud of me. They were discussing among themselves: disturbances, anti-Semitism, etc. I heard. I was living through the terrifying stories, but knowing for certain in my heart that none of this makes sense, "Can people in our times do such deeds?"

I was an independent teacher. I had my own *cheder*. I was only twelve years old. Can this be believed? I have a group of girls of my own age, some much taller than I. Some would cause disturbances. I especially remember Dinaka Chana's who wore down my patience.

It was the Sabbath evening. Father had come home for the Sabbath. He was a teacher in Horodok. At that time, my brother Hershel was among my students. Father and Mother were whispering, and were effusive in my praise: Hershel is very successful in his studies.

Mother had difficulty giving birth. I was in the synagogue, standing on a chair next to the holy ark, feeling Father's beard above my head. I heard the voice of the rebbetzin near us. She was comforting Father, "This will be a son, do not worry!" Ada was born on the eve of Passover before the Seder. Uhpeh Yitzkis was the midwife. "Uhpeh is a great expert. She did well with the physicians in Kiev. There in Kiev, they did not worry about a child." Then mother had a stillbirth.

I accompanied Ada to Uhpeh. Every year at Passover, we would bring her matzos and wine, a gift from the granddaughter.

I traveled to Dubrowna to study in the house of my uncle. I again sensed Father's beard above me. He kissed me. This was his last kiss. I never saw him again.

Years passed. I returned home excited for the meeting with my parents and the children. The wagon entered the village. That was the village, unchanged. Only the streets seemed smaller to me, and the distance from one end to the other seemed much smaller than that which was etched in my memory. We reached the home. I entered the dining room. That was again the *cheder*, and Father was at the head of the table. I ran to greet him, and suddenly stopped. "That is not Father!" It was Aharon the *melamed*. It was silent around.

They were looking at me. I was astonished. The door to the hallway opened. "Mother!" She had changed greatly; she was unrecognizably thin.

Slowly I found out everything. At that time, I found out about the disturbances that fate had kept from me in their time. Our village gave up five victims. Father was the last one.

Had Father stayed in Siman's barn for only a few more minutes – he would have been saved… How did Siman bang his head against the wall: "Murderers! He succeeded in hiding him for six days. The Balachowiczes had already left the village. The last two were already on the bridge, approaching the other side of the river. They returned, saw Father, and entered the house…"

He should have gone up to the roof. Leah sent me.

"Why specifically me, you go up."

"You go," Mother whispered to me, "It is hard for her."

"Yes, it happened there on the roof."

I traveled to Canada. There was a banquet. I bid farewell to my friends. In the morning, I was already on the carriage. Mother accompanied me to the train. My parting from Alta was difficult. I wept bitterly, and Uhpeh was also among those who accompanied me. I was very agonized that I did not kiss her as I did the Jewish neighbors. After some time, Mother and the children

[Page 268]

left Rubel. We continued to exchange letters with Alta, Noach-Leib and their son Baruch. We sent them money to erect a monument over Father's grave.

Dear Alta and Noach-Leib, pure, fine people, where is your gravestone?! The love of the entire village did not stand for you when the destruction came!

Tel Aviv, March 21, 1953

Translator's footnotes:

1. A difficult word to translate. In modern Hebrew, it refers to a prompter at a theatrical performance. Here it refers to an individual who recites incantations (Kabbalistic or simply superstitious) for various situations.
2. This is the Hebrew to Yiddish translation of Genesis 25:22 (And the children struggled within her – referring to Rebecca's pregnancy.) The common teaching method in *cheder*s involved reading Biblical verses word by word, with a Yiddish translation following each word.
3. Kohelet [Ecclesiastes] 4:8.
4. A Yiddish poem by Tchernichovsky.

The Balachowiczes in Rubel in 1928

by Yisrael Nachum Durchin

Translated by Jerrold Landau

Rubel had eighty Jewish families, comprising approximately five hundred individuals. Most were tradesmen: smiths, carpenters, builders, tailors, and shoemakers. There were six shopkeepers and three peddlers. The Jews earned their livelihoods in an ample fashion. Then pillage suddenly came. Already on the intermediate days of Sukkot, news reached us about the deeds and murderous activities of the Balachowiczes. We were astounded, but we hoped that we would be saved from them. The Balachowiczes arrived in our village on Shemini Atzeret. They began to make the rounds through the houses, and ordered the Jews to gather in the yard of the Christian school. Approximately forty Jews gathered there. The

Balachowiczes transported the Jews across the river, where they announced that the Jews of the village must give them a sum of 200,000 rubles as a punishment, and that they were hostages and prisoners until the money would be brought. They chose five Jews from among the hostages to go and collect that sum. The murderers said that if they give them the money, no harm will befall the Jews. The Jews collected 180,000 rubles and brought it to them. The pillagers took the money, removed the good boots from the Jews, and left. The Jews thought that the danger had passed, and they returned to being calm for a bit.

The following afternoon, news spread through the village that another band of Balachowiczes was approaching. Some hurried to escape to the forest or to hide in the houses of the farmers, while the brave ones remained in the village. Within a short time, thirteen Balachowiczes entered the village. One of them said that he was a legionnaire. They shot in the air several times as they entered, and announced that the Jews must gather in the large *Beis Midrash*. The Balachowiczes invaded the village and urged the Jews to go to the gathering. They mistreated the Jews along the way. They ordered Rabbi Moshe Chaim Hechtman to dance in the street, and they killed Mendel Nosanchuk, an elderly, sixty-year-old man. Fear and trepidation fell upon the Jews. They began to flee from the village. Approximately fifty Jews gathered in the *Beis Midrash*. The legionnaire demanded that they give him 200,000 rubles. The Jews claimed that it was impossible to collect such a hefty sum. Then, the legionnaire recorded the names of those gathered in the *Beis Midrash*, and listed on the side the sum of money that each one must give. From one of them, Aharon Tzvi Durchin, thirty years old, he demanded 10,000 rubles. Aharon Tzvi responded that he cannot afford such a hefty sum. The soldiers immediately took him out to the anteroom and murdered him. Then, the legionnaire demanded 1,000 rubles from Shalom Boyer. Boyer did not have such a sum in his pocket. They murdered him as well. The legionnaire turned to Yehuda Durchin, the uncle of Aharon Tzvi who had been murdered, and demanded 50,000 rubles from him. He did not have such a sum in his pocket. The legionnaire ordered that they place a rope on his neck, take him up to the bima and hang him. The unfortunate man requested that they allow him to bid farewell to his family. They sent a soldier with him to go to his house. When the wife and daughter of the unfortunate man saw that he was in danger, they spread out through the village, pawned off everything they had to the farmers, collected 50,000 rubles, and redeemed him from death. Yisrael Nachum (one of the two who told me everything) hid in the barn of a farmer across from the synagogue, for his brother Aharon Tzvi had been murdered. He left his hiding place and went to the *Beis Midrash* to see what was going on. They captured him as well and demanded 3,000 rubles from him. He was forced to give that sum. Then he asked the legionnaire: "Why were you so quick to kill my brother, for he too could have redeemed himself with money." The legionnaire responded that he could not wait long. The Balachowiczes volunteered for the war so that they could gather wealth, and if they did not kill the Jews, they would not give anything. The rest of the Jews who were in the *Beis Midrash* redeemed themselves with the sums that the legionnaire had designated for them. All of those who gave money received a receipt from

[Page 269]

the legionnaire with his signature (his name was Kaplinsky), as a certificate that it was forbidden to hurt them. Then, the legionnaire went with his deputy Smirnov and the *Poruchik* [lieutenant] Andreyev, accompanied by soldiers, to the house of Yehuda Durchin, who had redeemed himself with 50,000 rubles, and made themselves a sumptuous meal there. As they were eating, the legionnaire said that the money they had collected was very meager, and that 200,000 more must be collected for him. He demanded that he be given a list of all the wealthy Jews of the village. The head of the house responded that he could not give such a list. The legionnaire turned to the soldiers and said, "Make the rounds to the houses of the Jews and, for anyone who does not have a receipt that he paid the fine, pillage everything he has and kill him." The people in the house bowed down before the murderer, kissed his hands, and begged for mercy. Then he said that he was leaving now with his soldiers, and that he would return at noon the next day. The Jews have until that time to collect another 50,000 rubles for him. He added that he would also accept Polish marks, American dollars, and thousand-ruble notes. He would accept a mark for thirty-five kopecks, a dollar for seventy rubles, and a thousand ruble note for two hundred rubles. He would also accept ten-ruble gold dinar coins for two hundred rubles per dinar. The head of the house took it upon himself to fulfil the command. The legionnaire left the village with his brigade after midnight. Then the collection of money started. They collected 50,000 rubles. Those who did not have gave everything they had as a pledge.

Six Balachowiczes came the next day at noon and demanded 20,000 rubles from the Jews. The Jews asked the new robbers to wait a bit – they wished to continue on until the legionnaire would return with his troops. In the meantime, another feast was set up in the home of Yehuda Durchin in honor of the new guests. They were afraid to keep the 50,000 rubles that they had collected in the house, lest the new robbers find it. Therefore, they placed it under the bodies of the martyrs who were lying in the *Beis Midrash*. The new robbers did not grant any rest. They demanded money. They were given 1,000 marks at one time, four hundred rubles a second time, and then another two hundred rubles. In the meantime, the legionnaire returned with his troops. The Jews were glad to see him. Yehuda Durchin wept before him and said, "Behold, other soldiers came and demanded money. We made great efforts to ensure that they did not take the money that we collected for you with such great effort." He responded, "You are fortunate that you hid the money. I would not have accepted what you gave to them on the account." He sent for the six soldiers and ordered them to leave the village. He took the 50,000 rubles and complained that there were too few gold dinars. He was given another gold ring to appease him, and they asked him to leave a few of his soldiers in the village to protect the Jews from other soldiers. He agreed. He left five soldiers and gave a certificate to Yehuda Durchin with the following words:

"We command all soldiers who come from any place to not take any monetary fines from the Jews. Anyone violating our order will be given over to a field trial. Signed by Legionnaire Kaplinsky and *Poruchik* Andreyev."

After that, he gave a permit that the murdered people could be taken for a Jewish burial in David-Horodok. At that time, those six soldiers pillaged the Jews at the other edge of the village. After the legionnaire left, the five soldiers that he left to guard the Jews also began to dip into the booty, and to violate girls and young women. Then all the Jews of the village escaped. They left their houses and everything that they had, and fled from the sword. They hastened to find a hiding place in the forest. The soldiers pillaged all that day and all night. They pillaged clothing, pillows, blankets, and everything they could find. They left nothing.

New murderers came at night. When they saw that there were no Jews in the village and that there was nothing to take in the houses, they spread out to search for the hidden people. They found the *shochet* [ritual slaughterer] Chaim Cohen, a father of five young children, in the nearby village of Khotomel. This was in the morning, and he was wearing his tallis and tefillin, and standing in prayer. They grabbed him, took him out of the village, and murdered him. That day, they found Aryeh Leib Bukov, fifty years old and a father of seven children, in the forest. They murdered him in the house of a farmer without saying a word. They found the eighteen-year-old lad Moshe Lapkin, and he fell victim in their hands. The whole time, they raped women and girls. This continued until Wednesday of the second week. The Jews were in the forest the entire time. On

[Page 270]

Wednesday, when the village was somewhat calm, Nachum Stollman, a 45-year-old Jew, father of seven young children, went to his house to see what had taken place there. They murderers burst into the house. He went to hide in the attic. They found him and hanged him.

The situation of the Jews was terrible. Nothing remained of all their toil. Their houses were destroyed and they were all naked and barefoot. It was a complete destruction. Forty women had been raped. They had even raped thirteen-year-old girls. About fifteen innocent girls contracted venereal diseases, having been infected by the scoundrels.

The "Scroll of Tribulations" by Feinstein, published by *Hatzefirah* [a Hebrew-language newspaper published in Poland] and later in a booklet, describes at length the deeds of Balachowicz and the destruction that he brought throughout the region, and especially in David-Horodok and Rubel. It is clear that it is more

important to bring down an appropriate section as it was and in the name of the writer. Of course, it would be possible to write more than was mentioned here.

The David-Horodok Organization in Israel

by The Committee

Translated by Jerrold Landau

Fifteen years ago, at the beginning of the Second World War, a communal organization for the not insignificant number of David-Horodok natives in the Land did not exist yet.

When the tidings of Job regarding what was transpiring in Poland began to arrive, and when information about the refugees of David-Horodok in Russia became known, our member R. Mishalov approached our member Ch. Kolozny regarding the establishment of a committee for the natives of the town of David-Horodok in Israel, which would organize assistance activities and would remain in contact with the refugees.

The members A. Lachovsky, Y. Kashtan, D. Yudovitz, Y. Lifshitz, Dov Shafer, R. Mishalov, A. Sh. Friedman, M. Margolis, B. Slomiansky, Ch. Kolozny, and S. Kirzner were invited to the founding meeting of the committee.

Thanks to the activities of the committee, most of the addresses of the approximately two hundred natives of David-Horodok were obtained. The committee contacted them with a special flyer and with private visits requesting monetary assistance for the refugees.

The member Aryeh Dushnik was elected as head of the committee. He devoted a great deal of his time and efforts to the success of the activities of the committee.

After several addresses of the refugees in Russia were obtained, the committee began to send parcels and letters of encouragement to support the refugees during their time of tribulation. The parcels were sent in all sorts of ways by mail and by the Sochnut [Jewish Agency] with the assistance of the members Glinansky and Y. Kashtan. A substantial portion of them reached their destinations.

Approximately ten years ago, the first memorial day for the martyrs was arranged. From that time, a memorial day has been observed every year, with the participation of most of the natives of David-Horodok in the Land.

The committee was diligent in energetic efforts in all areas. Contact was made with the natives of David-Horodok in America. Financial support was received from them. A charitable fund in the name of the martyrs of David-Horodok was founded in 1949 through the mutual efforts of the Horodokers in America and the Land. It helped those in need by giving loans that were to be paid back.

With time, a substantial portion of the refugees of David-Horodok in Russia who had received full assistance from the committee arrived in the Land. The member Shmuel Zezik, who arrived from Russia, was accepted as a member of the committee, as were the brothers Eliyahu and Yitzchak Glinansky. They assisted greatly in increasing the activities of the committee.

Other meetings and celebrations dedicated to the mutual efforts were arranged, over and above the memorial gatherings. The guests from America, Y. Kitay, Chana Spielberg-Grenadier and others who participated in the meetings and gatherings of

[Page 271]

the natives of David-Horodok in the Land were very impressed with the activities of the committee. This increased the assistance of the David-Horodok natives in America for the charitable fund and for the publication of the Yizkor Book.

Four years ago, the members of the committee began diligent efforts for the memorial book of the martyrs of David Horodok. A great deal of valuable material for the book was gathered during those years due to the efforts of certain individuals.

This book is the crowning achievement of the activities of the committee. A very interesting and valuable period for the memory of the martyrs has concluded – and an eternal monument for our generations and those that will follow us has been established.

A gathering of David-Horodok natives in 1933

[Page 272]

The eleventh memorial gathering of the natives of David-Horodok in the Beit
Yisrael Hall in Tel Aviv, July 28, 1953

The presidium of the eleventh memorial gathering with the participation of
Yaakov Kitay, a guest from America

[Page 273]

The participants in the eleventh memorial gathering

[Page 274]

A portion of those present at the mourning gathering for the martyrs of David-Horodok in Tel Aviv, 5713 [1953] with the participation of Yaakov Kitay, the guest from America

Memorial Book

[Page 277]

A Candle for the Fallen

Translated by Jerrold Landau

Yitzchak Lipman the son of Leah, the grandson of Reb E. Y. Shafer. He was born on September 12, 1928, and fell in the battle near Tira, May 13, 1948.

Aharon Sherman the son of Moshe and Rachel nee Katzman. He was born in Rishon LeZion on September 4, 1927. He was educated in the school in Rishon LeZion. He joined the signal and communications unit of the Haganah at the age of fourteen. From 1942, he served as a guard in the police unit of the settlements centered in Afula. With the outbreak of the War of Independence, he was called to Unit 52 of the Givati Brigade, and participated in the conquest of Sarafand, and in the battles of Tel Arish, Gan Yavne, and Kfar Uriah. He also took part in the security of the road to Jerusalem. He fell on 3 Sivan 5708 [1948] when he penetrated with a squad to Nitzanim, which was in the hands of the Egyptians. He was injured by Egyptian bullets from a distance of a few meters. He was removed from there by his comrades as they retreated. He was buried in Rishon LeZion.

Aharon Sherman

Aryeh Shostakovsky - He was the son of Aharon and Pesia. He was born in David-Horodok on Kislev 5664 (December 10, 1904).[1] He made *aliya* in the year 5685 (1925). He obtained a high school education and was active in the Haganah. He fell in Wadi Rushmiyya, Haifa when a bomb exploded on 14 Tammuz 5698 (July 13, 1938).

Aryeh Shostakovsky

Pesia Lev - She[2] was the daughter of Zalman and Shoshana. She was born in Kfar Saba on Tammuz 5689 (June 17, 1929). She received public and high school education, continued her education and qualified as a nurse. She took care of babies. She was active in the Haganah. She fell in Sha'ar Hagai on a caravan from Jerusalem on 25 Kislev 5708 (December 7, 1948).[3]

Pesia Lev

[Page 278]

Shoshana Lev - She was the wife of Zalman, and the daughter of Yaakov and Pesha Ziporin. She was born in David- Horodok and made *aliya* to the Land in 1921. She was active in the Zionist movement, and a member of Kibbutz Merhavia. She became ill with a broken heart after her daughter Pesia fell, and she died on 17 Adar 5712 (March 14, 1952).

Shoshana Lev

Zeev Lachovsky - He was the son of Shalom and Batya, nee Rakow. He was born in Rubel on September 11, 1922, and was educated in David-Horodok. He was in Russia and Germany during the war years. He spent two years in Cyprus, and made *aliya* in 1947. He served in the Israel Defense Forces and fell in the battle of Sajara on 8 Tammuz 5708 (June 1948).[4]

In various places during the War of Independence, he concluded a sniper's course, and served as a squad leader in a battle unit. He participated in the defense of Tel Aviv and its boundaries, as well as the attacks on Yazur, Tel Arish, and Salma. Then he moved to the gateways of the Negev and participated in the defense of Negba. He fell during a heavy attack on June 21, 1941, and was buried on the spot.

Zeev Lachovsky

Zeev Virobnik - He was born in Tel Aviv to his father Zelig and his mother Leah Edel Dushnik. He was the first grandchild of his grandfather Aryeh Dushnik. He concluded his studies in a business school and worked as a government official. He was responsible, and faithfully conducted all tasks assigned to him. He was tall, and full of dedication and energy. Anyone in his presence felt that they were in the presence of an Israeli youth on whom they could depend.

During the disturbances of 1936, he participated in the defence of Tel Aviv and the Jews of Jaffa. He would return to his work after tense nights of guard duty, without uttering a word about what had taken place, as if nothing had happened. He was sent to a sniper's course, and he went to various places in his tour of duty when it concluded.

He was sent to Kibbutz Negba during the War of Independence along with sixty other lads in order to reinforce the locals in their defence of the passageways to the south. The Egyptians opened a heavy bombardment on June 2, 1948, with the aim of capturing the point. Zeev volunteered to stand on the water tower as a scout, to sound an alarm about approaching danger. Thanks to him, everyone knew the place of danger and was able to take precautions. The reaping of death by the enemy did not bother Zeev. He remained in his place, quiet and strong, until he was hit in his strong heart with a volley of bullets, and he fell victim.

May his memory be a blessing.

Zeev Virobnik

[Page 279]

Shulamit Durchin - The farther we are from the War of Independence, and as we bring to our memories the images of our sons and daughters who fell, with images peering at us from their literary legacy and their letters – we are enveloped with trembling of splendor over the human glory that they exemplified.

These images shall serve us in the future as a precious commodity for the education of future generations, as a form of a new chapter in our book of books...

The images of the daughters are particularly noble. Their numbers were fewer than the sons. Therefore, their value was at a higher level.

Without doubt, Shulamit stands in the ranks of those images.

She was the daughter of two well-pedigreed families of the town: from her father's side, the Durchin family, well known as people of deeds, and from her mother's side from the families of Shlomo Zingerman and Rabbi Dovidl of Horodok. She exemplified both sides together with her good soul, her deeds, her nobility, her understanding of people, and angelic splendor. Heaven and earth joined together in her. She had the character of an exceptional girl. We include here a few excerpts of her letters, and also an excerpt from the booklet that the Kibbutz published in memory of its members who fell during the War of Independence. Both of these present the image of Shulamit to us in her full human glory.

Shulamit Durchin

"Who is Preferable?"

Along the way from Siberia to the Land of Israel, there were, as is known, intermediate stations in the refugee camps in Germany.

Finally, the awaited day came, and the family was about to leave the camps and to make *aliya* to the Land, seemingly with "returnee" documents.

The girl did not agree to make *aliya* together with her parents. The reason was: "I am young and healthy, and I cannot make *aliya* on Aliya Bet. There are so many disabled people who do not have the strength to sneak across borders, and the like. Would it not be better if one of them received the certificate… and I will make *aliya* as many do… In the meantime, I will continue to take care of the youth in the camps."

"Who Will Build?"

In a letter to a friend who remained in Germany, she wrote the following from the port city, after she met with about a hundred youths who were ready to make *aliya* to the Land.

"All the youth who are traveling with me only want to continue with their studies. I discussed with them, and all of them are traveling only for the purpose of study and study."

"Who will build the Land?"

She asked, and she ended her letter, "I have already begun to think otherwise regarding my future…"

Fortunate Among the Fortunates

That is how she saw herself when the arrived in the kibbutz (Netzarim).

She had to conduct a difficult battle against the general consensus that pervaded among her circle of acquaintances in the city

[Page 280]

regarding the kibbutz. She had before her a "good" and sure path. From there, from Russia, she had brought a high school certificate confirming her good marks. Here in Jerusalem, the gates of the university were open wide before her. She entered in the middle of the year and passed the second course (physics – mathematics) with excellence. She also had a guaranteed stipend. However, "I was born to be a kibbutznik" she excused herself to her relatives regarding the direction she took in her life. "Only here have I begun to live," and the previous months were "months of decadence" and "it is left for me to regret the past greatly." For "to feel depression on the soil of the homeland – that is a sin like no other…"

One of the members of the kibbutz (Yissachar) writes in the booklet in memory of the fallen:

"Shulamit is not a common personality in our days. It was as if she belonged to an older era of pioneering Zionism…"

The girl absorbed her first sprouts of Zionist national idealism within the walls of the Tarbut School in the town (Stolin). Furthermore, the spirit of the Land of Israel pervaded in the home of her parents who were dedicated Zionists, and the spoken language in her home was Hebrew.

When the Soviet regime began, and the Hebrew school turned into a school in which the language of instruction was Yiddish and Russian, and the entire national spirit had been expunged from it with a cruel hand, Shulamit fought, as was her way, against the strange spirit, and did not give in…

The six years of exile in Siberia showed her how the Russian youth were raised and educated to love their land and regime. This further forged her spirit to merge completely with the Land and its soil. Therefore "it is a sin to feel depression here on the soil of the homeland" was a sort of echo of the poem of the poet:

"Behold, I desire and kiss your stones
And the taste of your clods of earth is sweeter than honey to me."

From the Siege

An excerpt from a letter:

"Tzvi (A friend who was about to graduate from the Technion, and later fell as a sapper in Sodom) indeed we knew that it would be our lot to participate in the War of Independence…"

"For me it was so good how I succeeded in escaping from the city. For at times, a heap of endless happiness fills my heart with the thought that I am here and am able to do what I am doing with my own hands."

"We have paid with precious victims (three members of the kibbutz fell from the incessant attacks of the neighbors, Yavne from the north and Ashdod from the south), and my hands have already been sullied with blood, with a great deal of blood of lads who had said a moment before: 'Shula you are iron' and then they ceased living… But we succeeded in overcoming. Our kibbutz stands strong. And I see my nation – a precious nation, desiring to be redeemed and prepared for redemption. I am beginning to be proud like my nation. Youth such as this will not succeeded in educating even one nation…"

From the echoes here, with these words, memories from there, from the spirit of the Komsomol[5] Russian youth – which Tzvi, to whom the letter, was addressed, also knew very well – the youth have been educated to dedicate everything for the homeland and the regime, even…

And in a letter to a brother: "It is true, Yossi, that we must be fortunate, for it is our lot to participate in the holy war, the War of Independence. I am satisfied with you, that you are in the ranks of the fighters. It is too bad, though, that we are in different corners."

After she told her brother about the status that she has in her group, that even their armed ones call her by her name "Shulamit" as a sister who wishes to make herself more prominent than her brother, and not without feelings of self pride – she adds at the end with precious humor: "Bow your head as you are reading, that my 'bluffs' pass over your precious head."

[Page 281]

And in another letter: "What took place this week – the week before Passover – was very serious. However, there is a G-d in Heaven! The villains discharged 5-10 thousand bullets from all types of weapons that we are familiar with, even anti-tank weapons, shells, and smoke bombs (such villains!) All this continued from 7:00 a.m. until 3:00 a.m. However, our group is wonderful. I am now in love with our soldiers. I am beginning to be proud of my nation!" (After the disappointment imparted to her by the civic and university surroundings, with which she was involved before her *aliya* to the Land.)

"We hope that all of this will soon end with a righteous and true victory, and we will meet healthy and whole."

However, fate had it differently. On June 6, one week after the final letter, thirty people fell in the final decisive battle from the murderous volley of fire that the Egyptians rained down when they broke into the weapons area. Half of the victims were members of the kibbutz. Shulamit was among them, as she was working in providing aid to the wounded members.

That kibbutz member who memorialized her above writes: "Shulamit encouraged us all during those difficult days. Her optimism did not abate until the final moment."

"She knew no weariness during the final ten days of siege. She was an unfailing wellspring of energy. Her main character trait was love of her fellow, a love that was especially displayed in guiding the youth. She first became involved in that role in the camps, and later with us." The friend concludes, "From this place, the institution for youth that will be founded on the land of Nitzanim in memory of its protector – is the most important actualization of the soul of Shulamit. It will be an appropriate monument to perpetuate her pioneering life." One from among many! There were such people.

Yitzchak Idan Zeldin

Tzvi Durchin

"We offer the money upon which we will resist for you, State of Israel."

(Natan Alterman)

I had the merit of knowing him from up close. We lived together in a single room in Haifa, and studied at the Technion. During the four months of our mutual life, until the War of Independence, I was impressed on many occasions with his personality and character.

The main trait of his personality was steadfastness and dedication. Those two traits accompanied Tzvi during all the periods of his life.

When the family was deported from Pinsk and came to Siberia – Tzvi separated from them and went to Leningrad, where he endured the entire period of terrible siege when the sword consumed outside and the hunger inside. He studied the building trade there at the engineering technical school. That profession guaranteed a bright future in Russia, especially to someone who was also a member of Komsomol. However, Tzvi was not enticed by the irritating lights of Russia. He escaped from there at the first opportunity and made *aliya* to the Land, to bind his fate with the fate of the nation that was renewing its life in the homeland.

He was accepted to the third course at the Technion. He would have graduated as a building engineer

Tzvi Durchin

within one year. In the interim, he had to sustain himself. His family was still wallowing in the camps in Germany, and the conditions of a student in Haifa were not simple. Tzvi studied and worked. He worked as a building worker, he worked at the port, he worked and studied, studied and worked. Despite his full days and nights, he also found time to help a floundering friend solve his problems, to finish the faculty work, etc.

Like all of us, Tzvi was not given the opportunity to study in peace. War was on the horizon. Around, there were preparations for a fateful event. Students of the Technion were taken to positions and training. They were sent to guard duty in various locales cut of from the city. However, they wished to discharge Tzvi. The large-scale draft had not yet taken place. Everything

[Page 282]

that was done, was done voluntarily. Tzvi did not have the obligation to volunteer. Since he had to sustain himself, he was freed from the partial draft. Nevertheless, Tzvi volunteered and participated in everything. He was once asked about this, and he responded:

'I have done more than enough for a land that is foreign to us. I have dug ditches, suffered, gone hungry. What did I not do there? Now, what is demanded of us – is the smallest of the small amount in comparison to our duty to our Land.'

The battles that preceded the declaration of the state began. The Technion was closed. The students were sent to various units. We were separated. I went to one of the units in the north, and Tzvi was given a responsible role in the engineering brigade. Tzvi excelled in his dedication to his role as a sniper. As the head of a squad of the engineering brigade, he participated in various actions. His life, the life of a 26-year-old student who was faithful and dedicated to the nation and the Land, was cut off as he was disarming a mine during one of the actions to liberate Sodom.

May his memory be a blessing.

Shlomo Idan

Tzvi was the son of Etel Olpiner of Horodok and Yisrael Nachum Durchin of Rubel.

Uri Weisberg, the
son of Yitzchak
and Sara, born
on August 5,
1938

Fell in the Sinai
Campaign,
October 31, 1956

Baruch Hochman,
the son of
Yehuda and
Zissel

Born on 26 Sivan
5681 [1921], fell
on 28 Elul 5711
[1951]

[Page 283]

Zalman Gloiberman of blessed memory.
One of the first pioneers of the Third Aliya.

Isser Barsky of blessed memory. One of the fallen of the War of Independence. Born on 13 Shvat 5688, January 24, 1929.[6] Fell in the battle of Hill 69 on June 27, 1948.

Zeev Gloiberman of blessed memory, the partisan, fell during the Second World War.

Translator's footnotes:

1. The Hebrew and English dates are off by one year, as Kislev 5664 would be at the end of 1903.
2. The text says "He," but this is clearly an error.
3. The Hebrew and English dates are off by one year, as Kislev 5708 would be at the end of 1947.
4. The text says "(June 1948)," but 8 Tammuz 5708 would be July 1948.
5. The Communist youth movement in Russia.
6. The Hebrew and English dates are off by one year, as January 24, 1929 would be 13 Shvat 5689.

[Pages 284-296]

List of the Martyrs From David-Horodok

Our sincere appreciation to Yad Vashem for the submission of this necrology for use by JewishGen.

Note: Page numbers refer to the original book.

Coordinator's note: The spelling of the first and last names in this list may not match the standardized spelling of names found elsewhere in this book.

Last Name	First Name	Gender	Father's First Name	Mother's First Name	Spouse's First Name	Profession	Page no.
ABERBUKH	Khaim	Male			Sara		284
ABERBUKH	Sara	Female			Khaim		284
ABRAMOVITZ	Sara	Female					284
ABRAMOVITZ	Zeev	Male					284
ANTL	Gershon	Male					292
ANTL	Khava	Female					292
ANTL	Shlomo	Male					292
ASHMAN	Henia	Female					284
ASHMAN	Khaia	Female			Yaakov		284
ASHMAN	Miriam	Female					284
ASHMAN	Yaakov	Male			Khaia		284
ASHMAN	Yisrael	Male					284
AVREKH	Braindel	Female					284
AVREKH	Sara	Female					284
AVROSHIN	Moshe Faivel	Male					284
AVROSHIN		Male			Moshe Faivel		284
BARASH	Teibel	Male					284
BARZIVIN		Male			Yaakov		285
BARZIVIN	Yaakov	Male					285
BASEVITZ	David	Male					285
BASEVITZ	Lipka	Female					284

BASEVITZ	Moshe	Male			Nekhama	285
BASEVITZ	Nekhama	Female			Moshe	285
BASEVITZ	Yaakov	Male				285
BEGUN	Mordekhai Yaakov	Male				285
BEGUN	Peshe	Female			Shlomo	285
BEGUN	Shlomo	Male			Peshe	285
BEGUN		Male			Yosef	285
BEGUN		Male			Mordekhai Yaakov	285
BEGUN	Yosef	Male				285
BEIGELMAN	Shlomo	Male				285
BEIGELMAN	Shlomo	Male				285
BEIGELMAN		Male			Yosef	285
BEIGELMAN		Male			Shlomo	285
BEIGELMAN	Yosef	Male				285
BEILIN	Barukh	Male				285
BEILIN	Meir	Male				285
BEILIN	Pesakh	Male				285
BEILIN	Sara	Female			Yaakov	285
BEILIN		Male			Pesakh	285
BEILIN	Yaakov	Male			Sara	285
BEKMAN	Rashke	Female			Shlomo Khaim	285
BEKMAN	Shlomo Khaim	Male			Rashke	285
BEKOV	Barukh Yeshayahu	Male				285
BEKOV		Male			Barukh Yeshayahu	285
BEREZNOGER	Alte	Female			Yitzkhak	285
BEREZNOGER	Barukh	Male	Pinkhas	Etil		285
BEREZNOGER	Breindil	Female	Pinkhas	Etil		285
BEREZNOGER	Etil	Female			Pinkhas	285
BEREZNOGER	Khaia	Female			Shlomo	285
BEREZNOGER	Khaia	Female				284

BEREZNOGER	Leizer	Male					284
BEREZNOGER	Libe	Female	Shlomo	Khaia			285
BEREZNOGER	Mikhaela	Female			Yosef		284
BEREZNOGER	Moshe	Male			Tzipora		285
BEREZNOGER	Motel	Male	Pinkhas	Etil			285
BEREZNOGER	Pinkhas	Male			Etil		285
BEREZNOGER	Reina	Female					285
BEREZNOGER	Rivka	Female					284
BEREZNOGER	Shaia	Male	Pinkhas	Etil			285
BEREZNOGER	Shlomo	Male			Khaia		285
BEREZNOGER	Tamara	Female					285
BEREZNOGER	Tzipora	Female			Moshe		285
BEREZNOGER	Yaakov	Male	Shlomo	Khaia			285
BEREZNOGER	Yerakhmiel	Male	Shlomo	Khaia			285
BEREZNOGER	Yitzkhak	Male			Alte		285
BEREZNOGER	Yosef	Male			Mikhaela		284
BERGMAN	Gitel	Female			Motel		285
BERGMAN	Gitel	Female			Motel		284
BERGMAN	Golda	Female			Pesakh		285
BERGMAN	Lea	Female			Yosef		284
BERGMAN	Motel	Male			Gitel		285
BERGMAN	Motel	Male			Gitel		284
BERGMAN	Pesakh	Male			Golda		285
BERGMAN	Rakhel	Female					284
BERGMAN	Yaakov	Male					285
BERGMAN	Yosef	Male			Lea		284
BERKOVITZ		Male			Yosef		285
BERKOVITZ	Yosef	Male					285
BERMAN	Beril	Male			Sheina		285
BERMAN	Beril	Male					285
BERMAN	Ester	Female					285
BERMAN	Gisia	Female					285
BERMAN	Lea	Female					285

BERMAN	Sheina	Female			Beril		285
BERMAN	Yudel	Male					285
BIGUN	Khaikel	Male			Tzirel		285
BIGUN	Tzirel	Female			Khaiakel		285
BLIZOVSKI	Nakhman	Male					285
BORUKHMAN	Gitel	Male					285
BORUKHMAN	Lea	Female					285
BORUKHMAN	Meir	Male					285
BORUKHMAN	Mordekhai	Male					285
BORUKHMAN	Moshe	Male					285
BORUKHMAN	Reuven	Male					285
BORUKHMAN	Sara	Female					285
BORUKHMAN	Shalom	Male					285
BORUKHMAN	Yehoshua	Male					285
BRANCHUK	Beniamin	Male	Khaim	Rivka			284
BRANCHUK	David	Male	Khaim	Rivka			284
BRANCHUK	Itka	Female	Khaim	Rivka			284
BRANCHUK	Khaim	Male			Rivka		284
BRANCHUK	Rivka	Female			Khaim		284
BRATZKER	Etil	Female	Mendil				285
BRATZKER	Mendil	Male					285
BRATZKER	Rakhel	Female	Mendil				285
BRATZKER		Male			Mendil		285
BRATZKER	Utka	Female	Mendil				285
BROKHMAN	Arie	Male			Fruma		285
BROKHMAN	Asher	Male					284
BROKHMAN	Barukh	Male	Khaim	Yekha			285
BROKHMAN	David	Male			Simkha		285
BROKHMAN	David	Male	Meir				285
BROKHMAN	David	Male					285
BROKHMAN	Fruma	Female			Arie		285
BROKHMAN	Khaim	Male			Yecha		285
BROKHMAN	Liba	Female			Moshe		285

BROKHMAN	Mania	Female	Moshe	Liba			285
BROKHMAN	Mikhael	Male	Moshe	Liba			285
BROKHMAN	Moshe	Male			Liba		285
BROKHMAN	Moshe	Male					285
BROKHMAN	Shalom	Male					285
BROKHMAN	Simkha	Female			David		285
BROKHMAN	Sonia	Female	Moshe	Liba			285
BROKHMAN	Sonia	Female					285
BROKHMAN	Tzipa	Female					285
BROKHMAN		Male			Asher		284
BROKHMAN		Male			David		285
BROKHMAN		Male			Moshe		285
BROKHMAN	Yecha	Female			Khaim		285
BROKHMAN	Yehuda	Male					285
BROKHMAN	Yosef	Male	Moshe	Liba			285
BROKHMAN	Yosef Zalman	Male	Khaim	Yekha			285
BRONSHTEIN	Lea	Female					284
BRONSHTEIN		Male			Yaakov		284
BRONSHTEIN	Yaakov	Male					284
BUKHLITZKI	Dov	Male	Nisan	Khaia			285
BUKHLITZKI	Khaia	Female			Nisan		285
BUKHLITZKI	Khaim	Male	Nisan	Khaia			285
BUKHLITZKI	Nisan	Male			Khaia		285
BUKHLITZKI	Zeev	Male	Nisan	Khaia			285
BUKOV	Lea	Female					285
BUKOV	Mindl	Female					285
BUKOV	Moshe	Male					285
BUKOV	Rivka	Female					285
BUKOV	Tilka	Female					285
BUKOV	Yitzkhak	Male					285
BURMAN	Yudel	Male	Meir				285
BURSHTEIN	Avraham	Male			Brakha		284
BURSHTEIN	Beilka	Female			Yosef		284

BURSHTEIN	Brakha	Female			Avraham		284
BURSHTEIN	Meir	Male	Avraham	Brakha			284
BURSHTEIN	Menakhem	Male					285
BURSHTEIN	Moshe	Male					285
BURSHTEIN	Moshe Khaim	Male					285
BURSHTEIN	Motel	Male					285
BURSHTEIN	Pesil	Female					284
BURSHTEIN	Rivka	Female	Avraham	Brakha			284
BURSHTEIN		Male			Motel		285
BURSHTEIN		Male			Menakhem		285
BURSHTEIN	Yosef	Male			Beilka		284
CHECHIK	Arie	Male	Herschil	Fredil			295
ZEZIK	Braindel	Female			Yudl		295
ZEZIK	Dvora	Female	Herschil	Fredil			295
ZEZIK	Eliahu	Male			Sheina Feigel		294
ZEZIK	Eliahu	Male		Sheindil			295
ZEZIK	Eliahu	Male					295
ZEZIK	Fradil	Female			Herschil		295
ZEZIK	Frodil	Female			Herschel		292
ZEZIK	Herschel	Male			Frodil		292
ZEZIK	Herschil	Male			Fradil		295
ZEZIK	Itka	Female		Sheindil			295
ZEZIK	Khaia	Female					295
ZEZIK	Khaia Elka	Female					295
ZEZIK	Khashke	Female					292
ZEZIK	Khashke	Female					295
ZEZIK	Moshe	Male					292
ZEZIK	Moshe	Male					295
ZEZIK	Sheina Feigel	Female			Eliahu		294
ZEZIK	Sheindil	Female					295
ZEZIK	Shmuel Leibel	Male					295

ZEZIK	Simkha	Male		Sheindil			295
ZEZIK		Male			Eliahu		295
ZEZIK	Yudel	Male			Breindil		295
ZEZIK	Zelda	Female	Herschil	Fredil			295
CHERTOK	Nakhum	Male					288
CHERTOK	Nekhama	Female					288
CHERTOK	Sara	Female					288
CHESNOK	Barukh	Male			Rakhel Lea		295
CHESNOK	David	Male			Tema		294
CHESNOK	Khaia	Female	Meir	Liba			294
CHESNOK	Liba	Female			Meir		294
CHESNOK	Meir	Male			Liba		294
CHESNOK	Moshe Ber	Male					294
CHESNOK	Rakhel Lea	Female			Barukh		295
CHESNOK	Sheina	Female	Meir	Liba			294
CHESNOK	Tema	Female			David		294
CHISNUK	David	Male					292
DANZIGER	Itka	Female			Yekhiel		286
DANZIGER	Yekhiel	Male			Itka		286
DIATLOVITZKI	Dov	Male					286
DIATLOVITZKI	Pinkhas	Male					286
DIATLOVITZKI		Male			Dov		286
DIATLOVITZKI		Male			Pinkhas		286
DIATLOVITZKI	Yosef	Male					286
DOBRUSHIN	Aharon	Male			Rakhel		287
DOBRUSHIN	Aharon	Male			Rakhel		287
DOBRUSHIN	Eliahu	Male	Noakh	Miriam			286
DOBRUSHIN	Faivel	Male					286
DOBRUSHIN	Faivel	Male					286
DOBRUSHIN	Khaia Elka	Female					286
DOBRUSHIN	Lea Fridl	Female	Noakh	Miriam			286
DOBRUSHIN	Mania	Female					286
DOBRUSHIN	Miriam	Female			Noakh		286

DOBRUSHIN	Noakh	Male			Miriam		286
DOBRUSHIN	Rakhel	Female			Aharon		287
DOBRUSHIN	Rakhel	Female			Aharon		287
DOBRUSHIN	Rozale	Female		Mania			286
DOBRUSHIN	Shimel	Male					286
DOBRUSHIN	Yosef	Male					286
DOLGOPIATI	David	Male			Itka		286
DOLGOPIATI	Itka	Female			David		286
DREBSKI	Matatiahu	Male			Pesil		286
DREBSKI	Pesil	Female			Matatiahu		286
DREIZEL	Rasel	Female					287
DREIZIN	Miriam	Female			Yosef		287
DREIZIN	Miriam	Female			Shlomo		287
DREIZIN	Sheindil	Female					287
DREIZIN	Shlomo	Male			Miriam		287
DREIZIN	Yosef	Male			Miriam	Scribe/Writer	287
DUBERSHTEIN	Mania	Female					287
DUBLIN	Metil	Male					287
DUBROVITZKI	Avraham	Male					287
DUBROVITZKI	Avraham	Male					287
DUBROVITZKI	Beniamin	Male					287
DUBROVITZKI	David	Male					287
DUBROVITZKI	Fradil	Female			Mordekhai Leib		287
DUBROVITZKI	Khashke	Female					287
DUBROVITZKI	Mordekhai	Male					287
DUBROVITZKI	Mordekhai Leib	Male			Fradil		287
DUBROVITZKI	Moshe	Male					287
DUBROVITZKI	Peshe Krina	Female					286
DUBROVITZKI	Sara	Female			Shepsil		287
DUBROVITZKI	Shepsil	Male			Sara		287
DUBROVITZKI	Shmuel	Male					287
DUBROVITZKI		Male			Avraham		287

DUBROVITZKI	Yisrael	Male				287
DUBROVITZKI	Yosef	Male				287
DUBROVITZKI	Zelig	Male				286
DURCHIN	Avraham	Male				287
DURCHIN	Hinda	Female				287
DURCHIN	Khana	Female			Yaakov	287
DURCHIN	Khana	Female				286
DURCHIN	Leibke	Male			Sara	287
DURCHIN	Rakhel Feiga	Female			Yitzkhak	287
DURCHIN	Sara	Female			Leibka	287
DURCHIN	Shimon	Male				287
DURCHIN		Male			Avraham	287
DURCHIN		Male			Velvel	286
DURCHIN		Male			Yitzkhak	287
DURCHIN	Velvel	Male				286
DURCHIN	Yaakov	Male			Khana	287
DURCHIN	Yehudit	Female				287
DURCHIN	Yitzkhak	Male			Rakhel Feiga	287
DURCHIN	Yitzkhak	Male				287
EDEL	Berta	Female			Yitzkhak	292
EDEL	Gedalyahu	Male				292
EDEL	Khaia	Female				292
EDEL	Roza	Female				292
EDEL	Yitzkhak	Male			Berta	292
EIZENBERG	Aharon	Male			Elka	284
EIZENBERG	Bashka	Male			Simka Broindel	284
EIZENBERG	Beril	Male				284
EIZENBERG	Elka	Female			Aharon	284
EIZENBERG	Gitel	Female	Aharon	Elka		284
EIZENBERG	Gitel	Female	Moshe Yitzkhak	Sara		284
EIZENBERG	Gudel	Male	Aharon	Elka		284

EIZENBERG	Miriam	Female	Aharon	Elka			284
EIZENBERG	Moshe Yitzkhak	Male			Sara		284
EIZENBERG	Motel	Male	Moshe Yitzkhak	Sara			284
EIZENBERG	Reizil	Female	Moshe Yitzkhak	Sara			284
EIZENBERG	Sara	Female			Moshe Yitzkhak		284
EIZENBERG	Shoshka	Female	Moshe Yitzkhak	Sara			284
EIZENBERG	Simka Broindel	Female			Bashke		284
EIZENBERG	Yaakov	Male	Moshe Yitzkhak	Sara			284
ELPINER	Aharon	Male	Avraham				284
ELPINER	Alte	Female					284
ELPINER	Avraham	Male					284
ELPINER	Gedalyahu	Male			Rakhel		284
ELPINER	Itzel	Male					284
ELPINER	Khaim	Male	Avraham				284
ELPINER	Meir	Male			Sara		284
ELPINER	Rakhel	Female			Gedaliyahu		284
ELPINER	Sara	Female			Meir		284
ELPINER	Sonia	Female			Yosef		284
ELPINER		Male			Itzil		284
ELPINER	Yosef	Male	Moshe Nisan		Sonia		284
EPSHTEIN	Moshe	Male					292
EPSHTEIN		Male			Moshe		292
EPSHTEIN		Male	Moshe				292
ERLIKH	Moshe	Male					284
FEIN	Barukh	Male					293
FEIN	Dvora	Female					294
FEIN	Ester	Female					293
FEIN	Lea	Female			Moshe		293
FEIN	Moshe	Male			Lea		293

FEIN	Rakhel	Female			Yekhiel		293
FEIN	Rakhel	Female			Yekhiel		294
FEIN	Yekhiel	Male			Rakhel		293
FEIN	Yekhiel	Male			Rakhel		294
FELDMAN	Akiva	Male			Dvora		293
FELDMAN	Barukh	Male					294
FELDMAN	Dvora	Female			Akiva		293
FELDMAN	Feigil	Female					294
FELDMAN	Khaia	Female					294
FELDMAN	Khaim	Male					294
FELDMAN	Khava	Female					293
FELDMAN	Mikhael	Male					294
FELDMAN	Shalom	Male					294
FELDMAN	Yitzkhak	Male					294
FERBER	Beril	Male			Ester		293
FERBER	Ester	Female			Beril		293
FERBER	Ester	Female			Leizer		293
FERBER	Leizer	Male			Ester		293
FERBER	Rivka	Female	Leizer	Ester			293
FERBER	Sara	Female	Leizer	Ester			293
FERBER	Shmuel	Male	Leizer	Ester			293
FERBER	Yosef	Male	Beril	Ester			293
FERMAN	Aizik	Male					293
FIALKOV	Beril	Male					294
FIALKOV		Male			Beril		294
FILBIN	Batze	Female					294
FILBIN	Bilka	Female			Leizer		293
FILBIN	Feigil	Female			Khaim		293
FILBIN	Herschil	Male			Rivka		293
FILBIN	Khaim	Male			Feigil		293
FILBIN	Leizer	Male			Bilka		293
FILBIN	Moshe	Male	Khaim	Feigil			293
FILBIN	Moshe	Male					294

FILBIN	Rivka	Female			Herschil		293
FILBIN		Male			Moshe		294
FINKELSHTEIN	Alter	Male					292
FINKELSHTEIN	Golda	Female			Khaim		293
FINKELSHTEIN	Khaia	Female			Shlomo		293
FINKELSHTEIN	Khaim	Male			Golda		293
FINKELSHTEIN	Khava	Female					292
FINKELSHTEIN	Lipa	Male	Khaim	Golda			293
FINKELSHTEIN	Mania	Female					293
FINKELSHTEIN	Rivka	Female					293
FINKELSHTEIN	Shimon	Male			Zelda		293
FINKELSHTEIN	Shlomo	Male			Khaia		293
FINKELSHTEIN		Male			Khava		292
FINKELSHTEIN		Male		Khava			292
FINKELSHTEIN	Yisrael	Male					293
FINKELSHTEIN	Zelda	Female			Shimon		293
FISHELOV	Sara	Female					294
FISHELOV	Zlatka	Female	Sara				294
FISHMAN	David	Male					293
FISHMAN	Doba	Female					293
FISHMAN	Feigel	Female			Moshe		292
FISHMAN	Feigil	Female					293
FISHMAN	Malka	Female					292
FISHMAN	Moshe	Male					293
FISHMAN	Rivka	Female					293
FISHMAN	Roshka	Female					293
FISHMAN	Sara Lea	Female			Zalman		293
FISHMAN	Simkha	Male					293
FISHMAN		Male			Yeshiyah		293
FISHMAN		Male		Doba			293
FISHMAN	Yeshiyah	Male					293
FISHMAN	Zalman	Male			Sara Lea		293
FISHMAN	Zelig	Male					293

FLEISHMAN	Aharon	Male			293
FLEISHMAN	Barukh	Male		Mania	293
FLEISHMAN	Mania	Female		Barukh	293
FLEISHMAN	Shlomo	Male			293
FLEISHMAN		Male		Aharon	293
FLEISHMAN		Male		Shlomo	293
FREIMAN	Feigel	Female	Khaikel		293
FREIMAN	Hodel	Female	Khaikel		293
FREIMAN	Khaikel	Male			293
FREIMAN	Khaim Yankel	Male			293
FREIMAN	Leibel	Male	Khaikel		293
FREIMAN		Male		Khaiakel	293
FREINKEL	Khinka	Female		Yosef	294
FREINKEL	Yosef	Male		Khinka	294
FRES	Eliezer	Male		Vichna	294
FRES	Vikhne	Female		Eliezer	294
FRIDMAN	Alter	Male		Yentil	293
FRIDMAN	Asher	Male			294
FRIDMAN	Barukh	Male		Kreina	294
FRIDMAN	Barukh	Male			294
FRIDMAN	Brakha	Female		Mikhael	294
FRIDMAN	Ester	Female		Mordekhai	294
FRIDMAN	Feigil	Female			293
FRIDMAN	Freidil	Female		Reuven	294
FRIDMAN	Golda	Female			294
FRIDMAN	Henia	Female		Yaakov	293
FRIDMAN	Henia	Female			293
FRIDMAN	Khaim	Male		Pril	294
FRIDMAN	Khaim	Male			293
FRIDMAN	Khana	Female		Yehuda	294
FRIDMAN	Kreina	Female		Barukh	294
FRIDMAN	Makhla	Female			293
FRIDMAN	Mania	Female			293

FRIDMAN	Meir	Male	Yaakov	Henia			293
FRIDMAN	Mikhael	Male			Brakha		294
FRIDMAN	Mindl	Female					293
FRIDMAN	Mordekhai	Male			Ester		294
FRIDMAN	Moshe	Male					293
FRIDMAN	Moshe	Male					293
FRIDMAN	Moshe	Male					293
FRIDMAN	Peril	Female			Khaim		294
FRIDMAN	Rakhela	Female	Yosef				293
FRIDMAN	Reizl	Female	Yosef				293
FRIDMAN	Reuven	Male			Freidil		294
FRIDMAN	Sara	Female	Yosef				293
FRIDMAN	Shmuel	Male					293
FRIDMAN		Male			Yaakov		293
FRIDMAN	Yaakov	Male	Moshe		Henia		293
FRIDMAN	Yaakov	Male					293
FRIDMAN	Yehuda	Male			Khana		294
FRIDMAN	Yehuda	Male					293
FRIDMAN	Yentil	Female			Alter		293
FRIDMAN	Yosef	Male					293
FRIDMAN	Yosef	Male					293
FRIDMAN	Yosel	Male			Zelda		293
FRIDMAN	Yudel	Male					293
FRIDMAN	Zelda	Female			Yosel		293
FRIDMAN	Zelda	Female					293
FRIMAN	Leibel	Male	Mordekhai	Vikhna			292
FRIMAN	Meir	Male	Mordekhai	Vikhna			292
FRIMAN	Mikhael	Male					292
FRIMAN	Mordekhai	Male			Vikhna		292
FRIMAN	Pesakh	Male	Mordekhai	Vikhna			292
FRIMAN	Vikhna	Female			Mordekhai		292
FRIMAN	Yentl	Female	Mordekhai	Vikhna			292
FRIMAN	Yosef	Male					292

FRIMUN	Entil	Female	Motel	Vikhna			294
FRIMUN	Leibel	Male	Motel	Vikhna			294
FRIMUN	Meir	Male	Motel	Vikhna			294
FRIMUN	Motel	Male			Vikhna		294
FRIMUN	Vikhna	Female			Motel		294
FUKSMAN	Moshe	Male					294
FUKSMAN		Male			Moshe		294
FURMAN	Blumka	Female			Yosef		293
FURMAN	Dina	Female			Shlomo		294
FURMAN	Golda	Female					294
FURMAN	Khashke	Female			Yosef		293
FURMAN	Meir	Male					294
FURMAN	Mikhael	Male					294
FURMAN	Motel	Male					294
FURMAN	Shaia	Male					294
FURMAN	Shimon	Male					293
FURMAN	Shimon	Male					294
FURMAN	Shlomo	Male			Dina		294
FURMAN		Male			Yosef		294
FURMAN		Male			Yosef		294
FURMAN		Male			Shimon		293
FURMAN		Male			Shimon		294
FURMAN		Male			Shaia		294
FURMAN	Yosef	Male			Blumka		293
FURMAN	Yosef	Male			Kheshka		293
FURMAN	Yosef	Male					294
FURMAN	Yosef	Male					294
GALINSKI	Sara Lea	Female			Shmuel		286
GALINSKI	Shmuel	Male			Sara Lea		286
GARTZULIN	Khana	Female			Yaakov		286
GARTZULIN	Yaakov	Male			Khana		286
GEIER	Asher	Male			Eidel		286
GEIER	Asher	Male			Rivka		286

GEIER	Avraham	Male	Asher	Eidel			286
GEIER	Eidel	Female			Asher		286
GEIER	Feigel	Female	Asher	Eidel			286
GEIER	Khaim	Male	Asher	Eidel			286
GEIER	Rivka	Female			Asher		286
GEIER	Shifra	Female	Asher	Eidel			286
GELBURT	Rishel	Female			Yekel		286
GELBURT	Yekl	Male			Rishel		286
GELMAN	Efraim	Male					285
GELMAN	Reizil	Female					285
GELMAN	Sara	Female			Yosef		286
GELMAN	Yosef	Male			Sara		286
GELMAN	Zysl	Female					285
GERSHINOVITZ	Shlomo	Male			Tzipora		286
GERSHINOVITZ	Tzipora	Female			Shlomo		286
GERSHTEIN	Boaz	Male					285
GERSHTEIN	Khaim	Male			Mania		285
GERSHTEIN	Mania	Female			Khaim		285
GERTZIK	Dovka	Female			Litman		286
GERTZIK	Litman	Male			Dovka		286
GINSBURG	Alte	Female			Moshe Yehoshua		286
GINSBURG	David	Male			Rakhel		286
GINSBURG	Feigele	Female	Moshe Yehoshua	Alte			286
GINSBURG	Khana	Female	Moshe Yehoshua	Alte			286
GINSBURG	Moshe Yehoshua	Male			Alte		286
GINSBURG	Rakhel	Female			David		286
GINSBURG	Yisrael	Male					286
GINSBURG	Zeev	Male	Moshe Yehoshua	Alte			286
GINTZBURG	Golda	Female			Itzil		286
GINTZBURG	Henia	Female			Yaakov David		286

GINTZBURG	Itzel	Male			Golda		286
GINTZBURG	Liba Reizl	Female					286
GINTZBURG	Miriam	Female	Yaakov David	Henia			286
GINTZBURG	Rakhel	Female	Yaakov David	Henia			286
GINTZBURG	Sara	Female	Yaakov David	Henia			286
GINTZBURG	Yaakov David	Male			Henia		286
GINTZBURG	Yisrael Yosef	Male					286
GITELMAN	Feigil	Female			Gershon		286
GITELMAN	Gershon	Male			Feigil		286
GITELMAN	Shlomo	Male					286
GITELMAN	Yehoshua	Male					286
GITELMAN	Yisrael	Male					286
GLEIBERZON	Malka	Female			Zalman		286
GLEIBERZON	Zalman	Male			Malka		286
GLOIBERMAN	Dvora	Female			Yosef		286
GLOIBERMAN	Leibel	Male			Pua		286
GLOIBERMAN	Pua	Female			Leibel		286
GLOIBERMAN	Roda	Female			Shimon		286
GLOIBERMAN	Shimon	Male			Roda		286
GLOIBERMAN	Yaakov	Male					286
GLOIBERMAN	Yosef	Male			Dvora		286
GLOIBERMAN	Zeev	Male	Yosef	Dvora			286
GLOIBERMAN	Zeev	Male	Leibel	Pua			286
GOLDHOR	Rivel	Male					286
GOLDHOR	Shimon	Male					286
GOLDHOR		Male			Yaakov		286
GOLDHOR	Yaakov	Male					286
GOLDHOR	Yehuda	Male					286
GOLDMAN	Sara	Female			Yehoshua		286
GOLDMAN	Shlomo	Male	Yehoshua	Sara			286
GOLDMAN	Vitka	Female	Yehoshua	Sara			286

GOLDMAN	Yehoshua	Male			Sara		286
GOLDMAN	Yisrael	Male	Yehoshua	Sara			286
GOLUBITZKI	Efraim	Male					286
GOLUBITZKI	Khana	Female					286
GOLUBITZKI		Male			Yosef		286
GOLUBITZKI	Yosef	Male					286
GONIN	Sheindil	Female			Yaakov Shlomo		286
GONIN	Yaakov Shlomo	Male			Sheindil		286
GORNSHTEIN	Mendel	Male					286
GORNSHTEIN		Male			Yisrael		286
GORNSHTEIN	Yisrael	Male					286
GORSKI	Rakhel	Female					286
GOSKEVITZ	Barukh	Male					286
GOSKEVITZ	David	Male					286
GOSKEVITZ	Fishel	Male					286
GOSKEVITZ	Golda	Female			Herschil		286
GOSKEVITZ	Golda	Female					286
GOSKEVITZ	Herschil	Male			Golda		286
GOSKEVITZ	Kalman	Male					286
GOSKEVITZ	Pesakhka	Male					286
GOSKEVITZ	Tentzer	Male					286
GOSKEVITZ	Tzeitl	Male					286
GOTLIB	Arie	Male	Yosef	Ester			286
GOTLIB	Ester	Female			Yosef		286
GOTLIB	Shakhna	Male	Yosef	Ester			286
GOTLIB	Yosef	Male			Ester		286
GRANADIR	Malka	Female			Meir		285
GRANADIR	Meir	Male			Malka		285
GRAVITZ GINSBURG	Yisrael	Male					286
GRECZNIK	Avraham	Male					286
GRECZNIK	Lipman	Male			Rashke		286
GRECZNIK	Rashke	Female			Lipman		286

GROSHKIN	Khana	Female					286
GRUSHKEVITZ	Barukh	Male					286
GRUSHKEVITZ		Male			Barukh		286
GUREVITZ	Bashia	Female					286
GUREVITZ	David	Male	Bashia				286
GUREVITZ	Fishka	Male			Yashka		286
GUREVITZ	Herschil	Male	Bashia				286
GUREVITZ	Hinda	Female			Zalman		286
GUREVITZ	Isser	Male	Bashia				286
GUREVITZ	Malka	Female	Pesakh	Nekhama			286
GUREVITZ	Meir	Male					286
GUREVITZ	Nekhama	Female			Pesakh		286
GUREVITZ	Pesakh	Male			Nekhama		286
GUREVITZ	Roni	Female	Pesakh	Nekhama			286
GUREVITZ		Male			Meir		286
GUREVITZ	Yashke	Male			Fishka		286
GUREVITZ	Yentil	Female					286
GUREVITZ	Yosef	Male	Bashia				286
GUREVITZ	Yuzhi	Male	Pesakh	Nekhama			286
GUREVITZ	Zalman	Male			Hinda		286
GURFINK	Khinka	Female					286
GURFINK		Male			Khinka		286
GUZ	Khaitze	Female			Mordekhai		286
GUZ	Mordekhai	Male			Khaitza		286
HADIUK	Aharon Volf	Male					287
HEDEK	Aba	Male			Tamara		287
HEDEK	Aharon	Male			Yentil		287
HEDEK	Alter	Male					287
HEDEK	Bashka	Female			Beril		287
HEDEK	Ben	Male	Beril	Bashke			287
HEDEK	Beril	Male			Bashke		287
HEDEK	Beril	Male			Drizel		287
HEDEK	Dreizel	Female			Beril		287

HEDEK	Leiba	Male			Tzipe		287
HEDEK	Mendil	Male	Beril	Bashke			287
HEDEK	Moshe	Male					287
HEDEK	Sheindil	Female					287
HEDEK	Tamara	Female			Aba		287
HEDEK	Tzipe	Female			Leiba		287
HEDEK		Male			Moshe		287
HEDEK	Yentil	Female			Aharon		287
HOKHMAN	Aharon	Male			Meril		287
HOKHMAN	Beilka	Female			Moshe		287
HOKHMAN	Meril	Female			Aharon		287
HOKHMAN	Moshe	Male			Beilka		287
HOLTZMAN	Asher	Male					287
HOLTZMAN	Gershon	Male			Mikhal		287
HOLTZMAN	Mikhal	Female			Gershon		287
HOLTZMAN	Shmuel	Male					287
HOLTZMAN	Yehuda	Male					287
IAKHNICH	Rakhel	Female					289
IANKELEVITZ	Khaim	Male			Reizil		289
IANKELEVITZ	Reizil	Female			Khaim		289
IANKELEVITZ	Todros	Male					289
IANKELEVITZ		Male			Todros		289
IANKELEVITZ	Velvel	Male					289
ILMAN	Brakha	Female			Yitzkhak		284
ILMAN	Kahat	Male			Sara		284
ILMAN	Sara	Female			Kahat		284
ILMAN	Yitzkhak	Male			Brakha		284
IONASH	Avraham Ezra	Male					289
IONASH	Bila	Female			Nekha		289
IONASH	Gitel	Female					289
IONASH	Leibel	Male			Tzipe		289
IONASH	Nekha	Female			Bila		289
IONASH	Tzipe	Female			Leibel		289

IONASH		Male			Yosef	289
IONASH	Yosef	Male				289
IUDOVITZ	Asher	Male				289
IUDOVITZ	Avraham	Male			Khana	289
IUDOVITZ	Avraham	Male		Khaia		288
IUDOVITZ	Barukh	Male				288
IUDOVITZ	Barukh	Male				289
IUDOVITZ	Beril	Male	Meir			288
IUDOVITZ	Betzalel	Male			Nekhama	289
IUDOVITZ	David	Male				289
IUDOVITZ	Ester	Female	Yosef	Margola		288
IUDOVITZ	Feigele	Female				288
IUDOVITZ	Hershel	Male	Betzalel	Nekhama		289
IUDOVITZ	Hershel	Male				289
IUDOVITZ	Herzl	Male				289
IUDOVITZ	Itzel	Male				289
IUDOVITZ	Khaia	Female				288
IUDOVITZ	Khana	Female			Avraham	289
IUDOVITZ	Khendel	Female			Zeev	289
IUDOVITZ	Leibel	Male				289
IUDOVITZ	Leizer	Male				288
IUDOVITZ	Levita	Female			Zelik	288
IUDOVITZ	Malka	Female			Yesha	288
IUDOVITZ	Malka	Female		Rivka		288
IUDOVITZ	Margola	Female			Yosef	288
IUDOVITZ	Meir	Male				288
IUDOVITZ	Meir	Male				289
IUDOVITZ	Mikhael	Male				288
IUDOVITZ	Miriam	Female			Tzvi	289
IUDOVITZ	Mordekhai	Male			Moshe Masha	289
IUDOVITZ	Moshe Masha	Male			Mordekhai	289
IUDOVITZ	Nekha	Female				289

IUDOVITZ	Nekhama	Female			Betzalel		289
IUDOVITZ	Nekhamka	Female			Shlomo		289
IUDOVITZ	Peshe	Female					288
IUDOVITZ	Rivka	Female					288
IUDOVITZ	Sala	Female					289
IUDOVITZ	Sheina Rakhel	Female					289
IUDOVITZ	Shlomo	Male			Nekhamka		289
IUDOVITZ	Shlomo	Male	Betzalel	Nekhama			289
IUDOVITZ	Tzvi	Male			Miriam		289
IUDOVITZ		Male			Itzil		289
IUDOVITZ		Male			Barukh		288
IUDOVITZ		Male			David		289
IUDOVITZ		Male			Zelig		289
IUDOVITZ		Male			Yosef		289
IUDOVITZ		Male			Leibel		289
IUDOVITZ		Male			Leizer		288
IUDOVITZ		Male			Meir		288
IUDOVITZ		Male			Mikhael		288
IUDOVITZ	Yasha	Male			Malka		288
IUDOVITZ	Yentil	Female		Rivka			288
IUDOVITZ	Yosef	Male			Margola		288
IUDOVITZ	Yosef	Male	Meir				289
IUDOVITZ	Zeev	Male			Khendel		289
IUDOVITZ	Zeev Tzvi	Male	Meir				288
IUDOVITZ	Zelig	Male					289
IUDOVITZ	Zelik	Male			Levita		288
KALOBNIK	Khana	Female			Velvel		296
KALOBNIK	Velvel	Male			Khana		296
KANCHIK	Avraham	Male					295
KANCHIK	Etil	Female					295
KANTOR	Ester	Female					296
KANTOR	Moshe	Male					296
KANTOR	Shulamit	Female		Ester			296

KANTOR	Sonia	Female		Ester			296
KANTOR		Male			Moshe		296
KAPLAN	Avraham	Male			Sheina		295
KAPLAN	Lea	Female			Shlomo Khaim		295
KAPLAN	Moshe Khaim	Male					295
KAPLAN	Sheina	Female			Avraham		295
KAPLAN	Shlomo Khaim	Male			Lea		295
KAPLAN	Yitzkhak	Male					295
KAPLINSKI	Mania	Female			Tzivi		296
KAPLINSKI	Tzivi	Male			Mania		296
KAPUSTA	Rakhel	Female					295
KAROLIN	Nakhum	Female	Yaakov	Sheina			295
KAROLIN	Pesil	Female	Yaakov	Sheina			295
KAROLIN	Sheina	Female			Yaakov		295
KAROLIN	Shlomo	Male	Yaakov	Sheina			295
KAROLIN	Stisha	Female	Yaakov	Sheina			295
KAROLIN	Yaakov	Male			Sheina		295
KARPEL	Moshe	Male			Rakhel		296
KARPEL	Rakhel	Female			Moshe		296
KARPEL	Velvel	Male			Zletka		296
KARPEL	Zlatka	Female			Velvel		296
KATZ	Avraham	Male	Beril	Vikhne			289
KATZ	Bebel	Female					289
KATZ	Beila	Female					289
KATZ	Beril	Male			Vichna		289
KATZ	Khaia	Female			Khaim David		289
KATZ	Khaim David	Male			Khaia		289
KATZ	Khana	Female					289
KATZ	Moshe	Male	Beril	Vikhne			289
KATZ	Nekha	Female					289
KATZ	Reizil	Female	Beril	Vikhne			289

KATZ		Male			Nekha		289
KATZ	Vikhne	Female			Beril		289
KATZ	Zysl	Male					289
KATZMAN	Ahuva	Female	Barukh Yosef	Tzirel			296
KATZMAN	Avraham	Male			Feigil		296
KATZMAN	Avraham	Male	Bunia	Teibel			296
KATZMAN	Avraham Aharon	Male			Khana Bila		296
KATZMAN	Barukh	Male					296
KATZMAN	Barukh Yosef	Male			Tzirel		296
KATZMAN	Beila	Female	Bunia	Teibel			296
KATZMAN	Breindil	Female					296
KATZMAN	Bunia	Male			Teibel		296
KATZMAN	Darne	Female					296
KATZMAN	David	Male			Henia		296
KATZMAN	David	Male	Meir				296
KATZMAN	Ester	Female			Yisrael Mordekhai		296
KATZMAN	Feigil	Female			Avraham		296
KATZMAN	Gertel	Female	Barukh Yosef	Tzirel			296
KATZMAN	Henia	Female			David		296
KATZMAN	Henia	Female			Moshe		296
KATZMAN	Hersh Leib	Male					296
KATZMAN	Khaim	Male	Shlomo	Yentil			296
KATZMAN	Khaim	Male	Barukh Yosef	Tzirel			296
KATZMAN	Khana Bila	Female			Avraham Aharon		296
KATZMAN	Leibel	Male			Peshe		296
KATZMAN	Mindil	Female					296
KATZMAN	Mindl	Female	Bunia	Teibel			296
KATZMAN	Mordekhai	Male					296
KATZMAN	Moshe	Male			Henia		296
KATZMAN	Noakh	Male					296

KATZMAN	Peshe	Female			Leibel		296
KATZMAN	Rivka	Female	Barukh Yosef	Tzirel			296
KATZMAN	Sheina	Female	Barukh Yosef	Tzirel			296
KATZMAN	Sheindil	Female					296
KATZMAN	Shlomo	Male			Yentil		296
KATZMAN	Shlomo	Male			Yentil		296
KATZMAN	Teibel	Female			Bunia		296
KATZMAN	Tzirel	Female			Barukh Yosef		296
KATZMAN		Male			Hersh Leib		296
KATZMAN	Velvel	Male					296
KATZMAN	Yehoshua	Male	Bunia	Teibel			296
KATZMAN	Yehuda	Male					296
KATZMAN	Yentil	Female			Shlomo		296
KATZMAN	Yentil	Female			Shlomo		296
KATZMAN	Yentil	Female	Bunia	Teibel			296
KATZMAN	Yisrael Mordekhai	Male			Ester		296
KATZMAN	Yitzkhak	Male					296
KATZMAN	Yudel	Male	Meir				296
KERTZMAN	Avraham	Male			Tzifka		295
KERTZMAN	Eliahu	Male					295
KERTZMAN	Henia	Female					295
KERTZMAN	Lea Sara	Female					295
KERTZMAN	Pinkhas	Male					295
KERTZMAN	Reuven	Male					295
KERTZMAN	Tzipka	Female			Avraham		295
KHASHIN	Asher	Male					288
KHASHIN	Herschil	Male					288
KHASHIN	Leizer	Male					288
KHASHIN	Motel	Male			Rakhel		288
KHASHIN	Rakhel	Female			Motel		288
KHASHIN		Male			Asher		288

KHASHIN		Male			Herschil		288
KHASHIN		Male			Yaakov		288
KHASHIN		Male			Leizer		288
KHASHIN	Yaakov	Male					288
KIRZHNER	Doba	Female	Yisakhar	Shushka			295
KIRZHNER	Leibel	Male	Yisakhar	Shushka			295
KIRZHNER	Shoshka	Female			Yisakhar		295
KIRZHNER	Yisakhar	Male			Shoshka		295
KITAI	Leibel	Male					296
KITAI		Male			Leibel		296
KITAIN	Khaia	Female					296
KLEINMAN	Khaike	Female			Yosef		295
KLEINMAN	Yosef	Male			Khaika		295
KNUBOVITZ	Bila	Female			Simkha		296
KNUBOVITZ	Simkha	Male			Bila		296
KOBRINCHUK	Bila	Female			Yitzkhak		296
KOBRINCHUK	Yitzkhak	Male			Bila		296
KOFMAN	Zlatka	Female					295
KOHEN	Aharon	Male			Golda		289
KOHEN	Avraham Yitzkhak	Male			Rakhel		289
KOHEN	Golda	Female			Aharon		289
KOHEN	Rakhel	Female			Avraham Yitzkhak		289
KOHEN	Ronia	Female			Yitzkhak		289
KOHEN	Yitzkhak	Male			Ronia		289
KOLODNI	Avraham	Male					296
KOLODNI	Avraham Yitzkhak	Male		Khava			296
KOLODNI	Beril	Male			Feigil		296
KOLODNI	Beril	Male	Yisrael	Liba			296
KOLODNI	Bilka	Female			Reuven		296
KOLODNI	Dora	Female	Yisrael	Liba			296
KOLODNI	Feigil	Female			Beril		296
KOLODNI	Gershon	Male					296

KOLODNI	Itel	Female			Litman		296
KOLODNI	Khaia Riva	Female			Leizer		296
KOLODNI	Khaim	Male			Malka		296
KOLODNI	Khava	Female					296
KOLODNI	Lea	Female					296
KOLODNI	Leika	Female					296
KOLODNI	Leizer	Male			Khaia Riva		296
KOLODNI	Liba	Female			Yisrael		296
KOLODNI	Litman	Male	Moshe		Itel		296
KOLODNI	Litman	Male	Yosef				296
KOLODNI	Malka	Female			Khaim		296
KOLODNI	Malka	Female	Reuven	Bilka			296
KOLODNI	Meir	Male					296
KOLODNI	Miriam	Female	Reuven	Bilka			296
KOLODNI	Moshe	Male	Reuven	Bilka			296
KOLODNI	Moshe	Male		Khava			296
KOLODNI	Nekhamka	Female					296
KOLODNI	Nitka	Female					296
KOLODNI	Rakhel	Female		Dora			296
KOLODNI	Reuven	Male			Bilka		296
KOLODNI	Rivka	Female	Reuven	Bilka			296
KOLODNI	Rodil	Female					296
KOLODNI	Sonia	Female			Yaakov		296
KOLODNI	Tzipora	Female		Khava			296
KOLODNI	Yaakov	Male			Sonia		296
KOLODNI	Yaakov	Male	Litman	Itel			296
KOLODNI	Yaakov Ezra	Male					296
KOLODNI	Yisrael	Male			Liba		296
KOLODNI	Yisrael	Male	Litman	Itel			296
KOLODNI	Yosef	Male	Reuven	Beilka			296
KOLODNI	Yosef	Male					296
KOLOTITZKI	Sara	Female			Akiva		296
KOLOTITZKI	Akiva	Male			Sara		296

KOLOTITZKI	Barukh Hirsh	Male					296
KOLOTITZKI	Bluma	Female					296
KOLOTITZKI	Disel	Female			Moshe		295
KOLOTITZKI	Dvora	Female			Meir		295
KOLOTITZKI	Eliahu	Male					296
KOLOTITZKI	Ester	Female	Moshe	Disel			295
KOLOTITZKI	Fradil	Female					296
KOLOTITZKI	Khaim	Male			Rivel		295
KOLOTITZKI	Khava Gitel	Female	Moshe	Disel			295
KOLOTITZKI	Khinka	Female					296
KOLOTITZKI	Lea	Female					296
KOLOTITZKI	Meir	Male			Dvora		295
KOLOTITZKI	Moshe	Male			Disel		295
KOLOTITZKI	Nekha	Female					296
KOLOTITZKI	Rivel	Female			Khaim		295
KOLOTITZKI	Sara	Female	Moshe	Disel			295
KOLOTITZKI		Male			Barukh Hirsh		296
KOLTUN	Beila	Female					296
KONDA	Avraham	Male					295
KONDA	Grunia	Female			Yitzkhak		295
KONDA	Yitzkhak	Male			Grunia		295
KORMAN	Avraham Beril	Male			Rakhel		295
KORMAN	Khaia	Female					295
KORMAN	Mendil	Male		Khaia			295
KORMAN	Metil	Male					295
KORMAN	Noakh	Male					295
KORMAN	Rakhel	Female			Avraham Beril		295
KORMAN	Sara	Female			Yaakov		295
KORMAN	Shoshka	Female					295
KORMAN	Simkha	Male					295
KORMAN	Yaakov	Male			Sara		295

KOSOVER	Khaia	Female				295
KRAVCHIK	Barukh	Male		Moshe Bila Masha		295
KRAVCHIK	Bila	Female				296
KRAVCHIK	Dvora	Female		Moshe Shlomo		295
KRAVCHIK	Khaim	Male				295
KRAVCHIK	Moshe	Male		Pril		295
KRAVCHIK	Moshe Bila Masha	Male		Barukh		295
KRAVCHIK	Moshe Shlomo	Male		Dvora		295
KRAVCHIK	Peril	Female		Moshe		295
KRAVCHIK	Sender	Male				295
KRAVCHIK	Simkha	Male				295
KRAVCHIK	Sonia	Female				296
KRAVCHIK		Male		Sender		295
KRAVCHIK	Yaakov	Male				295
KRAVCHIK	Yudel	Male				295
KREININ						296
KRIKUN	Aharon	Male		Khana		296
KRIKUN	Khana	Female		Aharon		296
KUMER						295
KUNIK	Shabtai	Male				296
KURTZ neé BRODER	Rivka	Female				295
KURTZNER	Khaim	Male		Nishka		295
KURTZNER	Nishka	Female		Khaim		295
KUSHNIR	Aizik	Male		Khaia		296
KUSHNIR	Golda Rakhel	Female				296
KUSHNIR	Khaia	Female		Aizik		296
KUSHNIR	Shmuel	Male				296
KUSHNIR	Teibel	Female		Zeev		296
KUSHNIR	Zeev	Male		Teibel		296
KUTNIK	Miriam	Female		Moshe		295

KUTNIK	Moshe	Male			Miriam	295
KVETNY	Aharon	Male			Golda	295
KVETNY	Golda	Female			Aharon	295
KVETNY	Liba	Female			Mordekhai	295
KVETNY	Mordekhai	Male			Liba	295
LADETZKI	Litman	Female			Getzil	289
LADETZKI	Getzil	Male			Litman	289
LADETZKI	Leibel	Male				290
LADETZKI	Moshe	Male			Shoshana	289
LADETZKI	Sara	Female				290
LADETZKI	Shoshana	Female			Moshe	289
LADETZKI	Ulia	Female				290
LAKHOVSKI	Abel	Male			Malka	290
LAKHOVSKI	Eliahu	Male				290
LAKHOVSKI	Hershel	Male				290
LAKHOVSKI	Malka	Female			Abel	290
LAKHOVSKI	Naomi	Female				290
LAKHOVSKI	Shalom	Male				289
LAKHOVSKI		Male			Shalom	289
LAKHOVSKI	Zlatka	Female				290
LAMDAN	Beril	Male	Nakhman	Sara		289
LAMDAN	Fruma	Female	Nakhman	Sara		289
LAMDAN	Guta	Female				289
LAMDAN	Itzel	Male				289
LAMDAN	Khaia	Female	Nakhman	Sara		289
LAMDAN	Khava	Female				289
LAMDAN	Lea	Female				289
LAMDAN	Nakhman	Male			Sara Lea	289
LAMDAN	Rakhel	Female	Nakhman	Sara		289
LAMDAN	Sara Lea	Female			Nakhman	289
LAMDAN	Sheindl	Female	Nakhman	Sara		289
LAMDAN		Male			Itzil	289
LAMDAN		Male			Zelik	289

LAMDAN	Zelik	Male	Nakhman	Sara		289
LAMDAN	Zelik	Male				289
LANSKI	Khaitzik	Male				290
LANSKI	Shmaria	Male				290
LANSKI		Male		Shmaria		290
LASOVSKI	Itka	Female		Khaim		289
LASOVSKI	Khaim	Male		Itka		289
LEIKHTMAN	Sheina	Female		Shimon		290
LEIKHTMAN	Shimon	Male		Sheina		290
LELCHITZKI	Ginsche	Female				289
LELCHITZKI	Khaia	Female		Yisrael Yosef		289
LELCHITZKI	Yisrael Yosef	Male		Khaia		289
LELCHITZKI	Zelde	Female				289
LENIN	Tzirel	Female		Shlomo		289
LENIN	Shlomo	Male		Tzirel		289
LEVIN	Moshe	Male		Peshka		290
LEVIN	Peshka	Female		Moshe		290
LEVIN	Rivka	Female				290
LEVIT	Avraham	Male				290
LIBERMAN	Avraham Moshe	Male		Hudes		290
LIBERMAN	Avraham Moshe	Male				289
LIBERMAN	Hudes	Female		Avraham Moshe		290
LIBERMAN	Itka	Female				290
LIBERMAN	Khava	Female	Avraham Moshe	Hudes		290
LIBERMAN	Sara	Female				289
LIBERMAN		Male		Avraham Moshe		289
LIFSHITZ	Aharon	Male		Etil		290
LIFSHITZ	Avraham	Male		Tzirel		289
LIFSHITZ	Avraham	Male	Yosef			289
LIFSHITZ	Bashka	Female		Yosef		289

LIFSHITZ	Beila	Female				289
LIFSHITZ	Beila Pesil	Female				289
LIFSHITZ	David Yosef	Male			Feigil	290
LIFSHITZ	Dvora	Female				290
LIFSHITZ	Eizel	Male			Hindel	289
LIFSHITZ	Etel	Female			Aharon	290
LIFSHITZ	Feigil	Female			David Yosef	290
LIFSHITZ	Fruma	Female			Yisrael Yosef	289
LIFSHITZ	Gershon	Male	Aharon	Etel		290
LIFSHITZ	Gershon	Male	Avraham	Tzirel		289
LIFSHITZ	Henia	Female				289
LIFSHITZ	Herschil	Male			Sonia	289
LIFSHITZ	Hindel	Female			Eizel	289
LIFSHITZ	Itzik	Male				290
LIFSHITZ	Khaia	Female				290
LIFSHITZ	Khaike	Female			Shmeril	289
LIFSHITZ	Khaike	Female				289
LIFSHITZ	Moshe Aharon	Male			Sara	289
LIFSHITZ	Moshe Feigel	Male				290
LIFSHITZ	Moshe Shlomo	Male				290
LIFSHITZ	Neta	Female				290
LIFSHITZ	Rishel	Female				290
LIFSHITZ	Sara	Female			Yitzkhak	290
LIFSHITZ	Sara	Female			Moshe Aharon	289
LIFSHITZ	Sara	Female	Aharon	Etel		290
LIFSHITZ	Seril	Female				290
LIFSHITZ	Shlomo	Male	Avraham	Tzirel		289
LIFSHITZ	Shmeril	Male			Khaika	289
LIFSHITZ	Shmuel	Male				290
LIFSHITZ	Shprintza	Female				290

LIFSHITZ	Shusha	Female					289
LIFSHITZ	Sonia	Female			Herschil		289
LIFSHITZ	Tzirel	Female			Avraham		289
LIFSHITZ		Male			Itzik		290
LIFSHITZ		Male			Yehuda		290
LIFSHITZ		Male			Moshe Feigel		290
LIFSHITZ		Male			Shmuel		290
LIFSHITZ	Yaakov	Male	Yosef	Bashke			289
LIFSHITZ	Yaakov	Male	Shmril	Khaika			289
LIFSHITZ	Yaakov	Male					290
LIFSHITZ	Yehuda	Male					290
LIFSHITZ	Yerakhmiel	Male					289
LIFSHITZ	Yisrael Yosef	Male			Fruma		289
LIFSHITZ	Yitzkhak	Male			Sara		290
LIFSHITZ	Yosef	Male			Bashke		289
LIFSHITZ	Yosef	Male	Avraham	Tzirel			289
LIFSHITZ	Yosef	Male					290
LIFSHITZ	Zeev	Male					290
LIKHTENSHTEIN	Tzipka	Female					290
LIKHTSHTEIN	Meir	Male			Zelda		290
LIKHTSHTEIN	Sara	Female	Meir	Zelda			290
LIKHTSHTEIN	Zelda	Female			Meir		290
LUBLINER	Barukh	Male		Teibel			289
LUBLINER	Brakha	Female		Teibel			289
LUBLINER	Teibel	Female					289
LURIE	Ester Reizl	Female			Herzl		289
LURIE	Herzl	Male			Ester Reizl		289
LUTZKI	Avraham Zeev	Male			Brakha		289
LUTZKI	Brakha	Female			Avraham Zeev		289
LUTZKI	Brakha	Female					289
LUTZKI	Henia	Female			Shmuel		289

LUTZKI	Shmuel	Male		Henia	289
LUTZKI		Male		Velvel	289
LUTZKI	Velvel	Male			289
MAGIDOVITZ	Avraham	Male		Miriam	291
MAGIDOVITZ	Miriam	Female		Avraham	291
MAGIDOVITZ	Rivka	Female		Yitzkhak	291
MAGIDOVITZ	Yitzkhak	Male		Rivka	291
MANISHUK	Golda	Female		Leibel	290
MANISHUK	Itzik	Male			290
MANISHUK	Leibel	Male		Golda	290
MANUSEVITZ	Avigdor	Male		Sheindl	291
MANUSEVITZ	Eliahu	Male			291
MANUSEVITZ	Khaim	Male			291
MANUSEVITZ	Sheindl	Female		Avigdor	291
MANUSEVITZ		Male		Eliahu	291
MANUSEVITZ		Male		Khaim	291
MANUSEVITZ		Male	Khaim		291
MARGOLIN	Aizik	Male			290
MARGOLIN	Asher	Male		Khaia	291
MARGOLIN	Khaia	Female		Asher	291
MARGOLIN	Khaim Leib	Male		Lea	290
MARGOLIN	Khashke	Female			291
MARGOLIN	Lea	Female		Khaim Leib	290
MARGOLIN	Moshe	Male			290
MARGOLIN	Pesil	Female			291
MARGOLIN	Rivka	Female			291
MARGOLIN	Sender	Male			291
MARGOLIN	Shoshana	Female			290
MARGOLIN		Male		Aizik	290
MATORIN	Betzalel	Male		Khaitza	291
MATORIN	Isser	Male		Sonia	291
MATORIN	Khaitze	Female		Betzalel	291
MATORIN	Moshe Yitzkhak	Male		Tzila	291

MATORIN	Rakhel	Female					291
MATORIN	Sonia	Female			Isser		291
MATORIN	Tzila	Female			Moshe Yitzkhak		291
MATORIN	Yisrael	Male					291
MEIDELOV	Liza	Female					291
MEIDELOV	Malka	Female					291
MEIDELOV	Pesil	Female					291
MEINKIN	Moshe	Male			Rivka		290
MEINKIN	Rivka	Female			Moshe		290
MEINKIN	Sara	Female	Moshe	Rivka			290
MEINKIN	Sheindl	Female	Moshe	Rivka			290
MEKLER	Braindel	Female					291
MEKLER	Efraim	Male					291
MEKLER	Elka	Female					291
MEKLER	Moshe	Male					291
MEKLER	Nakhum	Male					291
MEKLER		Male			Nakhum		291
MEKLER	Yaakov	Male					291
MEKLER	Yosef	Male					291
MENDELSBERN	Menus	Male					290
MESTER	Aharon	Male			Feigel		291
MESTER	Aizik	Male	Reuven	Sonia			290
MESTER	Anita	Female					290
MESTER	Feigel	Female			Aharon		291
MESTER	Khaitze	Female			Yaakov		291
MESTER	Pia	Female	Yaakov	Khaitza			291
MESTER	Reuven	Male			Sonia		290
MESTER	Sonia	Female			Reuven		290
MESTER	Tzvia	Female					290
MESTER	Yaakov	Male			Khaitza		291
MESTER	Yekhezkel	Male	Yaakov	Khaitza			291
MESTER	Yosef	Male	Reuven	Sonia			290
MIGDALOVITZ	Berl	Male			Itke		290

MIGDALOVITZ	Itke	Female			Berl		290
MILMAN	Asher	Male					290
MILMAN	Breindil	Female					291
MILMAN	Khaim	Male					291
MILMAN	Meir	Male			Tzirel		290
MILMAN	Motel	Male					291
MILMAN	Nekhama	Female					291
MILMAN	Pesil	Female			Shlomo		290
MILMAN	Roshke Bavel	Female					291
MILMAN	Sara	Female					290
MILMAN	Shlomo	Male			Pesil		290
MILMAN	Tzirel	Female			Meir		290
MILMAN		Male			Yosef		290
MILMAN		Male			Motel		291
MILMAN	Yosef	Male					290
MILRAN							291
MISHALOV	Batia	Female					290
MISHALOV	Miriam	Female	Simkha	Tzipa			291
MISHALOV	Noakh	Male	Simkha	Tzipa			291
MISHALOV	Simkha	Male			Tzipa		291
MISHALOV	Tzipa	Female			Simkha		291
MISHALOV	Yitzkhak	Male					290
MOGILEVSKI	Yosef	Male					291
MOGILOV	Ester	Female					291
MOGILOV	Moshe	Male		Ester			291
MOGILOV	Yosef	Male		Ester			291
MOLOCHNIK	Faivel	Male					291
MOLOCHNIK	Hershel	Male					291
MOLOCHNIK	Pesakh	Male					291
MOLOCHNIK	Shmuel	Male					291
MOLOCHNIK		Male			Hershel		291
MORAVCHIK	Aharon	Male			Fruma		290
MORAVCHIK	Aharon	Male		Lea			290

MORAVCHIK	Bashka	Female				290
MORAVCHIK	Beila	Female			Shmuel	290
MORAVCHIK	Beila	Female		Riva		290
MORAVCHIK	Beila	Female				290
MORAVCHIK	Beril	Male			Ester	290
MORAVCHIK	Beril	Male			Freidil	291
MORAVCHIK	Betzalel	Male			Ester	290
MORAVCHIK	Dov	Male			Nekhama	290
MORAVCHIK	Dvora	Female			Zeev	290
MORAVCHIK	Eidel	Male				291
MORAVCHIK	Eliezer	Male	Zeev	Dvora		290
MORAVCHIK	Ester	Female			Beril	290
MORAVCHIK	Ester	Female				290
MORAVCHIK	Ester	Female				291
MORAVCHIK	Ester	Female			Betzalel	290
MORAVCHIK	Etel	Female			Leizer	290
MORAVCHIK	Faivel	Male	Leibush	Reizl		291
MORAVCHIK	Feigel	Female			Mendel	290
MORAVCHIK	Fradil	Female				290
MORAVCHIK	Freidel	Female			Beril	291
MORAVCHIK	Fruma	Female			Aharon	290
MORAVCHIK	Golda	Female			Yosef	290
MORAVCHIK	Golda	Female				290
MORAVCHIK	Itka	Female			Meir	291
MORAVCHIK	Khaia	Female			Meir	291
MORAVCHIK	Khaim	Male		Lea		290
MORAVCHIK	Khaim	Male				290
MORAVCHIK	Khava	Female			Yisrael	290
MORAVCHIK	Kopil	Male				291
MORAVCHIK	Lea	Female				290
MORAVCHIK	Lea	Female				290
MORAVCHIK	Leibush	Male			Reizl	291
MORAVCHIK	Leizer	Male			Etil	290

MORAVCHIK	Malka	Female				291
MORAVCHIK	Mashka	Female			Shlomo	290
MORAVCHIK	Meir	Male			Itka	291
MORAVCHIK	Meir	Male			Khaia	291
MORAVCHIK	Meir	Male				290
MORAVCHIK	Mendel	Male			Feigel	290
MORAVCHIK	Mikhael	Male	Aharon	Fruma		290
MORAVCHIK	Motel	Male				291
MORAVCHIK	Nakhman	Male	Leibush	Reizl		291
MORAVCHIK	Nekhama	Female			Dov	290
MORAVCHIK	Nekhama	Female	Leibush	Reizl		291
MORAVCHIK	Nisan	Male	Yisrael	Khava		290
MORAVCHIK	Perel	Female			Yitzkhak	290
MORAVCHIK	Peshke	Female				290
MORAVCHIK	Pia	Female				290
MORAVCHIK	Reizl	Female			Leibush	291
MORAVCHIK	Riva	Female				290
MORAVCHIK	Rivka	Female	Yosef	Golda		290
MORAVCHIK	Sara	Female		Riva		290
MORAVCHIK	Shaia	Male				291
MORAVCHIK	Shakhna	Male	Yehuda	Khaia		290
MORAVCHIK	Shlomo	Male			Mashka	290
MORAVCHIK	Shlomo	Male				291
MORAVCHIK	Shmuel	Male			Beila	290
MORAVCHIK		Male			Motel	291
MORAVCHIK	Yehuda	Male			Lea	290
MORAVCHIK	Yisrael	Male			Khava	290
MORAVCHIK	Yitzkhak	Male			Perel	290
MORAVCHIK	Yitzkhak	Male	Shmuel	Beila		290
MORAVCHIK	Yitzkhak	Male		Lea		290
MORAVCHIK	Yitzkhak Kopel	Male		Riva		290
MORAVCHIK	Yosef	Male			Golda	290
MORAVCHIK	Yosef	Male				291

MORAVCHIK	Zeev	Male			Dvora		290
MORAVCHIK	#NAME?	Female			Yehuda		290
MUNUSVITZ	Khana	Female					291
MUTZULSKI	Alte	Female			Shmuel		290
MUTZULSKI	Berl	Male					290
MUTZULSKI	Hershel	Male			Miriam		291
MUTZULSKI	Miriam	Female			Hershel		291
MUTZULSKI	Shmuel	Male			Alte		290
MUTZULSKI	Yosef	Male					290
NAKHMANOVITZ	Lea	Female	David	Zelda			291
NAKHMANOVITZ	David	Male			Zelda		291
NAKHMANOVITZ	David	Male			Khana		291
NAKHMANOVITZ	Doba	Female	Shmuel	Khava			291
NAKHMANOVITZ	Eidel	Male					291
NAKHMANOVITZ	Eshke	Female					291
NAKHMANOVITZ	Feiga	Female			Lipman		291
NAKHMANOVITZ	Freidel	Female	David	Zelda			291
NAKHMANOVITZ	Hirschel	Male	Shmuel	Khava			291
NAKHMANOVITZ	Itke	Female					291
NAKHMANOVITZ	Khaia	Female			Moshe		291
NAKHMANOVITZ	Khaia	Female					291
NAKHMANOVITZ	Khana	Female			David		291
NAKHMANOVITZ	Khana	Female					291
NAKHMANOVITZ	Khava	Female			Shmuel		291
NAKHMANOVITZ	Lipman	Male			Feiga		291
NAKHMANOVITZ	Meir	Male	Shmuel	Khava			291
NAKHMANOVITZ	Moshe	Male			Khaia		291
NAKHMANOVITZ	Moshe	Male	David	Zelda			291
NAKHMANOVITZ	Moshe	Male	Shmuel	Khava			291
NAKHMANOVITZ	Naomi	Female	David	Zelda			291
NAKHMANOVITZ	Nekhama	Female	Moshe	Khaia			291
NAKHMANOVITZ	Pinkhas	Male	David	Zelda			291
NAKHMANOVITZ	Rakhel	Female	David	Zelda			291

Surname	Given	Sex	Father	Mother	Spouse	Page
NAKHMANOVITZ	Rivel	Male	Moshe	Khaia		291
NAKHMANOVITZ	Rivka	Female			Yudl	291
NAKHMANOVITZ	Shmuel	Male			Khava	291
NAKHMANOVITZ		Male			Yerakhmiel	291
NAKHMANOVITZ	Yerakhmiel	Male				291
NAKHMANOVITZ	Yudel	Male			Rivka	291
NAKHMANOVITZ	Yudel	Male	David	Zelda		291
NAKHMANOVITZ	Zelda	Female			David	291
NAKHMANOVITZ	Zelda	Female	Moshe	Khaia		291
NEIMAN	Avraham	Male			Dvora	291
NEIMAN	Avraham Yosef	Male			Rivka	291
NEIMAN	Dvora	Female			Avraham	291
NEIMAN	Henia	Female	Avraham Yosef	Rivka		291
NEIMAN	Khaia	Female		Khaia		292
NEIMAN	Khaia	Female				292
NEIMAN	Leibel	Male				291
NEIMAN	Miriam	Female	Avraham Yosef	Rivka		291
NEIMAN	Moshe	Male				291
NEIMAN	Rasel	Female				292
NEIMAN	Rivka	Female			Avraham Yosef	291
NEIMAN	Shmariahu	Male				291
NEIMAN	Tzirel	Female		Khaia		292
NEIMAN		Male			Leibel	291
NEIMAN		Male			Moshe	291
NEIMAN	Zelig	Male		Khaia		292
NOVAK	Meril	Female				292
NOVAK	Mikhael	Male				291
NOVAK	Nekhama	Female			Shlomo	291
NOVAK	Pinkhas	Male				291
NOVAK	Shlomo	Male			Nekhama	291
NOVAK		Male			Mikhael	291

NOVAK		Male			Pinkhas		291
OLPINER	Aharon	Male					284
OLPINER	Barukh	Male	Nekha				284
OLPINER	Beril	Male			Tzifka		284
OLPINER	Ester	Female			Yaakov		284
OLPINER	Khana	Female	Nekha				284
OLPINER	Mikhael	Male					284
OLPINER	Moshe Aharon	Male					284
OLPINER	Nekha	Female					284
OLPINER	Tzipka	Female			Beril		284
OLPINER		Male			Aharon		284
OLPINER		Male			Moshe Aharon		284
OLPINER	Yaakov	Male			Ester		284
OLPINER	Zelik	Male					284
OLSHANSKI	Asher	Male			Beila		284
OLSHANSKI	Avraham	Male			Lea		284
OLSHANSKI	Beila	Female			Asher		284
OLSHANSKI	Hilel	Male			Sara		284
OLSHANSKI	Khashke	Female			Nisel		284
OLSHANSKI	Lea	Female			Avraham		284
OLSHANSKI	Mordekhai	Male	Hilel	Sara			284
OLSHANSKI	Nisel	Male			Kheshka		284
OLSHANSKI	Rivka	Female					284
OLSHANSKI	Sara	Female			Hilel		284
OLSHANSKI	Sara Lea	Female			Yehuda		284
OLSHANSKI	Sara Malka	Female			Yosef		284
OLSHANSKI		Male			Yaakov		284
OLSHANSKI	Yaakov	Male	Nisel	Kheshka			284
OLSHANSKI	Yaakov	Male					284
OLSHANSKI	Yehuda	Male			Sara Lea		284
OLSHANSKI	Yisrael	Male					284
OLSHANSKI	Yona	Male					284

OLSHANSKI	Yosef	Male			Sara Malka		284
PAPISH							292
PAPISH	Aharon	Male	Litman	Nekhama			292
PAPISH	Beril	Male					292
PAPISH	Dashka	Female	Yitzkhak	Khana			292
PAPISH	Eliezer	Male	Litman	Nekhama			292
PAPISH	Ester	Female	Khaim Barukh	Reizil			292
PAPISH	Ester	Female	Khaim Barukh	Reizil			294
PAPISH	Feigel	Female	Yitzkhak	Khana			292
PAPISH	Fradil	Female	Khaim Barukh	Reizil			294
PAPISH	Freidel	Female	Khaim Barukh	Reizil			292
PAPISH	Khaim Barukh	Male			Reizil		294
PAPISH	Khana	Female			Yitzkhak		292
PAPISH	Khavale	Female			Mordekhai		292
PAPISH	Lea	Female	Litman	Nekhama			292
PAPISH	Lipa	Male	Tzvi	Mina			292
PAPISH	Litman	Male			Nekhama		292
PAPISH	Mina	Female			Tzvi		292
PAPISH	Mordekhai	Male	Khaim Barukh	Reizil			294
PAPISH	Moshe	Male	Litman	Nekhama			292
PAPISH	Motel	Male	Tzvi	Mina			292
PAPISH	Motel	Male	Khaim Barukh	Reizil			292
PAPISH	Nekhama	Female			Litman		292
PAPISH	Reizil	Female			Khaim Barukh		294
PAPISH	Reizl	Female			Khaim Barukh		292
PAPISH	Tzvi	Male			Mina		292
PAPISH	Yitzkhak	Male			Khana		292
PAPISH	Zelig	Male	Yitzkhak	Khana			292
PERBEROTZKI	Arie	Male			Golda		293

PERBEROTZKI	Arie	Male			Golda		292
PERBEROTZKI	Golda	Female			Arie		293
PERBEROTZKI	Golda	Female			Arie		292
PERBEROTZKI	Rakhel	Female			Shalom		293
PERBEROTZKI	Shalom	Male			Rakhel		293
PERTZOV	Aharon	Male					294
PERTZOV	Efraim	Male					293
PERTZOV	Faivel	Male					294
PERTZOV	Getzil	Male					293
PERTZOV	Golda	Female			Yaakov		293
PERTZOV	Khaim Itzik	Male			Teibel		294
PERTZOV	Nekhama Sara	Female					293
PERTZOV	Noakh	Male					293
PERTZOV	Rivka	Female					293
PERTZOV	Rivka	Female					294
PERTZOV	Teibel	Female			Khaim Itzik		294
PERTZOV	Yaakov	Male			Golda		293
PILCHIK	Leibel	Male					294
PILCHIK	Pesakh	Male					293
PILCHIK	Pesakh	Male					294
PINKEVITZ	Avraham	Male			Miriam		294
PINKEVITZ	Khava	Female	Avraham	Miriam			294
PINKEVITZ	Miriam	Female			Avraham		294
PINKEVITZ	Yosef	Male	Avraham	Miriam			294
PINSKER	Aharon	Male			Kheshka		294
PINSKER	Fruma	Female			Yoel		294
PINSKER	Khashke	Female			Aharon		294
PINSKER	Khashke	Female			Shmaria		294
PINSKER	Nekhama	Female			Yosef Efraim		294
PINSKER	Shmaria	Male			Kheshka		294
PINSKER	Yaakov	Male	Yoel	Fruma			294
PINSKER	Yoel	Male			Fruma		294

PINSKER	Yosef Efraim	Male		Nekhama	294
PISHCHANSKI	Reizil	Female		Zalman	293
PISHCHANSKI	Zalman	Male		Reizil	293
PITER	Shabtai	Male			292
PITNER	Beniamin	Male		Ester	294
PITNER	David	Male		Shoshka	294
PITNER	Dvora	Female		Shmuel	294
PITNER	Ester	Female		Beniamin	294
PITNER	Golda	Female		Leibel	294
PITNER	Khaim Aharon	Male			294
PITNER	Khana	Female			294
PITNER	Lea	Female			294
PITNER	Leibel	Male		Golda	294
PITNER	Malka Sara	Female			294
PITNER	Markel	Male			293
PITNER	Meril	Female			294
PITNER	Moshe	Male			293
PITNER	Sara	Female			293
PITNER	Shmuel	Male		Dvora	294
PITNER	Shoshka	Female		David	294
PITNER		Male		Yosef	293
PITNER	Yosef	Male			293
PLASKOWITZ	Dina	Female		Reuven	292
PLASKOWITZ	Eliezer	Male			292
PLASKOWITZ	Mendil	Male			294
PLASKOWITZ	Pesil	Female			294
PLASKOWITZ	Pesil	Female			292
PLASKOWITZ	Reuven	Male		Dina	292
PLASKOWITZ	Shlomo	Male			292
PLASKOWITZ	Shlomo Yitzkhak	Male			294
PLASKOWITZ		Male		Eliezer	294

PLASKOWITZ		Male			Yitzkhak		294
PLASKOWITZ	Yitzkhak	Male					294
PLOTNITZKI	Aharon	Male			Sara		293
PLOTNITZKI	Avraham	Male					293
PLOTNITZKI	Khaia	Female			Pinkhas		293
PLOTNITZKI	Khaim	Male	Aharon	Sara			293
PLOTNITZKI	Meir	Male	Aharon	Sara			293
PLOTNITZKI	Nekhama	Female	Aharon	Sara			293
PLOTNITZKI	Pinkhas	Male			Khaia		293
PLOTNITZKI	Sara	Female			Aharon		293
PLOTNITZKI		Male			Avraham		293
PLOTNITZKI	Yisrael	Male	Aharon	Sara			293
POLSKI	Khaia	Female			Zalman		293
POLSKI	Sara	Female			Zalman		294
POLSKI	Zalman	Male			Khaia		293
POLSKI	Zalman	Male			Sara		294
PORTNOI	Eidel	Female					293
PORTNOI	Herschil	Male					294
PORTNOI		Male			Herschil		294
PORTNOI	Yosef	Male					292
POSENITZKI	Avraham	Male			Menukhka		293
POSENITZKI	Menukhka	Female			Avraham		293
POTRUKH	Golda	Female			Yaakov		293
POTRUKH	Yaakov	Male			Golda		293
PROFES	Avraham	Male			Freidil		294
PROFES	Avraham	Male			Freidil		293
PROFES	Freidel	Female			Avraham		293
PROFES	Freidil	Female			Avraham		294
RABINSKI	Avraham	Male				Sheindl	297
RABINSKI	Sheindl	Female				Avraham	297
RAPOPORT	Roshka	Female				Yaakov	297
RAPOPORT	Yaakov	Male				Roshka	297
RATNER	Avraham	Male					297

RATNER	Khana	Female				297
RATNER	Khashke	Female			Yaakov	297
RATNER	Yaakov	Male			Kheshka	297
REIKHMAN	Khashke	Female			Sania	297
REIKHMAN	Leizer	Male				297
REIKHMAN	Senia	Male			Kheske	297
REIKHMAN	Shlomo	Male				297
REIKHMAN	Yehuda	Male				297
REITELMAN	Shlomo Pinkhas	Male			Tzvia	297
REITELMAN	Tzvia	Female			Shlomo Pinkhas	297
REIZIN	Miriam	Female			Shlomo	297
REIZIN	Shlomo	Male			Miriam	297
REZNIK	Aizik	Male			Khaia	297
REZNIK	Akiva	Male				297
REZNIK	Asher	Male			Khana	297
REZNIK	Batsheva	Female			David	297
REZNIK	Batsheva	Female			Mordekhai	297
REZNIK	Beril	Male				297
REZNIK	Bila	Female			Moshe	297
REZNIK	David	Male			Batsheva	297
REZNIK	David	Male			Lea	297
REZNIK	Dov	Male				297
REZNIK	Dunia	Female				297
REZNIK	Eliahu Meir	Male				297
REZNIK	Etil	Female				297
REZNIK	Feigil	Female	Moshe	Bila		297
REZNIK	Freidil	Female	Moshe	Bila		297
REZNIK	Hilel	Male				297
REZNIK	Itka	Female				297
REZNIK	Khaia	Female			Aizik	297
REZNIK	Khaike	Female			Shmariahu	297
REZNIK	Khana	Female			Asher	297

REZNIK	Lea	Female			David	297
REZNIK	Leibel	Male				297
REZNIK	Leibke	Male				297
REZNIK	Malka	Female			Yisrael	297
REZNIK	Malka	Female				297
REZNIK	Meir	Male			Peshe	297
REZNIK	Mendel	Male			Peshka	297
REZNIK	Mordekhai	Male			Batsheva	297
REZNIK	Moshe	Male			Bila	297
REZNIK	Moshe	Male			Rakhel	297
REZNIK	Moshe	Male				297
REZNIK	Peshe	Female			Meir	297
REZNIK	Peshka	Female			Mendel	297
REZNIK	Rakhel	Female			Moshe	297
REZNIK	Rivka	Female	Moshe	Bila		297
REZNIK	Sara	Female			Yisrael	297
REZNIK	Sara	Female				297
REZNIK	Shmariahu	Male			Khaika	297
REZNIK	Simkha	Male				297
REZNIK	Teibel	Female	Moshe	Bila		297
REZNIK		Male			Zelig	297
REZNIK	Yaakov	Male	Moshe	Bila		297
REZNIK	Yentil	Female				297
REZNIK	Yerakhmiel	Male				297
REZNIK	Yisrael	Male			Malka	297
REZNIK	Yisrael	Male			Sara	297
REZNIK	Yisrael	Male				297
REZNIK	Zelig	Male				297
RIMER	Anushka	Female			Shimon	296
RIMER	Bashka	Female			Yerakhmiel	297
RIMER	David	Male			Sonia	296
RIMER	Dov	Male			Sonia	296
RIMER	Naomi	Female				296

RIMER	Shimon	Male			Anushke	296
RIMER	Sonia	Female			Dov	296
RIMER	Sonia	Female			David	296
RIMER	Yerakhmiel	Male			Bashke	297
RIMER	Yosef	Male				297
RONKIN	Eliezer	Male			Reizil	297
RONKIN	Khaia	Female			Yehoshua	297
RONKIN	Moshe	Male			Tzvia	297
RONKIN	Reizil	Female			Eliezer	297
RONKIN	Reuven	Male				297
RONKIN	Tzvia	Female			Moshe	297
RONKIN	Yehoshua	Male			Khaia	297
ROTKIN	Asher	Male			Gitel	297
ROTKIN	Gitel	Female			Asher	297
ROTKIN	Itka	Female			Yudl	297
ROTKIN	Khaim Yaakov	Male				297
ROTKIN	Yehuda	Male				297
ROTKIN	Yudel	Male			Itka	297
ROZENBLUM	Fruma	Female				297
ROZENBLUM	Khaia	Female				297
ROZENBLUM	Yosef	Male				297
ROZENTZVEIG	Etil	Female			Yisrael	297
ROZENTZVEIG	Tzirel	Female				297
ROZENTZVEIG	Yisrael	Male			Etil	297
ROZMAN	David	Male				297
ROZMAN	David Moshe	Male			Tzila	297
ROZMAN	Lea	Female				297
ROZMAN	Reizil	Female				297
ROZMAN	Tzila	Female			David Moshe	297
SANDOMIRSKI	Avraham	Male				292
SANDOMIRSKI		Male			Avraham	292
SHAPOSHNIK	Freidil	Female				297

SHATZKI	Beniamin	Male			298
SHATZKI		Male		Yehuda	298
SHATZKI	Yehuda	Male			298
SHEFER	Velvel	Male			298
SHEINBERG	Alte	Female			297
SHEINBERG	Mikhael	Male			297
SHEINBERG	Nishka	Female			297
SHEINDELMAN	Bila	Female		Paltiel	298
SHEINDELMAN	Paltiel	Male		Bila	298
SHEKHTER	Bashke	Female		Pesakh	298
SHEKHTER	David	Male		Yenta Khana	298
SHEKHTER	Dina	Female		Volf	298
SHEKHTER	Dvushka	Female		Yudl	298
SHEKHTER	Golda	Female		Shmuel	298
SHEKHTER	Hilel	Male			298
SHEKHTER	Khana	Female	Volf		298
SHEKHTER	Moshe	Male			298
SHEKHTER	Pesakh	Male		Bashke	298
SHEKHTER	Shmuel	Male		Golda	298
SHEKHTER	Volf	Male		Dina	298
SHEKHTER	Yaakov	Male			298
SHEKHTER	Yenta Khana	Female		David	298
SHEKHTER	Yudel	Male		Dvushka	298
SHELUBSKI	Rashke	Female			298
SHERMAN	Faivel	Male			298
SHERMAN	Meir	Male			298
SHERMAN	Yisrael	Male			298
SHIFMAN	Arie	Male		Hinda	298
SHIFMAN	Benia	Male			298
SHIFMAN	Butza	Female			298
SHIFMAN	Elka	Female			298
SHIFMAN	Etil	Female		Shmuel	298

SHIFMAN	Feigil	Female				298
SHIFMAN	Hinda	Female			Arie	298
SHIFMAN	Khaia	Female				298
SHIFMAN	Malka	Female				298
SHIFMAN	Moshe	Male				298
SHIFMAN	Shmuel	Male			Etil	298
SHIFMAN	Zalman	Male				298
SHKLAVER	Alte	Female			Reuven	298
SHKLAVER	Moshe	Male			Yentil	298
SHKLAVER	Reuven	Male			Alte	298
SHKLAVER	Tzvi	Male				298
SHKLAVER	Yentil	Female			Moshe	298
SHKLAVER	Yisrael Mordekhai	Male				298
SHMUTZ	Beril	Male			Sara	298
SHMUTZ	Feigil	Female			Zeev	298
SHMUTZ	Moshe	Male				298
SHMUTZ	Sara	Female			Beril	298
SHMUTZ	Tulia	Female				298
SHMUTZ		Male			Yehoshua	298
SHMUTZ		Male			Yosef	298
SHMUTZ		Male			Moshe	298
SHMUTZ	Yehoshua	Male				298
SHMUTZ	Yitzkhak	Male				298
SHMUTZ	Yosef	Male				298
SHMUTZ	Zeev	Male			Feigil	298
SHNEIDMAN	Sara	Female			Meir	297
SHNEIDMAN	David	Male			Pia	298
SHNEIDMAN	Gitel	Female	Motel	Henia		297
SHNEIDMAN	Henia	Female			Motel	297
SHNEIDMAN	Meir	Male			Sara	297
SHNEIDMAN	Menakhem	Male	Motel	Henia		297
SHNEIDMAN	Motel	Male			Henia	297
SHNEIDMAN	Pia	Female			David	298

SHNEIDMAN	Rakheli	Female	Motel	Henia			297
SHNEIDMAN	Yaakov	Male	Motel	Henia			297
SHNUR	Ester	Female					297
SHOLOMOVITZ	Lea	Female					297
SHOSTAKOVSKI	Aharon	Male			Peshka		298
SHOSTAKOVSKI	Aizik	Male		Ester			298
SHOSTAKOVSKI	Aizik	Male					298
SHOSTAKOVSKI	Ester	Female					298
SHOSTAKOVSKI	Lea	Female	Leibel	Malka			298
SHOSTAKOVSKI	Leibel	Male			Malka		298
SHOSTAKOVSKI	Malka	Female			Leibel		298
SHOSTAKOVSKI	Nisan	Male	Leibel	Malka			298
SHOSTAKOVSKI	Peshka	Female			Aharon		298
SHREIBMAN	Beril	Male					297
SHREIBMAN	Khana	Female					297
SHREIBMAN	Leibel	Male			Michla		297
SHREIBMAN	Mikhla	Female			Leibel		297
SHREIBMAN		Male			Beril		297
SHULMAN	Mikhael	Male			Risha		297
SHULMAN	Mordekhai	Male					297
SHULMAN	Risha	Female			Mikhael		297
SHULMAN	Yaakov	Male			Zahava		297
SHULMAN	Zahava	Female			Yaakov		297
SHURMUK	Aharon Meir	Male					298
SHURMUK	Faivel	Male			Khana		298
SHURMUK	Feigil	Female			Yosef		298
SHURMUK	Hidil	Female					298
SHURMUK	Khaia	Female					298
SHURMUK	Khana	Female			Faivel		298
SHURMUK	Khana	Female					298
SHURMUK	Rakhel	Female					298
SHURMUK	Yisrael	Male					298
SHURMUK	Yosef	Male			Feigil		298

SHUSTER	Boaz	Male		Khaia	298
SHUSTER	Eizel	Male			298
SHUSTER	Eliahu	Male			298
SHUSTER	Eliahu Yona	Male			298
SHUSTER	Ester	Female			298
SHUSTER	Faivel	Male			298
SHUSTER	Feigil	Female		Yudl	298
SHUSTER	Grunia	Female		Leibel	298
SHUSTER	Herschil	Male		Sara	298
SHUSTER	Khaia	Female		Boaz	298
SHUSTER	Khana	Female			298
SHUSTER	Leibel	Male		Grunia	298
SHUSTER	Mendil	Male			298
SHUSTER	Moshe	Male			298
SHUSTER	Moshe Ester Masha	Male			298
SHUSTER	Sara	Female		Herschil	298
SHUSTER		Male		Eliahu Yona	298
SHUSTER		Male		Mendil	298
SHUSTER		Male	Ester		298
SHUSTER	Yudel	Male		Feigil	298
SHUSTER	Zlatka	Female			298
SHVARTZMAN	Alter	Male			298
SHVARTZMAN	Beril	Male			298
SHVARTZMAN	Doba	Female			298
SHVARTZMAN	Icie	Female			298
SHVARTZMAN	Itka	Female			298
SHVARTZMAN	Khaia	Female			298
SHVARTZMAN	Leibel	Male		Michla	298
SHVARTZMAN	Malka	Female		Simka	298
SHVARTZMAN	Meril	Female			298
SHVARTZMAN	Mikhla	Female		Leibel	298

SHVARTZMAN	Nitka	Female				298
SHVARTZMAN	Simka	Male			Malka	298
SHVARTZTUKH	Bashke	Female				297
SHVARTZTUKH	Berl	Male				297
SHVARTZTUKH	Yaakov	Male				297
SLOBODNIK	Avraham	Male			Lea	292
SLOBODNIK	Barukh Shlomo	Male			Meril	292
SLOBODNIK	Fruma	Female			Teibel	292
SLOBODNIK	Golda	Female			Yaakov	292
SLOBODNIK	Lea	Female			Avraham	292
SLOBODNIK	Meril	Female			Barukh Shlomo	292
SLOBODNIK	Teibel	Male			Fruma	292
SLOBODNIK	Yaakov	Male			Golda	292
SLOMINSKI	Aharon	Male			Rakhel	292
SLOMINSKI	Rakhel	Female			Aharon	292
SLOMINSKI	Sonia	Female				292
SLOMINSKI		Male			Zalman	292
SLOMINSKI		Male	Zalman			292
SLOMINSKI	Zalman	Male				292
SLUTZKI	Avraham	Male			Itsche	292
SLUTZKI	Efraim	Male	Nekha	Lea		292
SLUTZKI	Grunia	Female				292
SLUTZKI	Itsche	Female			Avraham	292
SLUTZKI	Lea	Female			Nekha	292
SLUTZKI	Nekha	Female			Lea	292
SLUTZKI	Sheindil	Female	Nekha	Lea		292
SMULIAR	Feigil	Female				292
SMULIAR	Herschil	Male				292
SMULIAR	Yehoshua	Male				292
SOLOMONIK	Ezra	Male				292
SOLOMONIK	Itke	Female			Mendil	292
SOLOMONIK	Mendil	Male			Itke	292

SOLOMONIK		Male			Ezra		292
SOLOMONIK		Male		Zlatke			292
SOLOMONIK	Zlatke	Female					292
SOSNIK	Bashka	Female			Moshe		292
SOSNIK	Felia	Female			Velvel		292
SOSNIK	Gitel	Female			Yaakov		292
SOSNIK	Khana Gitel	Female					292
SOSNIK	Leizer	Male					292
SOSNIK	Mikhael	Male	Moshe	Bashke			292
SOSNIK	Moshe	Male			Bashke		292
SOSNIK	Moshe	Male			Tzipora		292
SOSNIK	Motel	Male			Tzvia		292
SOSNIK	Rivka	Female			Shlomo		292
SOSNIK	Shlomo	Male			Rivka		292
SOSNIK	Tzipora	Female			Moshe		292
SOSNIK	Tzvia	Female			Yitzkhak Yaakov		292
SOSNIK	Tzvia	Female			Motel		292
SOSNIK		Male			Yehoshua		292
SOSNIK	Velvel	Male			Palia		292
SOSNIK	Yaakov	Male			Gitel		292
SOSNIK	Yehoshua	Male					292
SOSNIK	Yitzkhak Yaakov	Male			Tzvia		292
STASHEVSKI	Hadasa	Female			Meir		292
STASHEVSKI	Meir	Male			Hadasa		292
STOLINSKI	Rivka	Female					292
STOLINSKI		Male		Rivka			292
STOROVINSKI	Aviva	Female	Efraim	Sheindil			292
STOROVINSKI	Efraim	Male			Sheindil		292
STOROVINSKI	Lea	Female	Efraim	Sheindil			292
STOROVINSKI	Shindil	Female			Efraim		292
STOROVINSKI		Male			Yisrael		292
STOROVINSKI	Yisrael	Male					292

TILIN	Aizik	Male					288
TILIN	Bunim	Male					288
TILIN	Moshe Masha	Male	Aizik				288
TILIN		Male			Aizik		288
TILIN		Male			Bunim		288
TKACH	Bila	Female			Meir		288
TKACH	Itka	Female	Meir	Bila			288
TKACH	Meir	Male			Bila		288
TKACH	Moshe	Male	Meir	Bila			288
TOMARIN	Aharon	Male	Itzik	Yehudit			288
TOMARIN	Asher	Male	Beril	Rakhel			288
TOMARIN	Beril	Male			Rakhel		288
TOMARIN	Betzalel	Male	Beril	Rakhel			288
TOMARIN	Elke	Female					288
TOMARIN	Feigil	Female					288
TOMARIN	Herschil	Male	Itzik	Yehudit			288
TOMARIN	Itka	Female					288
TOMARIN	Itzik	Male			Yehudit		288
TOMARIN	Khana	Female			Mordekhai		288
TOMARIN	Mendel	Male			Sara		288
TOMARIN	Mordekhai	Male			Khana		288
TOMARIN	Moshe	Male					288
TOMARIN	Rakhel	Female			Beril		288
TOMARIN	Sara	Female			Mendel		288
TOMARIN	Sheindil	Female					288
TOMARIN		Male			Yisrael		288
TOMARIN	Yehudit	Female			Itzik		288
TOMARIN	Yisrael	Male					288
TREISTER	Khava	Female			Nisan Leib		288
TREISTER	Nisan Leib	Male			Khava		288
TUPLINKI	Aharon	Male	Avraham	Shushka			288
TUPLINKI	Avraham	Male			Shoshka		288
TUPLINKI	Khaim	Male	Avraham	Shushka			288

TUPLINKI	Khana	Female	Avraham	Shushka			288
TUPLINKI	Shoshka	Female			Avraham		288
TURKENITZ	Feigil	Female	Motel	Rivka			288
TURKENITZ	Golda	Female	Motel	Rivka			288
TURKENITZ	Herschil	Male			Lea		288
TURKENITZ	Lea	Female			Herschil		288
TURKENITZ	Motel	Male			Rivka		288
TURKENITZ	Rivka	Female			Motel		288
TURKENITZ	Shalom	Male					288
TURKENITZ		Male			Shalom		288
TUROVETZ	Feigil	Female			Volf		288
TUROVETZ	Volf	Male			Feigil		288
TURUSHKIN	Buna	Female			Tzvi		288
TURUSHKIN	Miriam	Female					288
TURUSHKIN	Tzvi	Male			Buna		288
TZFASMAN	Aizik	Male			Malka		295
TZFASMAN	Aizik	Male			Neta		295
TZFASMAN	Avraham Moshe	Male					295
TZFASMAN	Breindil	Female					295
TZFASMAN	Fruma	Female					295
TZFASMAN	Malka	Female			Aizik		295
TZFASMAN	Neta	Female			Aizik		295
TZFASMAN	Roshka	Female		Breindil			295
TZIPIN	Leib	Male			Shoshka		294
TZIPIN	Herzl	Male			Yentil		294
TZIPIN	Shoshka	Female			Leib		294
TZIPIN	Yentil	Female			Herzl		294
TZIPORIN	Bentzion	Male					295
TZIPORIN	Freidil	Female					295
TZIPORIN	Liba	Female					295
TZIPORIN	Meir Yosef	Male					295
TZIPORIN	Miriam	Female					295
TZIPORIN	Moshe	Male			Nekhama		295

TZIPORIN	Natan	Male					295
TZIPORIN	Natan	Male					295
TZIPORIN	Nekhama	Female			Moshe		295
TZIPORIN	Rakhel	Female					295
TZIPORIN	Sara	Female					295
TZIPORIN	Shmuel	Male					295
TZIPORIN	Simkha	Male					295
TZIPORIN	Tzeitil	Female					295
TZIPORIN	Velvel	Male					295
TZIRULNIK	Sheina Gitel	Female			Yosef		295
TZIRULNIK	Yosef	Male			Sheina Gitel		295
TZURNUMURITZ	Arie	Male			Sara		292
TZURNUMURITZ	Sara	Female			Arie		292
UKHST	Khaim	Male			Rozil		284
UKHST	Rodil	Female			Khaim		284
ULMAN	Alte	Female			Avraham		284
ULMAN	Avraham	Male			Alte		284
VAKS	Ester Lea	Female			Leibel		287
VAKS	Leibel	Male			Ester Lea		287
VAKS	Shabtai	Male					287
VAKS	Tzvi	Male	Leibel	Ester			287
VAKS	Tzvia	Female	Leibel	Ester			287
VAKS		Male			Velvel		287
VAKS	Velvel	Male					287
VAKS	Yosef	Male					287
VALPIN	Rakhel	Female					287
VALPIN	Aharon	Male					287
VALPIN	Aharon	Male					287
VALPIN	Arie	Male	Zelik	Kheshka			287
VALPIN	Asher	Male					287
VALPIN	David	Male	Zelik	Kheshka			287
VALPIN	David	Male					287

VALPIN	Ester	Female	Naftali	Golda		287
VALPIN	Gershon	Male				287
VALPIN	Golda	Female			Naftali	287
VALPIN	Khaia	Female			Yaakov	287
VALPIN	Khaia	Female				287
VALPIN	Khaim	Male			Rakhel	287
VALPIN	Khana	Female	Zelik	Kheshka		287
VALPIN	Khashke	Female			Zelig	287
VALPIN	Lea	Female	Naftali	Golda		287
VALPIN	Lea	Female	Pinkhas	Yentil		287
VALPIN	Malka	Female			Zalman	287
VALPIN	Mania	Female			Yaakov	287
VALPIN	Meir	Male	Zelik	Kheshka		287
VALPIN	Moshe	Male	Pinkhas	Yentil		287
VALPIN	Moshe	Male				287
VALPIN	Moshe Yaakov	Male				287
VALPIN	Naftali	Male			Golda	287
VALPIN	Pinkhas	Male			Yentil	287
VALPIN	Rakhel	Female			Khaim	287
VALPIN	Roshka	Female				287
VALPIN	Shoshka	Female				287
VALPIN	Tamar	Female	Zelik	Kheshka		287
VALPIN	Tamar	Female	Pinkhas	Yentil		287
VALPIN	Tzipora	Female				287
VALPIN		Male			Asher	287
VALPIN	Yaakov	Male			Khaia	287
VALPIN	Yaakov	Male			Mania	287
VALPIN	Yaakov	Male	Pinkhas	Yentil		287
VALPIN	Yentil	Female			Pinkhas	287
VALPIN	Zalman	Male			Malka	287
VALPIN	Zelik	Male			Kheshka	287
VARNIK	Khlavna	Male				287
VARNIK		Male			Khlavna	287

VAGER	Beril	Male			Khesha		287
VAGER	David	Male			Dvora		287
VAGER	Dvora	Female			David		287
VAGER	Feigil	Female			Herschil		287
VAGER	Freidil	Female	Herschil	Feigil			287
VAGER	Fridl	Female			Khaim		287
VAGER	Herschil	Male			Feigil		287
VAGER	Khaim	Male			Freidil		287
VAGER	Khasha	Female			Beril		287
VAGER	Kheshel	Male	David	Dvora			287
VAGER	Lea	Female	Khaim	Freidil			287
VAGER	Leizer Leib	Male	Khaim	Freidil			287
VAGER	Meir	Male	Khaim	Freidil			287
VAGER	Mordekhai	Male	Beril	Kheshe			287
VAGER	Moshe Aharon	Male	Beril	Kheshe			287
VAGER	Moshe Aharon	Male	Khaim	Freidil			287
VAGER	Nakhman	Male	David	Dvora			287
VAGER	Pesia	Female	Khaim	Freidil			287
VAGER	Rakhel	Female	David	Dvora			287
VAGER	Rakhel	Female	Beril	Kheshe			287
VAGER	Rivka	Female	Herschil	Feigil			287
VAGER	Rodil	Female	Khaim	Freidil			287
VAGER	Sara	Female	Khaim	Freidil			287
VAGER	Yosef	Male	Beril	Kheshe			287
VEINER	Aharon	Male			Rivka		287
VEINER	Beril	Male					287
VEINER	Faivel	Male					287
VEINER	Rivka	Female			Aharon		287
VEINER		Male			Beril		287
VEINER		Male			Faivel		287
VEINSHTEIN	Berele	Male					287
VEINSHTEIN	Eliahu	Male					287

VEINSHTEIN		Male			Cantor	287
VEINSHTEIN		Male				287
VINIK	Bashka	Female			Tuvia	287
VINIK	Tuvia	Male			Bashke	287
VISMAN	Shmariahu	Male			Sonia	287
VISMAN	Sonia	Female			Shmariahu	287
VISOTZKI	Eidel	Male			Malia	287
VISOTZKI	Melia	Female			Eizil	287
VISOTZKI	Sheina	Female			Zerakh	287
VISOTZKI		Male			Yosef	287
VISOTZKI	Yaakov	Male				287
VISOTZKI	Zerakh	Male			Sheina	287
ZAGRODSKI	Mari	Female			Shlomo	288
ZAGRODSKI	Shlomo	Male			Meri	288
ZEGER	Aharon	Male			Hudel	288
ZEGER	Are	Male				288
ZEGER	Asher	Male			Pesia	288
ZEGER	Eliahu	Male	Yaakov			288
ZEGER	Eliahu	Male				288
ZEGER	Ester	Female	Yaakov			288
ZEGER	Ester	Female				288
ZEGER	Golda	Female			Yeshiyah	288
ZEGER	Golda	Female				288
ZEGER	Hudel	Female			Aharon	288
ZEGER	Khaike	Female			Moshe Yitzkhak	288
ZEGER	Khendel	Female				288
ZEGER	Leibel	Male				288
ZEGER	Lipa	Male			Teibel	288
ZEGER	Meir	Male		Golda		288
ZEGER	Moshe Yitzkhak	Male			Khaika	288
ZEGER	Nakhum	Male				288
ZEGER	Pesia	Female			Asher	288

ZEGER	Pinkhas	Male					288
ZEGER	Sara Itka	Female					288
ZEGER	Shlomo	Male			Zelda		288
ZEGER	Shlomo	Male			Zelda		288
ZEGER	Shoshka	Female	Moshe Yitzkhak	Khaika			288
ZEGER	Shoshka	Female					288
ZEGER	Teibel	Female			Lipa		288
ZEGER		Male			Are		288
ZEGER		Male			Yehoshua		288
ZEGER		Male			Yaakov		288
ZEGER		Male			Leibel		288
ZEGER		Male			Pinkhas		288
ZEGER	Velvel	Male					288
ZEGER	Volf	Male					288
ZEGER	Yaakov	Male					288
ZEGER	Yaakov	Male					288
ZEGER	Yehoshua	Male					288
ZEGER	Yeshiyah	Male			Golda		288
ZEGER	Zeev	Male	Moshe Yitzkhak	Khaika			288
ZEGER	Zelda	Female			Shlomo		288
ZEGER	Zelda	Female			Shlomo		288
ZELDIN	Bila	Female					288
ZELDIN	Itsche	Male					288
ZIKLIK	Khana	Female					288
ZIKLIK	Miriam	Female					288
ZIKLIK	Yehoshua	Male					288
ZILBERMAN	Meir	Male			Rivka		288
ZILBERMAN	Rivka	Female			Meir		288
ZULKVER	Moshe	Male				Doctor	288
ZULKVER		Male			Moshe		288

[Page 299]

Natives of David-Horodok Who Died in the Land

Translated by Jerrold Landau

The list was arranged by Ch. Kolozny and E. Nachmanovitz

Afonhendin, Shimon	Lev, Shoshana (Ziporin)
Afonhendin, Yaakov	Lev, Pesia (daughter of Shoshana)
Afonhendin, Dvora	Lachovsky, Zeev Ben-Shalom
Aharoni, Rivka (Ziporin)	Lachovsky, Itka Rachel
Barsky, Isser	Lifshitz, Moshe-Yehuda
Blizhovsky, Tova (Cantor, Teibel)	Lifshitz, Chaya
Grenadier, Noach	Lichtenstein, Kopel
Grenadier, Riva	Lutzky, Shosha
Gdansky, Chaya (Grenadier)	Mishalov, Moshe-Aharon
Glinansky, Aharon	Mishalov, Toiva
Glinansky, Beila	Mekler, Mordechai
Gloiberman, Zalman	Finkelstein, Shraga
Gloiberman, Nota	Finkelstein, Beila
Dravsky, Daniel (from Olpen)	Ziporin, Mordechai
Durchin, Tzvi (son of Yisrael-Nachum and Etel)	Ziporin, Shalom
Hochman, Baruch (son of Yehuda and Zissel)	Kashtan, Yehuda
Virobnik, Zeev (grandson of Dushnik)	Kashtan, Yosef
Weisberg, Uri (son of Sara Grenadier)	Katzman, Malka
Vager, Rachel (wife of Leibel)	Ronkin, Shimon
Vager, Chaya, Vager, Tova (her daughters)	Reznik, Zeev Ben-David
Volpin, Yentl	Rabbi Shapira
Zagorodsky, Dr. M.	Shafer, Aharon Yonah
Zager, Yaakov	Shafer, Riva
Zager, Abba (from Tury)	Shafer, Rafael
Chover, Ester	Shostakovsky, Leibel
Turkenitz, Eliyahu	Yitzchak the son of Leah Shafer, Kfar Vitkin
Turkenitz, Chaya	Tzivia Kraus (Ziporin)
Lifshitz, Dov	

[Page 300]

Family Pictures

Translated by Jerrold Landau

Nachman Blizhovsky

Dvosha Afonhendin

Shimon Afonhendin

Yosef, Ester, Shachna and Aryeh Gotlieb

[Page 301]

Sonia Basevitz   Reizel Basevitz   Yosef Basevitz

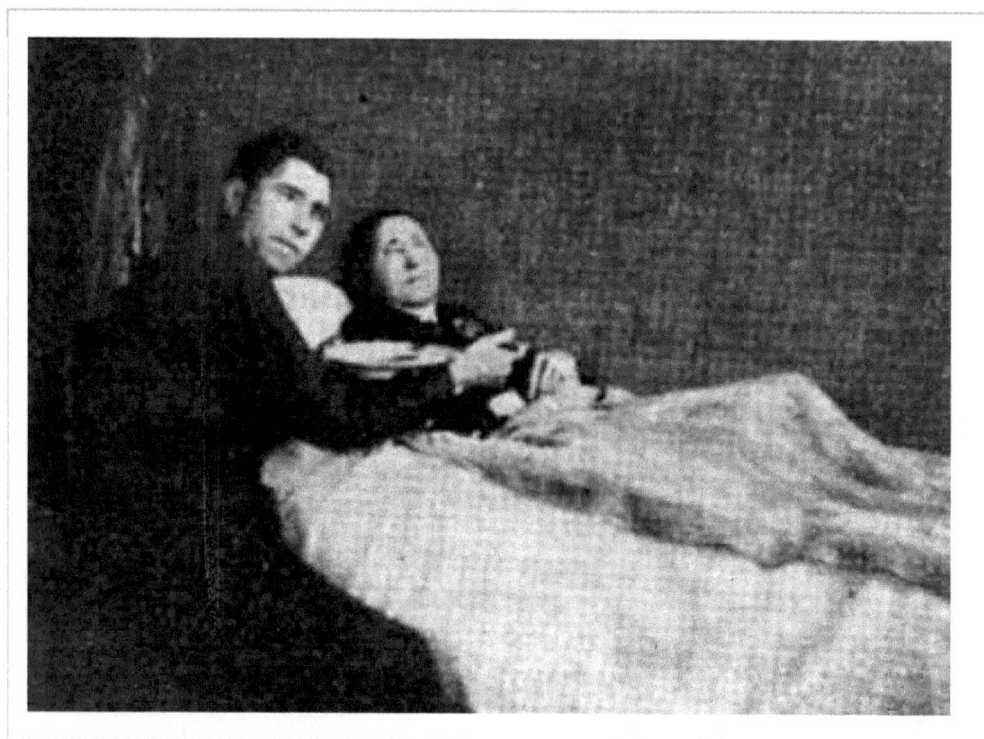

Yaakov Basevitz and his mother

Teibel Basevitz

David Basevitz

[Page 302]

Family of Shimon Dobrushin

Dobrushin Family

Sara Liberman

[Page 303]

Wife of E. Zeev Lutzky

Mordechai Mekler

Family of Noach Dobrushin

[Page 304]

Family of Leibel Gloiberman

Gloiberman family

[Page 305]

Gloiberman family

Eisenberg Lelzizky Family

[Page 306]

Dvora Vager

David Vager

Hershel, Rivka, Chashel Vager

Rachel Vager, Sara Vager

Nachman Vager

[Page 307]

Dov Meir Lifshitz

Eidel Lifshitz

Moshe Lifshitz

Shmuel and his wife Bracha Lifshitz

Chaim the son of Moshe Lifshitz

Eidel and Yaakov, the children of Moshe Lifshitz

[Page 308]

Family of Yaakov Sandberg.

Sender Margolin and his sister Masha and the children

Simcha Mishalov

Avrahan and Tzirel Lifshitz

Miriam and Noach Mishalov

[Page 309]

Roshka and Reitza Motzolsky

Yosef Motzolsky

Family of Dov Farber

[Page 310]

Dov Motzolsky

Rachel and Yechiel Pain

Family of Moshe Pain

[Page 311]

Yisrael Meir Lachovsky

Itka Rachel, Lachovsky's Wife

Finkelstein Family

[Page 312]

Yisroel Olshansky

Yaakov Olshansky

Yisrael Finkelstein

Chaya and Shlomo Finkelstein

Rivka and Lula Munbaz

Lipa Finkelstein

[Page 313]

Top right to left: Leibel, David, Zeev Berezdivin, Hinda, Perl
Bottom right to left: Eizel, Nishka, Baruch

[Page 314]

Mordechai Turkenitz

Chaya and Nissan Buchalitzky

Children of Chaya and Nissan Buchalitzky

Magidovitz Family

[Page 315]

Children of Yitzchak Magidovitz –
Gershon, Shaike, Elka, Faigele

Leah Kolozny

Family of Avraham Magidovitz

Family of Yitzchak Magidovitz

[Page 316]

Reizel and Leizer Ronkin*
* Coordinator's note: The text says "Roknin," but this is clearly an error.

Yoel Pinsky and his son

Fishman Family

[Page 317]

Yitzchak-Aryeh, Sara, Breindel

Getzel Perzov

Yaakov, Golda, Efraim, Noach, Nechama, Sara, Rivka Perzov

[Page 318]

Rashka and Yaakov Rappaport

Kravchik family: Mendel, Sheindel, Shlomo, Zelda, Dvora, Sender, Yentl, Tzipora, Eliezer

[Page 319]

Miriam Schwartzman

Itka and her daughter, Mirya Schwartzman

Family of Tzvi Zezik

[Page 320

Chava Kolozny

Shosha Lutzky

Kolozny Family

[Page 321]

Litman the son of Yosef Kolozny

Litman Kolozny

Chana Gittel Sosnik

Zeev Shafer

Mordechai Shafer

[Page 322]

Yisrael Shertok

Tzipora and Yosef Shertok

Shertok Family

[Unnumbered page following 322]

Martyrs of Rubel

Translated by Jerrold Landau

Coordinator's note: This list is not included in all printings of the original *Memorial Book of David-Horodok*.

Rabbi Youngstein, his wife Malka and three children

Bodomsky, Moshe, his wife Hinda and their daughter

Burshtein, Yehuda

Bigelman, Avraham Tzvi, his wife and their two children

Bigelman, Itzik, his wife and their children

Bashkin, Asher, his wife Miriam and their children

Gomer, Shmuel, his wife, their daughter Rachel and son Bora

Gomer, Yehuda and his wife

Ginzburg, Isser, his wife Malka, their son Meir Velveli and their daughter Reizel

Ginzburg, Boaz, his wife, their daughter Perl and her three children

Ginzburg, Litman, his wife Sheindel and their five children

Ginzburg, Meir, his wife and their children

Ginzburg, Moshe, his wife and their children

Ginzburg, Noach, his wife and their son Yaakov

Ginzburg, Shlomo, his wife Yonah and their two children

Ginendel, Zalman, his wife and their three children

Ginendel, Litman, his wife Sheindel and their five children

Zingerman, Mordechai, his wife Sara

Zingerman, Chaya Bracha, her husband Efraim Globerson and their daughters Gisha and Lifsha

Zingerman, Gittel, her husband Leibel Landau and their son Yoel, his wife Chishka and their three children

Cohen, Leah, the wife of the *shochet*

Marer, Shlomo the son of Tzvi, his wife Chava, their daughter Tzipora, their son Tzvi and two other children

Nosanchuk, Ben Zion, his wife and children

Nosanchuk, Genya and her children

Nosanchuk, Yosef, his wife Rivka, their children Golda and Yehoshua

Nosanchuk, Moshe, his wife and two children

Nosanchuk, Yehuda, his wife Eshka, their children Avraham and Peshka

Portnoy, Isser, his wife Rachel and their three children

Portnoy, David, his wife Sara and their children

Portnoy, Chana Feigel, their daughter Rivka and her children

Plotnitzky, Isser, his mother Beila, his wife Feigel, their daughters Zissel, Chava, and one more

Plotnitzky, Yisrael, his wife and three children

Plotnitzky, Yosef, his wife Vichna

Plotnitzky, Nachum, his wife Risha and their three children

Fishman, Zelig, his wife Sonia and their three children

Frumkin, Yehuda Baruch, his wife Chava and their daughter Reichel

Peres, Chaya Perl, Gnesha Dobrushka, Yitzchak, Yaakov, and Moshe

Friedman, Yaakov, his wife Michal and their two children

Zezik, Noach Leib, his wife Alta and their children

Konik, Asnat and her daughters

Rosenzweig, Chaim Leib, his wife Rivka, and their daughter Golda

Lifshitz, Aharon, his wife Feigel, and their son Meir
Lifshitz, Sunya, his wife Chaya and their children Sheindel, Beila, Zelda, Dvosha, Eshka, Yachna, Asher and one other child, his mother Dvora
Lemkovitz, Aharon, his wife Chaya Leah and their children Yaakov, Nachum and Grunya
Macherson family
Moravnik, Meir, his wife Pesha, and their three children
Marer, Shlomo, his wife Malka and their two children

Rimar, Yehuda
Rimar, Yaakov Michal and Chava
Rimar, Miriam and their daughter Chana
Rimar, Tzivia, her husband and their three children
Rimar, Moshe Feivel, his wife Chaya and their eight children
Shulman, Avraham, his daughter Pesil, her husband and three children
Shulman, Motel and his family

May G-d avenge their blood.

[Page 323]

G-d full of mercy, Creator of earth and heaven, Who hears the cries of the sorrowful, Judge of [injustice to] widows and Father of orphans: Do not keep silent and restrain Yourself when the blood of Your people is flowing like water. Grant perfect repose under the Wings of the Divine Presence in the holy and pure heights that shine as the brightness of the firmament, for the thousands of souls of holy [people of] Israel, men, women, boys, girls, infants, and children, who were murdered, slaughtered, strangled, drowned, burnt, and buried alive in the countries of: Poland, Austria, Bulgaria, Belgium, Bukovina, Bessarabia, Galicia, Germany, Denmark, Hungary, Holland, Yugoslavia, Greece, Latvia, Lithuania, Norway, Czechoslovakia, France, and other countries of Europe. All are holy and pure, and among them are spiritual personalities, *Gaonim*, *Tzadikim*, rabbis, Hassidim, and Yeshiva heads, cedars of Lebanon and mighty [Torah] scholars, and their students. May Our G-d remember them positively, and may their repose be in the Garden of Eden. The Master of Mercies shall shelter them in the protection of His Wings for eternity, and bind their souls in the bounds [of life]. G-d is their inheritance, and may He take revenge on their behalf, and may their sacrifice be remembered for us forever, and may their merit stand for us and for all of Israel.

Earth, do not cover their blood and do not be the place of their cries. By their merits, may the exiled of Israel return to their inheritance, and may these righteous ones be a perpetual remembrance before their Righteous G-d. May they come in peace and rest in their repose, and arise and live again at the End of Days, and let us say Amen.

From Childhood Years

[Page 405]

David-Horodok 50 Years Ago

by Motel Slutzky, New York

Translated by Norman Helman z"l

It is difficult to say how David-Horodok differed much from other small towns, stuck in the deep marshes of Polesye. They had the same style houses, streets, schools, shops, marketplace and the same livelihoods, troubles, cares and sorrows.

David-Horodok produced no famous men by whose merit a permanent light could be kindled in the history of Byelorussian Jewry. Kaidanov was renowned for the Kaidanover Rebbe – Avraham Reizin. Stolin had acquired a reputation with the Stoliner Rebbe. However, David-Horodok had no such luck. But, for those born and raised in David-Horodok, the town had a permanent charm. The *meshchane* [town citizens] would say: "Horodok solodok" – a sweet town.

Even having departed as a youth, as did most David-Horodokers who now live in America, one still carries a longing in his heart for the old home. No matter what different memories and impressions that each David-Horodoker brought with him

The Greble

[Page 406]

from his childhood years, everyone carried an exceptional love and memory for the Horyn River which flowed through the middle of town.

Not Yudovitz's wall, not the marketplace, the Olshaner Street, the marshes, the Olpener Street, the Velemitsher Street, the school yard or the various streets and byways round about, not the hill but only the river will be the subject of the first encounter and greeting: "from which side of the river did you come from?"

Wherever destiny takes you, whether to hot desert sands or to the shores of the Pacific or Atlantic, if you were born and raised in David-Horodok, the river will follow you wherever you go the rest of your life and take a prominent place in your memories.

The Horyn River in rising tides

The Horyn River is the true "woman of valor." She is the nourisher and supplier of almost the entire town. She makes many rich and others poor. For one, it tears up his yard and cattle stall, and for another on the opposite shore, it deposits soil for an orchard and garden. The river carries ships, barges, rafts and steamboats. It fills the fishermen's nets with the finest fish. It breeds flocks of geese whose meat and fat feed the town's inhabitants and whose down softens their bed covers.

How beautiful the river is in the summer time. On its shores there is ceaseless activity, both day and night.

[Page 407]

The shore of the Horyn River in David-Horodok

Here they build the magnificent ships. Piles of lumber go on ships to distant Prussia. The two small steamboats: *Vion* and *Strekaza* are going – one to Nirtcha and the other to Vidibor-Stolin. The steamboats are the pleasant intermediaries between David-Horodok and the outside world.

In the summer, we swim and play in and around the river. We walk along the large wooden bridge. We run to greet the incoming steamboat even if there is no one that we are waiting for.

At night, the town's youngsters strolled along the riverbank behind Mordechai-Zelig's orchard in Tchipovskes Street, from there around the church hill, along the dirt path to the Chovorsker windmill and on to the marshes.

We remember the town in its prosperous times. Famous for their wealth were such affluent men as: Yudovitz, the Bregmans, Lipman Ladezky, Aharon-Leib of Orly, Leibke Grushkin, Pesach Yashke's and many more. They were the "eastern wall" Jews of the "Great" and *"Nagid"* [rich man's] synagogues.

The greatest imprint on David-Horodok was left by Yudovitz. He had done much traveling in the outside world and he brought back European fashion to David-Horodok. He was less concerned with Europeanizing David-Horodok, as for example Peter the Great with Moscow, as he was interested in making improvements in the town.

[Page 408]

The Yudovitz wall

I see before my eyes the two things that he built. Yudovitz's two-story brick building with the spread-eagle wings on both sides contained walled shops on half the street, the Amalia Hotel and a large orchard surrounded by a brick wall which gave the building the appearance of a medieval baron's castle. A small bridge behind the orchard led to Zlodeyevka. Yudovitz also built the Great Synagogue in the school yard with great style and taste. It would have suited a German city rather than a town in the Polesye marshes. Yudovitz's masonry on the Olpener Road produced bricks impressed with the letters "YU." The beautiful idyllic water mill, called the Olpener mill, was an ideal model for a landscape painter. Lastly, there was Yudovitz himself, a tall frame and a well-fed belly; his stern and lordly face with cold, sharp gray eyes. He had pointed and thinly twisted whiskers which reminded people of the Baron Hirsch Ginzburg with his top hat and thick cane with a staghorn handle.

Yudovitz's time faded away and the Bregmans emerged on the scene with the berlina business. The berlinas [river barges] transported products from Polesye and Byelorussia to Ukraine and Great Russia and from the banks of the Dnieper back to Polesye.

The Bregmans built their warehouses from David-Horodok to Kremenchug and Ekaterinoslav. The berlinas transported wheat flour from Kiev, Poltava and Kharkov

[Page 409]

sugar, salt, barley grain, oil, coal and many other products over the waters of the Pripyat and Dnieper until their very ends.

Their tugboat steamboat *Montefiore* would visit the town once a year. In the fall, before winter froze the river, the steamboat would tow a long line of high-bellied berlinas and leave them for the winter on the banks of the Horyn River opposite Moche Rimar's dock where they were built.

With the berlinas came the owners, Yossel, Yankel and Motel Bregman. Their expensive skunk furs lined with cat skin gave a special dignity to the eastern wall of the Great Synagogue. Even the Slonimer rabbi with his long, red beard, in his nook next to the ark, acquired a certain distinction with the arrival of the Bregmans. Their time also passed and quickly faded. All that remained of them was the glory of Yossel Bregman's beautiful daughters: Golda Reina, Shifra Sarke and the prettiest of them all, Rivkele Bregman.

The subsequent tycoons who followed the Yudovitzes and the Bregmans, such as Leibke Grushkin, Pesach Yashke's, Lipman Ladezky and a few lesser people, were already Jews whose possessions were no longer as lavish as their predecessors.

New winds began blowing over Russia and they were also felt in our out-of-the-way town.

* * *

The turbulent months of the 1905 revolutionary upheaval pass through my mind like a kaleidoscope. The almost unlimited power of the wealthy disappeared. One then had to deal with the Eserists, Iskrists and Bundists.

After a while when the youth realized that they would never attain the right of direct and secret ballot, they resolved to leave the town. They began the great mass immigration to America after the Russo-Japanese War.

Except for Mordechai Laptchevan who would on no account, leave David-Horodok, all the other "brothers and sisters" began to leave the town. The town became impoverished and, if not for the help of the sons and daughters in far-off America, they would have starved to death.

No longer were the songs and laughter of the Jewish youth heard along the banks of the river on summer nights. The orphaned ships stood tied up at the river docks. As a boy or a girl grows up, they go off to America.

An echo of the horrible pogroms which had raged through the length and breadth of the Jewish cities and towns in Russia also reached David-Horodok. A Horodoker *meshchanin* [town citizen] named Zuchter murdered with an axe an entire Jewish family of seven souls in the nearby village of Orly.

[Page 410]

The murder was carried out at night when everyone was asleep. Terror fell on the town and the surrounding villages. Everyone prepared for pogroms and the horrible murder was regarded as a "down payment."

I remember as though it were now, the frightful funeral; the wagons with the massacred bodies and the blood-soaked bed clothes. That tragic night with the wagons and bodies is engraved in my memory to this day, like a horrible nightmare.

* * *

David-Horodok had many laborers, butchers, wagon drivers and, of course, peddlers, shopkeepers, fishmongers, brokers and religious article dealers.

In those days, the butcher carts stood in the middle of the marketplace where the church now stands. The sticks fastened to the edges of the stands on which hung the carts made the marketplace similar to a garden of babbling.

I can hear even now the clamor, cursing, screaming, the dull clang of the cleavers in the butcher stalls and the wild skirmishing of the dogs for a bone, a piece of meat or for a first claim at the butcher stall.

The butchers would come into our house for the evening prayers. Instead of a towel or handkerchief, they would use the window curtains to wipe their hands. After they had finished praying and left the house, the curtains remained hanging like pressed together horses tails. However, we couldn't complain too much because had they wished to wipe themselves on the lapels of their kaftans or on the sleeves of their jackets, they would on no account have succeeded. Their hands, covered with fat and blood, would slide off their clothing and remain as wet as ever.

Saturday night they would come to our house in order to settle up the jointly owned merchandise that they would purchase and slaughter during the week. The large black table in the dining room was covered with chalk marks of lines and circles. The corner of a half-circle was erased with a finger and a cat's ear placed above it. Such was the arithmetic which only the butchers understood. Often there would be a sudden shouting and dispute which would end in a fist fight. When they fought, they were not joking. They would try to hit each other on the full body and more than one butcher came away with a bruised chest and a nasty cough.

My father would buy the hides and the unkosher meat from the butchers and sent it to the regiment for the soldiers. Wagon drivers were frequent visitors in our house. They would transport the hides and the meat to the ships, steamboats and the train at Lakhva.

The wagon drivers were divided into groups. Each group had a monopoly on a certain route. Thus there were: "Lakhver," "Stoliner," "Turover" and "Pinsker" wagon drivers. One group would not trespass in another's territory. Besides these,

[Page 411]

there were "market wagon drivers." They would make deliveries from the wholesalers to the shops such as a sack of flour or a cask of gasoline, or they would transport a Jew to a neighboring village.

The town's butchers and wagon drivers were not what you would call "eastern wall sitters." For that reason, they were the only ones who were respected by the town and village gentiles.

If a gentile became drunk and unruly towards a Jew, whether in a tavern or in the marketplace, it was enough for Ezra the butcher to come over and lay his huge butcher hand on the nape of the gentile's neck and all became quiet and peaceful.

At the time when they anticipated pogroms in town, the butchers and wagon drivers comprised the greatest part of the self-defense organization. The wagon drivers prepared themselves with cleavers, revolvers and lead pipes. They had resolved that in case of a pogrom, the gentiles would pay dearly for such an endeavor and they would no longer start up with the Jews. The end result was that, despite the incitement of the priests, the gentiles did not venture to start a fight.

David-Horodok was rich in smiths who were divided into various categories. There were smiths who worked in shipbuilding at Moche Rimar's dock. They made *skabkes, zhabkes, yarshes* with heads like loaves of bread and *shvaranes* for the oars. There were those who made bells for the horses, knives for the gentiles, knives for the house, cleavers, door handles, hinges and iron doors for brick stores and cellars. There were smiths who only worked with copper. I remember one of them, Eizel the smith. Besides his work at the forge, he was an outstanding *baal tefillah* [prayer leader]. There were other smiths who would also belong to the burial society and catch a drink of whiskey at a burial, which was almost a daily event in town. Even in normal times, the town had more funerals than marriages. Fortunately, David-Horodoker women understood the situation and tried to compensate for the losses. A David-Horodoker woman who had no more than half-dozen children was considered barren.

The town carpenters would work with copperware. They would travel on the roads and sell the copper work and chests to the peasants. However, most of the carpenters produced furniture, doors, windows and other household items.

In normal times, drillers and sawyers worked at Moche Rimar's dock building barges. Other than this, they usually worked for the town only after a fire. Fires were frequent occurrences in our town and, if occasionally a fire was a little delayed, there were those who would "invite" this "guest."

Cobblers worked both for high quality and for second-rate. There were those fancy shoemakers who worked with very expensive leathers and others who worked with cowhide.

The tailors were also divided into categories. There were tailors for the wealthy and for the poor. There even were those who hardly earned the grain to put in the water for barley soup.

[Page 412]

The poor tailors earned their livelihood by remaking the clothing of older people for youngsters, from women's garments to men's, etc.

There were hat makers who sewed caps, one of whom I cannot forget to this day. Besides being a hat maker, he served as the "town clock." When one heard Moshe the hat maker's coughing as he came from the marketplace even before the cock had crowed, you knew that it was time for Jews to get up for the first minyan.

The only Jewish packer in town was Elya, son of Aharon Moshe the doctor. The old father Aharon also helped work in the yard. They would make various containers including long barrels in which they would pack red raspberries which the peasants would gather by the thousands of poods [1 pood equals about 36 pounds] in the forests of Polesye each fall season.

Masons and some cobblers had extra jobs to supplement their incomes. Thus, several cobblers were at the same time the town musicians. The "musician of musicians" had to supplement his income by working as a barber and photographer. The clarinetist of the band was a mason. The small trumpet, the large trumpet and the drummer would make the shoes for the bride and groom before playing at their wedding. The drummer also helped to carry *shalach manos* [Purim gifts], act as caller, etc.

The watchmaker also occupied with the production of galoshes. Once he was almost burnt to death when the gasoline suddenly ignited.

David-Horodok was rich in rabbis and ritual slaughterers, almost as many as Mozyr or even Pinsk. No town was more renowned than David-Horodok for starving so many rabbis. Why the rabbis picked just this town to conduct their fasts, G-d only knows!

Two of the ritual slaughterers were also cantors. The synagogue cantor, Reb Shmerl, prayed in the large choir synagogue with a choir that he trained and Reb Leibe was the cantor at the Great Synagogue.

* * *

David-Horodok had its own dynasty of "good Jews" [euphemism for Hassidic rabbis]. This was the family of the Alter Reb, Rabbi Yisrael Yosef who had come from Volhyn, from Koretz.

The street around the Alter Reb's study-house was occupied by his sons and daughters. They lived in want but warmed themselves under the broad but cooling rays of the bygone star of their grandfather, the Alter Reb.

In contrast, there was joy and liveliness in the Stoliner *shtibel*. They still talk about when the Stoliner Rebbe visited. Then, even the *Misnagdim* [scholastics who were anti-Hassidic] would go into their study-houses on the side streets and stick close to the walls in fear of receiving a smack in the neck and throat from a tipsy Stoliner Hassid. At that time the Alter Reb's Hasidim felt particularly abased and dejected.

David-Horodok was the capital for Reb Yisrael Yosef just as Stolin was the capital for Reb Ahrele.

[Page 413]

Reb Baruchl had his own study-house and his own Hassidim. Reb Baruchl's Hassidim were not rich Jews. They were small shop owners and laborers, but they did not let their rabbi down. Indeed, looking at the stateliness of Reb Baruchl, his beautiful long gray beard, his intelligent large deep eyes and his patriarchal Abraham-like appearance, no town would have allowed such a personage to go hungry all seven days of the week.

* * *

Between *Mincha* [afternoon prayer service] and *Maariv* [evening prayer service] in the Great Synagogue, the shadows would lengthen and darkness settled in. One hardly notices the man standing at the podium. Only his voice is heard with its own peculiar sad, sweet sounds filtering through the twilight. It is Yossel the butcher singing the Psalms.

Later, after the *Maariv* service, Berl the sexton teaches a portion of Talmud for the public. Then the eastern wall loses its privileged status. The wealthy, the merchants and the laborers mix together. Honor belongs to the one who can learn.

Indeed, they all sat together hand in hand; the aristocratic looking and affluent Pesach Yashke's, Yankel Shashe Gittel's, Velvel Ester Chaya's, Moshe Noah Leib's, along with the butchers Herzl the Pravik, Eizik Leibele's, Getzel and the Jewish wagon drivers such as the two brothers Wolf and Alter Archik's.

It is summer. The Pinsk wagon drivers drive to Pinsk with their sleighs only in the winter time when the steamboats are idle. The brothers Wolf and Alter earn their summer livelihood pulling lumber out of the river at Shlomo Feigele's dock where ships are built. The most they earn is 20 kopecks a day. In truth, this suffices only for sandy black bread, perhaps for a little barley to make soup or a piece of kishka. It was really a difficult and poor livelihood but all was forgotten in the evening at the Talmud lesson, for then, one was learning Torah!

The town of Slutsk took away Berl the *shamash* [beadle] who became their Yeshiva headmaster and Reb Dovidl took over the job of giving the public Talmud lessons. Noah Pinchas taught Ein Yaakov [a collection of legends in the Talmud] at the Alter Reb's study-house. The school teacher studied Bible and Rashi [biblical commentary] with the Jews at the Cold Synagogue. Only in the Stoliner *shtibel* did they revel, sing and dance because they "did not believe in sadness."

Soon the summer is over and the High Holy Days approach. The sexton knocks at dawn summoning people to rise and say *Selichot* [penitential prayers]. I go with my father to the *Nagid* [rich man's] Synagogue. At the podium Yankel Yeshias stands. His hoarse and tearful voice begs, demands and pleads. The congregants repeat after him with tears pouring from their eyes. I look at the Holy Ark and it seems to me that the cover flutters as the Holy Spirit in the Ark cries and bewails the bitter lot of the people of Israel.

* * *

A very good Jew arrived in town from abroad. He was dressed aristocratically with a cape, a soft hat and a cane in his hand. His handsome face was encircled by a broad black beard and his black eyes made him look like Dr. Herzl.

[Page 414]

This was Yashai Adler. He came from Krinki in the province of Grodno and he opened a school in David-Horodok where he taught the children Hebrew in Hebrew. Instead of the old familiar children's teacher with his whip, Adler typified the modern instructor who organized the school in the modern style – clean, neat and disciplined.

After a while there arrived in town the "crooked elephant" – Helfand. That was the real name given to the man who later became famous under his literary pseudonym, A. Litvak.

With Helfand, the Bund arrived in town. Thanks to the Bund, David-Horodoker boys and girls became "brothers and sisters." Students arrived in town to deliver speeches. They organized an illegal library, conspiratorial gatherings and divisions between the various doctrines of socialist and nationalist thought. In one word, things became very lively in our sleepy Polesyen town. Those were the years of the 1905 revolution.

On a cold and wintry Sabbath, Helfand was taken away from us by sleigh accompanied by a strong police guard to a distant prison or Siberia.

* * *

It is difficult to leave the town where one was born and raised. It is especially difficult to leave the beautiful river. This is where we played, bathed, floated in boats, slid on ice, played pranks with friends for which we were spanked and poked at by our fathers and teachers and beaten by the gentiles in the daily wars that we waged with them. It is still deeply engraved in our hearts for an entire lifetime.

Sabbath Evening

(Pictures of a Town)

by Berl Neuman

Translated by Norman Helman z"l

The clock strikes twelve. The day is half gone. The sun is in mid-sky. The aroma of the *pletzlach* [flat rolls] and fresh *bulkas* [baked rolls] has long since dissipated with the wind.

A new odor now emanates from the chimneys. Like the music of a stringed instrument, the aroma rises to the sky and the heavenly servants carry the "burnt offering" aloft on their wings to the Master of the World as a Sabbath gift. Thus the industrious housewives let the outside world taste the aroma of their cholent and noodle kugel.

Noah the blacksmith (he was a righteous Jew) had long since closed up his shop and walked home at a rapid pace in case he would be tardy in welcoming the Sabbath Queen. As it says in the verse: "Delay the end of the Sabbath and hasten its coming."

In the marketplace clanging of locks and bolts can be heard. At half-closed doors, the shopkeepers stand around glancing up and down the empty

[Page 415]

marketplace and one after another unhurriedly (perhaps another customer might come at the last moment) close up the shops.

When Nishka the proprietor begins to close her shop, Lipa the driver rubs his back on the wagon post, shrugs his shoulders to conclude his backscratching, gives a broad and resounding yawn, slowly climbs off the wagon and his white and skinny little horse, blind in one eye, barely drags its feet. "Nu," he says and the horse seems to understand that the day of rest is also arriving for him and he joyfully plods along.

First Lipa and then Eizik "the goat" on one side, "the brilliant" and his son Itzel (both in one wagon) on the other side, overworked Jews with hunched shoulders and formalized outfits, separate themselves one from the other. This is the way wagon drivers part, separating at the brick wall of the church on the way home for Sabbath.

On the other side of the marketplace near Kaplinsky's apothecary, the esteemed drivers returning from their trip to Lakhva begin to gather. They represent an entirely different world. The horses are healthy, well-fed and large. The wagons are tall with containers in the rear and filled with fragrant hay. They were outfitted with padded and comfortable covered seats for the convenience of their passengers. Arriving from the road, they stop to grab a quick chat.

Shaike "the kaiser" begins to tell of the "wonders" of his trip as he pulls hard on the reigns of his horse which at that moment begins to whine as if it understands the conversation.

"With my horse I don't have to be ashamed," says Benjamin the driver with a quiet voice, giving his horse a tickle under the belly with his whip. It appears that the horse is pleased with his owner's compliment and he rears up and industriously digs a hole in the ground with his hind legs.

Asherke "the deaf" with his black and playful horse "Pupike," which was tied with a rope, jumps down while holding up his pants. He does not hear the conversation but pokes his way into the middle staring with a pair of jovial, sparkling bright eyes. He shrugs his shoulders, pulls his right ear to the side and asks quietly, wanting to participate in the conversation: "Well? What? Are you talking about something?"

"Nothing, nothing," says Yossel "the blond" with a muffled voice. "Leibke doesn't mean you, he means the horse."

The resounding laughter of the drivers reverberates through the half-deserted marketplace. However, Asherke is not dismayed. He twists around, cracks his whip in the air and laughs good-naturedly together with all the others.

The old David Chesnok, who is a little late, comes along the road. He stops his horse and wagon awhile and, without getting down from his wagon, he says with dignity: "Jews, it is already late. There is no time. It is already Sabbath eve. We must give our horses some oats and drive home."

[Page 416]

Meanwhile, his horse takes advantage of the opportunity, raises his tail and empties his bowels. He swishes his tail right and left driving away the flies and he is ready to go into his stall for the Sabbath.

The drivers decide that it is definitely time to drive home when they see from a distance Shlomo Pinchas hurrying to the bathhouse with a pack of white linen under his arm.

There was a certain charm about the David-Horodoker bathhouse. I can see before my eyes the long building with red bricks and the high narrow windows with small square bracketed panes.

In the first anteroom, a pile of branches lay prepared. The oven was heating up so as to warm the water in the steam boiler which would convey the hot water through pipes into the two large casks which stood on high iron railings near the ceiling.

The dark corridor led into the first wardrobe room where, on the left side, stood a closet containing cubicles for the clothing. On the opposite side there were wooden benches for resting. From there, a door led to the "thrashing bath."

The bathhouse in David-Horodok

[Page 417]

The "thrashing bath" or, as others called it, the "sweat bath," constituted another world. The door opened with great difficulty because of two heavy stones bound to it with rope which held it back.

Not everyone could go in there because some could not tolerate the heat. Every once in a while, someone would pass out and they would pour a bucket of cold water on him and lead him by hand into the cold room where they would lay him on the cool concrete bench until he came to himself.

It is really no wonder. The thick steam was intermingled with the stench of dirty underwear hanging from sticks inserted in the overlying rafters. Not every heart could endure it. Indeed, this is the reason that such a frail Jew as Baruch "the healer" never experienced the zest of being steamed-out in the Jewish David-Horodoker "sweat bath."

The only one who felt better there than at home was Moshe Mordechai Zelig's "the digger." The heat was never enough for him. When he got together with Meir-Hersheln the butcher, things then really were spirited. First Meir-Hershel would shout in his husky voice, "Throw on another bucket!" To pour a bucket of water on the boiling hot stone in the oven required great skill and Moshe "the digger" was an expert.

One bucket after another and the heat increased. The steam could be cut with a knife as it was thick enough to simply choke a person. At this point they both climbed up to the highest step and their work began. They raised and lowered their branches to clear away the steam on all sides. One thrash and then another, a third, a fifth and a tenth.

"Ah, ah, ah," cried one of them with great pleasure – "a little higher…there, there, there…harder….even harder…good…good…ah!" Now the other one lies down and the first one gives him a double measure. Thus the two beaten Jews leave the "sweat bath" to the mikveh [ritual bath]. In the mikveh room it was a little quieter. Only the screaming of the small children, who were splashing in the water, disturbed the silence.

From the mikveh room a door led to another room which contained a row of white tubs intended for the wealthy.

And now we see a tall broad-boned Jew enter the mikveh room. This is Mordechai Leib "the general." He confidently descends step-by-step until he remains standing in the middle of the mikveh with the water reaching his chest. He puts his hands on his head, bends down, turns right and left in order to make circlets of waves which draw off the leaves still stuck to his body after the "sweat bath." He immerses himself three times then gets up and stretches his entire length and straightens his long yellow beard.

After him comes the old Rabbi Wolf Hillel's

[Page 418]

with careful steps, bent over almost to the ground. Before he descends the last step, he covers his ears, nose and eyes with the fingers of both hands. When he leaves the last step, he stands in the water with his head barely visible. He is immersed as he stands. Nevertheless, he bends three times and, barely catching his breath, he comes out cautiously wiping his face with one hand.

The day doesn't linger. Time flies. The bathhouse empties. The streets become filled with the Sabbath spirit. Through the windows the gleam of the brass candlesticks can be seen and the covered challahs on the clean, white tablecloths.

Washed and outfitted with shining shoes, the small children wander about the streets peeling kernels which their mothers have put in their pockets in honor of the Sabbath. Girls, with braided pigtails on their radiantly shampooed heads, show off to each other their pretty Sabbath clothes.

With white pressed shawls on their heads, the grandmothers go out on the porch to wait for Velvel Raishke's who walks along the streets with a stick in his hand knocking on the shutters and announcing that it is time to bless the candles.

The sun begins to set. The day departs giving away for the town's heartfelt Friday evening. From the synagogues one can hear the melody of "Come, let us sing to the Lord; let us shout with joy to the Rock of our salvation…

My Grandmother Told Me

(Memories)

by Berl Neuman

Translated by Norman Helman z"l

Long Tevet [December-January] evenings. Outside, the frost was burning cold. The window panes sprouted various snow-capped mountains and thick, deep birch forests through which you could barely see the street.

In the house by a small flickering kerosene lamp which threw shadows on the walls that children were afraid to look at because grandmother had said that one must not play with shadows because demons can give them nightmares, on such an evening, grandmother sat on a short footstool next to the stove, surrounded by her grandchildren and looked into the fire which danced cheerfully, throwing tongues of fire into the black soot-filled chimney. From time to time, grandmother threw a long thin piece of kindling into the fire, causing it to crackle, throwing sparks onto the wooden floor which was grooved with shadows.

From time to time the scraping of feet on the white, frozen snow could be heard, slowly receding into the stillness of the night.

[Page 419]

In such a dark and idyllic silence, Grandmother Bashe told her grandchildren that once…a long time ago…her grandmother had told her…that the Horyn River had been far…very far away from town…and year in and year out, the river with its ice flows slowly cut the banks and, with the slow pace of generations, it neared the town.

And the grandchildren swallowed the enchanting tale word-for-word from grandmother's mouth, and little children's heads could not understand how the river could move.

The rectangular clock with its ancient flowered dial and long brass chains with heavy weights which propelled the shiny pendulum back-and-forth with its never tardy tick-tock, tick-tock, put the children to sleep in grandmother's lap, dreaming sweet dreams of water fairies and with the question "how could it be..?" on their lips.

* * *

The years fly by and children grow up in naive, contented and quietly dignified simplicity. They grow up in streets where the puddles never dry out during the entire year, not having a chance to look even through the smallest window at the wide world and not knowing what is going on out there.

It is really no wonder that we grown children could not imagine a taller person than Itzik of Nirtcha, a richer Jew than Moche and a feebler man than Maltchik.

Could there possibly be a better matzo shmura baker than Shmerl Beyez's? And where could you find such a hearty singer, psalm-reciter and *hakofot*-distributor than Avraham Yossel?

What town in the entire world possesses a better cantor and choirboys than Shmerl Lansky and his choir?

And who can compare to the piety of Malachl who never complained, enduring the torments of Job with a constant smile?

What Jewish community was blessed with such a saint as Reb Dovidl?

Who else had the honor to taste the pleasure of a Hassidic melody on a Sabbath afternoon at the rebbe's table when Yossel Kolozny would roll his eyes upward and, with a thin voice, would fill the air of the Hassidic *shtibel* with Sabbath songs?

Who else could dance with such fervor at the rebbe's table than Shia the tourier?

Or does there exist anywhere a smarter cobbler than Eizel "Chupchik" and a better tailor than Yossel "Podrick?"

And more….and many, many more Jews, of blessed memory!....

That is how "far" children looked and how very much they understood…happy, naive, hearty childhood years.

* * *

[Page 420]

On spring days when the sun would emerge from its wintry mantle of clouds and warm up the winter-long cake of ice which had reached the open mouth of the well on the street, when the yellow icicles hanging from the straw roofs, which were shaped by the winter into various artistic forms, would begin dripping rapid drops into the container which would also serve as a sitting stool on summer nights – on such spring days, children with happy, smiling faces would go out to the Horyn River and watch how the river outgrows the banks and, with immense force, pulls hunks of ice which are split with a frightening noise and are drawn into a pile, one on top of another, to later slide off and disappear into the deep abyss only to be propelled later to the surface where they are eventually sliced by the ice cutters which protect the bridge from destruction.

Also torn along by the powerful current were bones from the graves of the old cemetery and wooden beams which were ripped out from the foundations of houses along "Egypt Street," leaving the houses precariously close to toppling into the water.

The river tears at the high bank making deeper and deeper inroads and then the children understood Grandmother Bashe's story of the past… that once… a very long time ago… the river was far away… very far.

* * *

Were it not for the dark black Hitlerian clouds which covered the skies of the Jewish communities, wiping them off the surface without leaving even a memory, then grandchildren in David-Horodok would still be telling their children today that once… a very long time ago… there was…

May G-d remember their sacred souls!

Our Shtetl

Berl Neuman

Translated by Norman Helman z"l

Would you like to become acquainted with our town? Would you like to get some its flavor?

In the books of Sholem Aleichem and Mendele Mocher Sforim, you will find a large part of what our town possessed.

After all, what didn't our town possess? Poor people, sextons, synagogue trustees and ordinary community workers; moneylenders, providers of orphans and ordinary benefactors; a poorhouse, a bathhouse, a ritual bath and above all… mud! A sea of mud! It seemed as if there was no spot in the entire world that was free of mud. Mud in the street, in the yard, on the sidewalk and mud right up to the house.

What wasn't done to try and get rid of the mud? In my time, I recall that they fixed the streets three times. And who doesn't remember how the gentiles would lay a thick cover of gravel along the length of the street and then overlay it with dirt? Do you think that it really helped? Forget it [literally: a yesterday day]!

[Page 421]

After all the gravel and dirt laying, when one had to cross the street, for example near Moshe Yehuda Lifshitz or Yudel Shatsky or Shimon Leichtman, it was truly deadly dangerous!

And if one of the residents was good-hearted enough to lay a couple of boards across the street, do you think it was already an easy matter [literally: Torah noodles]? Now you cross with dry feet? That is not the way it begins and that is not the way it ends! As soon as you put a foot on a board, it slides forward and sinks into the mud as the other end of the board rises up into the air and you remain stuck in the mud with your shoes. You lose your composure, no longer regarding the presence or absence of a board and you wade in the mud to get to the other side as quickly as possible. When you finally get to the other side, you look around to be sure that no one is looking and you anguish over your shoes and long trousers which are now covered with mud up to your knees.

Around Gittel Yonah's house, it was true chaos! If you recall, her house was next to the marketplace. There, at the marketplace, all the David-Horodoker Jews ran in the morning and there was real reason to run.

There were plenty of good things in the marketplace: pokers, water troughs, kneading troughs, shovels, tubs, pails, soaking dishes, shoes and boots – ask what not!

Today, who talks about food? Whatever the mouth could desire! As for example, Eizel Lubitsch loved big fish, so he ran to buy big fish… Mendel "the Bratsker" could only afford small flat cakes so he also ran to grab a pile of small flat cakes.

Very early, at dawn, the two brothers Eizik Berush's and Shmuel Michal are already walking on the street. They are coming from the first minyan with their prayer shawls under their arms. Where do you suppose they are going? To the marketplace!

One buys a bundle of hay for his cow and the other purchases a ball of plain thread to sew the clothing of the peasants.

Many Jews would often love to go to the marketplace and observe what was being bought and sold and perhaps they too would grab a bit of a bargain!

Just an example, Moshe'l "fyetshkalip" simply loved to go out with his cane and derive pleasure from everything; he always had plenty of time, blessed be the Name. Berl "fista-let" also didn't mind such pleasures. In fact, when they met each other at the marketplace with empty stomachs, they would pick out a convenient and strategic spot and trade witticisms, laughing at the world.

In such a manner, the entire town was there, some running and some walking.

Chaya-Leah Shmaya's ran to sell fried goose skin and fat; Shashke Korman ran to sell fresh bagels; Nache Sarainke's ran with a wagon of apples and Nache Katz went with quick steps perhaps to buy some boar bristles.

Just as in my father's vineyard, there flourished Simcha "the Japanese." A broad shouldered and big footed man with a pair of fisherman boots pulled up to the armpits, a rope tied around his coat from which hung two ends on either side like a Hassid's gartel [belt worn during prayer] – he would whirl around the marketplace looking for a livelihood. It seems that he had large lips while his nose was always a bit swollen

[Page 422]

and his speech was a little slurred. However, this didn't prevent him from carrying a sack of potatoes on his shoulders for someone, or Feigel Betzel's basket into her house. In truth, he was cut out to be a wagoner but he had never acquired a horse.

* * *

G-d forbid. I am not consumed with jealousy but the women had it better than everyone. First of all, a Horodoker Jew loved his wife and secondly, she did not work hard.

A sack of potatoes, a cask of cabbage and berries and a keg of sour pickles with dill were stored in the cellar. Millet, beans, barley, and buckwheat groats – everyone kept a supply. A kneading trough of bread was good for an entire week. Milk? What David-Horodoker Jew did not have is own cow in a stall? Well, besides bringing in an armload of wood, heating up the oven, warming up the food and sweeping the house, there was nothing to do.

There was plenty of time to stand at the window and look at who was passing by in the street. The mother stands at one window, the daughter stands at another and they gossip about the street. If the cantor passes with a few people, the daughter says: "You see mother, someone is probably having a bris." Yossel the smith with his patched eye passes by: "Mother, who died?" If they saw a policeman approaching from a distance, they both disappeared – mother and daughter, quickly away from the windows, rushing out through the back door with brooms in hand and they begin, whether they need to or not, sweeping the street because they are sure that he is coming to give them a citation.

There passes Elya Yafa's with a charity box, shivering from the cold. Israel "the lazy," a hat-maker by trade, carries a pair of hides to cut out warm jackets for the gentiles for the winter. He drags himself along, bent over like a barrel. Moshe'l Leizer's springs along continually shrugging his shoulders. He snorts and spits and talks to himself. Velvel Kushner strides along with his long legs, raising his head high. He hardly says good morning to anyone. He carries his fiddle along and goes to entertain Rivele Yudovitz with a concert.

Then Sara-Leah "the bride" passes by with a large pack under her shawl. She walks carefully, step-by-step, as if she were counting her footsteps. Her son Zelig follows her. He walks straight as a string on a violin, as though he had swallowed a stick. He doesn't bend at all. You could put a glass of water on his head.

And so they pass, young and old, men and women, idlers and workmen. Moshele Menachem's with a tool box and a saw in his hands; Shlomke Ben-Zion's carries a suit to take measurements on someone. David Bielke's hurries to the steamboat and the old "boy" has already put on his black winter overcoat with the yellow, worn-out skunk skin collar which dates back to Chmielnicki's times, sidling along with his hands

[Page 423]

pushed into his sleeves and shaking his head.

Understandably, there was something to say about each one: Chaim Yankel "the honey squeezer" is too short; Isser Gurevitz is too tall; Abrahaml Levin is too fat and Shmuel "the fetshkur" is too thin.

It was a unique and beloved occupation to stand at the window and it wasn't bad even standing there for hours. Occasionally the window-watchers would be saddened by the sight of Dr. Shalkaver running past with hurried strides. Probably someone is good and sick.

In all, we had only one doctor in town. What do you think? We had enough. First of all, God had bestowed him with strong legs so he was always running in order to satisfy everyone and secondly, everyone knew what to do for their sick.

If one of us became sick, we knew that the first thing was to withhold food. If he became weaker and feverish, the second step was to place an ice bag on his head.

As the patient became even weaker from hunger and properly chilled from the ice cap, the neighbors would then mix in with their advice – step number three was to apply leeches.

After the leeches had sucked up the last drop of blood and the Angel of Death was already standing at the head of the bed, we would then run to the synagogue and knock on the Holy Ark and beg for mercy. Afterwards, they would run to the doctor and ask him to save the moribund patient.

Nevertheless, Horodoker Jews were generally healthy and satisfied. Most of the illness was caused by the "evil eye." We had a special "doctor" for this – Feigl the blacksmith. She would continually talk and spit, snort and spit and her incantations really helped. Not only that but if someone had a swelling on the eye, a stye or some other such sore, Feigl the blacksmith would lick it with her tongue and her lick would really help. Nowadays, who still talks about cutting a rose? For that, there was no one like her! Whether it helped or not, the important thing is that they believed it would help. Horodoker Jews were believers!

Did not Horodoker mothers believe that there was a kind-hearted Sara sent down by heaven to protect the Jewish woman in childbirth and her newborn infant? And really, why should one not believe it? It is clearly written in the Yiddish Bible!

And one also believed in the devil's camp – Heaven protect us that would try by various means and tricks to entrap the child in sin. Indeed, there were Horodoker Jewish mothers who would routinely distribute goodies to small school children in order to encourage them to say their nightly prayers

[Page 424]

without fail. In addition, they would hang placards containing psalms on each window and door in order to prevent the entrance of imps and evil spirits.

Horodoker Jews believed in everything except one thing! They did not believe that there could come a time when beasts in the form of people would rise up against them and ruthlessly murder them.

Good-natured, naive, friendly Jewish mothers and fathers, children and old folk, merchants, artisans, laborers and toilers! With "I believe" on their lips, they were led to the mass slaughter.

How great is the calamity when we must write about them in the past tense!

David-Horodok Until the War

by Yitzchak Nachmanovitz

Translated by Norman Helman z"l

David-Horodok was a small town, a small island of culture in the black and remote sea of Polesye. Near to G-d and far from people, because getting there was no easy matter. With the wagon from the train station, it was a 25 kilometer journey over muddy roads, or with the steamboat from Pinsk in the summer, it was a 14-18 hour voyage through the wild dreamlike forests and swamps of Polesye.

A new arrival would notice nothing special. Small houses cling to the Mother Earth as if they want to unite with her. Incidentally, there was a street popularly called "Egypt Street" where the houses were sunk halfway into the ground.

Outwardly, the town had nothing to recommend it. But when one of its own people looked at it, an inhabitant who would have experienced the local way of life, the sweet kernel under the external gray husk, the life of the small houses with their cares and joys, it appealed to him with a special zest.

In general, David-Horodok was a unique and interesting town. There were about 18,000 inhabitants of which about 7,000-8,000 were Jews and the remainder were Byelorussians with a small number of Poles.

A hundred years would go by with many assaults and battles with various gangs who would pass, and the life of the town did not change. In general, the relationship between the inhabitants was not bad. During World War I, when Balachowicz and his band entered the town, the Byelorussians saved the Jews from death by hiding them in their own homes. The solidarity of the people was also demonstrated when the Red Army arrived and wanted to requisition the cattle of the Polish landowners. The Jews and the Byelorussians opposed this and they set up armed resistance. The town was

[Page 425]

then visited by a punishment expedition which shot to death the most distinguished people in town. This is how Betzel Yudovitz, of blessed memory, was killed. Later, when the first Poles came into town, also "fine young men," the Polish inhabitants hid many Jews.

Thus, many years passed. Lands were wiped out; regimes changed but in David-Horodok, life flowed on without alteration. Calm reigned – a pleasant calm. Even the "gods" lived at ease…next to the church stood the Jewish synagogues and study-houses and all was normal.

If there were positive qualities in Jewish community life, these were to be found in David-Horodok.

Politically active but with ethical content, all parties and organizations were permeated with feelings of brotherhood. The *Mizrachist* and the Communist would meet in the synagogue on Yom Kippur. There were no great "leaders" – all were equal; young and old stuck to their jobs. Everyone knew his place. It is truly a shame that Sholem Aleichem was never there because he could have found as many original folk themes as in Kasrilevke [Sholem Aleichem's fictional prototype of a shtetl]. Each and every individual was unique. Each one was a living Noah Pandre [heroic fictional character penned by Zalman Schneour] with many similar examples such as Abraml "the bastard," Shia "the kaiser," David "the brilliant," Yude "the scholar," etc. etc.

Simple, unassuming, poor but always cheerful, each with its own wit and mannerisms, one could write a book about them.

One cannot overemphasize their uniqueness and modesty; the most pious wore no ear locks or kaftans; the most intelligent spoke the mother tongue. There were two valuable libraries with the newest books which were read after a hard day's work. Work and culture went hand in hand.

An exemplary youth was brought up in the well-organized Tarbut School – all in the Hebrew language. After the eight classes of school, many of the graduates went elsewhere for higher education. In Pinsk and Vilna, some 100 David-Horodoker youth went to intermediate and high schools. That is the way it was until the war.

Rabbis & Community Leaders

[Page 429]

The Horodoker Dynasty
From the Book on Hassidism

by Dr. Rabinovitz

Translated by Norman Helman z"l

At about the beginning of the nineteenth century, an independent Hassidic dynasty was founded in David-Horodok which is near Pinsk and even nearer to Stolin. Its adherents were known in the vicinity of Pinsk as "Horodoker Hassidim" (to distinguish them from those of Rabbi Menahem Mendl of Vitebsk who went by the same name). This was the smallest branch of the Hassidic dynasties in Polesye and it had a small circle of Hassidim in David-Horodok, Lakve, Luniniatz, Pinsk and Kozanhorodok. Just as the Labashier Hassidim found their place west of Pinsk, between Pinsk and Kobrin, so did the small group of Horodoker Hassidim, east of Pinsk between Pinsk and Lakve. The founder of the dynasty was Rav Wolf who was called by his Hassidim name: Rav Wolftsi (Ginsburg), a son of the tsaddik Rav Shmuel Halevi of Kashivke, a town in Volin not far from the well-known Hassidic centre of Nasvizh.

Rav Schmuel was a close friend of the renowned tsaddik of Volin, Rav Mordehai of Nasvizh. This can be seen from a letter written by Rav Asher of Stolin sometime between 1802 and 1826 indicating that both tzadikim were on friendly terms and were in-laws.

There is no information as to how Rav Wolf founded an independent dynasty in the centre of the Karlin realm. The only Hassidic source that mentions Rav Wolf refers to him as Av Bet Din (head of the rabbinic court). It is also popularly believed that Rav Wolf was first designated as a rabbi in David-Horodok and later, probably because of his lineage, he became a rebbe (Hassidic designation of their rabbi). Details of his personality, life and the exact year of his death are unknown. There are various popular legends regarding his death which testify to his popularity and authority. The legacy of his rabbinical seat went to his son, Rav David. It appears that he had no great influence. For example, Rav David is not mentioned in the short family biography kept by Hassidic sources. Subsequently, Rav David's son, Rav Israel Yosef Halevi, became a central figure in the small Hassidic branch, and he was their rebbe until the end of the nineteenth century. He was a renowned scholar and he led his small congregation of Jews autocratically. Both his fellow townsmen and those from surrounding areas regarded him with great respect. In contrast to the Barazner Hassidim who were mostly common rabble, his Hassidim included many aristocrats, even some from misnagid (rationalists who were usually antagonists of Hassidim) homes. For example: when he would journey to the Horodoker synagogue in Pinsk, his 'table' would be visited by the then Hashuber rebbe, Rav Motis, the community heads, cultural leaders and others.

Rav Israel Yosef had personal dealings with the renowned tsaddik of Volin, Rav Itzhak of Nasvizh. From the letters which Rav Israel Yosef wrote to him (in 1856, 1861 and 1864),

[Page 430]

one can see his spiritual dependence on Rav Itzhak of Nasvizh. With the expression: "I pray and implore that his holiness (Rav Itzhak) not forget us in the future…so that I may rest peacefully in my house…" He refers undoubtedly to the controversy between his Hassidim and the Stolinr Hassidim who regarded the Horodoker Hassidim as inferior.

The liturgical melodies in his Horodok synagogue was called "the rebbe's study-house" were similar to the liturgy in Volin. Rav Israel Yosef died in 1899 and a common tomb enclosed his grave along with the graves of his father and grandfather in the Horodoker cemetery. His descendants had certain renown such as his grandson Rav Itzhak who died in 1908. Rav Itzhak's grandson, Rav Aharon, belonged to the last generation of the dynasty. He occupied the position of rebbe in the neighbouring town of Luniniatz. A second grandson, the last Horodoker rebbe, Rav Moshe was a student at the yeshivas of Volozhin and Lida and a gifted preacher. He was close to the Zionist movement and was held in great esteem by all. He died a martyr at the hands of the Nazi.

Of the writings of the Horodoker tzadikim, nothing remains except the few letters mentioned above. The establishment of a dynasty probably resulted from choosing the son of a Hassidic tzadik as a rabbi who then became both rabbi and rebbe together. This is similar to the manner in which the Libasheier dynasty was established. The small branch of Horodoker Hassidim were bound together solely by the personalities of the tzadikim Rav Wolf and Rav Israel Yosef who enlarged the small number of Hassidim in that narrow corner of Polesye. They remained the only disciples of the Hassidic movement.

[Page 430 - Yiddish] [Page 179 - Hebrew]

Yitzchak Leib Zager

Y. Lifshitz and Sh. Zezik

Translated by Norman Helman z"l

There stands in front of my eyes the small study-house on the "synagogue court" in which Y.L. Zager was raised and lived. A loving warmth would permeate you as you entered this little house. His simple parents would receive you with a permanent smile on their lips.

[Page 431]

The peacefulness, quiet and cleanliness; the love of the people would make you forget that you were in a small lowly house. You would get the feeling of spaciousness. His father, a blacksmith, was a scholar like many other laborers in David-Horodok, and he sent his only son to the *Yeshiva*.

He became instilled with the Zionist ideal along with his fellow *Yeshiva* students such as P. Novak, Sh. Reznik and others. When they organized the first group of the *Tzeirei Zion* movement in David-Horodok, Y.L. Zager proceeded to join them. His boundless devotion and enthusiastic activities soon put him at the head of the movement which he led until the last day of his life.

Y.L. Zager's activities in town were not limited only to the idealistic *Tzeirei Zion* movement and later the *Poalei Zion* party. There was hardly a social institution in the town in which he was not an active leader. In such manner, he devoted much time and energy to the public library named after Y.L. Peretz of which he was one of the founders. The *Keren Kayemet* fund, the charity boxes and especially the orphans' committees were able to exist until the last moment thanks to his ties with America and the trust they had in him.

Y.L. Zager did his communal work with no expectation of reward. His honesty was renowned throughout the town. Characteristically, in all the institutions where he was active, they gave him the office of treasurer. Everyone had complete trust in his notebook where he would inscribe with tiny Rashi script (biblical commentator who invented his own Hebrew script) the revenues and debits of those institutions.

Y.L. Zager knew everyone in town and everyone knew him. People would confide in him and they would come to ask him for help. He would manage the free loan funds and he was always ready to help when he was convinced that the involved individual was in a critical situation. He always knew who was really needy and who not. He was not a talker but a doer.

When in 1938 there was a local election in town, the natural candidate for community leader was Y.L. Zager. The *Poalei Zion* party and the artisans went to the polls with a joint list at the top of which was Y.L. Zager. His popularity in town insured the victory of that list in the balloting. Everyone wanted to see him head of the community. Unfortunately, certain circles paid off the proper people and the list was invalidated on the basis of the infamous paragraph 20 with the resultant embitterment and displeasure of the great majority of the Jewish population.

In the last years, he worked on steamships as agent of his brother-in-law in America. Even here he was the treasurer to the great satisfaction of the partners.

[Page 432]

He died at his work. He drowned while swimming in Nirtcha on Sabbath, August 1, 1939. His death caused great sadness throughout the town.

Funeral of Yitzchak Leib Zager in David-Horodok - 1939

A funeral committee was immediately organized by all the political parties and communal institutions. The funeral took place on the next day – Sunday, August 2 with a large procession composed of the entire Jewish population of the town. At the synagogue court, eulogies were given by representatives of all the parties and communal institutions. His grave was in the same section as all the departed greats of that generation in our town.

The organizational funeral committee selected three people who devised a plan to perpetuate his name by building in his name a house for the orphans' committee and the Y.L. Peretz public library. At the end of the thirty-day mourning period, on September 2, 1939, they proclaimed the campaign to accomplish this goal. Unfortunately, the outbreak of World War II on September 1, 1939 nullified all their plans and they were not even able to erect a stone over his grave.

Perhaps it is symbolic that such a pure and honest soul was not contaminated by the murderous Nazi and local criminal hands.

Yitzchak Leib Zager

[Page 179 – in the Hebrew section]

Eve of the War

[Page 435 - Yiddish] [Page 202 - Hebrew]

My Visit to David-Horodok
On the Eve of the Breaking of WWII

by M. Rappaport

Translated by Norman Helman z"l

I had a great longing to see my town again; visit my parents, relatives and friends, to stroll the streets and byways in the town of my birth and to meet face-to-face all those with whom I was raised, educated and worked many long years.

I had the opportunity just before the outbreak of World War II when I was visiting Poland. It was at the end of August, 1939. All of Europe was permeated with terror and fear of the approaching war. Polish Jewry was especially filled with anxiety and dread. No one knew what the next day would bring. The military censors were very strict and the Jewish press was barely able to inform with hints between the lines what might happen. No one's heart could have predicted how near the Holocaust was and how complete the calamity that was approaching.

We obtained more details at the English consulate in Warsaw including a stern warning that we must leave Poland within 24 hours. These instructions came as an unexpected blow. I asked myself what to do – return without seeing my home, my parents, my friends and acquaintances or to go the dangerous path and realize my dream to see all those that I loved and treasured.

I decided on the perilous course and I ventured to spend a few hours at home. It was dark when I arrived in David-Horodok. I left before dawn.

I will never forget those few hours when my parents' house suddenly became the focal point for all the David-Horodoker Jews. Some came to greet a relative or friend; others came to hear news of the Land. We all felt as if the floor was burning under our feet and a bitter lament was heard from all assembled: what next? How does one escape and where?

I recall how every face beamed when hearing a living greeting from the Land concerning our efforts and struggles, concerning the light and shadows that go along together, concerning ambitious construction work – everything that was being created in our Land. In my conversation, there was a touch of reproach to all those whose place should have been with us

[Page 436]

in our Land but who, unfortunately, had made short-sighted miscalculations which decided their fate.

It was a night of watching. Everyone talked and everyone asked, beginning with Rabbi Shapira of blessed memory, a devoted and faithful Zionist worker who lived to see the Land, and ending with many others. Every little detail interested them: the economic situation, current events, etc.

It was very difficult for me to answer all the questions. The excitement finally subsided when I promised to take part in a meeting the following day when I would discuss all the questions in greater breadth and depth. Unfortunately, this meeting did not take place just as the best dreams and aspirations of my dear countrymen were never realized. The meeting did not occur because I received a telegram at that moment from my wife and from my home authority which said briefly and simply: "because of the strained situation, return immediately".

* * *

There is no solace or compensation for the great calamity, for the killing of all these industrious people, toilers, people of religion and culture, of initiative and boundless devotion to Judaism and Zionism. They were cut off like young twigs by the foreign murderous hands.

The only consolation is the living monument which was established in our Land – in Israel – the hundreds of families of David-Horodoker Jews who were saved with their wives and children and who well up in full-blooded life in all the corners of our Land. They work, create and serve together with all Israeli citizens, like a living sturdy wall for the renewed state.

[Page 436 - Yiddish] [Page 203 - Hebrew]

My Last Days in David-Horodok

by M. Shur Ami

Translated by Norman Helman z"l

The Soviet occupation force had divided the inhabitants into three classes:
1. The trustworthy class: Ex-communists in whom there were found no deviations and those others who openly declared their sympathy for the Bolshevik authority with no one denouncing them.
2. The enemies of the regime: the wealthy and the Zionist activists.
3. Ordinary inhabitants: who would require prolonged re-education with the hope that they would become future citizens of the Soviet Union.

The majority of the David-Horodoker population belonged to the second and third categories. People in the second category who had not been denounced and had not been the subject of an official or unofficial complaint, were automatically transferred to the third category.

In the months of March and April, 1941, hundreds of young people

[Page 437]

were mobilized into "work battalions" and most were sent to construct evacuation centers near the borders of Byelorussia, as for example in Kobrin and Bialystok. I belonged to the Kobrin group.

On June 20, a Jewish lad happened to stand watch at one o'clock at night. He was five minutes late. The commander of the detachment, a Soviet citizen named Gur, quickly alerted the entire detachment and rebuked the lad publicly: "Traitor! If the war broke out tomorrow, would you still be sleeping? In three days, you will stand trial."

In 48 hours, the German-Russian War flared up. Air raids and artillery shelling accompanied us on our way back home. I tried to always be with other David-Horodokers. The confusion was great. We were given contradictory orders. Wherever we turned, there were Germans. We could not retreat during daylight and we were forced to lay in the forests and swamps and run at night. We only had one goal: home!

On June 26, 1941, Friday evening, I arrived in David-Horodok with my unforgettable friend, Moshe Schechter, David's son and Wolf the newspaper salesman's grandson. I did not recognize the town. What David-Horodoker does not recall the hours before the Sabbath? The shopkeepers rush to close their shops and the laborers end their work. The Sabbath candles are lit on all sides and everyone goes to the prayer house with the children. And now it is like the eve of Tisha B'Av. It is pitch black in the streets and on the face of every Jew is the dread of the approaching Germans.

We were soon surrounded by familiar faces and before we could change our filthy clothes, we had to answer all of their questions. They had thought that the entire mobilized group had fallen. The following day, on the Sabbath, others began arriving.

My family was no longer at home. It turned out that they had fled to the Russian border along with a few dozen other families. The following day, on Saturday night, they returned because they were forbidden to cross the border.

The town filled up with refugees from surrounding towns. The fear was intense. The gentiles taunted us: "Jews, your time has passed! The Soviets are leaving here."

Confusion reigned everywhere. One day the masses were mobilized and the next day they were all set free because of a lack of communication. The last mobilized group was sent to Minsk on June 28.

We friends met to decide on where to go next and the opinions were divided. Moshe Schechter was among those who decided to stay. Yitzchak Gelman and I decided to go. We informed our families and our former companions in the Zionist youth movement whose attitudes had not been swayed. The majority refused to go.

On July 6, the last Soviet officials left town. With no prearrangement, we 20 boys and girls found ourselves

[Page 438]

on Olshaner Street. Along the way, we met several other youth who did not want to join us, saying that "the Germans are no worse than the Russians. We will also adjust to the new regime."

When we reached the border, the guards refused to let us pass. No argument would help. Several became demoralized. Yitzchak Gelman, Miriam Frenkel, Tzirel Begun and Shoshana Eisenberg returned home.

One of our group, who was born in a border village, agreed to lead us by backroads and cross the border at night. Barely men, we went to the south of Malishev. At night, we encountered an armed patrol which happened to contain former officials from our town. The patrol commander was Rachlin, who had been the Communist Party secretary in David-Horodok. He wanted us to understand that he would agree to give us a place near his camp and he promised that he would give us a solution in the morning if he could get weapons for us.

It was a night of horror. We could see fires in our town in the distance. The Germans had already been there and had begun plundering.

In the morning, the droshke returned from Turov with the partisans. We were soon called to the commander. "I could not get any weapons," he said, "but you may pass. The matter has been arranged with the commander of the border guards."

We rushed forward and did not encounter a single living soldier.

Hearing the German advance, they had all run away. Within sight of Turov, we could see a truck coming towards us at a distance, loaded with soldiers and machine guns. We did not know if they were Russians or Germans. There was a cemetery to the left. We hid among the grave stones. After the truck had passed, we set forward again. By nightfall, we had arrived in Turov on genuine Soviet soil.

The Last Day and the Last Hour

[Page 441 - Yiddish] [Page 208 - Hebrew]

The Last Days and the Last Hours

Described by Bat-Sheva Kushnir and Gronim Pelavin

Translated by Norman Helman z"l

On July 5, 1941, the Germans entered David-Horodok. Several weeks before the capture of the town, local Christians headed by Maraiko, Kulaga and Latun, may their names be blotted out, succeeded in creating the impression that the town Jews were waiting for the Red Army to return. As a result, the Christians received permission from the SS headquarters in Pinsk to handle the Jews at their own discretion.

On August 10, at 4 o'clock in the morning, all the Jewish quarters were surrounded. All Jewish men and children eight years of age and older were brought forsaken and barefoot to the concentration point in the courtyard of the Catholic Church – and from there to their last journey.

Yaakov, Aba Gertzulin's son, the only Jew who had been forewarned by a Christian of the fate of those who were being sent away, tried to escape. A murderer's bullet stopped him and he died on the spot. All roads were blocked and there was no possibility of escape.

From the concentration point, the Jews were sent to two common graves which had previously been prepared. When the Jews came to the ditches, they were instructed to undress and climb down into the ditches where they were shot to death with machine guns.

A group of Jews were spared from the murder and they were used to sort the fallen bodies in the trenches. Afterwards, they were also murdered. After the murder, the trenches were filled in by the local people who took part in the killing.

Only a few managed to hide out by various means, but eventually they too met the same horrible fate.

Nachman Yonush, Yosef's son, Itche the milkman's grandson, succeeded in escaping through the village of Berezhnoye and reached Stolin. He hid in their ghetto for a year until he was killed along with the Jews of Stolin.

Yaakov, Litman Kolozny's son and Moshe Elianik's grandson, hid for several days until a Christian informed on him. They dragged him to the Gestapo and tortured him until he was finally relieved with a bullet.

Reb Aharon Slomiansky, who had been hidden several days by a Christian, was forced to leave his hiding place because the Christian was afraid they would kill him for hiding a Jew. Having no other alternative, Reb Aharon decided to return home. As he crossed the bridge, gentiles grabbed him and threw him into the river. He immediately drowned. Thanks to his wife Rachel who exerted superhuman efforts, he was buried in the Jewish cemetery.

Simcha, Moshe Aharon Mishalov's son, hid for two weeks in his cellar but the Christian servant gave him over to the gentiles. They dragged him out of the cellar

[Page 442]

and murdered him in his house in front of his wife and children.

Isser, Nissan Gurevitz's son, hid in a clothing closet. The local citizens found him, pulled him out and dragged him into the marketplace. They beat him and tortured him viciously and put out his eyes. His inhuman screaming was heard from one end of the town to the other. He pleaded with his murderers to end his life.

Reb Kahas, Reb Sander Belohousky's son, and Reb Moshe, Reb Avraham Baruchin the Choromsker's son, hid until 1943 in a nearby village with a Christian peasant. They dreamt that Rabbi Moshele, the

Stoliner Rebbe, was yet alive. They crawled out of their hiding place and they went off to Stolin. Gentiles killed them along the way.

Reuven, Chaim Kolozny's son, hid in his yard. The gentiles found him, killed him and threw him into the outdoor privy.

Baruch-Yosef, Moshe Katzman's son, and his two sons hid out somewhere. They had nothing to eat and so they presented themselves to the Gestapo. There they were told that the Gestapo had no liquidation decree concerning them and they could go where they wished! However, the local citizens beat them to death with sticks in the marketplace.

Yitzchak, the son of Shlomo the Ozdanicher, remained alive thanks to a Christian who hid him after he promised to marry her. When the Red Army returned, he fulfilled his promise.

* * *

After the mass murder and on a cold and rainy day, they also drove the women and children out of the town. The local citizens chased after them for several kilometers with shouts of "Get out! We don't need you!"

Amongst the women there were several men who dressed in women's clothes. One of these was Rabbi Moshele, Rabbi Velvele Ginzburg's son. The local citizens, who were examining the faces of the refugees, recognized him. They pulled him out and murdered him.

Vigdor's daughter Leah, Reb Moshe Kolozny's wife, no longer had the strength to go on with the exiles and she sat down next to Chaim Baruchin's house. She was killed on the spot.

Chaya, Reb Asher Yudovitz's daughter, seeing what was happening, picked her child up and jumped with him into the Horyn River.

Feigele, Betzel Yudovitz's wife, and Rivka, Motel Bregman's wife, and her daughters remained almost to the end. But as soon as they had given up all their gold and silver, they were chased to the Olshaner Bridge and were murdered there.

A portion of the exiles arrived at the ghettos in Lakhva, Stolin and Visotzk. They had drunk their cups of bitterness and they were liquidated along with all the Jews in these ghettos.

[Page 443]

Three weeks after the women were driven from town, they were allowed to return into a newly created ghetto which existed for a year. Afterwards, they were sent to the same place where the men had been killed and they were murdered.

A Visit to the *Shtetl* After the Holocaust

Yitzchak Nachmanovitz

Translated by Norman Helman z"l

The year 1939 arrived. The town was taken by the Soviets. Many Jewish refugees from western Poland settled in David-Horodok.

In 1940, they began arresting and exiling Zionists and others. The town shuddered. The mood was strained. Still, there was the motto: "All for one and one for all."

Then July 6, 1941 arrived. The town was captured by Hitler's troops. Many Jews wanted to save themselves in Russia but the NKVD and the border guards would not let them pass and so they were forced to remain under Nazi rule. Then began the horror and the murderous faces of the Byelorussians were shown. They began catching Jews in the streets and forcing them to do labor.

Many of Hitler's troops passed through the streets of the town heading east. A few days later, they returned because of the bad roads intending to find another path through the marshes. In town, it was rumored that the Germans had been driven back by the Red Army. This was exploited by the newly proclaimed mayor, the villainous *feldsher* (medic) Ivan Maraiko who went to Gestapo headquarters in Pinsk and reported that the Jews were spreading the rumors and that they – the Jews – were attacking the German army. This vile slander brought on the bloody 17th of Av of 1941, about one month after the Germans had captured the town. In the beginning of August, about 50 SS murderers arrived unexpectedly. At 4 o'clock in the morning they surrounded the town and later began their bloody work with the help of the local Byelorussian underworld that had enlisted as police. Anticipating abundant booty, they began driving together all the Jewish men. They gathered everyone at the courtyard of the church and accompanied them with frightful beatings with sticks and guns.

There, they were forced to remain on their knees with their hands upraised for an hour until all the houses were searched. Whoever was found hiding was shot to death on the spot. That was the fate of the brothers Isser and Hershel Gurevitz – two healthy and sturdy young men who were pulled out of a hiding place. As they were led away, their ribs were broken and their eyes gouged out.

After all the men were assembled, they were arranged in columns and led out

[Page 444]

of the town. No one knew where they were going. They presumed that they were being led to work. However, the question was quickly answered.

Three kilometers beyond the town on the Olshaner road, on a hill of sand, the peasants had prepared a freshly dug trench. It was already too late to consider resistance. Besides, in 1941, there had not yet been any mass murders of Jews so that quiet and respectable, decent people could not believe that such a thing could occur. But it did – the last word belonged to the machine guns… and then, with a last breath, each sent a curse…

A policeman tried to pull the ring off the hand of Leizer Ronkin thinking that he was already dead. But the latter was able to raise himself up and spat at the murderer's face. With a curse on his lips, he fell dead.

So did the Mother Earth take in and hide you in eternal rest.

Honor to your memory, my brothers!

For your unassuming, difficult but decent lives, the "civilized" world has rewarded you with "a quick death."

* * *

That same afternoon, after the murderers had completed their "little job", they again went to "work". All the remaining women and children received an order that they were to immediately leave town. In this particular "holy" work, the entire Christian population took part. Young and old, all like wild specters, they went to the Jewish houses with sticks and they drove out the housewives and their children with beatings, expecting to rob them of their possessions.

They drove them out of town with beatings and verbal abuse. "Despised Jews," raged the aroused, looting crowd. Many of them stood at the bridge checking each Jewish woman to see if they could find a man disguised in women's clothing.

In such fashion, they discovered several men in women's clothes including Rabbi Moshele, Berl Migdalovitz and others who were viciously beaten by the wild mob and then shot to death. The women and children were accompanied with beatings until they reached the outskirts.

The unfortunates went as far as the first village of Choromsk after which they strayed through the fields, hungry, beaten and exhausted, many of them pregnant, sick and old, women with suckling babies, torn away from their husbands and fathers, desolate and forsaken in a land of wild animals. One of the better peasants would occasionally give a piece of bread or a potato.

[Page 445]

Some of them went to new towns such as Stolin, Lakhva, Visotzk and others. There they shared the bitter fate of those Jewish inhabitants. The remainder strayed and wandered over the dirty and muddy roads of Polesye. There was the constant danger of encountering further mental humiliation and physical abuse.

Autumn arrived with its damp and cold weather. Many women and children died along the roads. Every bush and tree along the way knew of their suffering. Finally, at the end of autumn, they were allowed back into David-Horodok where a ghetto had been created for them. Life in this ghetto was appalling. The entire population of the ghetto received ten kilos of bread per day and most of them had to work for the German army. They were forced to do a variety of jobs.

Many working women and children were overcome by hunger and inhuman conditions and they died. Those that remained hardly resembled human beings.

They were isolated, swollen with hunger, encircled by barbed wire in a small part of a filthy quarter, guarded by the murderous police who was headed by a creature with a rotten soul – Liava Kasarev – may his name be blotted out. He worshipped many gods. But he was particularly attracted to "shiny buttons" [officers] for whom this beast in the form of a person was prepared to do anything.

So the ghetto existed until the eve of Rosh Hashanah in 1942. On that day, the ghetto was liquidated.

All the women and children, the number was no longer very great, no more than 1600 souls – accompanied by beatings from the police as well as a special group of SS horsemen, were driven to the same trench on the Olshaner hill. There, everyone was stripped naked and shot to death.

Once again, Mother Earth opened her arms and received for the men their wives and children.

Thus was the innocent Jewish David-Horodok taken from the earth and ceased to exist.

The abandoned homes were taken possession by their "new owners", but not for long. For later, when large partisan bands began to operate in the vicinity, they assaulted the town a few times and burnt most of the Jewish houses.

* * *

I came to David-Horodok in August, 1944. I found mounds with overgrown grass in place of the houses. Instead of joyous laughter and childish playful screaming, places that once had beckoned with the glow of their homely warmth, now presented a fierce and frightening picture.

Every remaining house, every tree that stood like a solitary wounded limb – cries, screams, laments and anxiously asks: Where are the gray and respectable old folks who would rest in our shade? Where has the happy laughter fled,

[Page 446]

the tender feelings, the curlyheaded children? Why is all that was beautiful and loving gone? And many, many more whys?

No answer came. I cannot find it. From the dentist Edel's house to the church hill – not one remaining house, only wild grass… mounds and grass.

Someone appeared… moving about like a wild apparition… he doesn't look me in the eyes… with dirty bare feet in a good black pullover with silk lapels. He doesn't speak... no one here talks now… They know nothing... They did hear about something but they don't remember exactly…

What's the use of talking? It is better to be quiet in a cemetery. A woman sells second-hand children's clothes in the marketplace. The woman keeps silent but the clothing cries – cries with pitiful tears!

I came to the holiest place for me in the entire world – to the mass grave. A smooth, sandy field – four years later! Four long years after fire and blood. Years of home-sickness close by; for finally coming to the home which was so near... Where are the loving mother's arms? Where are the coveted friendly faces – gleaming with pleasure at each encounter?

Member of our town Yitzchak Nachmanovitz is digging a pit to bury the bones of the martyrs found in the common grave

[Page 447]

No one kisses. No one shakes my hand. I stand shattered, dismayed and waiting, but in vain in this small arid field – a town is hidden. No markers, no monument tablets, no inscriptions, no flowers. A strange and heart-rending silence.

It remains a secret of nature. How much human beauty and dignity, how much love and friendship, how much creative initiative and talent was so cruelly, murderously and prematurely transported to eternal rest? Here, thousands of women, men and children released their pure souls and under the noise of the murderers' machine guns they sounded their last protest – a curse – a curse on the "culture" and the heads of the murderers as well as on the leaders and presidents, socialists and democrats, in uniforms and in dress coats. A curse on the heads of those who travelled to Munich, London, Paris or Moscow in white gloves, selling children's souls and trading with the blood and flesh of innocent people.

* * *

The 17th of Av! Today is the sad day of your downfall, my David-Horodok. Your life was unassuming and full of service and perhaps that is why you were "rewarded" with a quick demise. You went like a pioneer to the sacrifice on the altar of the people. The number of your fortuitously spared sons is small. There are approximately 100 men who are now widely separated. In bitter spirit, we kneel and bow our heads in deep sorrow for you, our beloved and unforgettable David-Horodok.

Dear martyrs! Mothers, fathers, sisters and brothers as well as your beloved children! The 17th of Av is engrained deep into my heart, never to be forgotten. On that day, no smile is seen and joy vanishes from the heart. My mind burns with the realization of helplessness and the lost opportunity for a full revenge.

Rest forever, my dear ones.

May your holy memory be forever.No one kisses. No one shakes my hand. I stand shattered, dismayed and waiting, but in vain in this small arid field – a town is hidden. No markers, no monument tablets, no inscriptions, no flowers. A strange and heart-rending silence.

It remains a secret of nature. How much human beauty and dignity, how much love and friendship, how much creative initiative and talent was so cruelly, murderously and prematurely transported to eternal rest? Here, thousands of women, men and children released their pure souls and under the noise of the murderers' machine guns they sounded their last protest – a curse – a curse on the "culture" and the heads of the murderers as well as on the leaders and presidents, socialists and democrats, in uniforms and in dress coats. A curse on the heads of those who travelled to Munich, London, Paris or Moscow in white gloves, selling children's souls and trading with the blood and flesh of innocent people.

* * *

The 17th of Av! Today is the sad day of your downfall, my David-Horodok. Your life was unassuming and full of service and perhaps that is why you were "rewarded" with a quick demise. You went like a pioneer to the sacrifice on the altar of the people. The number of your fortuitously spared sons is small. There are approximately 100 men who are now widely separated. In bitter spirit, we kneel and bow our heads in deep sorrow for you, our beloved and unforgettable David-Horodok.

Dear martyrs! Mothers, fathers, sisters and brothers as well as your beloved children! The 17th of Av is engrained deep into my heart, never to be forgotten. On that day, no smile is seen and joy vanishes from the heart. My mind burns with the realization of helplessness and the lost opportunity for a full revenge.

Rest forever, my dear ones.

May your holy memory be forever.

Editor's note:

Yitzchak (Itzl) Nachmanovitz was in the Soviet Union during World War II. Immediately after the end of the war, he visited David-Horodok as a Red Army soldier and he saw the destruction of the town with his own eyes. He now lives in the United States of America. The above description was written in 1946 on the fifth anniversary of the destruction of David-Horodok Jewry. At that time, he was visiting the German concentration camps and in September, 1946, he published "A Home" in the Yiddish paper. We republish this description with small deletions.

Impressions

Reported by Meir Hershel Korman[i]

Translated by Norman Helman z"l

Bas-Sheva Lin, Meir Eliyahu Kushnir's niece, was the only one of all the David-Horodokers who I found in David-Horodok when I returned after Rosh Hashanah 5705 [1944].

The water carrier who had worked for me for four years did not recognize me. Her house was filled with Jewish goods.

The water carrier sent me to

[Page 448]

a second gentile who had taken possession of Litman Nachmanowitz's house. The gentile told me that the David-Horodoker gentiles had received awards from the German authorities for their part in killing and exterminating the Jewish population.

On the following day, I requested a home from the local authorities. When they suggested that I live in a Jewish house, I rejected the idea and I requested permission to live in my former butcher shop. My request was rejected. Not knowing this, I fixed up my butcher shop as a home. Later, the authorities helped me to set up a grocery store.

Also later, Noach, the son of Bezalel Yudovitz, came to David-Horodok. He had been wounded and walked on crutches. He received material and medical help from the Soviets and he helped me personally.

Later on, Zeev Shalom Lachovsky and Moshe, son of Yisrael Reznik, returned to Horodok.

* * *

The first Jewish victim in David-Horodok was Meir Eliyahu Kushnir who had lived in Raditch [the gentile section of David-Horodok]. After they had driven him out of his house, the *Horodtchukas* [Christians of Tartar descent from David-Horodok] attacked him and murdered him in the marketplace in the middle of the day.

The second victim was Zeev, the son of Grunya Kunda, a grandson of Velvel the blacksmith. The gentiles murdered him on Olshan Street next to Shlomo Fleishman's house.

On the 17th of Av, 5701, the Jewish men were concentrated in front of the church and they were sent from there to a place where the *Horodtchukas* had prepared a common grave. It is very difficult to imagine the brutal acts and the atrocities that the *Horodtchukas* carried out against the Jews in the last minutes before they murdered them.

They stripped the clothes off the victims, smashed heads, cut off limbs and slaughtered with whatever came to hand: sticks, stones, iron bars and guns. Afterwards, they threw them into the trenches and buried them alive! Three days after the mass murder, the ground still stirred.

The leader of the pogrom was the medic, Ivan Maraiko, who made a special trip to Pinsk in order to bring back the SS. Before traveling to Pinsk, he gathered gold and silver from the Jews who entrusted him to hide their valuables.

After the aktion, the gentiles began searching for Jews in hiding. The first to be discovered was Avraham Slutzky, the wagon driver, and next was Mendel the Bratsker's son, who had hidden in the garden amongst the beans. They were both immediately murdered.

Reuven Kolozny hid in the closet of his gentile neighbor, Markovitz. He was murdered on the spot and remained there.

[Page 449]

Baruch Katzman and his two sons were found and killed by Dimitry Pozik.

Isser, son of Nissan Gurevitz, had his eyes gouged out by the *Horodtchukas* and his limbs severed one by one!

Yehoshua Zager of Tury, who had hidden in an oven, was pulled out and murdered.

Aharon Slomiansky was thrown into the Horyn River. Thanks to the efforts of his wife Rachel, he was pulled out by hired gentiles and merited burial in the Jewish cemetery.

My two children, Bracha and Baruch, who, thanks to a gentile woman, had fled to the Dubinitz Forest, were returned to town by the gentiles and cut to pieces in the middle of the marketplace. My son Yaakov succeeded in escaping.

Simcha Mishalov hid four months in his own cellar. His gentile maid fed him the entire four months. She then informed on him and he was murdered on Greble Street. Before his soul returned to G-d he was heard to cry out: "Scoundrels, what are you doing?

A son of Berl Schmutz, who was dressed as a woman, was recognized by the gentiles and murdered by them.

After the men had been slaughtered, the Jewish women of David-Horodok were driven out of town. A portion died along the way. The remnant that later returned to Horodok were murdered by the gentiles a year later and they were thrown into the same trenches as the men.

The daughter of Rabbi Moshele became a partisan in the forests of Wysokie. She fell in battle.

Golda Rachel, Meir Eliyahu Kirzner's wife, hid in the chapel in the village of Choromsk where she was later killed.

Shmuel Katzman, a son of Leibel Katzman, moved about in the forest of Orly for four months. The gentiles caught him there and hacked him to pieces.

Nishka, Chaim Kirzner's wife, along with three other women hid themselves in a stable and that is where they were killed.

Leah, Moshe Kolozny's wife, was killed by the gentiles on the Greble Bridge. The gentiles planned to kill me. One night, a representative of the gentiles came to kill me. I began to scream and the police soon came and saved me.

At last, I could no longer stay in David-Horodok because of the hatred of the gentiles and I ran away.

Coordinator's Footnote:

i. This article is very similar to the article "In David-Horodok in 1945" by Meir Tzvi Korman on pages 229-230 in the Hebrew section. Both were written by the same person (Tzvi in Hebrew and Hershel in Yiddish are equivalent names.) However, each article contains unique information, so both have been included.

Partisan Stories

[Page 453 - Yiddish] [Page 215 - Hebrew]

1. Colonel Satanovski [i]

by Chaim Hochman

Translated by Norman Helman z"l

Chaim Hochman

[Page 215 - in the Hebrew section]

We found ourselves in the vicinity of the village of Kripna not far from Pinsk, in thick forests. We had been prepared for many days to move to another spot but meanwhile, we did not move.

Where were we moving and, most important, what were we waiting for? This apparently was the commander's secret.

Our woman officer, for whom I was the driver, told me the deepest secret; that we were waiting for an airplane coming here from Moscow with important people. They should have been here four days ago and no one knew why they were late.

What had happened? Did they meet with some misfortune? A few hours after the lady officer told me this story, our detachment began to move out. We traveled the entire night and by day; we remained in a large and thick forest containing deep mud. This was our provisional headquarters and residence.

We received the order to set up cabins and although it was already late autumn (a month after Sukkot 1943), we were not allowed to light a fire. An officer, husband of the lady officer, came to our wagon with their child and told us that the parachutists had finally arrived but that they had met with misfortune. Three of them died on their way to join the detachment. A peasant from the village of Tereblichi had betrayed them.

The forest in which our detachment now stood was near the large village of Karatzke-Valya. The population of the village were friendly to the partisans and headquarters gave permission to light fires during the day for cooking and baking.

That same day, there was an assembly and the commander of the detachment, Colonel Satanovski, gave the partisans and the refugees instructions concerning their behavior. The chief directive was that, with the exception of those partisans who were sent on terrorist actions against the Germans, no one was to leave the area. Whoever disobeyed the command would be shot on the spot, without a trial.

Before finishing these instructions, he turned to the assembly: "Comrades, whoever comes from or is familiar with the region of David-Horodok, Stolin and Turov, let him report to me in my headquarters after the assembly."

I went into staff headquarters and reported to the commander that I knew David-Horodok well, as well as a little of the vicinity.

"Tell me comrade Hochman, do you know where the villages of Ozdanichi, Tereblichi and Korotichi are located?"

"Yes," I answer. He asked me to stand aside and he interrogated the second partisan who entered headquarters right after me.

[Page 454]

"Where are you from, comrade?" "From the village of Bukcha," answered the partisan. "It is far from David-Horodok, but we peasants often went there and that is why I know the region."

"Why did you join our detachment?" continued the commander in his line of questioning.

"Because I want to fight the Germans," was the partisan's answer. "Listen, comrade!" as the commander turned to the partisan, "perhaps there is a Jew in our detachment who knows you?" "Not in our detachment," again replied the partisan, "but there are Jews in Fyodorov's detachment nearby who know me from home. Ask them about me."

Contact was quickly made with Fyodorov's detachment and the answer returned that the partisan was a fine and upstanding man and that there was no danger of his being a traitor.

After a brief interval, there came 10 young men into the commander's headquarters. They were strong and jovial partisans. Later, German battle uniforms were brought in. All the partisans except for me took off their partisan clothes and donned the sparkling new German battle uniforms. They even had not forgotten to put crosses on their necks. One of the partisans put on the uniform of a German officer. He was one of the ten who had come from Moscow and had perfect command of the German language.

All the weapons – rifles, machine guns and grenades – with which these "Germans" were armed were German-made. Even the cigarettes were German. I dressed up in traditional Jewish clothes concealing a revolver and several hand grenades. The "German officer" gave me the following directions:

"In case we encounter Germans or police along the way, we will say that we caught you hiding out in the forest. After we beat you up (signs of the beating were immediately provided. They cut one of my fingers and smeared the blood on my face and hair), you are taking us to the place where many other Jews are hidden."

The commander ordered us not to leave headquarters and not to show ourselves to anyone. Halfway through the night, we were ready for our journey. The "German officer" turned to us with the following words: "Comrade partisans! A short time ago we were boarding an airplane in Moscow to come and join your partisan detachment. Along with the pilot, we were thirteen men.

[Page 455]

Near the Pripyat River, not far from Mikashevitz, we were chased and shot at by German airplanes. When our plane was set on fire, we jumped out with our parachutes. Luckily, we all landed safely near the village of Tereblichi. After we searched and found each other, we went into a peasant's hut in the village and we asked him for the way to the hamlet of Mairlin. The peasant showed us the way assuring us that there were no Germans or police in the entire region. While we were checking the route with our map, it turned out that the peasant was at that moment informing on us. We started along the road, thanking and blessing the peasant and his family.

In half an hour, we were accosted by men who called out: 'Halt! Put your hands up' and they began shouting at us. Three of our comrades were killed on the spot. We immediately opened fire and heard the screaming and groaning from the wounded on their side.

With that, the clash in the small forest ended. Crawling on all fours, we tried to reach a different and larger forest. Along the way, we stumbled on a body that was choking with pain cause by one of our bullets. He was wounded on both feet. This wounded policeman irately cursed the peasant Karp who had awaked the police from sleep and chased after the partisans along with them. We choked the policeman to death," continued the "German officer", "and after several days of wandering through swamps and forests, we reached your detachment, exhausted. Now," proposed the "officer", "we are going to bring that peasant back here. We must take revenge against such a cowardly dog!

"In truth, there are more important targets for our partisans," noted the "officer". "Our entire energy must be concentrated against the accursed Germans but we are consumed with resentment and anger that one of our own peasants, flesh of our flesh, spilled the blood of his own brothers and betrayed his own people to the German murderers like a servile dog. We will bring him back here to the detachment. We will bring him back here dead or alive, that traitor-murderer, so that partisan blood will not be spilled wantonly."

Following the words of our group leader, we set out on our way. We wandered through forests, swamps and fields for three nights until we arrived at the village of Korotichi.

After our "Germans" found out that there were only five policemen in the village, we all went into the police station. Our "officer" informed the policemen that his group was specially selected to

[Page 456]

effect the liquidation of the remaining Jews who were hiding in the forests. Pointing at me, the "officer" said that his captured Jew would show us the place where many Jews were hiding.

In order to undertake such a holy task, they would have to mobilize the police of Korotichi, Tereblichi and Ozdanichi.

After all the policemen of Korotichi had been mustered together, we all went to Tereblichi. In the Tereblichi police station, which was a private house, all the Tereblichi policemen were assembled, including the peasant Karp. Two policemen were dispatched by the "officer" to Ozdanichi with orders to return with that village's police.

The "officer" spoke Russian amongst the policemen and scolded them for their lack of vigilance. "It appears," he roared with a thundering voice, "that within 10 kilometers or so from your posts there are so many Jews still hidden. How is it possible? No small thing – so many Jews!" he repeated.

Concluding his talk to the police he turned to his "German" comrades and talked to them in German.

The policemen began to reply saying that it was not their fault that there were still a few living Jews hidden here or there. Each one of them had done his utmost to exterminate the hated Jews. They hadn't rested day or night, searching very corner, catching women, children and men, murdering all without mercy.

They then described a litany of gruesome acts which each one had performed. Each story was more horrible and appalling than the preceding one. In such manner, listening to these vile tales of murder, we passed the time. The night was dark and cloudy but it was coming to an end.

We partisans shivered; the ground was burning under our feet. We were anxious to get back into the forest before they found out that we were partisans. Everyone held his weapon tightly in his hand. Everyone was restless and impatient.

Only the "officer", the oldest of the group, was calm and in no hurry. He alone was smoking and he offered cigarettes, German cigarettes, to all the police. He listened patiently to all of their horror stories, kept company with them and, at the same time, he threw in "innocent" questions: "Well, and what have you been doing about partisans? You eat, drink and sleep and you don't catch partisans? Shame on you!"

Then the peasant Karp spoke. He told how approximately 10 days previously he delivered a group of partisans into the hands of the police. "Unfortunately," he said, "there were not enough police and only three partisans were killed while the others managed to escape into the forest. Four policemen fell in this matter. As for myself," boasted the peasant Karp, "I barely escaped with my life.

[Page 457]

I hid in a ditch and laid there until the partisans had left. For this deed of mine," he explained, "I received a beautiful reward from the town commandant in David-Horodok: two milk-cows and much clothing from the dead Jews."

Outside, daylight appeared. The peasant woman was already up and her children were beginning to awaken. The peasant woman took a pot of soup out of the oven and she and the children began to eat. I stretched out my hand to the woman and begged her for a little soup. She poured a full bowl of warm soup and gave it to me. Just as I began to eat, the eldest of the group, the "German officer", came over to me, pulled the bowl out of my hands and said: "Did the good woman give this to you? In that case, eat!" Having finished speaking, he poured the entire bowl of soup over my head. The "Germans" and policemen responded to this "heroic" act with shrills of laughter. There was indescribable joy and cheer. All were pleased with the "brilliant" occurrence.

Abruptly, we heard the sound of voices. The door swung open and the two messengers entered along with the eight policemen from Ozdanichi. The policemen greeted each other joyfully. They shook hands, chatted and eventually told the story of how the "German group leader" had poured the bowl of soup over my head.

I sat in a corner, covered from head to foot with the remains of the flour and potato soup. My face and hands were streaked with blood and I made myself cry …

Our group leader, the "officer" whispered secretive orders to the police commanders and the peasant Karp …

The peasants of the village on learning that we were going on such a holy mission to catch Jews, brought us considerable food such as eggs, butter, pork, bread and a considerable number of whiskey flasks. The "officer" ordered us to begin our journey.

Each man quickly packed a share of the food into his rucksack and began walking along the road which led to the right of the woods of the village of Kalk.

We went through thick forests of small trees. Along the way, the police asked me about the hidden Jews. They were interested to know if there were any rich ones and if there were any young women. They were greatly encouraged and pleased by my answers. I told them that they would find everything there: much money, gold, jewels and especially young and beautiful women …

[Page 458]

After having marched for three hours, our "officer" told us to stop. "We must," he said, "have a rest and a bite to eat." All the weapons were stacked together in piles of three. We sat down and began to feast. They ate and drank whiskey without end and "out of the goodness of their hearts", they even gave me plenty to eat. Meanwhile, the "officer" took out a map and showed the already half-drunk policemen the place where they would find the Jews with their cabins. Naturally, this place was very, very near …

Encouraged that they were very close to their goal, and imagining the "juicy morsel" that awaited them, the policemen again renewed their drinking. At the end of the meal, the policemen laid down to rest on one side and all the "Germans" on the opposite side. Peasant Karp and a completely inebriated policeman were sent to guard me and the weapons … In a few minutes, all the police fell into a deep sleep.

The "Germans" quickly awoke from their "sleep". They took up the loaded guns and in seconds all the policemen were shot to death. Only one person was "spared" – peasant Karp. He was to be brought back alive to the detachment in order to hand him over to the parachutists whose three companions had been killed through Karp's treachery.

On the tenth day we returned to our detachment. The same day that we returned, Karp was hung. On searching his belongings, we found a pocket watch with a Hebrew inscription. The inscription read: "In memory of the wedding of Dov Farber". This watch was a wedding gift to Berl Farber from his father-in-law.

* * *

The detachment commander Satanovski was happy at our return. He received us joyfully and said that he had had a premonition that our mission would succeed.

He said that our group leader, the "officer", was one of our best and cleverest sons of Russia. He knew ten languages including perfect German, he was an able diplomat and well-qualified for such missions.

"Yet," said the commander Satanovski, "during the entire ten days that you were away, I was restless and could not sleep. Who knows – war is war and anything can happen!"

"Friends," said our commander, "you are tired from the strain and from the journey. Each of you gets three days furlough. However, I am also giving you the following order: No one is to know where you have been and what you have done. For disobeying this order, you will receive the severest of war-time punishment."

Coordinator's footnote:

i.   This article is equivalent to the article in the Hebrew section "Among the Partisans in the Vicinity of David-Horodok" on pages 215-217.

[Page 459 -Yiddish] [Page 222 - Hebrew]

2. Rosh Hashanah of 1943 in the Partisan Detachment[i]

by Chaim Hochman

Translated by Norman Helman z"l

The Polish partisan detachment "Kościuszko" which numbered some 300 Poles and 8 Jews, was in the vicinity of the large village of Molczyca (about eighty kilometers from Pinsk) in large and thick forests deep with swamps.

The detachment had under its protection a camp of relatives consisting of about one hundred Polish families who had fled the slaughters caused by the Ukrainians. There were also a number of Jewish souls in the camp, unfortunate remnants of the tens of thousands of Jews who were cruelly murdered by the Germans along with the Ukrainians and Byelorussians.

I was appointed by the staff to act as driver for the families of the partisan fighters. The detachment would not stay in one place for very long. We would often change locations in the forests.

On the eve of Rosh Hashanah 1943, a camp Jew came to the commander of the detachment with a request that they be allowed to hold communal services on the following day in a nearby barn in the forest. The commander was a young, healthy and handsome man who spoke and wrote Polish well and who had arrived by airplane from Moscow a month earlier with the ten other Polish parachutists.

The commander spoke little and was unusually stern. No one had yet seen a smile on his handsome face. His orders to the partisans as well as to the camp refugees were always brief and curt. He had traitors and informers shot without mercy. We Jews began to notice a good streak in his character as soon as he arrived at the detachment. That is, he ordered that his food and kitchen overseers should not abuse anyone by lessening their food rations so that the Jewish refugees would receive just as much as the Polish and Russian refugees.

On the morning of Rosh Hashanah, the commander sent for the Jews who had asked him permission on the previous day to pray together in congregation. He answered with a smile that had not been seen on his face since his arrival:

"If you think that your G-d will help you as a result of your prayers, then go entreat him. My god," he said holding his weapon against his heart, "is my gun and my grenade. The German murderers understand that language better and it reaches them faster. Your pleas and prayers reach your G-d just about as much as they reach the Germans. But pray, and entreat your G-d as much as your hearts' desire. I have no right to hinder your religious feelings. Pray as much as you like, but let it be quiet."

All the Jews, except for the Jewish partisans on duty, came to pray. There was only one tallis and one *machzor* which a Plotnitzer Jew had taken along with

[Page 460]

him when he fled from the slaughter. He wrapped himself in the tallis and prayed while the others, the remnant of tens of thousands of Jews who were murdered, slaughtered and buried alive, were choked with tears, pounding their heads against the walls and sobbing in violent spasms.

Human words are too poor to describe these heart-rending scenes, when close to thirty unfortunate Jews, men, women and children, desolate, lonely and orphaned, vented their tears and their rage over their great misfortune.

Many Polish refugees from the camp and partisans from the detachment gathered around the barn. Many of them cried along with the Jews. Who knows what was oppressing them? Perhaps they were regretting what role they may have had in helping the Germans kill the parents, husbands, wives and children of these Jews that were here and praying now.

When the cantor, a good singer with a hearty voice and a pained heart, began saying the *Hineni heani* prayer, the tears literally flooded the barn. At that moment, the detachment commander, Colonel Satanovski, came riding up quickly on his horse. He requested a short intermission in the prayers and, seated on his horse, he said the following:

"Comrades! Why are you crying? We are still alive, so what is there to cry about? The Germans are retreating thanks to the severe beatings rendered by the brave Red Army on all fronts. It won't be long now before Russian soldiers will be strolling the streets of Berlin, over the entire accursed German land and over the dead bodies of the German murderers. The day of vengeance is near! However, our partisan situation today is not better but somewhat worse than before. We must increase our vigilance. The Germans will be hard to displace. We and all the other courageous partisan detachments have destroyed all the bridges and railway lines. The Germans find themselves in a desperate situation. They know that the partisans are now their greatest danger. Therefore, they have dispatched special divisions to destroy us. Also from the west, from Germany, they have sent out German divisions to help. We are in the middle. However, all the roads are blocked. For the time being, they cannot get to us. Every night, large Russian partisan groups are dropped by airplane. They are mining the roads in the path of the retreating Germans. They are being torn to pieces in the fields and in the forests. As long as we don't fight them in open battle, the brave Russian

Army is doing that with great success, we can avoid great casualties. Whether all of us who are here will survive is hard to know. Perhaps we can hope."

"The Germans have burnt down everything from Pinsk to Mozyr and Zhitomir. We have a directive from the highest command in Moscow to destroy, without mercy, all German followers and traitors. In my refugee camp, we uncovered an entire family of German spies. Over ten of my dear partisan lads were killed because of them. Tonight, the entire family of eight will be hung. Although only the daughter was actually guilty, the entire cowardly family knew about her treachery. Let us hope that we will endure all hardships. Long live the Red Army!"

[Page 461]

After finishing his speech, the commander turned to the cantor wrapped in his tallis, and said the following: "Listen now, continue your prayers. Say what you were saying before I came to the barn."

The cantor covered his head with his old shredded tallis, leaned his thin and dried hands against the eastern wall of the barn and began to tearfully intone the words of *Hineni heani.*

The commander got off his horse, smoked a cigarette, leaned his left shoulder against his horse, looked the entire time in the direction of the forest and, with quiet attention, listened to the sad and tearful melody. I noticed that tears were in his eyes…

* * *

The war was over. I returned to my hometown and encountered destruction and a huge mass grave. All was lost. I was sent to Rovno where there was a job opportunity.

In the administrative office of the town commandant, I met a man dressed in a handsome black suit with carefully combed hair. He was conversing with the commandant. I could not take my eyes off him. I had seen this man somewhere before and I could not remember where. The man noticed that I was looking at him with special interest, and he abruptly asked me: "Don't you recognize me, comrade? Well, my friend," he said, "if you don't remember, it doesn't matter. It is not necessary, my friend. Everything evil must belong to the past, to history."

When he left the administrative office, the town commandant of Rovno asked me: "Comrade Hochman, were you in his Polish detachment called Kościuszko during the war?" I didn't let him go any further: "Yes, yes, that's right! He is the commander of my detachment, the Polish Colonel Satanovski!"

"No, no," interrupted the Rovno town commandant, "No, not the Pole Satanovski but the courageous hero of the Soviet Union, organizer of all the Polish partisan units on Soviet soil who is now decorated with all the highest medals by comrade Stalin himself and who is now a frequent guest, along with all the other distinguished personalities in the Kremlin – a colonel and heroic partisan, the Jew Moshe Satanovski!"

Coordinator's footnote:

i.   This article is equivalent to the article in the Hebrew section "Colonel Satanovski" on pages 222-224.

[Page 462 - Yiddish] [Page 218 - Hebrew]

Miriam Bregman Tells of Her Partisan Activities

Translated by Norman Helman z"l

In mid-July, 1941, towards the end of the week when the Germans had been in David-Horodok for several days, a rumor spread that the Russians were returning. The Germans retreated along with their town helpers.

Miriam Bregman

[Page 218 - in the Hebrew section]

The murderer, I. Maraiko, who stood at the head of the local authorities, fled to Pinsk with his cohorts. When they asked him why he abandoned the town without an organized management, he replied that he had fled because of shooting from the Jews and Russians. Sunday, the Germans returned, bringing the murderer and his henchmen with them.

They soon ordered the Jews to wear a blue Star of David on a white band on their sleeves. That same day, they took the men "to work" beyond the town. Several hours later, we heard shooting from the direction that the men had gone. Who and what? No one knew. We had hidden our father in the cellar and when the gentiles entered to look for men, we created an uproar to divert their attention.

That same night, in pouring rain, I suddenly heard crying. I saw through the window women and children with sacks on their backs. In reply to my question, they told me that all the Jews were being driven across the bridge and out of town. My father quickly put on women's clothes and we all stood together in the crowd: my mother, my father, my sister Feigele and I. Along the road, we encountered a gentile who was inspecting the crowd and he recognized my father. Words were of no avail. He returned with him to the town.

The rain poured. The women and children were brought to a manor alongside the river on the way to Stolin. They assured us that they would return us home just as soon as they had completed their search for weapons in our houses. Meanwhile, the gentiles from the vicinity arrived and they began to plunder and grab whatever came to hand. One of them struggled with me, threatening me with a knife if I would not give him my coat. However, I did not give it to him and he left.

At night, the murderer Maraiko came and took away Rivka, Yossel Yudovitz's wife; her two daughters, Malle and Yentl; Leah, Elya Bregman's daughter; and Malka, the pharmacist Yashe Yudovitz's wife. He also wanted to take my sister Feigele. "Why should she have to suffer here?" he said. But I refused to part with her under any conditions.

In the morning, Vanke and a band of cohorts drove us off the manor towards Stolin. They shot into the air, pushed and chased us. The older ones could not hold up and fell along the way. When we were not far from Stolin, they turned us back toward David-Horodok.

One kindly gentile, who had known my maternal grandfather, Herzl

[Page 463]

Luria the timber merchant, took us away to his farm at the time that the others were returning to David-Horodok. I learned later that they were crammed into a ghetto in the town which they had surrounded with barbed wire.

According to his plan, Feigele and I would work in the field and my mother would stay in the house.

He treated us very well. However, two days later, when he went with us into the field, a neighbor from the village passed us. "Now that you've been seen, you can no longer remain with us," said the gentile, "because my life is also now in jeopardy." He brought us to some relatives on another farm and he went alone to Stolin to get yellow patches, which was his usual routine.

When he returned, he drove us in his wagon through the forests near Stolin, where he let us off. He took our belongings in his wagon and transported them to Stolin. We walked the rest of the way to Stolin. The gentile refused to take any gift or money from us.

In Stolin, we hid several days with Ester Blizhovsky, but our goal was Sarny. My aunt, my mother's sister, lived there. We walked to Dombrovitz and we drove from there to Sarny by wagon. We stayed in Sarny for five months until they established a ghetto in the Jewish quarter. It is noteworthy that certain Sarny gentiles did not want to leave the border region of the ghetto. Most of the Jews survived in the ghetto by selling their belongings and utensils. We did not want our aunt to have to support us so we moved to other lodgings which were provided by the communal committee.

There were several David-Horodokers with us in the ghetto: Golda Finkelstein and her mother Yentl, Zelda Finkelstein and her daughter Sara, and Chaike Finkelstein with her two daughters Mania and Rivka. Golda Finkelstein had her personal problem to add to the general woe. During the days of the Holocaust, she gave birth to a daughter on her twelfth wedding anniversary.

All the Jews were required to register on two separate occasions over a six-month period. At the second registration, they established a ghetto for recently arrived Jews from Dombrovitz and the surrounding region. Then, the killing began. Every day, five hundred men were transported to the trenches which had been prepared in the forest outside of town.

When our transport arrived at the spot, we all began running away from the trenches towards a hill over near Sarny – a splendid target for the German guns. My sister Feigele was wounded. While running, I heard a voice: "Run daughter!" To this day I don't know if that was my mother's voice. In any case, I never saw her again.

We came to a stream and I washed Feigele's foot.

[Page 464]

We spent the entire night alone in the forest, terrified by horrible visions. In the morning, we discovered a small house in the forest and we went inside. Feigele's foot had become swollen and so she lay down and quickly fell asleep. I went outside to look around and to try and find some Jews. When I returned to get Feigele, people in the house told that she had gone with the shepherds. I later learned from the village teacher that Feigele had been dragged into the woods and forced to lay on the ground while they drove back and forth over her with a bicycle until, with terrible pain and suffering, she gave up her pure and innocent soul.

I went off on the pathway crying bitterly until I finally dropped off into an exhausted sleep. A gentile woke me, brought me into the forest and succeeded in finding me a hiding place. Early next morning, I set off walking again until a wagon stopped and gave me a ride to a nearby farm. I went into a house and asked for a drink. I found two Jews there. After I ate and drank, the Jews showed me the road and warned me to hide from wagons. I went on, but suddenly I heard the sound of an approaching wagon. I quickly hid in the bushes. To my great terror, the wagon stopped near my hiding place. My soul nearly left my body before I realized that the wagon contained my friends from the farm. They drove me in their wagon to the family of a Jewish doctor who lived in the forest. I stayed with them for a month. At night, we would go to the gentile houses to beg for food, even a dry crust of bread. The trees served as hiding places during the night.

One gentile woman treated me very kindly and invited me into her home once a week. There I would wash my hair. She gave me a cooking pot and some salt – a very scarce commodity. The pot had two advantages. One was that I could eat warm cooked food after having wandered for weeks through the cold forest. Most important was that potatoes, which were half-burnt when roasted over a fire, could now be eaten entirely without any waste.

Another gentile woman hid me in the forest when the Germans appeared once. Afterwards, she brought me back to my friends. One night, while we were warming ourselves by a fire that we lit in the forest, a man with a gun suddenly appeared and said, "I am a partisan. We have a wounded man." By the light of the flames he examined each one of us until he came next to me and stared at me. Suddenly we heard a shot and a cry, "Get going!"

Everyone ran away, but one by one, they returned. The doctor called his daughters to come back, saying that they would "take care of him" if they did not return. Afterwards, they all searched for me, calling me by name again and again, but I lay the entire night hidden in the bushes. In the morning I returned to the group.

The doctor praised me and said: "You were smart not to come..."

That is how things were for several months until the outlaws, whose leader was Bandera and who called themselves *Banderovtzes*, began catching Jews. At that time, the partisans showed up. I begged them to take me with them,

[Page 465]

but they refused. Then I said to them: "Finish me off if you won't honor my wish." They finally consented.

At the beginning, I worked for several months in the medicine section, accompanying the wounded in wagons and nursing them. Later, when I had proven myself courageous and bold, I was assigned to the information service. My job was to go to the villages, find out the number of German soldiers in each place, how many weapons they possessed and where their commander was located. When I brought back the accurate information, the partisans would attack each place and destroy it.

There was a landing strip built near Zhitomir where the Soviets landed airplanes of the Red Army, evacuating our severely wounded and providing us with supplies and weapons. The airplanes would come at night and we would light fires to guide them in their landing. Once an enemy airplane circled overhead. Thinking it was one of ours, we lit the fires. The airplane veered off and headed towards Kiev. A few hours later, it returned and gave us a "present" of bombs.

In one of our raids, we overran the village of Emilchino near Zhitomir. The retreating Germans were convinced that they were opposing soldiers of the Red Army. While we held the village, we ate and drank ceaselessly. We followed the system of "take from this one and give to the next one". We would take from one person and then repay him with what we took from the next person.

One of my jobs was observation. Once, while I was sitting at my post, I didn't notice that our people had left the area and the Germans were coming up. However, I wasn't abandoned. A horse and rider were sent to retrieve me and we succeeded in escaping in the last minute before the Germans marched in.

This was but only one of the many miracles that happened to me.

After we had extricated ourselves from Emilchino, I was again assigned as an observer. About a kilometer away from me, deep in the forest, our people were stationed with a cannon. I was to warn them when the enemy approached. To lose a cannon was for us a far greater tragedy than to lose one of our own people, and I was no exception. I suddenly heard the sound of horse's hooves. "Halt," I shouted. "Who's there?" and I whispered the password. My situation was intolerable. Whoever did not carry out his duty, even when guiltless, the penalty was death. With my luck, they were our men. In recognition, I was given a medal.

[Page 466]

One night, we were riding our horses near a train station. We watched over our horses as if they were our own eyes because they were our most important means of communication. We handled them properly, as best we could. When we saw that their strength was exhausted, we would confiscate fresher and stronger horses along the way.

At crossroads, we would separate and ride in various directions back and forth in order to confuse the enemy. At one time, we passed the train station and I became separated from my unit in order to change my horse. When I returned, no one was there. I had indeed acquired a fresh horse and I had a gun. But, I was alone. I wandered alone for a week without seeing a single soul. I was so weary that the gun became too much of a burden for me and I parted with it as a "friend". On the eighth day, I came to a village. I entered a cabin and asked the residents if they had seen horses and riders in the vicinity. "Yes, yes! I saw them," answered the man of the house. "Sit a while. Relax. I'll come right back." I decided that he was a village official and I used the moment of his departure to get out of there. I left my horse and all my belongings.

I later went into several houses and ordered the residents to give me food and to do me no harm if they didn't want to deal with the partisans who were coming after me. At last, I went into a small house and again asked if they had seen horses and riders in the region. After I had promised a proper reward, the resident went with me to show the way. On the tenth day of my wanderings, I was reunited with my people.

Once, we were surrounded by the Germans and they shot at us from all sides. Our situation was hopeless and we began to say farewell to each other. A portion of us succeeded in breaking through the enemy line and escaped, leaving the wounded behind. We were soon given the order to turn back and rescue the wounded. Many fell in the renewed skirmish. Many of our people also died at Brody, especially a number of Jews from Dombrovitz.

The enemy had a widespread espionage network. Not infrequently, we would arrive at a certain place and come under attack by enemy planes. We would always withdraw in the direction taken by the enemy airplanes.

In Lemberg [Lvov], we came in contact with the Red Army. I was appointed head nurse for a transport of wounded and typhus victims to the rear area. A number of them were lying on the ground. I fulfilled this function for the Red Army for one week. That same week, we dug a grave for a partisan who had survived many battles, but died in an accident. I said a short eulogy over his grave. After that, I resolved to leave the partisans and do something for myself. At the time we captured Emilchino, I became a close friend

[Page 467]

of one of the village girls. Now that the region had been cleared of the enemy, I came to her house. We were joined by several wagoners and young people who were going the same way. My girlfriend's house had

remained intact and her family unharmed. I was there scarcely a month when I began working in the office of a large sawmill. I had to change my residence, but I returned each Sunday to spend time with my companions.

So I spent several months until I heard the news that Pinsk had been liberated. I decided to return home. I procured a passport and traveled to Sarny. I wanted to continue on my way to David-Horodok but I met friends in Sarny who wouldn't let me go because "there is not even the memory of a Jew there." I reluctantly remained in Sarny and took up the offer to work as a clerk for the commissar of the military stationed in Sarny. The NKVD also offered me a job, which I refused. A short time later, when I was ordered to the front with my military unit, I decided to remain with the NKVD.

I was awarded the rank of an officer and I was quartered next to the residence of the commissar. Before I started working, I was given the longest detailed questionnaire I had ever seen. I kept that job for several months. During that period, there were still marauding bands that pillaged and staged pogroms. The NKVD uniform protected me. I was also saved by the fact that I often appeared together with the commissar, just the two of us, and each such appearance had a powerful impression on everyone, especially those who planned to harm me.

My closeness to the public prosecutor also enabled me to arrest several gentiles who I recognized as murderers of Jews.

On a certain day, I decided to travel to Emilchino for a farewell visit. Since I could not afford to travel on my salary, I was forced to sell paper at a high price to cover my travel expenses. However, I was caught and arrested.

An NKVD employee, who was arrested for a similar crime, was punished by taking twenty-five percent of his wages until he had completed his obligation. I was freed after much effort and a report was sent concerning me to Sarny. When I returned to Sarny, I again enjoyed the commissar's trust and he never deducted a *groschen* from my wages.

The transports of supplies and troops all passed through Sarny which also served as a military camp. When a troop train would stop, I would put two or three bottles of whiskey in my rucksack and go to the station to trade with the soldiers for clothing, which was plentiful on the trains. Once, I came there and the railroad NKVD policemen surrounded the train and started a search.

[Page 468]

Before they searched me, I succeeded in getting rid of the whiskey. When they brought me to my commissar, I feigned ignorance, saying that I was there as an NKVD officer.

Half a month later, I requested a release from the NKVD and an emigration permit. My commissar reminded me of my arrest. Nevertheless, he sent me with a letter, whose contents I do not know to this day, to the commissar of Rovno.

The guards would not let me see him and they tried to get rid of me with various excuses. I would not be put off and I went in. He read the letter and sent me back with another sealed letter, whose contents were also unknown to me. I gave this letter to the commissar of Sarny and all the obstacles in my path were set aside.

I drove to freedom.

The Horrible Ghetto Slaughter
in Rubiel [Rubel], David-Horodok and Stolin

Translated by Norman Helman z"l

A Letter to Detroit

Michael Nosanchuk of Rubiel describes the horrible events in a letter to his brother Berl Nosanchuk of Windsor. The letter writer escaped from Rubiel, joined the anti-Nazi partisans and later joined the Red Army. The letter was published in The Forward by Yaakov Nosanchuk of Detroit.

The letter writer is the only one of his family that was saved and one of the few survivors of Rubiel, David-Horodok and Stolin. He escaped in the midst of the slaughter as if by a miracle and joined the ranks of the partisans. Later, he joined the Red Army.

Mr. Yaakov Nosanchuk gave us two letters to publish. The first letter gives us a general overview of the conditions that the Red Army soldier endured and the second letter describes the details of the horrible slaughter.

He writes in the first letter:

Today is the happiest day of my life. That is how I feel as I read a letter written in my brother's hand. How many days and nights did I think

[Page 469]

of only one thing, that you should only know of the dark fate that had overtaken us. Escaping from the dark ghetto, from the murderous hands of the Germans, wandering around in the mud, swamps, woods and marshes alone and forlorn, worse off than a dog. I had only one thought – how can I let my brother and sister know? Will someone in my family even know of my death, of what I endured? More than once I wanted to end my life, but remembering you, I encouraged myself. I kept up my hope and, with all my strength, I endured everything. My only aspiration was to get hold of a gun and take revenge. It was not easy for me to decide to join a partisan detachment. From the detachment, I went on to join the Red Army. I was in Lithuania, Latvia, later on the front lines outside of Warsaw, and I ended in the darkness of Berlin. I took revenge for our innocent spilt blood. But the great wound will not heal.

In the second letter, written five days later (January 15, 1946), the writer gives the following details of the bloody slaughter:

In 1941, around the 16th of Av (I remember it was a Sunday), the horrible slaughter occurred in David-Horodok. With the pretext that they were being sent to work, everyone was gathered outside of Horodok and shot to death.

I was in Rubiel at the time, unaware of anything. I had a passion for fishing and so I went out to the river. Yaakov, our Golda's husband, sat at home around the table with his fellow Hassidim. I called for him to come with me. But he only joked that he would come later with a wagon to get the fish. I went alone.

At around five o'clock in the afternoon, I heard guns shooting, one after another. I settled deeper in the bushes and waited until someone came from the village. The first to announce the bitter news was the shameless Marko.

Just two hours earlier, everything was peaceful. Everyone sat at his work, whether at the forge or at sewing. Suddenly everyone was dead! Including Yaakov. A short time ago he was telling jokes and now he lays dead. Why? Fifty-three martyrs were murdered with Chanale's father and Gittel's husband among them.

Before he died, Yaakov said a few words. They had taken them out, bound together in groups of three, into barns and there they shot them. Soon came the realization that all were gone in Horodok as well.

I managed to get away unnoticed to Avdeus in Horisha [Hotomel]. The murderers soon realized that I was not amongst the bodies and they began searching for me. However, Avdeus knew how to hide me. In Stolin, the black SS were not yet active. They had seized only David-Horodok. In Rubiel, the perpetrators were local gentiles. I received a message from our Moshe Chaim, may he rest in peace, that I should come to Stolin. I went there. The unfortunate women of Horodok and Rubiel had been driven out of the villages of Horisha [Hotomel] and they were robbed of their belongings before their eyes. The gentile Nikolai Pusiks pulled Yaakov's boots off Chaya's feet (our Golda's daughter). (I later saw him while with the partisans, and we killed him.) The unfortunates then wandered through the Brezno forest. Nowhere would anyone let them in.

[Page 470]

They created a communal organization in Stolin and with much money and sacrifice; they worked to allow the unfortunates to enter Stolin.

On the second day of Rosh Hashanah, I sat with our brother Moshe Chaim. Suddenly two thugs burst into the house and took Moshele away forever. Three days later, we learned that they had tortured him to death. They had stuck him with prods and tore pieces off him. On the second day of Rosh Hashanah, 1941, at 12 midnight, he gave up his holy soul in a Stolin jail. I found his body six months later and I buried him wrapped in his tallis near Aunt Golda's grave.

Lyova, covered in tears, said the graveside Kaddish. Zelig Fishman was with me. He helped me. The face of our holy brother was already decomposed but I recognized him anyway. Frumke, Genya, Chaya and Rachel also came running to help. We made the funeral without the knowledge of the Germans.

After Moshele's death, I began a different life. I became a part of a family of orphans and widows. I would look at the children, especially Avivale, and my heart would nearly break. Aunt Golda held out well but then the light began to go out. At Chanukah, she breathed her last in our house. All the Rubiel widows wept for her. We made a quiet funeral because the Germans forbade funerals.

But we didn't have much time to think of the dead. The great burden of all the orphans and widows fell on me. I turned in every direction trying to keep them from starving. We had a minyan in our house. Father, may he rest in peace, would say Kaddish with Lyova. The first Kaddish was for the Rubiel martyrs, next for our brother and then for Aunt Golda. Father would say little, just bite his lips and keep silent. Often, he would scold the women when they began to cry and then he would begin to shed tears too. I was forced to play the role of a hero, but at the same time shed my own tears.

One could not appear on the street after seven o'clock in the evening. We would sit behind closed shutters. Often Genya and her children would come through the garden and we would sit together. Not infrequently, we would talk about you, whether you knew what was happening here and what you would think when you found out?

Thus we sat in the house the entire winter.

On the eve of Passover, they drove Genya out of her house and then us as well. At that time Zelig Fishman, may he rest in peace, gave us considerable aid. There then began rumors that they would make a ghetto in Stolin. How many trials could we endure? How many tribulations? They were flaying our skins. By the eve of Shavuot, they had completed encircling the ghetto with a fence of 15 wires, one post every two or three meters.

We received the order to move to the ghetto. It is impossible to describe the picture. Everyone carried what they could – one must live. Father, may he rest in peace, took his cane and went into the ghetto. We were assigned a small room: me, Golda's Shia, cousin Yaakov's

[Page 471]

five-year old son Michalke and our parents. Not far from us was Genya with her children and Frumke.

In the ghetto it was forbidden to take anything in or out. The death rate reached twelve a day. People became swollen. I would look at mother's feet and I would shudder. We talked of nothing but eating. We found ways of smuggling food into the ghetto. Then came the terrible knowledge that they were shooting all the Jews. We couldn't believe it. What does it mean? How could they? Small children? Old people? It cannot be.

Until the black day came, on the eve of Rosh Hashanah 1942, there had been 7,000 souls in Stolin and all were killed. The graves were prepared. They were first stripped naked and then forced to lie down in the graves, then shot in rows.

I will never forget the last night in the ghetto. I stayed with mother until 3 o'clock. We kissed and kissed, cried and cried with your photographs pressed to our hearts, we said our farewell to you. Father recited the confessional prayer. Mother bathed and put on clean clothes, preparing for her death. She then drove me out of the house: "Go away from us! You will survive. Hide yourself. Don't stay with us! Perhaps you will be able to avenge us and tell of our fate."

At that moment I didn't believe mother's words. How can I survive when we are surrounded on all sides? I went away with the idea that our parents last minutes would be easier if they thought I had survived.

So I left the dearest and most treasured, forever! A thousand times I cursed that moment when I left. I often wished that I had lain down with them and embraced them as all the martyrs did before they died.

I stayed in a cellar with Valyen Molochnik for 18 days after the slaughter in the ghetto. I thought of everything, looking for ways to get out. My heart told me that if I could only get out of the ghetto I would know how to get along. I tried to get Valyen to go along with me. However, at that time, his wife was also alive and in hiding. Others who were still alive included: Beila Molochnik, Nissel, their daughter Bashale, Shalom Durchin with his wife and child. Their family was still intact and I was already an orphan. I would meet them at night and try to convince them to try to find a way to escape with me. They decided to wait for a miracle and they remained there.

I began to search for a way out by myself. On the 18th night after the slaughter, I groped around in the dark ghetto – doors, windows, all were broken. All the houses were vacant and I thought I had stumbled over the dead body of a martyr – my hair shuddered. I had only one thought – life, life! How to get out of there?

At that moment, I encountered another living person. I quickly went over to him. I thought that he was another unfortunate like me, trying to find a way out. How shocked was I to see

[Page 472]

a tall gentile standing before me – the biggest thief in Stolin (he now sits in jail) and he led me out of the ghetto.

Valyen, Beila, Nissel, and Shalom were found and shot to death several days after my escape.

I then began to live my golden days. A lone survivor in the world, wandering about. I owe gratitude to Avdeus and Chvedar Siroshik, Levan Malak Mamanovich – they helped me out until I could fend for myself. That is to say, I joined a partisan detachment. I will not describe my further experiences. They are not important. I believe that what I have written will give you more-or-less a clear picture of what happened to us.

We have with us here from Rubiel, Avraham Shulman, the Levite's two sons. They are longing for their aunt Eydel Shulman in New York and they do not have her address. If you can, dear brother, find out her address from the Rubiel people and let her know about the two boys. Let her write to them to my address.

[Page 475 - Yiddish] [Page 231 - Hebrew]

My Small Revenge for the Heinous Crime
(A Chapter From My Memoirs)

by Aharon Moravchik

Text translated by Norman Helman z"l

Yiddish captions translated by Jerrold Landau

Coordinator's note: This article is repeated on pages 231-238 in the Hebrew section and on page 475-486 in the Yiddish section. The articles are equivalent, except for a difference in the number of illustrations. Photos of the author (page 231) and of two of his four children (page 237) only appear in the Hebrew section. Also, the Hebrew section has one additional document on page 236.

May, 1946. The transport that drove the repatriates (Polish citizens who spent World War II in the Red Army), including me, to the Polish People's Republic stopped at Kielce, a small town in lower Silesia. There, we all had to begin to build a new life.

Should I anchor myself here or search for a more central town? Was it more important to be here or in a large city? Naturally, I was lonesome and forlorn, without a relative, a helper or a friend. I decided to settle where fate had led me and I stayed in that town.

I had in my possession the list of names of the David-Horodoker murderers which I had succeeded in acquiring while riding in the transport. From time to time, I took out the list and read through the names of the murderers who had killed the Jews of David-Horodok. There was the name of the father of sinners, the most to blame and chief murderer, the medic Ivan Maraiko, may his name be blotted out, and after him, his trusted accomplices: the lawyer, Ivgeny Yavplov and his wife Marusya; Kasarev and his three sons; Siamyon; Kulaga and his son Grigory; Damyon Maraiko; Straiko; Hantshl; Krim Levkovski; Polukoshka; Kazalovski; Gritzkavitch and a lot more – may their names and memories be blotted out.

They are probably even now going about – these murderers – free as can be in the Polish People's Republic and they are comfortably enjoying themselves with the robbed possessions of the Jews. That thought would not leave me alone. I resolved that I must find and unmask them at any cost. Jewish blood must not be spilled wantonly! I must be the blood-avenger for my David-Horodoker brothers and sisters.

A few weeks after my arrival in Poland, the Kielce pogrom broke out.

Turmoil seized the survivors and the Jews began a mass exodus from the country whose soil had absorbed the blood of millions of guiltless Jewish victims and was still not sated.

It was natural for me to be carried along by the great stream of survivors. My friends tried to convince me to go. However, a hidden power would not let me leave the place. I stayed to search for the murderers despite the fact that many of my friends thought it was madness.

* * *

[Page 476]

I decided to get a job in the district ministry where they had offered me a responsible post. In a short time, I had won the trust of the director himself.

The ministry director was a middle-aged man with an authentic Polish moustache and whiskers. He was easy-going and direct. Every word that came from his mouth was first considered, weighed and measured.

His relations with people as well as his general appearance was sympathetic. The man was highly honorable, a devout communist and an outspoken idealist. His pure Aryan outward appearance, his authentic Polish family name, his wonderful Polish literate speech and his pure Polish accent all indicated that here was a Pole of many generations. It is interesting to note that later, and under different circumstances with this "authentic Pole", I found out that he was a good-hearted Jew.

One morning, the director invited me into his office and requested that I travel with an expert to Breslau [in Polish: Wrocław] to purchase a taxi for the ministry. He added discreetly: "I know that you are a Jew and I am sure that you will carry out this mission successfully."

I thanked him for his confidence and I willingly accepted the mission, hoping without any foundation for it that I might find traces of the David-Horodoker murderers in that large city.

* * *

I carried out my mission in Breslau, purchasing the taxi and its necessary accessories and I had to wait another three days so that I could take everything together back to Kielce. I decided to utilize those three days to search for traces of the murderers.

Wandering through the streets of Breslau, I chanced to run into my friend Avraham Moshe Greenberg, a Jew from Lomzhe who was now the community leader in our new town. He told me that his object was to purchase poultry in Breslau for the kaporos ceremony for the Jews of Kielce. He suggested that I come along with him and help him buy the poultry. I took up his proposition with pleasure thus becoming a partner in a good deed.

We went to the marketplace which was filled with thousands of people and hundreds of kiosks with their proprietors. I recalled the time when there were millions of Jews in Poland and I imagined that same marketplace filled with Jewish merchants and peddlers, without whom it would have been impossible to conceive of such a market day. Who have believed, I thought, that this all had disappeared so quickly?

Walking along side Greenberg and absorbed in my thoughts, the unbelievable suddenly occurred: a gentile, who was selling herring at his

[Page 477]

stand, began to stare at me. Instinctively our eyes met. Abruptly, he asked me in Russian: "Are you a compatriot?" A few seconds later he added: "Are you Moravchik?"

I was startled as if by an electric shock when I unexpectedly heard my family name spoken in the Russian language in a foreign city amongst strangers. I thought I was dreaming or that I was hearing a voice from another world.

Fortunately, I did not lose my presence of mind and I quickly reasoned that this person might have something to do with David-Horodok and perhaps he was one of those that I was seeking. "And who are you?" I asked him in Russian.

Instead of a reply, the unknown person began to draw back and stammer: "Excuse me. Perhaps I made a mistake. I didn't mean you." "Say who you are!" I began to shout nervously: "Just now you called me by my name. You certainly know me from before." A crowd of people gathered. My agitation grew from moment to moment as I continued to demand that he tell me who he was.

The unknown man remained silent. He bowed his head as if he were searching for something on the ground. He realized that he had given himself away. "Militia, militia," I began shouting in a shrill voice which I myself did not recognize.

In a few minutes, two militia men arrived. I explained to them that I suspected this person of collaborating with the German occupation forces during the war and participation in the extermination of the Jews of David-Horodok. The militia men ordered the gentile to lock his stall and they took us both to the police station. After inspecting his documents, it became apparent that he was one of the David-Horodoker citizens whose name figured in the murderous regime.

At the time of the first inquest, which was made on the spot in my presence, the murderer turned to me and said: "Moravchik, who are you arresting? I had an unimportant position with the Germans. Why don't you arrest Ivan Maraiko who was mayor of David-Horodok under the Germans? He was responsible for the killing of all the David-Horodoker Jews and despite that, he is now a free man in Warsaw."

Thus, I was set on the trail of the chief murderer Maraiko and I understood that this beginning would eventually lead to the arrest of all the remaining murderers who were on Polish soil. I do not exaggerate when I say that this day was the happiest day of my life since the beginning of the war in 1939.

I had lived to see the fruition of my dedicated work. I was proud of my achievement

[Page 478]

even though I knew that the vengeance would not return my dear David-Horodoker brothers and sisters to life. At the same time, I took stock of the situation and realized that the basic groundwork would have to be done first and that it would not be easy.

My resolution to carry out the holy work to the end became even firmer and the beginning gave me the courage, strength and enduring vigor to continue my efforts to find the remaining murderers.

* * *

The medic Ivan Maraiko, who had many Jewish clientele, had immediately put himself in the service of the Germans and was appointed town mayor by them. From the first day, a terror campaign was waged against the Jewish inhabitants. One of the most valuable men in town, the dentist Yitzchak Edel, was shot with his son Gedalyahu on that day.

Aharon Slomiansky, a respected Hassidic Jew, was thrown from the bridge into the Horyn River. Simcha Mishalov and Motel Kvetny hid themselves with their "good friend" Ivan Maraiko, who took plenty of gold and silver for his services. A few days later, Ivan Maraiko drove them out of hiding, ordering the citizenry to kill them. Simcha Mishalov was killed before his own house in front of his wife and children.

The Finkelstein family, who were valued by the citizenry, especially the Christian shoemakers, were murdered along with all the other Jews despite their having paid a huge ransom and despite the pleas of the Christian shoemakers to the authorities to let them live as good Jews.

Rabbi Moshele demonstrated unusual courage and selflessness on behalf of his community. Every day he would come to intercede with the murderer Ivan Maraiko and try to affect the repeal of the decrees against the Jews. Finally, he was driven to the slaughter along with all the other men. Wrapped in his tallis and tefillin, he gave a sermon to the doomed Jews before he was killed with them.

Baruch-Yosef Katzman and his sons managed to avoid the execution by hiding in a barn. They had provided themselves with food for two weeks and they hoped that they could escape into the forest.

Two weeks later, when the food had run out, they came out of hiding. Afraid to go to the local gentiles for help, they went straight to German headquarters which was in Yudovitz's house. They explained to the Germans how they had managed to hide and they pleaded with the Germans to spare their lives.

[Page 479]

To their great surprise, they received the following reply from the Germans which was characteristic of German precision:

"We received the command to kill the Jews on August 10. Since that deadline has passed and we have no further orders, we will do you no harm and you are free." As soon as Katzman and his sons went out of the German headquarters, they ran into the drunkard and murderer Elia Stavro (Stadnik) on the street. He took an iron bar and murdered them on the spot! It is interesting that, the same night of the murder, he went berserk, set his own house on fire and was burnt alive.

Ezra Solomonik also hid from the slaughter. A couple of days later, his neighbor Yasip Dubok (Matusiavitch) discovered him and murdered him.

The "most important" work of the murderer Maraiko was his provocations against the David-Horodoker Jews, that is, against his patients from whom he had earned a living all of his life.

He and his accomplices had hidden iron bars, axes and several revolvers in the large synagogue and he then reported to the German headquarters in Luninets that they had uncovered a weapons arsenal in the synagogue with which the Jews were planning an uprising against the Germans. On the basis of the provocation, the Germans ordered that all the Jewish men of David-Horodok be killed.

Over 3,000 Jews, all the men over the age of 14, were murdered on August 10. They were buried in large mass graves which had been prepared ahead of time along the road between Chinovsk and Olshan.

In the last moment before the horrible slaughter, Maraiko pretended to intercede, letting it be known that he was working on the Germans to allow the Jews to ransom their lives with money or valuables. Many of the unfortunate victims believed him and they led the murderers to where they had hidden gold, silver and other valuables.

After several crates were filled with Jewish belongings, the Jews were led back to the place of execution where they were killed along with all the others. Maraiko personally took part in the killing, shooting the Jews with a revolver.

It is said that the cries of the unfortunate victims were heard many kilometers away. The covered mass graves were seen to move for three days because many of the Jews had been buried while still alive.

The women and children remaining in town were driven out of town by the murderers on the night after the mass murder. They were not allowed to take anything with them. There were cases where women were driven out of their homes in their nightgowns.

[Page 480]

After driving the women and children out, the local citizens and peasants from surrounding villages plundered all the Jewish belongings left behind.

* * *

The arrested David-Horodoker citizen did not know the current Warsaw address of Ivan Maraiko. Finding him would not be an easy task. I traveled to Warsaw several times to search for him. Unfortunately, my efforts were not crowned with success. I had almost given up the idea of finding him. However, as luck would have it, on one of my trips to Warsaw, I met a Jewish secret agent (Yehuda Spivak-Zinger, now in Israel) on a train. On learning of my mission, he took upon himself the task of finding Maraiko.

After long efforts and searching, he finally found him in a small town near Warsaw where he was working as a doctor using a falsified diploma. Maraiko had grown a beard so as not to be recognized. I was overwhelmed with joy when I received the telegram from Spivak-Zinger with the happy news of Maraiko's arrest. A short time later, his wife Darya came to me in Kielce (to this day I am puzzled as to how she got my address) to beg for mercy, forgiveness and pardon.

My encounter with her was rich with dramatic moments: "Get out of my house, murderess. I don't want to see you and I don't want to hear about your husband," I said to her and spat in her face. "I will not take offence because I was expecting such a reception," she replied, adding at the same time that it was worth it

if only I would listen to what she had to say.

At that moment the idea occurred to me that maybe it really was worthwhile to restrain myself despite my aversion and for the sake of the benefit which I might derive from listening to the murderess. Perhaps that way I could get her to give me the addresses of the other murderers. I told her to go down and wait for me in the street. I did not want to have that defiled person in my home.

Her entire conversation was an attempt to whitewash her husband of all sins, and thereby to convince me to drop my charges against him. Among other things, she told me that her son Misha had returned to Poland from England after the war (he was an officer on the Polish ship Pilsudski during the Polish-German war which had been sunk in battle), and he brought back with him a very charming Jewish woman who he had married in England and whom Darya loved like her own daughter. Later, I established that the information was unfortunately correct and that a Jewish woman had married the son of the murderer of the David-Horodoker Jews.

[Page 481]

She contended that her husband unfortunately had had no choice and was forced to take the post of David-Horodoker town mayor by the Germans. Acting as mayor naturally he had tried to find ways and means of revoking the decrees against the Jews. In general he, Ivan Maraiko, was completely innocent though he was forced to carry out the orders of Ivgeny Yavplov who was appointed district commissioner by the Germans.

My patient listening encouraged Darya and, in the course of the conversation, she let me know that she understood that I was in difficult material circumstances and that, as old friends, they were prepared to help me.

Her impertinent proposal so upset me that I began to shout and I spat in her face again as I started to go back into my residence. She began to run after me with apologies, pleading with me that I should listen to her again. In the meantime, I reminded myself that I had not yet accomplished my purpose in this conversation. I did not have a single address of the remaining murderers and so I remained listening to her again.

The conversation lasted six hours. They were six painful hours for me because I did not forget for a single moment that I was conversing with a beast in human form whose hands had dipped in the blood of thousands of my dear brothers and sisters, including my beloved wife and my four dear little children.

Yet, the entire effort had been worthwhile because I came away from the conversation knowing the place of residence of Ivgeny Yavplov and his sadistic criminal wife Marusya.

* * *

Before the outbreak of the Soviet-German war, the murderer Ivgeny Yavplov was arrested by the Soviet authorities for his White Guard past and put into prison in Brisk.

When the war between Germany and Russia broke out, the Russians evacuated the prisoners in special transports deep into Russia. He and Leizer Ronkin escaped the transport. A few days later, after their arrival in David-Horodok, Leizer Ronkin was killed by the local citizens by order of his prison mate, the same Yavplov.

Arriving in David-Horodok, Yavplov immediately placed himself in the service of the Germans who appointed him district commissioner. In revenge for his arrest by an NKVD officer who happened to be Jewish, he was determined to kill all the Jews in town. His wife, the sadistic murderess Marusya, right after her husband's arrest, threatened, in my presence, that "there will come a day when I'll take revenge on the Jews because a Jew arrested my husband."

[Page 482]

Both Yavplov and his wife Marusya fulfilled their pledges. In a letter sent to me in Poland by Milke Stollman-Russman and her daughter Nina from Detroit, there is a precise description of the ruthless acts of Ivan Maraiko, Ivgeny Yavplov and his wife Marusya.

Marusya particularly stood out because of her sadism. She murdered Yaakov Gertzulin by herself when she found him hiding. She threw living Jewish children into the Horyn River.

The arrest of the Yavplovs was accomplished with great difficulty. Sensing that the ground was burning under their feet, they fled the town of Zielona Góra where they had lived and, for weeks, they hid as fishermen in a small and secluded village.

Secret agents watched their house in Zielona Góra and at long last they were arrested.

At the time of the inquiry, a hoard of gold, silver and valuables was found and confiscated from them. Of course, this was all stolen from the David-Horodoker Jews. Amongst other things in their possessions, there was a photograph of my two children, Sarale and Yitzchakl, with a Polish inscription. This was written by my little girl in her childish handwriting to their daughter Zoaye who had been her girlfriend before the war. In the seven-year period before the outbreak of World War II, Yavplov and I had worked together in a bureau for pleas, translations and other office work.

The murderess Marusya wanted to use this photograph to show me what dear friends we had been, indicated by her having kept the picture with her the entire time without destroying it, and she tried to work on me to cancel their arrest.

She also told me that she knew that the Christian Alexandra Agradzinska had hidden a Jewish girl and that she had not informed on her to the authorities.

However, when I took out the material in my possession which detailed her and her husband's "fine activities", the murderess said not a word.

And I? I began looking at the photograph and I could not take my eyes away from my children. I realized that I had lost my entire family, my wife, my four children, my parents, brothers and sisters, the entire Jewish community of my hometown, all those who had been and had died so tragically. I looked and cried and looked. A torrent of tears flowed unceasingly from my eyes.

After a while, I found out that the murderess Marusya was trying to fool the investigating judge by pretending that she was gravely ill, hoping to get a medical release.

[Page 483]

I immediately traveled to Zielona Góra and showed the prosecutor the letter of Mrs. Milke Stollman-Russman and her daughter Nina which detailed the sadistic activities of the murderess Marusya Yavplov.

The prosecutor was so overcome and moved that in my presence he ordered the arrest of the "invalid", declaring that there was no place on free soil in the Polish People's Republic for such contemptible people.

In the course of the investigation, the Yavplovs revealed the residence of the murderer Levkovski from the village of Syamihostsichy.

When I arrived at Zgazshaletz and turned to the secret police to secure Levkovski's arrest, the commandant, who happened to be a Jew, was on furlough. When he was informed by telephone of my mission, he canceled his furlough and returned to personally expedite and assist me in my task. In such a manner, one murderer implicated the next and, in a short time, they arrested Krim, Damyon Maraiko, Babka and others.

Understandably, each arrest was a story in itself, filled with dramatic moments, enormous efforts, with searching and traveling and even with personal danger.

It is interesting to note that the Polish security police warned me to be careful because my life was in danger. They told me not to go out alone at night, not to open my door until I was certain who was on the other side, not to go among strangers, etc. I paid no attention to their warnings as I energetically carried out my holy work.

The Polish security police appropriately valued my achievements and, in gratitude, they sent me a letter of appreciation which gave me a certain moral satisfaction for my untiring holy work. Understandably, my greatest satisfaction came from the arrest of the murderers.

From unofficial sources, I learnt that Maraiko's daughter Ella was later arrested. She had worked with the Germans as an interpreter. Also arrested were his two sons-in-law, Vaitavitch and Vialavaiski, who were officers in the pre-war Polish army and his son Misha with his Jewish wife from England. Misha had taken a high position in the Polish security ministry.

* * *

My turn had come to immigrate to Israel. Unfortunately, I could no longer delay my departure. With pain in my heart, I was forced to tear myself away from my personal involvement and leave the finishing work to the Polish security organization.

Before I left Poland, I visited the secret police in Warsaw where I knew that all the arrested murderers were detained and were awaiting extradition to David-Horodok (which was now in the Soviet Union) where they were to be prosecuted at the site of their crimes.

[Page 484]

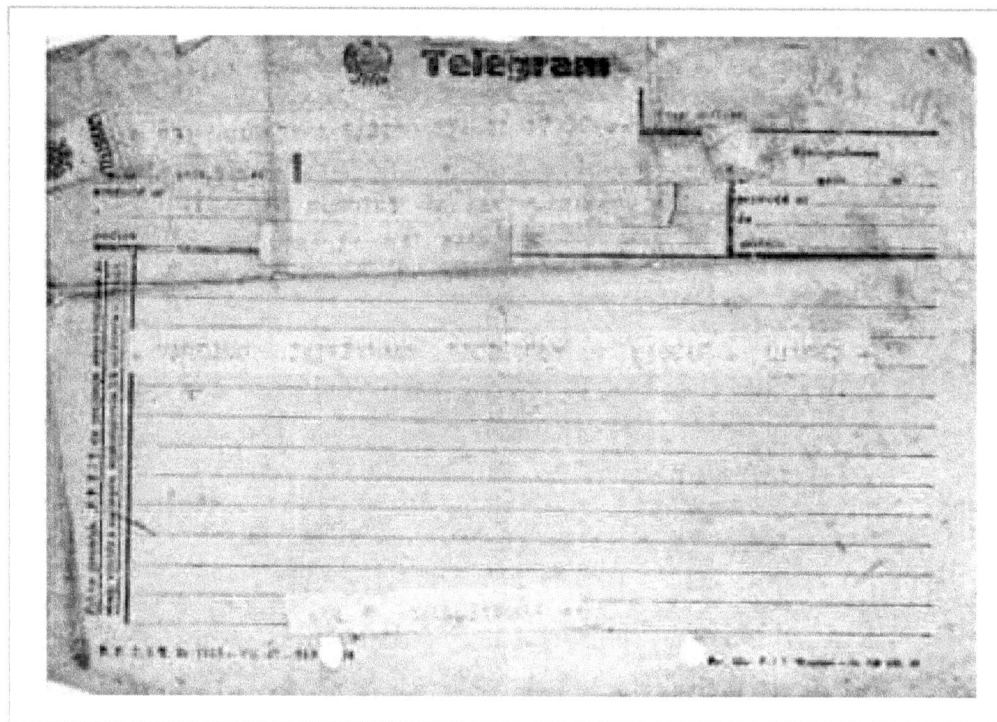

A telegram from Zinger to Aharon Moravchik
informing him of the arrest of the murderer Maraiko

[repeated on Page 234 - in the Hebrew section]

The investigating magistrate Major Piontkovski offered to take me into the prison or to bring the murderer Ivan Maraiko into his chamber so that I could confront him. I did not avail myself of the opportunity, not wanting to look at his murderous face. In truth, there are times that I regret not taking advantage of this opportunity to see that murderer at the time he was suffering punishment for his sins.

At the same trip to Warsaw, I paid a visit to the Soviet Embassy and they promised me their full support in handling the case.

I would like to take the opportunity to stress the unusual interest taken in the case by the Central Committee of Polish Jews in Warsaw, who provided legal (they supplied two lawyers to assist) and financial support.

I would also like to bring into the open a fact that shines a ray of light in the vast darkness that encompassed David-Horodok. A Christian with a noble spirit, Alexandra Agradzinska, was the only one in town to hide (at risk of her own life), a Jewish girl named Golda Kuzniatz (now in Haifa) through the entire time of the German occupation.

This fact is particularly noteworthy because all of the other Christians

[Page 485]

of David-Horodok, without exception, were crueler than the Germans towards the Jews. Alexandra Agradzinska was the only bright spot in the vast black blot that was the tragic David-Horodoker reality of those times.

I would like to take this opportunity to express our sincere appreciation and thanks to Mrs. Agradzinska who still lives in Poland. In gratitude, I have sent her the gift of a crate of oranges from Israel.

* * *

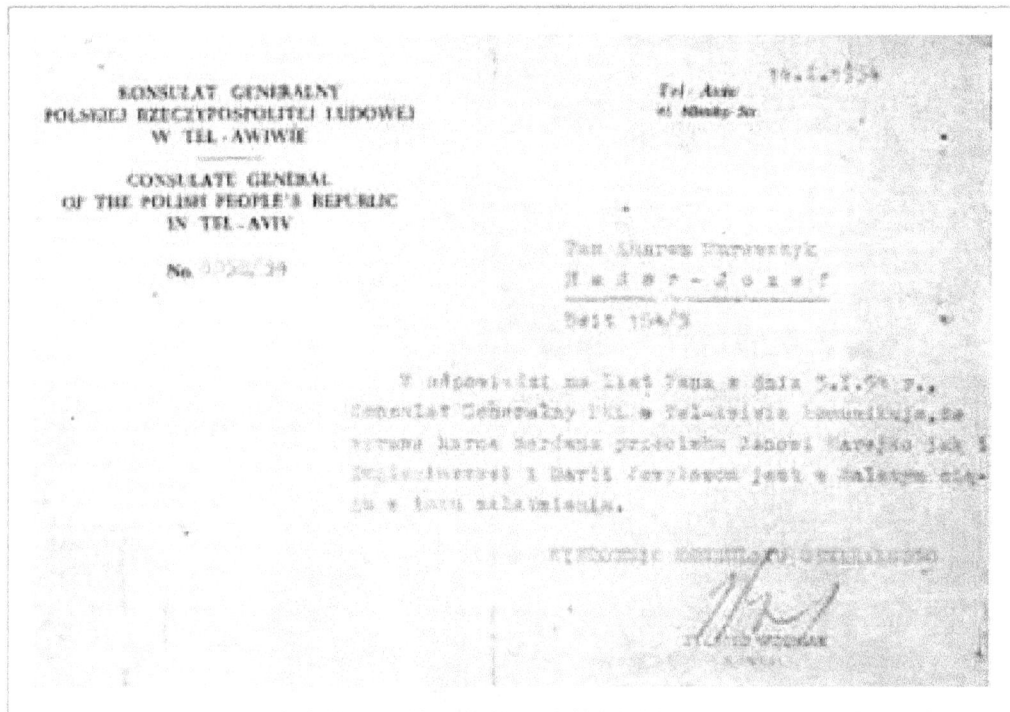

A letter from the Polish embassy in Tel Aviv to Aharon Moravchik,
informing him of the accused who were arrested in Poland

[repeated on Page 236 - in the Hebrew section]

After my arrival in Israel, I proceeded with the case. I got in touch with the Polish Embassy in Tel Aviv and I received verbal and written clarifications from them. At my request, the Warsaw prosecutor sent a number of affidavit forms to a court in Tel Aviv in order to get the testimony of witnesses that were now living in Israel. In 1953, the testimony was taken in Tel Aviv and then the documents were returned to Warsaw.

In August 1954, I revisited the Polish embassy. I feel it necessary to relate to my countrymen their answers to my questions.

[Page 486]

I was told: "All of the arrested criminals are confined. How many murderers were arrested, where they are confined and whether they have stood trial yet – we cannot give you answers to these questions, yet."

As compensation for these evasive answers, I received the following promise: "Patience, dear sir; a day will come when you will know everything."

Unfortunately, at the time of this writing, that promise has not yet been fulfilled.

Uncaptioned. Aharon Moravchik

[Page 231 - in the Hebrew section]

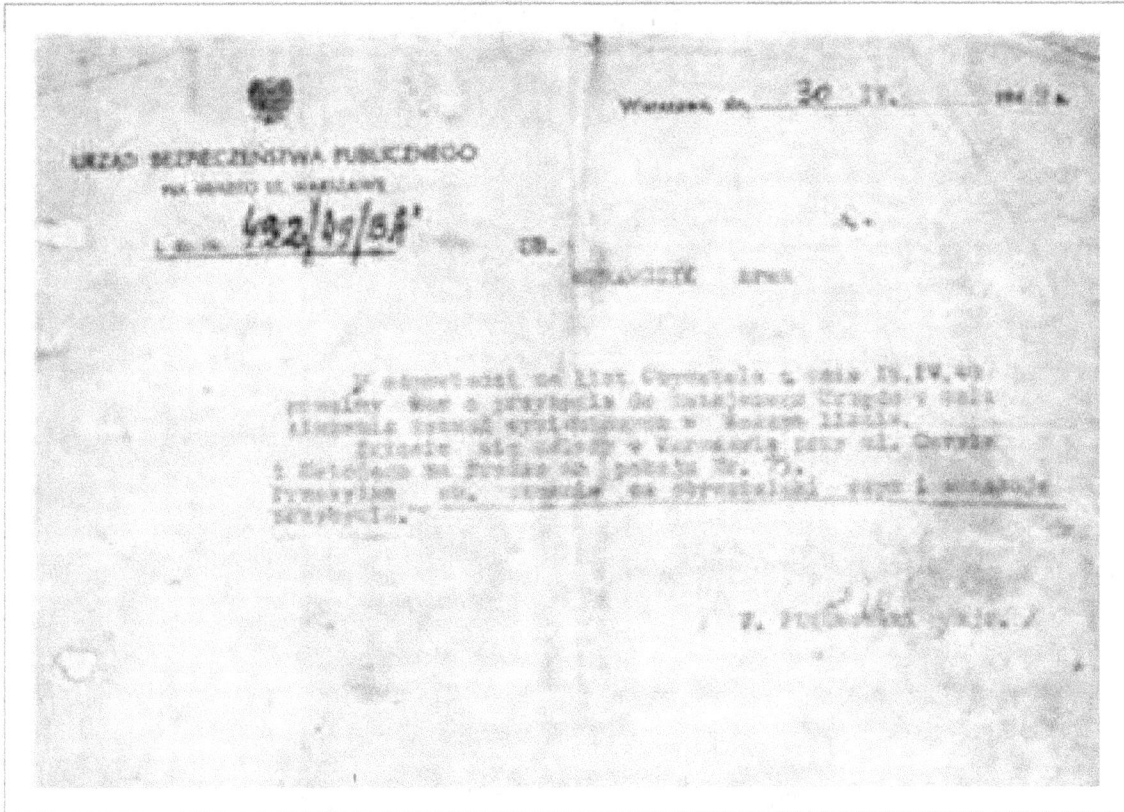

A letter from the commander of the U. B. [Ministry of Public Security] in Warsaw,
Major Piontkovski, expressing recognition to Aharon Moravchik for his deeds

[Page 235 - in the Hebrew section]

Sarale and Izi [Yitzhak] Moravchik, children of Aharon Moravchik. The photo was taken by Archik [Aharon] Moravchik from the murderess Marusya Yavplov.

[Page 237 - in the Hebrew section]

[Page 486]

Tzivia Kraus (Ziporin), z"l

by Reuven Mishalov

Translated by Ala Gamulka

At the Shiva

In 1923, I, together with interested parents and ardent Zionist leaders, took part in the founding (later the establishment) of the Tarbut School in David-Horodok.

I remember exactly when, during student registration, there was a large group of young women. Were they themselves candidates for the school or did they come to register someone younger than they? Bashfully, she supplied the required details – Tzivia Ziporin, 11 years old.

At first, the teaching staff believed her height (which surpassed all other students) caused her bashfulness. However, already in the first days of school, we felt that this was her positive and natural quality.

This asset and many others with which Tzivia was blessed, helped her to quickly hold an important position in school life. She was loved by her classmates. Schoolmates and teachers always saw her as studious, tidy, punctual, correct and dependable and it was not difficult for her to please others and for them to have a warm memory of her.

Due to the unsatisfactory economic situation at home, it was, sadly, not always easy for her to study in peace. She had much heartache. However, her positive character traits remained unshakable. On the contrary, they became stronger and became, with age, even better.

Later, when she had the position, in the same school, of teacher's aide in the kindergarten, her concern for the children bound them to her. The parents were grateful and the administration was appreciative.

Years later, when I met Tzivia in the Land of Israel – she was Mrs. Kraus by then – I, happily, was able to see again the previous quiet admiration of the infinite tenderness, caring and love which she gave to her husband and frail parents. She never forgot anyone. She always remembered every good deed done to her.

Tzivia did not like a job half done. She believed in doing it well. She helped with love and warmth.

Who knows if these properties, valued by everyone, did not affect her health? This was so to the bitter end which came – for us all – so suddenly.

The bright light was snuffed forever from the dark eyes.

May her soul be bound with the bond of life.

Haifa 7.2.57

Remarks: Since the Hebrew section of the book had already been closed, these final words were written in Yiddish.

Name Index

Kashtan, 33, 62, 137, 156, 226, 242, 243, 244, 245, 246, 247, 248, 249, 317, 318, 396
Kastutovich, 9
Katz, 114, 118, 127, 157, 158, 184, 440
Katz, 357, 358
Katzman, 49, 59, 74, 75, 77, 98, 128, 129, 148, 156, 198, 279, 323, 358, 359, 396, 455, 460, 461, 480
Katznelson, 165
Kazalovski, 478
Kerensky, 15, 30, 32, 39, 60, 76
Kertzman, 359
Kesler, 204
Khashin, 359, 360
King John Casimir, 20
King Sigismund Iii, 10
Kirzhner, 360
Kirzner, 175, 268, 269, 279, 317, 461
Kitai, 360
Kitain, 173, 360
Kitay, 6, 318, 319, 321
Kleinman, 360
Knubovitz, 360
Kobrinchuk, 360
Kofman, 360
Kohen, 360
Kolodni, 360, 361
Kolodny, 121, 287, 308
Kolotitzki, 361, 362
Kolozizky, 49
Kolozny, 49, 112, 127, 138, 139, 145, 146, 148, 149, 157, 158, 172, 175, 211, 229, 230, 233, 235, 247, 251, 252, 264, 266, 279, 317, 396, 415, 420, 421, 438, 454, 455, 460, 461
Koltin, 211, 229
Koltun, 362
Kon, 98
Konda, 362
Konik, 424
Korman, 87, 277, 278, 279, 280, 362, 440, 459, 461
Kościuszko, 467, 469
Kosover, 363
Kotsh, 295, 305
Kotzikovitz, 200, 202
Kozak, 150
Kraus, 396, 489
Kravchik, 82, 83, 87, 160, 175, 191, 275, 363, 418
Kreines, 204
Kreinin, 363

Krikun, 363
Krim, 478, 483
Kula, 208
Kuloga, 85
Kumer, 363
Kunda, 133, 278, 460
Kunem, 91
Kunik, 363
Kurtz, 363
Kurtzner, 363
Kushner, 441
Kushnir, 86, 128, 277, 278, 454, 459, 460
Kushnir, 363
Kutnik, 363, 364
Kvetny, 42, 52, 73, 76, 107, 142, 144, 148, 149, 268, 364, 480

L

Lachovsky, 40, 42, 49, 52, 75, 76, 77, 126, 127, 177, 223, 227, 231, 278, 317, 325, 326, 396, 410, 460
Ladetzki, 364
Ladezky, 117, 153, 429, 431
Lakhovski, 364
Lamdan, 364, 365
Lanski, 365
Lansky, 44, 46, 57, 58, 127, 137, 145, 149, 220, 438
Lapkin, 316
Laptchevan, 431
Lasovski, 365
Leibele's, 434
Leib's, 434
Leichtman, 39, 51, 61, 104, 127, 185, 440
Leikhtman, 365
Lelchitzki, 365
Lelzizky, 268, 403
Lemkovitz, 424
Lenin, 164, 365
Lev, 324
Levin, 365
Levinsky, 288
Levit, 365
Levkovski, 478, 483
Liberman, 365
Lichtenstein, 173, 204, 276, 396
Lifshitz, 6, 7, 44, 46, 53, 57, 58, 61, 75, 77, 82, 83, 105, 112, 121, 127, 144, 156, 158, 159, 160, 170, 174, 197, 206, 214, 216, 217, 222,

228, 287, 310, 311, 317, 365, 366, 367, 396,
   405, 406, 408, 424, 440, 446
Likhtenshtein, 367
Likhtshtein, 367
Lipman, 127, 323, 352, 373, 429, 431
Litvak, 60, 162, 434
Lubliner, 367
Lurie, 367
Lutzki, 367, 368
Lutzky, 59, 118, 121, 127, 139, 148, 156, 210,
   211, 396, 400, 420

M

Macherson, 424
Magidovitz, 46, 146, 232, 414, 415
Magidovitz, 368
Maltchik, 438
Mamanovich, 477
Manevitz, 62, 156
Manishuk, 368
Manoach, 40, 53, 158
Manusevitz, 368
Mapu, 39, 285
Maraiko, 85, 279, 454, 456, 460, 470, 471, 478,
   480, 481, 482, 483, 484
Marer, 424
Margolin, 62, 127, 156, 172, 173, 266, 368, 407
Margolis, 317
Markovitz, 279, 460
Massey, 75
Matorin, 42, 118, 368, 369
Matosvitz, 150
Matusiavitch, 480
Mazer, 175
Meidelov, 369
Meinkin, 369
Meiri, 109, 165, 167, 187, 263
Mekler, 127, 173, 369, 396, 400
Mendele, 100, 118, 216, 282, 288, 300, 439
Mendelsbern, 369
Mester, 40, 53, 57, 58, 149, 157, 158, 369
Metman, 301, 302
Migdalovitz, 369, 370
Milman, 127, 148, 149, 276, 294, 370
Milran, 370
Minkovitz, 282
Mishalov, 42, 63, 68, 75, 76, 118, 127, 145, 149,
   150, 156, 157, 158, 172, 177, 182, 266, 279,
   317, 370, 396, 407, 408, 454, 460, 480, 489

Moche, 81, 84, 127, 148, 150, 267, 431, 432,
   438
Mogilevski, 370
Mogilov, 370
Molochnik, 230, 370, 477
Mor, 6, 83, 160
Moravchik, 6, 24, 42, 52, 53, 59, 77, 82, 83, 86,
   87, 109, 118, 121, 127, 129, 149, 150, 157,
   158, 159, 160, 165, 167, 170, 174, 175, 187,
   193, 210, 263, 268, 279, 370, 371, 372, 373,
   478, 479, 480, 484, 485, 486, 487, 488
Moravnik, 424
Morel, 148
Morgenstein, 174
Morgenthau, 35
Morstein, 190
Motzani, 59
Motzny, 145
Motzolsky, 130, 139, 408, 409
Munbaz, 413
Munusvitz, 373
Mutzulski, 373
Muzikant, 121

N

Nachmanovitz, 87, 88, 277, 396, 442, 455, 458,
   459, 460
Nakhmanovitz, 373, 374
Neiditz, 285
Neidos, 157
Neiman, 374
Neuman, 435, 438, 439
Nikolaevich, 29, 136
Nosanchuk, 270, 289, 291, 305, 307, 308, 313,
   315, 424, 475
Novak, 53, 118, 121, 127, 158, 374, 375, 446

O

Olpiner, 41, 44, 46, 52, 53, 57, 59, 73, 107, 113,
   117, 118, 122, 145, 146, 148, 157, 159, 170,
   174, 175, 216, 331, 375
Olpiner-Beit Aryeh, 41
Olshanski, 28, 375, 376
Olshansky, 9, 59, 63, 64, 65, 118, 145, 157, 183,
   187, 188, 189, 194, 412
Oltz, 145
Onoshko, 31
Opingandin, 66, 127
Ovchinnikov, 15, 30

www.ingramcontent.com/pod-product-compliance
Lightning Source LLC
Chambersburg PA
CBHW062018090426

42811CB00005B/894